Marshall and His Generals

Marshall and His Generals

U.S. Army Commanders in World War II

Stephen R. Taaffe

University Press of Kansas

© 2011 by the University Press of Kansas

Published by the University Press of Kansas (Lawrence, Kansas 66045),
which was organized by the Kansas Board of Regents and is operated and
funded by Emporia State University, Fort Hays State University, Kansas
State University, Pittsburg State University, the University of Kansas, and
Wichita State University

Library of Congress Cataloging-in-Publication Data

Taaffe, Stephen R.
  Marshall and his generals : U.S. Army commanders in World War II /
Stephen R. Taaffe.
    p. cm. — (Modern war studies)
  Includes bibliographical references and index.
  ISBN 978-0-7006-1812-5 (cloth : acid-free paper)
1. World War, 1939–1945—Campaigns—Europe. 2. World War,
1939–1945—Campaigns—Pacific Area. 3. Generals—United States—
History—20th century. 4. United States. Army—Officers—History—
20th century. 5. United States. Army—History—World War, 1939–1945.
6. Generals—United States—Biography. 7. United States. Army—
Officers—Biography. 8. Marshall, George C. (George Catlett), 1880–1959.
9. World War, 1939–1945—Biography. I. Title.
  D756.3.T33 2011
  940.54'12730922—dc23   2011018954

British Library Cataloguing-in-Publication Data is available.

Printed in the United States of America

10 9 8 7 6 5 4 3 2

The paper used in this publication is recycled and contains 30 percent
postconsumer waste. It is acid free and meets the minimum requirements
of the American National Standard for Permanence of Paper for Printed
Library Materials z39.48-1992.

To my in-laws, Tom and Joan Phillips
For their kindness to my family over the years

Contents

Acknowledgments

I am grateful for all the help that I had in writing this book. My wife, Cynthia, not only read through the manuscript, but also left me alone when I needed to work. My unexpectedly growing family, now containing four children, was a constant reminder of my need to finish this project and move on with my life. I received considerable assistance from the archivists and librarians at the Ralph W. Steen Library, the United States Army Heritage and Education Center, the Dwight D. Eisenhower Library, and especially the George C. Marshall Foundation. Paul Barron, the director of library and archives at the Marshall Foundation, helped make my research trip there the most pleasant and productive I have ever undertaken. My department chair and friend, Dr. Troy Davis, secured me a course reduction one semester to facilitate my research, and Stephen F. Austin State University's administration later gave me a faculty development leave to finish the manuscript. Dr. Philip Catton, another friend and colleague, critiqued the manuscript and offered his usual sage and astute advice. Ken Arbogast-Wilson once again created maps for me and tolerated my ignorance about cartography with his usual good humor. Finally, I want to thank Mike Briggs and the good folks at the University Press of Kansas for their kindness and patience.

Marshall and His Generals

Introduction

World War Two was by definition global in scope, and its reach eventually extended to even some of the earth's most remote places. The conflict seeped into the American heartland, touching every community to one degree or another. This was as true of Roanoke, Virginia, as any other place. Nestled in the Shenandoah Valley between the Blue Ridge and Appalachian mountains, Roanoke contained a prewar population of almost 70,000. The war changed the city in all sorts of noticeable and subtle ways. Gasoline, sugar, and meat were merely among the more obvious rationed goods. City leaders organized a civilian defense program that ultimately enrolled 6,700 people as air raid wardens, auxiliary firemen, and clearance and demolition workers. These enthusiastic volunteers never had the chance to put their new skills into practice against German or Japanese bombers, but they found other ways to contribute to the war effort. Periodic collection drives gathered scrap metal and even the old cannon at Elmwood Park for conversion into implements of destruction. In 1943 Mayor Walter Wood kicked off a million-dollar bond campaign by buying a bond from a member of the Junior Chamber of Commerce while a formation of bombers roared overhead to encourage everyone to invest in the common cause. Although these and other events brought home the war's reality to everyone, perhaps the biggest reminder of its omnipresence was the conspicuous absence of 7,500 Roanoke men and women who had enlisted in or been drafted into the army and navy to fight fascism throughout the world—of whom 224 never returned.[1]

The pupils in Lillian Craig's remedial class of nine- to twelve-year-olds at Roanoke's Virginia Heights Elementary School were among those interested in the conflict and the changes it brought to their city. Discussion of the war ranged from the mundane to the weighty, but the one topic that generated the most curiosity in her class was the criteria the army used to select its generals. Rather than waste time in idle speculation, the students decided to go straight to the top for the answer. On 2 March 1944, they wrote a letter to General George C. Marshall, who ran the army as its redoubtable chief of staff, to ask him exactly how he chose those he wanted the Senate to confirm as generals.[2]

George Catlett Marshall was one of the leading architects of the colossal American war effort that had consumed cities such as Roanoke. Born in Uniontown, Pennsylvania, in 1880, Marshall attended the Virginia Military Institute and was commissioned in the infantry in 1902. He received the usual assignments for a junior turn-of-the-century American army officer, but from the start he impressed almost everyone with his ability and potential. His performance during maneuvers on Luzon in the Philippines in 1914, for example, convinced fellow lieutenant Henry Arnold, future commander of the Army Air Force, that Marshall was destined to become chief of staff. After the United States entered World War One in April 1917, Marshall sailed to France as a staff officer in the First Infantry Division as part of General John Pershing's American Expeditionary Force. There Marshall came to Pershing's attention during an inspection by boldly and angrily defending his division commander from Pershing's criticisms. Pershing appreciated Marshall's honesty and forthrightness, and in July 1918 he transferred Marshall to the Operations Section at his Chaumont headquarters. Although he yearned for a combat command, Marshall brilliantly executed his new responsibilities. He planned and oversaw the preparations for the St. Mihiel and Argonne operations, which involved moving more than a half million men, 2,700 guns, and 900,000 tons of supplies over a few congested roads and railroads in the space of several weeks. After the war Marshall gained valuable insight into the War Department's workings as Pershing's aide and troubleshooter during Pershing's tenure as chief of staff. Upon Pershing's retirement in 1924, Marshall went to China as executive officer for the Fifteenth Regiment, and then spent five years as assistant commandant of the Infantry School at Fort Benning, Georgia. At Fort Benning he instituted valuable reforms designed to encourage officer initiative, independence, and flexibility. He also had the opportunity there to meet and evaluate innumerable younger officers who later played important roles in World War Two. Marshall's slow but steady rise through the army's hierarchy, however, was interrupted after General Douglas MacArthur became chief of staff in 1930. MacArthur disliked the Pershing clique for slights real and imagined that he had suffered at its hands during and after World War One. He did nothing to secure Marshall's promotion to brigadier general, but instead assigned him to a dead-end job as instructor of the Illinois National Guard. Fortunately for Marshall and his career aspirations, his internal exile ended in 1936 after General Malin Craig succeeded MacArthur as chief of staff. Craig admired Marshall and put his career back on track by getting him his first star and placing him in charge of a brigade. In the summer of 1938, Craig brought Marshall to Washington first as head of the War Plans Division and shortly thereafter as deputy chief of staff.

Chiefs of staff were like generals appointed by the president with the Senate's consent. They generally, though not always, served for four years. Marshall understood that his last opportunity to become chief of staff would occur when Craig's tenure ended in 1939. Despite his accomplishments and ability, his chances of succeeding Craig appeared slim. For one thing, he was still a very junior general in an organization that valued seniority. There were twenty-one major generals and eleven brigadier generals ahead of him on the army register. In addition, the War Department was wracked by a feud between Secretary of War Henry Woodring and Assistant Secretary Louis Johnson that politicized and complicated all issues involving the army and made it difficult to evaluate people strictly on their merits. Finally, Marshall had alienated President Franklin Roosevelt during a White House meeting in late 1938 by flatly and bluntly condemning as impractical the president's plan to build thousands of airplanes. Roosevelt was so angry at Marshall that he refused to speak to him at a reception several days later.

Despite these drawbacks, Marshall had a number of advantages that ultimately persuaded the president to nominate him for the job. He was not as junior in rank as it initially seemed. Recent army tradition limited chiefs of staff to those officers who would be younger than the mandatory retirement age of sixty-four when their terms ended. By that criterion, there were only four eligible officers with more seniority than Marshall, all of whom were major generals: John DeWitt, Hugh Drum, Walter Krueger, and Frank Rowell. Marshall also had plenty of support for his candidacy. Woodring and Johnson, for instance, both backed him despite their hatred for each other, as did Craig. Marshall's most important booster, however, was Harry Hopkins, Roosevelt's closest adviser. Marshall had impressed Hopkins with his competence and bearing, and Marshall later speculated that it was Hopkins's endorsement that put him over the top. Marshall may have angered Roosevelt, but, like Pershing a quarter of a century earlier, the president respected Marshall's willingness to speak up. Moreover, unlike Hugh Drum, Marshall did not actively campaign for the post, but instead conducted himself with a modesty and discretion that indicated that he would perform the chief of staff duties in a low-key nonpartisan fashion. These factors convinced Roosevelt that Marshall was the right person for the post. After a private meeting between the two men in which Marshall warned the president that he would often have to tell him unpleasant things, Roosevelt announced his decision on 27 April 1939. Marshall officially assumed his new post on 1 September, the same day, coincidentally, that World War Two began in Europe.[3]

In postwar interviews and memoirs, many of Marshall's contemporaries lauded him as World War Two's greatest general. For example, Omar Bradley, who himself established an enviable war record, called Marshall "the most impressive man I ever knew, one of the greatest military minds the world has ever produced."[4] As chief of staff, Marshall oversaw the army's dramatic transformation from a small constabulary to the world's most powerful military force in six short years. Honorable, direct, and self-disciplined, Marshall possessed the extraordinary organizational and administrative skills that constructing a modern army required. His incisive mind enabled him to spot the weaknesses in any report or presentation and to ask probing questions that got to the heart of the problem. He dominated meetings and conferences with his obvious integrity, clarity in speech, and forceful manner, and used these talents to reach decisions and get things done. He possessed a keen understanding of the relationship between ends and means and worked hard to overcome the red tape that plagued the army's obdurate bureaucracy. Because he understood that any chief of staff had limited time, stamina, and knowledge, he looked for ways to compensate for these deficiencies. He established a strict routine to conserve energy, which included leaving the office by 6 P.M. and avoiding after-hours shop talk. Indeed, he refused to take his job home with him and accepted phone calls there only from the White House and secretary of war. He and his wife relaxed by riding horseback, canoeing down the Potomac River, and gardening. At the same time, though, he kept in touch with the far-flung war effort through frequent inspection trips and encouraged frank and open communication with his subordinates. Finally, he relied heavily on his staff to relieve him of many of the burdens of his office. He encouraged staffers to disagree with him if they thought he was wrong, delegated as much authority to them as possible, and supported their decisions. Although he was quick to transfer those staffers who failed to measure up to his high expectations, his confidence in them and in the United States' ultimate victory won their loyalty and admiration. Even those who personally disliked Marshall or questioned his grasp of grand strategy acknowledged his abilities as chief of staff.

In fact, Marshall had enemies in part because there was something intimidating and cold-blooded in his manner. On the outside, he was distant, austere, formal, and humorless. He disliked excessive drinking, marital infidelity, immature behavior, and off-color humor. Almost no one addressed him by his first name, and he rarely called anyone by theirs. As chief of staff, Marshall deliberately banished friendship and sentiment from his calculations and cultivated an aura of aloofness. He once explained to his wife that making good decisions required him to keep a clear mind, so he did not have the luxury of emotions such as anger, worry, or frustration. With such a stern persona, it was hardly surprising that many officers making presentations before him found the experience thoroughly nerve-wracking. There was, however, just beneath the surface a gentler and more human side to Marshall that endeared him to others. He was kind and considerate, and possessed a quiet sense of humor. He frequently gave enlisted men rides on his way back to his Fort Myers quarters and once ordered 40,000 cases of beer shipped immediately to soldiers in Iceland when he learned that they had run out. After overseas inspection trips, Marshall personally contacted the wives of the generals he had met to update them on their husbands' circumstances. He also arranged—sometimes most insistently—for generals returning from the front to spend time with their wives. Because Marshall understood that loyalty was a two-way street, he stood by those who did their duty, no matter how unpopular their decisions. Small wonder that Bradley also wrote, "In the army we often scoff at the myth of the indispensable man, for we have always maintained that Arlington Cemetery is filled with indispensable men. General Marshall, however, was an exception, for if ever a man was indispensable in a time of national crisis, he was that man."[5]

Marshall had countless responsibilities as chief of staff, but he believed that his most significant and difficult task was recommending officers for the president to nominate as generals and assigning them to their posts. Although Roosevelt was commander in chief of the American military and ultimately responsible for its personnel, he rarely interfered with Marshall's decisions once the United States entered the war. There was a lot at stake because an army is no better than its leadership, so poor generals, or poorly placed ones, could cost the country the war. Marshall understood this as well as anyone. Discussing the army's generals with a group of governors, Marshall said, "*The man has to have it or he doesn't stay*. And we listen to no excuses of any kind. . . . We must have the very best leadership we can possibly give these men and we've stopped at nothing to produce that leadership."[6] No doubt because he considered the issue so important, Marshall was intrigued with the letter from Lillian Craig's class. In fact, he not only responded to it, but he also did so in a manner that demonstrated that he had put considerable thought into the matter.[7]

Marshall was a product of late-Victorian, small-town America, so it is hardly surprising that he valued character more than anything else in his generals. To Marshall, character was fate, something that indicated a man's potential and capabilities. As he explained in his 15 March 1944 response to Lillian Craig's students: "The most important factor of all is character, which involves integrity, unselfish and devoted purpose, a sturdiness of bearing when everything goes wrong and all are critical, and a willingness to sacrifice self in the interest of the common good."[8] Conversely, Marshall hated cant, grandstanding, indecisiveness, pessimism, a refusal to accept responsibility, and deliberate discourtesy. Whatever prejudices Marshall may have harbored in his subconscious, he was convinced that a man's character trumped all else in determining his destiny. Throughout his career, Marshall carefully evaluated the character of promising young officers he encountered at postings such as Fort Benning. Although he may have had difficulty remembering names—he often referred to people by some distinguishing characteristic, such as "Red Eyes"—Marshall rarely forgot a brilliant or dismal performance, and he made it his business to keep track of and cultivate those officers he believed could someday serve the army and their country well in wartime. To be sure, Marshall occasionally promoted and appointed people whose character he doubted, but he did so reluctantly, and it went against his grain. As Dwight Eisenhower later noted,

"But when he made exceptions it was clear that General Marshall always maintained a positive, and permanent, mental reservation [about the person]."[9]

Despite all his years in the small prewar army, it was impossible for Marshall to personally meet and evaluate every officer eligible for the highest ranks and positions. This became even truer after thousands of National Guard and reserve officers flooded into the mobilized army. Consequently, as Marshall admitted to Lillian Craig's students, he had to depend increasingly upon the recommendations of others. Initially his mainstays were his three chief lieutenants: General Henry Arnold of the Army Air Force, General Brehon Somervell of Army Service Forces, and especially General Lesley McNair of Army Ground Forces. Once the army began deploying overseas, however, Marshall more and more relied upon the suggestions of the various American theater commanders. Marshall firmly believed that theater commanders should have men of their own choosing, so he was reluctant to force personnel upon them. Dwight Eisenhower, for instance, later quoted Marshall as saying, "You do not need to take or keep any commander in whom you do not have full confidence. So long as he holds a command in your theater it is evidence to me of your satisfaction with him. The lives of too many are at stake; I will not have you operating under any misunderstanding as to your authority, and your duty, to reject or remove any that fails to satisfy you completely."[10] Therefore, as the war progressed many high-ranking combat assignments resulted not from Marshall's fiat, but rather from discussions between the chief of staff and his theater commanders. Although the extent of the negotiations varied according to the theater's importance and Marshall's relationship with its commander, there was an unmistakable give-and-take to the process. Marshall consequently usually applied a surprisingly light touch on personnel matters, considering his strong opinions on the subject. If he often seemed reactive in the selection process, it was because he had confidence in those officers who made their recommendations to him.

Whatever Marshall's commitment to character, he was not about to rely upon it entirely when there was so much at stake. Although he did not mention it to Lillian Craig's students, Marshall applied other criteria as well in selecting his generals and making his appointments. One of the most significant was education. The army had developed a full-fledged educational system during the turn-of-the-century Progressive era, and by World War Two schooling had become an integral and necessary part of an ambitious officer's career. The most promising officers attended the Command and General Staff School at Fort Leavenworth in Kansas and the Army War College at Washington Barracks in the nation's capital. The former trained mid-level officers to serve as division and corps staffers, while the latter taught majors and colonels to command large units. Both schools were open to National Guard officers, but these part-time soldiers rarely had the time to take advantage of the opportunity, so the vast majority of the graduates were Regular Army. Although some have criticized these schools for inculcating conformity and failing to accommodate new technology, they were important for several reasons. For one thing, the schools provided officers with a common playbook with which to ply their trade. Officers learned to speak the same professional language, follow identical procedures, and operate according to common doctrine. This ensured greater coordination and simplified communications during the war. In addition, the schools introduced the army's elite officers to each other. As one such officer later explained:

> These personal relationships that are established at West Point, and in the Army schools to which a career officer is sent thereafter, are a vital factor in the cohesiveness, the team spirit of the professional Army. A career officer is going to school as long as he lives, and in the close associations of the barracks and the classroom, he unconsciously makes his estimates of the character, the integrity, and the competence of his fellows. And they make their estimates of him. In time of battle, therefore, top commanders know the characteristics of their immediate subordinates. They know which ones are by nature bold and reckless, and must be restrained a little, which ones are by temperament cautious, and must be prodded. They are aware of the traits of their opposite numbers, commanding other corps and divisions in the line, and can anticipate how their units will fight.[11]

These relationships invariably contributed to recommendations officers made to Marshall on assignments because people usually want to work with or for those with whom they are familiar and in whom they have confidence. Finally, the educational system screened the officer corps by filtering out the inefficient, degenerate, lazy, and stupid, leaving behind in theory only the best and brightest. Generally speaking, it was extremely difficult for officers to rise to the highest combat commands in World War Two unless they had attended and done well at the Command and General Staff School and the Army War College because Marshall and others customarily checked their educational records as part of the evaluation process.[12]

Finally, Marshall looked at an officer's age when making promotions and assignments, especially for combat commands. Marshall's World War One experiences convinced him that leading soldiers in combat was a job for younger men because they had the necessary energy, stamina, and vigor. When he became chief of staff, Marshall was dismayed that elderly officers past their prime led so many field armies, corps, and divisions. To rectify this, in 1940 a new War Department policy limited the maximum age of officers serving with troops to sixty-two for major generals and sixty for brigadier generals. Marshall applied this new rule in a tenacious and cold-blooded campaign to supplant overage officers with younger men in their fifties and even forties. Although these efforts often aroused the resentment of those displaced, Marshall usually tried to be as considerate of their feelings as possible. He explained to one relieved corps commander:

> We have had to be absolutely firm on the question of age for command. Not only that, but we must go much lower in the age groups for division and corps commanders than we are now doing. Every bit of data we receive from the fighting fronts clearly shows that this is a young man's war except in rare instances and then only in the highest command. . . . I hope you will not be too much disappointed and that you will feel certain that there is nothing of reflection on you in this affair other than your birthday.[13]

There was nevertheless no mistaking his intent; on one occasion he bluntly told a group of officers, "All four of you are too old to command divisions in combat."[14] Despite his efforts, a frustrated Marshall often complained that he was not getting sufficient support from the War Department in removing some of the army's deadwood. Even so, he persevered, though on occasion he was willing to compromise if a theater commander insisted on obtaining the services of an older general. For Marshall, however, youthfulness remained an important prerequisite in promotions and appointments to high combat commands.[15]

While character, education, and age were Marshall's key criteria, he ignored several issues that had in the past sometimes played important roles in determining promotions and assignments in the army. He displayed little interest in an officer's family background, service branch, political connections, or membership in any of the army's innumerable cliques. Nor did he care much about ethnicity or creed, though the army's institutionalized racism and regimentation had largely homogenized the officer corps in those respects for him. Significantly, he did not consider a lack of World War One combat experience a disqualifying factor for high combat command. Some of the army's greatest World War Two generals, such as Dwight Eisenhower and Omar Bradley, never heard a shot fired in anger before the conflict. Once the United States entered the war, Marshall gave mental points to high-ranking officers who had already led men against the Germans and Japanese, but he remained reluctant to penalize those who had done well in stateside training assignments by denying them the chance to prove themselves in action. Lastly, although Marshall placed great emphasis on an officer's character, he did not mind eccentric personalities. Indeed, he had a soft spot for some of the army's talented unconventional-thinking oddballs such as George Patton.[16]

Generally speaking, Marshall sought certain kinds of officers as his senior combat commanders. Almost all were Regular Army men with good records at either the Command and General Staff School or the Army War College, preferably both. They were usually in their forties and fifties and had somewhere along the line attracted the attention of Marshall or some other high-ranking officer who had Marshall's ear and wanted their services. Although Marshall was a big believer in character, as the conflict progressed he increasingly redefined character as those traits generals needed to wage war successfully. He wanted his combat commanders to possess cool professional detachment, energy, resilience, concern for their men, and drive. Five days after he dictated his letter to Lillian Craig's class, he elaborated to Eisenhower, "I wasn't so much interested in . . . [generals'] tactical skills as I was in having sturdy, aggressive fighters who would stand up during moments of adversity."[17] Fortunately, even the most dysfunctional, inbred, and backward organizations have the kind of men Marshal wanted. Marshall's challenge was to identify these officers, place them into responsible positions, and help them fulfill their various missions.[18]

Although the army had to compete with the navy, industry, and agriculture for the country's finite manpower pool during World War Two, its growth was still impressive. The Regular Army contained only 175,000 men when Germany invaded Poland in 1939, and its responsibilities were limited mostly to protecting the Western Hemisphere and the Philippines. Conscription and the mobilization of the National Guard and reserves increased its strength to 1.6 million soldiers organized into thirty-seven combat divisions by the time the Japanese attacked Pearl Harbor, but this was only a harbinger of things to come. The army ultimately expanded into a huge force of 10.4 million troops. By comparison, the army had only 3.7 million men at its World War One peak. Of these more than 10 million soldiers, Brehon Somervell's Army Service Forces employed 3 million of them, and Henry Arnold's Army Air Force skimmed off another 2.3 million for its operations. This still left approximately 5.3 million men for Lesley McNair's Army Ground Forces to bear the brunt of the actual fighting, out of which he created eighty-nine 15,000-man combat divisions. In the end, the army deployed about 3 million soldiers to Europe and another 1.36 million troops to the Pacific. Unfortunately, the army's losses, while nowhere near as heavy as those sustained by Germany or Japan or the Soviet Union, were still substantial. The army suffered 936,000 battle casualties during the war, of whom 235,000 died. Another 83,400 soldiers succumbed to accidents, illness, and various other misfortunes.

The army's enormous size during the war required the creation of units rarely seen in its history. Allied leaders divided the globe into theaters of war whose commanders oversaw millions of men from many different countries. Marshall and McNair also organized their eighty-nine divisions into corps, their corps into field armies, and their field armies into gargantuan army groups. An army group contained two or more field armies, sometimes of different nationalities, and during World War Two its size could exceed a million men. Theoretically, army groups had few administrative and logistical responsibilities, so their commanders could concentrate on conducting large-scale operations determined at the theater level, but the degree of bureaucratic overhead usually depended more upon the personality of its commander than organizational doctrine. Army group commanders were supposed to assign their field armies specific combat and administrative tasks, but leave it up to their subordinates to plan and execute their missions. In reality, however, some army group commanders were more hands-on than others. Although the Americans and British deployed five army groups in Europe, there were none in the Pacific because the theater commanders there did not see a need for them.

Field armies, for their part, consisted of two or more corps led by a full or lieutenant general. Unlike army groups, field armies were self-contained units with substantial administrative, logistical, and even territorial responsibilities. Their commanders designed and implemented army group directives by giving broad orders to their constituent corps. As with army groups, field armies tended to reflect the personalities and proclivities of their commanders. Some shunted their administrative responsibilities off on their chief of staff so they could focus on overseeing combat operations, whereas others had a more holistic view of their duties. During World War Two, the army deployed eight field armies overseas that saw significant action—three in the Pacific and five in Europe.

Army groups and field armies were important, but perhaps the large unit most overlooked by historians is the corps. A World War Two corps was a flexible entity containing two or more divisions. It consisted of little more than a headquarters to which army group or field army commanders assigned various divisions depending upon its mission. The army deployed twenty of them overseas that saw combat during the conflict. Theoretically, their commanders had few administrative responsibilities, so they could concentrate exclusively on combat operations. As one corps commander, Matthew Ridgway, later explained:

> The function of the corps in the chain of command has never been properly appreciated. The public knows of armies, and of divisions, but the intermediate headquarters, the corps, is generally less fully understood. The fact is the corps commander is the highest commander in the military hierarchy who is solely a battle leader, a tactical commander. The division commander has a great logistical responsibility; the army commander is primarily concerned with logistics and territorial matters. But the corps commander is almost exclusively concerned with battle tactics. He is

responsible for a large sector of a battle area, and all he must worry about in that zone is fighting. He must be a man of great flexibility of mind, for he may be fighting [with] six divisions one day and one division the next as the higher commanders transfer divisions to and from his corps. He must be a man of tremendous physical stamina, too, for his battle zone may cover a front of one hundred miles or more, with a depth of fifty to sixty miles, and by plane and jeep he must cover this area, day and night, anticipating where the hardest fighting is to come, and being there in person, ready to help his division commanders in any way he can.[19]

As Ridgway implied, history has with a few exceptions all but forgotten not only the war's corps commanders, but most of the field army and even army group commanders as well.[20] Nevertheless, these men played a vital role in winning the conflict. Like any other military unit, army groups, field armies, and corps were no better than their leaders who imprinted their personalities on their subordinates, staffers, and rank-and-file. As Eisenhower put it:

I have developed almost an obsession as to the certainty with which you can judge a division, or any other large unit, merely by knowing its commander intimately. Of course, we have had pounded into us all throughout school courses that the exact level of a commander's personality and ability is always reflected in his unit—but I did not realize, until opportunity came for comparisons on a rather large scale, how infallibly the commander and unit are almost one and the same thing.[21]

Therefore, the quality of a unit, even a big one, was usually directly proportional to the quality of its leader. Army group, field army, and corps commanders were also relevant because they planned and implemented many of the war's large-scale operations based on the objectives developed at higher levels. Finally, these commanders provided a pool from which Marshall could draw men for other, even more important, assignments. Several of the army's highest-ranking World War Two generals cut their teeth at the head of corps or field armies before Marshall gave them greater responsibilities.

The quality of high-ranking American combat commanders tells a lot about the army's performance in World War Two. On the whole these officers fought well and contributed significantly to American victory over both Germany and Japan. Although only a few were truly brilliant, most were competent and capable men who used the resources at their disposal to prosecute the war in a cost-effective manner. Only thirty-eight officers commanded the army groups, field armies, and corps in combat, of whom seventeen led their units from their deployment overseas until the end of hostilities. Most of those replaced were relieved because of illness or promotion, not failure on the battlefield. Such a low turnover rate indicates Marshall's satisfaction with these men. Moreover, the leaders of the various American theaters, army groups, and field armies almost always praised their subordinate commanders individually and collectively in their wartime reports and postwar reminiscences. Finally, the very fact that the army triumphed over the Germans and Japanese serves as confirmation of the value of its large-unit commanders. Some argue that American wartime success was due primarily to allies and overwhelming numerical and materiel superiority, but this is a long way from the complete story.[22] In fact, the United States' resources were finite, and its allies were themselves able to remain in the war only due to extensive American assistance. There were instead other factors in play, one of which was high-level leadership. Had army group, field army, and corps commanders been incompetent, it is hard to see how the United States could have helped to defeat the Axis. To be sure, these men sometimes committed errors and missed opportunities, but this should not detract from their wartime achievements.

1

Stopping the Japanese Offensive

An Unexpectedly Large Commitment to an Unexpectedly Large War

For the United States, World War Two was really two conflicts waged simultaneously, one in Europe and North Africa against Germany and Italy, and the other in the Pacific Ocean and East Asia against Japan. Such a war required the dispersal of American resources and the careful allocation of priorities. To their credit, American policymakers had foreseen this possibility. Even before the Japanese attack on Pearl Harbor they had decided to give precedence to destroying Adolf Hitler's Nazi regime because they concluded that Germany's economic, technological, and scientific capabilities posed the greater threat to the United States and its presumptive allies. War with Japan, if and when it came to that, would be a secondary concern addressed only after Germany had been defeated. And, in the grand scheme of things, this was more or less how it worked out. Most American military assets flowed across the Atlantic for use against Germany, which surrendered five months before Japan. The details governing the relationship between the two wars, however, were far more complicated and messy than they initially appeared. In fact, the Pacific War consumed greater resources than expected and developed in ways unanticipated by American military planners for several interrelated reasons.

The Pacific War's enormous geographic expanse provided one of these reasons. The Pacific Ocean covers approximately 64 million square miles, making it roughly half again as big as its Atlantic counterpart and more than twenty times larger than the contiguous United States. Although prewar American naval strategists expected to battle Japan roughly along the central Pacific axis from the Philippines to Hawaii, Japan's initial multipronged offensive extended the zone of conflict far beyond that. As a result, the Pacific War was fought not only on and between the tiny and barren central Pacific atolls, but also in geographically and topographically diverse places such as the frozen and foggy Aleutians, the jungle-ridden islands of the Southwest Pacific, Manila's urban environment, and the volcanic ash of Iwo Jima. The United States also committed significant resources, though few combat troops, to the Asian mainland in China, Burma, and India. The distances involved were staggering. It was 2,100 miles from San Francisco to Pearl Harbor, and from there an additional 3,400 miles to Tokyo, 4,770 miles to Manila, and 4,200 miles to Brisbane, Australia. By contrast, it was only 3,100 miles from New York City to London. New Guinea alone, the biggest of the thousands of islands dotting the Pacific, would if superimposed over the United States stretch from the North Carolina sounds to western Nebraska. Manning and supplying such a vast battlefield involving several fronts necessitated a greater commitment of American military resources than anyone predicted.

Logistics also forced the Americans to assign additional resources to the Pacific War. Not only were the distances involved huge, but the infrastructure in most places ranged from primitive to nonexistent. There were simply not enough airfields, port facilities, warehouses, power plants, paved roads, and so on that the motorized American military required to function properly. To support their activities, the army and navy brought in large numbers of service personnel to construct and maintain the necessary facilities, but they could never quite keep up with the logistical demands placed on them. At one point in early 1944, for example, more than 140 ships of all kinds crowded Milne Bay harbor in New Guinea waiting to be unloaded. Moving and caring for all these men, their supplies, and their equipment strained limited shipping resources that local commanders wanted to use to sustain their combat operations, and the problem only got worse as the Americans advanced across the Pacific toward Japan and stretched their supply lines even further.

Australia and New Zealand were two of the United States' most important Pacific War allies. Australian troops in particular played a crucial role in stopping the Japanese offensive in the Southwest Pacific and bore the brunt of the fighting there until 1944. The two nations also provided significant logistical support for local American forces. Although both countries contributed to Japan's defeat in vital ways, their participation complicated American military planning. Securing Australia's and New Zealand's communications and supply lines to the United States entailed a far greater resource commitment than American military strategists ever anticipated. Indeed, doing so initially required more men and material than the European War, which theoretically had top priority. The first ad hoc American counterattacks against Japan in the Solomon Islands and New Guinea were designed as much to safeguard Australia and New Zealand as anything else. Even after the Japanese threat there had receded, American personnel continued to stream into the region as further operations there developed a momentum of their own.

Competing interservice priorities also accounted for the Pacific War's unexpected prominence. The Pacific Ocean's peculiar geography—vast stretches of water sprinkled by thousands of islands of varying sizes—required close army and navy cooperation. The American military, though, was not a unitary actor. Instead, the army and navy were separate and independent branches constitutionally answerable only to the president as commander in chief. Fortunately, the Joint Chiefs of Staff (JCS) provided a coordinating mechanism for the two services. Created early in the war at Marshall's urging, the Joint Chiefs consisted of Marshall, Army Air Force chief General Henry Arnold, chief of naval operations Admiral Ernest King, and William Leahy, a retired naval officer and former chief of naval operations who chaired the JCS meetings and liaised with the president. The JCS made decisions by consensus, which under normal circumstances might have resulted— and sometimes in fact did result—in gridlock and irresolution. The Joint Chiefs, however, had a powerful incentive to settle disputes among themselves. If they were unable to agree, their only recourse was to appeal to the president, but none of them wanted to abdicate their strategic responsibilities to the unpredictable Roosevelt, who on several occasions showed a positive genius for disrupting American grand strategy. As a result, many strategic judgments flowed from complicated compromises that worked to the advantage of those favoring a greater commitment to the Pacific War—meaning especially Ernest King. While Marshall was steadfast in his support for crushing Germany first, King was less so. King and many of his navy colleagues saw the Pacific War as *their* war. After all, they had planned for it for generations, and the Pacific's wide oceanic expanses were ideal for the deployment of the navy's fleets. Besides, naval officers were eager to exact retribution for the damage the Japanese had inflicted on their pride and ships at Pearl Harbor. King's problem was that although he had the marines at his disposal for amphibious operations, it was soon apparent that the navy still needed the army's help to prosecute the war against Japan effectively. King constantly pressured Marshall to divert more resources to the Pacific War. Marshall was willing to go along with King up to a point, first to stop the initial Japanese offensive and then to maintain the strategic initiative that American and Australian forces had so painfully seized. In return, King loyally supported Marshall in his strategic disputes with the British over the conduct of the European War.

These interservice rivalries manifested themselves in the conduct of the Pacific War as well. Army and navy officers often disagreed on the best strategic path to the Japanese homeland. Most naval officers, as well as a good many of their Army Air Force colleagues, advocated advancing on Japan via the central Pacific route from Hawaii. Doing so would give the navy plenty of space to maneuver its warships for the climactic battle that it sought with its Japanese counterpart. It would also provide the Army Air Force with the bases it needed for its long-range bombers to pound Japanese cities and employ the marines in their specialized role as amphibious shock troops against the small Japanese-held atolls in the area.

PACIFIC OCEAN AREAS

Many army officers, on the other hand, backed the Southwest Pacific route from Australia. They argued that this approach would allow them to use Australia's resources and manpower, afford them enough room to deploy their troops in the area's big islands, sever Japan's supply lines with the oil-rich Dutch East Indies, and reclaim American honor by liberating the Philippines. Both routes had merit, but the real issue was whether the army or navy would be in overall command of the Pacific War. As one general later put it, "I felt that the discussion really wasn't basically concerned about the best way to [win the war]. It was who was going to do it, and who was going to be in command, and who was going to be involved."[1] The JCS was unable to conclusively settle the issue, so it instead compromised by dividing the Pacific War into two theaters, the Pacific Ocean Area (POA) under Admiral Chester Nimitz and the Southwest Pacific Area (SWPA) under General Douglas MacArthur, and authorizing each officer to conduct offensive operations. Although this resulting Dual Drive Offensive violated the American military's emphasis on concentration of force, the JCS was willing to pay this price to preserve interservice harmony. Sanctioning the Dual Drive Offensive, however, required a corresponding increase in the amount of men, supplies, and equipment allotted to the Pacific War to sustain operations in both theaters.

Finally, the Japanese themselves compelled a larger-than-expected American investment in the Pacific War. Although the United States dwarfed Japan in economic productivity, racism and strategic myopia prevented American policymakers from recognizing Japan's early military capabilities. Japan's initial multipronged offensive netted it a quarter of the globe in six short months, and stopping it initially required American military planners to assign more men, supplies, and equipment to the Pacific than to Europe, where there was less immediate urgency for them. Once there, it was logistically and bureaucratically impossible to transfer all those assets across the Atlantic. Moreover, waging war against the Japanese proved more difficult than anticipated. As part of their Bushido code, Japanese servicemen saw surrender as dishonorable and often fought to the death. Prying them out of their well-defended positions entailed the overwhelming application of American firepower. Mustering and supporting such firepower, however, meant a massive commitment in manpower and materiel. Even worse, the Japanese battled with increasing ferocity as the American juggernaut approached their Home Islands, necessitating even more American resources.

For all these reasons, the American investment in the war with Japan was considerable. Indeed, because of the navy's fixation with the conflict, nearly half of all American servicemen deployed overseas during World War Two went to the Pacific. The army did a better job of living up to the Germany First policy, but even it diverted substantial resources across the Pacific. By the time Germany surrendered in the spring of 1945, there were 1.36 million soldiers and airmen in the Pacific, about half as many as there were across the Atlantic.[2] In terms of combat units, the army deployed twenty-one of its eighty-nine divisions, five of its twenty corps, and three of its eight field armies that saw significant action against Japan. Unlike in Europe, there were no army groups in the Pacific, mostly because Douglas MacArthur acted as his own army group commander.

Most of the combat units the army sent to the Pacific—fifteen of the divisions, four of the corps, and two of the field armies—spent the bulk of their time in action in MacArthur's SWPA theater. Marshall permitted MacArthur considerable leeway in selecting his field army and corps commanders. Whenever Marshall dispatched a new field army or corps headquarters to SWPA, he usually gave MacArthur a list of possible commanders to choose from, and almost always mentioned his favorite based on his criteria. MacArthur might or might not accept Marshall's suggestions, but he rarely asked for an officer by name from the States, perhaps because after retiring from the army in 1937 he simply no longer knew the eligible and available high-ranking personnel. Instead, MacArthur usually preferred to promote from within SWPA because he was more familiar and comfortable with those officers who had served with him there. He and General Walter Krueger, head of the Sixth Army and MacArthur's chief ground forces commander, picked their corps commanders from those divisional leaders who had proven themselves as skillful and aggressive officers in independent offensive missions. In the rest of the Pacific, on the other hand, Marshall generally appointed the field army and corps commanders after consultations with General Millard Harmon and General Robert Richardson, the army's highest-ranking officers in the central and southern Pacific.[3]

History has all but forgotten the Pacific War's field army and corps commanders, in large part because of the long shadow that MacArthur cast over everyone and everything associated with the conflict in that part of the globe. At first glance the caliber of these men seems lower than that of their European War counterparts. Although many have heralded MacArthur as a strategic and operational genius, most of his army subordinates demonstrated little imagination at the tactical level. They frequently resorted to set-piece assaults that relied on massive firepower to overcome Japanese defenses. It is, however, important to place their collective record in context. In his mania for self-promotion, MacArthur intentionally denied his generals the kind of publicity that other theater commanders accorded their subordinates. As a result, the press rarely noticed even exceptional performances by most Pacific War generals. Moreover, American field army and corps commanders usually did not have the opportunity to engage in the kind of swift and sweeping flanking and exploitation maneuvers that sometimes characterized the European War because of the Pacific Ocean's geographic, climactic, and logistical constraints. Pacific War generals may have been conventional and solid rather than dazzling and slashing, but they got the job done despite tenuous logistics, dissension within MacArthur's military family and with the navy and marines, and stiff Japanese resistance. None was relieved due to incompetence, and one of the corps commanders went on to lead a field army before the war ended. While it is possible to criticize individual actions, these men never lost a major battle on their amphibious march to Japan.

Douglas MacArthur's World

On the evening of 21 March 1942, a curious crowd in Adelaide, Australia, turned out to meet a train carrying the United States' most famous general. Douglas MacArthur's unlikely presence Down Under resulted from a series of unhappy and unforeseen occurrences. Just ten days previously he, his wife and young son and amah, and selected staff officers had on President Roosevelt's orders slipped away from the besieged island fortress of Corregidor in Manila Bay on a PT boat. After a harrowing 500-mile journey through enemy-infested waters to the southern Philippines island of Mindanao, they boarded a ramshackle B-17 Flying Fortress bomber for a dangerous flight to Alice Springs in remote central Australia. From there they took a train to Melbourne via Adelaide. Along the way MacArthur learned that the American reinforcements he had expected in Australia were not there. Without them, there was no way he could rescue the beleaguered soldiers he had left behind—or, as some claimed, abandoned—in the Philippines. Exhausted by the strain of his long and dangerous journey, and burdened by his growing realization that he had played a major role in what was shaping up to be one of the biggest military defeats in American military history, MacArthur was depressed and discouraged by the time his train pulled into the Adelaide station. He was, however, not the type to flinch in the face of adversity. After greeting the assembled onlookers, MacArthur pulled a rumpled sheet of paper out and in a subdued, flat, and quiet voice read one of World War Two's most famous speeches, in which he concluded, "The President of the United States ordered me to break through the Japanese lines and proceed from Corregidor to Australia for the purpose, as I understand it, of organizing the American offensive against Japan, a primary object of which is the relief of the Philippines. I came through, and I shall return."[4]

For all of MacArthur's grim determination, the fact remained that the United States had suffered one military disaster after another in the first months of the Pacific War. Japan's unexpected attack on the naval base at Pearl Harbor on the morning of 7 December 1941 crippled the American fleet there and temporarily removed it from the strategic chessboard. By the end of the year, the Japanese had also stormed Guam and Wake islands, isolating the Philippines from Hawaii and the American mainland. Roosevelt had recalled MacArthur to duty the previous July to command all the American and Filipino troops in the Philippines. MacArthur's claims that he could successfully defend the archipelago helped persuade Marshall to send reinforcements there before war broke out, but things had not turned out as MacArthur planned. Hours after the Japanese raided Pearl Harbor, they also surprised MacArthur's air force and destroyed most of its planes on the ground. On 22 December, Japanese soldiers landed at Lingayen Bay on Luzon and rapidly drove MacArthur's ill-trained and -equipped American and Filipino soldiers out of Manila and into the nearby Bataan Peninsula. Although MacArthur's men fought valiantly, the 76,000 troops on Bataan surrendered on 9 April 1942, followed by the capitulation of Corregidor and the rest of the Philippines on 6 May. These American defeats were bad enough, but they were just one part of an unhappy Allied tapestry. The Japanese also seized the oil-rich Dutch East Indies, Hong Kong, Burma, Malaya, and, perhaps worst of all, Singapore and its 65,000 British Empire defenders. Through skillful fighting and with minimal losses, the Japanese controlled one quarter of the globe by the end of May 1942.

Nine days after MacArthur made his celebrated speech, the Joint Chiefs of Staff put him in charge of the newly created Southwest Pacific Area theater. In doing so, the JCS gave MacArthur the opportunity to fulfill his pledge—and to cause them no end of strategic trouble in the process. Indeed, Douglas MacArthur was one of the most baffling men to ever wear an American military uniform. He was born on an army post in Little Rock, Arkansas, in 1880, the son of Arthur MacArthur, a Union Civil War hero and veteran of the Philippines Insurrection. After graduating first from his West Point class of 1903, he served in the Philippines, as an aide to his father and then to President Theodore Roosevelt, and on the General Staff. He participated in the American occupation of Veracruz, Mexico, in 1914, and later went to France as chief of staff for the Forty-second "Rainbow" Division during World War One. MacArthur fought gallantly in the trenches, was gassed twice, and was awarded seven Silver Stars. After the conflict he became superintendent of West Point, where he modernized the place and instituted important reforms. He later oversaw the Philippines Department before President Herbert Hoover appointed him chief of staff in 1930. He played a controversial and important role in dispersing the Bonus Army in 1932 and later clashed repeatedly with Roosevelt over the army's budget. He retired in 1937 to take a lucrative job preparing the Filipino army for independence. Despite insufficient funds, dialect problems, and President Manuel Quezon's growing hostility, MacArthur constantly insisted that he was making substantial progress. Unfortunately, Japan's startlingly successful invasion showed that these claims were at best exaggerated and at worst deceptive.

Despite his inaccurate assertions about the Philippines' defenses, there was in fact much to admire about MacArthur. He impressed people with his forceful personality, winning charisma, and physical courage. Erudite and possessing a phenomenal memory, he could expound intelligently on a wide variety of topics ranging from East Asian philosophy to atomic warfare. One observer noted, "There's nobody in our age who had more stuff stored away up here that he could use from the English language to football statistics; information would come out of that head like an encyclopedia. He just had the cerebrum to go with the personality and the physical appearance."[5] Moreover, he combined his intellectual prowess with formidable persuasive powers that charmed even those predisposed to dislike him and his ideas. Pacing his office as he made his points, he often seemed to speak beyond his immediate audience, as if trying to rally future generations to his posthumous banner. As a strategist, MacArthur rarely took counsel of his fears in the ruthless execution of his plans. He once admitted that he did not know much about the minutiae of soldiering—he attended neither the Command and General Staff School nor the Army War College—so he gave his subordinates considerable leeway in implementing his directives. At the same time, though, he was always impatient for success and intolerant of failure. These traits, combined with the natural leadership skills of a gentleman aristocrat and an absolute certainty in whatever cause he advocated, inspired intense loyalty from many of those drawn into his orbit.

This was all well and good, but there was also a dark side to MacArthur that undermined his effectiveness as a general. His total commitment to his causes often degenerated into self-righteousness, pomposity, self-deception, and egomania. To achieve his goals, which he all too often confused with his country's, MacArthur sometimes lied and manipulated those around him. He did so by transforming conversations into long-winded monologues that gave listeners no opportunity to express their views, ask questions, or raise important issues. MacArthur was more than willing to pull strings to get what he wanted, but his clumsy and amateurish forays into domestic politics backfired on him more than once. In his mania for publicity and the limelight, he often denied his subordinates the credit they deserved, leading to hurt feelings. Although quick to reciprocate loyalty, he was very reluctant to remove or replace the incompetent sycophants who clustered around him. Finally, he cared little about enemy intentions and capabilities, resulting in a strategic recklessness that contributed to some of his greatest military defeats. Lieutenant Colonel Gerald Wilkinson, Britain's liaison officer to SWPA, probably described MacArthur best: "He is shrewd, proud, remote, highly strung and vastly vain. He has imagination, self-confidence, physical courage and charm, but no humor about himself, no regard to truth, and is unaware of these defects. He mistakes his emotions and ambitions for principles. With moral depth he would be a great man; as it is he is a near miss which may be worse than a mile."[6]

Although personnel from all the relevant allied nations were supposed to staff theater commands, MacArthur gave the Dutch and Australians little say in his SWPA General Headquarters (GHQ). Instead, he built GHQ around those officers who escaped with him from the Philippines, the so-called Bataan Gang. The most important of these men was his chief of staff, Major General Richard Sutherland. Born in Maryland in 1893, the son of a future West Virginia senator, Sutherland graduated from Yale in 1916 before accepting an army commission. He fought in France in World War One and opted to remain in the army after the conflict ended. After occupation duty, he taught at the Infantry School at Fort Benning and then at the Shattuck Military Academy in Minnesota. He attended the Command and General Staff School from 1927 to 1928, the French École Su-perieure de Guerre in 1930, and the Army War College from 1932 to 1933 before working on the General Staff during MacArthur's tenure there as army chief of staff. He and MacArthur were reunited when Sutherland was sent to the Philippines in 1938, and the following year he succeeded Dwight Eisenhower as MacArthur's chief of staff.

Brusque, smart, and seemingly emotionless, Sutherland was MacArthur's efficient hatchet man, who was capable of dressing down or relieving a subordinate without sympathy or explanation. Not surprisingly, Sutherland made his share of enemies. Detractors claimed he was mean-spirited, untrustworthy, and cold-hearted. Well aware of the enmity he generated, Sutherland resigned himself to it, saying, "Somebody around here has got to be the SOB. General MacArthur is not going to be . . . so I guess I'm it."[7] In fact, Sutherland was no martinet, but rather like Marshall he recognized that he could not permit sentimentality or feelings to cloud his thinking. Unlike Marshall, however, Sutherland was a brittle man without the chief of staff's generosity and humanity. While he and MacArthur were not personally close and did not socialize, Sutherland served MacArthur well as a sounding board because he gave honest and informed feedback. He ran the GHQ staff ably enough, enabling MacArthur to focus on the big strategic picture, and he did a good job translating MacArthur's broad ideas into implementable directives. Sutherland seemed the epitome of self-control, but the stress of his job took a toll on his health. During the war he suffered from stress-induced teeth grinding and high blood pressure, which may have affected his judgment. General George Kenney, SWPA's air force commander, later wrote:

> While a brilliant, hard-working officer, Sutherland had always rubbed people the wrong way. He was egotistic, like most people, but an unfortunate bit of arrogance combined with egotism had made him almost universally disliked.

However, he was smart, capable of a lot of work, and from my contacts with him I had found that he knew so many of the answers that I could understand why General MacArthur had picked him for his chief of staff.[8]

As with Sutherland, MacArthur's relationship with Marshall was more professional than friendly. MacArthur had never thought much of Marshall, probably because Marshall was a Pershing man. Pershing had after World War One squashed MacArthur's efforts to secure a Medal of Honor, and MacArthur's resulting enmity was broad enough to encompass those such as Marshall within Pershing's circle. Indeed, Robert Eichelberger claimed that MacArthur once told him, "George Catlett Marshall is the most overrated officer in the United States Army. He'll never be a general officer as long as I am Chief of Staff."[9] That had been true enough, but the army continued to churn out promotions after MacArthur's tenure ended. Now, in a twist of fate, the man MacArthur once denigrated was his superior, with substantial power over his future. MacArthur may or may not have fully grasped the concept of the chain of command, but he knew Marshall well enough to understand that he had to treat him respectfully if he wanted to attain the authorization and resources necessary for him to return to the Philippines and redeem his pledge to liberate the archipelago. Although he did not always heed Marshall's advice, MacArthur was during the conflict invariably civil toward him and rarely denigrated him behind his back.

As for Marshall, he realized from the war's start that managing MacArthur would be a challenge. He disliked MacArthur's penchant for publicity, his refusal to give his subordinates adequate recognition, his oft-repeated suspicions that the navy and other shadowy forces were conspiring against him, and his meddling in politics. Nor did Marshall think much of Sutherland. Marshall strongly suspected that Sutherland fed MacArthur's paranoia by withholding important information from him. Marshall, however, not only respected MacArthur's intellect, but also recognized that MacArthur's status in the army, popularity, and national prominence made it unlikely that Roosevelt would remove him from his command. As a result, Marshall was determined to set aside personal feelings for the common good. He worked hard to placate MacArthur and prevent any misunderstandings between them. He carefully perused all messages his staffers sent to MacArthur and presented many of his notions as suggestions rather than orders. He also defended MacArthur from his detractors. For example, during one JCS meeting he cut off Ernest King's anti MacArthur tirade by thumping the table and exclaiming, "I will not have the meetings of the Joint Chiefs of Staff dominated by a policy of hatred. I will not have any meetings carried on with hatred."[10] Besides, Marshall sympathized with MacArthur's difficult circumstances, agreed with many of his strategic ideas, and regretted that he could not provide him with

NEW GUINEA AND SOLOMON ISLANDS

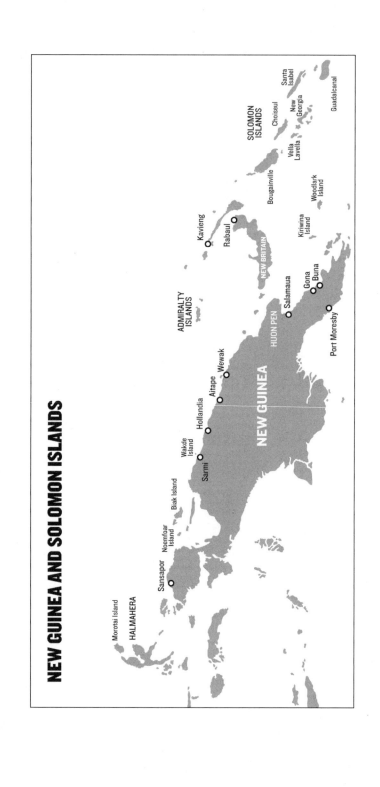

more resources. Their one wartime meeting, at Goodenough Island in December 1943, was formal and restrained rather than tense and rancorous, and they addressed each other by first names. This mutual courtesy meant that while Marshall and MacArthur did not always see eye to eye on personnel issues, they were still able to work out mutually acceptable solutions.[11]

Indeed, MacArthur's criteria for selecting high-ranking personnel such as field army and corps commanders were somewhat different from Marshall's. Both men valued boldness, energy, toughness, and determination. MacArthur, however, saw his generals as members of his military family, not as interchangeable cogs in a massive bureaucracy. As such, he prized personal loyalty more than did other generals. He expected his lieutenants to stay out of his limelight, support or at least tacitly accept his views on all subjects, and remain dependent upon his good graces. Like Marshall, MacArthur believed in giving officers considerable autonomy to complete their missions, so he rarely interfered in their day-to-day operations unless their actions endangered his strategic timetable. Unlike the chief of staff, MacArthur was reluctant to elevate officers to corps or field armies until they had proven themselves in combat at the division level by successfully completing an independent mission. He usually liked to promote from within his organization so he could rely on his own observations of a man's qualities and value. At the same time, he was often reluctant to relieve generals who failed to measure up to his standards, especially men of proven fidelity. For all these reasons, the turnover rate among his highest-ranking ground forces commanders during the war was very low. If MacArthur's personnel policy meant that he sometimes tolerated a certain amount of mediocrity, it also gave his subordinates time to develop and improve in their jobs.[12]

The war continued while MacArthur organized his GHQ. To complete their conquest of New Guinea, in late April the Japanese launched a seaborne offensive toward Port Moresby, the nexus of Allied activity on the big island. In the ensuing Battle of the Coral Sea on 4–8 May, the intercepting American naval forces suffered heavier losses than their Japanese counterparts, but the Japanese turned their tactical victory into a strategic defeat by withdrawing northwestward. The following month the Americans shattered an all-out Japanese effort to seize Midway Island and destroy the remainder of the United States' Pacific fleet. The American navy not only sank four enemy aircraft carriers, but also decimated their all-but-irreplaceable air crews. Although in retrospect Coral Sea and Midway marked a turning point in the Pacific War, the Japanese did not immediately surrender the strategic initiative. Thwarted at sea, in July the Japanese embarked on an overland effort to capture Port Moresby. After taking the villages of Buna and Gona on New Guinea's north coast, Japanese soldiers streamed along the Kokoda Trail across the towering Owen Stanley Mountains toward Port Moresby, brushing aside sporadic and ineffective Australian opposition. Increasing deprivation and stiffening Australian resistance finally brought the Japanese to a halt only thirty miles from Port Moresby in mid-September. Exhausted, the Japanese retreated back over the Owen Stanleys and dug in at Buna-Gona. At about the same time, Australian troops and American engineers repulsed a Japanese amphibious assault on Milne Bay at New Guinea's southeastern tip. By mid-November, after tremendous exertions and considerable losses, the Japanese were back where they started, with little to show for their efforts.

This back-and-forth fighting across the Owen Stanley Mountains did not prevent MacArthur from focusing on the big picture. He was determined to assume the strategic offensive as soon as possible with the Australians and the two American divisions at his disposal. He thought that doing so required a corps headquarters from the States to organize and train these American units because he did not have sufficient staffers at GHQ for the job. On 2 July he radioed Marshall to ask for a corps commander and staff. He did not have anyone in particular in mind, but only wanted someone "fully qualified." Marshall responded by offering him General Robert "Nelly" Richardson, with General Oscar Griswold and General Robert Eichelberger as alternates. Marshall selected Richardson for two reasons. For one thing, Richardson currently commanded the Seventh Corps in California, from which Marshall intended to create the new corps headquarters in Australia, so he was familiar with the personnel involved. Moreover, Richardson was at that very moment Down Under on an inspection trip for Marshall. Marshall figured he would therefore be familiar with SWPA and could quickly and efficiently assume his new duties. MacArthur for his part was delighted with the choice because he believed Richardson was an efficient officer. Richardson too was happy for the opportunity to lead a corps into combat.

Unfortunately for Richardson, his assignment unexpectedly fell through. In his report to Marshall on his inspection trip, Richardson argued strenuously against placing American troops under Australian control. Marshall, however, believed that this was a necessary facet of coalition warfare in SWPA, and if Richardson was unable to accept it, then he should not go there. Besides, Marshall did not understand why Richardson felt it necessary to return to Washington to hand-deliver his report when he had more urgent matters to attend to. Marshall consequently rescinded Richardson's appointment on 30 July, though he made it clear to MacArthur that it was in no way his fault. Stunned by this sudden reversal of fortune, Richardson hurried to the War Department to explain to Marshall that his report was his objective assessment of the situation only, not the conditions under which he would serve. But by then Marshall had already moved on to someone else. Richardson would have to bide his time until Marshall gave him another overseas post, one that would prove both frustrating and bittersweet.[13]

With Richardson out of the picture, Marshall offered MacArthur either of the original alternatives for the job: Oscar Griswold or Robert Eichelberger. MacArthur though remained content to leave the selection in Marshall's hands, probably because he knew and respected both men. Although Griswold had been a stateside corps commander longer than Eichelberger, Eichelberger had impressed Marshall more. Indeed, Eichelberger had been on Marshall's radar screen for some time. The previous January, Marshall had considered sending Eichelberger to China as Chiang Kai-shek's military adviser before opting to dispatch General Joseph Stilwell instead. Eichelberger had not only trained the Seventy-seventh Division well enough to earn a promotion to corps command, but also earned Marshall's admiration by organizing a first-rate demonstration for Winston Churchill at Fort Jackson, South Carolina, on 24 June during the British prime minister's visit to the United States. Marshall had been toying with the idea of giving Eichelberger a prominent role in the planned invasion of North Africa, but now decided that he would be more useful in Australia with MacArthur. Upon receiving his new orders, Eichelberger flew to San Francisco to prepare his First Corps staff for deployment overseas, and he reached Australia via Honolulu, Palmyra Atoll, and Fiji on 25 August. Before he left for SWPA, he wrote to his wife, "'Defense of country' seems a trite phrase in peace time and yet as a professional soldier it must be near and dear to us when our country is in danger."[14]

Bob Eichelberger was a very popular man. Affable, genial, cheerful, and easygoing, he was a wonderful conversationalist full of good stories, so he always had a big crowd at his mess. His smooth and polished manner ingratiated him with his superiors, but his equal friendliness toward subordinates won their unwavering loyalty and devotion. His chief of staff, for example, wrote, "He is such a big person. It is no wonder everyone loves working for him!"[15] Fortunately for the war effort, there was more to Eichelberger than mere sociability. He possessed that unmistakable command presence that made leadership look easy. Although he appreciated the finer things in life and availed himself of them without guilt, he was also tough enough to withstand the rigors and deprivations of the front without complaint. As a capable administrator, he was accustomed to leading by suggestion rather than coercion and to seeing the big picture without getting bogged down in petty details. Like Marshall and MacArthur, he believed in giving a man a job and letting him do it his own way. His meetings often seemed rambling and unstructured, but at the end all the important questions got answered and everyone knew what was expected of him. Journalists found him as appealing as everyone else, and he was not averse to their attentions—at least not at first. He was not as expert in tactics or weaponry as some of his colleagues, but his innate common sense compensated for these deficiencies on the battlefield. On the other side of the Eichelberger ledger, he was sensitive to slights real or imagined, and often felt unappreciated. Eichelberger treated people warmly, honestly, and openly, and expected such treatment in return. When it was not forthcoming, he became resentful, self-pitying, and suspicious. He was not, in short, likely to adjust easily to the backbiting, intrigue, and manipulation that swirled around MacArthur's GHQ.[16]

Eichelberger had made his mark in the army almost exclusively as a staffer and administrator. Born in Ohio in 1886, he transferred to West Point from Ohio State University and graduated in 1909. As a young officer he was stationed in Panama—he was onboard the first boat to steam through the new Panama Canal—and along the Mexican border, but missed the fighting in France in World War One. Instead, he served in Russia as General William Graves's assistant chief of staff in the Siberian Expedition. During that time he gained insights into the Japanese Army that he would put to good use during the Pacific War. After returning home, he worked with the American delegation at the Washington Naval Conference as part of the General Staff's intelligence division. He attended the Command and General Staff School from 1925 to 1926 and the Army War College from 1929 to 1930 before becoming adjutant and secretary at West Point from 1931 to 1935 and then secretary to the General Staff from 1935 to 1938. Along the way he gained innumerable boosters, including chief of staff Malin Craig and Roosevelt's military aide, Edwin "Pa" Watson. He capped his prewar career by returning to West Point as its superintendent, from where Marshall assigned him to command and train the Seventy-seventh Division. Commenting somewhat resentfully on Eichelberger's seemingly effortless progression up the chain of command, one of MacArthur's staffers later noted, "Eichelberger was for many years the secretary of the General Staff in Washington. That was a powerful position and a position which helped him to make friends in the political field. He was also superintendent of West Point. He got that job because he had the other job. He was good-looking, smooth, polished, and socially just the thing for Washington."[17]

Once Down Under, Eichelberger quickly got to work at Rockhampton organizing and training his First Corps and its two divisions, the Thirty-second and Forty-first. During his occasional visits to GHQ at Brisbane, he got along all right with MacArthur, with whom he shared an interest in West Point athletics. He was happy with his headquarters, especially his chief of staff and old friend, Colonel Clovis Byers. Unfortunately, Eichelberger's good mood did not last, and he became increasingly disenchanted as the weeks passed. Pugnacious as ever, MacArthur had assumed the offensive by sending one of Eichelberger's divisions, General Edwin Harding's untried Thirty-second, to New Guinea in late September to join Australian forces in an assault on the Japanese stronghold at Buna-Gona on the big island's north coast. Eichelberger wanted to take his First Corps headquarters there to supervise and participate in the attack. In mid-November he flew to Port Moresby to seek MacArthur's approval. MacArthur was sympathetic, but told him to consult Sutherland. Abrasive as ever, Sutherland brusquely rejected the idea and peremptorily ordered Eichelberger back to Australia on the first available plane. To complete Eichelberger's humiliation, Sutherland added that his primary responsibility would be training American soldiers, not leading them into action. An angry Eichelberger felt as if Sutherland was treating him like an upstart lieutenant, not a lieutenant general. To top it all off, MacArthur had concluded that Eichelberger's staff was too large and wanted to strip it of a quarter of its personnel for other units. Small wonder Eichelberger noted morosely that he might have participated in Dwight Eisenhower's North African invasion had things worked out differently.[18]

Happily for Eichelberger, though not for the American war effort, his luck was about to change. A couple of days after Sutherland threw Eichelberger out of New Guinea, two regiments of Harding's Thirty-second Division joined Australian forces in assailing Buna-Gona. The assault quickly degenerated into a nightmarish stalemate. The inexperienced GIs floundered in the swamps and jungle in their attempts to come to grips with the entrenched Japanese. Inadequate supplies, equipment, and air and artillery support hindered American efforts to push forward. The soldiers became demoralized, command and control broke down, and disease and enemy fire decimated the units. MacArthur's disappointment with the failed offensive turned into shock and anger when he received reports that some American soldiers had thrown down their weapons and run away under fire. He dispatched Sutherland for a firsthand look at the situation. Although Sutherland did not actually travel to the front, he did talk with Harding at his Dobodura command post. Sutherland did not like what he heard, and upon his return to Port Moresby he recommended Harding's removal from command. Even before he sent Sutherland on his inspection trip, though, MacArthur had already concluded that some changes were necessary. "Dick," he had said, "I think you had better bring Bob Eichelberger up here. We are going to need him."[19]

Eichelberger received his summons from MacArthur just before midnight on 29 November. Next morning he and Byers flew from Rockhampton to Port Moresby, and they arrived at MacArthur's command post in the late afternoon. MacArthur was pacing on the sweeping veranda, discussing the situation with several of his subordinates, while Sutherland sat glumly at a desk, his eyes nervously following MacArthur. Only General George Kenney, SWPA's aggressive and ebullient air chief, had a smile for the two visitors. MacArthur turned to Eichelberger and said abruptly, "Bob, I'm putting you in command at Buna. Relieve Harding. I am sending you in, Bob, and I want you to remove all officers who won't fight. Relieve regimental and battalion commanders; if necessary, put sergeants in charge of battalions and corporals in charge of companies—anyone who will fight. Time is of the essence; the Japs may land reinforcements any night." After giving Eichelberger a moment to absorb the information, MacArthur continued, "Bob, I want you to take Buna, or not come back alive." Turning to Byers, MacArthur added, "And that goes for your chief of staff too. Do you understand?" To sweeten the deal, such as it was, MacArthur also promised to award Eichelberger the Distinguished Service Medal and release his name to the press if he succeeded in his mission. Such incentives, though, apparently did not apply to Byers, whose motivation was limited to ensuring that MacArthur's threats did not become reality.[20]

Eichelberger and Byers reached the Buna front the next day, 1 December. There they discovered intermingled units, insufficient discipline, minimal communications with division headquarters, and demoralized troops living in squalor. The GIs had adopted a live-and-let-live attitude toward the Japanese, which, while minimizing losses, was unlikely to end the battle anytime soon. Eichelberger did not gut the division's leadership from top to bottom as MacArthur recommended, but he did relieve a disgruntled Harding and several other high-ranking officers. Eichelberger rested his men for a couple of days while he acquainted himself with the situation, brought up additional supplies and equipment, and reorganized the two exhausted regiments. On 5 December, he ordered an all-out attack that achieved little beyond swelling the American casualty list. Disappointed but undaunted by the setback, Eichelberger resorted to brutal attrition to grind down Japanese resistance. He frequently visited the front lines to encourage his tired soldiers and repeatedly exposed himself to enemy fire. These tactics, however, took time that Eichelberger did not have because a frustrated MacArthur was applying increasing pressure on him to finish the operation. As the days turned to weeks without much progress, MacArthur seriously considered removing Eichelberger from his new command and replacing him with Sutherland. Sutherland visited the front twice to browbeat and bully Eichelberger, but this did little to advance the timetable. An angry Eichelberger responded by writing, "The fighting part of the job, I like. It is the other side of it that has been my difficult problem."[21] In the end, though, American firepower and numbers won the day by grinding the Japanese down. Buna fell on 2 January 1943, nearly a month after the Australians overran nearby Gona. Although MacArthur declared the fighting over on 8 January, mopping up around nearby Sanananda continued for two more weeks.[22]

Eichelberger could be, and was, proud of his accomplishment. He had after all almost singlehandedly jumpstarted a stalled American offensive and led his bleddown and demoralized soldiers to victory. In seizing Buna-Gona and destroying its defenders, the Allies gained an important foothold across the Owen Stanley Mountains that MacArthur would use as a springboard for further operations against the big Japanese base at Rabaul on New Britain. The price, however, had been high. Eight thousand Australian and American troops had fallen in the battle, more than the number killed and wounded during concurrent operations at Guadalcanal. MacArthur lived up to his word by releasing Eichelberger's name to the press and securing him a Distinguished Service Medal. As a result, Eichelberger not only received a slew of laudatory letters from friends and well-wishers, but also got his picture on the cover of *Life* and *Time* magazines.

Having won the army's first major Pacific War engagement, Eichelberger was the logical choice to lead SWPA's ground forces in the campaign against Rabaul. Unfortunately for Eichelberger, though, MacArthur saw things through a different lens. While he congratulated Eichelberger, he was not altogether pleased with his First Corps commander's leadership or belligerent attitude at Buna. More significantly, MacArthur disliked the idea of sharing SWPA's limelight with a new hero who might conceivably supplant him someday. Indeed, during a meeting after Buna MacArthur alluded to Eichelberger's popularity and said, "Do you realize I could reduce you to the grade of colonel tomorrow and send you home?"[23] As SWPA's chief of amphibious forces, Admiral Daniel Barbey, later put it, "There was no place in the Southwest Pacific for two glamorous officers."[24] Instead of rewarding Eichelberger with increased responsibilities for a job well done, MacArthur exiled him to Australia to resume his former duties training American units Down Under for future missions someone else would conduct in New Guinea.[25]

It only gradually dawned on Eichelberger that he had been sidelined. He had difficulty reconciling MacArthur's actions with his syrupy words. During their occasional meetings in 1943, MacArthur invariably praised Eichelberger's work, kept him up to date on current operations, and hinted at his involvement in future plans. Like so many others, Eichelberger was mesmerized by MacArthur's rhetoric and only dimly realized that MacArthur was stringing him along. Instead of blaming MacArthur for his plight, Eichelberger rationalized that he lacked sufficient rank to command American troops in New Guinea, or that there were not enough units there to justify committing his corps. As far as Eichelberger was concerned, if anyone was at fault for his plight, it was probably the untrustworthy Sutherland. Despite his frustrations and insomnia, Eichelberger tried to be upbeat and philosophical, but it was not easy when the war was obviously passing him by, and his bitterness often seeped through. He could, however, take pride and comfort in his good relationship with the Australians, his staff's growing proficiency, and his skillful handling of Eleanor Roosevelt during her trip to the Southwest Pacific. He adopted as his mantra, "As long as I keep my sense of humor they can't get me down."[26]

Despite his efforts to remain upbeat, Eichelberger could not help but feel that he had entered a Kafkaesque and surreal world in which the ordinary rules did not apply. Although MacArthur seemed in no hurry to utilize Eichelberger's hard-earned combat skills, he refused to let him go elsewhere to ply his trade. Marshall had always thought highly of Eichelberger and recognized that his recent combat experience made him a valuable commodity in an army that did not yet possess many battle-tested leaders. He tried three times in 1943 to pry Eichelberger out of SWPA for a more active assignment. In March he suggested that MacArthur send Eichelberger back to the States to train a field army. That August, Marshall seized upon MacArthur's recommendation against awarding Eichelberger a Medal of Honor for his actions at Buna as evidence that he lacked confidence in his First Corps commander. That being the case, Marshall noted, perhaps MacArthur would be willing to part with Eichelberger. Finally, in December Marshall directly asked MacArthur to transfer Eichelberger to Europe so he could lead a field army in the D-Day invasion of France. In return, he offered to dispatch one of the army's most aggressive division commanders, General J. Lawton Collins, as his replacement. Eichelberger never received any official notification of these machinations, but he was well aware of them through his GHQ contacts. He was eager to leave SWPA for a more active post in Europe—or anywhere else for that matter. To smooth the way, he lobbied on his own behalf by keeping in touch with his War Department friends and even asking his wife to talk with Lesley McNair's wife and Pa Watson and see what information about his future prospects she could inveigle from them.

Unfortunately for Eichelberger, all these efforts came to nothing. Although Marshall believed that Eichelberger could be put to better use in Europe, he refused to transfer him out of SWPA without MacArthur's approval. MacArthur may have disliked the publicity Eichelberger garnered after Buna and questioned his performance there, but he still valued Eichelberger as a capable officer whose talents he planned to employ eventually. As he explained somewhat disingenuously to Marshall:

> I hold Eichelberger in highest esteem both professionally and personally. He is entirely happy in his present command and I am very desirous in keeping him. His experience in the Papuan [New Guinea] Campaign has increased his command ability[,] strengthened his weak points and generally enhanced his value to this area. I feel that his services are of more value here than they could be in any assignment to which he could aspire in the United States and recommend most earnestly against his relief.[27]

MacArthur eventually informed Eichelberger of Marshall's attempts to procure his services, but coupled this information with vague assurances that he intended to give him a combat assignment sooner or later that would surpass any he might receive in Europe. Eichelberger was dubious about that, but hardly in any position to argue the point. Instead, he complained of his mistreatment at Sutherland's hands and bluntly told MacArthur that 1943 had been the most miserable year of his life. MacArthur nodded his head knowingly and gave Eichelberger a leave of absence to return to San Francisco to see his wife and cool off. Eichelberger lamented his inability to shake free of SWPA, but he continued to work hard to keep a positive attitude and perform well at his present assignment in the hopes that his fortunes would take a turn for the better.[28]

With Eichelberger out of the picture, at least temporarily, MacArthur now sought out a new leader for American ground forces in New Guinea. Since asking for another corps commander would be redundant and arouse Marshall's suspicions, MacArthur instead requested a field army to relieve GHQ of some of the burden of overseeing the fighting. MacArthur wanted a capable officer with whom he was familiar, with sufficient seniority to outrank any Australian generals who might otherwise claim authority over American troops, and with enough perspicacity to stay out of the limelight. Good field army commanders, though, were a rare breed. As MacArthur later explained, "An army commander had to divorce himself from the men of his division or the men of the other divisions, had to work with his staff, relate to them in an entirely different way. His work was more on an intellectual level; he couldn't think of individuals. Emotions or spirit had to be downplayed. . . . It's hard to find such a man."[29] Happily, MacArthur knew just such a man. On 11 January 1943, he asked Marshall for the services of General Walter Krueger, an old friend and current chief of the stateside Third Army.[30]

Walter Krueger's background was unusual for a high-ranking American army officer in that he was neither native born nor a West Pointer. Instead, he had been born in Germany in 1881 and emigrated to Ohio with his family when he was eight years old. He enlisted in the army in 1898 and fought in both the Spanish-American War and the Philippines Insurrection. After rising to sergeant, Krueger passed the qualifying exam and was commissioned as an officer in 1901. A young Douglas MacArthur was among the first to befriend the new second lieutenant. Krueger graduated from the Infantry-Cavalry School in 1906 and the Command and General Staff School a year later. He participated in Pershing's 1916–1917 Punitive Expedition to Mexico and then served in France as a staffer during World War One. After the conflict and occupation duty he returned to the States and attended the Army War College from 1920 to 1921 and was then assigned to the General Staff. Crossing interservice boundaries, Krueger worked at the Naval War College as both a student and teacher, giving him a unique perspective for an army officer that paid big dividends during his amphibious operations in the Pacific. He also became something of an expert on the Wehrmacht because he translated so many German army texts. He renewed his acquaintance with MacArthur, now chief of staff, during a tour of duty as head of the War Plans Division in the mid-1930s. After that he became, successively, commander of a brigade, a division, a corps, and finally, in May 1941, a field army. He led the Third Army in the famous Louisiana maneuvers that summer, though most of the credit for its success went, unfairly, to his chief of staff, Dwight Eisenhower.

Unsmiling, hard-bitten, direct, and stubborn, Krueger fit the stereotype of a tough Prussian officer. He overcame his lack of a West Point education to rise to the top of the army's hierarchy through his unwavering ambition, keen intellect, iron self-discipline, and prodigious work ethic. As a former enlisted man, he appreciated the needs of the rank-and-file more than most generals. Indeed, nothing irked him more than officers who failed to look after their men. He never yelled at or mistreated an enlisted man, but rather responded to their shortcomings by chewing out their officers. He seemed to have little use for officers as a class and once exclaimed, "You know the trouble with the Army is the officers. They're a necessary evil."[31] As a result, he inspired fear and dread in some, and bemused irritation in others, but rarely affection. During the war, for example, Dwight Eisenhower sent Eichelberger a clipping of a braying donkey and likened it to an angry Krueger. Although some said he possessed a good heart and desperately wanted to be liked, he was unpopular because he rarely showed much warmth or empathy. When one general thanked Krueger for a leave home, Krueger barked, "Don't thank me! When one general officer says he feels another deserves leave and can be spared it is my duty to approve."[32] His taciturnity, dourness, loud opinions, and humorlessness did not help matters. One officer noted that Krueger reminded him of a long-suffering high school principal, and another referred to him as the meanest man alive with a heart of gold. No doubt Krueger was sensitive to criticism, demanding, critical, unimaginative, easily irritated, and sometimes overly cautious, but he compensated for these drawbacks with a relentless pursuit of his objectives and a firm grasp of small-unit tactics. Whatever his sins and shortcomings, few people ever accused Walter Krueger of incompetence.[33]

Just because MacArthur wanted Krueger did not mean that Marshall would send him. Marshall had met Krueger in the Philippines in 1903 when they were both young lieutenants in the same regiment, and over the years he had gained a pretty good understanding of the man. Marshall lauded Krueger's diligence, energy, aggressiveness, and intelligence, but knew of his failings. In fact, in April 1941 Marshall had written Krueger a private letter expressing concerns about Krueger's stubbornness, hypersensitivity, resistance to ideas not his own, and reluctance to accept blame and admit wrongdoing. As usual with Krueger, he accepted his superior's views without complaint or excuse and promised to profit from Marshall's advice that he work on his flaws. In addition, Krueger was at sixty-two too old to lead a field army overseas, according to Marshall's rigorous standards. Despite such concerns, Marshall gave way and ordered Krueger to SWPA because he believed that theater commanders should have subordinates of their own choosing. Besides, McNair thought a lot of Krueger, as did Henry Stimson, the secretary of war and Krueger's old friend. On 23 January, MacArthur cabled Krueger, who was inspecting a division at Camp Carson in Colorado, that he had requested his services. Next day McNair telephoned him with official confirmation and ordered him to Washington for consultations. As McNair was hard of hearing, Krueger had to shoo everyone out of divisional headquarters so he could shout back in private. Although not the most demonstrative of men, Krueger was still excited and pleased at the news. After all, Marshall's mania for youth had condemned most officers Krueger's age to stateside training assignments. Now, however, he had the opportunity to be in the thick of things in a prominent role. Krueger was disappointed to learn that he could not bring the Third Army moniker with him; instead, he would activate a new army, the Sixth, for operations in SWPA, largely with staffers taken with him from the Third. Krueger arrived in Australia on 7 February, and his Sixth Army became operational nine days later at Camp Columbia outside Brisbane.[34]

Not only did Krueger and MacArthur personally like each other, but they usually worked well together. Krueger's nuts-and-bolts conception of tactical warfare complemented MacArthur's emphasis on the big strategic picture. This did not, however, mean that the relationship was trouble free. During the war MacArthur complained that Krueger's slow and methodical methods delayed GHQ's timetables. Krueger for his part grumbled about MacArthur's unwarranted and unrealistic pressure to seize objectives, and likened GHQ to a needle constantly prodding him from behind. Although Krueger believed in obeying orders without question, even his deference had limits. For instance, after MacArthur complained that one of SWPA's divisions had never learned to fight, Krueger barked back that all of his men were fine soldiers. MacArthur gave Krueger considerable autonomy to fulfill GHQ's strategic plans, and Krueger used this leeway now and then to twist and modify his orders to suit his purposes without MacArthur's knowledge. Krueger was not much of a publicity hound—in fact, this was one reason why MacArthur wanted him—but it sometimes irked him that he was not getting the credit he felt he deserved. He once lamented to Eichelberger, "I don't get any of the glory—just the responsibility."[35] Australian General Thomas Blamey was technically commander of all SWPA ground forces, but MacArthur did not want to place American soldiers under foreign control. To circumvent Blamey, MacArthur renamed the Sixth Army "Alamo Force" and used it to conduct operations in New Guinea independently of the Australians, which further reduced Krueger's profile, though not his workload. Finally, Krueger hated Sutherland and ignored him whenever possible. He tried to avoid GHQ, but when he had to go there he marched straight into MacArthur's office without saying a word to Sutherland. Despite these difficulties, Krueger always completed his missions, so that MacArthur wrote melodramatically years later, "Swift and sure in attack, tenacious and determined in defense, modest and restrained in victory—I do not know what he would have been in defeat, because he was never defeated."[36]

To neutralize the big Japanese base at Rabaul, the Joint Chiefs of Staff authorized Operation Cartwheel. As its name suggests, Cartwheel envisioned SWPA working in conjunction with the neighboring South Pacific Area Command (SOPAC) in an elaborate series of maneuvers against Rabaul. While SOPAC clawed its way up the Solomon Islands chain, SWPA would seize part of the New Guinea coast and clear both sides of the Vitiaz Strait. Completing Cartwheel took nearly a year, and there was nothing easy about it. The Australians did most of SWPA's ground fighting, but Alamo Force played an increasingly important role. Krueger oversaw the campaign from his headquarters first at Milne Bay, then Goodenough Island, and finally Cape Cretin. While the Australians struggled to conquer the Huon Peninsula with some American support, Alamo Force conducted unopposed amphibious assaults on Kiriwina and Woodlark islands in the Trobriands on 23 June and Nassau Bay in New Guinea a week later. In subsequent operations, Krueger's men crossed the Vitiaz Strait to establish footholds in New Britain at Arawe on 30 November and Cape Gloucester on 26 December, followed by a seaborne attack on Saidor in New Guinea on 2 January 1944. Finally, on 29 February, General Innis Palmer Swift's First Cavalry Division launched a bold assault on the Admiralty Islands. Clearing them of the enemy took until mid-April, but by then it was apparent that the Japanese in the region had been so battered that storming Rabaul was no longer necessary. Instead, the JCS decided to simply bypass the place and leave its 100,000 defenders isolated and cut off—prisoners, as it were, in their own camp. There were many reasons for this impressive victory, including the valor displayed by the Australian troops and officers, who bore the brunt of the fighting, but MacArthur and the command team he put together deserve their share of the credit.

Climbing the Solomons Ladder

While the fighting raged in and around eastern New Guinea, there was another, equally important and bloody struggle occurring across the Solomon Sea in the Solomon Islands. The Solomons were a 930-mile-long chain of islands extending ladder-like southeastward from Rabaul. Under normal circumstances, the

Solomons had little strategic value, but all that changed in early July 1942 when the Japanese began constructing an airfield on Guadalcanal. Planes from this airfield could endanger Australia's supply and communications lines with the United States, isolating the country from the Allied war effort. Ernest King, the navy's hard-driving chief of naval operations, certainly saw it this way, and he persuaded the JCS to authorize a limited offensive, called Operation Watchtower, to seize the island. On 7 August, the First Marine Division stormed ashore at Guadalcanal. The marines quickly scattered the Japanese construction crews and occupied the airfield, which they subsequently renamed Henderson Field. Unfortunately, their initial success was deceptively easy. The attack provoked a violent Japanese response that engulfed the island and its surrounding waters in six months of heavy combat. Guadalcanal became a vortex that sucked in Japanese and American resources at an alarming rate. The result was a brutal war of attrition in the air, at sea, and on land. Although the campaign seesawed back and forth for the rest of the year, the Americans continued to maintain their foothold at the all-important airstrip.

Initially the Guadalcanal campaign was primarily a navy affair. The navy ran the theater and of course protected the sea-lanes to the island, and the marines in the beginning furnished the vast majority of the troops committed there. Marshall and the army were focused on the European War in general and, as time went on, the North African invasion in particular. The army's main contribution was at first aerial. This was evidenced in Marshall's 26 July selection of General Millard "Miff" Harmon as the commander of SOPAC's army forces. Harmon was an Army Air Force general and Henry Arnold's friend. Born in 1888 into a military family, Harmon graduated from West Point in 1912, was commissioned in the infantry, and joined the Signal Corps's fledgling Aviation Section four years later in time to participate in Pershing's Punitive Expedition into Mexico. He saw air combat in World War One, and afterward attended the Command and General Staff School from 1922 to 1923 and the Army War College from 1924 to 1925. He went to Britain as an observer after World War Two broke out, and a year later Arnold made him his chief of staff, from which position Marshall sent him to the South Pacific. As Marshall explained to him shortly thereafter, "You have an important and interesting assignment, and I want you to know that I have full confidence in you."[37] Although Harmon was a peppery and opinionated man, he retained the ability to get along with others, including the irascible Admiral William Halsey, the eventual SOPAC commander. Able and devoted, Harmon recognized immediately the necessity for interservice coordination in the South Pacific and acted accordingly, earning kudos from almost everyone in the theater. He did irk Arnold by asking for far more air resources for the region than were readily available, but this was an indication that Harmon recognized before his superiors back in Washington did that the Guadalcanal campaign was likely to be long and difficult. Despite Harmon's air background, Marshall still respected him enough to consult him about the selection and performance of high-ranking army ground forces officers in the theater.[38]

The First Marine Division bore the brunt of the early fighting at Guadalcanal, doggedly repelling a series of ferocious Japanese attacks under trying conditions, but by November it was clearly time to withdraw the exhausted outfit. It was equally obvious that securing the island required substantial army resources despite the commitment of the Second Marine Division there. Elements of General Alexander Patch's Americal Division—so-called because it was formed the previous May from a conglomeration of American units on New Caledonia—had already arrived in mid-October, and by the end of November the entire division was on hand. In addition, General J. Lawton Collins's Twenty-fifth Division started disembarking in mid-December. To direct all these forces, Harmon recommended the establishment of a corps headquarters. Marshall agreed, and on 2 January 1943 the new Fourteenth Corps became operational. Its headquarters personnel were taken from the Americal Division, not transferred in from the States, so its size was relatively small throughout the remainder of the campaign. To command the corps, Marshall turned to Sandy Patch.

Patch was born into an army family at remote Fort Huachuca, Arizona, in 1889, but was raised in Pennsylvania. He went to Lehigh University for a year before transferring to West Point, from which he received his degree and an infantry commission in 1913. He was stationed on the Mexican border before going overseas to France in World War One. There he ran the army's Machine Gun School and saw action at Second Marne, St. Mihiel, and the Argonne. After occupation duty in Germany, Patch returned home and attended the Command and General Staff School from 1924 to 1925 and the War College from 1930 to 1931. He also taught at the Staunton Military Academy in Virginia on two different occasions for a total of seven years. He helped organize the army's new triangular divisions, commanded a regiment, and was directing the Infantry Replacement Center in South Carolina when the Japanese bombed Pearl Harbor. Soon afterward, Marshall dispatched him with a task force to French-owned New Caledonia in the Pacific to protect the strategically located island from any possible Japanese assault.

The thin, spare, and wiry Patch did not often make a very good first impression. Taciturn, enigmatic, and ascetic, he was so full of nervous energy that he had a hard time expressing himself. Secretary of War Henry Stimson liked him, but noted that he was "rather difficult in speech."[39] Those who knew him well, on the other hand, lauded his modesty and selflessness that made it possible for him to cooperate easily with the French, the navy, and even George Patton. He charmed people with his dry and understated Scottish sense of humor and an eccentric streak that included proficiency with the accordion. He possessed a sensitivity toward the war and its victims that separated him from his more dispassionate colleagues. Despite this empathy, Patch after a somewhat rocky start eventually developed into a cool, balanced, resolute, and aggressive commander fully capable of making big decisions deftly and decisively. Unfortunately, he was also subject to lung problems that occasionally sidelined him and limited his effectiveness. Lucian Truscott, a superb battlefield general in his own right with high standards, later summed up Patch's attributes: "I came to regard him highly as a man of outstanding integrity, a courageous and competent leader, and an unselfish comrade-in-arms."[40]

Marshall's decision to assign the new Fourteenth Corps to Patch was based as much on following the path of least resistance to the common-sense solution as anything else. After all, Patch was already on Guadalcanal and was thoroughly familiar with the new corps's personnel because they were largely drawn from his Americal Division. There was, however, more to it than that. Patch had done well up to his sojourn on Guadalcanal. On New Caledonia he had successfully organized and trained his jury-rigged division, charmed the prickly French there, and cooperated effectively with the navy. Harmon saw it that way and had recommended Patch for a Distinguished Service Medal. Kudos came from other sources as well. McNair had always been a booster, and both Robert Richardson and Henry Arnold had extolled Patch's efforts on New Caledonia during their inspection tours of the South Pacific. The only potential red flag was Patch's delicate health. Guadalcanal taxed the constitution of even the most robust people, and Patch had already come down with pneumonia en route to the South Pacific the previous February during a layover in Trinidad. Marshall had been concerned enough to ask the doctors there for a confidential report, but they had assured him that Patch was recovering rapidly, and there had been no recurrence at New Caledonia. Considering all these factors, it would have been odd had Marshall *not* given the corps to Patch.[41]

Although elements of the Second Marine Division remained on Guadalcanal, the army gradually took over the campaign even before the Fourteenth Corps was officially created. In mid-December, Patch's Americal Division began an offensive against Japanese-held Mount Austen, which overlooked Henderson Field. Patch recognized and was concerned about the losses that Guadalcanal's harsh environment could inflict on men and materiel, but Harmon assured him that he would make up any shortages. The arrival of Collins's Twenty-fifth Division enabled Patch to expand his operations significantly. Starting on 10 January 1943, Collins aggressively spearheaded a series of attacks against Japanese positions at the Galloping Horse Hills, the Sea Horse, and Gifu strongpoint. American numbers and firepower steadily forced the Japanese westward. Unfortunately, Patch then mistakenly concluded that the Japanese might assail Henderson Airfield again, so he redeployed the Twenty-fifth Division to face this illusionary threat, weakening his remaining forces. As a result, the Japanese not only escaped to Cape Esperance, but also successfully evacuated their remaining 13,000 personnel on the island on successive nights ending on 7–8 February.[42]

Patch could take pride in his accomplishments. In six weeks of tough fighting, he had performed ably and professionally in driving the Japanese from the island and terminating six brutal months of heavy combat in the area. Collins, for instance, recalled that at his arrival on Guadalcanal, an air raid siren wailed as Patch escorted him to the command post. "Don't let that disturb you, Collins," Patch said nonchalantly. "Happens all the time."[43] Of the 36,000 men the Japanese committed to the island, nearly 25,000 became casualties. They had also lost 24 warships and 600 aircraft that Japanese industry could replace only with great difficulty, if at all. The Americans for their part suffered 1,600 killed and 4,200 wounded out of the 60,000 troops they deployed to Guadalcanal. The campaign secured Australia's communications and supply lines with the United States and provided the Americans with a springboard for further operations up the Solomons toward Rabaul. It was, in short, a tremendous American victory. Marshall for one saw it that way. SOPAC commander Admiral William Halsey did too, and expressed his satisfaction with Patch in his usual jovial and hackneyed manner: "When I sent Patch to act as tailor for Guadalcanal, I did not expect him to remove the enemy's pants and sew it on so quickly."[44]

A closer look at the campaign's conclusion, on the other hand, casts some doubts on these positive evaluations. Patch cannot be held responsible for the larger-than-expected commitment of scarce American resources to Guadalcanal, but his cautiousness enabled the Japanese to slip away to fight another day despite American superiority by land, sea, and air. Furthermore, Patch's normal congeniality did not prevent him from quarreling with the brash Collins. Collins believed that Patch was too timid, whereas Patch resented Collins's tendency to exceed his orders. Although Collins later downplayed their disagreements, Patch found them serious enough to complain about Collins to Marshall. Indeed, from that point on Patch detested Collins and did not want to work with him. Unfortunately for Patch, Marshall thought a lot of Collins and responded to Patch's evaluation by questioning *Patch's* judgment. Finally, and most seriously, Patch was ill throughout much of his time on Guadalcanal. He came down with malaria and dysentery soon after he arrived, and later suffered from a recurrence of pneumonia. One officer later recalled:

I came in his bed room which was partitioned off at the rear of the shack. I found General Patch lying on an iron bunk. He was very sick. He was suffering from tropical dysentery, I believe, and he had a fever. His eyes looked terrible. The lower lids seemed to be about a quarter inch lower than they ordinarily would be. He was practically skin and bones and his face plainly showed the effect of his illness.[45]

Notwithstanding his afflictions, Patch refused to be evacuated, but instead saw the campaign through to its conclusion. Even so, there is little doubt that his illness sapped his strength, impaired his efficiency, and contributed to the conservative tactics Collins lamented.[46]

Harmon was among those who recognized at least some of Patch's problems. While he believed that Patch had done a fine job on Guadalcanal and hated to lose him, Harmon had for several months been concerned about Patch's uncertain health. Harmon felt that Patch's persistent illnesses were undermining his effectiveness by lessening his stamina and contributing to an unwarranted nervousness. By way of solution, Harmon suggested to Marshall that he bring Patch back to the States temporarily for a rest. Doing so, Harmon continued, would also enable McNair to use Patch's new combat experience in organizing and training troops for overseas operations. Marshall took the hint and on 19 March ordered Patch home. Marshall was careful, though, to praise Patch for a job well done and assure him that his relief was not due to any loss of confidence in him. Patch responded that he wanted to remain in an active combat theater, but that as a soldier he would of course obey Marshall's directive. Patch left Guadalcanal in April and assumed command of the Fourth Corps in Washington State. Despite Marshall's implied assurances, Patch never returned to the Pacific theater, but would instead go on to play an important part in the European War.[47]

To replace Patch, Marshall sent General Oscar "Griz" Griswold. The fifty-six-year-old, Nevada-born Griswold had graduated from West Point in 1910 and spent several years in China before going to France as a machine gun officer in World War One. After returning to the States, Griswold attended the Command and General Staff School from 1924 to 1925 and the Army War College four years later. Unlike all but two others of the army's World War Two corps commanders who saw much action, Griswold performed poorly at the Command and General Staff School, ranking in the bottom half of his class. He subsequently served in the Air Corps, on the General Staff, with the Infantry Board, and in the Office of the Chief of Infantry. After World War Two began in Europe, Griswold successively commanded a regiment, the Infantry Replacement Training Center, the Fourth Division, and finally, starting in October 1941, the Fourth Corps. Although McNair had only reluctantly recommended Griswold as head of a division in July 1941, he had been more positive in suggesting him for a stateside corps three months later. Marshall did not have much of a personal connection with Griswold, but was impressed with the positive reports he received about him. Marshall had on at least two occasions tried to get Griswold overseas into the fighting because Griswold was one of the more experienced corps commanders and had played a prominent role in the November 1941 Carolina maneuvers. He had offered Griswold to MacArthur for the First Corps in July 1942, and two months later had placed him third on a list of possible task force commanders for the invasion of North Africa. Now, however, Marshall took matters into his own hands and ordered Griswold to the South Pacific to lead the Fourteenth Corps.

The tall and bespectacled Griswold was highly esteemed in the prewar army as an infantry expert who preached the virtues of flexibility and firepower. Moreover, officers and the rank-and-file admired him personally. He won the respect of his subordinates by praising them in public and reserving his criticisms for behind closed doors. Clovis Byers, Eichelberger's loyal chief of staff, referred to Griswold as the most immediately likable man he had ever met. Griswold brought to the Fourteenth Corps an uncomplicated and practical approach to military problems, a calmness and grace under pressure, and a realistic understanding of twentieth-century warfare and its practitioners. Unlike many Regular Army officers such as Krueger, Griswold valued national guardsmen and gave them every chance to succeed. It was no coincidence that one of the war's most successful National Guard division commanders, General Robert Beightler of the Thirty-seventh, served under Griswold throughout much of the Pacific War. Although matter-of-fact, wry, and down-to-earth, Griswold also possessed a philosophical outlook toward life in general and the war in particular. Such characteristics indicated his capacity for leadership and responsibility. Finally, he was willing to speak his mind in defense of friends and ideas regardless of the consequences, a trait that later in the conflict did not endear him to the hard-nosed Krueger.[48]

While MacArthur and Krueger cleared the northeastern New Guinea coast, Halsey prepared to carry out SOPAC's part in Operation Cartwheel. SOPAC's role in the two-pronged drive toward Rabaul was to climb the Solomons ladder toward the big Japanese fortress. Even before the fighting on Guadalcanal had ended, SOPAC had drawn up plans to assault New Georgia, a swampy and jungle-ridden island in the center of the Solomons chain. SOPAC valued New Georgia because it contained a Japanese airfield at Munda Point on the island's west coast. In American hands, planes flying from Munda could not only strike Rabaul, but also support and protect further offensives in the region. The army's main contribution to the operation, dubbed "Toenails," was General John Hester's rookie Forty-third Division. Since Toenails was supposed to be a one-division job, Halsey—or, more specifically, Admiral Richard Turner, the hot-tempered and intrusive head of the South Pacific Amphibious Force and the man responsible for shepherding the soldiers to the island—decided not to use Griswold's Fourteenth

Corps headquarters for the mission. Harmon, however, was from the start concerned that Hester lacked the staff to command both his division and all the necessary supporting troops, so he warned Griswold to be ready to move to the island at a moment's notice.[49]

The initial assault on New Georgia consisted of a complicated series of landings in late June and early July 1943, the most important of which was at Zanana, 5 miles from Munda. Although the Japanese had only 5,000 men to oppose Hester's two regiments attacking southwestward from Zanana, they fought with their customary skill and tenacity from well-camouflaged positions. The dense jungle, hilly terrain, and inexperience quickly stymied Hester's advance. American casualties were not prohibitively high, but increasing numbers of soldiers succumbed to combat fatigue, friendly fire, and physical exhaustion, all symptoms of the poor leadership sometimes present in National Guard divisions in their first actions during the war. Within days it was clear that the operation was in trouble and that Hester would not seize Munda anytime soon.

Back at Guadalcanal, Griswold was gradually adjusting to the alien environment Marshall had thrust him into. Logistics had taken a backseat to combat operations during the fighting there, so Griswold's first mission was establishing some logistical orderliness. He might have blamed some of the confusion on Patch, but a tour of the island right after his arrival convinced him that Patch deserved all the credit he could get for his performance there. Equally enlightening was a terrible cloudburst after an all-night downpour on 7–8 May that nearly washed away his headquarters. There was of course little Griswold could do about mother nature's machinations, but he was less accepting of the growing crisis on New Georgia. A quick visit to the island on 5 July with Harmon and Turner persuaded him that Hester lacked the resources for the task. Harmon agreed that Hester needed assistance, but Turner insisted otherwise. Although Turner often operated through intimidation and browbeating, Harmon was hardly the kind of man to meekly accept such bullying. He instead flew to Halsey's headquarters at New Caledonia and got him not only to order Griswold and his Fourteenth Corps headquarters to New Georgia, but also to dispatch substantial reinforcements from Beightler's Thirty-seventh and Collins's Twenty-fifth divisions to help wrap up the operation as soon as possible.

Griswold arrived on 15 July and got to work reorganizing, untangling, and supplying the various forces there or on the way. On 24 July, the night before he launched his offensive, Griswold confided in his diary, "I face tomorrow my first test in battle leadership. I bow my head in humility and pray I may have what it takes to properly lead my troops. God with us, we will win the victory."[50] Griswold's big push made only slow progress, but American numerical superiority and firepower—especially flamethrowers and tanks—gradually wore down Japanese resistance. Griswold quickly concluded that the lackluster Hester was not measuring up and attained Harmon's permission to replace him with General John Hodge, assistant commander of the Twenty-fifth Division. Hester was an old friend, though, so Griswold sent his chief of staff, General William Arnold, to do the deed for him. Griswold was also so unhappy with Joe Collins's bossy and imperious attitude that he recommended to Marshall that he not be promoted to the corps level. Despite these personnel problems, the Fourteenth Corps slowly advanced. Munda fell on 5 July, but mopping up remaining Japanese opposition continued for several more weeks.[51]

Like Guadalcanal, New Georgia was an important American victory that fell short of what might have been achieved. In seizing New Georgia, the Americans took a big step toward Rabaul, and planes flying from Munda and other airfields carved out of the jungle could more easily pound the Japanese island fortress. On the other hand, there were plenty of things about Toenails that gave American planners pause. The operation required far more time and resources than expected. SOPAC invested elements of three divisions and suffered 1,094 killed and 3,873 wounded to occupy New Georgia. It would take months to refit the Forty-third and Twenty-fifth divisions. Finally, a good many Japanese troops slipped away. At this rate, SOPAC would not get to Rabaul anytime soon. In response to these concerns, Halsey decided to take advantage of his growing mobility to bypass Kolombangara Island and its 12,000-man garrison to strike instead at lightly defended Vella Lavella. A regiment of the Twenty-fifth Division landed there on 15 August and quickly occupied the place. Although the Japanese managed to evacuate their troops from Kolombangara, the Americans still took another leap toward Rabaul, only this time with substantially fewer casualties than they sustained on New Georgia.

Although Griswold was a dispassionate man, he was proud of his victory on New Georgia even though he displayed little tactical finesse. Marshall was less impressed with the accomplishment and in fact asked Harmon for a confidential assessment of Griswold's effectiveness. Fortunately for Griswold, Harmon's positive evaluation convinced Marshall that no change was necessary in the Fourteenth Corps. By way of reward for his solid performance, Harmon also sent Griswold on ten days' leave to Australia. Griswold was happy to get out of the fetid Solomons for a while to a more conducive climate, and to see and swap war stories with old friends such as Eichelberger and MacArthur. On the other hand, he also faced some physical problems. Griswold had had a hernia operation before he left the States, and in the Solomons his eye began to bother him. After his leave was up, Griswold flew to an army hospital in Aukland, New Zealand, to have a cyst removed from his eye. The doctors were concerned enough with his overall condition to keep him there for more tests. In the end, they gave him a clean bill of health, but the whole experience rattled and embarrassed him. Perhaps this was what he meant when he told Eichelberger that generals are like monkeys because "the higher up the pole we go the more of our ass we show."[52]

While Griswold was recreating and fretting about his health, SOPAC put into motion its last major offensive. In August the Joint Chiefs of Staff concluded that since it lacked sufficient resources to storm Rabaul, it would be best to simply bypass it. SOPAC's role in Rabaul's isolation was to seize the large northern Solomon island of Bougainville. Rather than assail the well-defended Japanese airstrip at Buin on Bougainville's southern tip, Halsey chose to land instead at Empress Augusta Bay on the island's isolated west coast and build an airfield there from scratch. To carry out the mission, Halsey planned to use the First Marine Amphibious Corps, containing the Third Marine and Thirty-seventh divisions. The Third Marine Division came ashore without serious opposition on 1 November and quickly set about establishing a defense perimeter with the Thirty-seventh Division after its arrival. Halsey, however, decided that he needed the Third Marine Division for other operations, so he ordered Griswold and his Fourteenth Corps, as well as the Americal Division, to take over from the First Marine Amphibious Corps. Griswold established his headquarters on Bougainville on 15 December.

Griswold's first job was once again logistical. The marines and Thirty-seventh Division had already set up a defensive perimeter, but Griswold turned it into a truly fortified position by carving roads through the jungle so he could better supply his forces and take advantage of his interior lines to shuffle troops from place to place if the enemy attacked. In fact, the Japanese were determined to do just that. More than 15,000 Japanese soldiers painstakingly hacked their way from Buin to launch an all-out assault on the Americans at Empress Augusta Bay. They estimated that there were 30,000 Americans waiting for them, when in fact there were twice as many well-equipped and -supplied GIs dug in there. Moreover, Griswold knew the enemy was on its way. When the Japanese charged out of the jungle on 8 March 1944, the Americans greeted them with overwhelming firepower. Griswold needed little tactical skill to wage the battle, which mostly involved committing his reserves to threatened parts of the line. The only real crisis occurred when General John Hodge, the Americal Division's new forceful and feisty commander, evacuated his men from Hill 260. Griswold thought this was a mistake because it enabled the Japanese to look down upon the American perimeter, so he ordered Hodge to retake the hill. Doing so led to an inconclusive back-and-forth struggle in which neither side gained a decisive advantage. The Japanese offensive petered out by 24 March, and three days later the survivors began to retreat through the jungle back to Buin. They had lost more than 5,000 killed and 3,000 wounded, far more than the 263 American dead.[53]

Although the exhausted GIs on Bougainville would have disagreed, Griswold's victory there had been easy compared to his ordeal on New Georgia the previous July. This was in no small part due to Griswold's thorough preparations and competent handling of his forces. This was Marshall's interpretation, and on 3 April he congratulated Griswold through Halsey on a job well done. Unhappily for Griswold, Marshall subsequently forgot about him when Bougainville was overshadowed by bigger events in Europe, such as the Normandy invasion. In the meantime, Griswold stayed on Bougainville to keep an eye on the remaining Japanese and attend to administrative matters as the war passed him by. Fortunately for him, he retained Harmon's confidence, and in fact Harmon wrote General Thomas Handy, Marshall's chief of operations, extolling Griswold's tenacity, diligence, and ability in both combat and logistical operations. Harmon explained:

> I feel that Griswold, during his thirteen months' tour of duty in this area, has been subjected to continuous, exacting pressure greatly beyond that normally anticipated for an officer of similar command responsibilities. Every task to which he has been assigned he has carried through in a superior manner. . . . He is one of those rarities among our senior combat commanders who has a thorough and sound sense and knowledge of the implications of logistics and its co-relation with combat operations.[54]

On 5 July 1944, a navy request to award Griswold a Distinguished Service Medal for his work in the Solomons jogged Marshall's memory. Marshall realized that Griswold had been in the Solomons for more than a year, time enough to physically wear down even the sturdiest of generals. As far as Marshall knew, Griswold was a skilled and experienced corps commander whose services could be put to better use than on backwater Bougainville, so he toyed with the idea of transferring him back to the States, giving him another corps, and shipping him off to Europe to fight the Germans. Since the Fourteenth Corps was now part of SWPA, Marshall solicited MacArthur to see if he was willing to part with Griswold. MacArthur was not and radioed Marshall, "General Griswold is entirely satisfactory as a corps commander and performing an excellent job on Bougainville. There remains a considerable clean up operation on that island in which Griswold is eminently qualified to carry through."[55] So Griswold remained marooned on Bougainville. In September Marshall again contemplated reassigning him, this time to China to serve under General Joe Stilwell, but nothing came of that either. By that time, however, MacArthur had big plans for Griswold and his corps.[56]

Conclusions

The Pacific War consumed far more resources than the army anticipated or wanted. Stopping the initial Japanese offensive required the army to commit not just combat divisions, but corps and a field army as well. Fortunately, the first corps commanders performed credibly despite significant obstacles. The local army theater leaders, MacArthur in SWPA and Harmon in SOPAC, played a passive role while Marshall selected these men based on his criteria. Each corps commander overcame difficult circumstances—Eichelberger at Buna, Patch on Guadalcanal, and Griswold on New Georgia—to win at a time when American experience and materiel superiority could not be taken for granted. Ironically enough, all three corps commanders found their victories bittersweet. MacArthur subsequently sidelined Eichelberger out of jealousy, Patch left the theater due to illness, and Griswold was stranded on Bougainville. On the other hand, the only field army commander dispatched to the Pacific in the first year of the war, Walter Krueger, followed a different trajectory. In his case, Marshall sent him overseas reluctantly and only at MacArthur's specific request. Krueger subsequently led the Sixth Army/Alamo Force successfully through Operation Cartwheel, and at its conclusion there was little doubt that he would continue to play a major role in MacArthur's war.

2
The North African Campaign

Another European War

Unlike the Pacific War, with its peculiar geography and remote Asiatic foe, the European War against Germany and Italy seemed recognizable. Europeans had after all colonized and settled the United States, and almost all army officers and policy makers traced their lineage back to the continent. Despite long-standing isolationist sentiment, the social, political, and economic links between the United States and Europe were strong and durable. The United States had even waged war in France a generation earlier with a mass conscript–based army against the German empire. Indeed, many high-ranking World War Two army commanders cut their military teeth in the Western Front's trenches. Those who missed overseas deployment still studied the conflict's campaigns and toured its battlefields in their serene interwar years. This familiarity helped compensate for the European War's impressive scope and scale. In terms of geography, ideology, and technology, the European War dwarfed its World War One predecessor. In World War One the army limited its deployment mostly to France and was seriously engaged for only six months or so. In World War Two the army's efforts across the Atlantic lasted two and a half years and included armored combat, amphibious operations, and strategic bombing in areas as diverse as the North African deserts, the Italian mountains, and the Belgian forests. Moreover, in this case the enemy was not an atavistic and insecure kaiser, but a fascist regime whose wickedness propagandists did not need to exaggerate.

The United States was not alone in its war against Germany and Italy. Although it had fought with other countries in previous conflicts dating back to the American Revolution, its European War allies were dissimilar in terms of their numbers, strength, and varied circumstances. Each ally presented its own unique set of problems, and dealing with them sometimes seemed to confirm the old adage that war with allies was worse than without them. These allies included a gaggle of governments-in-exile seeking to reclaim their countries from German occupation, among which the Free French were the most prominent. The French were sensitive to slights, contentious, eager to restore their glory and erase the stain of their humiliating defeat in 1940, and disinclined to take direction from anyone. The communist Soviet Union was in a different category altogether. Working with the Soviets required overlooking and downplaying the uncomfortable fact that they were every bit as evil as the Nazi Germans and had joined the Grand Alliance only because their mutually beneficial relationship with Adolf Hitler did not pan out as they hoped. The Soviets bore the brunt of the European War and suffered accordingly. This meant not only that the United States needed them to remain in the conflict to keep American casualties at an acceptable level, but also that the Soviets had a psychological edge in negotiations that they did not fail to utilize. The Soviets were comparatively remote and cooperated only grudgingly with the Americans and British. The Anglo-American alliance, on the other hand, became the most intimate partnership in modern history. The two countries were united by language and culture, and their governments made a conscious decision to collaborate as much as possible on military issues. This included integrated headquarters and staffs down to the field army level, coordinated strategic planning, and the sharing of intelligence and technology. This often caused difficulties because the two nations possessed separate military philosophies, traditions, national goals, and standard operating procedures. Preserving the coalition required strategic compromises that occasionally contradicted army doctrine and created trouble for those army officers forced to navigate between maintaining the all-important alliance and doing what they believed to be militarily sound.

The United States and its new allies confronted the greatest threat to European freedom and security since Napoleon Bonaparte sought to unite the continent under his rule. Despite its defeat twenty years earlier, Germany began World War Two with an advanced economy, reservoirs of scientific talent available to develop new technology, an educated populace, and a formidable army with a long history of prevailing against heavy odds. These assets enabled the Nazis to conquer much of Europe from 1939 to 1941. Indeed, by the time the United States entered the conflict in December 1941, the Germans had occupied Austria, Czechoslovakia, Poland, Denmark and Norway, the Low Countries, France, much of the Balkans, the Baltic States, and the western Soviet Union from the outskirts of Leningrad to Ukraine. Germany therefore had at its disposal a vast region with actual and potential resources comparable to those the Allies possessed. German scientists were also conducting research in areas such as rocketry, jet aircraft, and submarine propulsion that if realized would provide additional advantages for its military. As it was, after two years of war Germany's enemies were barely holding out. The British were fighting desperately to preserve their empire and had no chance of returning to the European mainland on their own, most Europeans were cowed or collaborating, and the Soviets had sustained millions of casualties and lost thousands of square miles of territory.

American involvement held out the hope of eventual German defeat, but its initial efforts generated more heat than light. The same Japanese offensive that brought the United States into the conflict also diverted its attention and assets away from Europe to the Pacific. Moreover, German submarine warfare threatened to derail the United States' efforts to exert its nascent power overseas and aid its British and Soviet allies. None of this boded well for the shaky alliance among the three countries that was based primarily on their common hatred of the Germans. To be sure, by then the Germans had serious problems of their own. Their Italian allies were proving more trouble than they were worth. The Italian people had been unenthusiastic about the war from the start, and dictator Benito Mussolini's foolhardy actions in the Balkans and North Africa required the deployment of scarce German resources to these regions to bolster foundering Italian efforts there. The British were unexpectedly stubborn and resilient, and the war with the Soviets was appallingly bloody, vicious, and unending. Finally, although the Nazis had set Germany's startlingly successful war machine in motion, their inefficient, immoral, and counterproductive policies were already undermining their accomplishments. Even so, the Germans remained redoubtable opponents, so there was nothing inevitable about Allied victory.

In the Pacific War interservice rivalries played a predominant, if not determining, role in strategic planning and the allocation of resources. This was not the case in the European War because geography, doctrine, and politics precluded significant navy involvement. As a continental power, Germany was far less dependent on the ocean for commerce and resources than was Japan. Although the American navy played a vital role in securing the Atlantic sea-lanes and cooperating in amphibious operations, it was the American army that destroyed the German army in western Europe. In addition to these geographic facts of life, army doctrine also pointed it toward Europe. Whereas navy doctrine pushed it toward war with Japan, army doctrine called for a concentration of force against the main enemy target, which when translated into reality meant engaging the Germans on the European continent. Finally, political decisions gave the army good reason to wage war in Europe. Even before American entry into World War Two, the Roosevelt administration decided on a Germany First policy in the event that the United States found itself in a global conflict with multiple enemies. In short, focusing on Germany was natural and politically expedient for the army. As a result, during World War Two the army sent the vast majority of its ground forces across the Atlantic. Of its eighty-nine divisions, sixty-two of them, or more than three-quarters, went to Europe. This was also true of fifteen of its twenty corps and five of its eight field armies dispatched overseas that saw serious action. Only in Europe was the army so big that it needed to form army groups to coordinate and control its larger units. It took time, though, to deploy such enormous forces. Not until the summer of 1944, two and a half years after Pearl Harbor, was the army able to employ sufficient strength to really engage the Germans on the scale necessary for victory. Only eight divisions in one corps fought in North Africa and Sicily in 1942–1943. As late as the spring of 1944, the Fifth Army in Italy, which then constituted the army's main European effort, contained no more than seven American divisions organized into two corps. Not until the Allied invasion of German-occupied France in June 1944 could the army really flex its muscles, so that by the time Germany surrendered the following May there were two American-dominated army groups, four field armies, thirteen corps, and fifty-five divisions actively engaged in northwest Europe.

As in the Pacific War, assigning leaders for these large units was one of Marshall's most important responsibilities. He did so not unilaterally, but rather in consultation with the local army theater commanders. Just as Douglas MacArthur dominated the army's Pacific War efforts, General Dwight Eisenhower was the army's most significant European War personality. Eisenhower was one of Marshall's protégés, and the two men developed a close professional relationship that made their selection process of personnel more informal, open, and reciprocal than the one between Marshall and MacArthur. Generally speaking, Marshall discussed an officer's abilities with McNair before radioing his recommendation to Eisenhower. Although Marshall as chief of staff could have simply ordered Eisenhower to accept an officer as a corps or field army commander, he did not believe in forcing men on his lieutenants. He therefore gave Eisenhower the right to veto his suggestions, and in fact as the war went on and his confidence in Eisenhower grew, he granted him virtual carte blanche over personnel picks. Eisenhower for his part was always solicitous and respectful of Marshall's views, but as time went on he and his right-hand man, General Omar Bradley, developed some definite ideas of their own. Marshall and Eisenhower both agreed that corps and field army commanders should be energetic, tough, selfless, and youthful, and that political connections and other factors unrelated to character and record had no place in their deliberations. Unlike Marshall, Eisenhower emphasized recent combat experience and downplayed education. Eisenhower claimed to be as cold-blooded as Marshall in removing or rejecting inefficient officers, but in reality he was often reluctant to do so with old friends or people with whom he had previously worked. Finally, Eisenhower looked to the past to determine a candidate's future potential. Writing to his son in early 1944, Eisenhower noted, "One thing that has struck me very forcibly, and through conversation I have learned that other old grads have been impressed in the same way, is the frequency with which one finds the older officer of today to be merely a more mature edition of the kid he knew as a Cadet. This is not always so and sometimes the exceptions are so glaring as to prove the rule."[1]

On the surface, the quality of the European War corps and field army commanders appears higher than that of their Pacific War counterparts. European War generals such as Lucian Truscott, J. Lawton Collins, Matthew Ridgway, and of course George Patton are familiar to World War Two aficionados, but almost no one remembers Douglas MacArthur's chief lieutenants. It was, after all, the European War generals who landed at D-Day, broke through enemy lines in Normandy, raced across France, won the bitter Battle of the Bulge, and leapfrogged across the Rhine River into Germany. However, since Marshall and his theater commanders selected their corps and field army commanders from the same pool in roughly the same manner, there are other reasons for the apparent superior generalship displayed in the European War. First of all, Eisenhower raised his officers' profile among contemporaries and historians by giving them credit and press for their accomplishments. This differentiated him from the egotistical MacArthur, who deliberately denied his subordinates much public recognition. Moreover, there were more opportunities to engage in the grand maneuvers and big battles that win renown in the wide expanses of western Europe than on the cramped and jungle-ridden Pacific islands. American field army and corps commanders in both parts of World War Two were as a group generally solid and competent rather than brilliant and innovative. This was perfectly consistent with the army's emphasis on professionalism and convention, and conformed with the realities of the global conflict that tested these men. With its enormous resources, the United States did not need military geniuses capable of overcoming huge odds, but rather proficient generals who could apply American power with minimal risk and casualties. Whatever their missed opportunities and set-piece thinking, European War field army and corps commanders, like their Pacific War colleagues, attained this standard and won the war.

Operation Torch

One afternoon in April 1942, Marshall and General Dwight "Ike" Eisenhower, the assistant chief of the War Plans Division, were in Marshall's War Department office discussing the promotion of another officer. Although Marshall was as usual keeping closely to his regular schedule, the bleary-eyed Eisenhower had, like most General Staff personnel, been working long hours to mobilize and deploy the army for the war all too suddenly upon it. The first months of the conflict had brought little but bad news as the Japanese gobbled up American, British, and Dutch possessions in the Pacific and Southeast Asia one after another. In the course of their conversation, Marshall mentioned that in this war, unlike the last one, he would make sure that promotions went to field commanders instead of staffers. By way of illustration, Marshall explained, "Take your case. I know that you were recommended by one general for a division command and by another for corps command. That's all very well. I'm glad that they have that opinion of you, but you are going to stay right here and fill your position, and that's that! While this may seem a sacrifice to you, that's the way it must be." Eisenhower was an ambitious officer with a temper, and he was not surprisingly unhappy to learn that Marshall intended to imprison him in Washington while his colleagues were leading men into battle. "General," he responded, "I'm interested in what you say, but I want you to know that I don't give a damn about your promotion plans as far as I'm concerned. I came into this office from the field and I am trying to do my duty. I expect to do so as long as you want me here. If that locks me to a desk for the rest of the war, so be it!" Having vented his spleen, Eisenhower stormed toward the door. However, embarrassment overtook him as he walked across the office, so he sheepishly turned back to Marshall and grinned weakly. The chief of staff said nothing, but Eisenhower detected a flicker of a smile cross his face. Three days later, upon receiving word of his elevation to major general, Eisenhower wondered if Marshall had manufactured the incident as some sort of test.[2]

In fact, Marshall had been watching Eisenhower's career for some time and had included him among a group of younger officers he was systematically grooming for important wartime posts. Marshall had not known Eisenhower well personally before the war, but was aware of his stellar reputation. In fact, Marshall had years earlier as assistant commandant of the Infantry School tried unsuccessfully to procure Eisenhower's services. Eisenhower reappeared on Marshall's radar screen in 1939 after his return from a four-year stint in the Philippines. In the summer of 1941, Eisenhower made a name for himself as Walter Krueger's chief of staff during the Louisiana maneuvers. Krueger, not normally one to indulge in effusive praise for anyone, lauded Eisenhower to Marshall as "a man possessing broad vision, progressive ideas, a thorough grasp of the magnitude of the problems involved in handling an Army, and lots of initiative and resourcefulness."[3] Lesley McNair, the head of Army Ground Forces, thought enough of Eisenhower to recommend him for a division command in October 1941. When Marshall asked McNair's assistant, General Mark Clark, for a list of ten candidates to take over as assistant chief of the War Plans Division, Clark responded that Eisenhower was the only person he would suggest. The man Eisenhower would replace, General Leonard Gerow, said the same thing. Marshall made the appointment probably as much to have a look at Eisenhower as anything else. During their time together, Marshall liked what he saw and made a mental note to move Eisenhower up when the right job presented itself.[4]

Like most of Marshall's staffers, Eisenhower quickly developed a deep reverence for the chief of staff. One of Eisenhower's sponsors, General Fox Connor, had told him during their time together in Panama in the 1920s that he should serve with Marshall if he ever got the opportunity. Connor explained to Eisenhower that Marshall was a genius with a greater understanding of the intricacies of coalition warfare than anyone else in the army. Eisenhower remembered the advice, but he was still unhappy with his assignment to the War Plans Division because he desperately wanted a troop command, not another desk job. Although he quickly determined that Marshall was an austere and stern man, he concluded, "I knew about his reputation, of course, but before long I had conceived for him unlimited admiration and respect for my own reasons. He inspired affection in me because I realized the burden he was uncomplainingly carrying. He never seemed to doubt that we would win, even when the Philippines had fallen."[5] Eisenhower extolled Marshall's toughness, stamina, loyalty, and decisiveness. He adopted Marshall as another of his mentors, and the good working relationship they developed eventually played an important role in the selection of many of the field army and corps commanders in the war with Germany.[6]

While Marshall was impressed and pleased with Eisenhower, as time went on he grew increasingly concerned that the long hours Eisenhower worked were taking a toll on his efficiency and making him stale. This perhaps contributed to Marshall's decision to send Eisenhower on an inspection trip to England with Henry Arnold and Mark Clark to check on early American preparations for Operation Roundup, the proposed Allied invasion of German-occupied France tentatively scheduled for the spring of 1943. Eisenhower and his colleagues left on 23 May 1942 and returned twelve days later. Eisenhower concluded that General James Chaney, the Army Air Force commander in London more or less supervising the buildup, was out of touch and lacked sufficient drive. He recommended that all American forces—ground, naval, and air—be placed under one man, and suggested General Joseph McNarney for the position. Marshall, however, had already slated McNarney for his deputy chief of staff. Instead, he gave the post to Eisenhower. As the head of the newly dubbed European Theater of Operations, Eisenhower would oversee American deployments in England until, presumably, Marshall arrived to lead American troops in the cross-channel assault. Eisenhower was elated to get a field command and grateful for Marshall's vote of confidence in him. He was back in England on 24 June.[7]

Eisenhower's biography demonstrates the army's twentieth-century role as a vehicle for social mobility. He was born into a poor family in Texas in 1890 and grew up in Abilene, Kansas. Eisenhower sought an appointment to West Point mostly because it would provide him with a free college education he could not have otherwise afforded. Although he devoted little time to studying, he still managed to graduate in the upper half of his 1915 class. Much to his chagrin, he did not get overseas in World War One, but instead spent the conflict stateside training troops, during which time he became one of the army's few armored experts. After the war, he was assigned to Panama as General Fox Connor's executive officer. Connor took Eisenhower under his wing and exposed him to important works in military science and history. From that point on Eisenhower began to make his mark in the army. He graduated at the top of his 1926 Command and General Staff School class and attended the Army War College two years later. After touring Europe to gather information for a report for the American Battle Monuments Commission, Eisenhower transferred to the War Department to work as chief of staff General Douglas MacArthur's aide. He then accompanied MacArthur to the Philippines as his assistant military adviser. His relationship with MacArthur, always ambiguous and tenuous, gradually deteriorated, and he was happy to return home in late 1939. From that point he entered Marshall's gravitational field, and after the Japanese attack on Pearl Harbor he found himself in the War Plans Division.

Marshall may or may not have yet sensed it, but Eisenhower's greatest attribute, and the one that would most benefit the Allied cause, was his ability to get along with people and persuade them to work together for the common good. He was a charming, popular, and immensely likable man without a trace of phoniness, and possessed a magnetic personality that attracted people to him. One officer noted that within twenty minutes of Eisenhower's walking into a room full of strangers, a good many of them would be calling him by his nickname. Fortunately, there was much more to him than mere affability. He was ambitious without being cloying and underhanded, intelligent rather than scholarly, and eminently practical. His directness, integrity, and modesty enabled him to give credit to others without resentment or jealousy, which went a long way toward winning their loyalty. At the same time, though, Eisenhower was beneath the surface a tough and taut man who, like Marshall, possessed a towering temper he tried hard to control. He chain-smoked constantly, worked hard, and put enormous pressure on himself. Finally, Eisenhower saw and understood the big picture. Some of his contemporaries later claimed that he was not much of a tactician or even a strategist, but this must be placed in context. Because Marshall moved him up so quickly, he never had the opportunity to lead an army group, a field army, a corps, or even a division. Consequently, he was unable to accrue the kind of nuts-and-bolts military knowledge that his colleagues gained through rigorous combat experience. In fact, Eisenhower became primarily a military manager and diplomat, not a battlefield commander. He recognized more clearly than his more parochial subordinates that maintaining the Anglo-American alliance was vital to Allied success. To do so, he made compromises that were not always militarily sound, but that were necessary to preserve the interallied harmony upon which victory depended.[8]

Eisenhower's mission changed dramatically within two months of his arrival in London. The British did not believe that Operation Roundup was then practicable and advocated an Anglo-American landing in North Africa instead as part of an effort to clear the continent of Axis forces. The Joint Chiefs of Staff opposed such a dispersal of Allied resources to a secondary target, but British Prime Minister Churchill circumvented them by appealing directly to President Roosevelt. Roosevelt was eager to see American troops in action, preferably before the November midterm elections, and gave his approval over the JCS's objections. The plan, initially dubbed "Super Gymnast" but later changed to the more inspiring "Torch," called for an Allied amphibious assault against the pro-German Vichy French possessions of Morocco and Algeria. Once safely secured, the Allies could then push eastward and cut off from Europe the German and Italian army operating in Egypt. Because of French antipathy toward the British, stemming from the Royal Navy's sinking of the French fleet at Mers-el-Kabir in July 1940 to keep it out of German hands, Allied leaders concluded that Torch required an American commander to give it an American hue. While batting around prospective candidates, Ernest King suggested Eisenhower. King liked Eisenhower for all the usual reasons, but also respected him because during his time in the War Plans Division Eisenhower had stood up to him. Marshall and Arnold were also predisposed toward Eisenhower. Of equal importance, Eisenhower had during his short time in England thoroughly charmed a good many British leaders, including Churchill, so he was acceptable to them too. Eisenhower was surprised by his sudden change of venue. Indeed, he initially condemned Torch as an unwise diffusion of American resources and doubted it would succeed. Still, orders were orders, and he immediately got to work after receiving word of his new mission on 14 August. As he saw it, effective interallied cooperation was a key to success, so he established an integrated Allied Force Headquarters (AFHQ) to plan and implement Torch. After a prolonged, maddening, and often confusing debate with the War Department, Eisenhower's staff planned to throw 107,000 men—three-quarters of whom were American—at three targets along the North African coast: Casablanca, Oran, and Algiers. The Allies hoped that the French would offer little or no resistance to an American-dominated operation.[9]

Selecting his subordinate commanders was among the many responsibilities Eisenhower faced in planning for Torch. He did so in consultation with Marshall. Marshall did not force anyone or anything on Eisenhower, but he had his opinions and expected Eisenhower to hear them and take them into account. At the same time, he asked Eisenhower to be completely open and honest with him in all areas. In a late September message to Eisenhower, for example, Marshall wrote:

I can't think of any other matters to bring up at this time except to tell you again to deal with me on the frankest possible basis. When you disagree with my point of view, say so, without an apologetic approach; when you want something that you aren't getting, tell me and I will try to get it for you. I have complete confidence in your management of the affair and want to support you in every way practicable.[10]

As it was, Eisenhower was already developing some ideas about the kind of officers he wanted working for him, ideas that subsequently hardened under the stress of war. Eisenhower shared Marshall's disdain for connections and superficiality, as well as his emphasis on leadership, sound judgment, selflessness, and determination in the face of adversity. Although Eisenhower, like Marshall, sought men of character, he defined the term somewhat differently than did the chief of staff. Eisenhower placed more emphasis on imagination and a man's single-minded desire for combat duty. He also expected his lieutenants to understand their subordinates and respect their judgment. Finally, Eisenhower claimed that he intended to be ruthless toward his subordinates. In an August 1942 letter to a friend he wrote:

The men that can do things are going to be sought out just as surely as the sun rises in the morning. Fake reputations, habits of glib and clever speech, and glittering surface performance are going to be discovered and kicked overboard. Solid, sound leadership, with inexhaustible nervous energy to spur on the efforts of lesser men, and iron-clad determination to face discouragement, risk and increasing work without flinching, will always characterize the man who has a sure-enough, bang-up fighting unit. Added to this he must have a darned strong tinge of imagination—I am continuously astounded by the utter lack of imaginative thinking among so many of our people that have reputations for being really good officers. Finally, the man has to be able to forget himself and personal fortunes. I've relieved two seniors here because they got to worrying about "injustice," "unfairness," "prestige," and—oh, what the hell![11]

In fact, Eisenhower was not initially as callous as he claimed, and only gradually developed the ability to separate his personal feelings from a dispassionate analysis of an officer's performance.[12]

During the planning for Torch, Eisenhower worked most closely with General Mark "Wayne" Clark. Clark initially served as the European Theater of Operations' ground forces and Second Corps commander until Eisenhower made him his deputy. Like Eisenhower, Clark was at forty-six comparatively young for his

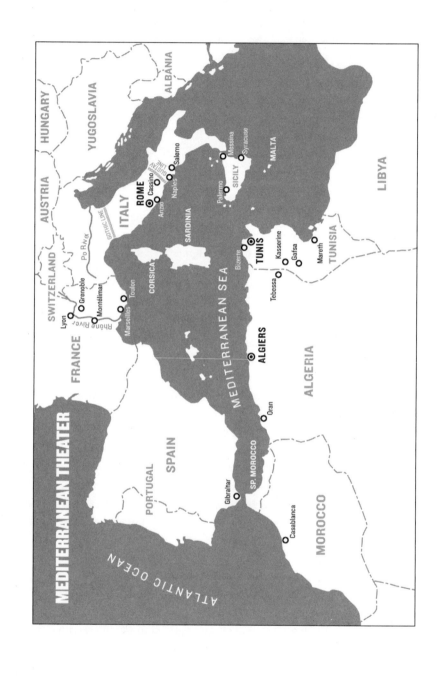

MEDITERRANEAN THEATER

ATLANTIC OCEAN

PORTUGAL

SPAIN

SP. MOROCCO

MOROCCO

Gibraltar

Casablanca

FRANCE

SWITZERLAND

Lyon

Rhône River

Grenoble

Montélimar

Marseilles

Toulon

CORSICA

SARDINIA

MEDITERRANEAN SEA

ALGIERS

Oran

ALGERIA

Tebessa

Kasserine

Gafsa

Mareth

TUNISIA

TUNIS

Bizerte

AUSTRIA

SWITZERLAND

HUNGARY

YUGOSLAVIA

ALBANIA

ITALY

Po River

GOTHIC LINE

ROME

Cassino

Anzio

GUSTAV LINE

Naples

Salerno

Palermo

SICILY

Messina

Syracuse

MALTA

LIBYA

new and immense responsibilities. The son of a career army officer, Clark had been born in 1896 at Madison Barracks in Sackets Harbor, New York. He graduated from West Point just in time to participate in World War One. Although wounded at the head of a battalion in the Aisne-Marne campaign, he recovered soon enough to take part in the St. Mihiel and Argonne offensives. He spent most of the interwar years as a staff officer, interspersed with stints at the Infantry School in 1925, the Command and General Staff School from 1933 to 1935, and the Army War College from 1936 to 1937. He came to Marshall's attention first as the Third Division's operations officer during Marshall's tenure as a brigade commander in that division, and then while overseeing the same unit's amphibious training in Monterrey, California, as its deputy chief of staff in 1940. Marshall initially contemplated sending Clark to teach at the Army War College, but ended up appointing him McNair's deputy for training. Clark often antagonized McNair with his high-handedness, but there is no doubt that he also played a pivotal role in organizing and training the rapidly expanding army and won kudos from almost everyone with whom he came into contact. Marshall decided to make Clark the ground forces commander in England for a number of reasons. For one thing, Marshall felt that Clark's training background would be useful in preparing the American units on their way to England for Operation Roundup. Moreover, Clark had impressed the British, and it seemed a good idea to build upon that sentiment by keeping him there. Finally, Clark's old friend Eisenhower recognized talent when he saw it and specifically asked for him. McNair and Marshall both alluded to the new job after Clark returned from his inspection trip to England, but he did not get his official orders until 10 June. Clark was elated but sobered by this momentous assignment, which catapulted him to the top of the American war effort in Europe.[13]

As Marshall and Eisenhower realized, Clark was a valuable and impressive officer for many reasons. Tall, impeccably dressed, and with a lean and hungry face behind a big Roman nose—Churchill referred to him affectionately as the "American Eagle"—Clark conveyed intelligence, energy, and determination. He made his mark as an organizer, trainer, and planner by pitilessly cutting away the bureaucratic weeds that so often choked innovation and creativity in the army. He could, in short, get things done. Unfortunately, there was an off-putting side to Clark that hindered his effectiveness throughout the war. Whereas no one held Eisenhower's ambition against him, Clark's seemed underhanded and self-serving. He craved the limelight and was a shameless self-promoter, often at the expense of others. His temper, vanity, chauvinism, and aloofness toward subordinates worked against him too, so that more than one officer later called Clark his own worst enemy. For all his ability, Clark lacked sufficient introspection to recognize and correct these foibles. Many of his colleagues, including George Patton and

Omar Bradley, viewed him warily and never quite trusted him. Eisenhower also came to see Clark somewhat balefully, but found him so indispensable during the planning for Torch that he eventually made him his deputy commander and gave him considerable autonomy to act as he saw fit. Eisenhower wanted a knowledgeable American on deck in case anything happened to him, and doing so also made organizational sense. Clark was reluctant to surrender his corps, but did so out of a sense of duty and also because he hoped his new job would get him into action sooner rather than later. He found his experience as deputy commander akin to "sitting on a thousand volcanoes." Clark got his first taste of the fame he sought when he secretly traveled to Algiers on a British submarine to meet with a pro-Allied French party on 22 October to discuss the possibilities of cooperation. Although he did not achieve much, and in fact in retrospect the entire mission seemed unwise, the drama associated with his getaway eventually garnered considerable attention from the press.[14]

Even with Clark's help, Eisenhower remained overwhelmed with the enormous demands on his time that preparing for Torch required. There simply were not enough hours in the day for all the necessary paperwork and meetings. Eisenhower realized that he needed a chief of staff to relieve him of some of the burden, and he knew just the man for the job: General Walter Bedell "Beetle" Smith. The Indiana-born Smith trained as a machinist and worked in an automobile plant when he was young, but his first love was soldiering. In 1911, at age sixteen, he joined the Indiana National Guard, and he received his commission when the United States entered World War One. He was wounded in France and ended the conflict on the General Staff in Washington. He opted to remain in the army after the war, and attended both the Command and General Staff School and Army War College. He spent most of the interwar years, however, as an instructor. After World War Two began in Europe, Omar Bradley, then assistant secretary of the General Staff, was so frustrated that Marshall devoted so much time editing his staff officers' outgoing letters that he suggested to Marshall that he bring in the erudite Smith to do the job. Bradley later joked that although Marshall had a high opinion of Smith, he had to be reminded of it. Marshall made the appointment, but Smith eventually ended up serving as liaison to the White House and Treasury Department. Marshall found him so valuable that he only reluctantly surrendered him to Eisenhower. At the same time, Marshall for some reason enjoyed needling Smith. During the North African campaign, for example, he repeatedly complained to a busy Smith that the army band in the theater was not receiving enough publicity, and threatened to put a marine in charge unless Smith attained better results.[15]

Smith was a lean man with a square jaw and deeply dimpled chin. Almost everyone praised his sharp intellect, eloquence, and ability to cut through red tape. He was in fact direct, abrupt, hard-boiled, and brutally blunt to the point of tactlessness. He intimidated people with his sarcasm and intensity. For instance, he once called his female secretary an idiot in her presence and that of several other officers. On the other hand, he was considerably nicer and more diplomatic after hours. As chief of staff, Smith served ably as Eisenhower's hatchet man, gatekeeper, and paper pusher, freeing up Eisenhower's time for more important activities. By assuming the role of the bad cop, Smith helped protect and preserve Eisenhower's genial image that was a key to interallied cooperation. Eisenhower was very pleased with Smith's work, and within two weeks of his arrival wrote, "I wish I had a dozen like him."[16] Unfortunately for Smith, the stress of his new job exacerbated his chronic ulcer and reduced him to a dairy diet. He became so ill that at the end of September Eisenhower ordered him to a hospital, where he received an immediate blood transfusion. Smith feared Eisenhower would send him home, but he recovered and remained Eisenhower's chief of staff until the end of the war.[17]

Eisenhower also had to select the leaders for the three task forces slated to land on the North African coast. The Eastern Task Force, targeting Algiers, went to General Charles "Doc" Ryder because his Thirty-fourth Division was spearheading the assault. Choosing the Central Task Force commander for the attack on Oran was more difficult. Eisenhower originally planned to give the assignment to General Russell "Scrappy" Hartle, the head of the Fifth Corps. Hartle and his Fifth Corps headquarters were already in Britain, and Eisenhower felt that he had done a good workmanlike job. If this contradicted the tough standard for leadership Eisenhower frequently espoused in his correspondence, he did not recognize it as such. Marshall, however, identified the problem immediately when in late September Clark flew to Washington to update him on Torch's progress. Marshall may or may not have been aware that Hartle was overly fond of the bottle, but he stated plainly that Hartle's mediocrity should disqualify him from such an important undertaking. While Marshall preferred that Clark take over the Central Task Force, he added that he was willing to give Eisenhower almost any officer he might want for the mission. Indeed, the list Marshall provided was a veritable who's who of the army's most distinguished generals, including Lesley McNair, Jacob Devers, Ernest Dawley, William Simpson, Oscar Griswold, Courtney Hodges, John Lucas, Lloyd Fredendall, and Robert Richardson. He specifically singled out Dawley as a man who had impressed McNair.[18]

As soon as Clark returned to Britain, he and Eisenhower huddled to discuss among other things the Central Task Force command. Eisenhower decided to heed Marshall's advice and jettison Hartle, but also concluded that Clark was too important to Torch's overall success to take a lesser role, much to Clark's chagrin. Despite Marshall's obvious hint about Dawley, Eisenhower instead opted to ask for Lloyd Fredendall to lead the Central Task Force, which included elements of the Ninth, Thirty-fourth, and First Armored divisions. Later, when it was time to distribute credit and blame for the North African campaign, both Marshall and Eisenhower claimed they had been unfamiliar with Fredendall and distanced themselves from his selection. In fact, Fredendall owed his high standing to Lesley McNair's sponsorship. McNair appreciated Fredendall's solid performance in the 1941 Carolina maneuvers and had written Marshall shortly afterward, "I feel strongly that you have something in Fredendall. I wish that there were more like him."[19] Both Marshall and Clark took their cue from McNair, and transmitted McNair's high opinion of Fredendall to Eisenhower. To Eisenhower, Fredendall sounded like the kind of tough and hard-driving general he was looking for.[20]

Like Clark, Fredendall was the son of a career army officer. Born in Cheyenne, Wyoming, in 1883, Fredendall heeded his parents' wishes and secured an appointment to West Point. Unfortunately, he failed out of the academy twice because he could not grasp trigonometry and analytical geometry. Undaunted, he enrolled in the Massachusetts Institute of Technology to bring his mathematical skills up to speed, and then successfully passed the officer's qualifying exam and got commissioned in 1906. As a young officer he served in the Philippines and Hawaii. Although he managed to get to France in World War One, he spent the conflict as commandant of a training camp and saw no action. Afterward, he attended the Infantry School in 1922, the Command and General Staff School from 1922 to 1923, and the Army War College from 1924 to 1925. He taught military science and tactics at the University of Minnesota and led a regiment in the Philippines. He also worked in the Statistics Branch, the Inspector General's Department, and the Office of the Chief of Infantry. Marshall appointed him commander of the Fourth Division in October 1940, and less than a year later moved him up to the Second Corps. Marshall subsequently transferred him to the newly created Eleventh Corps to make room for Clark to take over the Second, but assured Fredendall that it was no reflection on his abilities. On 9 October, only a week after Eisenhower requested his services, Fredendall was in Britain preparing for his part in Torch.[21]

On the surface, there was much to admire about Fredendall. He was a small, tough, self-confident, and feisty man who looked younger than his fifty-nine years. Although a strict disciplinarian and fine trainer with a well-deserved reputation for profanity, he was also something of an intellectual. Perhaps because of his insomnia, he read widely, and when he did not feel like doing that he passed his nights sitting cross-legged on the floor playing solitaire. His hard-driving and direct manner had worked well for him in prewar maneuvers, but unfortunately he had only affected the mannerisms of a successful can-do general, not absorbed the essence. There was in fact a certain brittleness to Fredendall's character that hardly boded well. He was extremely critical of almost everyone, including subordinates, superiors, and allies, so he did not always take advice even if it was obviously in his best interests to do so. Worse yet, he tended to jump to conclusions without sufficient evidence. These traits were unlikely to endear him to those working for or with him, and would instead undermine the teamwork upon which military success depended. His deficiencies, as of yet undetected, would manifest themselves with tragic results in the barren wastes of central Tunisia.[22]

Finally, Eisenhower procured the services of an old friend, General George Patton, to head the Western Task Force, containing elements of the Third and Second Armored divisions. Born in California in 1885, Patton spent a year at the Virginia Military Institute before transferring to West Point, from which he graduated in 1909 and was commissioned in the cavalry branch. He attended and then taught at the Mounted Service School and competed in the Pentathlon in the 1912 Stockholm Olympics. He later wheedled his way onto General John Pershing's staff to participate in the 1916–1917 Punitive Expedition into northern Mexico, during which he killed one of Pancho Villa's lieutenants in a shoot-out. After the United States entered World War One, Patton accompanied Pershing to Europe. In France he was put in charge of a tank school, and he was later wounded leading an armored brigade in the St. Mihiel operation. Although he recognized the tank's potential, he returned to the cavalry after the war because there seemed no future for armor in the postwar army. He held a variety of staff and line positions in the interwar years, and punched his ticket at the Command and General Staff School from 1922 to 1923 and the Army War College nine years later. When the German conquest of Poland, the Low Countries, and France proved to everyone the tank's value, Patton re-embraced armored warfare. He commanded in succession an armored brigade, the Second Armored Division, the First Armored Corps, and the Desert Training Center before Marshall assigned him to Torch.

Patton was a complicated man. Perhaps to compensate for an unusually high and squeaky voice or some deep-seated insecurity, he cultivated a flamboyant and boastful persona. He was known for his outspokenness, outlandish and profane stories, and colorful garb. For example, he once claimed to have discovered a drowned Mexican floating in a cask while sampling a California wine, and said that his grandfather had killed the governor of the Bahamas with a decanter. Small wonder that more than one person thought he was crazy. His marriage into a wealthy family provided him with a standard of living far above that of other officers and enabled him to indulge in polo and yachting. Although he enjoyed such activities, he was a terrible sport who did not know how to lose gracefully. Whether on the battlefield, playing field, or high seas, Patton sought to attract attention to himself by demonstrating his reckless courage. His example inspired some and annoyed others. Indeed, he was as sycophantic and ingratiating toward his superiors as he was demanding and mercurial toward his subordinates. Fantastic statements, undeniable charisma, buffoonish behavior, bizarre mannerisms, and independent wealth made him a standout in the prewar officer corps. Just beneath the surface, though, Patton was much different. He was so sensitive, emotional, and soft-hearted that he was easily moved to tears. Although he seemed to value impulsiveness, he was actually a thoughtful man well-versed in topics as diverse as Scripture, Shakespeare, military leadership, and history. For instance, he would frequently praise enlisted men for seemingly mundane work—digging a ditch, directing traffic, or so forth—knowing that word would get around and improve morale. As one officer explained, "Georgie always gave you the impression that he didn't have any brains, he was just one of those fellows that drove ahead; far from it, he was a very shrewd and a very confident man. . . . He was an extremely able tactician, and strategist too."[23] American World War Two generals tended to be cautious men who sought to use their military power to win with minimum risk and loss, but Patton was an exception. He believed in seizing the initiative, maintaining maximum pressure on the enemy, and ruthlessly exploiting whatever opportunities presented themselves regardless of the dangers involved. If his judgment was sometimes questionable, his willingness to fight was not.[24]

Considering the controversy Patton invariably generated, it was hardly surprising that some of Eisenhower's staffers doubted the wisdom of assigning such a loose cannon to lead the Western Task Force. Happily for Patton, Eisenhower disagreed. Eisenhower and Patton were old friends. They shared an interest in armored warfare, and during their time together at Fort Meade after World War One had stripped an entire tank down to its component parts and then reassembled it. Indeed, Patton had served as one of Eisenhower's many mentors. Clark also wanted Patton for the job. When Clark was a teenager at Fort Sheridan, Illinois, a dashing and newly commissioned Patton had impressed him as the ideal cavalry officer, and the intervening years had not diminished Clark's opinion. Eisenhower asked for Patton for Torch, but he was not sure that Marshall would go along with the application because of his seniority. Marshall, however, was not one to worry about such formalities. Marshall had a soft spot for eccentric officers such as Patton who marched to their own tune. He was familiar with Patton and had been keeping an eye on his career even before Patton distinguished himself in the 1941 Louisiana maneuvers. In fact, Marshall and his wife had temporarily stayed with the Pattons at their Fort Myers, Virginia, quarters after Marshall became chief of staff. Although Marshall did not approve of Patton's often immature behavior, he recognized the man's ability and wanted to put him to good use. Secretary of War Stimson was another of Patton's supporters. On the other hand, McNair was less enthusiastic and had opined to Marshall that division command was probably Patton's limit. Despite McNair's reservations, on 11 August Marshall acceded to Eisenhower's request and appointed Patton to the Western Task Force.[25]

Torch was a complicated operation for all sorts of reasons. Logistically, it involved transporting and escorting over 100,000 Allied troops with all their supplies and equipment across the U-boat–infested Atlantic from starting points as diverse as Virginia, Maine, and Scotland. In an effort to secure Vichy French support—or at least acquiescence—for the invasion, Eisenhower and Clark entered into protracted and difficult negotiations with French officials that Clark later described as "perfect hell." Finally, there were some personnel problems. Fredendall caused little trouble and as time went on grew on Eisenhower, but Patton was another matter. As soon as Patton returned to the States from his mid-August consultations with Eisenhower in England, he so alienated the naval officers with whom he was cooperating that Eisenhower heard rumors that Marshall was considering relieving him of his command. Eisenhower figured that the navy did not understand Patton's peculiar personality and successfully discouraged such efforts, and in the end Patton and his naval counterpart managed to hammer out their differences. Patton and Eisenhower agreed that Torch was bad strategy, but were determined to make it work. Patton believed that speed, drive, and especially leadership were the keys to victory. He worried that his old friend Eisenhower was becoming too self-important, and concluded that Clark was more interested in furthering his own career than the war effort.

Unfortunately for Patton's disposition, there was not much he could do about his superiors. On the other hand, he was in a position to select some of his subordinates. He secured the services of General Geoffrey Keyes as his deputy, General Lucian Truscott to lead one of his assault forces, and General Ernest Harmon as commander of the Second Armored Division. Marshall was not sure that Harmon was up to the job, but gave way when Patton insisted on including him. Although Patton continued to have nagging doubts about the operation, he felt he had done all he could by the time his convoy set sail from Norfolk, Virginia, on 23 October. From then until the soldiers hit their beaches, the operation was out of his hands. Mulling things over on the cruiser USS *Augusta*, Patton wrote in his diary, "Every once in a while the tremendous responsibility of this job lands on me like a ton of bricks, but mostly I am not in the least worried. I can't decide logically if I am a man of destiny or a lucky fool, but I think I am destined."[26]

At dawn on 8 November, American and British forces descended into their landing craft and stormed the North African beaches. Resistance from Vichy French troops varied from place to place depending mostly upon the inclinations of local military leaders. Pro-American elements at Algiers made the Eastern Task Force's job comparatively easy. Most of its units faced little or no opposition as they splashed ashore, and a negotiated ceasefire at the end of the day enabled the

Americans to occupy the city with scarcely a shot fired. By then Doc Ryder was so thoroughly exhausted from days without sleep that he was barely able to function, but fortunately his best was not necessary on that occasion. The fighting was heavier at Oran and required a major American attack before the French surrendered on 10 November. Finally, Patton's Western Task Force had the most difficult time of all. Heavy surf and communications snafus turned the beaches into a chaotic mess, and some French soldiers fought fiercely. Just as Patton was preparing an all-out assault on Casablanca on 11 November, though, he received word that the French had capitulated throughout North Africa the previous day, rendering an attack unnecessary. Allied casualties for Torch were approximately 2,200. Although French losses were less certain, they probably topped 3,000. For this bargain price, the Allies secured a foothold in northwest Africa from which they could launch an offensive into Tunisia and hopefully trap Field Marshall Erwin Rommel's German-Italian army fleeing westward after its defeat at the hands of the British at the Battle of El Alamein in late October.[27]

Eisenhower began distributing credit for Torch's victory even before the fighting ended. He did so not only out of his generous nature, but also no doubt to justify his and Marshall's personnel selections. He did not assess his subordinates according to the rigorous and unforgiving criteria he frequently referred to in his correspondence, but rather on the basis of secondhand information and snap judgments. Although he recommended both Patton and Fredendall for promotions to lieutenant general, he lavished most of his praise on the latter officer in his cables to Marshall. On 11 November, only three days after the landings, he wrote to the chief of staff, "I bless the day you urged Fredendall upon me and cheerfully acknowledge that my earlier doubts of him were completely unfounded."[28] These words would later prove quite embarrassing to Eisenhower, but at the time they made perfect sense. Almost everyone commended Fredendall's efforts at Oran, including even the high-handed British. He had, after all, fulfilled his mission in seventy-two hours with minimal losses. In addition, Eisenhower lauded Patton, Ryder, Harmon, Smith, and Truscott for their efforts. He specifically noted that Truscott had conducted Torch's stiffest engagement in seizing Port Lyautey. In terms of concrete awards, though, the biggest prize went to the man who had not fought at all: Mark Clark. Eisenhower placed Clark in charge of a new American field army—the Fifth—he was creating for future operations. Eisenhower's peculiar reasoning was that Clark deserved to lead the outfit because he was most familiar with American resources, plans, and prospects in the Mediterranean, and should therefore outrank all other officers in the region. If Eisenhower was a man going places—and, after Torch, he clearly was—then he was bringing along most of the high-ranking ground forces commanders who had made his initial success possible.[29]

Rocky Victory in North Africa

Unhappily for the Allies, exploiting Torch's success proved far more problematic than anyone anticipated. Eisenhower's initial optimism rapidly crumbled under the weight of the seemingly intractable difficulties he faced. For one thing, the logistics involved in an Allied advance to Tunisia were formidable. There were no usable railroads to Tunisia, and the mountainous region's few roads turned to mud holes when the winter rains arrived. As a result, it was much easier for the Germans to rush reinforcements to Tunisia through the ports of Tunis and Bizerte than for the Allies to get there. Moreover, a continuing fear that fascist Spain might enter the war on the side of the Axis compelled Eisenhower to keep substantial forces in Morocco that he could otherwise have deployed eastward. Not only were the Americans new to war, but the British and Americans were unaccustomed to working together, leading to innumerable misunderstandings and mistakes for Eisenhower's inexperienced headquarters to sort out. Finally, although dealing with local French officials was clearly necessary to maintain control over northwest Africa, doing so exposed Eisenhower to severe criticism back home for negotiating with collaborators. Considering these obstacles, it was hardly surprising that the Allies failed to push toward Tunisia with sufficient strength. Those troops whom British First Army commander General Kenneth Anderson managed to get across the mountains ran into heavy opposition at Longstop Hill, only 25 miles from Tunis, in late December. The Germans drove the British and Americans off the hill and inflicted more than 500 casualties on them. This setback, along with worsening rains that all but immobilized the mechanized Allied armies, persuaded Eisenhower to suspend his offensive. The Allies had lost the race for Tunisia.

Not surprisingly, criticism of Eisenhower increased in proportion to his setbacks. Some American officers grumbled that he was too pro-British, and attributed his Anglophilia at least in part to an affair he may have been having with his English driver, Kay Summersby. Some British officers, on the other hand, focused on his inexperience and supposed incompetence. For instance, General Alan Brooke, the chief of the Imperial General Staff, complained that Eisenhower devoted too much time to political affairs, and snidely noted that it was just as well because he was such a poor strategist. Indeed, the British successfully inserted between Eisenhower and his combat generals British General Harold Alexander as Allied ground forces commander in part to isolate Eisenhower from the day-to-day military matters that they felt he was too inept to handle himself. Others found fault with Eisenhower's disorganized headquarters and the logistical mess behind the lines. This carping took a toll on Eisenhower, who was learning that leadership often required waiting for subordinates to do their jobs while those without all the facts offered unsolicited advice and criticism. He smoked more than ever, contracted pneumonia, was depressed, and frequently lost his temper. After one particularly difficult meeting he exclaimed, "Anyone who wants my job as commander of the North African Theater of Operations can damned well have it!"[30] Rumors spread that he would be relieved of his command, and he himself sometimes feared that it was just a matter of time.

Fortunately for Eisenhower, he retained Marshall's confidence. In late January 1943, after the Casablanca Conference, Marshall visited Eisenhower at his Algiers headquarters. He urged Eisenhower to concentrate on the immediate military situation, leave mundane matters to his staff, and relax more. His attitude, one observer noted, was akin to that of a father to a son, though Marshall was always careful not to refer to Eisenhower by his nickname. Remaining in Marshall's good graces was of course important, but Eisenhower knew as well as anyone that Marshall's continued support depended on his ability to deliver victory in North Africa.[31]

The fluid military situation in North Africa required some changes in the American command structure. The biggest question was who would lead American ground forces in Tunisia. Not surprisingly, Eisenhower first turned to Mark Clark, with whom he had worked closely for months. Eisenhower had already slated Clark to command the new Fifth Army, and Clark hoped to deploy that unit's headquarters to Tunisia with him. The problem was that there were not enough American troops in Tunisia to warrant anything more than a corps, and Clark was reluctant to step down to that level. Eisenhower was already getting a little put out with Clark's overweening ambition and self-centeredness, so in response to this recalcitrance he removed Clark as his deputy and sent him to Oujda to train and organize the Fifth Army. As Eisenhower noted months later:

> [Clark's] only drawback now is a lack of combat experience in a high
> command position. This I tried to give him in the early days of organizing an
> American Task Force in the central Tunisian front. He rather resented taking
> any title except that of Army Commander, and since I would not at that time
> establish an American Army Command on the Tunisian front, I had to place
> another in charge of the American effort.[32]

Eisenhower somewhat disingenuously explained to Clark that his new job would play to his organizational strengths and make it easier for the Allies to keep an eye on the Spanish and French. Clark claimed to see Eisenhower's logic, but he was deeply disappointed with this inactive assignment far from the combat and glory that the Tunisian front offered. For this he had no one to blame but himself, though he did not see it this way. In fact, he began badmouthing Eisenhower to fellow officers such as Patton, who saw these denunciations as more evidence of Clark's underhandedness. He became so difficult that in late January Eisenhower summoned him to Algiers for a "very frank" discussion about his poor attitude.

With Clark eliminated from contention, Eisenhower's choices for the Tunisian front narrowed to Fredendall and Patton. Although Eisenhower respected Patton and contemplated making him his deputy ground forces commander, he selected Fredendall instead. Eisenhower reasoned that since most of the troops and staffers in western Tunisia currently belonged to Fredendall anyway, he should logically command there. And so Fredendall, not Patton, took over the Second Corps in western Tunisia shortly after the new year began.[33]

By early February 1943, Anderson's British First Army held a line through Tunisia stretching from the Mediterranean to El Guettar. To fill it, Eisenhower deployed the British Fifth Corps to the north, Fredendall's Second Corps in the center, and the poorly equipped French Nineteenth Corps to the south. While the Allies got their military ducks in a row, German strength in Tunisia increased. In addition to the 111,000 German and Italian troops rushed to Tunisia after Torch, Rommel's 78,000 men finally arrived following their 1,400-mile retreat from Egypt after the Battle of El Alamein. Rommel left some of his men at the Mareth Line in southern Tunisia to thwart General Bernard Montgomery's pursuing British Eighth Army and moved the remainder to central Tunisia. Unfortunately, Fredendall had difficulty deploying his mostly green and inexperienced Americans. Although Eisenhower had praised Fredendall's energy and ability, some of his less admirable traits manifested themselves in the Tunisian highlands. Fredendall was a xenophobic man who distrusted the British in general and Anderson in particular. The previous November he had told Patton that he feared that the British would dominate the war effort and leave the Americans out in the cold. His staff picked up on and disseminated this anti-British sentiment. Not only did Fredendall dislike the British, but he did not get along with some of his subordinates either. In particular, he and General Orlando "Pinky" Ward, the scholarly and reserved commander of the First Armored Division, were at loggerheads. Fredendall concluded that Ward was incompetent and disloyal, and Ward felt that Fredendall did not know how to handle armor. The two men barely communicated with each other, and in fact Fredendall began bypassing Ward and issuing orders directly to his subordinates. Finally, Fredendall rarely left his isolated headquarters about 8 miles from Tebessa, but he was still suspicious of reports from officers who had been to the front. As a result, Fredendall scattered his units across the Tunisian mountains and did not provide an adequate reserve. He seemed to believe that he was waging the static warfare that had characterized World War One. Eisenhower was aware of some of these problems, and on 4 February he sent Fredendall an unofficial letter urging him to get along with the British and to keep his subordinates on their toes. Eleven days later, he assured Marshall that Fredendall was doing well, writing, "He is working incessantly and for the past few days has had little rest. Yet he seems keen and fit, and I am placing a lot of confidence in him."[34]

In fact, Fredendall had good reason to work hard. On 13 February, Rommel launched an all-out offensive against the Second Corps. The Germans charged through the Faid Pass in the eastern Dorsal Mountains and caught the First Armored Division by surprise at the town of Sidi Bou Zid. With air superiority, better equipment, and greater experience, the Germans shattered the American line. After two days of fighting, Anderson ordered a retreat fifty miles westward behind the western Dorsal Mountains, the last substantial natural barrier between the Germans and the Allied logistical nexus along the Algerian coast. The Germans assailed Kasserine Pass on 19 February and broke through the next day. Then, however, Rommel paused. The Germans had overextended themselves with their rapid advance, and Allied reinforcements were flooding into the region. American artillery in particular was playing an increasingly decisive role in disrupting German dispositions. Finally, Montgomery's British Eighth Army was threatening the Mareth Line to the south. Mulling things over, Rommel responded with uncharacteristic restraint and opted to suspend the operation. On 23 February, the Germans fell back through Kasserine Pass to the eastern Dorsal Mountains. At the cost of only 2,000 men, Rommel had inflicted more than 10,000 casualties—6,500 of them American—captured a lot of equipment, and humiliated the American army.

Regrettably, Fredendall did not rise to the occasion during the German offensive. He rarely left his isolated headquarters, but instead tried to fight the battle over the telephone and radio. As a result, he failed to deploy and maneuver his troops effectively. By now Fredendall had so little confidence in Ward that he dealt with him as infrequently as possible. His habit of circumventing Ward contributed to the First Armored Division's woes. On 19 February, Fredendall told Lucian Truscott, now serving as Eisenhower's special representative, that Ward should be relieved of his command. Truscott believed that Fredendall and Ward were both at fault and obviously could not work together, and told Eisenhower as much when he returned to Algiers. Eisenhower was unsure what to do. He liked and respected Ward and had no desire to ruin his career by acceding to Fredendall's request. He responded to Fredendall by lauding Ward's performance so far and attributing Ward's problems to exhaustion and overwork. Fredendall got the hint and replied that he had no desire to remove Ward. Safeguarding Ward's future, though, perpetuated rather than resolved the personality differences that were handicapping American efforts to stop the German attack. To remedy and clarify the situation, Eisenhower resorted to a stratagem he and Truscott had previously discussed. On 20 February, Eisenhower ordered Ernest Harmon, current commander of the Second Armored Division in Morocco, to report to Algiers. When Harmon arrived, Eisenhower informed him that he would go to the front to serve as Fredendall's deputy in whatever capacity Fredendall thought necessary.[35]

Harmon would play an important if often unheralded role in the war against Germany in North Africa, Italy, and northwestern Europe. Born in Massachusetts in 1894, he went to Norwich University for a year before transferring to West Point, from where he graduated in 1917. During World War One he fought at St. Mihiel and in the Argonne Forest. After the conflict he went to the Cavalry School and then taught at West Point and Norwich. He attended the Command and General Staff School from 1931 to 1933 and the Army War College from 1933 to 1934 before serving a four-year stint on the General Staff. Although—or perhaps because—he was a cavalryman, he gravitated toward the armor after World War Two began in Europe and rose to lead the Second Armored Division. Harmon was a colorful, tough, and energetic man who smoked constantly and possessed a low gravelly voice. Like Patton, he enjoyed combat and once exclaimed to a subordinate, "By God! I got everything in the division shooting, including all the tank dozers."[36] Terse and profane in speech, he had a coarseness that separated him from many of his more sophisticated colleagues. At the same time, he possessed a certain introspection that gave him a philosophical outlook toward life. He was in many respects cut from the same cloth as his mentor Patton. Unlike the more ingratiating and sycophantic Patton, however, the blunt Harmon was more inclined to talk back to his superiors, making him difficult to handle. Perhaps for this reason, Marshall had his doubts about Harmon and let him participate in Torch only at Patton's insistence. He won Patton's and Eisenhower's praise for his actions at Casablanca, so it was hardly surprising that when Eisenhower needed help reconciling Fredendall's and Ward's differing views of the proper employment of armor in Tunisia, he turned to Harmon.[37]

Harmon flew to Algiers from Rabat in Morocco on 21 February and met with Eisenhower that afternoon. A dour and depressed Eisenhower outlined the military situation, discussed the ongoing personality conflict between Fredendall and Ward, and gave Harmon his orders. While Eisenhower authorized Harmon to relieve Fredendall or Ward if he felt it necessary, the main thrust of his directive was that he should help Fredendall in any way possible. Such broad and vague instructions made Harmon so nervous that he tossed and turned all night. Indeed, Eisenhower and his aide could only with difficulty awaken Harmon at 3 A.M. the next morning. In one of the war's more incongruous scenes, Eisenhower laced up a semiconscious Harmon's boots, bundled him into a car, and then guided him to a bomb shelter during a German air raid. When Harmon arrived at Second Corps headquarters after threading his way through trucks and men fleeing the battle, one of Fredendall's first questions was whether they should evacuate to a safer location. Harmon had only the sketchiest understanding of current conditions, but he was a pugnacious man who did not like to retreat unless absolutely necessary, so he recommended against pulling out. In fact, Harmon had already decided to do whatever he thought was best because he figured he would get little credit if successful and considerable blame if things went wrong. After listening to Fredendall complain about Ward, Harmon asked if he could act as he saw fit. When Fredendall answered yes, Harmon said, "Well, here, give me that phone." Although he was supposedly supervising Ward, Harmon spent the next few days doing Fredendall's job. He got out in the field, untangled and deployed and coordinated units, and reestablished the tattered American lines. The Germans certainly made his task much easier by withdrawing, but Harmon still deserved credit for bringing order to the chaos. When he finally returned to Second Corps headquarters, he found Fredendall asleep. Harmon later wrote that Fredendall had had a few too many drinks and had called Anderson to give him a piece of his mind before turning in. At any rate, after Harmon woke him and reviewed his actions, Fredendall asked Harmon if he intended to remove Ward. Harmon responded that he felt that Ward was doing a good job and that Fredendall should leave him alone. If that was the case, said Fredendall, then Harmon may as well go home. This was fine with Harmon, and, after stopping at Constantine to see his friend Truscott, he reported to Eisenhower in Algiers on 28 February.[38]

Harmon was just about the only American to emerge from the Kasserine Pass debacle with an enhanced reputation. His fine performance elicited a congratulatory letter from Eisenhower, but Harmon was most proud of the reception he received from his division when he returned to Morocco. Word of his arrival spread beforehand, and thousands of waving and cheering GIs lined the road as he drove by. For most high-ranking American officers, though, Kasserine Pass was a painful and humiliating memory. Omar Bradley, for example, wrote shortly before he died, "Even these many years later, it pains me to reflect on that disaster."[39] Eisenhower was of a similar mind. He was aware that he had hardly lived up to the promotion to full general he obtained just before the German offensive, and had a difficult time keeping cheerful and optimistic in the difficult days that followed. Fortunately for Eisenhower, he retained Marshall's confidence. Marshall was of course deeply concerned about the army's poor performance at Kasserine Pass, but he did not intend to pull the rug out from under Eisenhower. Knowing this helped sustain Eisenhower through the crisis.[40]

Eisenhower was willing to accept some of the responsibility for the Kasserine Pass debacle, but in truth there was plenty of blame to go around. Not surprisingly, though, most observers traced the defeat directly back to the unpopular

Fredendall and were not shy about saying so. In the aftermath of the battle, innumerable high-ranking officers such as Anderson, Alexander, Beetle Smith, Omar Bradley, Truscott, and Harmon all recommended to Eisenhower that he replace Fredendall because he simply was not up to the job of running an army corps. For example, when Eisenhower asked Harmon after his short sojourn to the front for his opinion on Fredendall, Harmon responded bluntly, "He's no damned good. You ought to get rid of him."[41] Alexander, on the other hand, expressed his views more diplomatically by telling Eisenhower, "I'm sure you must have better men than that."[42] Although the Second Corps staff loyally defended him, Fredendall's chief lieutenants had all lost confidence in him. This included Ward of course, but also General Terry Allen of the First Division and Doc Ryder of the Thirth-fourth Division. All of them had seen firsthand the tragic results of Fredendall's generalship and had no desire to participate in another operation under his command.

Despite these testimonials against Fredendall, Eisenhower hesitated to remove him. After all, he had appointed Fredendall to the position he had failed to fill effectively and had on several occasions during and after the battle pledged his continuing support, so he had a certain proprietary interest in him. For all his rhetoric about ruthlessly judging subordinates solely on the basis of their performance—indeed, at about this time Eisenhower wrote a friend, "For God's sake don't keep anybody around that you say to yourself, 'He may get by'—he won't."[43]—Eisenhower was still too soft-hearted to put his tough words into practice. He worried about Fredendall's weak staff and reluctance to prepare to assume the offensive. At first he considered merely bolstering Fredendall with some more capable assistants. However, when it became clear to Eisenhower that Fredendall no longer had the support of his subordinates, colleagues, and the British, he finally decided to relieve him. Eisenhower was probably also aware that firing Fredendall would help everyone place the sad Kasserine Pass episode behind them. On 5 March, Eisenhower traveled to Second Corps headquarters near Tebessa to deliver the bad news to Fredendall personally. Fortunately for Fredendall, Marshall felt that he could still play a useful role in the war and brought him back to the States to lead a training army.[44]

Eisenhower put considerable thought into Fredendall's replacement. After Harmon returned from the front and denounced Fredendall, Eisenhower had offered him command of the Second Corps in recognition of his clutch performance at Kasserine Pass. Harmon was tempted, but demurred because he did not think it would be proper for him to replace a superior whose removal he helped engineer. Instead, he recommended his friend George Patton for the job. He was not the first to do so; Truscott had made the same suggestion earlier. Indeed, it was a logical choice that had already occurred to Eisenhower. Patton was familiar with the general situation in the theater, had proven himself capable of leading large units in combat, and was one of Eisenhower's oldest friends. Moreover, now that Clark's vanity had removed him from contention, Patton was really the only general on hand qualified for the position. Eisenhower concluded that Patton had the necessary leadership skills, experience, and reputation to revitalize the demoralized Second Corps. There were, however, two obstacles to appointing Patton. The first was that Patton was currently busy planning the proposed invasion of Sicily that his First Armored Corps would conduct. Eisenhower's solution was to make Patton's assignment to the Second Corps temporary until he got the unit back on its feet, which should take about a month. After that, he could return to Morocco to continue preparations for the Sicily campaign. The second problem was Patton's personality. For all his positive attributes that Eisenhower was counting on, Patton was also unpredictable, reckless, and almost as Anglophobic as Fredendall. To neutralize these character deficiencies, Eisenhower made it clear to Patton that he had to get along with the British and not needlessly expose himself to enemy fire.[45]

For Patton, the previous four months had been a purgatory. Although he capably oversaw the military occupation of Morocco and worked surprisingly well with local leaders, he did not see this as his destiny in the war. Patton was a man of action who craved combat, and without its stimulus he became increasingly frustrated and miserable. The war, it seemed, was leaving him behind. Indeed, there was plenty of evidence that his inactive status might stretch on indefinitely, such as Eisenhower's decision to appoint Clark head of the new Fifth Army. Patton could not understand how Clark, whom he saw as an insincere, self-centered, and duplicitous man without much leadership experience, was more qualified for the job than he was. Patton attributed Clark's good fortune solely to his sycophantic relationship with Eisenhower. Morocco reminded Patton of his California childhood, making him homesick. Critical as ever, Patton condemned Eisenhower's strategy, predicted disaster, and complained that no one paid any attention to him. To be sure, Eisenhower at one point talked of making Patton his deputy, but Patton was not too keen on the idea because he would not actually direct anyone under fire. In early February things began to look up for Patton when Eisenhower informed him that he would command American forces in the invasion of Sicily. When Eisenhower summoned him to take over the Second Corps a month later, Patton realized that he was inheriting a military mess, but also recognized the opportunity to get back into the thick of the action and hoped to make the best of it. In fact, he commented with his usual self-confidence that he should have gotten the job sooner because he was the logical man to run Rommel to ground.[46]

Late in the morning of 7 March, General Omar Bradley was one of innumerable curious onlookers who gathered outside Second Corps headquarters at Djebel Kouif to greet the procession of scout cars and halftracks that barreled into the dingy square, sirens wailing. After the vehicles screeched to a halt, Patton leaped from the lead car to survey the scene and strike a pose for his new command. Although Bradley and Patton would be closely associated for the remainder of the war, they were two very different kinds of personalities. Bradley was almost stereotypically Midwestern in his speech and mannerisms. He did not smoke, rarely swore or drank alcohol, and disliked attention. Unpretentious and unfailingly polite, Bradley was a quiet, simple, and unflappable man. He did not look much like a soldier, and one colleague said he could easily be mistaken for a university arts and sciences dean. In fact, there was a distinctly scholarly hue to Bradley. He possessed a first-rate mind, was self-disciplined, and weighed matters carefully before making decisions. Other generals called him "Brad" and respected him immensely for his intellect, clarity, and management skills. He invariably treated his subordinates respectfully and attentively in an almost fatherly way, and never resorted to intimidation or humiliation to motivate them. One of his corps commanders compared Bradley to a comfortable and familiar old shoe. Bradley later explained, "Throughout the war I deliberately avoided intervening in a subordinate's duties. When an officer performed as I expected him to, I gave him a free hand. When he hesitated, I tried to help him. And when he failed, I relieved him."[47] In reality, though, he interfered more than he was willing to admit, but did so in a subtle and helpful manner that rarely antagonized his subordinates. He had none of Patton's brashness and outlandishness, but was instead unassuming, matter-of-fact, and considerate. One general later said about Bradley: "His rough-hewn features bespeak a deep-seated integrity, along with an uncommon feeling for his associates and the men under him, and a rare ability to gauge their fine qualities as well as their human frailties. He is one of the most genuinely modest men I have ever known, but back of his somewhat retiring nature is a keen mind and a toughness in making decisions that engenders confidence."[48]

Bradley was born into a poor rural Missouri family in 1893. As with his classmate Eisenhower, West Point attracted Bradley because it promised a free education. Bradley enjoyed West Point's discipline and camaraderie, and opted to make a career out of the army after he graduated in 1915. Much to his chagrin, he spent World War One not in the trenches of France, but policing Montana copper mines. After the conflict he taught mathematics at West Point for four years, attended the Infantry School, and served in Hawaii. He ranked first in his 1928 Command and General Staff School class, the only World War Two corps or field army commander to achieve that standing. Even more important for his career, he subsequently met and impressed Marshall as an instructor at the Infantry School from 1929 to 1933. Tours of duty at the Army War College and West Point followed, and in 1938 he went to work in Washington in the personnel office. The following year Marshall made Bradley an assistant secretary of the General Staff.

Marshall also secured Bradley's promotion from lieutenant colonel to brigadier general and appointed him head of the Infantry School. There Bradley played a prominent role in developing the officer candidate school model. After the United States entered World War Two, Bradley led the Eighty-second Division and then the Twenty-eighth Division. He did a fine job with both units and was by way of reward slated to take over the Tenth Corps when Marshall dispatched him instead to North Africa on a vague mission to help Eisenhower.

Bradley was no doubt a capable man, but he owed a good bit of his professional success to Marshall's tutelage. Although not personally close—Bradley was, like so many officers, somewhat intimidated and uncomfortable around the formidable Marshall—the two men developed considerable respect for each other. Bradley considered his time at the Infantry School with Marshall the highpoint of his education as a soldier, and later wrote of Marshall, "No man had a greater influence over me personally or professionally."[49] Marshall for his part saw something special in Bradley and thereafter tracked and cultivated his career. Once he became chief of staff, Marshall systematically moved Bradley from one important post to another to give him as much experience and preparation as possible for the big responsibilities he envisioned for him. On 11 February 1943, Eisenhower asked Marshall to send someone to North Africa to serve as his eyes and ears at the front, and placed Bradley at the top of his list of possibilities. Marshall wanted to be helpful, and as Bradley was just then between jobs, he was the logical choice. Bradley's gratitude for being sent overseas to Europe instead of the Pacific was counterbalanced by his concerns that he might end up riding a desk. Upon reaching cold and windy Algiers on 24 February, he drove to Eisenhower's headquarters and was startled by the grim atmosphere there. Bradley did not know Eisenhower well, and in fact their wives did not get along, but he was impressed with Eisenhower's maturity and grasp of the situation. His dejection increased, though, when Eisenhower spelled out his mission because he knew that Fredendall and his staff would view him as Eisenhower's spy. As things turned out, Bradley neither liked nor respected Fredendall and became one of many officers who recommended his dismissal to Eisenhower. After Patton took over the Second Corps, Eisenhower offered Bradley to him in whatever capacity he wanted. Patton did not want Bradley operating in his headquarters outside his authority—"I'm not going to have any goddam spies running around my headquarters," he explained to Bradley—so he opted to make Bradley his deputy. Eisenhower agreed, though he told Bradley to continue to report his observations directly to him. Since Patton's tenure as Second Corps commander was temporary, Eisenhower decided that Bradley would then assume command of the unit if he performed well as Patton's deputy. There was some talk of having Bradley take over the planning for the invasion of Sicily instead, but Bradley successfully lobbied Eisenhower to remain with the Second Corps because he wanted to see some action. Besides, with Clark and Harmon out of contention, Bradley was really the only high-ranking officer in the theater eligible to run the Second Corps after Patton left.[50]

Bradley and Patton complemented each other in many ways. Patton then was not much interested in logistics, administration, personal feelings, diplomacy, and the innumerable other noncombat facets of generalship. Bradley, on the other hand, believed that mastering these often mundane and tedious chores was a professional responsibility. Bradley's methodical and sympathetic leadership style soothed the rough seas Patton left in his wake and permitted Patton to focus on fighting. In North Africa Patton was very pleased with Bradley's work and appreciated his efforts, though he became more critical of him when their roles were reversed in northwest Europe. As for Bradley, he had a pretty good understanding of Patton's value and idiosyncrasies. He had first encountered Patton back in Hawaii in the mid-1920s, but they did not interact much because they ran in different social circles. While Bradley learned to appreciate Patton's aggressiveness, tactical skill, and initiative, he was disturbed with his lack of self-control, profanity, and poor treatment of subordinates. He recognized that there were different leadership styles, but wondered if Patton did not alienate as much as he inspired. Bradley later wrote, "Patton was a superb field general and leader—perhaps our very best—but a man with many human and professional flaws. Those flaws held the potential for danger, even disaster, so much so that Marshall and Ike felt Patton had to be continuously watched and tethered. I was aware of these reservations about Patton on the higher level and, in fact, I shared them."[51]

Patton viewed whipping the demoralized Second Corps into fighting shape as a big part of his job. To emphasize that there was a new sheriff in town with new and greater expectations, Patton strictly enforced uniform regulations and even broke into latrines to see if the startled soldiers were properly attired. Soldiers accustomed to the informality of a combat zone were shocked to learn that Patton expected them to wear their helmets, leggings, and neckties at all times, or face hefty fines. Needless to say, this generated considerable anger toward Patton, but also drove his point home. Patton, however, knew that restoring discipline was merely preparatory to the larger goal of leading the Second Corps to victory in the next big Allied offensive. Because Alexander distrusted the American army's combat prowess, he assigned the Second Corps the minor mission of diverting Axis forces away from the British Eighth Army's main assault on the Mareth Line by attacking in the Gafsa area. In the second half of March and early April, the Second Corps sought to force its way through the passes at El Guettar and Maknassy. The battle seesawed back and forth with neither side gaining an advantage, but on 7 April the Germans and Italians, having been outflanked from the Mareth Line, retreated northward to make their last stand at a bridgehead around Bizerte and Tunis.

Patton believed that the army lacked sufficient good leaders because most people were not ruthless, direct, and aggressive enough. As a result, he was as tough on his high-ranking officers as he was on everyone else, and refused to accept even reasonable excuses for failure. As Harmon later explained, "While Patton's relentless, driving determination to maintain constant pressure on the enemy was a power restorative to sagging American morale, it sometimes led him to wreak cruel and unjustified vengeance on his subordinates."[52] This did not include Bradley, with whose performance Patton was well pleased and upon whom he relied more and more. Patton, however, had a different view of his divisional commanders. He was especially unhappy with Pinky Ward and his First Armored Division. Patton felt that Ward was too pessimistic, cautious, and lazy. After Ward encountered heavy rains and stiff enemy opposition near Maknassy, Patton repeatedly pressured him to seize his objectives. At one point Patton ordered him to personally lead an assault on a hill, and not to return alive if he failed. As it was, Ward was slightly wounded in the unsuccessful attempt. Shortly thereafter Patton sent Bradley to relieve Ward of his command. Bradley personally thought that Ward had done as well as could be expected under the circumstances, but admitted that he was no longer effective now that he had lost Patton's confidence. To replace Ward, Eisenhower dispatched Harmon from Morocco. Patton was no more understanding of him than he had been of Ward. When Harmon reported to Patton, the latter had just awakened from his afternoon nap and was in a surly mood. Harmon asked if he should attack or defend with his new unit, and Patton growled, "What have you come here for, asking me a lot of Goddamned stupid questions. Get the hell out of here and get with what I told you to do or I will send you back to Morocco."[53] Nor was Patton any more sympathetic toward General Terry Allen and General Manton Eddy, commanders of the First Division and Ninth Division, respectively. Although Patton praised the First Division—the famous "Big Red One"—in his diary, he publicly humiliated Allen by urinating in his slit trench and implying he was a coward. Harmon and Allen were among the army's most aggressive officers, so it is hard to see that Patton's browbeating served much purpose.[54]

The German and Italian retreat northward coincided with the end of Patton's tenure with the Second Corps. On 15 April, Patton surrendered the outfit to Bradley and returned to planning the invasion of Sicily. While Bradley got comfortable with his new post, Alexander placed the finishing touches on his plan for the final assault on Axis forces in North Africa. Alexander initially relegated the Second Corps to a secondary role because of his continuing doubts about American soldiers. Patton and Bradley, however, successfully lobbied Eisenhower to order Alexander to alter his arrangements and deploy the Second Corps to the north along the Mediterranean, pointed toward Bizerte. Doing so required considerable logistical finessing, but the Second Corps headquarters was up to the challenge and got its troops in position by mid-April. The British Eighth Army launched its attack on 19 April, followed by the Second Corps four days later.

Bradley ran the corps much less flamboyantly and belligerently than Patton had done. He eliminated many of the rules and regulations Patton had instituted and encouraged his lieutenants to solve their own problems. When he was not out in the field, he often sat on a metal seat in front of a big map in his tent plotting strategy and bantering with his staffers. His division commanders responded to his folksy, calm, and reassuring demeanor much better than to Patton's forceful leadership style. For example, Harmon at one point complained about the British habit of stopping for tea every afternoon, seemingly regardless of circumstances. Bradley replied, "Relax, Ernie. The British have been drinking tea every afternoon, war or no war, for three hundred years. They'll be doing it for another thousand. You can't buck all that tradition. Next time they stop, you stop too, and go up and have some tea with them."[55] The key to the Second Corps's battle was Hill 609, which dominated the route to Bizerte. Bradley gave the job of seizing it to Doc Ryder's Thirty-fourth Division. The Thirty-fourth Division had fought poorly since its successful landing at Algiers, but Bradley hoped the outfit could redeem itself here. Ryder's men battered away at the hill for five days and sustained heavy casualties until they finally occupied it on 1 May, opening the door for the rest of the corps to flood toward Bizerte. Harmon's First Armored Division played an especially important part in breaking through German lines. The Americans entered Bizerte on 7 May at about the same time Tunis fell to the British. The last resisting Axis troops on the Cape Bon peninsula surrendered six days later, ending the North African campaign in Allied victory.[56]

The North African campaign was important for all sorts of reasons. Most obviously, it expelled Axis forces from the continent, enabling the Allies to use it as a springboard and staging base for further operations in the Mediterranean and southern Europe. Not only were Sardinia, Sicily, the Italian mainland, and Greece now vulnerable to Allied invasion, but Allied bombers flying from North African bases could range as far as the Romanian oilfields that helped fuel the German war machine. The Axis powers also sustained heavy materiel and manpower losses in North Africa. In addition to the 40,000 killed and wounded the Germans and Italians suffered in Tunisia, another 275,000 of them became prisoners of war. Allied casualties in Tunisia, on the other hand, totaled 70,300, of whom approximately 18,200 were American, 16,100 Free French, and the balance British Empire. The defeat weakened Italy's means and will to continue the conflict, thus crippling its alliance with Germany. The campaign correspondingly lifted Allied morale and helped solidify the Anglo-American coalition. In sum, the North African campaign was the first giant leap toward victory for the British and Americans.

A Testing Ground for Personnel

For the American army, the North African campaign had the benefit of providing it with the valuable and comparatively low-risk experience it needed to successfully conduct future operations. This was especially true of senior commanders, beginning with Eisenhower. After an admittedly rocky start, he ultimately proved himself capable of fulfilling his primary mission of melding and maintaining the Anglo-American alliance. Despite occasional and inevitable tension between American and British officers, Eisenhower's determined insistence on portraying himself more as an impartial ally than as an American set an example that served as much-needed glue for the coalition. Such actions, however, did not always earn the respect of his more chauvinistic and parochial subordinates. During the 20 May victory parade in Tunis, an angry Bradley and Patton were relegated to an inconspicuous viewing stand while Eisenhower ignored them and hobnobbed elsewhere with British and Free French officials. To Bradley and Patton, this symbolized an unhealthy Anglophilia on Eisenhower's part that undermined and denigrated the American army's contributions. Nor were they especially impressed with Eisenhower's battlefield expertise. Marshall, on the other hand, understood Eisenhower's role and praised him for his outstanding leadership in effectively coordinating Allied air, ground, and naval forces. As for Eisenhower, he was largely unaware of the resentment some American officers felt toward him. He was grateful for Marshall's kind words and continuing support, but found victory in North Africa anticlimactic and unfulfilling. He had recognized for some time that vanquishing the Axis there was merely a matter of time and had mentally moved on to preparing for other campaigns that everyone expected to be more challenging than the one just completed.[57]

Patton regretted leaving an active assignment in Tunisia for an inactive one, but felt that he had done a good job under difficult circumstances. After all, he had taken the corps into battle only ten days after assuming command, and had in six short weeks done a lot to restore the unit's morale. He noted in his diary, "I have been gone forty-three days, fought several successful battles, commanded 95,800 men, lost about ten pounds, gained a third star and a hell of a lot of poise and confidence, and am otherwise the same."[58] Among those unchanging qualities was a smug satisfaction that he had outshone his nemesis Mark Clark. To Patton, one-upping his rival was as rewarding as the congratulatory letters he received from Eisenhower and Marshall. Patton's accomplishments, though, were in many ways more apparent than real. Bradley for one later noted that the Second Corps under Patton's command fought comparatively minor engagements and achieved no decisive breakthroughs. Moreover, Patton exhibited a questionable leadership style that alienated more than encouraged subordinates. Eisenhower shared Bradley's reservations about Patton's handling of personnel. While he continued to respect Patton's generalship, he wrote in a personal memo, "He talks too much and too quickly and sometimes creates a very bad impression. Moreover, I fear that he is not always a good example to subordinates, who may be guided by only his surface actions without understanding the deep sense of duty, courage, and service that make up his real personality."[59] Fortunately for Patton, Eisenhower was prepared to overlook these quirks and gave him a prominent role in future operations.[60]

Despite the attention Patton garnered from the press, Omar Bradley emerged from the campaign with the best reputation within the American army in Africa. Patton may have deserved credit for restoring Second Corps morale, but Bradley actually led the unit to victory in northern Tunisia. People lauded his tactical skills, his ability to manage personnel, and especially his calm professionalism. Marshall was pleased that his long-standing confidence in Bradley had been justified. Eisenhower referred to Bradley as a "godsend" even before he took over the Second Corps, and after the campaign ended he wrote:

This officer [Bradley] is about the best rounded, well balanced, senior officer that we have in the service. His judgments are always sound and everything he does is accomplished in such a manner as to fit in well with all other operations. He is respected by British and Americans alike. I have not a single word of criticism of his actions to date and do not expect to have any in the future. I feel that there is no position in the Army that he could not fill with success.[61]

Not surprisingly, Eisenhower enthusiastically recommended Bradley's promotion to lieutenant general. Even Patton and Clark, two men not normally inclined to praise rivals, were complimentary. With references like these, there was little doubt that Bradley was a man going places.[62]

The North African campaign also served as a training ground for several future corps commanders such as Manton Eddy, Ernie Harmon, and Doc Ryder. Ryder led the Eastern Task Force to victory at Algiers, but his Thirty-fourth Division's subsequent performance in central Tunisia left much to be desired. Ryder, however, managed to nurse his unit along until it proved itself by storming Hill 609. Bradley was grateful for Ryder's success, but he was not as impressed with him as he was with Eddy and Harmon. Eddy's professionalism and bearing appealed to Bradley, who called Eddy his most balanced and tactically skillful division commander. On the other hand, Bradley complained that Eddy was often too cautious and required periodic reassurance. Finally, both Bradley and Eisenhower were very pleased with Harmon. In fact, Eisenhower referred to Harmon as the army's outstanding divisional chief in North Africa. Harmon took the demoralized First Armored Division and turned it into an effective outfit with his aggressive and energetic leadership, even though he alienated much of its officer corps in the process with his belligerent style. It was the First Armored Division that made the Second Corps's decisive breakthrough that opened the door for the Americans to drive toward Bizerte. Harmon knew this as well as anyone, and shortly after the Germans and Italians surrendered he got drunk at a dinner at Bradley's headquarters and insisted that his division had played the key role in American victory. Despite this indiscretion, Harmon was clearly a candidate to take over a corps.[63]

Unfortunately for Harmon, by the end of the summer his chances of leading a corps declined precipitously. In early June Harmon attended a dinner with Marshall, who was visiting North Africa after the Trident Conference in Washington. Patton warned Harmon to be on his best behavior because Marshall was looking him over as a possible candidate for corps command. During the meal Harmon impressed Marshall so much that afterward Marshall apologized to Patton for questioning his decision to use Harmon in Torch. Next morning, though, Harmon innocently asked Marshall if he had received a letter of recommendation he had written for one of his divisional officers. Harmon did not know it, but the man had gotten into trouble some time earlier for trying unsuccessfully to circumvent army censorship rules by sending a letter to his wife via a State Department diplomatic pouch. Marshall snarled at Harmon that he should know better than to vouch for someone like that, and that he was therefore obviously unfit for greater responsibilities. He then drove away before a speechless Harmon could respond. Subsequent events did little to help Harmon's cause. A little more than a week later, General Ernest Dawley, commander of the Sixth Corps, contemplated relieving Harmon from his First Armored Division because the outfit's ill-disciplined GIs were causing so much trouble at Rabat by, among other things, beating up the military police there. Finally, in early July Harmon gave a speech to selected officers of the First Armored and Thirty-sixth divisions on his battle experiences in Tunisia. With his usual dry and tart humor he introduced the topic by saying, "My talk has to do principally with the stupidity of high command. I say stupidity, because there are times when the higher commanders were stupid as hell."[64] Such bluntness was typical of Harmon, but it hardly endeared him to his superiors. Small wonder that on 24 August Eisenhower noted to Marshall that although he valued Harmon's combat leadership enough to include him as a possible corps commander, he did not have much faith in his common sense and good judgment.[65]

Harmon's career setbacks, while demoralizing for him, were temporary, and he would continue to play an important role in the European War. On the other hand, the North African campaign adversely impacted the careers of several other important American combat commanders. The first and most obvious was Lloyd Fredendall's. Fredendall's timidity, ineptness, and tactical myopia contributed significantly to American defeat at Kasserine Pass. No doubt Fredendall faced serious obstacles—inferior equipment, poor coordination with the Army Air Force, inexperienced troops, and an unhappy relationship with Anderson and the British—but he lost his grip on the Second Corps when the Germans launched their offensive. Although both Marshall and Eisenhower were responsible for Fredendall's appointment, Eisenhower compounded the mistake by retaining him even after it was clear he was no longer effective. Fredendall was therefore Marshall's and Eisenhower's most glaring personnel blunder. As for Mark Clark, Eisenhower had nothing but good things to say about his contribution to Torch's success. After that, though, Clark's insistence on leading a field army raised doubts in Eisenhower's mind about his commitment to the common cause, and he relegated Clark to the inactive Fifth Army for the remainder of the campaign. Eisenhower still valued Clark, but obviously wanted to send him a message about selflessness. Lastly, Terry Allen's career was jeopardized in North Africa. Allen was one of those eccentric oddballs who appealed to Marshall, and on one level he had fought very well throughout the campaign at the head of the First Division. Unfortunately, he alienated Bradley with his independent and impulsive nature, surliness toward superiors, and inability to maintain discipline over his proud and freewheeling outfit. Bradley was especially upset with an unauthorized and unsuccessful assault Allen initiated against the Germans during the Second Corps' push on Bizerte. Bradley later regretted that he did not relieve Allen then and there. He did, however, conclude that it was simply a question of when, not whether, he removed Allen from his division. With these notable exceptions, Eisenhower was on the whole pleased with his senior commanders.[66]

3
The Long and Frustrating Italian Campaign

Sicily

In January 1943, more than three months before the Germans and Italians surrendered in North Africa, Allied leaders met in Casablanca to plot their next moves. Marshall and his JCS colleagues remained committed to a cross-Channel assault on German-occupied Europe, but it was clear that the Allies still lacked the necessary resources for such an undertaking in the immediate future. Rather than let the war stagnate, the Anglo-American Combined Chiefs of Staff—so-called because it consisted of the American Joint Chiefs of Staff and its British equivalent—opted to continue the conflict in the Mediterranean by authorizing an attack on Sicily. They hoped that seizing the triangular island would secure Allied shipping lanes through the Mediterranean, put to good use all the battle-hardened British and American troops currently in North Africa, divert German forces away from the Eastern Front with the Soviet Union, and further weaken Italy's war effort. Moreover, Sicily could serve as a stepping-stone to the Italian mainland should that prove necessary. To command the invasion, the Combined Chiefs turned again to Eisenhower. Although some British leaders, such as Alan Brooke, had serious doubts about Eisenhower's military abilities, no one could gainsay his knack for getting Britons and Americans to work together harmoniously. Still, the British tried to compensate for his supposed military shortcomings by successfully arguing for the appointment of British generals as his air, ground, and naval deputies, including Harold Alexander as head of the Fifteenth Army Group. The Combined Chiefs slated the operation, code-named "Husky," for June or July.[1]

Before Marshall returned to the States, he and Eisenhower met in Algiers in late January to, among other things, discuss Husky's command structure. There they decided that Patton should lead Husky's American ground forces. Both men recognized Patton's eccentricities, but respected his military acumen. After all,

Patton had successfully organized and led the Western Task Force in its assault on Casablanca, making him one of the few American generals with such a line on his military résumé. As Eisenhower had put it a month earlier, "Patton I think comes closest to meeting every requirement made on a commander."[2] Moreover, Fredendall was currently preoccupied in Tunisia, and Eisenhower did not believe Clark was ready for such a mission. In short, Patton's experience, knowledge, familiarity, and availability made him the best candidate for the job. Patton originally commanded the First Armored Corps, but in May Marshall and Eisenhower chose for prestige purposes to elevate his force and rename it the Seventh Army. Marshall worried that invading Sicily with a corps while the British used Montgomery's Eighth Army might imply that the Americans were not pulling their weight. Eisenhower agreed with Marshall's logic, but opted to wait until just before the invasion to make the change official.[3]

Patton was pleased with both his force's new designation and the quality of the units and officers under his command. Eisenhower originally planned for Patton to fight in Sicily with General Ernest "Mike" Dawley's recently arrived Sixth Corps. Dawley had led the unit for about a year, and Marshall, McNair, and Eisenhower all rated him highly. Patton, on the other hand, was more ambivalent because Dawley had not yet seen action. In fact, Patton sent him to Tunisia toward the end of the fighting there and asked Bradley to make sure he was shot at. The more Patton thought about it, the more he disliked the idea of relying so heavily on an untried man. Fortunately for Patton, a solution presented itself. Now that the North African campaign was coming to an end, Bradley and his Second Corps headquarters were available for a new mission. Like everyone else, Patton had been impressed with Bradley's performance there. He believed they made a good team and decided to secure Bradley's services for Husky if possible. During a meeting in Gafsa, Patton buttonholed Bradley and said, "I've worked with you and I've got confidence in you. On the other hand I don't know what in hell Dawley can do. If you've got no objection, I'm going to ask Ike to fix it up."[4] Bradley was amenable to the idea and told Patton to go ahead. Eisenhower saw Patton's logic and agreed to the change in mid-May. Although Marshall then suggested sending Dawley and his corps headquarters to England, Eisenhower persuaded him to keep the outfit in North Africa as part of Clark's Fifth Army in case an invasion of the Italian mainland proved necessary. And so it was Bradley, not Dawley, who accompanied Patton to Sicily.[5]

Patton was also happy with his other lieutenants. Geoffrey Keyes had been Patton's deputy for Torch and had overseen the planning for Husky while Patton was busy straightening out the Second Corps in Tunisia. Although Marshall questioned Keyes's organizational and training skills, Eisenhower and Patton were both happy to have him continue as Patton's second-in-command. Eisenhower slated elements of three American infantry divisions to storm Sicily on the first day of the invasion, one of which was General Frederick Walker's rookie Thirty-sixth Division. Patton, though, was not quite sure what to make of Walker, so he traded his outfit for Terry Allen's veteran and prima donna First Division. When Walker asked him about the switch, Patton lied that it was not his idea. Patton and Bradley may have had their doubts about Allen, but he was a proven fighter who shared Patton's aggressive instincts. No one, on the other hand, had any qualms about Lucian Truscott's Third Division. Truscott had fought well enough at Casablanca during Torch to win Patton's and Eisenhower's praise. Unfortunately, after the operation was over Patton did not have a post commensurate with Trus-cott's rank and abilities, so he suggested that Truscott seek employment else-where. Truscott traveled to Algiers and talked with Eisenhower, who made him first his deputy and then in March 1943 the head of the Third Division. Truscott did such a good job whipping the Third Division into fighting shape that ob-servers soon called it the best-trained division in the theater. He insisted that his men march faster than any other outfit, and his "Truscott Trot" became famous. In fact, Eisenhower told Marshall a week before Husky began, "If his command does not give a splendid account of itself, then all signs by which I know how to judge an organization are completely false."[6] Finally, General Troy Middleton's in-experienced Forty-fifth Division was en route to the Mediterranean from the States to participate in Husky's initial landings. Ordinarily Eisenhower and Patton would have been concerned to give such an important role to an unknown divi-sion, but not in this case. Middleton was universally respected by the army's high-ranking officers, having taught a good many of them at the Command and General Staff School. Marshall thought a lot of him, and McNair believed that the Forty-fifth Division was the best division to that point to leave the States. The Second Armored Division and Eighty-second Airborne Division under, respec-tively, General Hugh Gaffey and General Matthew Ridgway were also scheduled to join the opening operations on Sicily. Both were led by well-qualified officers destined to make their marks in the war. Patton therefore had just about as good a collection of divisional generals at his disposal as the army could then muster.[7]

Patton's satisfaction with his subordinates contrasted sharply with his frustra-tions with other aspects of Husky. For one thing, he intensely disliked British General Bernard Montgomery and his plan to conquer the island. Montgomery proposed that both American and British forces land on the southeastern part of Sicily. Once ashore, Montgomery's Eighth Army would thrust northward toward Messina to cut off the Axis escape route while Patton's Seventh Army covered and protected the British left flank. Not surprisingly, Patton objected to assuming such a secondary and cautious role. He attributed Eisenhower's acceptance of Montgomery's scheme to his continuing and unfathomable Anglophilia. Indeed, this was only one aspect of Eisenhower's leadership that bothered Patton. Patton complained that Eisenhower's obsession with military minutiae diverted him from more important tasks, worried that Eisenhower and Clark were undercutting him, and felt that Eisenhower failed to appreciate his talents. Patton grumbled that Eisenhower never even invited him to dinner despite their long-standing friendship. Shortly before Patton embarked, Eisenhower told him that he was a great fighter, but not much of a planner. Patton retorted that the only operation he had so far planned, the Western Task Force's assault on Casablanca during Torch, had worked out well enough. In spite of these and other aggravations, Patton tried hard to remain positive and upbeat. He maintained his health by getting plenty of sleep, exercising, eating sensibly, and drinking moderately. He also attempted to be nice to his colleagues, including even the detested Clark. Most important, he reminded himself that it was his destiny to do great things. All this helped Patton keep periodic depression at bay, and in fact one observer remarked that Patton was not as irritable as circumstances warranted. Less than a week before the invasion Patton wrote to an old friend, "I have a great optimism about this operation, springing largely from the heart rather than the head."[8]

Although Patton was unaware of it, Bradley was also unhappy with parts of Husky, albeit for different reasons. Bradley's biggest concern was not Eisenhower or even so much the British, but rather George Patton. Bradley and Patton had worked well together in Tunisia, and continued to cooperate in planning for Husky, but Bradley was questioning Patton's unconventional behavior. On 25 June, for example, a gaggle of officers including Marshall, Eisenhower, and Bradley watched in shocked and embarrassed silence during a landing exercise near Oran as an outraged Patton strode into the surf and chewed out some soldiers as only he could for failing to fix their bayonets before they hit the beach. Patton also offended Bradley by relegating him and his Second Corps headquarters to the fly-infested, fetid, and hot village of Relizane, 30 miles south of Patton's more comfortable headquarters at Mostaganem. An angry and humiliated Bradley attributed the slight to Patton's reluctance to share center stage with another lieutenant general. Nor was Bradley, a meticulous and nuts-and-bolts general, altogether comfortable with Patton's habit of delegating so much of the planning details for Husky to Keyes. Bradley's misgivings, though, extended beyond Patton. He understood Patton's rationale for procuring the veteran First Division for Husky, but continued to harbor serious doubts about Terry Allen's ability to maintain discipline over his flinty Big Red One—doubts that were confirmed when First Division soldiers rioted upon learning that they would not be rotated home. Finally, Bradley's knowledge of Troy Middleton's stellar reputation failed to completely overcome his unease at committing the untried and unknown Forty-fifth Division to the initial assault on Sicily.[9]

Husky began on the night of 9–10 July when American paratroopers and British glider-borne soldiers descended onto Sicily. A few hours later, the first of 150,000 Allied troops boarded their landing craft and headed for the beach from the huge armada that had transported and escorted them from a half dozen points along the North African coast. The Americans came ashore at three beaches along southern Sicily at Licata, Gela, and Scoglitti. Truscott's Third Division at Licata and Middleton's Forty-fifth Division at Scoglitti met little opposition—one officer remembered Middleton as "a heroic looking fellow sitting on the hood of his jeep in the landing boat"—but the Germans and Italians launched a strong counterattack against Allen's First Division at Gela. Over the course of the next two days it was touch-and-go, but Allen's veterans managed to repel the assault with the help of offshore naval gunfire. After they occupied Syracuse, the British Eighth Army's advance northward toward Messina ran into heavy resistance from Germans dug in south of Catania that brought it to a halt. Unlike the approximately 200,000 demoralized Italians whose will to fight rapidly disappeared, the Germans increased their strength on Sicily from 30,000 to 50,000 and waged a fierce and effective rear-guard action. In an unsuccessful effort to outflank the Germans, Montgomery expropriated a road originally assigned to the Seventh Army, further marginalizing it from the action.[10]

Whatever his role, Patton was happy to be back in the war. He was especially pleased that Truscott's Third Division was living up to its pre-campaign billing. On the other hand, he resented Eisenhower's treatment of him. Eisenhower seemed to have concluded that the best way to handle Patton was with a professional aloofness and coolness, and rarely displayed toward Patton the graciousness and good humor that made him such an effective interallied supreme commander. Eisenhower had little positive to say to Patton during a 13 July visit to the Seventh Army; quite to the contrary. Two nights previously, Patton had ordered elements of the Eighty-second Airborne Division parachuted into Sicily as reinforcements. Although various headquarters from the Seventh Army down issued orders to the troops prohibiting them from firing on any overhead planes that night, most either did not get the word or ignored it. Of the 144 planes carrying 2,000 paratroopers, friendly fire shot down 23 planes and killed or wounded 229 men. Eisenhower was furious and held Patton accountable. Nor was Eisenhower satisfied with the dearth of information Patton was sending him. Eisenhower was so critical that an angry and upset Patton wondered if Eisenhower was laying the groundwork to remove him from his post. This was not the case—indeed, on 17 July Eisenhower assured Marshall that Patton was doing a good job—but Eisenhower's heavy-handed approach was hardly the acme of personnel management. Patton was nothing if not resilient, though, and opted to accept such criticism as one of the prices he had to pay for the privilege of waging war.

Indeed, a week later Patton's old friend, General Everett Hughes, wrote, "Geo[rge] says it is a good war, best he was ever in—thinks he is doing okay."[11]

By then Patton had a concrete reason for his good mood. Perhaps because he felt he was already on thin ice with Eisenhower, Patton did not initially protest Montgomery's occupation of the road originally allotted to the Seventh Army, even though this shunted the Americans even further to Husky's periphery. When Alexander made the confiscation official, though, Patton decided that enough was enough. He boarded a plane and flew to Alexander's headquarters in Tunis to protest. Patton sought from Alexander more than just a road; he wanted the opportunity to play a greater role in the campaign. Specifically, Patton asked Alexander's permission to cut across Sicily and seize the northern city of Palermo. Doing so would give him the port he needed to support his own offensive eastward toward Messina. Alexander was not the type of general to stand in the way of his lieutenants' requests, so he agreed to the proposal. Patton hurried back to Sicily and formed a provisional corps under Jeff Keyes consisting of Gaffey's Second Armored and Truscott's Third divisions. On 19 July Keyes pushed northward toward Palermo against little opposition, and the hard-marching Third Division entered the city just three days later. Patton arrived after dusk and discovered Keyes and Gaffey asleep in the Royal Palace. He woke them up and congratulated them on a job well done, and the three generals shared swigs from a small flask. He also praised Truscott, exclaiming, "The Truscott Trot sure got us here in a damn hurry."[12] Although Bradley later sourly referred to the Palermo operation as a publicity stunt that diverted part of the Seventh Army from its main job of fighting the Germans, Patton was elated. He believed that his coup not only put the Seventh Army in position to race Montgomery to Messina, but also demonstrated the proper application of armor. Patton wrote in his diary, "I feel that future students of the Command and General Staff School will study the campaign of Palermo as a classic example of the use of tanks."[13] He gave Keyes credit for the successful implementation of his plan and urged Eisenhower to release Keyes's name to the press.[14]

Patton was determined to beat Montgomery to Messina, but redeploying his army for such a race took a week. He brought in Eddy's Ninth Division, replaced Middleton's tired Forty-fifth Division with Truscott's Third, sent Keyes to clear out western Sicily with his provisional corps, and ordered Bradley to prepare to push eastward with his Second Corps. Despite the delays, the mercurial Patton was in a good mood because of his recent successes. Even Eisenhower refrained from his usual criticisms during a 31 July visit. Patton's offensive began on 1 August, but it was tough going in the mountainous terrain against the usual ferocious German resistance. The German defense line was anchored on the town of Troina, and Bradley had to commit the entire First Division, as well as elements of the Ninth, before the Germans pulled out five days later. Patton personally promoted a buck sergeant who took over his bled-down company after its officers had been killed or wounded and led the outfit in a successful attack on a German-held ridge. Truscott had an equally difficult time advancing along the northern Sicilian coast. In an effort to shake things loose, Patton three times launched small-scale amphibious assaults behind German lines, but with only marginal success. When Patton learned that Truscott wanted to postpone one such landing he raced to the Third Division command post to make sure the operation went on as scheduled. There he shouted and screamed at Truscott, questioned his courage, and threatened to relieve him of his command. Truscott, whose aggressive instincts rivaled Patton's, coolly replied that he served at Patton's pleasure and that removing him was Patton's prerogative. Patton immediately calmed down and suggested that they share a drink, but he refused to sanction any delay. Unfortunately, the Third Division suffered heavy losses for little gain in the undertaking. On 16 August, the Third Division reached Messina just ahead of the British, who had had their own hard fight up the east coast. Next day Patton and Keyes triumphantly entered Messina and took possession of the city.[15]

Bradley was not among the high-ranking officers who accompanied Patton's victorious procession into Messina. Although Patton regretted his absence and attributed it to a communication snafu, a disgruntled Bradley interpreted it as a personal slight. Indeed, it had been a difficult campaign for Bradley. En route to Sicily, he suffered so severely from hemorrhoids that he feared he might be invalided home. On the advice of the shipboard doctor, he underwent local surgery shortly before the amphibious assault began. Throughout the first weeks of Husky, Bradley endured considerable pain riding around in a jeep over Sicily's stony roads, even though he sat on an inflatable lifejacket. Small wonder that one aide observed that he always looked tired. Bradley generally got along well with his subordinates, but not Terry Allen. Bradley had had his doubts about Allen's generalship back in Tunisia, and events in Sicily exacerbated them. He believed that Allen not only mishandled the First Division's initial unsuccessful attack on Troina, but also failed to obey orders in a timely fashion. As soon as he pulled the First Division out of the line, Bradley, with Patton's and Eisenhower's approval, relieved Allen and sent him back to the States. Although Patton and Allen were in many ways cut from the same rebellious cloth, Patton too had soured on Allen, and had in fact scribbled in his diary even before Husky, "General Allen . . . is in a bad state of mind. He finds fault with everything and was totally ignorant of the plan for the landing of his own division."[16]

Bradley's difficulties with Allen, though, paled in comparison to his frustrations with Patton. As a down-to-earth man, Bradley had little patience for or understanding of Patton's theatrics and showmanship, believing that they alienated both the average GI and officers. Indeed, Bradley saw himself as a case in point because he felt unappreciated and put-upon by Patton. On the first day of the campaign, for example, Patton countermanded one of Bradley's orders without informing him and issued instructions directly to Allen. Patton apologized when Bradley confronted him about his actions, but Bradley's anger returned when he heard rumors that Patton was badmouthing him to Eisenhower as too cautious. As far as Bradley was concerned, his methodical tactics were far superior to Patton's suggestion that he forgo maneuvering and charge straight for Messina. Finally, Bradley complained that Patton and his staff paid insufficient attention to logistics. As a result, the Second Corps had to deal with poor coordination with the Army Air Force, artillery ammunition shortages, and communications problems. From Bradley's perspective, he did all the heavy lifting on Sicily while Patton gallivanted around the island garnering cheap publicity.[17]

Sicily was a qualified and flawed Allied victory. Seizing the island opened the Mediterranean to Allied shipping and weakened Italy's resolve to continue the war, but a closer look showed that the British and Americans did not fight especially well. For all of Patton's chest-thumping, it was the Germans who demonstrated superior generalship. Although heavily outnumbered and outgunned from the beginning of the campaign to the end, the Germans not only inflicted greater losses than they sustained—the final numbers were 16,500 German casualties, 11,500 British, and 7,500 American—but also managed to evacuate most of their men and equipment to the Italian mainland in the face of Allied naval and air superiority. Despite enormous Allied advantages, it still took the British and Americans nearly forty days to push the Germans off the island. Throughout the campaign the Germans exhibited a flexibility, resilience, and tactical ingenuity that the Allies failed to match. Husky also revealed serious problems in the Allied command structure that went beyond the personal antipathy between Patton and Montgomery. Eisenhower had little direct control over ground operations because he had to work through Alexander, so he often acted more as an interested observer than as a supreme commander. Alexander for his part took a hands-off approach that permitted Patton and Montgomery to do whatever they wanted with minimum coordination between their armies. Clearly, the Anglo-American alliance remained a work in progress.

In the warm glow generated by victory on Sicily, there was little critical self-analysis of their performances by the army's senior ground forces officers. In fact, the division, corps, and field army commanders had with a few exceptions avoided any serious tactical errors and fought in a competent, albeit conventional, manner. What aggressiveness they demonstrated was often the result of Patton's prodding. Marshall dispatched another round of congratulatory messages, in which he lauded Eisenhower's "brilliant success" and Patton's "grand job of leadership." He also called for the permanent promotions of Patton and Bradley to, respectively, major general and brigadier general. Secretary of War Stimson visited the theater at about that time and was impressed with Eisenhower's growing maturity and gravitas. Eisenhower shared his superiors' satisfaction with his lieutenants. He especially showered Bradley with praise, informing Marshall:

> There is very little I need to tell you about him [Bradley] because he is running absolutely true to form all the time. He has brains, a fine capacity for leadership and a thorough understanding of the requirements of modern battle. He has never caused me one moment of worry. He is perfectly capable of commanding an Army. He has the respect of all his associates, including all the British officers that have met him.[18]

Eisenhower, however, was probably motivated as much by his personal fondness for Bradley as by an objective assessment of his military abilities. Eisenhower also recommended Middleton and Truscott as corps commanders, and added that he had very favorable reports about Keyes. As for Patton, Eisenhower extolled his combativeness and aggressiveness to Marshall, but expressed vague concern with his poor judgment in handling his subordinates, his difficulty in controlling his temper, and his weakness as a planner. Patton for his part singled out Bradley and Keyes for commendation, and added that Keyes and Middleton would both make good corps commanders.[19]

Eisenhower's concerns about Patton stemmed in part from his knowledge of the infamous slapping incidents. On 3 August Patton visited an evacuation hospital where he verbally and physically abused a soldier suffering from combat fatigue because he believed the man was shirking his duty. A week later he repeated the performance at another hospital, only this time he also took out his revolver and threatened to shoot the traumatized and frightened victim.

Word of these events spread rapidly through Sicily, and Eisenhower learned of them on 13 August. Eisenhower was appalled by Patton's callous behavior, but unsure how to respond. On the one hand, he felt that in striking enlisted men Patton had committed a serious transgression that demonstrated the lack of judgment and self-control to which he alluded in his message to Marshall. It was in fact a court-martial offense that could end Patton's career. On the other hand, Patton was not only one of Eisenhower's oldest friends, but also his most successful general. Patton had more victories under his belt than any other American general in the theater, and his aggressiveness placed him in a league of his own. Removing him from his command and sending him home might do great harm to the Allied war effort.

After several nights of tossing and turning, Eisenhower opted to deal with the matter as quietly and discreetly as possible, but in such a way that Patton under-stood that his conduct was unacceptable. He pleaded with war correspondents to refrain from mentioning Patton's misdeeds and did not even refer to them to Marshall except in the vaguest and most general manner. In a 17 August private letter to Patton, Eisenhower deplored Patton's actions, but hoped that they were attributable to thoughtlessness and the strain of the campaign. He also dispatched General John Lucas, one of his deputies and Patton's close friend, to deliver a harsher and blunter message. Lucas informed Patton that Eisenhower expected him to personally apologize to the soldiers he mistreated, the hospital personnel, and as many of his Seventh Army units as possible. Unfortunately for Eisenhower, his efforts to keep the affair out of the press failed, and it became a public scandal back in the States in late November and December. Although Marshall asked for the details, he and Stimson were content to leave Patton's fate in Eisenhower's hands. Eisenhower assured them that Patton remained a useful officer, but he was very angry with him.[20]

Patton initially failed to recognize the seriousness of his actions. As far as he was concerned, he was simply maintaining discipline by discouraging the lolly-gagging that if left unchecked would spread like a communicable disease through any army. Nevertheless, he still felt bad about letting Eisenhower down and ad-mitted that perhaps his methods were not the best. He dutifully made the apolo-gies that Eisenhower demanded, but they were vague and lacking in sincere remorse. The rank-and-file's responses ran the gamut from enthusiastic adulation to surly resentment. It only gradually dawned on Patton that his misdeeds could imperil his career. His original expectations that he would soon fight in Italy or go to England to prepare for the invasion of German-occupied France did not pan out, and instead his Seventh Army degenerated into a hollow force without any attached combat units. At the same time, Patton's colleagues and rivals one by one left for new and important assignments elsewhere—Clark to the Italian mainland with his Fifth Army and Bradley to England to take over a new field army there. Although in late September Eisenhower promised to recommend Patton for an important combat command in an active theater, Eisenhower's own status was then uncertain, and nothing immediately came of his pledge. Besides, he was not inclined to do Patton any favors after the criticism he received for his handling of the slapping incidents. Stuck in Sicily without the stimulus of combat or plan-ning, Patton became bored, frustrated, and depressed. He felt unappreciated, con-spired against, resentful, and victimized. When he learned that Marshall had criticized him and his staff for their alleged logistical incompetence, he guessed correctly that his erstwhile loyal subordinate Bradley had been badmouthing him. He could not sleep at night, but was tired all day. On Thanksgiving he confided in his diary, "I had nothing to be thankful for so I did not give thanks."[21] Patton was, however, comforted that his loyal staff chose to remain with him, and he maintained his faith that it was his destiny to play an important part in the war. For right now, though, Sicily had become more of a miserable exile to be endured than an island fortress he had conquered.[22]

Salerno and the Invasion of the Italian Mainland

In one of its innumerable compromises designed to reconcile divergent British and American strategic thinking, the Combined Chiefs of Staff had given Eisenhower broad authority to use his forces in the Mediterranean to take advantage of any opportunities to knock Italy out of the war. Eisenhower, though, was initially pessimistic that he could accomplish much. Seven of his divisions and a good number of his landing craft were scheduled to go to England to prepare for the assault on German-occupied France, seriously depleting his strength. He figured that he might be able to seize Sardinia and Corsica, and perhaps even put troops onto the tip of Italy's toe, but that was it. He lamented that he had hitherto been too cautious and had permitted the North African campaign to drag on longer than was necessary, and hoped that a more aggressive approach might work better in the future. Happily for the Allies, that summer a series of events gave Eisenhower the chance to demonstrate his boldness and advance the war effort in the region. The invasion of Sicily completely discredited Italian dictator Benito Mussolini's tottering regime, and on 25 July Italian king Victor Emmanuel III ordered his dismissal and arrest. The king also directed Marshal Pietro Badoglio to establish a new government. Like most Italians, Badoglio wanted out of the war, and on 31 July he entered into secret and complicated negotiations with the Allies for Italy's surrender. Italy's possible withdrawal from the conflict presented the Allies with an opportunity to roll back German power to the Alps with minimal resources and losses. The British of course were all for the idea. Marshall was more reluctant, but acquiesced to appease the British and because the troops used would be those already on hand in the theater. Eisenhower's plan was for two of Montgomery's British Eighth Army divisions to cross the Straits of Messina and land in southern Italy in early September. Then on 9 September, the day after the Allies officially announced Italy's capitulation to the world, Wayne Clark's Fifth Army would storm ashore at Salerno, a port about 40 miles south of Naples, in Operation Avalanche. The hope was that these two blows would so stun the Germans in Italy that they would offer little resistance to an Allied advance on Rome and points northward.

Clark's frustrations since Torch were if anything worse than Patton's. While not as mystical as Patton, Clark too considered it his destiny to play an important part in the war. Unfortunately, his ego and pride had almost short-circuited him right out of the conflict. The previous December he had rejected Eisenhower's offer to lead the Second Corps in Tunisia and instead lobbied to take over the Fifth Army in Morocco because he liked the prestige involved in commanding a field army. Eisenhower was disappointed that Clark placed his ambition ahead of the war effort, and warned him that his initial responsibilities with the Fifth would be limited to organizing and training incoming units to the theater. Within a month Clark realized that the drawn-out North African campaign and Eisenhower's decision to entrust Husky to Patton meant he would not see action for the foreseeable future. Clark hand-picked a capable staff and did a good job at his assigned task, but began badgering Eisenhower for a more active role. In fact, Eisenhower had to make a special trip to Oujda to reassure Clark and his staff that they would not be sidelined forever. Despite his misgivings about Clark's vanity, Eisenhower continued to value Clark's more positive attributes. When in mid-June Marshall alluded to bringing Clark home to become head of Army Ground Forces, Eisenhower responded that he needed Clark where he was. Clark hoped that his Fifth Army headquarters might get transferred to England to participate in the cross-Channel assault on German-occupied France, or might be used to assail Sardinia. Instead, Eisenhower tapped him for Avalanche. Eisenhower wanted an American field army for the operation, and Clark's was the only one readily available. Although Eisenhower acknowledged that Bradley had more experience and even briefly considered giving him the job, Bradley was too busy on Sicily to undertake the necessary preparations. Besides, Eisenhower felt that Clark's energy, quality staff, organizational skills, and familiarity with amphibious warfare planning more than made up for his combat inexperience. As for Clark's narcissism, Eisenhower assured Marshall that he had outgrown this regrettable trait and was ready to contribute any way he could.[23]

To implement Avalanche, Eisenhower gave Clark the British Tenth Corps and Mike Dawley's Sixth Corps. Dawley and his Sixth Corps headquarters had arrived in the Mediterranean the previous spring, but had not yet seen action. Eisenhower had slated the Sixth Corps for Husky, but Patton had balked at conducting the campaign with an untried corps and had successfully lobbied Eisenhower to substitute Bradley's battle-tested Second Corps instead. Now Clark, who had never led large formations in combat, had to pay the price for Patton's persuasiveness by embarking on Avalanche with an inexperienced army headquarters and an equally inexperienced corps. Greenness aside, Dawley came highly recommended. The fifty-seven-year-old Wisconsin-born Dawley had graduated from West Point in 1910 and entered the artillery branch. He did two tours of duty in the Philippines and then participated in World War One as executive officer of an artillery school in France, where he met Marshall. In the interwar years he taught at West Point from 1919 to 1924, attended the Command and General Staff School from 1926 to 1927, served in the office of the chief of field artillery from 1927 to 1930, went to the Army War College from 1933 to 1934, and instructed at the Infantry School from 1934 to 1939. After he commanded a field artillery regiment and the Seventh Division's artillery, Marshall appointed him to lead the Fortieth Division two months before the United States entered World War Two. He greatly impressed McNair with his handling of the division and with his performance in the Carolina maneuvers. McNair's endorsement no doubt helped Dawley secure the Sixth Corps in April 1942. Marshall strongly recommended Dawley to Eisenhower as Central Task Force commander for Torch, but Eisenhower opted for Fredendall instead. Although Eisenhower in mid-May 1943 praised Dawley to Marshall as a "splendid officer," Clark later claimed that Eisenhower had had his doubts about Dawley from the start. Patton for his part had a difficult time figuring out Dawley. Clark did not know Dawley well, but was willing to give him the benefit of the doubt because he placed so much stock in McNair's judgment. Dawley was in fact an intelligent, earnest, and knowledgeable man, but also so quiet and reserved that it was hard for people to know him well.[24]

Montgomery's two divisions crossed over to Italy's toe without opposition on 3 September and began moving northward. They met little resistance, but the Germans slowed their march by creating as many obstacles as possible before falling back. As a result, the British had to overcome destroyed bridges, tunnels, culverts, and so on. While the British Eighth Army pushed on, more than 500 Allied vessels carried elements of five divisions to Salerno. Eisenhower had selected Salerno, a crescent-shaped bay bisected by the Sele River and overlooked by mountains, because it was the northernmost landing site available within range of Allied fighter planes in Sicily. The main American contributions consisted of Fred Walker's untried Thirty-sixth Division and two regiments from Troy Middleton's veteran Forty-fifth Division. Clark planned to put the two British divisions ashore north of the Sele and Walker's men to the south of the river on the first day. The Allies announced Italy's surrender on 8 September, but the unsurprised Germans quickly and efficiently disarmed the Italians and took over their defensive posts. Therefore, British and American soldiers ran into heavy fire when they assailed the Salerno shoreline next morning. They managed to secure a foothold, but the Sele River continued to separate the British and American beaches. The Germans rushed reinforcements to the area while Clark struggled to consolidate the beachhead and land Middleton's two regiments. On 12 September, the Germans launched a heavy counterattack down the Sele that wrecked an American battalion and almost reached the sea. Clark rushed every available man to the front regardless of specialty—cooks, clerks, mechanics, drivers, orderlies, and so on—and courageously motored up and down his tattered American line encouraging the

GIs. In the end, American artillery ashore and afloat carried the day and forced the Germans back. Meanwhile, a worried Eisenhower—he believed that if Avalanche failed Marshall would relieve him of his command—hurried as much help as he could to the beleaguered Fifth Army in response to the precarious situation there. Every available warplane flew northward to strike German positions inland. On 13 September a battalion from the Eighty-second Airborne Division parachuted in, and the next day the Forty-fifth Division's remaining regiment arrived. Clark finally united the two parts of his beachhead on 16 September at about the same time American patrols encountered Montgomery's men from the south. Two days later the Germans sullenly withdrew from the overlying mountains, bringing Avalanche to a close. Establishing themselves on the European continent cost the Allies 9,000 casualties, of whom 5,500 were British.[25]

For Clark, Avalanche was a traumatic baptism of fire as an army commander. The night before he departed for Italy, he was so nervous that he could not concentrate on a game of bridge he played with Eisenhower and two other officers in Algiers. Clark discovered that perhaps the worst thing about being a commander was watching events unfold over which he had little control. As far as Clark was concerned, the first three days ashore at Salerno went relatively smoothly. For example, on 10 September he described conditions at the beachhead as "well in hand." He did not conclude until an early morning meeting with Dawley two days later that the Thirty-sixth Division was in serious trouble. Clark thereupon undertook herculean efforts to rectify a situation so serious that he made contingency plans to evacuate his headquarters by sea. Not until the sixteenth did he breathe easy and conclude that the worst was over. Despite Clark's pre-invasion jitters, his calmness and serenity in adversity made a good impression. Alexander visited on 15 September and was struck by Clark's controlled demeanor, as was Eisenhower during his inspection two days later. On the other hand, when the cool and professional Truscott arrived on the fourteenth to prepare for his division's commitment, he immediately recognized that Clark had spread his units so thinly that the German threat seemed worse than was actually the case. This may have been true, but Eisenhower's opinion was the one that mattered most. On 20 September Eisenhower radioed to Marshall his qualified endorsement of Clark. Eisenhower noted that although Clark was not as good at gaining people's confidence as Bradley and lacked Patton's single-minded determination to win at all costs, he had done well enough to justify keeping him as head of the Fifth Army. It was now apparent that the fighting in Italy would continue through the fall and winter, and Eisenhower intended Clark to lead the American effort there.[26]

Clark's composure around his superiors helped him escape blame for an operation that, while successful, came a lot closer to failure than previous amphibious landings in North Africa and Sicily. Unhappily for Mike Dawley, his obvious nervousness throughout the operation made him the perfect scapegoat for the close call. Although Clark later claimed that he had had serious doubts about Dawley all along, he did not express them until after the Fifth Army repulsed the ferocious German counterattack. Clark disliked Dawley's anxious behavior and actions and asked Alexander to look in on him during the latter's 15 September visit to the beachhead. Alexander did so, and afterward took Clark aside and said with his usual unobtrusiveness, "I do not want to interfere with your business, but I have had some ten years' experience in this game of sizing up commanders. I can tell you definitely have a broken reed on your hands and I suggest you replace him immediately."[27] Alexander was especially concerned with Dawley's palpable jumpiness. Clark agreed with Alexander's assessment and asked Alexander to bring up the matter with Eisenhower when he saw him at Amilcar in Tunisia. Clark also appointed General Matthew Ridgway, commander of the Eighty-second Airborne Division, as Dawley's deputy to help him and keep an eye on him. Upon hearing Alexander's report, Eisenhower decided to go to Salerno for a firsthand look at the situation. Eisenhower arrived on a British warship on the seventeenth, and after talking with Dawley and Clark determined that Clark and Alexander were right that Dawley had to go. Eisenhower listened to Walker explain the situation, and then asked Dawley, "How'd you ever get the troops into such a mess?"[28] He issued the necessary orders before he left. Eisenhower admitted that his investigation was cursory, but he had concluded that Dawley was simply too indecisive, uncontrolled, and anxious to lead a corps, and that these unfortunate and hitherto unknown traits had contributed to Avalanche's difficulties. After Eisenhower departed, Clark, Dawley, Walker, and Ridgway took a trip to the front, and on the way back Dawley antagonized Clark by criticizing him and Eisenhower for *their* skittishness. Three days later, no doubt to bolster the record against Dawley should it prove necessary, Clark elaborated on and specified Dawley's sins. He claimed that Dawley created no corps reserve, left his left flank in the air and took no steps to protect it, showed insufficient initiative, possessed an incompetent and unhappy staff, failed to keep the British informed of his activities, located his headquarters poorly, and lost the confidence of subordinates such as Ridgway.[29]

Clark sent a Fifth Army staff officer to bring Dawley official word of his relief. The staffer reached Dawley's headquarters around midnight and discovered the Sixth Corps headquarters personnel standing around with long faces, having already heard the news. Upon being awakened, Dawley said to the staff officer, "I know what you are going to say. When do I leave?" He talked with Patton in Sicily on his way home and blamed his discomfiture on the interference and vacillation of Clark and his chief of staff, General Al Gruenther. Patton enjoyed any gossip that reflected poorly on Clark, but could not help but comment that for all the manliness and restraint Dawley displayed, he did not seem particularly gung-ho. After returning to the States, Dawley traveled to Washington to explain to Marshall what had happened. Marshall listened sympathetically, but as he showed Dawley to the door he unkindly noted that after hearing his story he had concluded that Dawley should have been removed from his command much sooner.

No doubt Dawley's performance left much to be desired, but some credible observers felt that many of the problems he confronted at Salerno were beyond his control and not attributable to him. Truscott, for instance, pointed out that Clark had unexpectedly ordered Dawley ashore on the first day of the Salerno landing. As a result, Dawley had to set up his headquarters without sufficient staff and communications. In fact, he had to share the Thirty-sixth Division's communications network, complicating his and Walker's operations. Colonel James Gavin, a young and aggressive paratrooper who later rose to command the Eighty-second Airborne Division, spent a good deal of time with Dawley at Salerno and later claimed that Dawley did as well as could be expected under difficult circumstances. Others were more inclined to blame Walker for the Thirty-sixth Division's problems than Dawley, but Walker had the advantage of Clark's friendship. Walker for his part believed that Clark exaggerated his division's woes during the fighting and felt he and Dawley had done good jobs under trying conditions. Later Walker sardonically noted, "[Dawley] handled his job as well or better than Clark handled his."[30] In brief, some people felt that Dawley's relief was as much about preserving Clark's reputation as anything else.[31]

Eisenhower and Clark had no difficulty in settling on General John Lucas as Dawley's replacement. The previous May Marshall had grown concerned that Eisenhower was devoting too much time to political affairs at the expense of military matters, and had sent Lucas to the Mediterranean to assist him on the military side of the equation. Eisenhower found Lucas very useful and dispatched him to Sicily during Husky to serve as his eyes and ears. Although Patton ordinarily would have resented one of Eisenhower's minions looking over his shoulder, he made an exception in this case because Lucas was an old friend. Lucas not only won everyone's respect in Sicily, but he also successfully completed the delicate and difficult mission of delivering Eisenhower's oral message to Patton after the slapping incidents without antagonizing either party. In late August Marshall ordered Omar Bradley to England to take over a field army there, opening up a slot at corps command. Marshall guessed correctly that Eisenhower would choose Lucas, and was not surprised when on 24 August Eisenhower wrote to him, "He [Lucas] has not had combat responsibility but he has had combat experience. He spent the entire month in Sicily, and is well-acquainted with battlefield conditions and requirements. I think he would command a combat corps most successfully."[32] There were several division commanders whose selection seemed more obvious—Truscott and Middleton, most prominently—but Eisenhower did not want to take them away from their outfits on the eve of a new campaign. Lucas had not anticipated Bradley's departure, so he was surprised but delighted when on 2 September Eisenhower offered him the Second Corps. He was less happy when Bradley skimmed off the best staffers before leaving, but was willing to pay that price to get the most battle-tested corps in the American Army. Less than three weeks later, though, Eisenhower suddenly directed Lucas to report to Clark at Salerno. Since Lucas had already secured a corps that was scheduled to go to Italy anyway, Eisenhower and Clark figured that it made sense to simply transfer Lucas to the Sixth Corps in place of Dawley. In fact, before Avalanche Clark had made it clear to Lucas that he hoped he would receive the Second Corps and looked forward to serving with him in Italy. Clark had also promised Walker that he would get a corps command, but he apparently valued Lucas's abilities more and opted to fulfill that pledge first. Lucas took a minesweeper to Salerno on 24 September, where Clark informed him that he would lead the Sixth Corps.[33]

Lucas was a cavalryman turned artilleryman. Born in West Virginia in 1890, he graduated from West Point in 1911 and went overseas to the Philippines. Upon his return he was sent to the Mexican border and stationed in Columbus, New Mexico. There he played an important role in repelling Pancho Villa's attack on the town in 1916. He participated in Pershing's Punitive Expedition into Mexico and fought in France in World War One, where he was wounded at the head of a battalion at Amiens and invalided home. After the conflict he attended the Field Artillery School in 1921, the Command and General Staff School from 1923 to 1924, and the Army War College a decade later. In between these tours he spent much of his time teaching military science at various universities. He served in the Personnel Division in the mid-thirties, and then on the Field Artillery Board. After World War Two began in Europe, he commanded first the Second Division and then the Third Division. He impressed McNair, which no doubt contributed to Marshall's decision to promote him to lead the stateside Third Corps and place his name on the list of possible Central Task Force commanders for Torch. Lucas was admired in the prewar officer corps for his integrity, intelligence, breadth of knowledge, and compassion. He read widely and particularly enjoyed Rudyard Kipling's poetry. His thoughtfulness was real enough, but rarely transcendent. He was in fact thoroughly capable in an ordinary sort of way, the type of combat officer who would fulfill the letter of his orders but not go much beyond that. Lucas's men called him "Foxy Grandpa" in part because he looked older than his years, but also because the corncob pipe he constantly smoked and his bushy gray mustache implied cleverness. Although competent and methodical, he possessed little of the energy, aggressiveness, and drive that made generals such as Patton and

Truscott so successful on the battlefield. Nevertheless, Clark was glad to have him as the Fifth Army undertook its long campaign against Rome.[34]

Lucas's transfer to the Sixth Corps meant that Eisenhower had to find someone else to lead the Second Corps. Since he did not want to use any of his division commanders, there was really only one senior officer in the theater with the requisite experience for the job: Jeff Keyes, Patton's current Seventh Army deputy. Moreover, now that the Seventh Army was inactive while Patton cooled his heels in his Sicilian exile, Keyes was underemployed and available. Patton and Keyes were old friends, and Patton had secured Keyes's services for the Western Task Force during Torch. Later Keyes oversaw the preparations for Husky while Patton was busy in Tunisia, and even after Patton returned he left most of Husky's planning in Keyes's hands. On Sicily Keyes successfully led Patton's hastily improvised provisional corps against Palermo. Patton respected Keyes's drive, nerve, and his determination to obey even difficult orders. He gave Keyes most of the credit for seizing Palermo so quickly, and communicated as much to Eisenhower on several occasions. Patton saw Keyes as his protégé and believed he was fully qualified to move up to a corps. Eisenhower needed little persuading as to Keyes's usefulness. The previous year, before Marshall put him in charge of Torch, Eisenhower had suggested Keyes as a good candidate to take an armored corps to North Africa. Eisenhower admired Keyes's tactical knowledge, combativeness, and loyalty. His only concern was that Keyes was often too chary in praising his subordinates, which Eisenhower believed might undermine morale and reduce his effectiveness. Indeed, Eisenhower wrote Keyes a letter pointing out this problem and encouraging him to address it. As for Clark, he did not seem to have strong feelings for Keyes one way or another, though he acknowledged his tactical prowess. The big obstacle to Keyes's elevation was Marshall. Marshall for some reason did not think much of him, and in fact the previous March had in a cable to Eisenhower questioned not only Keyes's training skills, but also his ability to fill *any* important position. Patton's efforts to talk Keyes up to Marshall during the chief of staff's visit to the theater in May did not erase Marshall's doubts. Eisenhower initially made Keyes's appointment temporary in case Marshall protested, but in the end Marshall raised no objections. Despite his reservations, he wanted Eisenhower to have officers of his own choosing under him. Both Patton and Keyes were delighted with the news, and Keyes and his Second Corps headquarters entered the lines in mid-October.[35]

Jeff Keyes would lead the Second Corps in Italy for the remaining twenty-one months of the European War, making him the army's longest-serving World War Two corps commander in an active theater. Keyes was a cavalryman by training. Born in New Mexico in 1886, the son of an army officer, he graduated from West Point in 1913 and then spent World War One teaching there. After the conflict he attended the Cavalry School in 1925, the Command and General Staff School from 1925 to 1926, and the War College from 1936 to 1937. His most interesting assignment was a year at the French École de Guerre in 1933, which later contributed to his good relationships with French officers in North Africa and Italy. He was in the General Staff's Supply and Transportation Branch when World War Two broke out in Europe, and became the Second Armored Division's chief of staff when Patton selected him as his Western Task Force deputy. Keyes was a gentlemanly, hard-driving officer with a strong personality and plenty of initiative. People remarked on his common sense and level-headedness, traits that came in handy in dealing with the German foe, the cold and rainy Italian mountains and the logistical problems they caused, his French and British allies—and Wayne Clark. He accepted Eisenhower's advice and became more attentive to and considerate of his subordinates after he took over the Second Corps, frequently visiting them at the front to keep tabs on them. One officer remembered returning to his regiment during a rough battle in the northern Italian mountains after recovering from a wound. Keyes greeted him, explained the difficult situation into which he was about to be thrust, and added, "It's a tough fight, but it's going well. You are here."[36]

The Italian campaign was always a tough fight. Shortly after the Allies established themselves ashore, Eisenhower directed Alexander's Fifteenth Army Group to seize Rome. Doing so, however, turned out to be far more difficult than anyone expected. Italy was an awful place to wage war. The narrow Italian peninsula was intersected by rivers and covered with mountains that contained poor roads unsuitable for the mechanized British and American forces. Autumn rains that gradually turned to sleet and then snow churned the countryside into a muddy mess. Worst of all, the Germans decided to hold on to as much of the peninsula as possible and conducted a skillful retreat by demolishing bridges, sowing mines, and fighting from defensive positions until the last possible moment. The Allies discovered all these problems during their attempt to grab Naples, through which they hoped to supply their armies. The British undertook the main effort against the port while the Americans drove across the mountains to approach it from the northeast. The Germans evacuated the city on 1 October and fell back to the Volturno River. Although the Germans completely wrecked everything of military value in Naples, Allied engineers had the port unloading 7,000 tons of cargo a day by early November. Meanwhile, Lucas pushed Truscott's Third Division and Ryder's Thirty-fourth Division across the Volturno in mid-October, and from there the Allies slowly and painfully advanced northward until they ran into the formidable Gustav Line, from which the Germans planned to make their stand. Merely approaching the Gustav Line cost the Allies considerable casualties and time, and in late December Clark called a halt so his tired soldiers could catch their breath.

The Italian campaign was not shaping up as Clark wanted or expected. He was an ambitious man who had sacrificed much to secure command of a field army, and he was well aware that stalemate promoted neither his nor the Allies' purposes. Despite his lack of progress, Clark tried to remain upbeat and put the best spin on things. In an assessment based in part on presuppositions and hypotheticals, Clark wrote his wife in mid-November:

There is no question but that it [the Italian campaign] has been completely successful. We facilitated the advance of the Eighth Army by our landing, and we have captured the great port of Naples, and will capture Rome. We have drawn many divisions from the Russian front, which has helped them materially. Being in Italy, we threatened Southern Europe, which has necessitated the Germans moving more divisions to this area, thereby weakening the Russian front or depleting their reserves. I am surprised that the press has questioned the decision of our Supreme Commander in taking on this Italian adventure. There is no question but that it was the right thing to do.[37]

Clark initially assured Eisenhower that he was working well with the British, but as time went on he increasingly saw the British as a convenient scapegoat for his problems, and criticized them as slow and timid. On the other hand, Clark was happy with his hand-picked staff. He and Fifth Army chief of staff Gruenther were not personally close—indeed, Clark kept his distance from everyone in the Fifth Army—but the two men worked well together. Gruenther often served as a buffer between Fifth Army officers and the demanding Clark. Clark was an able executive and administrator capable of great charm. To his credit, he insisted that his headquarters do whatever it could to support his lieutenants in the field. One officer remembered, "No representative of a troop unit, no commander or staff officer from a troops unit ever went to General Clark's headquarters with a request without being warmly received and being provided with what he needed to the extent it was available. The personnel administration and logistic support provided by Fifth Army headquarters was superb."[38] Notwithstanding this generosity, Clark's subordinates remained leery of him and never really warmed to him because he seemed too cloying and vainglorious. His entourage in his frequent trips to the front invariably included journalists and photographers, and his public relations officers publicized Clark at the expense of everyone else. Truscott later referred to Clark's mania for self-promotion as his greatest weakness, one that prevented him from getting the good feel for the battlefield that separates great generals from merely competent ones. Another officer attributed Clark's shortcomings to the fact that he never led a division or corps in combat before taking over the Fifth Army and therefore did not understand the problems involved in running such units.[39]

As for his corps commanders, Clark was on the whole satisfied with their performances that autumn. He praised Lucas's ability to wage mountain warfare and publicly congratulated Keyes for successfully leading the Second Corps in its first major action in Italy. Lucas and Keyes, though, were increasingly unhappy with the campaign. Lucas resented Clark's interference in all areas and found it unhelpful. He was grateful that he got along with Clark, but was under no illusions as to the reasons, confiding in his diary, "Our relations have been very pleasant. As long as I win battles, I imagine they will be."[40] Lucas was an old artilleryman, so he was especially irked by the Germans' ability to fire a few rounds, displace, and then open up again before the Americans spotted them. As the campaign dragged on, he became very pessimistic about the prospects of achieving much in the theater. On the other hand, he was pleased with his three division commanders. He had good reason for this; all three of them—Truscott, Ryder, and Middleton—were extremely competent men who went on to lead corps of their own. Keyes for his part was deployed to Italy after Lucas, so it took him somewhat longer to become disenchanted with the place. Besides, he was an aggressive man who disliked backing away from any obstacles, so he had a difficult time understanding why his GIs were making so little progress. Clark rode herd over him too, but it was no worse than Patton's browbeating. By the end of the year, though, even Keyes grew discouraged as bad weather set in and the German resistance gelled along the Gustav Line.[41]

The fighting that autumn even took a toll on the Fifth Army's capable division commanders. Middleton was an astute man who quickly recognized that the campaign was unlikely to yield many strategic benefits anytime soon. He was, like Lucas, unhappy with Clark's excessive interference and in mid-October complained to Lucas that his Forty-fifth Division was just butting its head against a German stone wall. By November he was exhausted and dispirited, conditions no doubt exacerbated by an arthritic knee that kept him in constant pain. It was not so much climbing the steep Italian mountains that hurt him, but rather the long jeep rides that immobilized his knee. He tried to keep his affliction secret from Lucas, but Lucas eventually found out and sent him to a hospital in Naples. Lucas noted that it was difficult to remain cheerful while hurting, and Middleton's despondency was infecting his staff. When Middleton failed to improve, Clark and Lucas reluctantly removed him from his division and replaced him with General William Eagles.

Unfortunately, Middleton was not alone in his difficulties. In late November Doc Ryder came down with some sort of painful facial neuralgia that put him out of action for several weeks. His division, the once sturdy and dependable Thirty-fourth, was in little better shape. For this Clark blamed Ryder. He thought that Ryder was a good combat commander, but weak in administration. In particular, Clark believed that Ryder had not been sufficiently ruthless in removing under-performing subordinates who hurt divisional morale. Clark drove to the hospital and warned Ryder that he would lose his division unless he shaped up. Clark was not alone in his evaluation; Patton agreed with him. After an early January visit to the Thirty-fourth Division headquarters Patton noted that while Ryder was un-doubtedly a brave man, he was not a good soldier.

Fred Walker's health was fine, but he was growing disenchanted not only with the developing military stalemate, but also with Clark's and Keyes's meddling in divisional operations. He felt that both men were too jumpy and prone to exag-gerate German capabilities, and told his staffers not to send alarming news to them unless he okayed it. Even Clark's most aggressive subordinates were dissatis-fied. Clark was not surprisingly very pleased to get Truscott's crack Third Divi-sion, which he considered the best outfit in the entire army. Lucas agreed and wrote of its commander, "Truscott is one of the greatest soldiers in the Army. He never complains and nothing 'can't be done.'"[42] Truscott arrived with his usual fidgety combativeness, but within a short time he too protested Clark's unwar-ranted intrusions because he did not think that Clark had a particularly good grasp of the military situation. Truscott did not like anyone telling him what to do, and once informed Lucas he would take Berlin if everyone just left him alone. By November, however, even Truscott admitted that he was tired and that his fine division needed a break. His health was also breaking down. Truscott at least had the opportunity to make a difference, but the same could not be said of Ernie Harmon, who was perhaps the most dissatisfied and frustrated of all. Harmon understood that his First Armored Division's tanks were unsuited for Italy's mountainous terrain and objected to the dispersal of his unit on unimportant missions. As a result, he figured that he was wasting his time in Italy, though he did his best to maintain his sense of humor and spirits.[43]

The invasion of southern Italy was different from previous American army campaigns in Europe. Operation Torch took just three days. The fighting in Tunisia lasted longer, but once the Allies got their ducks in a row they required only thirty-one days to push the Germans and Italians into an enclave around Tu-nis and Bizerte, and, after a short break, another twenty-five days to compel their surrender. Finally, conquering Sicily necessitated thirty-eight days. In all these cases, the Allies faced limited numbers of German troops and reaped important strategic gains. In southern Italy, though, the Allies achieved less than they had hoped by the end of the year. To be sure, they had knocked Italy out of the war, es-tablished a beachhead on the European continent, and tied down significant Ger-man forces, but Rome remained in German hands. After 113 days of grueling combat, the Allies were only now approaching the main German line of resistance. Merely coping with the skillful German fighting retreat required overwhelming artillery support and thoroughly exhausted the Fifth Army and the British Eighth Army. The British and Americans in Italy would have been even more demoralized had they known that the worst was yet to come.

Piercing the Gustav Line

The solidification of German defenses along the Gustav Line made it increasingly clear that the Allies' current strategy in Italy would not yield significant results anytime soon. One obvious solution to this conundrum was for the Allies to use their naval superiority to launch an amphibious landing somewhere up the Italian coast behind the Gustav Line. Doing so would compel the Germans to either evacuate their positions and retreat northward to protect their supply and communications lines or else stay put and be destroyed. The idea occurred to Eisenhower among others. It seemed like an ideal solution, but there were serious difficulties in implementing it that the Allies had to confront and overcome. For one thing, Salerno demonstrated that amphibious operations were not sure bets because the Germans could rush reinforcements overland to the beachhead as fast as or faster than the Allies could by sea. Also, conducting such a landing required resources not necessarily on hand, especially the vital landing ships tanks (LSTs) required to supply troops ashore. The Americans were putting enormous pressure on the British to focus Allied men and materiel on German-occupied France, and in fact would at the Teheran Conference in November–December 1943 finally pin the British down on a rough date for the invasion, dubbed "Overlord." Even before that Allied resources had already begun flowing out of the Mediterranean to England. Despite these limitations, Eisenhower decided to risk an amphibious assault and persuaded the Combined Chiefs of Staff to delay moving sixty-eight of the precious LSTs from the Mediterranean until 15 December, and later got it to extend the deadline by a month. Unfortunately, the Fifth Army and British Eighth Army failed to achieve sufficient progress to make an amphibious attack practical, so Clark and Alexander reluctantly scrubbed it. In mid-December, though, Winston Churchill almost single-handedly resurrected the proposal on his way home from the Teheran Conference. Churchill fell ill in Tunis, and while recovering he lamented the lack of progress in Italy and the downgrading of the Mediterranean theater. To Churchill, only Rome's occupation would satisfy the Allied investment in the campaign, and the key to taking the Italian capital was an amphibious operation ultimately labeled "Shingle." To that end, he inveigled Roosevelt and the Combined Chiefs to keep the LSTs in the theater until mid-February, and then persuaded Alexander and Clark to take their recently canceled plan off the shelf. Their target was Anzio, on the west Italian coast about 35 miles south of Rome and 70 miles north of the Gustav Line.

Major changes in the American command structure in the Mediterranean complicated the planning for the Anzio landing. On 31 December Eisenhower left Algiers to visit the States before recrossing the Atlantic to assume command of Allied forces preparing for Overlord. With Eisenhower's departure, the Mediterranean became a British-dominated theater under British General Henry "Jumbo" Wilson. Before he closed up shop, Eisenhower had recommended to Marshall General Jacob Devers as Wilson's deputy and senior American officer in the theater. Devers was, like Eisenhower, a Marshall protégé. He was one of the first younger officers whom Marshall elevated to general and had justified Marshall's confidence in him during his stint as Ninth Division commander at Fort Bragg in 1941. There were almost no accommodations ready for a National Guard division on its way to the post ahead of schedule, so Devers hurriedly scrounged up enough men and lumber to construct barracks for the troops, earning him a reputation as a man who could get things done. After the United States entered the war, Marshall recommended Devers to Eisenhower as a possible candidate to lead the Central Task Force in Torch. When that did not pan out, Marshall sent Devers to England in May 1943 to supervise the American buildup there. Marshall believed that Devers had done a good job in England and hoped that Eisenhower would find a suitable role for him in Overlord. Eisenhower, though, pointed out that once he took over as supreme commander for Overlord, Devers would become somewhat superfluous in England. Instead, he felt that Devers could better serve the Allied cause in the Mediterranean as Wilson's deputy. Devers had no battle experience, but Eisenhower did not see that as a disqualifying factor because Clark would continue to oversee combat operations in Italy. Devers could use his administrative abilities to relieve Clark of some of the paperwork that took up so much of his time so he could focus on the fighting. Finally, Eisenhower informed Marshall that he had spoken with high-ranking British officers and found them amenable to Devers's appointment. Deferential to the chief of staff as always, Eisenhower stated that he was willing to make room for Devers in Overlord as a field army commander if Marshall could satisfactorily arrange all the personnel pieces. Although Marshall was disappointed, he went along with the proposal because he did not want to force anyone on Eisenhower. On 29 December Marshall issued orders transferring Devers to a post that Bradley, for one, later asserted was almost tailor-made for him. That same day Eisenhower radioed Devers to congratulate him on his new job and assure him that he would find it important and interesting.[44]

Eisenhower was not being completely honest with Marshall in his reasons for recommending Devers as Wilson's deputy. Although he assured Marshall he had nothing against Devers, the truth was that Eisenhower disliked the man. Their relationship had been cordial enough at the war's start, but in the summer of 1943 Devers denied Eisenhower's request to send four medium bomber groups from England to the Mediterranean. From that point on Eisenhower denigrated Devers as a lightweight in over his head. Many of Eisenhower's staffers and subordinates were quick to embrace this evaluation of Devers. Omar Bradley, for example, later admitted that Eisenhower prejudiced him against Devers, but added that after renewing his relationship with Devers in England he was inclined to agree with Eisenhower's characterizations. Bradley found Devers "overly garrulous (saying little of importance), egotistical, shallow, intolerant, not very smart, and much too inclined to rush off half-cocked."[45] Patton agreed. When Devers's career trajectory was steeper than his own, Patton had as usual resorted to ingratiation, referring to Devers as one of his dearest friends. Later, however, Patton maligned Devers's abilities. With unconscious irony, he stated that Devers was too bombastic and full of himself. Like so many veterans, Patton had a hard time listening to a combat virgin like Devers expound on strategy and tactics. He fully agreed with Eisenhower's assertion that Devers was ".22 caliber"—though he also snidely noted that this was a case of the pot calling the kettle black. Even after Eisenhower and Devers switched places in early 1944, Eisenhower continued to find fault with Devers. In particular, he complained that Devers was too slow and chary in sending him the personnel from the Mediterranean he asked for.[46]

These negative depictions of Devers were one-sided and unfair. In fact, Devers was considerably more astute and effective than Eisenhower and his colleagues believed. For every Eisenhower and Bradley who dismissed Devers, there were others such as J. Lawton Collins and Ernie Harmon who praised his virtues. Devers had been born in Pennsylvania in 1889 and graduated from West Point in 1909. He taught mathematics at West Point and then served as a field artillery instructor at Fort Sill during World War One. Like Eisenhower and Bradley, he thereafter worried that his lack of combat experience in the conflict would hobble his career. He spent much of the interwar years back at West Point teaching, and eventually rose to become executive officer there. He also attended the Command and General Staff School from 1924 to 1925 and the Army War College from 1932 to 1933. After World War Two broke out in Europe, Marshall sent him to the Panama Canal Zone to bolster its defenses. His performance there contributed to Marshall's decision to elevate him to brigadier general over hundreds of other more senior officers, and to eventually assign him to lead the Ninth Division. In July 1941 Marshall put Devers in charge of armored forces at Fort Knox, Kentucky, and during his time there he contributed to the development of the Sherman tank. Marshall then dispatched him to England in May 1943, from where he went to the Mediterranean. There was an element of truth to the unflattering descriptions of Devers. He was indeed glib, serenely and often obliviously self-confident—he once claimed to know more about armor than either Patton or Eisenhower—ambitious, and somewhat superficial. On the other hand, he was an energetic man who looked much younger than his years, with a cheerful grin and plenty of charm and enthusiasm. If he was not necessarily a deep thinker, he possessed considerable common sense and could see to the heart of problems. Observers invariably noted his can-do attitude. When one fellow officer marveled at his ability to cut through red tape and get things done, Devers responded that the key to his success was that he was more interested in results than procedure. He hated paperwork and strived to keep it to a minimum, and treated his subordinates with a respect Patton for one would have found hard to understand. Devers invariably looked hard for the good in people and took it for granted that others acted in a similar manner. During the war he eventually rose to command an army group and successfully completed his missions despite troublesome allies, limited resources, difficult terrain, and Eisenhower's hostility.[47]

Devers was an unhappy and disappointed man when he arrived in Algiers to assume his new duties. He had hoped to lead a field army in Overlord, but had instead been kicked upstairs to an administrative post that promised little by way of glory and recognition. There were, however, plenty of problems for him to address. He liked most of his staffers, but they were scattered across the Mediterranean and hard to coordinate. Moreover, Eisenhower and others tried to cherry-pick the best ones for their own headquarters, and Devers's efforts to accommodate everyone seemed to satisfy no one. Nor did he and Clark get along with each other. There had been bad blood between them back in the States when Clark tried unsuccessfully to restrict Devers's access to McNair. Ever the optimist, Devers tried to find the best in Clark and years later even acknowledged his brilliance, but he became increasingly disenchanted with him during their time together in the Mediterranean. He developed serious doubts about Clark's generalship soon after he arrived in the theater, and used Clark's inability to end the stalemate in Italy as his main piece of evidence. As far as Devers was concerned, Clark was a bad officer and difficult subordinate whom he would have relieved if Marshall had let him. Clark for his part thought that Devers did not ever understand or care about the Italian campaign and that Devers's criticisms were based on ignorance rather than military acumen. Finally, no sooner had Devers arrived in Algiers from England than he fell ill with the flu and was bedridden for about a week. As a result, he played no part in Shingle's planning and raised no red flags—and therefore escaped much of the opprobrium attached to the operation.[48]

Clark on the other hand was much more involved, and therefore much more culpable, than Devers for Shingle. He was initially enthusiastic about the idea of an amphibious assault behind German lines and assigned the job to the dependable John Lucas, whose corps was not then seriously engaged. He began to have doubts, though, when he learned that the resources at his disposal were so limited as to preclude the landing force from doing much more than establishing a beachhead, but decided that he was in no position to protest orders that originated with the prime minister. Resorting to mixed metaphors and passive voice, Clark later wrote:

> I felt that I had a pistol pointed at my head. I had been told to make an end run to Anzio, but now I was told that it would have to be done without sufficient craft and that virtually all those craft would be withdrawn a few days after we hit the beaches with two divisions. Since it would obviously take much longer than that for the beachhead troops to join up with the balance of the Fifth Army, I would have two divisions left high and dry at the end of a long limb.[49]

He was not alone in his assessment. Before Eisenhower left for England, he asked Troy Middleton to look over the Shingle plans. Middleton did so and concluded that Lucas needed more troops to do the job envisioned for him. Despite Clark's reservations, he maintained a positive attitude in his conversations with Alexander, whom he did not much like, and did not call attention to the plan's obvious flaws. Rather than argue against what he believed was a militarily unfeasible operation, Clark passed the buck to Lucas by giving him vague instructions that left it up to him whether to push inland toward Rome after the landing or to stop and dig in. Or, to use Clark's own analogy, he redirected the pistol pointed at his head toward Lucas's instead. In his private conversations with Lucas, Clark reminded him of his own close call at Salerno and encouraged him not to do anything rash at Anzio. "Don't stick your neck out, Johnny," Clark said. "I did at Salerno and got into trouble."[50]

Lucas was an intelligent man who recognized immediately the untenable position into which he had been placed. Churchill and Alexander expected him to land at Anzio and then thrust inland toward Rome to cut off those Germans manning the Gustav Line, but Lucas realized that he did not have sufficient resources for the job. Lucas fretted about the lack of preparation and rehearsal time, the shipping shortage, the small number of troops at his disposal, and the necessity for him to use a British division. Worst of all, Clark seemed to be setting Lucas up as the fall guy by issuing him contradictory and unclear orders. To Lucas it appeared that he could either obey Churchill's and Alexander's wishes by risking his corps in a militarily unsound march on Rome or jeopardize his career by acting in a prudent fashion. When Lucas expressed his apprehensions to Clark and his Fifth

Army staffers, they told him that the decisions had already been made and he should get on with the operation. It was therefore small wonder that Lucas questioned Clark's moral courage. After a 10 January conference, Lucas wrote in his diary, "I feel like a lamb being led to slaughter."[51] Nor was Lucas alone in his concerns. Truscott, whose Third Division constituted the American contribution to Shingle and whose aggressive instincts were beyond reproach, shared Lucas's doubts. He later claimed that no one below Clark's headquarters believed that the Sixth Corps could do more than land, establish a beachhead, and hold on until the rest of the Fifth Army broke through the Gustav Line and rescued it, which would take at least a month. Anyone who thought differently, Truscott concluded, was no military expert. In fact, Truscott expected to meet heavy opposition at the water's edge and to face German counterattacks from the start. Even Patton was troubled when during a trip to Naples he learned Shingle's details from a clearly worried Lucas. He doubted that Lucas possessed sufficient drive for such a flawed operation. In a clumsy effort to buck Lucas up, Patton said, "John, there is no one in the Army I hate to see killed as much as you, but you can't get out of this alive. Of course, you might be only badly wounded. No one ever blames a wounded general for anything."[52] Lucas later learned that before Patton left he took one of Lucas's aides aside and told him to shoot Lucas if things got rough. Lucas joked that he was from then on leery of turning his back on the aide. It was a rare moment of levity for Lucas, whose reservations only increased as the big day approached.[53]

On the morning of 22 January, Lucas's two divisions landed practically unopposed along three beaches at Anzio after a short preliminary bombardment. The Germans had committed most of their reserves to the Gustav Line to confront the latest Allied offensive there, so Shingle caught them completely by surprise. By the end of the day Lucas had 36,000 troops ashore. There were in fact almost no Germans between Anzio and Rome, presenting Lucas with the opportunity to seize the Italian capital. Instead, Lucas followed his instincts and his interpretation of his ambiguous orders by instructing his men to dig in along a defensive perimeter. His cautiousness gave the Germans time to summon reinforcements from throughout southern Europe to confront the Sixth Corps. Clark visited the beachhead the day after the landing and said he was pleased with the way things were going. He decided to send Lucas additional soldiers, and wrote that after they arrived, "I will then strike out and cut the German lines of communications, forcing his withdrawal out of the Cassino area [at the Gustav Line]. Then I will turn my attention to Rome."[54] Although Allied reinforcements arrived in the form of William Eagles's Forty-fifth Division and Harmon's First Armored Division, they failed to keep pace with growing German strength in the area. Nor did they contribute much to the half-hearted and unsuccessful offensive Lucas initiated on 30

January. By the time the Germans launched their all-out counterattack on 16 February, they had 125,000 men to throw at Lucas's 100,000. The German assault focused on the British First Division and Forty-fifth Division. Soldiers fought through heavy rains, along deep gullies, and often at night. Each side resorted to infiltration tactics that all but negated the idea of a "front line." As at Salerno, the veteran Forty-fifth bent but did not break, and after five days the Germans fell back. By then each side had lost approximately 19,000 men since Shingle began.

For Winston Churchill, the stalemate at Anzio was unhappily reminiscent of the Gallipoli disaster he authored during the First World War, which almost ruined his career. With his usual apt turn of phrase, he said of Anzio, "I had hoped we were hurling a wildcat into the shore, but all we got was a stranded whale."[55] Churchill was never one to leave military affairs to the generals, so he demanded corrective action from Alexander. Alexander visited the beachhead twice and was not pleased with what he found. Based on his personal observations and the reports of British officers, especially British First Division commander General William Penny, Alexander concluded that Lucas was too old, tired, out-of-touch, uninformed, and uninspiring for his job, traits that caused him to squander a golden opportunity to seize Rome. After complaining to Clark several times about Lucas, on 16 February Alexander resorted to an out-of-channels appeal to Eisenhower in England via Alan Brooke. He probably did so because he had a good relationship with Eisenhower, whereas he barely knew Devers. Through Brooke, Alexander asked Eisenhower to use his influence to secure Lucas's relief, and suggested replacing him with a British corps commander, one of the American divisional commanders, or perhaps a "thruster" such as George Patton.

Eisenhower was startled by this unorthodox plea. As far as he was concerned, Alexander ought to take up his problems regarding Lucas with Clark and Devers, not him. The fact that he had not, Eisenhower snidely noted, was more evidence of Devers's incompetence. Still, Eisenhower wanted to be helpful. He rejected the idea of a British corps headquarters for Anzio, but noted that of the American divisional commanders available at the beachhead, he preferred Truscott, Eagles, and Harmon in that order as Lucas's replacement. He also offered Patton's services for a month if Devers was agreeable. Patton had recently arrived in England, but was not yet doing much, so he was available for a short-term mission. To lay the groundwork for a Patton rescue, should it be necessary, Eisenhower ordered him to his headquarters next morning to explain the situation. Although Eisenhower apologized to Patton for the potential change in plans, Patton was elated by the opportunity to lead soldiers in a desperate battle. In fact, he told Eisenhower he would command anything from a platoon up to get into a fight. Unfortunately for Patton, Clark had by then come up with another solution, so Patton ended up staying in England. As for Devers, he had already been to Anzio twice, and was, like Alexander, unhappy with the situation there. He felt that Lucas should have marched on Rome when he had the chance. He did not know Lucas well, but was unimpressed with what he had seen. Somewhat contradictorily, Devers also noted that Lucas had done as well as could be expected with the means at his disposal. After a week of defending Lucas, though, Devers finally agreed with Alexander that Lucas was mentally and physically exhausted and should be removed. As a result, by 17 February a consensus had emerged among Churchill, Alexander, and Devers that Lucas was unfit for his post and should be reassigned.[56]

By that point Clark had reached the same conclusion. Clark had never believed that Lucas could have reached Rome on his own with the resources initially placed at his disposal, and in fact called such an idea "ridiculous." He also personally liked Lucas and felt that he had done a good job in the fighting in southern Italy. At the same time, though, Clark had during his frequent visits to Anzio developed serious reservations about Lucas. He concluded that Lucas could have been more aggressive in expanding and consolidating the beachhead, and was concerned that Lucas did not keep in close enough touch with his subordinates. He was also unhappy that Lucas asked for an additional division on 9 February because Clark had neither a division to spare nor the logistical capability to support one at Anzio. To Clark, Lucas seemed tired and worn out. Therefore, when on 16 February Alexander again expressed his dissatisfaction with Lucas, Clark was not in the mood to strongly defend his Sixth Corps commander, especially when Alexander told him, "You know, the position is serious. We may be pushed back into the sea. That would be very bad for both of us—and you would certainly be relieved of your command."[57] This disinclination was no doubt reinforced by Clark's knowledge that the prime minister wanted Lucas out of the way too. Instead of protecting Lucas, Clark focused on manufacturing a graceful exit for him that would preserve his career and dignity. He did not want to relieve Lucas in the middle of the German counterattack because it might lower morale and disrupt Sixth Corps operations. By way of compromise, he opted to assign Truscott as Lucas's deputy until the situation calmed down, after which he would kick Lucas upstairs to become the Fifth Army's deputy commander. One potential problem was that Truscott was not particularly enthusiastic about his proposed new role. While he was aware of Lucas's limitations, the two men were old friends who had worked well together, and Truscott did not think Lucas deserved to be replaced. Moreover, Truscott did not relish trading his important and active assignment with the Third Division for one without many command responsibilities. Despite these reservations, Truscott's soldierly instincts prevailed, and he said he would obey his orders. After the big German counteroffensive petered out several days later, Clark traveled to the beachhead and removed Lucas from the Sixth Corps.[58]

Lucas was disappointed but hardly surprised by his dismissal. As early as 29 January he had suspected that some senior officers were unhappy with his decision to forgo a drive to Rome for the sake of establishing a defensive perimeter at Anzio. While Lucas admitted that Clark had been very helpful in bolstering the beleaguered beachhead's defenses, he resented Clark's intimations that he should have pushed toward Rome because he thought Clark ought to know better. Nor did Lucas appreciate Clark's decision to cramp his command style by establishing an advanced army headquarters at Anzio. As far as Lucas was concerned, he had followed Clark's instructions and was doing as well as—indeed, probably better than—could be expected under the difficult circumstances into which he had been thrust. On 16 February, the same day Alexander and Devers were nosing around the beachhead and finding fault with his actions, Lucas confided in his diary, "Had I done so [assaulted Rome] I would have lost my corps and nothing would have been accomplished except to raise the prestige and morale of the enemy. Besides, my orders didn't read that way."[59] Lucas strongly and correctly suspected that Truscott's promotion to his deputy foreshadowed his relief, and was deeply hurt when the axe fell right after he had successfully repulsed the ferocious German counterattack five days later. Lucas's appointment as the Fifth Army's deputy commander did nothing to allay the bitterness he felt toward Clark and the British.

Because Clark believed that Lucas was thoroughly exhausted, he brought him out of Anzio with him on 23 February and sent him to Sorrento for a rest. Marshall and McNair wanted to preserve Lucas's dignity and take advantage of his experience, so Marshall ordered him back to the States via England a month later to lead a training army, and Lucas played no further active role in the war. Lucas was well-liked and respected in the army, so many officers sympathized with his plight. Some argued that Clark had placed him in an untenable situation and then scapegoated him when Shingle did not turn out as Churchill and Alexander envisioned. By this line of reasoning, Lucas paid the price for Clark's inability to muster sufficient moral courage to tell Alexander and Churchill that Shingle lacked the resources to succeed. Dwight Eisenhower, however, was not among those who interpreted things this way. He rejected Marshall's offer to use Lucas as a corps commander or as his eyes and ears. Eisenhower, whose perspective was different from most, commented that Lucas got a fair chance to satisfy his superiors, and his failure to fulfill his assigned mission justified his relief.[60]

Clark's selection of Lucian Truscott as Lucas's replacement was unsurprising. Truscott had a well-deserved reputation as a hard fighter and had probably seen more action than any other American division commander up to that point. He had participated in the Canadian raid on Dieppe in August 1942 at the head of an army ranger unit, landed with Patton in Torch, and led the Third Division through Sicily, southern Italy, and now Anzio. Superiors such as Patton, Eisenhower, and Devers lauded his abilities and admired the work he had done turning the Third Division into the best American division in the Mediterranean. Moreover, he was already on the scene at Anzio and understood the problems there. Although he later claimed that Anzio was impractical, at the time he maintained his aggressive reputation by telling Devers that Clark had overruled him and prevented him from advancing toward Rome. Clark recognized that the combative Truscott could sometimes be troublesome, but he also acknowledged his merits. Years later, Clark explained his decision: "I selected Truscott to become the new Sixth Corps commander because of all the division commanders available to me in the Anzio beachhead who were familiar with the situation, he was the most outstanding."[61] Of the other two American division leaders at Anzio, William Eagles was new to his position and therefore unready for greater responsibilities. On the other hand, Ernie Harmon's combat record was almost as impressive as Truscott's, and he had twice been considered for his own corps. Despite Harmon's impressive résumé, though, Clark opted to go with Truscott. Clark may have shared Eisenhower's reservations about Harmon's judgment and common sense. Truscott might be touchy, but Harmon was a bona fide loose cannon. Tactless, impatient, and direct, he was known to yell at his superiors up to and including Clark if he disliked their decisions. Besides, Clark believed he would lose Harmon's undeniable armored warfare talents if he took over the Sixth Corps. As a result, a deeply disappointed Harmon lost another chance at a promotion to corps command.[62]

Truscott was one of the two or three best corps commanders the army produced during World War Two, even though he was not a West Pointer and did not go to the Army War College. He had been born in Texas in 1895 and spent six years teaching in Oklahoma before enlisting in the army when the United States entered World War One. He was commissioned as a cavalry officer, and although he spent the conflict along the Mexican border and saw no combat, he still liked the army enough to stay in after Germany surrendered. He graduated from the Cavalry School in 1926 and then served as an instructor there from 1926 to 1931. He did well in the Command and General Staff School from 1934 to 1936, and later taught there. Fortunately for Truscott, his force of personality and acknowledged ability compensated for his lack of the usual credentials for high-ranking officers. He was assigned to the Thirteenth Armored Regiment in 1940, and the following year worked as a staff officer in the Ninth Corps. After the Japanese bombed Pearl Harbor, Truscott went to England to study the British commandos and develop an American equivalent. He and some of his new rangers participated in the Dieppe debacle, and then Patton recruited him for Torch. Eisenhower recognized his talents and put him in charge of the Third Division, from which he ascended to lead the Sixth Corps. Truscott was a distinctive general for a number of reasons. He possessed a gravelly voice, supposedly because he accidentally ingested acid as a child. He wanted his men to recognize him instantly, so he wore a rust-colored leather jacket, shiny lacquered helmet, light khaki pants, white scarf, and cavalry breeches and boots. Whether riding on the polo field, swearing at his soldiers, or spitting tobacco juice with old cavalry sergeants, Truscott projected toughness and drive and inspired people with his attitude and leadership, for example, by insisting that his division march faster than regulations called for. No-nonsense, practical, blunt, and self-confident, Truscott disliked excessive interference from his superiors and wanted to do things his own way. He led from the front and was frequently under fire. Like Patton, Truscott also possessed a thoughtful streak that belied his dynamism and increased his effectiveness. He paid close attention to such military minutiae as traffic patterns, vehicle use, headquarters organization, interallied cooperation, infantry replacements, and morale. His solutions were both astute and commonsensical. In the Italian mountains he used mules for transportation, and he made sure that every soldier in his unit got an hour a day for himself whenever possible. Small wonder that in his correspondence Eisenhower almost always coupled Truscott's name with some superlative adjective, and later wrote, "I have always had such tremendous confidence in him as a fighting leader."[63]

Truscott took over what had become, and would remain for the next three months, a besieged and beleaguered beachhead. It was a difficult situation for an officer with Truscott's aggressive instincts who was accustomed to taking the battle to the enemy. Moreover, Truscott was plagued by additional problems that made leading the Sixth Corps difficult for him. For one thing, he was not in the best physical condition. His leg was in a cast due to injuries sustained by a bursting German shell during a 24 January air raid, he suffered so severely from laryngitis that he could barely speak above a whisper, and he had an abscessed tooth. As for his mental state, his satisfaction in his promotion was counterbalanced by his regret in leaving his beloved Third Division. Nevertheless, Truscott was not about to let his personal woes interfere with his duty. He immediately set about bolstering the Allied lines by instilling pride and resilience in his American and British troops. On his first day as Sixth Corps commander, he visited almost every single unit at Anzio, exhorting and encouraging the men by word and deed. Knowing that soldiers become stale and dispirited under siege, he instituted a vigorous retraining program to keep their combat skills honed. He concluded that the Sixth Corps staffers possessed too much of a bunker mentality, and urged them to emulate his example by getting away from headquarters more often. He got rid of some of them and molded the rest into his own hard-driving image. He also went out of his way to mend relations with the British. Lucas had never really understood or liked the British troops under his command and rarely interacted with them. British officers in turn distrusted Lucas and badmouthed him to Alexander. Truscott, on the other hand, regularly invited British officers to his headquarters for drinks and informal discussions. Truscott's success was due in no small part to his sterling reputation as a general. Indeed, he inspired loyalty and was respected by both superiors and subordinates. Although the siege continued under appalling conditions as German artillery ranged over every acre of the beachhead, by force of personality Truscott succeeded in restoring Allied morale and confidence.[64]

Unfortunately, Truscott was unable to establish a good working relationship with the one person who mattered most: Wayne Clark. Clark had assured Truscott of his total support and confidence, but Truscott had reasons to doubt Clark's commitment. Clark had after all twice sacrificed corps commanders to preserve his own position and reputation, so it was hard to blame Truscott for wondering about his own future should the siege drag on without resolution. Indeed, Truscott had had a jaded view of Clark even before Anzio. As a tough and hard-bitten officer who cared little for other people's opinions of him or his methods, Truscott had small respect for Clark's pontifical and vainglorious manner. Although Clark promised Truscott complete control over Anzio, Truscott was dismayed that this did not include army supply officers succoring the beachhead. In response to these and other problems with Clark, Truscott was careful to put his side of the story on the record and kept the lines of communications open with Devers. Clark for his part was unhappy with Truscott. He had known Truscott for a long time and realized from the start that he was a difficult subordinate to handle. Still, Clark was disturbed with what he saw as Truscott's whiny attitude and habit of making demands he knew Clark could not immediately fulfill. As a skilled bureaucratic infighter, Clark recognized that Truscott was building a record to deflect blame should things go wrong at Anzio. Clark, however, had promised Truscott that he would take full responsibility for the beachhead, so he could not understand Truscott's concerns. Nor was Clark pleased that Truscott was bypassing Fifth Army headquarters to correspond with Devers over things such as tactical air support and personnel assignments. During an early March trip to Anzio, Clark told Truscott to cease his detrimental activities, and he was outraged when later in the month he learned that Sixth Corps staffers were still talking with Devers's people. To Clark, Truscott was behaving more like a prima donna than a professional soldier.[65]

One of Operation Shingle's bitter ironies was that it was designed to relieve pressure on Allied soldiers butting their heads against the formidable Gustav Line stretching across the Italian peninsula south of Rome. Instead, the perilous circumstances in which the Sixth Corps found itself compelled the rest of troops in the Fifth Army and the British Eighth Army to redouble their efforts to fight through the Gustav Line and rescue their comrades at Anzio. They had to do so under the worst possible conditions in the worst possible time of the year, climbing snow-covered mountains under heavy fire. The Germans had taken advantage of the local topography to make the Gustav Line extraordinarily formidable. They placed it behind steep-banked and rain-swollen rivers and on mountains that dominated the surrounding countryside. The Gustav Line bristled with concrete bunkers and pillboxes that dotted the landscape, gun positions blasted out of solid rock that were impenetrable to Allied counterbattery fire, hundreds of thousands of mines and booby traps, and miles of barbed wire. It was impossible to deploy much armor in the mountains, so the depleted and exhausted Allied infantry units bore the brunt of the combat. For the Allied infantrymen climbing up one cold and barren mountainside after another, often under fire and without adequate cover, it was a miserable way to wage war.

Shingle made life difficult for Clark too, though for different reasons. Most obviously, he was unable to devote his full attention to the Gustav Line because he spent so much time dealing with the crisis at Anzio. Interallied and personnel problems complicated Clark's difficulties. Although he and Devers were outwardly cordial to each other, their relationship was deteriorating. Devers readily admitted that Clark's staff was first rate, but he had growing doubts about Clark's generalship. In particular, he disliked Clark's chauvinism. Clark's regular denunciations of the British contribution to the Italian campaign often reached British ears. British officers complained to Wilson, who raised the issue with Devers. Devers understood the importance of interallied harmony to the Allied war effort and was not at all amused with Clark's counterproductive attitude. Like other officers exposed to Clark, Devers later called Clark his own worst enemy. As for Clark, he did not believe that Devers understood the problems caused by bad weather, horrible terrain, tough German defenses, insufficient resources, and recalcitrant allies. He grumbled that his inability to get British commanders in the Fifth Army to obey orders retarded his operations. Indeed, he wanted to purge the Fifth Army of all foreign elements except for the hard-fighting Free French. One thing both Devers and Clark agreed upon, however, was the need for additional reinforcements so the Allies could break the current unhappy stalemate and seize Rome.[66]

While Lucas and Truscott fought at Anzio, Jeff Keyes undertook the equally difficult job of spearheading the Fifth Army's offensive through the Gustav Line. Keyes was a tough soldier accustomed to getting things done, but he had little success that winter, in part because of the limited resources at his disposal. In an effort to divert German attention from the upcoming Anzio landing, Clark ordered Fred Walker's Thirty-sixth Division to cross the Rapido River. Walker's two attempts to get over the river on 20–21 January 1944 failed miserably in the face of intense German opposition and cost the Thirty-sixth Division over a thousand casualties. Walker had argued against the assault from the start because he recognized the futility of confronting the Germans in that area, so he was unsurprised by the defeat. Keyes had had his doubts too, but gritted his teeth and tried to carry out Clark's instructions. Although Clark accepted full responsibility for the debacle at the time, the failed operation ruined Walker's relationship with both Clark and Keyes, the former for ordering it in the first place and the latter for insisting on its implementation. In the ensuing months, Clark gradually eased Walker out. Clark unilaterally replaced many of the Thirty-sixth Division's staffers and then persuaded Marshall to offer Walker a stateside job as commandant of the Infantry School. Walker saw the writing on the wall and accepted the post before Clark could relieve him of his command. After the Rapido River fiasco, Clark focused on forcing his way through the Liri Valley to rescue the beleaguered Sixth Corps at Anzio. Unfortunately, the Liri Valley was dominated by 1,700-foot-high Monte Cassino, atop of which sat an old Benedictine monastery. Doc Ryder initially impressed Clark by getting his Thirty-fourth Division over the Rapido, but his subsequent efforts to seize Monte Cassino stalled within 400 yards of the monastery in mid-February. Throughout the long and frustrating winter, Clark's attitude toward Keyes waxed and waned according to the Second Corps's progress. Clark may have complained that Devers did not understand the obstacles he faced in Italy, but he accepted no such excuses from Keyes. It was a situation Keyes could scarcely have enjoyed. To complicate matters, Keyes clashed with General Bernard Freyberg over the proper deployment of his New Zealand troops. On the other hand, Keyes got along well with the French forces under his control. He knew many of them from his time at the École de Guerre in the mid-thirties, and in fact their commander, General Alphonse Juin, had been one of his instructors there. Finally, in February Marshall informed Devers that he had received negative reports about Keyes's performance. Marshall had never thought much of Keyes and was therefore predisposed to believe the worst about his generalship. To counterbalance Clark's ambivalence, Marshall's hostility, and continuing disappointment on the battlefield, Keyes could count only on Devers's support.[67]

As winter ended, Alexander decided to use overwhelming force to break the stalemate in Italy in an operation he dubbed "Diadem." He redeployed most of the British Eighth Army opposite the Liri Valley, leaving only one corps to screen the eastern side of the peninsula along the Adriatic Sea. This reduced Clark's responsibilities to Anzio and the west Italian coast. Not only did Clark now have less ground to cover, but he also received two new divisions, the Eighty-fifth and Eighty-eighth, to strengthen his army. In early April Marshall ordered Clark home for rest and consultations, during which he stressed that Clark needed to seize

Rome before Overlord began. Despite his reservations, Clark apparently vouched for all the high-ranking American officers in the Mediterranean theater, because on 22 April Marshall assured Devers that he had complete confidence in him, Clark, and their American corps and division commanders. Alexander's basic plan was to assail the Gustav Line first, and then launch an offensive from the Anzio beachhead. On 11 May some 1,600 Allied artillery pieces opened up on the Gustav Line before the infantry advanced. The Germans fought hard as usual, but Juin's French Expeditionary Corps broke through in the lightly defended Aurunci Mountains. Polish soldiers stormed Monte Cassino on 23 May, the same day Truscott's Sixth Corps attacked from Anzio. Two days later troops from Keyes's Second Corps reached Truscott's men after attacking up the Italian coast. This was of course good news, but Truscott was focused mostly on seizing Valmontone and cutting off the German retreat from the Gustav Line toward Rome. At this point, though, Clark intervened and without immediately informing Alexander ordered Truscott to send most of his forces toward Rome instead. As a result, the Germans managed to escape to fight another day. By way of compensation, on 4 June Clark entered Rome in triumph, and the next day he, Keyes, Truscott, Juin, and other high-ranking Fifth Army officers met at the Capitoline Hill to discuss their next moves and savor their victory. Alexander had shattered the logjam in Italy, but the price had been high; some 40,000 Allied soldiers had been killed and wounded, compared to 38,000 German casualties. Among the American dead was Marshall's stepson, Lieutenant Allen Brown, shot by a German sniper near Campoleone on 29 May as he stood in his tank turret.[68]

Clark's decision to target Rome instead of the retreating German forces generated considerable controversy. Had Clark succeeded in destroying much of the German army in Italy, it is possible that the Allies might have advanced rapidly up the peninsula that summer and reached the Danubian Plains, perhaps shortening the war and limiting Soviet expansion into eastern Europe. Many observers felt that Clark was more interested in cheap glory than in sound military tactics. Although Clark later defended his actions on military grounds, he admitted that he was determined to enter the Italian capital first and was overly sensitive about sharing the credit with his allies. On 31 May, for instance, he complained that he was under indirect pressure—he did not say from whom or how—to permit the British Eighth Army to participate in Rome's liberation. Alexander, though, later claimed that he had made it clear to Clark before the offensive began that the Fifth Army would have the honor of seizing Rome. Alluding to Clark's abandonment of the drive toward Valmontone, Alexander noted, "I can only assume that the immediate lure of Rome for its publicity value persuaded him to switch the direction of his advance."[69] Alexander was hardly alone in regretting Clark's judgment. Truscott argued strenuously with Clark to stick to the original plan and focus on Valmontone, and Harmon and Eagles were appalled with Clark's choices. One First Armored Division officer later summed up such feelings in a postwar interview: "I told you I was not uncritical of Clark in all respects, although I do think he was a good soldier. But that was one of the worst decisions I ever knew. At the time I thought so, and in retrospect, I still think so. And I think that that history of the events as they transpired rather backs up my feeling."[70] Whatever the contemporary or historical consensus, Clark's actions that spring did not seem to damage his standing with Marshall or retard his career. Marshall lamented Clark's mania for publicity, but appreciated his persistence, aggressiveness, dignity in the face of criticism, and organizing ability.[71]

Clark's uneasy relationship with his American corps commanders continued throughout Diadem. Keyes's standing in Clark's eyes had always been contingent upon his battlefield achievements, regardless of extenuating circumstances. Not surprisingly, Clark's initial criticisms of Keyes for his slow start at the beginning of the offensive turned to praise when Keyes aggressively pushed his troops up the Italian coast to the Anzio beachhead. Clark later pointed out that Keyes advanced 60 miles through the mountains in two short weeks, a remarkable accomplishment by Italian campaign standards. On the other hand, Clark's somewhat negative opinion of Truscott did not change much. He chastised Truscott—as well as Harmon, Ryder, and Eagles—when their attacks out of Anzio did not at first meet the kind of success Clark expected. Even after the Sixth Corps broke out of Anzio, Clark did not commend Truscott as much as he did Keyes. In fact, Clark was more convinced than ever that Truscott and his staffers were difficult and uncooperative people. Truscott's vocal opposition to Clark's decision to abandon the full-fledged drive on Valmontone no doubt contributed to this evaluation. Despite such reservations, Clark had good reason to feel triumphant as he and his corps commanders gathered at the Capitoline Hill. Rome, the Italian campaign's biggest prize and the recipient of so much Allied attention, had finally fallen to his Fifth Army, and the German army in Italy was in full retreat.[72]

A Backwater Campaign in Northern Italy

One of Mark Clark's distinguishing World War Two characteristics was his unhealthy craving for glory, attention, and recognition. In this respect he was rivaled only by Douglas MacArthur among high-ranking American army combat commanders. His ego overshadowed his undoubted organizational and administrative skills, persistency, physical courage, and charm. It also hindered the American war effort in ways big and small. It alienated subordinates who felt that Clark denied them the support and publicity they deserved, contributed to Clark's unwillingness to stand up for Dawley and Lucas, and caused him to throw away a chance to destroy the German army in Italy during Operation Diadem. None of this, however, mattered much to Clark as he stood on the Capitoline Hill in Rome and discussed the military situation with the gaggle of journalists who had accompanied him there. As a member of the small and exclusive list of generals who had conquered the Eternal City, Clark had good reason to be proud of the fruits of months of arduous labor. Unfortunately for Clark, his moment in the spotlight proved disconcertingly brief; within forty-eight hours worldwide attention dramatically shifted from Rome to the beaches of Normandy. There on the morning of 6 June, Eisenhower's Allied forces landed in Operation Overlord to begin the liberation of German-occupied western Europe. From that point on the Italian campaign became secondary and peripheral to the Allied war effort, and Clark's main task devolved into tying down enemy troops that the Germans might otherwise deploy to more important fronts. It was a thankless job that promised little time in the limelight. Not surprisingly, it took a toll on the morale of Allied soldiers in Italy, who understood that risking their lives for another mountain or river crossing was unlikely to make much of a difference in the conflict's outcome. Moreover, the British and Americans regularly raided Italy for resources to use in other, more significant, areas. It was therefore ironic—some would call it poetic justice—that Clark spent the remaining eleven months of the war laboring in relative obscurity.

Despite innumerable difficulties, the Fifth Army and British Eighth Army doggedly and dutifully soldiered on against the usual adroit German opposition. After evacuating Rome, the Germans conducted a skillful rearguard action designed to buy them sufficient time to finish constructing their new Gothic Line across the peninsula in the northern Apennine Mountains. There they hoped to replicate the previous winter's experience by forcing the Allies to wage war under circumstances that would dilute their advantages in air and artillery support. Throughout the summer, the Germans made temporary stands at various intermediary lines that compelled the Allies to stop, deploy, and launch time-consuming assaults. Not until mid-September did the Allies finally encounter the Gothic Line. The new Ninety-first Division managed to break through at Il Giogo Pass, but autumn rains stopped the Fifth Army's promising advance 10 miles shy of the Po River Valley. To the east, the British Eighth Army continued its attacks until December, but it too finally bogged down in the rain and mud. Although victory was tantalizingly close, the Germans in each case managed to maintain the integrity of their overall positions, thus obliging the Allies to spend a second long winter in the Italian mountains. Without a capital to seize or beachhead to rescue, though, this winter lacked the last one's sense of urgency. As a result, the Allies suspended major ground operations and relied on airstrikes and growing partisan activity to sap German strength. In April 1945, the Allies initiated a full-scale offensive that shattered the German lines once and for all. Allied units were well into the Po Valley when Germany surrendered early next month.

General Willis "Crit" Crittenberger was among the high-ranking commanders with Clark on Capitoline Hill that memorable June day right after Rome fell. Crittenberger led the recently deployed Fourth Corps and had been in the Mediterranean since the previous March. The Indiana-born Crittenberger had graduated from West Point in 1913, but like many of his contemporaries did not see overseas service in World War One. Instead, he spent the conflict back at West Point as an instructor. Afterward he graduated from the Cavalry School and later taught there. He attended the Command and General Staff School from 1924 to 1925 and the Army War College five years later. During the 1930s he was stationed in the Philippines and later with the Chief of Cavalry. From there he became a noted tanker and worked on the mechanization of the army. After a stint as chief of staff for the First Armored Division, he became successively a brigade, division, and finally corps commander. He took his Nineteenth Corps to England in January 1944 and was subsequently transferred to the Mediterranean. Crittenberger owed his advancement primarily to Marshall's support. During an inspection trip in the spring of 1942, Crittenberger greatly impressed Marshall by marching almost his entire Second Armored Division past the reviewing stand in less than twenty-five minutes. To Marshall this was a sure sign of an efficient unit with high morale, for which Crittenberger deserved the credit. Much like his friend Patton, Crittenberger was a showman enamored of spit and polish. Also like Patton, he won his subordinates' loyalty and superiors' support with dollops of exaggerated praise. Conscientious, hardworking, loyal, and able, if somewhat remote from the rank-in-file, Crittenberger was certainly no military genius, but during his eleven months in action in Italy he demonstrated the kind of skill and aggressiveness that won the respect of most observers, including Clark, Devers, and Truscott.[73]

Crittenberger came to Italy and the Fourth Corps in a roundabout manner. As soon as he took over as senior American officer in the Mediterranean, Devers asked Marshall for a spare corps commander. Marshall in response offered him the services of Crittenberger, Wade Haislip, Emil Reinhardt, Roscoe Woodruff, or Walton Walker, all of whom either already were corps commanders in England or were slated for deployment there. When Eisenhower learned of Marshall's proposal, he wrote frankly to him, "I hope that he [Devers] will pick Crittenberger. I understand, from what I am told here, that Devers considers Crittenberger a top-flighter, whereas my feeling is that he is the least able of the men now available to us."[74] Eisenhower did not elaborate, but his negative evaluation was probably due in part to Crittenberger's lack of combat experience. It is also likely that Eisenhower's antipathy was motivated somewhat by his knowledge of Devers's partiality toward Crittenberger. Indeed, Eisenhower's hatred of Devers was broad enough to also include some of those whom Devers respected. Fortunately for Eisenhower, Devers did in fact ask for Crittenberger's services. Soon after Crittenberger reached the Mediterranean, a slot at corps command opened up for him. Eisenhower had the previous October recommended that Marshall send an additional corps headquarters to the Mediterranean to encompass the new American divisions on their way and perhaps the French ones already in the theater as well. Marshall thereupon dispatched the Fourth Corps headquarters under Alexander Patch. Even before Patch arrived, though, Devers tapped him to lead the Seventh Army in the invasion of southern France. To replace him, Devers turned to Crittenberger. There was more to Devers's decision than mere convenience. Devers greatly respected Crittenberger and was happy to have him in his theater. After observing Crittenberger in action in Italy that summer, Devers recommended his promotion and wrote, "I consider Crittenberger one of my best commanders."[75] Devers of course had a proprietary interest in Crittenberger that may have colored his views, but Clark was under no such constraints. In fact, as a hard-bitten combat veteran and Eisenhower protégé, Clark might have been predisposed against Crittenberger. Instead, Clark praised Crittenberger for his celerity, initiative, and tactical acumen. Although Crittenberger was a headquarters operator who did not visit the front as often as Clark or Keyes, his subordinates appreciated his patience and understanding of their difficulties. Eisenhower may have been right that his corps commanders in England were better than Crittenberger—most notably, Haislip and Walker were capable men who gave good accounts of themselves in the fighting in northwest Europe—but Crittenberger had little to be ashamed of when he looked back at his wartime record. Whatever pride he felt, however, could not erase the sadness at the news of the death of his son, Corporal Townsend Crittenberger, who was killed in action in late March 1945 while helping to secure the Rhine River crossing.[76]

Crittenberger's appearance in the Mediterranean was counterbalanced by the departures that summer of some of the theater's most long-standing and important personalities. Truscott was the first to go. Soon after Rome fell, Clark pulled Truscott's Sixth Corps out of the line to prepare it for Operation Anvil-Dragoon, the invasion of southern France. Clark regretted parting with Truscott's three veteran divisions—the Third, Thirty-sixth, and Forty-fifth—but was not unhappy to lose Truscott. Although Clark sent Truscott a gracious letter of appreciation for his services and respected his combativeness at Anzio and elsewhere, he also felt that Truscott and his staffers were troublesome and difficult people. In fact, Clark preferred to give up the Sixth Corps rather than the Second or Fourth. Later that summer, the Thirty-fourth Division's Doc Ryder and the First Armored Division's Ernie Harmon also left Italy. Marshall was looking for combat-hardened division commanders with the potential to lead corps, and Devers believed that Harmon and Ryder fit the bill. Both men had been in action since North Africa and had accumulated a wealth of experience, and their units were among the most sturdy and reliable around. Harmon had performed particularly well at Anzio, where his division served as the fire brigade that Truscott used in emergencies. Clark had had his problems with them—Harmon was often disrespectful and insubordinate, and Ryder sometimes failed to take his division housekeeping duties seriously—but he agreed with the transfer and Devers's rationale. Leaving his outfit came hard to Harmon in particular, but he recognized that Italy was a backwater theater that offered few opportunities for him to employ either his talents or his beloved tanks.[77]

For Clark, the months following Rome's fall were full of frustration, contention, and bitterness. He believed that he had had the resources necessary to destroy the German army in Italy once and for all, but political decisions and circumstances beyond his control conspired to prevent him from doing so. First of all, Operation Anvil-Dragoon siphoned off not only three of the Fifth Army's veteran American divisions, but the four French ones as well. This reduction in strength of course weakened his army and narrowed his options. He expressed his objections to Marshall during the chief of staff's June visit, but also endorsed Anvil-Dragoon when he realized that Marshall and Eisenhower supported it. Like the good political operator he was, Clark recognized which way the strategic winds were blowing and acted accordingly.

Clark's unhappiness, however, extended beyond losing seven good divisions. He did not feel that the British were sufficiently committed to the campaign to wage the kind of warfare necessary to achieve the results he sought. Instead, the British seemed more interested in keeping their casualties low and protecting their empire. Clark understood neither the manpower constraints under which the bled-down and tired British army operated nor Britain's imperial obligations in the Balkans. Clark's loud and persistent denunciations of the British also undermined the Anglo-American coalition upon which the Italian campaign was built, though he did not seem to recognize the connection.

Finally, Clark faced and lamented the usual problems that fighting on the Italian peninsula entailed: rains and snows that washed out roads and bridges, inadequate room to maneuver, difficult terrain, and so on. As an ambitious man, Clark was demoralized by his inability to attain his objectives. He lacked close friends in the theater to share his burdens and was reluctant to impose his company on his subordinates. He was also saddened by the death of his mentor, Lesley McNair, in Normandy in July. Clark spent his evenings alone doing paperwork, reading, listening to the radio, writing letters to his wife, and playing with the headquarters dog. No doubt he questioned his decision to stay with the Fifth Army when he could have taken over the Seventh Army for the invasion of southern France, but at the time he preferred to concentrate his energies on seizing Rome. The Seventh Army was now near the center of the action in central Europe, whereas he was trapped in a strategically remote theater doing little more than tying down German troops. As the campaign season drew to a close, Clark concluded that despite the limitations under which he labored, he had come within an ace of breaking through the German lines once and for all. As he remembered in his memoirs:

> We had failed, and of course, failure is a bitter tea for any commander, regardless of the circumstances that made it inevitable. But that was now a secondary consideration. We were stuck in the high Apennines for the winter. Looking out from an observation post near Futa Pass I could see the snow sweeping across the dark crown of Mount Grande, and I knew that for the men of the Fifth Army it was going to be a hard winter, even if nobody fired a shot.[78]

Clark's continuing poor relationship with Devers compounded his gloom. Clark had months earlier decided that Devers did not understand the Italian campaign, but now he leveled the additional charge of neglect. On 15 August Devers's new Sixth Army Group landed in southern France for Operation Anvil-Dragoon and began moving northward. From that point on Devers invested most of his time and energy there, even though he was still Wilson's deputy and the senior American officer in the Mediterranean theater. Clark complained that Devers discriminated against Fifth Army operations in Italy in favor of those in southern France for personal and selfish reasons. Clark accused Devers of unwisely diverting troops from Italy to southern France, of trying to expropriate the Fifth Army's heavy artillery, of denying him the replacements he desperately needed, and of ignoring his recommendations for promotions. Clark was not the kind of man to keep his opinions to himself, so he angrily protested Devers's decisions to friends and colleagues. He even resorted to an out-of-channels appeal to Eisenhower for help in securing replacements. At one point he cabled Devers, "Your radio indicates a lack of appreciation of our tactical situation, the terrain, enemy resistance, and my mission. Unfortunately, you have not been able to visit this front in approximately two months."[79]

Devers for his part considered Clark's allegations unfair, inaccurate, and indicative of Clark's failings as a general. Devers did not believe that Clark was fighting effectively, for which he blamed Clark's vocal Anglophobia and military ineptitude. Indeed, Devers felt that he had bent over backward to avoid discriminating against the Fifth Army in favor of the forces in southern France. With his usual self-assurance, Devers observed that although the Fifth Army's corps commanders were aggressive men, they needed constant prodding that only he could provide. Clark's obstinacy and interference, however, prevented him from doing so. Devers noted that Clark's petulant cables "show quite well his lack of judgment and tact and indicate definitely that he is not a team player, nor has he the instincts of a fighting soldier and a gentleman. I shall take no action at this time but my judgment is that I should reprimand him. Both of his telegrams are inaccurate and stupid."[80] Considering Clark's incompetence, Devers believed that most American forces in Italy should be moved to southern France to fight there. Devers probably recognized that taking his dispute with Clark directly to Marshall was unlikely to redound in his favor, and might instead cost him his current job right when it was finally becoming something more than a mere administrative post.[81]

As things turned out, circumstances ultimately resolved the Clark-Devers feud to everyone's satisfaction. Marshall not only was well aware of the antagonism between the two men, but also realized that Devers could not serve simultaneously as deputy theater commander in the Mediterranean and as head of the Sixth Army Group in southern France. Devers recognized the incongruity too, and was more than willing to give up his administrative responsibilities in the Mediterranean to hold onto his new combat position. Marshall's initial inclination was to elevate Clark in place of Devers. Although Marshall continued to deplore Clark's self-aggrandizement and Anglophobia, he also respected his organizational abilities and aggressiveness. Besides, he would be the senior American officer in the region if Devers moved on. Devers not surprisingly recommended against this course of action. In a damning letter to General Tom Handy, Marshall's chief of operations, that undoubtedly reached Marshall's hands, Devers wrote, "[Clark] is not an inspirational leader and he does not get along well with the British. He has been a problem child to me ever since I have been in the theater. Furthermore, he is very selfish and sees all his problems through himself and how it will affect him. I have known for some time that General Wilson does not think any more of him than I do."[82] Instead, Devers recommended that Marshall appoint General Ira Eaker, who led the Army Air Force in the Mediterranean. Marshall, however, believed that Eaker was too pliant and would not stand up for American interests. As evidence, he referenced an incident in which Eaker followed the British lead in claiming that he could not spare any warplanes from the theater even though he had over 5,000 at his disposal and German air opposition was by then practically nil.

In the end, Marshall opted to send General Joseph McNarney to replace Devers. McNarney had served loyally and well as Marshall's deputy chief of staff. He had done the near impossible by quickly reorganizing and streamlining the army's labyrinthine bureaucracy at the war's start, and had a reputation as a clear-headed, cold-blooded, and hardworking officer with all the finesse of a sledgehammer. Moreover, he wanted to get out of Washington to see service overseas before the war ended. McNarney assumed his new duties in November and occupied the post until the end of the conflict. During his tenure, he won the respect of most observers with his unexpectedly cooperative attitude. Beetle Smith, for example, was shocked when McNarney offered Eisenhower's exhausted armies in northwestern Europe several thousand additional infantry replacements, and added, "This is a perfect Godsend, and I must say that ever since Joe has been on the job in the Mediterranean we have had nothing but the most thorough and complete cooperation and understanding. Any hard words I ever said about him in the past I hereby publicly and privately revoke. He may have a cynical attitude, but believe me, 'underneath that rugged exterior beats a heart of gold.'"[83] As for Clark, he was unaware of these machinations that might have changed his status and would not have wanted the administrative post anyway. In his memoirs he expressed his gratitude toward McNarney for his stalwart support, though Keyes remarked that this was because Clark pushed McNarney around. Whatever the truth of the matter, Clark was happy to be rid of Devers.[84]

Not long after McNarney arrived in the Mediterranean to replace the detested Devers, Clark got a second piece of good news. Early on Thanksgiving morning an orderly woke him up with word that the British signals officer attached to the Fifth Army had an urgent message for him. As Clark hurriedly dressed, he noted the dark, gloomy, windy, and drizzly weather outside. In his experience, such messages were usually from Churchill and usually contained bad news. When he got to headquarters, though, the smiling British officer told him that Churchill had recommended his promotion to lead the Fifteenth Army Group. General John Dill, head of the British military mission to Washington and Marshall's close friend, had recently died, and Churchill had decided to send Jumbo Wilson across the Atlantic to take his place. To fill Wilson's slot as Mediterranean theater commander, Churchill elevated Alexander. Since it was a British-dominated region, Churchill could have appointed a British general to replace Alexander, but he opted for Clark instead. Although Clark's Anglophobia was well known in British army circles, Churchill had had a soft spot for Clark ever since he and Eisenhower came to England to prepare for the invasion of North Africa. In words that many British officers would have found ironic, if not disingenuous, Churchill radioed Clark, "I am sure we could not be placing our troops, who form the large majority of your command, in better hands, and that your friendship, of which you told me, with General Alexander will be at once smooth and propel the course of operations. . . . We have the utmost confidence in you and in the goodwill which has always guided your conduct with your British comrades and Allies."[85] With the British onboard, it was easy for Marshall to go along with a plan that put an American in such an important position. Clark was of course pleased with this turn of events, which more or less placed him in charge of all Allied operations in Italy. He recognized that he needed to establish a harmonious interallied head-quarters for the Fifteenth Army Group, but true to form he was also determined to break up what he considered the British domination of the outfit by importing some of his Fifth Army staffers.[86]

Clark's elevation meant that the Fifth Army needed a new commander. On the morning of 21 November, Marshall and some of his staffers met for their daily discussion of the worldwide military situation, during which General John "Ed" Hull, chief of the operations division, brought up the issue of Clark's replace-ment. Hull reviewed the recent personnel changes in the Mediterranean and opined that Clark would probably recommend Jeff Keyes as his successor. Mar-shall had never thought much of Keyes, but happenstance had placed an alterna-tive candidate in the room that very day. After leading the Sixth Corps from the invasion of southern France to the German border, Eisenhower had in mid-October tapped Lucian Truscott to take over the new Fifteenth Army. Although Eisen-hower rated Truscott highly, he told him that he based his decision mostly on the fact that Truscott was, unlike all his other corps commanders, a lieutenant gen-eral. Whatever joy Truscott felt about his promotion evaporated when Eisen-hower informed him that the Fifteenth Army's primary responsibilities would be training and administration, not combat. Truscott immediately offered to take a demotion to major general if he could remain in action with the Sixth Corps, but Eisenhower terminated the discussion by stating evasively that Truscott's sugges-tion was not practicable.

In fact, Truscott's appointment to the Fifteenth Army was more Marshall's idea than Eisenhower's. A few months earlier, Marshall had talked with Truscott during a drive to Algiers and had been impressed with Truscott's observations about Anzio and American soldiers, weapons, and equipment. Considering his exem-plary record and obvious acumen, Marshall believed that Truscott deserved the next available field army in Europe. Before Truscott took up his new job, Eisen-hower sent him home for a well-deserved rest. Truscott had been either campaign-ing or planning for two long years, and was so exhausted that he slept for twenty-four straight hours before flying back to the States. Truscott traveled to Washington when his leave ended to wrap up some loose ends before returning to Europe, which was how he found himself invited to observe Marshall's daily meet-ing. After absorbing Hull's brief, Marshall turned abruptly to Truscott and asked him if he would like to go to Italy as head of the Fifth Army. Like the good soldier he was, Truscott replied that he would go wherever Marshall sent him. Marshall snorted, "I know that. That is not what I asked you. How do you feel about going back to Italy?" Put on the spot, Truscott stated that he preferred to stay with Eisen-hower. By way of justification, he noted that Keyes and Crittenberger had been his prewar seniors and agreed with Marshall that the important battles were being waged in northwest Europe. Marshall heard Truscott out and abruptly ended the conversation by saying to Hull, "Query General Eisenhower on this subject."

As soon as the conference ended, Truscott hustled to the airport in an effort to get to Europe to plead his case to Eisenhower before he had a chance to reply to Marshall's cable. Truscott did not want to go to Italy for all the reasons he and Marshall discussed, but especially because he did not want to serve under Wayne Clark again. Clark and Truscott did not get along particularly well. Clark considered Truscott a prima donna, and Truscott believed that Clark was more interested in furthering his own career than the war effort. Unhappily for Truscott, delays in departure and en route prevented him from reaching France until 24 November. Nevertheless, he rushed to Eisenhower's Versailles headquarters and explained the situation to Beetle Smith. Smith heard him out and responded, "Not a chance. The PM [Churchill] asked for you." This was true enough; Churchill had on Alexander's recommendation requested Truscott as Clark's replacement in the same message in which he suggested that Clark lead the Fifteenth Army Group. In his response to Marshall's message, Eisenhower expressed his high opinion of Truscott, noted that all his current field army commanders were currently preoccupied, and pointed out that Truscott got along well with the British and was familiar with the Italian campaign. Eisenhower hated to let Truscott go, but believed that doing so was the best solution to this particular problem. Although Truscott was unhappy with his new assignment, he reconciled himself to it and eventually told Marshall that he was happy to be back with the Fifth Army.[87]

Truscott's elevation was almost universally acclaimed within the army because no other officer in Europe had served as long and as well at the division and corps levels. Indeed, he and Alexander Patch were the only American World War Two generals to lead a division, a corps, and a field army in combat. Devers, for instance, noted that Truscott was exactly what the Fifth Army needed—implying that Clark was not. Even Patton, not one to distribute much praise in the privacy of his diary, admitted that Truscott deserved the post because he had done a good, though not brilliant, job. With his usual contrariness, though, Patton added that Keyes probably merited the post even more. Oddly enough, while Marshall had consulted Eisenhower on Truscott's appointment, he did not discuss the matter with Clark, who learned the news over the radio like most everyone else. Despite the serious misgivings Clark had had toward Truscott during their previous stint together, he was surprisingly blasé about his return to the theater. Moreover, Clark had very few complaints about Truscott's performance during the war's remaining six months. Not only did Clark's other responsibilities prevent him from riding herd over Truscott, but Truscott also succeeded in breaking through German lines once the Fifteenth Army Group's spring offensive got under way. As

John Lucas noted earlier, winning generals had an easier time getting along with Clark than those who failed to deliver victory.[88]

Truscott got along well with his subordinates and was impressed with their abilities. His concerns that his two corps commanders, Keyes and Crittenberger, would resent taking orders from someone who had once been their junior proved unfounded. Both men served him loyally and ably for the remainder of the conflict. Despite Eisenhower's doubts about Crittenberger, he waged an aggressive and intelligent war against the Germans. In particular, he worked hard to improve coordination between his ground units and the Army Air Force. Truscott wrote, "He has been outstanding during my entire time with the Fifth Army. He is in my opinion a better corps commander and a better battlefield leader than Geoff [Keyes]."[89] This did not mean that Truscott denigrated Keyes's abilities. Keyes not only gained both Truscott's and McNarney's respect, but Clark ultimately decided that his merits outweighed whatever shortcomings he displayed throughout the campaign. Keyes himself focused most of his disgruntlement on Clark and the British, both of whom he held responsible for the slow pace of operations. As for his divisional commanders, they too were pleased with Truscott. One noted that he was a fine leader who knew how to inspire troops, and another appreciated his patience and support. Still another summed up Truscott's attributes as an army commander by writing to him after the war:

As I have told you before, one of my treasured recollections of my service in Italy is your fine leadership and understanding as a commander. Your cooperation and insight made my tasks easier. Besides battlefield courage, you always have shown rare judgment and my brief personal acquaintance has heightened my admiration. I shall never ask more than to serve under your command again. I recognized in you the many qualities that I always sought for myself but rarely attained. My service in Italy and in preparation therefore was my duty as a soldier and if it contributed to your success in war I am satisfied.[90]

Although most of the Italian campaign had been characterized by contention and stress among its high-ranking American officers, it ended on a comparatively quiet note in this respect.[91]

A Long and Bitter Campaign

In February 1945, Marshall visited Italy on his way back to the States after the Yalta Conference in the Crimea in the Soviet Union. Marshall always insisted that his commanders refrain from ceremonial displays of pomp and pageantry during his inspections because they wasted time and interfered with the objective discussion of the military situation. Therefore, he was unhappy to see that Clark had an honor guard drawn up to greet him. When he expressed his displeasure, Clark assured him that reviewing the honor guard would only take a few minutes and would be well worth the effort. The honor guard consisted of troops drawn from fifteen different nationalities serving in the Fifteenth Army Group, including Americans, Englishmen, Indians, and so on. Clark's point, which Marshall immediately grasped, was "to show him how by team play, understanding and cooperation we of the 15th Army Group overcame the difficulties of having so many Allies."[92] This was true enough, but the incident also said more about Clark than he meant to convey. Most obviously, it demonstrated Clark's ability to pull and manipulate the levers of power in the American army to suit his own purposes and show himself in the best light. Before he became Fifth Army commander, Clark had led neither a corps nor a division, but served exclusively as a staff officer. He owed his rise to field army command primarily to McNair's, Marshall's, and finally Eisenhower's tutelage. As Clark himself later put it, "I got it because I happened to be at the right spot, at the right time, and was serving with the people who were making the decisions."[93] To be sure, Clark possessed many admirable qualities that justified his elevation, including organizational and administrative talent, the ability to select and cultivate a fine staff, and cool aggressiveness in battle. Unfortunately, Clark also had some negative traits that hindered the prosecution of the Italian campaign and cast doubt on Eisenhower's decision to assign him to the Fifth Army. These included vanity, self-centeredness, and chauvinism. There is no doubt that Clark faced some formidable obstacles in waging war in Italy—difficult terrain, abominable weather, troublesome allies, insufficient resources, canny opponents—but his less commendable characteristics only compounded these problems. For example, Clark failed to express his doubts about Anzio to Alexander because he feared that doing so would damage his standing and jeopardize his career. For the same reason he also sacrificed Dawley and Lucas rather than share the responsibility for their failures. He was unsympathetic toward the problems and concerns of superiors and allies who did not share his views, and his overweening desire to conquer Rome blinded him to the opportunity to destroy the German army in Italy. Whatever Clark's shortcomings, though, his high-ranking presence in Italy from Salerno to Germany's surrender made him the campaign's dominant American.

Few high-ranking American army officers augmented their military reputations during their time in Italy. Omar Bradley and Lucian Truscott were exceptions to this rule. Bradley won accolades for his performance in Sicily that helped secure him a prominent role in the invasion of German-occupied France, and Truscott's record at Anzio and elsewhere persuaded Marshall to eventually appoint him chief of the Fifth Army. On the other hand, Italy was hardly a high point in the careers of Eisenhower, Devers, and Patton, though they escaped the theater and went on to do good work in subsequent campaigns. Dawley and Lucas lost their corps, and Keyes and Crittenberger sank into obscurity. No doubt the difficulties of waging war in Italy contributed to the troubles the Fifth Army's corps commanders faced, but so did Clark's leadership style. Clark's personality not only handicapped his own efforts to wage war in Italy, but also made the campaign difficult for his lieutenants. Although Clark provided his corps commanders with as much materiel support as he could, he was considerably charier with his moral support. Throughout the campaign he showed little sympathy with their often legitimate problems, so his opinions of his corps commanders generally fluctuated according to their military fortunes. There is something to be said for a general who judges his subordinates strictly on the harsh criteria of success, but Clark often made demands on his corps commanders without understanding their limitations and obstacles. Jeff Keyes, for instance, was a steady and combative officer from the start of the Italian campaign to its finish. Clark's opinion of him, however, waxed and waned. Moreover, most of Clark's corps commanders entered the campaign with comparatively little combat experience and owed their appointments to their success in other areas. Truscott and Keyes had fought in Sicily, but Dawley, Lucas, and Crittenberger all went into action for the first time under Clark. Clark's inability to nurture and empathize with his green lieutenants made their tough assignment even more trying, and his ambitiousness and refusal to share credit with them fed the distrust most of them developed toward him. It would be an exaggeration to say that contention within the Fifth Army's officer corps prevented the Allies from winning the Italian campaign as quickly as they might have, but it is certainly true that it made the fighting in Italy more onerous than necessary.

4
The Dual Drive Offensive

Racing across New Guinea

For MacArthur, the Pacific War was as much about redeeming his promise to free the Philippines as about defeating Japan. The loss of the Philippines, with his humiliating departure from Corregidor, haunted him, and he pursued the archipelago's liberation with a resolution bordering on fanaticism. He once said he would fulfill his pledge even if he was "down to one canoe paddled by Douglas MacArthur and supported by one Taylor cub [plane]."[1] He saw the conflict through that lens and geared his strategic ideas to that end. Unfortunately for MacArthur, he did not determine American grand strategy; that was the Joint Chiefs of Staff's prerogative. The problem was that the navy also viewed the Pacific War as a redemptive crusade, only in its case Pearl Harbor, not Bataan, was the wrong to be righted. Naval officers had spent a generation studying war with Japan, and they firmly believed that the Central Pacific route from Hawaii, not MacArthur's Southwest Pacific route from Australia, was the most cost-effective way to reach the Japanese Home Islands. This strategic debate continued throughout Operation Cartwheel, with MacArthur and the navy using every persuasive weapon at their disposal to make their points to the Joint Chiefs. In March 1944, the JCS compromised by authorizing the Dual Drive Offensive, which called for simultaneous advances by Southwest Pacific Area and the Pacific Ocean Area forces toward the vaguely defined China-Formosa-Luzon region. While the JCS stated that the navy's Central Pacific route would have top priority, it bought MacArthur's cooperation by stating that he could assault the southernmost Philippines island of Mindanao preparatory to a possible attack on Luzon. The Dual Drive Offensive violated American military doctrine that emphasized concentration of force, but the JCS was willing to pay that price to preserve interservice harmony. As MacArthur interpreted the directive, he could still convince the JCS to let him assail the Philippines provided that he reached the China-Formosa-Luzon region ahead of the navy. To do that, he had to get across New Guinea's northern coast as rapidly as possible. New Guinea, therefore, was more than just a road to the Philippines; it was a racetrack as well, with the navy running hard on a parallel lane to the north. To complicate matters for MacArthur, at the same time he was moving across New Guinea, he also had to organize and assign commanders to a steady stream of reinforcements that the JCS allotted to SWPA.

Despite MacArthur's best efforts, SWPA had advanced less than 300 miles up the New Guinea coast in 1943, and at the end of the year was still 1,600 miles from the Philippines. If MacArthur planned to reach the China-Formosa-Luzon region ahead of the navy, he obviously had to pick up the pace. Therefore, he was attentive to a staffer's suggestion that SWPA exploit its superior mobility to bypass the strong Japanese defenses in the Hansa Bay–Wewak area and instead strike 500 miles to the west at Hollandia. Hollandia possessed two harbors and three airfields that SWPA could use to support further offensives toward the Philippines, and it was scantly defended. The JCS not only went along with MacArthur's proposal, but also ordered the navy to provide carrier support. To assail Hollandia, MacArthur planned to use 84,000 troops centered around General Frederick Irving's Twenty-fourth Division and General Horace Fuller's Forty-first Division. Such a large force, along with the logistical support required to move and supply it, was evidence of SWPA's growing strength. Indeed, MacArthur concluded that the operation—dubbed "Reckless"—called for the services of both Krueger's Sixth Army/Alamo Force and Eichelberger's First Corps.

While MacArthur and Krueger waged war against the Japanese in New Guinea as part of Operation Cartwheel, Bob Eichelberger remained in Rockhampton training troops. Eichelberger tried his best to remain positive and upbeat, but watching the conflict move northward without him had made 1943 the most miserable year of his life. During their occasional meetings MacArthur assured Eichelberger that the First Corps would see action again. But as the months dragged on and he remained in exile at Rockhampton, Eichelberger developed an increasingly jaded view of MacArthur's promises. MacArthur's refusal to let him go command a field army elsewhere was both comforting in that it seemed proof of MacArthur's confidence in him and maddening because it underscored his professional helplessness. As the year drew to a close, evidence mounted that Eichelberger's status really was going to change for the better. In mid-November, Krueger told him that the First Corps headquarters would be heading for New Guinea sometime after Christmas. There was a delay while GHQ reformulated its plans to attack Hollandia instead of Hansa Bay–Wewak, but on 6 February 1944 an excited Clovis Byers, Eichelberger's devoted chief of staff and boon companion, phoned from Brisbane with news that First Corps would soon get a combat mission. Four days later, Krueger flew to Rockhampton to explain to Eichelberger his role in Reckless. Now that he had a fighting assignment, Eichelberger's discouragement and unhappiness evaporated and he became his usual cheerful self.

He was pleased with his staff and delighted to work with Irving and Fuller. He lost weight playing badminton, swimming, doing calisthenics, and eating right. He even began thinking that perhaps it was for the best that MacArthur had kept him in SWPA, although he was far from reconciled with the way GHQ had treated him. As he explained to his wife, "This does not mean I have changed my mind for a minute about many things . . . but from a *military* standpoint I guess I am more happy than I have been at any time since I declared the battle of Sanananda officially at an end."[2]

Operation Reckless forced Eichelberger and Krueger to work closely together for the first time. During Krueger's occasional visits to Rockhampton in 1943, the two men got along reasonably well. Krueger enjoyed himself as much as everyone else at Eichelberger's convivial headquarters and unwound with jokes, stories, and gossip. Indeed, Krueger could use whatever relaxation he could get because he bore a heavy burden planning and leading Alamo Force in New Guinea. Although Krueger believed that a soldier's first job was to obey, he resented the pressure that MacArthur exerted on him for more rapid advances. For example, Krueger so strenuously protested MacArthur's decision in February 1944 to invade the Admiralty Islands ahead of schedule with a hastily organized reconnaissance-in-force that MacArthur had to take him aside for a private chat. Small wonder that Krueger confessed to Eichelberger and Byers that he felt unappreciated and lonely. Eichelberger for his part was initially amused by Krueger, but as their time together increased during the planning for the Hollandia assault, Krueger began to grate on his nerves. Eichelberger grew irritated with Krueger's presumptuous, tedious, and long-winded anecdotes about such things as the Louisiana maneuvers. As Eichelberger sarcastically explained to his wife, "Walter is a very interesting talker and knows much of the world. . . . I always find when I am thrown with him very closely that it really amounts to hard work."[3] Unhappily, Eichelberger's bemused annoyance with Krueger would metastasize into hatred and contempt under the stress of upcoming operations.[4]

Eichelberger's relationships with Sutherland and MacArthur, on the other hand, were more distant. He remained jaded and disillusioned with GHQ after his experiences at Buna, but he was now too busy planning the Hollandia operation to nurse those grudges that had tormented him the previous year. Although he still distrusted Sutherland and speculated that he was badmouthing him to MacArthur, he tried not to worry because there was little he could do about it. In fact, there is no evidence that Sutherland was undermining Eichelberger; Eichelberger had simply misinterpreted Sutherland's browbeating at Buna and elsewhere as an effort to destroy his career. As for MacArthur, Eichelberger claimed that he was neither impressed nor fooled by him, but in reality he remained susceptible to MacArthur's manipulation. For example, MacArthur told a very intrigued Eichelberger that he expected SWPA to receive enough reinforcements to warrant the creation of additional field armies and corps, and broadly hinted that Eichelberger was in line for a field army command if he performed well at Hollandia.[5]

At dawn on 22 April, Irving's and Fuller's soldiers splashed ashore at Tanahmerah and Humboldt bays at Hollandia. To Eichelberger's great relief, they met almost no resistance, so the GIs secured their beachheads and pushed inland with little difficulty. Amidst the organized chaos and confusion, MacArthur, Krueger, and Eichelberger visited the beaches to have a look around. MacArthur was elated with the evidence that his gamble had paid off. He congratulated Eichelberger on a job well done and told him he would give him a field army if he finished his mission as successfully as he had begun it. MacArthur's praise and pledges were not limited to Eichelberger. Of Irving he exclaimed, "Irving's plan wouldn't be called good—it was brilliant."[6] As for the more battle-tested Fuller, MacArthur promised to appoint him First Corps commander when Eichelberger moved up. Krueger was less demonstrative, but he too commended Eichelberger for his work. MacArthur subsequently invited Krueger and Eichelberger aboard the light cruiser USS *Nashville* for ice-cream sodas, and reinforced his approval by giving Eichelberger his untouched glass after Eichelberger wolfed down his own soda.

In fact, MacArthur was so sure of victory that he proposed sending the Reckless reserves up the coast to seize the airstrip on Wakde Island. Doing so would accelerate SWPA's timetable and push American forces closer to the Philippines. Krueger was noncommittal, but Eichelberger protested strongly. The reserve troops were not combat-loaded, he stated, so the landing would succeed only if there was no Japanese opposition, and no one could guarantee that. MacArthur backed down and permitted the operation to go on as planned, but he did not let this discordant note ruin his good mood as he headed back to Brisbane via Port Moresby on *Nashville*. Meanwhile, despite horrendous jungle terrain, Irving's and Fuller's men made good progress against the unorganized and scattered Japanese, and on 26 April they seized all three of Hollandia's airfields. When all was said and done, the Americans suffered only 152 killed and 1,057 wounded. By way of return on his investment, MacArthur leaped halfway up the New Guinea coast, gained airfields necessary for further operations westward, and isolated some 55,000 Japanese in the Hansa Bay–Wewak region.[7]

For Eichelberger, seizing Hollandia was merely the first, and in some ways the less complicated, part of his assignment. His next challenge was turning Hollandia into a major base containing five airdromes and capable of quartering 200,000 men. And as usual MacArthur wanted the job done quickly to keep to his ambitious timetable of reaching the China-Formosa-Luzon region ahead of the navy.

Eichelberger and his staffers called this the "Big Engineering Phase." There was nothing easy about it. Scattered Japanese opposition, pilfering soldiers, the appallingly poor road network from the airfields to Humboldt Bay, soggy terrain, and congested beaches all slowed progress. In fact, SWPA eventually scaled back its plans, but Eichelberger still oversaw the construction of three airdromes, 3 million square feet of covered storage, and facilities for 140,000 men. As far as Eichelberger was concerned, his biggest problem, or anyhow his most aggravating one, was not logistical but personal: Walter Krueger. Eichelberger and Krueger were both capable men, but whereas Eichelberger used charm and persuasion to get things done, Krueger had a less subtle leadership style that did not endear him to Eichelberger. As early as the day of the Hollandia landings, Eichelberger complained to MacArthur that Krueger was breathing down his neck. In the following weeks, Krueger mixed occasional praise with tart complaints that Eichelberger was falling behind schedule, and on 28 May he chewed out Eichelberger for his performance. Krueger later fumed to a staffer, "In my more than forty years as an officer I have never raised my voice to an enlisted man, but a Corps commander should know better."[8] Eichelberger deeply resented such criticisms, which he considered unfair and disrespectful, and increasingly dreaded wasting time listening to the grumpy Krueger's tedious stories.[9]

Although Eichelberger felt that Krueger was unjustly singling him out for persecution, there is nothing to support this. Krueger used this same direct method of motivation on all his subordinates. For example, two weeks after Krueger yelled at Eichelberger, Clovis Byers traveled to Alamo Force's advanced headquarters at Hollekang on Humboldt Bay on business. There he found Krueger berating one of his division commanders, General Franklin Sibert, in words almost identical to those he used with Eichelberger. Byers could not suppress a smile, to which Krueger retorted, "Sounds serious, doesn't it? Well, it is!" It was clear to Byers, however, that it was an act. Indeed, there is no evidence that Krueger hated Eichelberger or did anything to sabotage his career. Eichelberger mistakenly personalized Krueger's overbearing leadership style. If Krueger was laying it on a bit thick these days, it was in response to the strain he was under. For one thing, he was uncertain of his professional future. He would turn sixty-four in January—coincidentally, he and MacArthur shared the same birthday—and he worried that he might be forcibly retired and sent home. More seriously, at least for the present, MacArthur was exerting greater pressure than usual on him to accelerate operations along the New Guinea coast—that needle from behind.[10]

In this case, the bone of contention was Biak Island, off of New Guinea's north coast, where Fuller's Forty-first Division had landed on 27 May. MacArthur wanted Biak's three airstrips to dominate the skies over western New Guinea. Unfortunately, GHQ underestimated Japanese strength there, so Fuller's men found themselves engaged in a bigger fight than anticipated. Worse yet, the island's narrow coral ridges were tailor-made for defense. Although MacArthur publicly declared the operation practically over on 28 May, the fighting dragged on as Fuller's soldiers struggled through the jungle and up and down ridges to seize the airfields. MacArthur applied increasing pressure on Krueger to win the battle, and Krueger in turn leaned on Fuller. Finally, on 14 June, MacArthur bluntly radioed Krueger, "The situation on Biak is unsatisfactory. The strategic purpose of the operation is being jeopardized by the failure to establish without delay an operating airfield for aircraft."[11] In response to this not-so-subtle hint for faster results, Krueger decided not only to send reinforcements to Biak from the Twenty-fourth Division, but to also dispatch Eichelberger there to assume overall command of what would now become a corps operation.[12]

Although he hoped it would not come to it, Krueger had warned Eichelberger that he might have to send him to Biak, so Eichelberger was hardly surprised when on 14 June he received the summons. As Eichelberger hastily prepared to leave, he recalled a similar scene a year and a half earlier when MacArthur suddenly called on him to go to Buna to retrieve that battle. This time, though, Krueger showed more sympathy for Eichelberger's well-being than MacArthur had. Before boarding the plane that flew him to Biak, Krueger said, "Now, don't go and get yourself killed."[13] Upon reaching the island, Eichelberger discovered an extremely unhappy and angry Fuller. Fuller was furious with Krueger's constant badgering and did not want to be supplanted with a corps headquarters. As far as he was concerned, Krueger was asking him to do too much with too little. In fact, he was so fed up that he had already submitted his resignation before Eichelberger arrived and insisted that he would continue to do so every half hour until it was accepted. Eichelberger had the authority to relieve Fuller, but he did not want to. Instead, he joined the chorus of staffers who over the next two days urged him to stay. Fuller, however, refused to change his mind. He was clearly distraught and, as things turned out, ill with appendicitis, and left on a destroyer on 18 June.

Fuller's departure enabled Eichelberger to devote his full attention to the matter at hand. While Eichelberger felt sorry for Fuller, the more he looked over the military state of affairs, the more convinced he became that Fuller had failed to deploy and use his soldiers wisely. Eichelberger believed that Fuller had wasted his division on nibbling attacks that had not accomplished much. After a day of rest, on 19 June Eichelberger ordered a sweeping all-out offensive against the Japanese. Under Eichelberger's firm grip, which included enough yelling at people to make Krueger proud, the Americans quickly secured the airfields and ground down Japanese resistance. By 29 June the situation was sufficiently settled for Eichelberger to return to Hollandia. He was proud of his accomplishment and, recalling the events that had transpired after Buna, grateful that he had not garnered any publicity in the process. When he reached Hollandia, he and Krueger took a boat for the forty-five-minute ride to First Corps headquarters. Krueger spoke hardly a word to Eichelberger during the trip and upon their arrival merely stated, "Congratulations on the fine work you did." When Eichelberger offered to discuss the operation further, Krueger said, "I shall be too busy to talk to you," and drove away in a jeep.[14]

Krueger was certainly distracted by his many responsibilities. Not only was he overseeing several simultaneous ongoing operations in New Guinea and preparing for future campaigns, but he was also responsible for providing accommodations for a new field army headquarters, the Eighth, en route to SWPA. With reinforcements arriving in the theater, MacArthur believed he needed an additional field army with which to wage war. He no doubt had discussed the issue with Marshall at their Goodenough Island meeting the previous December and most likely agreed with him that Eichelberger should lead the new army. Krueger opposed the idea, probably because two armies would complicate planning and dilute his authority. However, if MacArthur insisted on another field army, then Krueger felt that Eichelberger was the right man for it. Indeed, Eichelberger was the logical choice. MacArthur preferred to work with people with whom he was familiar, and Eichelberger had served with him as SWPA's only corps commander since August 1942. Eichelberger also possessed a winning record, having defeated the Japanese at Buna, Hollandia, and now Biak. During that time, Eichelberger had learned the hard way to avoid publicity, so there was little chance of him horning in on MacArthur's limelight. Finally, MacArthur was beginning to realize that he could play Krueger and Eichelberger off against each other for his own benefit. He could through manipulation use one to goad the other into greater military efforts that would serve SWPA's cause well. MacArthur had hinted at his intentions to Eichelberger on several occasions starting back the previous January, but seemed in no hurry to make the appointment official.[15]

For Eichelberger, waiting for official word of his appointment to field army command was another long purgatory. He knew as early as May that the Eighth Army headquarters was on its way to SWPA from the States and that all indications were that MacArthur planned to place him in charge of it. Unfortunately, although plenty of GHQ and Sixth Army staffers told Eichelberger that the Eighth Army would be his, neither MacArthur nor Krueger confirmed it. Eichelberger speculated endlessly on the reasons for the delay and analyzed Krueger's motives in particular from every conceivable angle. He was convinced that Krueger's continued discourteousness was somehow related to his possible promotion. Then, suddenly, during a 6 July meeting, Krueger was all sweetness and light—"Butter wouldn't melt in his mouth," Eichelberger wrote. In the following weeks, Krueger became increasingly open with Eichelberger about his imminent new responsibilities. On 21 August, Eichelberger was removed from the First Corps. Saying his goodbyes was difficult for him because he had spent more than two years with the outfit. Two weeks later, on 11 September, he finally took over the Eighth Army in a ceremony before its staffers. Irving had his divisional band play a concert beforehand, after which Eichelberger gave a speech. Now that he was a field army commander, Eichelberger noted that he had all sorts of privileges he had not known while with the First Corps. On the other hand, he had to fight a sharp skirmish with Sutherland to get Byers as his chief of staff. But for Eichelberger perhaps the most pleasing perk was MacArthur's promise that he and his new army would play an important role in the upcoming liberation of the Philippines.[16]

Eichelberger may have disliked Krueger, but he disliked *and* distrusted Sutherland. Although Sutherland was very pleasant during his occasional visits to First Corps, Eichelberger remained suspicious of his motives and eventually developed the theory that Sutherland was trying to get the Eighth Army for himself. There is no evidence that this was in fact the case. Indeed, Sutherland respected and supported Eichelberger. As usual, Eichelberger misinterpreted abrasiveness as persecution. If Sutherland was in a good mood, he had his reasons that went beyond SWPA's recent military successes. He was then at the peak of his power and influence. Sutherland had served ably and well as SWPA chief of staff, running GHQ headquarters with such efficiency that MacArthur rarely interfered with him. In February 1944, MacArthur wrote to Marshall to recommend Sutherland's elevation to lieutenant general. MacArthur argued that Sutherland deserved the promotion not only because of his obvious executive ability, but also because he acted more like a deputy commander than a mere chief of staff. Considering such praise, it was hardly surprising that Sutherland began to envision a greater role for himself. According to his secretary, one day at GHQ's advanced headquarters at Hollandia, Sutherland gazed out over Lake Sentani from a veranda and said, "I am in command now. I am running this show. The General is an old man. He can't operate any more."[17]

Unfortunately for Sutherland, he failed to realize that his power depended almost entirely upon MacArthur's good graces. MacArthur was aware of the animosity Sutherland generated, but was willing to tolerate it because his efficiency more than compensated for his shortcomings, especially during the war's early dark days. As SWPA's resources and successes increased, though, MacArthur's need for Sutherland declined. Observers noticed that MacArthur started complaining about Sutherland behind his back. It was, however, a woman that served as the catalyst that disrupted their relationship. Soon after MacArthur and his entourage reached Australia in 1942, Sutherland initiated an affair with an Australian named Elaine Clarke. He got her a job as a receptionist at GHQ and eventually secured her a commission in the Women's Army Corps. There was nothing unusual about high-ranking SWPA officers taking up with mistresses, but Clarke was particularly irksome. Not only was she bossy and intrusive, but her infidelity while her husband, a British officer, languished in a Japanese prison camp disturbed many people. Although MacArthur normally turned a blind eye to such shenanigans, it was hard to overlook Clarke. One morning in late April 1944 at GHQ headquarters in Port Moresby, for example, MacArthur walked into Sutherland's office in his underwear to pitch an idea, and was startled and embarrassed to find her there. After dressing, he ordered her sent back to Australia. Later, in Brisbane, he clarified his directive, stating, "Dick, that woman must not go to the forward areas again. I want that understood. Under no circumstances is that woman to be taken to the forward areas."[18] Nevertheless, for whatever reason Sutherland brought her to Hollandia when GHQ moved its operations there, and MacArthur was annoyed to discover her serving as a hostess. Upon his return from observing the invasion of Morotai Island in September, MacArthur rebuked Sutherland again and insisted on shipping Clarke back to Australia. He also criticized Sutherland's decision to respond to the Joint Chiefs in favor of an assault on Leyte while MacArthur was traveling under radio silence to observe the Morotai operation. MacArthur had certainly not opposed invading Leyte, but he did not want people thinking that Sutherland was the power behind the SWPA throne making the important decisions. Sutherland protested that if MacArthur distrusted his judgment, then perhaps he ought to resign as chief of staff. MacArthur refused and stated that Sutherland would remain in SWPA and do his duty. Their relationship, formal enough to begin with, never recovered. In fact, it only got worse.[19]

Eichelberger's elevation to the Eighth Army meant that the First Corps needed a new leader. Marshall left the decision up to MacArthur, who decided to promote from within SWPA. Doing so, however, was more complicated than expected. MacArthur had promised the outfit to Fuller for his good work at Hollandia and elsewhere, but Japanese opposition and Krueger's badgering at Biak removed him from contention. Although MacArthur consulted Sutherland, Krueger's opinion carried the most weight. As Krueger saw things, corps commanders should be major generals who had aggressively led troops to victory in an independent capacity. By these criteria, there were only two candidates for the job: General Franklin Sibert and General Innis Palmer Swift. Of the two, Krueger preferred his old friend Palmer Swift. Under Swift's tutelage the First Cavalry Division had become the best division in SWPA, although the fact that the unit had not been cannibalized for cadres back in the States certainly helped. Unlike some of his contemporaries, Swift had recognized that the day of the horse in combat was over and had embraced mechanization. Swift and the First Cavalry Division proved themselves to MacArthur's and Krueger's satisfaction in their assault on the Admiralty Islands in February 1944. Despite their inexperience, Swift and his men fought well and cleared the islands of Japanese resistance in two months of sharp fighting. MacArthur originally intended to give Swift the new Tenth Corps, but Fuller's resignation changed that, so Swift got the First Corps instead. Normally Marshall would have protested the sixty-three-year-old Swift taking a corps into combat, but in this case he raised no objections, probably because he wanted MacArthur to have men of his own choosing and because McNair had evaluated Swift as a forceful officer who was "reasonably heady."[20]

Palmer Swift was in fact the oldest American World War Two corps commander deployed overseas who saw action. Born into an army family at Fort Laramie, Wyoming, in 1882, Swift graduated from West Point in 1904 near the very bottom of his class. Afterward he served in Pershing's Punitive Expedition to Mexico and went overseas to France at the tail end of World War One, though he did not see any combat. In the interwar years he attended the Command and General Staff School from 1922 to 1923, the Army War College from 1929 to 1930, and the Army Industrial College in 1931. Although he ranked near the bottom of his Command and General Staff School class too, he ended up teaching there for six years in the late 1920s. His first love was the cavalry, and from 1936 he systematically worked his way up through the First Cavalry Division's ranks as a regimental, brigade, and, finally, division commander by the time the United States entered the war.

Notwithstanding his poor academic record and lack of combat experience, Swift had a reputation as a good officer and a soldier's soldier. One staffer who first saw Swift when he assumed command of the First Corps on 22 August 1944 remembered, "A heavy-set, commanding figure, above average height, past sixty, hard and vigorous, strode the length of the dock followed by an aide. A heavy face, the unsmiling lips a mere line above a square jaw; eyes small, blue, and direct. A tough hombre, I said to myself, and knew that I was not alone in this estimate."[21] Swift combined this toughness with a certain flair for the dramatic. In the prewar days he had been famous in the cavalry for riding around his troopers at full gallop during reviews. In most respects, Swift was nothing like Eichelberger. If Swift was less sophisticated, genial, and sensitive than the man he was replacing, he was also more direct, respectful of authority, and empathetic toward the rank and file. Swift was in many ways cut from the same cloth as his friend Krueger, toward whom he was grateful for procuring his services overseas in spite of his age. As Swift explained it after he reached the Pacific, "If Krueger told me to cut my left arm up to the elbow, I cut it off. He got me out here. I am sixty-two years of age and General Krueger got the 1st Cavalry Division and got me out here."[22] Despite his affinity toward and debt to Krueger, Swift nevertheless found himself drawn into Eichelberger's convivial orbit, and frequently dropped in on Eichelberger's headquarters for dinner. Eichelberger liked Swift in part because he was a fighter, but also because, unlike Krueger, he told lively stories. Indeed, Swift possessed enough of a sense of humor under his rough exterior that his successor as head of the First Cavalry Division, General Verne Mudge, told him upon hearing of his promotion to First Corps, "They are sure scraping the bottom of the barrel, General."[23]

Swift's appointment did not solve MacArthur's personnel problems. The previous April Marshall had informed him that he would deploy the Tenth Corps headquarters to SWPA in July. He offered MacArthur a choice of four stateside generals as its commander—John Millikin, Frank Milburn, Louis Craig, or John B. Anderson, of whom Marshall recommended Craig because he seemed the most aggressive—but added that MacArthur could select his own man if he wanted. As usual, MacArthur opted to promote from within the SWPA family. He originally slated Swift for the post, but Eichelberger's elevation and Fuller's discomfiture changed that. To take the Tenth Corps, MacArthur and Krueger turned to General Franklin Sibert, current commander of the Sixth Division and runner-up for the First Corps. Sibert met all of Krueger's qualifications. He had successfully led his untried division in June and July in a tough fight against a series of well-defended Japanese positions in and around Lone Tree Hill at Sarmi, 125 miles up the New Guinea coast from Hollandia. Krueger liked what he saw, and on 2 July radioed MacArthur, "During a visit the Wakde–Maffin Bay area a few days ago, I was impressed with Sibert's skillful handling of his troops. He is cool and very aggressive and his troops reflect that spirit. . . . He is aggressive and has the punch to be expected of a corps commander who may at any time be required to command a large, independent task force in action."[24] In talking to Sibert, though, Krueger was more succinct, stating, "Well, I know you've got a fighting unit now."[25] Later that month, on 30 July, Sibert confirmed Krueger's convictions by conducting a successful, if unopposed, landing at Sansapor-Mar on New Guinea's Vogelkop Peninsula. With all this evidence and Krueger's recommendation in hand, MacArthur made the assignment official in August.[26]

Like Swift and Patch, Sibert was from an army family. His father was a general and his brother later became one too. Sibert had been born in Bowling Green, Kentucky, in 1891 and graduated from West Point in 1912. During World War One, Sibert served as an aide to his father, who commanded the famous First Division, and later led a machine-gun battalion. After the conflict he attended the Infantry School in 1924, the Command and General Staff School from 1924 to 1925, and the Army War College four years later. He thereafter held a variety of teaching and staff assignments, including stints back at the Command and General Staff School as an instructor and with the General Staff. Although he was slated for divisional command before Pearl Harbor, Marshall instead sent him to the China-Burma-India theater as a member of General Joseph Stilwell's staff. There he participated in Stilwell's famous retreat from Burma to India, but he annoyed Vinegar Joe because he had trouble keeping up with the column. Once in India, Sibert's relationship with Stilwell deteriorated further. Stilwell ordered Sibert to train Chinese troops in India, but Sibert did not feel that Stilwell had confidence in him. Besides, Sibert's health was poor, and he really wanted to take American soldiers into action, not train Chinese ones, so in September 1942 he asked Stilwell for a transfer home. Stilwell granted it, but not before sending Marshall a negative evaluation that stated that Sibert lacked "alert intelligence necessary for the work here." Despite this indictment from a trusted friend, Marshall gave Sibert the Sixth Division, which he trained and then took to New Guinea in January 1944.[27]

Sibert was probably the weakest of the Pacific War corps commanders. Although he made a good first impression with his friendliness and enthusiasm, the longer people were around him the less they thought of his abilities and judgment. There was, in short, less to him than initially met the eye. He was a phlegmatic, steady, and dogged officer unlikely to engage in much original thinking. Sibert hated to back down from a fight, but he also possessed a stubborn streak and sometimes seemed more interested in fulfilling his own agenda than in following plans determined by his superiors. While at the Infantry School, for example, he became so obsessed with bridge that he carried a lap board on the train that daily transported officers to and from Fort Benning. If he was unable to easily round up volunteers for a game, he walked up and down the aisle recruiting people. Finally, poor health plagued him throughout the war and may have impaired his efficiency. For now, however, most observers thought he was a good choice to lead the Tenth Corps.[28]

While Sibert was proving himself to Krueger's satisfaction at Lone Tree Hill, another potential corps commander was eliminating himself from contention on the other side of Hollandia. The isolated Japanese at Hansa Bay–Wewak decided to assume the offensive against SWPA instead of meekly accepting their fate. Their target was the American base at Aitape, halfway between Hollandia and Wewak. Starting in May, some 20,000 Japanese soldiers began hacking their way through the jungle toward Aitape. Krueger had worried about just such an attack, so he had sent General William Gill's Thirty-second Division to Aitape to defend it. Gill was an efficient and overbearing officer who had led the Thirty-second since February 1943. After he reached Aitape and sized up the situation, he dug in his division and called for reinforcements. Although Krueger sent help, neither he nor MacArthur was happy with Gill's actions because every soldier dispatched to Aitape diverted resources from SWPA's westward race to the China-Formosa-Luzon region. Krueger wanted Gill to assail the Japanese in the jungle and eradicate the threat as soon as possible, not wait around for the Japanese to seize the initiative. Krueger expressed his concerns about Gill's passivity as early as 19 June. When Gill remained ensconced behind his fortifications, Krueger on 2 July wrote him off as a potential corps commander.[29]

To command all the reinforcements streaming into Aitape, and to remove the responsibility for the operation's outcome from Gill's lackluster hands, Krueger dispatched General Charles "Chink" Hall and his Eleventh Corps headquarters, which had arrived in SWPA the previous February. Born in Mississippi in 1886, Hall went to the University of Mississippi for two years before transferring to West Point. He graduated in 1911 with a higher class standing than any other World War Two corps commander who saw action. After teaching at West Point for three years, Hall sailed for France after the United States entered World War One. There he saw considerable action in the fighting along the Marne, at St. Mihiel, and in the Argonne Forest. After participating in the occupation of the Rhineland, he returned to the States and attended the Command and General Staff School from 1924 to 1925 and the Army War College four years later. He served in the Philippines in the early 1930s and by the end of the decade had a regiment of his own. From there he progressed to assistant commander of the Third Division and then commander of the Ninety-third Division, and, finally, in October 1942, he took over the Eleventh Corps. Although he had not yet led troops in the war, he had impressed McNair and had observed the fighting in North Africa. In January 1944, Marshall informed MacArthur that he was sending the Eleventh Corps headquarters to SWPA. He noted that Hall was McNair's number-one choice for the corps in part because he had led the unit for more than a year, but presented MacArthur with the names of five other stateside generals if Hall was not suitable: John W. Anderson, John Millikin, John B. Anderson, Frank Milburn, Frederick Terrill, and Louis Craig. MacArthur probably accepted Hall, whom he deemed "entirely satisfactory," because at that point none of SWPA's division commanders had yet proven themselves in an independent capacity.[30]

Hall was a small, taciturn, and somewhat remote man well respected in the prewar army. He was not above twisting orders when it suited his purposes, but he usually tried hard to get along with his superiors. When he arrived in SWPA, he was surprised and impressed with everyone's serious sense of urgency. After four months in the theater, Krueger directed Hall to Aitape to take charge of the various units there or on their way. Despite Krueger's orders to the contrary, Hall brought his entire Eleventh Corps staff with him because he sensed he would need them. Hall knew that Krueger wanted quick action and was closely monitoring events at Aitape, so he was displeased with Gill's passive strategy. When he assumed command on 28 June, he dispatched part of his troops to the Driniumor River, east of

Aitape, to keep an eye out for the Japanese. Hall's analysis of the situation convinced him that the Japanese stood little chance of storming Aitape, and he was confident he could handle whatever they threw at him. Gill, on the other hand, did not share Hall's confidence. Gill was unhappy at being superseded and had little respect for Hall and his greenhorn staff. As he saw things, the Eleventh Corps personnel were in over their heads and out of touch. Years later, Gill wrote that the Eleventh Corps was "untrained in this thing from the top down. They had never been in any combat like that and they didn't know anything about jungle fighting."[31] Gill was partially right. Hall's efforts to square Krueger's demands for action with Gill's earlier defensive plan by dividing his forces in two contributed to the initial success of the Japanese assault across the Driniumor River on the night of 10–11 July. An angry Krueger arrived the next day to apply his direct form of motivation, but Hall appeased him with a plan to regain the initiative and wrap up the operation. A strong American counterattack pushed the enemy back to the Driniumor, and after several weeks of heavy fighting the Japanese gave up and retreated to Wewak. They sustained over 8,800 casualties in their desperate undertaking. The Americans for their part lost 597 killed, 1,691 wounded, and 85 missing. Hall's performance, while hardly stellar at the start of the operation, was good enough by the end to warrant Krueger's praise. Six weeks later, Hall justified Krueger's confidence in him with a successful, albeit unopposed, landing on Morotai Island between New Guinea and the Philippines.[32]

The Morotai operation marked the end of MacArthur's New Guinea campaign. In just five months and at the cost of only 11,300 casualties, SWPA forces had streaked 800 miles across the big island's north coast and reached the China-Formosa-Luzon region at the same time as the navy's concurrent central Pacific offensive. MacArthur did so by taking advantage of SWPA's superior airpower and naval mobility to bypass and isolate Japanese strongpoints along the coast and strike at relatively undefended areas. Once ashore, the Americans seized or constructed airfields that enabled them to project their power further to the north and west. From a strategic perspective, these operations pretty much ended as soon as SWPA had an airfield in hand, but at a tactical level they often continued long afterward because the Americans had to clear out die-hard Japanese defenders in the vicinity. This difficult and unheralded job went to Krueger's corps and division commanders, men such as Eichelberger, Hall, Sibert, and Swift. Although they had little opportunity to maneuver much in New Guinea's dense jungle, they used their superior firepower, equipment, and logistical support to attrit the weakened and outnumbered Japanese rapidly enough for MacArthur to keep to his stringent timetable. For this team that MacArthur put together on the fly, the New Guinea campaign served as a dress rehearsal for bigger and bloodier battles yet to come.

The Central Pacific Offensive

While MacArthur raced along the New Guinea coast, the navy was conducting its own offensive to the north across the Central Pacific. These operations differed from MacArthur's in all sorts of ways, but two in particular stood out. For one thing, whereas SWPA's fighting took place mostly in steamy, jungle-ridden environments, the navy's initially occurred on small, flat, and barren lagoon-enclosing reefs called atolls. These atolls presented military challenges every bit as difficult as those encountered in SWPA. For another, the army played a significant but secondary and often subordinate role in the Central Pacific offensive. The POA was led by the folksy, tough, and understated Admiral Chester Nimitz, and most of the important positions were held by naval officers who saw the Pacific War as primarily a naval conflict. The army had to work not only with these men, but also with the large Marine Corps contingent in the theater. As events proved, interservice cooperation was one of the biggest challenges in the POA's war against Japan.

Marshall appointed General Robert "Nelly" Richardson to lead the army's contribution to the Central Pacific offensive as head of the Hawaiian Department and military governor of the islands. On paper, Richardson's eclectic career made him an excellent selection to run the so-called Pineapple Army. Born in Charleston, South Carolina, in 1882, Richardson graduated from West Point in 1904 and was wounded the following year while fighting the Moros in the Philippines. He taught at West Point for eight years before going to France as part of Pershing's staff in World War One. After the conflict he returned to the Philippines for two years. He then attended the Command and General Staff School from 1923 to 1924, the École Superieure de Guerre in Paris from 1924 to 1926, and the Army War College from 1933 to 1934. In between these assignments, he served as military attaché in Rome from 1926 to 1928 and as executive officer and commandant of cadets at West Point from 1926 to 1933. Up until the mid-1930s Richardson occupied mostly administrative, teaching, and staff posts, but from that point on he increasingly held line positions. He commanded successively a cavalry regiment, a brigade, and, finally, the First Cavalry Division in 1940–1941. He was director of the Bureau of Public Relations for a short time in 1941 until Marshall, on McNair's recommendation, sent him to Birmingham, Alabama, to take over the Seventh Corps, from which he went to Hawaii in June 1943.[33]

Richardson was widely admired in the prewar army for his broad education, emphasis on discipline, and gentlemanly qualities. However, the general feeling that he was at heart a staffer generated scorn from those who saw themselves as combat officers and looked down upon those who were not. For example, when he learned that he and Richardson had both been promoted to lieutenant general, a contemptuous George Patton scrawled in his diary, "When Nelly got three stars it almost took the pleasure out of mine."[34] There were of course plenty of officers who rarely served with troops before the war who went on to become capable and respected combat commanders, but Richardson possessed the aura of a staffer no matter what job he held. Another hard-fighting general, J. Lawton Collins, was referring to Richardson when he wrote, "I have often been impressed with how accurately the nickname that an officer acquires in the Army portrays his characteristics, if not his character."[35] In fact, Nelly Richardson could be pompous, finicky, inordinately sensitive to slights real and perceived, and a stickler for protocol regardless of the circumstances. Eichelberger remembered that Richardson would always dash out of his office to impress people with his energy and importance. In short, Richardson was certainly an able and useful man, but only within certain limits.[36]

Marshall's motivations for selecting Richardson to lead the army's forces in the Central Pacific offensive are unclear. Marshall was initially so impressed with Richardson that in the first year of the war he considered him for several high-level missions—Chiang Kai-shek's military adviser in China, MacArthur's corps commander in Australia, and commander of the Central Task Force in Operation Torch—but for one reason or another none of these opportunities panned out. In October 1942, though, Marshall's opinion of Richardson took a dramatic turn for the worse. Marshall learned that during maneuvers at the Desert Training Center in California, Richardson failed to read all his instructions and seemed to resent taking orders from a former junior officer, General Alvan Gillem. Such carelessness and pettiness did not sit well with the meticulous and by-the-book chief of staff. "All this accumulation of the sensitive business is causing me to lose confidence and certainly to be extremely reluctant to give him any advance command," Marshall complained to McNair. "We haven't got time for this sort of personal business. When I think of full Generals and full Admirals in the British Army and Navy placing themselves subordinate to Eisenhower and working in complete loyalty to him, this business of Richardson does not set well."[37] McNair agreed and recommended that Marshall relieve Richardson from the Seventh Corps and give him an administrative job, or simply retire him once and for all. Marshall was unwilling to resort to anything as drastic as forced retirement, but Richardson's removal from the Seventh Corps and appointment as head of the Hawaiian Department and military governor of the territory no doubt stemmed from Richardson's uncooperative attitude. Overseeing Hawaii was one thing, but Marshall's subsequent decision to assign Richardson to lead the army's contribution to the POA's Central Pacific offensive was something else. To be sure, Richardson possessed the necessary administrative skills, rank, and self-confidence for this important job, but he had not so far demonstrated the tact, cooperation, and self-lessness required for such a post. It is possible that Marshall believed that

Richardson's prickly personality would help protect the army's prerogatives in a navy-dominated theater or that he felt that the position was a change in title only. Whatever the reason, Richardson activated his new command on 14 August 1943.[38]

Richardson's new job sounded important, and in many respects it was, but there was rather less to it than initially met the eye. Although Richardson was responsible for training, administering, and supplying the theater's army contingent, he did not have the authority to actually take these soldiers into battle. Nimitz gave that task to the marines over Richardson's objections partially because they were the amphibious warfare experts, but also no doubt because they were more subject to navy control. For Richardson, this was akin to a cuckold man living in an unconsummated marriage. Moreover, he did not much like the navy's and marines' way of doing things. Richardson complained about the navy's inflexible procedures, its misuse of Army Air Force units under its control, its interference with army prerogatives on Hawaii and elsewhere, its refusal to put army generals in command of the various island garrisons in the region, and its failure to give the army sufficient input into important operations. As for the marines, Richardson did not believe that they understood army doctrine well enough to command soldiers in combat. Finally, Richardson felt that he lacked sufficient staff to fulfill his myriad responsibilities and keep track of the navy's shenanigans. To his credit, he tried to be dispassionate and objective about his grievances. He got along well personally with Nimitz, with whom he met almost daily, and they kept their disputes on a professional level. Richardson's staff, on the other hand, failed to develop an easygoing relationship with Nimitz's counterpart because they communicated mostly by letter, even though only a few miles separated their headquarters. Through it all, Richardson pledged to Marshall, "You may rest assured that the fullest support and cooperation has been given [to the navy] in the past and will be given in the future to help win the war just as quickly as possible. My policy, in which the staff is fully indoctrinated, is that nothing must interfere with the full support of the operations in the Pacific."[39] Even so, Richardson was very unhappy in his limited role. He served so well as Hawaii's military governor that the locals sent a petition to Marshall lauding his work and urging his promotion, but this was not the same as leading troops under fire. Richardson had a big house, a nice car, and all the pomp and circumstance an officious officer could want, but he was in a gilded cage, and he knew it.[40]

Unfortunately for Richardson, his efforts to defend the army's rights in the POA often got little support or sympathy from Marshall. When Richardson cited examples he considered indicative of the navy's theater-wide attempt to marginalize the army, the chief of staff interpreted his comments as nitpicking. For instance, at one point Richardson complained that the navy was trying to gain control over dredges in the South Pacific. In August 1944 Marshall grew so exasperated with Richardson's carping over such minor details that he contemplated relieving him of his command. In the end, he refrained from doing so and instead ordered him to Washington for consultation, but his attitude toward most of Richardson's complaints did not change much. In December 1944, Richardson was so concerned that the navy was exceeding its authority that he asked Marshall to place the issue before the Joint Chiefs of Staff for adjudication. Marshall refused to do so, and summed up his philosophy about such interservice disagreements within the POA by noting that it was after all a navy-dominated theater by presidential fiat. "I realize," he stated, "that there must be constantly arising questions of authority but I feel that for the most part you and Admiral Nimitz can satisfactorily adjust them."[41] To Richardson, however, this was cold comfort because while he could protest and bargain with Nimitz, he had to do so from a subordinate position.[42]

Such disagreements might seem silly and irrelevant, but the serious consequences that sometimes grew out of them cost lives and threatened to disrupt the close cooperation between the army and navy that Marshall wanted to foster. The seeds of serious interservice discontent were first sewn during the operation to seize the Gilbert Islands. The Joint Chiefs of Staff authorized their occupation in July 1943 as a stepping-stone to the more strategically important Marshall Islands. The operation, christened "Galvanic," called for simultaneous assaults on two atolls, Tarawa and Makin, on 20 November by units that were part of marine General Holland "Howlin' Mad" Smith's Fifth Amphibious Corps. The Second Marine Division would storm Tarawa while a regiment from General Ralph Smith's rookie Twenty-seventh Division took care of Makin. The marines ran into such stiff resistance from Tarawa's 5,000 defenders that they were almost eliminated at the water's edge. After four days of bitter fighting, however, the marines managed to take the island and kill almost all of the Japanese there, but the battle cost them a thousand dead and twice as many wounded. The Twenty-seventh Division's attack on weakly defended Makin took just as long, but the army sustained only 218 casualties in the process.

The heavy losses sustained at Tarawa—Richardson said after visiting the atoll that it reminded him of the World War One battlefield at Ypres—tainted the victory in the Gilberts and convinced the navy and marines to take a hard look at their tactics, weaponry, and procedures. The army, however, also came under scrutiny for its actions. Although observers had praised the Twenty-seventh Division before the operation, its sluggish performance at Makin raised doubts as to its effectiveness. These concerns were underscored when a Japanese submarine sank the escort carrier USS *Liscome Bay* off Makin on the last day of the battle, killing 644 sailors, or almost three times as many Americans as fell on the island.

Navy and marine officers pointed out that if the army had seized Makin on schedule, then *Liscome Bay* would not have been there when the Japanese submarine put in its appearance. Holland Smith certainly viewed it in this light. He angrily criticized the Twenty-seventh Division and later claimed that he would have relieved Ralph Smith had he been a marine. Holland Smith traced the division's problems back to Richardson, a desk soldier for whom he had little respect. Richardson for his part believed that Holland Smith was a typical Marine Corps officer ignorant of army doctrine and unable to handle the large units the army was increasingly deploying. He also pointed out that the marines lacked sufficient trained officers to oversee the kind of big operations the Pacific War entailed. His proposed solution was to organize an army corps for the army's divisions in the POA that would operate independently from Smith's Fifth's Amphibious Corps.[43]

Whatever its merits, Richardson's recommendation to organize an army corps came too late to impact the POA's next operation, dubbed "Flintlock," against the Marshall Islands. Nimitz's headquarters took the lessons of Tarawa to heart and made all sorts of changes and modifications to its plans. Basically, it provided for more of everything—more assault troops, more landing craft, more equipment, a longer and heavier preliminary bombardment by more warships and bombers, and so on. Nimitz's target was Kwajalein, in the heart of the island group. Kwajalein, the world's largest atoll, contained nearly a hundred islands surrounding a huge lagoon, and it possessed more Japanese defenders than the marines had faced at Tarawa. On 1 February 1944 the Fourth Marine Division assailed the islands of Roi and Namur, 44 miles from Kwajalein proper, and crushed the Japanese there in two days of sharp fighting at the cost of 737 casualties, 190 of whom died. At the same time, to the south, General Charles "Pete" Corlett's Seventh Division, veterans of the assault on Attu in the Aleutians the previous May, stormed Kwajalein itself. Corlett's innovative use of artillery on offshore islets that had been seized the day before provided additional fire support for the infantry. Even so, the Seventh Division still required four days and 987 casualties to clear the island. Such losses were certainly regrettable, but they were much lighter than those sustained in the Gilberts, despite the large number of Japanese troops defending the atoll. Local navy commanders were so elated that they persuaded Nimitz to let them move against Eniwetok in the western Marshalls immediately with Flintlock's unused reserves, while the Japanese were still off balance. After the marines did some preliminary work in the area, a regiment from the Twenty-seventh Division landed on Eniwetok on 19 February. It encountered stiff enough resistance to require marine reinforcements, but the island fell after only two days.

Success in the Marshalls failed to shake Richardson's conviction that the army needed its own corps in the POA for its divisions there. He pleaded his case not only with Nimitz, but also directly with Marshall during the chief of staff's visit to

Hawaii at the end of 1943. Both Nimitz and Marshall were amenable to the idea, though Nimitz still insisted that the Fifth Amphibious Corps lead any amphibious assaults. To command this new corps, numbered the Twenty-fourth, Marshall initially suggested Troy Middleton. Middleton had ably led the Forty-fifth Division in Sicily and on the Italian mainland until invalided home by an arthritic knee. Marshall had deemed Middleton's combat record brilliant and wanted to find a proper venue for him to exercise his talents. The POA, with its flat atolls, seemed just the place for Middleton to wage war without aggravating his tender knee. Richardson countered by recommending Pete Corlett for the job. Corlett had fought well at Kwajalein, where his decision to emplace artillery on offshore islets for fire support had caught people's attention. Marshall was sympathetic to Richardson's suggestion. Although he did not know Corlett well personally, before Pearl Harbor he had been impressed that five officers requested Corlett's services. Marshall saw Corlett as a "strong character" and had gone out of his way to get him a combat assignment. In return, Corlett had repaid the chief of staff with impressive performances in the POA. Corlett started to put the corps headquarters together, but in the end neither he nor Middleton ended up with the outfit. The more Marshall thought about it, the more convinced he became that Eisenhower could use both Middleton and Corlett for the upcoming invasion of France. Eisenhower had recently complained that he lacked experienced high-ranking commanders, and sending Middleton and Corlett to England would help remedy the problem. Corlett's wealth of amphibious knowledge would be especially useful there. As a result, both officers wound up leading corps in northwest Europe, not in the POA.[44]

With Middleton and Corlett removed from contention, Richardson set his sights on General John Hodge for the new Twenty-fourth Corps. Hodge was unusual in that he was not a West Pointer. He had been born in Illinois in 1893 and attended Southern Illinois Teachers College and the University of Illinois before entering a reserve officer training program at Fort Sheridan, from where he went to France in World War One. He remained in the army after the conflict, teaching military science at Mississippi State University. Then he went to the Infantry School, the Command and General Staff School—he graduated fifth out of 118 in his 1934 class, the highest standing of any active World War Two corps commander except Omar Bradley—and the Army War College. He spent the late 1930s on the General Staff before transferring to the Seventh Corps, of which he became chief of staff shortly after Pearl Harbor. J. Lawton Collins asked for him as deputy commander of the Twenty-fifth Division, and Hodge performed well enough in that capacity at Guadalcanal to suit even Collins's exacting standards. Thereafter he was assigned to lead the American Division and, except for a short stint in which he took over the Forty-third Division during its debacle on New

Georgia, stayed with the outfit through Bougainville. After Collins left for the European theater, Hodge was probably the most combat-experienced army general in the POA, with three operations under his belt. Richardson knew and respected him from their time together in the Seventh Corps, and Hodge got along well with navy and marine officers. It was for these reasons, and because the European War was siphoning off most of the capable stateside corps commanders, that Hodge got the post. Since Eisenhower had recently taken Collins from SOPAC, Marshall was reluctant to deprive Harmon of yet another quality officer. Instead, he recommended Oscar Griswold, which was odd since he was also a valuable officer currently residing in Harmon's bailiwick. Richardson, however, insisted on Hodge, and Marshall gave way.[45]

Hodge was admired by almost everyone as a tough soldier and skillful officer, and by the time he took over the Twenty-fourth Corps he had the record to prove it. He initially made his mark as a good troop trainer and strict disciplinarian, but there was more to him than that. He was a forceful, analytical, and effervescent man willing to speak his mind. A year and a half of combat had sharpened his common sense and honed his combat skills. On the other hand, as a soldier's soldier Hodge had little understanding of the nonmilitary responsibilities that occasionally came an officer's way. The complexities and subtleties of diplomacy and politics were in particular beyond his ken. As a corps commander waging total war, though, he was in his element. His first challenge with the Twenty-fourth Corps was organizing its headquarters. Unlike almost all the other army corps during the war, the Twenty-fourth was pieced together with personnel on hand, not transferred intact and ready to go from the States. Hodge did his best, and there is no evidence that the Twenty-fourth's headquarters was any worse than that of other Pacific War corps.[46]

Regrettably, the establishment of the Twenty-fourth Corps came too late to prevent the interservice conflicts and misunderstandings it was supposed to help avert. Tension between the marines and army had manifested itself back in the Gilberts, and was still present to a lesser degree in the Marshalls. However, in the POA's next operation, against the Mariana Islands, it bubbled to the surface and threatened to irretrievably disrupt interservice harmony in the theater. Unlike the Gilberts and Marshalls, the Marianas had strategic relevance beyond merely pushing the POA closer to the China-Formosa-Luzon region. In American hands the islands could provide the Army Air Force with airfields that its new B-29 bombers could use to pound Japanese cities. The Marianas were also important enough to tempt the Japanese fleet into a big climactic battle with its American counterpart that navy officers craved. The assault on the Marianas, codenamed "Forager," would be the biggest POA operation to date. Forager called for the commitment of five divisions, two of which were army, against Saipan, Tinian, and Guam. On this occasion, Holland Smith and his Fifth Amphibious Corps would actually command these units in battle, making it the first time so many soldiers would be under direct marine control.

On the morning of 15 June, two marine divisions landed on Saipan and immediately ran into heavy opposition from the island's 32,000 Japanese defenders. However, the marines managed to carve out a beachhead and hold on. Next morning, though, Admiral Raymond Spruance, commander of the enormous armada assailing the Marianas, learned that the Japanese fleet was on its way for a showdown battle with his Fifth Fleet. To clear the decks for the upcoming fight, Spruance ordered Ralph Smith's Twenty-seventh Division put ashore and the transports and cargo vessels out of the way. Ralph Smith's troops began disembarking on 16–17 June, but Holland Smith's Fifth Amphibious Corps handled and deployed them carelessly by not giving them adequate guidance. Indeed, Holland Smith had never liked the Twenty-seventh Division and had complained about its sluggish performance at Makin. Its initial actions on Saipan did nothing to change his mind. In particular, the division got bogged down assailing a well-fortified area called Death Valley, holding up the marine advance on its flanks. Holland Smith fumed that the soldiers were not trying hard enough and pressured Ralph Smith to get his men moving. When the Twenty-seventh Division continued to stall, Holland Smith finally decided that Ralph Smith had to go. On 24 June, he and Admiral Kelly Turner, head of the amphibious forces, visited Spruance on his flagship, the cruiser USS *Indianapolis*. "Ralph Smith has shown that he lacks aggressive spirit," Holland Smith declared, "and his division is slowing down our advance. He should be relieved."[47] Spruance agreed and authorized Holland Smith to make the change. Although Holland Smith knew his decision would generate considerable controversy, he believed it was necessary to win the battle. The Twenty-seventh Division did not improve appreciably under new leadership, but American firepower and numbers gradually wore down Japanese resistance. By the time Saipan was secured on 9 July, the Americans had suffered 14,111 casualties, of which 3,674 were sustained by the army. To the south, the marines and General Andrew Bruce's rookie Seventy-seventh Division invaded Guam on 21 July and crushed its Japanese defenders in three weeks of fighting, at the cost of 7,800 killed and wounded. Finally, on 24 July a marine force seized Tinian after a week of combat. By the end of July, the Marianas were in American hands.

American victory in the Marianas was important for several reasons. For one thing, the islands were not even secured before aviation engineers moved in to build and improve airfields for the B-29 bombers that would eventually rain awful destruction on Japanese cities. The campaign also provoked the Japanese fleet into a ruinous engagement with its American counterpart at the Battle of the

Philippine Sea. Unfortunately, Holland Smith's relief of Ralph Smith tainted these benefits by sparking a serious interservice squabble. It started on Saipan, where army officers felt that their marine counterparts treated the Twenty-seventh Division with ill-disguised contempt for the remainder of the fighting on the island. Ralph Smith's eventual successor, General George Griner, quarreled with Holland Smith and stated that Smith was hopelessly prejudiced against the army. Back in Hawaii, Richardson was not surprisingly outraged by Holland Smith's actions. As soon as he had digested the news, Richardson flew to Saipan and decorated some Twenty-seventh Division soldiers without informing Holland Smith, even though the unit was still under Smith's command. Later Richardson berated Smith, saying that he had no right to relieve Ralph Smith and was biased against the army. Holland Smith quoted Richardson as saying, "You and your Corps commanders aren't as well qualified to lead large bodies of troops as general officers in the Army. We've had more experience in handling troops than you've had and yet you dare remove one of my generals. You marines are nothing but a bunch of beach runners anyway. What do you know about land warfare?"[48] Smith claimed that he managed to hold his tongue, but noted approvingly that Kelly Turner gave Richardson both barrels in another conversation shortly thereafter.

Unhappily, the interservice recriminations did not end there. To make his case, on 4 July Richardson established an army board of inquiry to investigate Holland Smith's relief of Ralph Smith. Dubbed the Buckner Board after its chairman, recently arrived General Simon Buckner, the board consisted of four army officers, one of whom was John Hodge. Meeting throughout July and August, the board took testimony and examined documents. Its credibility was undermined from the start not only because it did not interview any marine and navy personnel, but also because Richardson pressured Buckner and his colleagues to attribute Holland Smith's actions to a navy plot to circumvent the army and wage the POA war with marines only. Buckner's political sensitivities, though, were much keener than Richardson's, and he worked hard to moderate the board's findings so they did not irretrievably alienate navy officers. In the end, the Buckner Board concluded that although Holland Smith had the right to fire Ralph Smith, Ralph Smith's removal was "not justified by the facts" because Holland Smith was ignorant as to the Twenty-seventh Division's circumstances and conditions.[49]

Richardson and Holland Smith were both angered by this interservice brouhaha and sought their own interpretation of justice, but their superiors wanted the incident to disappear so they could focus on waging war against Japan. Nimitz argued that Buckner's report should be restricted lest its widespread release exacerbate interservice tension. Back in Washington, Marshall and King reached the same conclusion and came to a tacit agreement to simply move on and put the controversy behind them. As for the instigators of the ruckus, they all suffered professionally. While Marshall had no desire to fan the interservice flames created on Saipan, he also made it clear to King that in the future he did not want army units to operate under Holland Smith's command. In response, the marines kicked Holland Smith upstairs to the newly created Fleet Marine Force, and he never again led either soldiers or marines in combat. The incident also ruined Richardson's standing with the navy and marines and underscored his powerlessness in the navy-dominated POA. He thereafter sought to ingratiate himself with MacArthur's GHQ in the hope of securing a more lucrative assignment there, but nothing came of that either, so he had to remain in the POA.[50]

Conclusions

The Dual Drive Offensive was made possible by American materiel superiority that gave the JCS the luxury not only of waging war aggressively in Europe and the Pacific, but also of attacking Japan from two directions simultaneously. The additional resources the army dispatched to the Pacific for the Dual Drive Offensive required the deployment of new units and commanders, including one field army and three corps. In SWPA, MacArthur chose all but one of his new field army and corps commanders from within the theater, based on their records as aggressive fighters who had proven themselves in independent capacities. MacArthur accepted the one exception, Chink Hall, only because at that time there were no division commanders in SWPA who met his and Krueger's criteria. On the other hand, John Hodge's presence as head of the Twenty-fourth Corps in the POA was due to Hodge's obvious qualification, the increased number of army divisions in the theater, the lack of available stateside corps commanders, and, not least, the army's growing consensus that marine generals should not take soldiers into battle. All these generals would get their chance to justify their selections in the Pacific War's next big campaign in the Philippines.

5
Liberation of France

A Supreme Commander

Although American, British, and Soviet leaders had reasons for optimism when they met at the Teheran Conference in November and December 1943, Allied victory was by no means certain. In the Pacific, the Joint Chiefs had not yet authorized the Dual Drive Offensive, but limited American counterattacks had driven the Japanese out of eastern New Guinea, the central Solomon Islands, the Gilbert Islands, and the Aleutian Islands. The Japanese nevertheless retained control over Burma, the Dutch East Indies, eastern China, the Mariana Islands, their important bases at Rabaul and Truk, and of course Manchuria and Japan itself. The obliteration of Japanese cities by B-29 bombers and the systematic destruction of the Japanese merchant marine by submarines had barely begun, and the Americans were just learning to use their superior naval mobility to bypass and isolate Japanese strongpoints. On the Eastern Front the Soviets had won two colossal battles at Stalingrad and Kursk, inflicted hundreds of thousands of casualties on the Wehrmacht, and driven the Germans out of Ukraine and back to the Polish border. Unfortunately, Soviet losses had also been enormous, and the German army in the east still contained nearly 200 divisions guarding Poland, the Baltics, and the Balkans. Finally, the Americans and British had neutralized the U-boat threat in the North Atlantic, undertaken a sustained bomber offensive against Germany, seized North Africa and Sicily, and landed in southern Italy. On the other hand, they had not yet engaged a significant number of German troops, seriously crippled German industry, or established a foothold in Europe within striking distance of Germany itself. After more than two years of world war, the German and Japanese empires continued to provide their militaries with the resources they needed to prosecute the conflict. In sum, the Allies had a long way to go to win the war, but if victory was not exactly a foregone conclusion, it was definitely within the realm of possibility.

Marshall had always believed that an Anglo-American attack on German-occupied western Europe was the fastest and surest way to defeat Germany. Doing so would enable the army to deploy its growing strength for a decisive and hopefully victorious battle with the Wehrmacht, after which it could go full force to the Pacific to wreak vengeance on the Japanese. Unhappily for Allied harmony, the British saw things differently. They advocated an indirect and peripheral strategy of combating the Germans in the Mediterranean. By 1942 the British were running out of men, and they wanted to avoid a repetition of the enormous casualties they sustained on the Western Front in World War One. The British already had significant resources in the Mediterranean, and they hoped that fighting there would minimize British losses and safeguard their postwar empire. Although Churchill persuaded Roosevelt to undertake the North African campaign over Marshall's strident objections, the chief of staff continued to insist throughout 1943 on a cross-Channel assault. He was willing to compromise to gain the necessary consensus. He bought Ernest King's and the navy's support by agreeing to a limited counteroffensive against Japan, and placated the British by going along with continuing operations in the Mediterranean even though both undertakings dispersed army assets. At the Trident Conference in Washington in May 1943, Marshall finally gained a definite British pledge to assail western Europe the following spring, and at subsequent conferences he fought off Churchill's stubborn efforts to obfuscate his previous commitment. Not until the Soviets came out in favor of the American plan at the Teheran Conference did Churchill finally abandon his attempts to focus the main Anglo-American effort on the Mediterranean and reconcile himself to Operation Overlord, the massive Allied invasion of Germany's Fortress Europe.

The initial assumption was that the British would supply the supreme commander for the assault on western Europe because the early plans called for them to provide the bulk of the troops. In fact, after the Trident Conference Churchill confidentially promised the job to Field Marshall Alan Brooke, the chief of the Imperial General Staff. By the time of the Quadrant Conference in Quebec in August, however, Roosevelt had concluded that an American should lead the operation. The United States' military power was growing so rapidly that it was obvious by then that most of the men allotted to Overlord would be American. That being the case, Roosevelt doubted that his electorate would tolerate a foreigner directing so many American soldiers in such an important campaign. Churchill realized this as well, and at Quadrant told Roosevelt that although it would cause him embarrassment with Brooke, he believed that an American, preferably Marshall or Eisenhower, should be in charge. When he broke the news to Brooke, though, Churchill claimed that Roosevelt and his chief adviser, Harry Hopkins, strongarmed him into accepting an American for Overlord. Whatever the truth of the matter, Brooke was understandably disappointed, especially because he had little respect for either Marshall's or Eisenhower's military abilities.[1]

For those in the loop, the consensus was that Roosevelt would appoint Marshall to lead Overlord. Harry Hopkins, for example, had always been a big Marshall booster and believed that only he had the necessary prestige and qualifications for such an important job. Secretary of War Henry Stimson concurred wholeheartedly and later explained:

> Marshall towers above everybody else in the strength of his character and in the wisdom and tactfulness of his handling of himself and handling of his plan. He is by far the biggest man that I have met in Washington and although, as a loyal soldier, he does not seek exhibitions of his qualities as a civil character, yet he has them. He is selfless, tactful, careful in his detail work of planning, very conciliatory in negotiations, and yet capable of terrific force in carrying through a decision that he has fully made up his mind about.[2]

Hopkins and Stimson could recommend, but of course it was Roosevelt's decision. Roosevelt was initially inclined to agree with his advisers, telling one person that Marshall had earned the right to this prominent field command. As for Marshall, he no doubt wanted the position as a fitting culmination of his career, but characteristically declined to lobby for it or even express an opinion one way or another on the matter. He was, however, confident enough about his chances that his wife began quietly moving furniture out of the chief of staff's quarters at Fort McNair to their Leesburg, Virginia, home. For his replacement as chief of staff, Roosevelt at first suggested Douglas MacArthur to Stimson. MacArthur certainly possessed the necessary stature for the post, but Stimson pointed out that whatever his other attributes, MacArthur lacked the requisite disinterestedness for such a responsibility. Instead, he and Roosevelt quickly settled on Eisenhower. Eisenhower might not have Marshall's force of character, but he had in North Africa demonstrated many of the other qualities a wartime chief of staff needed. By the time of the Cairo Conference in November, these personnel decisions seemed so inevitable that Ernest King expounded upon them to Eisenhower and a clearly embarrassed Marshall when the three of them were together in Eisenhower's quarters. Most of the speculation centered on whom Marshall would select as his army group and field army commanders, with McNair, Devers, Courtney Hodges, and Bradley as the leading candidates.[3]

Despite the almost universal recognition by those Americans in the know that Marshall was the most qualified man to lead Overlord, Roosevelt hesitated to make the appointment. He did not doubt Marshall's competence, but instead worried that Marshall was too valuable as chief of staff to assume another post. He was not alone in this assessment. In mid-September, World War One hero General John Pershing wrote Roosevelt that Marshall's global responsibilities as chief of staff outweighed any tactical job, no matter how prestigious it might be. Pershing concluded, "I have written this, Mr. President, because it is my deep conviction that the suggested transfer of General Marshall would be a fundamental and very grave error in our military policy."[4] Such strong words from the highest-ranking officer in American history caught Roosevelt's attention. So did a conversation Stimson had with a group of prominent congressional Republicans at about the same time. These men were concerned that Marshall's transfer might hurt Congress's relationship with the White House on military matters because Marshall's endorsement gave Roosevelt administration proposals credibility among otherwise recalcitrant congressmen. Finally, the chairman of the Joint Chiefs of Staff, Admiral William Leahy, informed Roosevelt that although he and the other members of the JCS believed that Marshall deserved the Overlord command, they hated to break up the winning team that had so far overseen the American war effort.

In an effort to reconcile the problem, Roosevelt, Stimson, and Hopkins batted around various ideas that would enable Marshall to maintain his worldwide strategic duties and assume a more tactical role in Overlord. They discussed combining all of Europe in one big theater under Marshall's aegis, promoting him to a six-star general with authority over the entire army, and assigning an acting chief of staff subordinate to him to watch the army store in Washington while he campaigned in Europe. None of these ideas, though, proved feasible. The British, for instance, balked at surrendering their domination of the Mediterranean to a new gigantic theater under American control. As he so often did when confronted with thorny quandaries, Roosevelt vacillated and delayed in the hopes that a solution would present itself, even though Stimson and others warned him that he had to make his selection soon. At the Teheran Conference Stalin repeatedly asked who would be in charge of Overlord, as if this were a barometer of Anglo-American seriousness about the project. On their way back from the conference, the American and British delegations again stopped at Cairo. There Roosevelt summoned Marshall to his villa for lunch and bluntly asked his preference. Marshall explained that his personal feelings were irrelevant and he would wholeheartedly support whatever decision the president made. After hearing Marshall out, Roosevelt declined to give the job to him. He later explained to Stimson that relieving Marshall as chief of staff would hurt congressional relations and the war effort as a whole because his replacement, no matter how capable, would lack Marshall's experience and depth of knowledge about the plethora of complicated and interrelated subjects the chief of staff had to deal with on a daily basis. To Marshall, though, Roosevelt put the matter more simply: "I feel that I could not sleep at night with you out of the country." If Marshall was disappointed, he did not show it; shortly after he returned to the States General J. Lawton Collins visited him at his Pentagon office and found him relaxed, fit, confident, and seemingly without a trace of regret. For Marshall, who had sacrificed so much for his country and would give up even more in the coming years, this was just another measure of his devotion.[5]

With Marshall eliminated from contention, Eisenhower was the logical choice to lead Overlord. In fact, Churchill had stated previously that Marshall and Eisenhower were the only American officers he would accept for the job. Although he therefore got the post by default, there was much to commend in Eisenhower. He was experienced in coalition warfare, having successfully commanded Allied forces in campaigns in North Africa, in Sicily, and to a lesser extent in southern Italy. He understood the importance in maintaining the Anglo-American alliance and had made that a priority. His winning record and personality enabled him to get along with British and Americans of all stripes, giving him a popular appeal that transcended nationality. His expertise in amphibious warfare would also come in handy for Overlord. To be sure, Eisenhower had made his share of mistakes and had a number of enemies and doubters—Brooke being among the most prominent—but except for Marshall no one else had the necessary qualifications for an enormous undertaking such as Overlord. During a stopover in Oran on his way to Cairo and Teheran, Roosevelt spent some time with Eisenhower and was obviously impressed with him. Eisenhower then accompanied the British and American delegations to Cairo and made an equally good impression on the Combined Chiefs of Staff during their meetings. Arnold and King were already boosters anyway, and even Brooke recognized that Eisenhower possessed some of the traits that made him an ideal pick. On 6 December, just as the second Cairo Conference was breaking up, Roosevelt made the selection official.[6]

Eisenhower was a frustrated and unhappy man in the last months of 1943. After a promising start, the Italian campaign had bogged down and failed to yield the anticipated strategic benefits—meaning Rome. Worse yet, the Mediterranean theater's command structure diluted his authority by forcing him to work through his British ground, air, and naval deputies. Finally, he was worried about his future. A long stream of visitors from the States, including Secretary of the Navy William Frank Knox, opined that Eisenhower would replace Marshall as chief of staff when Marshall took over Overlord. Eisenhower did not want to return to the War Department with its paperwork, red tape, and bureaucratic rigmarole, and predicted that if he did he would be carried to Arlington Cemetery within six months. Instead, he hoped to remain in the field, even if his current job was more managerial than combative. Although he wished he might retain command of the Mediterranean theater or take over an army group under Marshall in England, this seemed increasingly unlikely. By the time the Cairo Conference convened, Eisenhower felt like a quarterback about to be benched halfway through the big game. He gloomily contemplated flying back to Washington via the Pacific so he could consult MacArthur and get up to speed on the war with Japan before he assumed his new duties as chief of staff. Then everything changed. On 7 December Eisenhower traveled to Tunis to meet Roosevelt, who was on his way home from Cairo. As soon as he was placed in Eisenhower's car, Roosevelt airily told him that he would lead Overlord and explained why. Eisenhower was of course thrilled by this sudden and unexpected turn of events that had rescued him from possible obscurity and put him back in the center of the war. As his aide noted, "For the first time since we learned of the possibility of Ike's transfer, we now feel that we have a definite and concrete mission. This adds zest to living and interest in pursuing the objective. It has already made a remarkable difference in Ike. Now he is back to his old system of incessant planning and thinking out loud of qualifications of this or that man for certain jobs."[7]

Before assuming his new duties in England, Marshall ordered Eisenhower back to the States to get some rest. There he spent some time with his family and tried without much success to forget about the war. On 3 January 1944 Marshall invited Eisenhower to dinner at Washington's exclusive Alibi Club with a group of the country's most powerful congressmen. Eisenhower gave a half-hour overview of his war while the men shucked steamed oysters and tossed the shells into large wooden bowls in the middle of the tables. Eisenhower's charm and sincerity worked as well here as elsewhere, and at the end of his speech one observer noted that the congressmen were ready to elect him president by acclamation. Marshall then bestowed his public blessing on Eisenhower by proposing a toast to him. By the time Eisenhower reached England on 16 January, he could be certain that whatever challenges and difficulties he faced in Europe, he had the support of the American political and military establishments back home.[8]

Overlord Lineup

As Marshall recognized in ordering Eisenhower home for a rest, commanding Allied forces for Overlord was a stressful, exhausting, complicated, and almost overwhelming task. The burden of responsibility alone was sufficient to crush even someone with Eisenhower's sturdy constitution. In the Mediterranean Eisenhower's authority was limited and circumscribed by British deputies such as Alexander who oversaw most air, naval, and ground operations. For Overlord, however, Eisenhower, with the War Department's backing, insisted on working directly with his subordinates. As a result, Overlord bore his imprint to a far greater extent than Husky or Avalanche. Unfortunately, this also increased Eisenhower's already heavy workload. Although he remained genial, sharp, and direct,

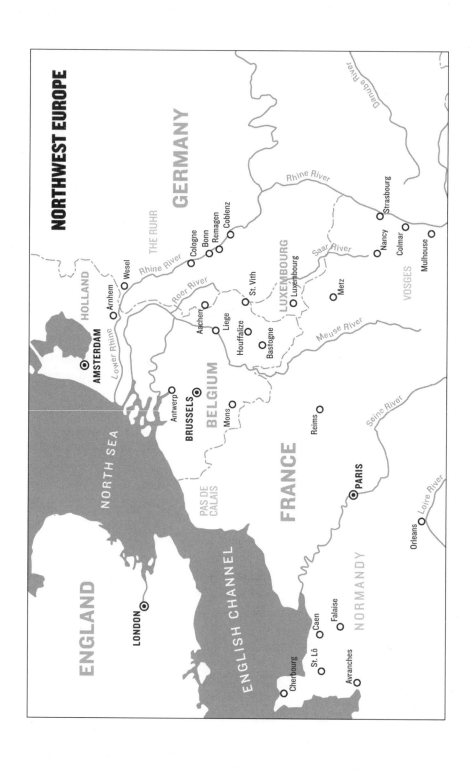

NORTHWEST EUROPE

as the weeks went on Eisenhower's health suffered. He complained of fatigue, eye-strain, and a nonstop ringing in his ear caused by high blood pressure. There was never enough time and resources to satisfy everyone. His military family could not compensate for the loneliness he often felt, and in fact he asked Marshall to send his son, a West Point cadet, over to keep him company because his popularity precluded him from enjoying recreational diversions such as the theater. Despite these and other problems, Eisenhower worked constantly and often traveled around England visiting the troops whose lives depended on his decisions.[9]

One of Eisenhower's most important tasks was reviewing the American ground forces commanders Marshall and McNair had assigned to Overlord. Some of them were already in England as part of Operation Bolero, the American buildup for Overlord that had begun long before Roosevelt appointed Eisenhower to his new post. Others were still stateside, waiting to cross the Atlantic with their headquarters. Fortunately, Marshall gave Eisenhower a free hand to accept or reject these men for any reason. Although Eisenhower joked that Marshall did so to avoid the responsibility for officers who failed, both men understood the seriousness of the issue. After all, Overlord would rise or fall based on the men charged with its implementation. Looking over his ground forces roster, Eisenhower was most concerned with the lack of recent combat experience among so many of his division and corps commanders. Part of the problem was that the army had not yet deployed many divisions and corps overseas, so it did not possess a cadre of high-ranking battle-hardened officers capable of leading large units. Many of the men who did meet this standard were busy fighting in Italy or in the Pacific. As a result, Marshall had been sending corps and division commanders to England who had not yet seen action. He did so partly out of necessity and partly because displacing those who had done good jobs stateside but had not had an opportunity to prove themselves in battle seemed arbitrary and unfair. Eisenhower understood Marshall's reasoning, but two years of warfare in the Mediterranean had convinced him that the more veterans he had in important positions, the better the chances of success. He was especially hesitant toward those rookies with whom he was not personally acquainted from his prewar days. Not surprisingly, then, he made it clear that he would apply the most rigorous standards toward his subordinates, and would relieve immediately those who did not measure up.[10]

Fortunately for Eisenhower, he had no reason to question the competence of his primary American ground forces subordinate. Six months earlier, in July 1943, Eisenhower's predecessor in England, Jake Devers, had asked Marshall to appoint a field army commander to keep pace with British preparations for the cross-Channel assault. Marshall delayed for more than a month, but in late August he decided to act. As far as he was concerned, Omar Bradley was the man most qualified for such an important job. Patton was another possibility, but although Marshall was as of yet unaware of the details of the slapping incidents, Eisenhower had expressed serious enough reservations about Patton's character and judgment for Marshall to pass him over. On the other hand, Eisenhower had nothing but effusive praise for Bradley, and had repeatedly called him the best combat leader he had. These sentiments reflected Marshall's own. Marshall had been a Bradley booster even before the war began, and Bradley had lived up to Marshall's expectations by leading the Second Corps to victory in North Africa and Sicily. Eisenhower was naturally reluctant to surrender his star lieutenant, and in fact initially suggested that Clark go to England instead. In the end, though, Eisenhower's selflessness asserted itself and he agreed to the transfer. Bradley's surprise and pleasure at his promotion more than compensated for the sorrow he felt in leaving the Second Corps. Before traveling to England to assume his new duties, he flew to the States for a brief visit. There he consulted with Marshall and impressed Stimson. By the time he got to work in England, Marshall had entrusted to him the additional chore of setting up an army group headquarters there as well. Marshall at first contemplated assigning McNair or Devers to command this army group, but Eisenhower pushed successfully to give Bradley the army group as soon as it was activated in France, though he did not make his decision official yet. Eisenhower explained to Marshall that he was not familiar with Devers and McNair, whereas Bradley was a known entity of proven value. Indeed, Eisenhower looked forward to working with him again.[11]

By now Bradley had become famous, with a *Time* magazine cover and stories about him in *Life* and *Newsweek* to prove it. None of this made the bashful general very comfortable, so he was happy to concentrate on his work after he reached England. Unfortunately, the rigors of campaigning in the Mediterranean had taken a greater toll on him than he realized. On 10 November a British lorry crashed into Bradley's car on his way to Bristol. The impact threw Bradley to the front of his vehicle, but except for shattered eyeglasses and a gash on his cheek he escaped serious injury. When he went to a nearby American army hospital as a precaution, though, doctors discovered that he suffered so badly from a cold and exhaustion that they kept him there for five days. One of his first responsibilities after he returned to duty was establishing the First Army's headquarters. Most of it arrived from the States in October, but Bradley was not about to rely solely on a bunch of greenhorns. He had instead brought the best staffers from the Second Corps with him and used them to form the nucleus of his First Army headquarters. Although a minority, these Second Corps veterans gave the First Army the tone and character it maintained for the remainder of the conflict. Bradley himself called the First Army staffers tough, arrogant, and impatient men with minimal respect for everyone else. Others noted that the First Army staff always seemed to have a collective chip on its shoulder. For now, however, Bradley managed to smooth their rough edges with his homey personality. One observer noted, "General Bradley is cool, logical, measured and sure of himself and his force. His staff have complete confidence in him. All of the key members went through the African and Sicilian campaigns with him. They are a well integrated, happy and informal lot. They know each other extremely well, work well together, and should do well. They all are completely devoted to General Bradley."[12] As for the army group headquarters, organizing it was not as difficult as Bradley feared because Devers had already done much of the groundwork. In addition to constant meetings and planning, Bradley made continuous inspections of the American units assigned to Overlord and consulted with Eisenhower on their commanders. His calm demeanor, obvious integrity, sympathy, and unflappability, along with the unmistakable competence of someone who had seen considerable action, inspired confidence among his subordinates. One remembered, "I could talk and reason with Bradley, and I had from him a warm feeling that he was supporting me in every way he could at all times."[13]

Once Bradley moved up to army group—assuming of course that the Allies succeeded in establishing themselves in France—someone would have to run the First Army. Eisenhower's initial inclination was to give the job to some deserving corps commander, but he mentioned to Marshall that he was willing to accept a younger stateside field army commander if he came across the Atlantic soon to get up to speed as Bradley's deputy. Marshall in turn recommended General Courtney Hodges, current head of the stateside Third Army. Eisenhower barely knew Hodges, but Marshall assured him, "He is exactly the same class of man as Bradley in practically every respect. Wonderful shot, great hunter, quiet, self-effacing. Thorough understanding of ground fighting."[14] In fact, Marshall had been cultivating Hodges's career for some time. The two men had served together at Fort Benning in the late 1920s and early 1930s when Marshall was assistant commandant there. After World War Two began in Europe, Hodges impressed Marshall with his work with National Guard generals at the Infantry School. Marshall appointed Hodges chief of infantry, secured his promotion to major general, and eventually put him in charge of the Third Army. Along the way he had offered Hodges to Eisenhower as a possible candidate to lead the Central Task Force in the North Africa invasion, and had recently sent him to Italy to observe the fighting there. Although Marshall made it clear to Eisenhower that the decision was his, Eisenhower got the unmistakable hint that Marshall wanted Hodges gainfully employed. On 29 December, Eisenhower radioed Marshall that he would take Hodges as Bradley's understudy and assign him to lead the First Army as soon as Bradley's army group became operational.[15]

Courtney Hodges followed an unconventional path to field army command.

Born in Georgia in 1887, Hodges aspired to be a soldier from an early age. He secured an appointment to West Point in 1904, but washed out in a year because he failed geometry. Undaunted, he enlisted as a private and rose to sergeant two and a half years later. He then passed a competitive exam and was commissioned as a second lieutenant in 1909. After stints in Kansas, Texas, and the Philippines, he participated in Pershing's Punitive Expedition into Mexico in 1916. He saw considerable combat in World War One, and his bravery in France earned him a Distinguished Service Medal, Bronze Star, and Silver Star. After brief occupation duty, he returned to the States and graduated from the Field Artillery School in 1920. He subsequently taught at West Point with Bradley from 1920 to 1924, attended the Command and General Staff School from 1924 to 1925, and worked as an instructor at the Infantry School and Air Corps Tactical School before becoming a member of the Infantry Board in 1929. He punched his ticket at the Army War College from 1933 to 1934, and after that served with the troops for several years before returning to Fort Benning as commandant of the Infantry School. He was chief of infantry when the Japanese bombed Pearl Harbor, and then successively headed the Replacement and Command School, activated the Tenth Corps, and was leading the Third Army when Marshall ordered him to England.

As Marshall informed Eisenhower, Hodges and Bradley were similar in their modesty, shyness, and unpretentiousness. If anything, Hodges's reticence was even more pronounced than Bradley's. He was well respected in the army for his methodical and detail-oriented approach to tactics and training. Marshall and Bradley were among his stoutest admirers, and Eisenhower eventually embraced their evaluation. All of them later lamented that Hodges's taciturn nature prevented him from receiving the credit he deserved for his wartime contributions. Bradley especially lauded Hodges's dependability and steadiness, and wrote in his memoirs:

> A spare, soft-voiced Georgian without temper, drama, or visible emotion, Hodges was left behind in the European headline sweepstakes. He was essentially a military technician whose faultless techniques and tactical knowledge made him one of the most skilled craftsmen of my entire command. . . . Hodges successfully blended dexterity and common sense in such equal portions as to produce a magnificently balanced command. I had implicit faith in his judgment, in his skill and restraint. Of all my Army commanders he required the least supervision.[16]

Others had a different take on Hodges. Patton considered him dumb, but of course he denigrated almost all of his competitors in the privacy of his diary. More credible observers commented that Hodges was only superficially like

Bradley. Both were self-effacing, but Bradley's folksy and empathetic manner inspired confidence in those around him and contributed greatly to his success in managing people. Hodges's colorless reserve, on the other hand, bespoke a secretive, brittle, cold-hearted, and impersonal man with limited imagination. He simply lacked that human touch that made Bradley so effective. Even in good times he came across as remote, cautious, and uninspiring. Hodges worked through a small group of advisers and relied on his forceful and abrasive chief of staff, General William Kean, to explain and enforce his directives. As a result, the First Army headquarters was under Hodges's tutelage a tense and difficult place. Hodges spread this anxiety to the rest of his army by blatantly playing favorites among his corps commanders. He and J. Lawton Collins liked and respected each other, so Hodges gave Collins considerable leeway in developing and implementing plans. On the other hand, Hodges had little faith in most of his remaining corps commanders and rode herd over them in such a way as to smother whatever initiative they brought to the First Army. As an old-fashioned infantryman, Hodges embraced straight-up fighting that sometimes led to unnecessary casualties and was reminiscent of World War One. Ernie Harmon, for example, found Hodges slow, timid, and unoriginal, and attributed whatever success he had to Collins's brilliance. Harmon remembered that after he was relieved from his armored division he stopped by First Army headquarters to see Hodges. Hodges greeted him without enthusiasm and sourly chastised him for not wearing the mandatory green patches on his uniform that identified high-ranking officers. Nor did he respond well to Harmon's flippant comment that he did not need the patches because his men knew who he was. Such an attitude was unlikely to encourage aggressiveness and support. Although Bradley ladled generous praise on Hodges in his memoirs, he later admitted that after observing Hodges in England before D-Day he privately fretted that Hodges was too indecisive and hesitant, and hoped that Kean could compensate for these shortcomings. It is, however, worth noting that during the campaigning in northwest Europe Hodges's First Army fought the hardest battles, inflicted and sustained the highest casualties, and gained the most ground of any of Eisenhower's field armies, including Patton's Third Army. It was Hodges who became the workhorse in Eisenhower's military stable.[17]

Eisenhower's worries about his large number of inexperienced commanders applied particularly to those officers slated to lead Overlord's initial assault waves. The plan called for General Leonard Gerow's Fifth Corps and General Roscoe Woodruff's Seventh Corps to make the first landings, with General Willis Crittenberger's Nineteenth Corps acting as a floating reserve and General Emil Reinhardt's Eighth Corps to follow up. None of these men had yet seen action in the war, and they were therefore bound to make at least some rookie mistakes. In an effort to leaven his roster with some veterans, Eisenhower asked Jacob Devers, now running American affairs in the Mediterranean theater, to transfer Lucian Truscott to England for Overlord. Eisenhower thought a lot of Truscott and had several months earlier recommended his elevation to corps commander. Truscott was an experienced, aggressive, and intelligent general who had fought well in North Africa, Sicily, and southern Italy. As Eisenhower explained to Devers, "This officer and I have been together a long time and I would particularly desire him as an assault corps commander. . . . He is exceptionally well-experienced in planning and executing an amphibious assault."[18] In exchange, Eisenhower offered to give Devers almost any of his corps commanders in England or en route there. Devers, however, knew talent when he saw it, so he turned Eisenhower down. His excuse was that Truscott was scheduled to take over the Sixth Corps when John Lucas moved up to Fifth Army command and Mark Clark left to lead the proposed invasion of southern France. Thoroughly miffed, Eisenhower appealed to Marshall for his help, and added that the months of preparation for Overlord would give Truscott a well-earned rest. Marshall in turn reiterated Eisenhower's request to Devers in a message of his own. This time Devers played the trump card of military necessity by noting that he could not spare Truscott from the imminent Anzio operation. Marshall was unwilling to deprive a subordinate of a qualified division commander on the eve of battle, so he did not insist. Eisenhower was deeply disappointed and lamented Truscott's absence for months. He was also further embittered toward Devers, who had once again outmaneuvered him in a bureaucratic skirmish. As for Truscott, he had no idea about these machinations and did not learn of them until months later.[19]

As it was, Marshall had been thinking about Eisenhower's shortage of experienced officers for some time, and had undertaken steps to alleviate the problem. On 20 December he asked MacArthur to transfer Bob Eichelberger to Europe to take over a field army. Eichelberger had won the United States' first victory on land over the Japanese at Buna in January 1943, but since then a jealous MacArthur had relegated him and his First Corps headquarters to training duties in Australia. Marshall respected Eichelberger and felt that he was wasting his talents Down Under, so he offered to swap him for General J. Lawton Collins, current chief of the crack Twenty-fifth Division in the South Pacific theater. As usual with such personnel issues, Marshall left the decision up to MacArthur. MacArthur turned Marshall down by claiming that he needed Eichelberger's services for future operations. He also stated that although he respected Collins, giving him the First Corps would alienate other, more senior and equally capable, division commanders in the Southwest Pacific theater.

Thus stymied, Marshall took a closer look at Collins. Like Bradley and Hodges, Collins was a Marshall protégé from his Fort Benning days. Marshall had appointed Collins head of the Twenty-fifth Division as part of his effort to place younger men in the war's more responsible positions, and in return Collins had justified Marshall's selection by turning the Twenty-fifth into a first-rate outfit that had performed well at Guadalcanal and New Georgia. After he returned to the States from the Cairo and Teheran conferences, Marshall summoned Collins to his Pentagon office for a chat right after Christmas. Marshall received him cordially, congratulated him on the fine job he had done in the Solomon Islands, and asked him about his time in the Pacific. After Collins finished his narration he brashly reminded Marshall that he had been leading his division for a year now and felt that he was ready to move up to a corps. Marshall had already been thinking along the same lines, but did not want to make any commitments until he consulted Eisenhower. Instead, he replied enigmatically, "Maybe you will." Considerate as ever, Marshall arranged for Collins and his wife, who had been apart for two years, to spend a week at the army resort at White Sulphur Springs in West Virginia to rest and forget about the war for awhile. While they were there the local hospital commander invited Collins to a small dinner at his house and warned him to be on time. When he arrived, Collins was surprised to discover Eisenhower there. Eisenhower said to Collins, "Well, hello Joe, I understand you are coming over to join us." Eisenhower did not elaborate as to any specific assignment, but instead spent the evening talking to Collins about mutual friends. In fact, Marshall had already sold Eisenhower on Collins, but Eisenhower wanted to run the idea past Bradley before making it official. When Collins flew to England in late January, he met with Eisenhower and Bradley and discussed his Pacific War experiences, during which Collins emphasized that he always seized the high ground. When he finished Bradley turned to Eisenhower and said, "He speaks our language." Less than two weeks later, on 12 February, Eisenhower and Bradley gave Collins the Seventh Corps to spearhead the assault on German-occupied France. Explaining the series of events that plucked him from the remote South Pacific jungle and transported him to a primary role in the war against Germany, Collins later declared that he was just lucky to be in the right place at the right time.[20]

In fact, Collins was being uncharacteristically modest; there was a good deal more to his success than mere luck. Born into a large Louisiana family in 1896 that included a brother who also commanded a division in World War Two, Collins graduated from West Point in 1917. He did not get overseas to participate in World War One, but served in the German occupation from 1919 to 1921 before returning to West Point as an instructor for three years. He attended and then taught at the Infantry School from 1925 to 1931, during which time he made Marshall's acquaintance. Stints at the Command and General Staff School, in the Philippines, at the Army Industrial College, and finally at the Army War College followed. Collins had spent almost all of his career in army education, so after the Japanese attacked Pearl Harbor he understandably feared that he would spend the war riding a desk. When he was ordered to the General Staff, he reminded Marshall that back at Fort Benning Marshall had once warned him to avoid staff positions in wartime. Marshall heard him out and roared, "Okay Collins, I'll let you go." In order to get away from Washington as quickly as possible, Collins jumped at the chance to become the Seventh Corps's chief of staff, from which he took over the Twenty-fifth Division. During the Guadalcanal campaign he received the nickname "Lightning Joe" for his aggressiveness and dash. He also contracted malaria at Guadalcanal, but refused to go to the hospital for treatment. His malaria resurfaced in New Georgia, along with a nasty case of gastroenteritis, making the operation his most miserable of the war. Once he was back in Washington, his malaria flared up for a third time, but he hid it from the doctors so they could not stop him from going to Europe.[21]

Collins was, like Truscott, one of the two or three best corps commanders the army produced in World War Two, and in fact Bradley later claimed that he relied on him more than on anyone else at his level. At forty-eight years old, he was younger than most men of his rank, with slicked-back hair and a cowlick, a set chin, and an uneasy smile. Brash, opinionated, energetic, and hard-driving, Collins was one of those subordinates who had to be reined in. When one division commander told him that he was holding the enemy in check, Collins exclaimed, "Hold the enemy in check? I knew you could do that, I want you to advance. This is an offensive."[22] There was, however, more to Collins than raw aggression. Again like Truscott, he put considerable thought into the nuts and bolts of waging war. He emphasized being flexible in planning and execution, gaining accurate intelligence about enemy strength and intentions, and keeping in constant touch with subordinates so they understood the situation. He had high standards and was ruthless toward those who failed to measure up to them. He combined his forcefulness with an eloquence he had cultivated as an interwar instructor to make even his boldest proposals sound reasonable. Not surprisingly, his bravado, overly smooth and polished manner, obvious ambition, independent attitude, and appreciation for publicity rubbed some people the wrong way. Sandy Patch, eventual commander of the Seventh Army, detested Collins from their days together on Guadalcanal. Oscar Griswold, under whom Collins served on New Georgia, recommended against ever elevating Collins to a corps because of his excessive assertiveness. Patton disliked him as well. Most of his American colleagues, though, welcomed him to the European theater and looked forward to working with him. This was especially true of Courtney Hodges. Collins and Hodges had known each other at Fort Benning, and although they had very different temperaments, they established a close and mutually beneficial relationship that paid big dividends in the war in northwestern Europe.[23]

In addition to Collins, Marshall procured for Eisenhower one other high-ranking combat veteran from the Pacific War. On 1 February Pete Corlett's Seventh Division landed on Kwajalein in the Marshall Islands as part of Operation Flintlock. The day before elements of the Seventh Division had seized a couple of lightly held islets offshore, enabling Corlett to emplace artillery there to support the main attack by pounding Kwajalein's Japanese defenders from a secure position. This proved one of the keys to the operation's success. Kwajalein fell after four days of combat and less than a thousand American casualties. As a reward for a job well done, Nelly Richardson, commander of the army's Pacific Ocean Area forces, elevated Corlett to lead the newly formed Twenty-fourth Corps and lauded him in a dispatch to Marshall. Marshall did not know Corlett well, but had heard good things about him since before Pearl Harbor. His successful assault at Kwajalein gave him the kind of amphibious warfare experience that Marshall felt could be put to good use in Europe. In a 17 February message to Eisenhower, Marshall praised Corlett's training, planning, and cooperation with the navy. He would, continued Marshall, make a fine corps commander if Eisenhower wanted him. After consulting with Bradley, Eisenhower responded two days later that he would take Corlett. He added, however, that planning was too far advanced to give him one of the corps slated to go ashore on D-Day, but he would instead assign him to the Nineteenth Corps. Eisenhower also promised to utilize whatever amphibious advice Corlett cared to impart. Corlett stopped in Washington en route to England and talked with Marshall, Stimson, and others. He found everyone enthusiastic about the contribution that they believed he could make to Overlord.[24]

The Colorado-born Corlett earned his nickname "Cowboy Pete" at West Point because of his western rancher background. After graduating near the bottom of his West Point class in 1913, he was posted first to remote Alaska, and then to New York and the Mexican border. He served with the signal corps in France in World War One, during which he contracted chronic bronchitis. After the conflict he attended the Command and General Staff School and Army War College in quick succession. He was one of only three World War Two corps commanders—Oscar Griswold and Palmer Swift were the others—who ranked in the bottom half of his Command and General Staff School class. He was also one of the few corps commanders who never went to one of the branch schools. Instead, he taught at the Coastal Artillery School and then the Command and General Staff School in the late 1920s. After running a battalion he worked with the Civilian Conservation Corps in Oregon before a stint at the General Staff in Washington in the mid-1930s. He subsequently became provost martial at Schofield Barracks in Hawaii, commander of a regiment, and was finally sent to Alaska after the war began. He participated in the bloodless occupation of Kiska in the spring of 1943, from which he ascended to the Seventh Division.

Although Eisenhower greeted Corlett with his customary warmth, the same could not be said of the rest of Eisenhower's entourage. This was partially due to personality. Corlett was an abrasive, high-strung, short-tempered, and unpolished officer whom Bradley later referred to as his own worst enemy. Equally free with his opinions and emotions, Corlett rarely fit in well with any team. Tact and discretion were simply not part of his interpersonal toolkit. Once he reached England, Corlett was deeply disturbed that no one seemed interested in taking advantage of his amphibious expertise, even though he had just gone through a big amphibious operation in the Marshall Islands. The only exception was Sandy Patch, who flew to England from the Mediterranean specifically to pick Corlett's brain for ideas for the invasion of southern France. Being an outspoken man, Corlett offered his unsolicited advice anyway. He repeatedly and presciently warned that Allied planners were not stockpiling enough artillery ammunition for such a big campaign and stated that the Americans needed to use more specialized landing craft called Alligators to reach the beach quickly and intact on D-Day. Corlett estimated that in the European War Americans were six months behind their Pacific War counterparts in amphibious knowledge, yet they seemed to treat him like an interloper and bush leaguer. At one point, for instance, an angry Beetle Smith cut off one of Corlett's litanies by exclaiming, "Do I have to defend the plan to you?"[25]

Marshall procured one other combat veteran for Eisenhower: Troy Middleton. Unlike the case with Collins and Corlett, Eisenhower was thoroughly familiar with Middleton, who had ably led the Forty-fifth Division at Sicily, Salerno, and southern Italy. Mark Clark and John Lucas had relieved Middleton of his command the previous November because Middleton's arthritic knee rendered him ineffective in the Italian mountains. When Middleton first returned to the States, Marshall considered sending him to Hawaii to take over the new Twenty-fourth Corps because he figured there would be little need for mountain climbing in the Central Pacific. Marshall reconsidered, however, after Eisenhower complained about his dearth of experienced leaders for Overlord. Marshall had met Middleton immediately after World War One. In their first encounter, he noticed that some of Middleton's men were struggling to help a hungover comrade march down a road. A puzzled Marshall suggested that Middleton simply place the troublesome soldier into an ambulance, but Middleton refused because it would lower the morale of his comrades. Marshall later called Middleton the army's outstanding World War One regimental commander, and his performance in the Mediterranean did nothing to alter Marshall's opinion. The problem was whether Middleton's weak knee could withstand the rigors of another campaign. In late February Marshall phoned Middleton, then leading the stateside Twelfth Corps on maneuvers in Tennessee, and explained the situation. Middleton claimed that his knee was fine now that he was away from the Italian mountains. In fact, he had joked to Jacob Devers a few months earlier that his knee hurt only when he was doing what he should not be doing—sitting around. Even after Marshall emphasized the seriousness of a corps commander being unable to physically fulfill his duties, Middleton insisted he could do the job Marshall had in mind. In response, Marshall cabled Eisenhower that although he was not altogether comfortable about dispatching a potential invalid on such an important mission, Middleton was head and shoulders above all other stateside corps commanders. Eisenhower and Bradley, on the other hand, had no such reservations. Eisenhower had recommended Middleton as a corps commander the previous August and was happy to secure his services now. He supposedly said, "I'd rather have Troy Middleton on crutches than most of these people."[26] Just to make sure this did not happen, Marshall assigned to Middleton a sergeant who had been a prewar physical therapist and ordered him to massage Middleton's knee twice a day. There was some talk of making Middleton Patton's Third Army chief of staff, but Patton stated that he preferred to pick his own man, and anyway Middleton wanted a combat job. He took over the Eighth Corps when he arrived in England in early March.[27]

Middleton was born in Mississippi in 1889. His hopes of attending West Point and becoming an officer failed when he did not get an appointment to the military academy, but instead of giving up he enlisted in the army in 1910 and received a commission two years later. He participated in the Veracruz operation in 1914 and then went overseas to France in World War One. He rose rapidly in the ranks and ended the conflict as the youngest regimental commander in the American Expeditionary Force, seeing action at the Second Marne, St. Mihiel, and the Argonne. After postwar duty in occupied Germany he returned to the United States and graduated from the Infantry School in 1921 and the Command and General Staff School in 1924. He subsequently taught at the Command and General Staff School for four years, during which he instructed almost every American army World War Two field army and corps commander at one time or another. He went to the Army War College in 1928 and then became commandant of Louisiana State University's Reserve Officer Training Corps for six years. He was in the Philippines when he got an offer from Louisiana State to rejoin the school as its dean of administration. His friend Eisenhower recommended against it because he believed a war was coming and Middleton would surely be a general in it, but Middleton retired from the army and took the job anyway. He offered his services to the army after the Japanese bombed Pearl Harbor, but insisted on a combat post. Marshall complied, and Middleton ended up with the Forty-fifth Division, which according to McNair was the best-trained division to leave the States when it went overseas to the Mediterranean for the invasion of Sicily. Middleton's performances at Sicily, Salerno, and southern Italy impressed Eisenhower,

Bradley, Clark, Lucas, and even Patton. He was, however, thoroughly disillusioned and unhappy with the progress of the Italian campaign when Lucas and Clark relieved him of his command. After Middleton examined the Shingle operation and started the preparations for the invasion of southern France, Marshall brought him back to America.[28]

Middleton was not an unfriendly person, but he came across to others as somewhat distant and restrained. He was a calm, straightforward, and down-to-earth man who reminded people more of a college professor than a soldier. Indeed, he possessed an academic's dispassion and frequently seemed to lack the enthusiasm of other generals. He often did not appear to care what others thought of him. He instead projected an aura of quiet professional efficiency. He expressed his wishes clearly and reasonably and without ever raising his voice. His World War One record and years as an instructor at the Command and General Staff School gave him a reputation as a master tactician even before Pearl Harbor that his time as a division and corps commander did nothing to tarnish. He developed intelligent, commonsensical, and methodical plans appropriate to the military situation, but was also capable of adapting and reacting to the enemy. There was, however, more to Middleton than mere tactical acumen. He was in fact a serious student of all things military, so that even Patton borrowed some of his ideas. For example, he noted that once an officer had gained his men's respect, all things from discipline on became possible. For all his diffidence and detachment, Middleton also possessed an iron resolve and mental toughness that served him well. He later noted:

> I think you have to like [war]. I hate to say this, but frankly I liked it. I enjoyed it. I got pleasure out of it. There's nothing more satisfying to me than working with people, no matter what they're doing! If they're fighting, be a fighter. I think I can truthfully say that I had reason to believe that I would be killed and so, what of it? You might as well give them your best while you're living and forget about that. That sounds silly, but death never occurred to me in war. I was thinking about getting the other fellow.[29]

To make way for Collins, Corlett, and Middleton, Eisenhower and Bradley decided to rid themselves of Crittenberger, Reinhardt, and Woodruff. Here Devers proved helpful by asking for Crittenberger as a spare corps commander in the Mediterranean. Eisenhower did not think much of Crittenberger, so he was happy to let him go. Nor was he especially enamored with Reinhardt, whom Patton disliked because of his lack of combat experience. Eisenhower transferred him back to the States, from where he eventually returned to Europe at the head of a division. As for Woodruff, Devers had brought him over to England the previous summer to lead the Seventh Corps. Eisenhower and Bradley had both gone to West Point with Woodruff, were personally fond of him, and believed he had done a fine job training the Seventh Corps. However, he had not yet seen action in the war, and Eisenhower and Bradley were deeply concerned about giving such an important job to an untested man. They initially transferred him to the Nineteenth Corps in place of Crittenberger, but after they secured Corlett, Bradley drove to see Woodruff and personally broke the bad news that they were sending him home. Woodruff was not surprisingly confused and heartbroken. He later wrote, "I was completely crushed. I hadn't the foggiest idea of what the hell had been going on. Nobody had made the suggestion to me, 'Woody you ought to be doing this,' 'You ought to be doing that.'"[30]Eisenhower's and Bradley's sympathy did not overcome their desire to do what they considered militarily sound. On the other hand, Eisenhower pointed out to Marshall that Woodruff had not really done anything wrong and asked him to give Woodruff Corlett's new Twenty-fourth Corps in the Pacific. Unfortunately for Woodruff, McNair for some reason decided that Woodruff was now tainted goods and as such was ineligible for another corps. After Woodruff spent several months in the States, Marshall sent him to the Philippines on a vague mission that would eventually turn his career around.[31]

Woodruff later grumbled quite accurately that Eisenhower's and Bradley's concerns about inexperienced corps commanders in important positions did not apply to General Leonard "Gee" Gerow, head of the Fifth Corps. There were, however, reasons for this apparent inconsistency. For one thing, Gerow had for some time been an integral part of Overlord planning, so removing him at this late date would complicate and perhaps compromise the entire operation. Of perhaps greater importance, Gerow was good friends with both Bradley and Eisenhower. Gerow and Bradley had attended the Infantry School together in the mid-twenties and had remained close since. Gerow and Eisenhower had met along the Mexican border before World War One and were later study partners at the Command and General Staff School. According to Gerow, their relationship at that time was akin to that of brothers. From this perspective, it was hardly surprising that Eisenhower and Bradley had complete confidence in Gerow's abilities, even though he had not yet heard a shot fired in anger in the war. On the other hand, Marshall had his reservations about Gerow. He had been sufficiently impressed with Gerow to appoint him his chief of war plans in December 1940, but felt that Gerow gradually grew stale from overwork and eventually ceased to be useful. Indeed, when Gerow turned the War Plans Division over to Eisenhower, Gerow said to him, "Well, I got Pearl Harbor on the book; lost the PI [Philippine Islands], Sumatra and all the NEI [Netherlands East Indies] north of the barrier. Let's see what you can do."[32] Although Marshall agreed to McNair's recommendation to elevate Gerow to division command in February 1942, his doubts remained. He did not believe that Gerow possessed sufficient drive to be an effective combat commander. Gerow did a good job training the Twenty-ninth Division in England, and ascended to lead the Fifth Corps after Devers removed Scrappy Hartle for excessive drinking and partying. McNair gave Devers a list of candidates to succeed Hartle, from which Devers selected Gerow because he had proven himself with the Twenty-ninth and because he was already on hand and knew the situation.[33]

Fortunately for the American cause, there was more to Gerow than connections and availability. Born in 1888, he was the only active World War Two corps commander who graduated from the Virginia Military Institute. He was commissioned in 1911, participated in the Veracruz occupation, and was after that stationed along the Mexican border. He went overseas to France in World War One as a signal corps officer and took part in the Second Marne, St. Mihiel, and Argonne campaigns. After the conflict he commanded the Signal Corps School from 1919 to 1921 before attending the Infantry School in 1924, the Command and General Staff School from 1925 to 1926, and the Army War College from 1930 to 1931. He then served in the Philippines and China before going to the War Plans Division in 1935, where he remained in one capacity or another until after Pearl Harbor. Gerow was the quintessential southern gentleman officer—courtly, considerate, and restrained. One observer recalled:

> General Gerow never called anybody by their first name. That was too familiar. And, the only people who called him anything but General that I ran across, were either Bradley or Eisenhower. . . . But, the division commanders in the Corps never called General Gerow anything but General Gerow, and he would call them by their last names. So, he was pretty strict, out of the old school-type soldier, not that he was nasty. He was just that way.[34]

Eisenhower valued him for his steadiness, loyalty, common sense, work ethic, and conscientiousness. He was also intelligent, precise, organized, and calm under pressure. If he lacked dynamism and passion and possessed the aura of a perpetual staff officer, his equanimity enabled him to listen to both sides of an argument without prejudice and respond objectively. He was well aware of the dangers his corps would face landing at Omaha beach on D-Day, but tried to remain optimistic and not let the aggravating bursitis in his shoulder that plagued him that spring bother him.[35]

Fitting George Patton into the upcoming campaign was perhaps Eisenhower's thorniest personnel problem. Although angered and disappointed by Patton's personal behavior on Sicily, Eisenhower remained fond of Patton and continued to respect his undeniable military abilities. Therefore, Eisenhower was throughout the winter of 1943–1944 adamant that Patton receive an assignment some-where commensurate with his talents. In late September, for example, Eisenhower had recommended Patton to Marshall as a field army commander for the cross-Channel assault everyone at that point assumed Marshall would lead. Eisenhower's appointment to command Overlord did not, however, automatically secure Patton a prominent position in the operation. Eisenhower stated that he wanted Patton for a field army in England, but was willing to give him up if there was good military reason to use him elsewhere. Marshall and Stimson, for their part, continued to value Patton, but did not want to force him on anyone, especially Eisenhower. As a result, Marshall and Eisenhower danced tentatively around the issue for several weeks. In January there was some talk of leaving Patton in the Mediterranean to head the invasion of southern France. Eisenhower opined to Marshall that Patton was familiar with the theater and the Seventh Army, got along well with the French who would play an integral role in the operation, and was readily available for the mission. In the end, the plan fell through because the slapping incidents had so soured Devers on Patton that he did not want Patton in his theater. This cleared the way for Patton to take over the new Third Army in England. Whatever the complexities of using or not using Patton, it was one of the army's intellectuals who cut to the heart of the matter. When Eisenhower so-licited Troy Middleton's opinion, Middleton replied, "Hell, I would have him up here. He is a fighter and that's what you pay an officer to do, is fight. . . . Get him up here Ike."[36] In asking for Patton, though, Eisenhower made it clear to Marshall that he would never advance him beyond the field army level. By the time Patton arrived in England, it was too late to employ him in the initial attack on the conti-nent. Instead, Overlord planners integrated him into Operation Fortitude, in which the Allies sought to convince the Germans that a largely fictitious army group under Patton was preparing for an invasion of Pas-de-Calais and that any other landing was merely secondary or diversionary. Not until the Allies had firmly established themselves on the continent would Patton and his Third Army enter the campaign.[37]

Eisenhower did not consult Bradley about his decision to assign Patton to the Third Army. He foresaw the possibility of conflict between the two men now that their roles were reversed, but hoped that Patton would reconcile himself to the new arrangement. Eisenhower guessed correctly that Patton would be so grateful for a chance to get back into the war that he would set aside his pride and loyally serve his former subordinate. Just to make sure, though, as soon as Patton reached England Eisenhower called him in for a blunt talk about his expectations. As for Bradley, he later stated frankly that he would not have recommended Patton's ap-pointment because he questioned Patton's conduct during the Sicily campaign. Before Bradley had left the Mediterranean the previous September to assume his new duties in England he had visited Patton at his headquarters in Sicily to say goodbye. Patton was in the doghouse after the slapping incidents and was deeply dejected by news that his Seventh Army would be practically disbanded, leaving him without a clear role. The stark contrast between the two men's futures made Bradley uncomfortable. Patton spent much of the evening giving Bradley ideas for Overlord to pass along to Marshall, who both men assumed would lead the operation. When Bradley met with Marshall in the States, he did not put in a good word for Patton. Instead, he voiced his unhappiness with the Seventh Army's performance in Sicily. Although he later claimed he avoided personalities, Marshall could hardly have missed Bradley's implied condemnation of Patton. Bradley was unhappy when he learned of Eisenhower's decision, but hoped for the best and did not complain. Like the good soldier he was, he opted to suppress his feelings, obey his orders, and work with Patton.[38]

It was a changed Patton who arrived in England on 26 January to assume his new duties. After the slapping incident the previous August, he had endured several months of disgrace, uncertainty, and forced inactivity. Eisenhower took away almost all of his troops and left him in virtual exile at his Seventh Army headquarters in Sicily to contemplate his behavior and future. During that time he heard various and unspecific rumors about a new assignment that merely exacerbated his insecurities. His hopes of becoming an army group commander evaporated when Bradley got the job, and Patton worried that Eisenhower would put him in charge of a training army in England, in which case he decided he would resign his commission rather than suffer such an inglorious fate. Eisenhower instead gave him the Third Army after delivering a stern lecture on self-control. Leading a follow-up field army was not Patton's ideal mission, but it was better than nothing, and he opted to make the best of it. The slapping incidents had done little to damage irretrievably Patton's faith in his own destiny, and he also retained his penchant for flattery, his self-confidence, his philosophical bent, and his habit of denigrating most of his competitors in the privacy of his diary. On the other hand, he now felt like a man under siege who had to constantly prove himself despite an exemplary combat record. He believed he was surrounded by enemies, or anyhow by people who did not necessarily have his best interests at heart. Even his erstwhile friend Bradley, Patton learned, had badmouthed him to the chief of staff. This compelled Patton to denounce his new boss in his diary in an unfair and oft-quoted tirade:

> Bradley is a man of great mediocrity. At Benning in command, he failed to get discipline. At Gafsa, when it looked as though the Germans might turn our right flank he suggested that we withdraw corps headquarters to Feriana. I refused to move. In Sicily, when the 45th Division approached Cefalu, he

halted them for fear of a possible German landing east of Termini. I had to order him to move and told him that I would be responsible for his rear, and that his timidity had lost us one day. He tried to stop the landing operation #2 east of Cap d'Orlando because he thought it was dangerous. I told him I would take the blame if it failed and that he could have the credit if it was a success. Finally, on the night of August 16–17, he asked me to call off the landing east of Milazzo for fear our troops might shoot at each other. He also failed to get word to all units of the II Corps on the second paratroop landing.[39]

Whatever his mindset toward his former star lieutenant, Patton was determined to keep his mouth shut and his head down if that was what it took to get back into the war. He said nothing to Bradley about his betrayal and instead pledged whole-hearted cooperation. He also swallowed Eisenhower's periodic Dutch uncle speeches about proper conduct. In fact, months of reflection had given Patton a degree of circumspection and self-awareness he hitherto had lacked, so much so that he wrote in his diary, "I have grown in stature, in poise, in self-confidence, and in self-control very much."[40] This hard-earned wisdom manifested itself in all sorts of ways, including in his dealings with his subordinates. Patton realized that in North Africa and Sicily his frequent use of public humiliation and unconstructive browbeating generated considerable resentment and hurt feelings among them. Shouting remained an integral part of Patton's interpersonal communications arsenal, but he now coupled it with a new sense of understanding and forgiveness. For instance, he emphasized to his corps commanders that he would not relieve them for occasional mistakes, especially if those errors resulted from their boldness and initiative. In so doing, he provided them with a sense of security that encouraged them to take risks that paid big dividends in the fighting in northwestern Europe. Small wonder that Bradley later observed that in some ways the slapping incidents were the best thing that ever happened to Patton.[41]

Unhappily for Patton, he had to surmount one more hurdle before he could return to the war. On 25 April he made a short speech to a crowd in Knutsford. Patton incorrectly believed that no reporters were present when he joked about "English ladies" and "American dames" and added, "Since it is the evident destiny of the British and Americans, and, of course, the Russians to rule the world, the better we know each other, the better job we will do."[42] Stateside newspapers immediately condemned Patton for his comments. The *Washington Post*, for example, opined that Patton's remarks demonstrated a lack of dignity that undermined his ability to lead regardless of his military talents. Marshall was especially upset because the hullabaloo threatened to derail his efforts to get the Senate to confirm a slate of promotions that included Patton's to permanent major general. Eisenhower was furious with Patton when he heard the news. To Eisenhower, this was conclusive evidence that Patton lacked sufficient self-control for his position, and he cabled Marshall that he was considering drastic measures—meaning removing Patton from his command. Before he acted, though, Eisenhower opted to talk with Patton and hear his side of the story. Marshall left the matter in Eisenhower's hands, but noted that as a battle-tested leader, Patton was a rare commodity. Patton was not surprisingly confused and angry at the hubbub and concluded that a vindictive journalist had set him up. As the seriousness of the situation sank in, he feared that he would lose his new job and even wrote to his wife that they might get the opportunity to go sailing in the Chesapeake soon.

By the time Patton drove to Eisenhower's headquarters on 1 May for their meeting, Eisenhower's anger had cooled somewhat for several reasons. For one thing, Eisenhower and Bradley were unsure with whom to replace Patton, and again lamented their inability to secure Truscott's services. In addition, Marshall hinted that he preferred that Eisenhower hold onto Patton. Marshall radioed that while it was Eisenhower's call, "My view, and it is merely that, is that you should not weaken your hand for Overlord. . . . Consider only Overlord and your own heavy burden of responsibility for its success. Everything else is of minor importance."[43] Finally, Eisenhower received evidence that Patton was unaware of the presence of the reporter when he made his observations. When Patton arrived he offered to resign for the good of the cause and/or have his name withdrawn from the promotions list. As he made his apology, he placed his forehead on Eisenhower's shoulder. Eisenhower felt ridiculous when Patton's helmet fell off his head and rolled across the room. Without a trace of embarrassment of his own, Patton picked up his helmet, put it on and adjusted it, saluted, and asked, "Sir, could I now go back to my headquarters?" Eisenhower made no commitments one way or another, so a dejected Patton recited poetry to himself during the long drive back to his headquarters and tried to remember that it was his destiny to do great things in the conflict. Two days later, Eisenhower told him that he had decided to retain him. Eisenhower explained to Marshall that he did not want to lose Patton's undoubted experience and skills. A grateful and relieved Patton noted in his diary, "Sometimes I am very fond of him [Eisenhower], and this is one of the times."[44]

Overlord was the most complicated military operation in history. The basic idea was to establish a foothold on the European continent from which the Allies could march on Germany itself. The Allied plan called for landing 160,000 American, British, and Canadian soldiers at five Normandy beaches on the first day, and then reinforcing them as rapidly as possible. Coordinating the various Allied air, ground, and naval units was extraordinarily difficult. The navy alone allotted 5,300 vessels of various kinds to Overlord. As the big day—D-Day—approached, the stress took a toll on some high-ranking Allied officers responsible for organizing the operation. Beetle Smith was so exhausted by the constant paperwork and meetings that he claimed he would never thereafter be an effective chief of staff, and he looked forward to retiring from the army immediately after the war ended. The strain got to Eisenhower too, but he continued to project an easygoing confidence and reassurance during his innumerable inspection trips. As he mingled with the troops, he invariably asked the GIs for their hometowns in the hopes of finding someone from Abilene, Kansas. He usually traveled by train, and after visiting each camp he invited the senior officers aboard for a fine dinner in an informal setting.

In early June thousands of soldiers began boarding the transports that would take them across the English Channel to France, while thousands more moved southward to take over the now-abandoned assembly areas to wait their turns. There were the usual last-minute loading problems and snafus, but the process went relatively smoothly. As the troops made themselves as comfortable as they could in their cramped quarters, Bradley summoned his top lieutenants to his Bristol headquarters for one final conference. Using a pointer and a map of France, Bradley in his usual quiet and professional manner explained the mission of each American corps and division so everyone would be working from the same page. When he finished, he dismissed the assemblage with a simple, "Good luck, men." Patton was, on the other hand, a good deal more emotional when he saw Bradley off a little later. Clenching Bradley's hands, Patton said, "Brad, the best of luck to you. We'll be meeting again—soon, I hope." Now that the preparations were over, Bradley was relaxed as he boarded the cruiser USS *Augusta*. He was also so embarrassed by a large bandage on his nose covering a recently lanced boil that he prohibited photographers from taking his picture. While he settled in on *Augusta*, his staffers joked nervously about the numerous "one-way" signs dotting the docks. Hodges was there too, looking jaunty and upbeat as he puffed a cigarette on the end of a holder. Unfortunately, storms delayed the armada's departure by a day, but Eisenhower made the tough decision to take advantage of a forecasted break in the weather to order the landing on 6 June. On the amphibious command ship USS *Ancon*, Gee Gerow chatted amiably with his friend General Tom Handy, Marshall's operations officer, who had crossed the Atlantic to watch the campaign unfold. Over on the attack transport USS *Bayfield*, Joe Collins was nervous about the poor weather and the accompanying delay, but when Admiral Don Moon woke him in the middle of the night to tell him that the operation was on again, Collins found the scene so surreal that he had no trouble falling back to sleep. Thousands of other soldiers, most much younger and less experienced than Collins, tried with varying success to calm their nerves, settle their stomachs, and get some rest.[45]

Victory in France

Allied planners dubbed the easternmost American beach "Omaha" and assigned its seizure to Gerow's Fifth Corps. Gerow in turn gave the job to elements of the First and Twenty-ninth divisions. Although before the invasion Gerow had been so deeply concerned about underwater obstacles at Omaha that Eisenhower had had to buck him up, these were the least of his problems on D-Day. The surrounding heights at Omaha provided excellent defensive positions for the German division that had, unbeknownst to Allied intelligence, recently taken up residence there. Preliminary naval bombardment did insufficient damage to the German defenders, and the infantry did not get the armored support it needed because many of the amphibious tanks were launched too far out in the sea and foundered in the choppy Channel waters. Finally, Corlett's prediction that the lack of specialized landing craft would handicap operations proved true. As a result, the first waves of assaulting infantry ran into heavy opposition and were roughly handled. Indeed, it initially appeared that German fire would destroy the Americans at the water's edge. Fortunately, the First Division was a veteran outfit that had seen action at North Africa and Sicily. Its commander, General Clarence Huebner, had taken over after Terry Allen's relief and had put considerable effort into instilling some discipline into the prima donna Big Red One that paid off on D-Day. Individual soldiers took the initiative to get off the beach and push inland. The accompanying Twenty-ninth Division was a rookie unit and therefore lacked the First Division's combat savvy, but assistant commander General Norman "Dutch" Cota ranged up and down the line inspiring his frightened GIs to move forward. Offshore, some of the smaller warships closed in to pulverize German gun emplacements. As the morning wore on and Allied firepower and numbers came into play, the Americans gradually carved out a shallow toehold.

On *Acton*, Gerow nervously listened to the sketchy and discouraging reports from Omaha. In an effort to secure more information, he dispatched his chief of staff and Tom Handy to the beach to take a look. By the time the officers arrived many of the surviving troops had advanced inland, but German artillery continued to pound the shoreline, and death and destruction were everywhere. To the visiting officers, the GIs seemed in good spirits, and Cota was positive. When they returned to *Acton*, Handy told Gerow that there was little he could do except to continue to send men ashore as quickly as possible. Gerow himself landed later in the day and spent the night sleeping in a ditch like everyone else. By then the blown and bloodied Americans had secured a precarious beachhead at the cost of 2,000 casualties. Considering the mayhem around them, it was hardly surprising that Gerow and Huebner were somewhat depressed when Bradley visited them the next day. Bradley had actually considered evacuating Omaha on D-Day, so he was relieved to see that the situation was improving and did his best to cheer up the two disconsolate generals. The situation remained touch and go for several days, though, and as late as 12 June Gerow told Bradley that he was worried because he had no reserves with which to repel a serious German counterattack.[46]

The other American beach was "Utah," located on the eastern side of the Cotentin Peninsula. Allied planners selected Utah to facilitate a drive on the city of Cherbourg at the top of the peninsula. In American hands, Cherbourg's port would greatly alleviate the Allies' logistical needs. Here things went much more smoothly for the GIs in Joe Collins's Seventh Corps than at Omaha because German defenses were weak. The first waves of General Ray "Tubby" Barton's Fourth Division landed in the wrong place, but found almost no Germans there. Rather than look this gift horse in the mouth, assistant division commander General Theodore Roosevelt Jr., the son of the twenty-sixth president, opted to start the war from there. By the end of D-Day the Fourth Division had secured the beachhead while losing fewer than 200 men, and elements of the Ninetieth Division were already coming ashore. Although Bradley encouraged a trim and confident Collins to get moving to take some pressure off of Gerow's beleaguered corps, Collins needed little urging. Moreover, General Maxwell Taylor's 101st Airborne Division had already seized many of the causeways over the swamps leading inland from Utah after its jump into Normandy during the night of 5–6 June. Consequently, Collins broke out of the beachhead on 8 June. Stiffening German opposition and broken terrain slowed the Americans down, but Collins was everywhere, prodding his subordinates to advance. Collins was fortunate to have some of the best American divisions available, including especially General Manton Eddy's crack Ninth Division, veterans of North Africa and Sicily. The Ninth drove across the base of the Cotentin and sealed it off on 18 June. With scarcely a pause, Eddy turned his division ninety degrees to the north and pressed toward Cherbourg. On 21 June Collins's three divisions—the Fourth, the Ninth, and General Ira Wyche's Seventy-ninth—launched an all-out attack on the city. Despite considerable air and naval support, the Seventh Corps still had to fight hard to overcome Cherbourg's defenders, but organized resistance ended on 27 June. Unfortunately, German demolition teams so wrecked the port that it was months before it was operating at full capacity. As for Collins, he chose not to rest on his laurels, but instead looked forward to reengaging the Germans to the south.[47]

Cherbourg's fall was a bright spot in a generally frustrating and unfulfilling military picture for the Allies in Normandy throughout June and most of July. The British, led by General Bernard Montgomery, had gotten ashore on D-Day more easily than the Americans, but their repeated attempts in the ensuing weeks to seize Caen and break out of their bridgehead failed. Their efforts, however, benefited the Americans by siphoning off the bulk of German armor in Normandy. Unfortunately, the Americans were unable to take advantage of this German weakness in their sector for several reasons. One big and mostly unanticipated problem was the terrain. Western Normandy was dotted with hedgerows—large earthen walls full of interconnected tree branches and roots that surrounded fields. The hedgerows turned every field into a miniature fortress from which well-concealed German soldiers could shoot at advancing GIs. Tanks lacked the power to plow through the hedgerows, and the Germans often destroyed those attempting to do so by targeting their exposed underbellies. Collins observed that the topography was even worse than Guadalcanal's. This spooky combat environment unnerved even veteran troops, of which Bradley's First Army contained painfully few. Except for the First, Ninth, Second Armored, and Eighty-second Airborne divisions, none of the large units in Normandy had yet seen action, so they made plenty of rookie mistakes. Frightened GIs froze under fire, relied excessively on artillery support, and were reluctant to take the initiative. The result was stalemate in Normandy. Bradley activated Corlett's Nineteenth Corps and Middleton's Eighth Corps on 14 June and 15 June, respectively, but kept them and Gerow's Fifth Corps on the defensive until Collins stormed Cherbourg because he lacked the ammunition to support more than one major operation. After Cherbourg fell, Bradley on 3 July unleashed Middleton for an all-out attack to the south. Although he threw Collins's Seventh Corps and Corlett's Nineteenth Corps into the fray, the offensive sputtered to a halt. Corlett managed to take St. Lo on 18 July, but this was short of the breakthrough Bradley had hoped for. By the end of the month the First Army had suffered over 100,000 casualties in Normandy. Bradley no doubt had these frustrating days in mind when he later wrote:

Incentive is not ordinarily part of an infantryman's life. For him there are not 25 or 50 missions to be completed for a ticket home. Instead the rifleman trudges into battle knowing that statistics are stacked against his survival. He fights without promise of either reward or relief. Beyond every river, there's another hill—and behind that hill, another river. After weeks or months in the line only a wound can offer him the comfort of safety, shelter, and a bed. Those who are left to fight, fight on, evading death but knowing that with each day of evasion they have exhausted one more chance for survival. Sooner or later, unless victory comes, the chase must end on the litter or in the grave.[48]

During the difficult Normandy campaign the American high command remained remarkably cohesive and united down to the corps level. Marshall visited London and Normandy shortly after D-Day, and upon his return to the States he wrote the president and secretary of war that Eisenhower and his staffers were confident, efficient, and in control of the situation. After Cherbourg fell Marshall sent a cheering note to Bradley praising his "great battle management" and extending his congratulations to his corps commanders, especially Collins. Eisenhower was equally satisfied with Bradley. He recognized Bradley's problems, but lauded his steadfastness and urged him to keep fighting hard. Eisenhower and Bradley in turn supported their corps commanders despite their collective inability to deliver decisive battlefield results. Bradley called on them frequently and encouraged them in his quiet and folksy way. When Gerow at one point noted that his corps had achieved all its objectives, Bradley smiled and reminded him that Berlin was the objective. On 5 July Eisenhower observed to Marshall, "Our Corps Commanders are all doing splendidly."[49] He elaborated that Middleton lacked the enthusiastic leadership others displayed, but made up for it with his tactical ability and straightforward workmanship. He did not mention Collins, probably because he felt no need to sell Marshall on him. On the other hand, a few weeks later he heaped exaggerated praise on Gerow, in whom Marshall had expressed doubts. As for Corlett, his impatience with the lack of military progress and eagerness to fight compensated for his more grating personality traits. The corps commanders for their part appreciated Bradley's help and understanding in the face of their tactical difficulties. Shortly after the Nineteenth Corps became operational, for instance, Corlett contracted a severe cold and kidney infection and was hospitalized for two days. Even after he was discharged, he remained sick for a couple weeks. To his surprise and relief, Eisenhower and Bradley did not remove him from his post, but instead brought the commander of the Twentieth Corps, General Walton Walker, over from England to serve temporarily as his deputy until he had fully recovered.[50]

On the other hand, the situation was more tempestuous at the division level. All the divisional commanders, with the exception of Manton Eddy and Matthew Ridgway, either were new to World War Two combat or new to their positions. Moreover, almost all of them were leading green outfits into action. It was therefore hardly surprising that many of them and their men performed poorly in their initial engagements. Since these outfits were so obviously at fault, Eisenhower and Bradley were more inclined to blame division rather than corps commanders for these difficulties. As a somewhat defensive Bradley recalled in his memoirs:

> There were instances in Europe where I relieved commanders for their failure
> to move fast enough. And it is possible that some were victims of
> circumstance. For how can the blame for failure be laid fairly on a single man
> when there are in reality so many factors that can affect the outcome of any
> battle? Yet each commander must always assume total responsibility for every

individual in his command. If his battalion or regimental commanders fail him in the attack, then he must relieve them or be relieved himself. Many a division commander has failed not because he lacked the capacity for command but only because he declined to be hard enough on his subordinate commanders.[51]

Eisenhower and Bradley had high hopes for General William McMahon's Eighth Division, which Eisenhower called the best-trained division in England. They were therefore surprised and dismayed when the outfit fought badly in its first battles. McMahon seemed mentally paralyzed when Bradley visited him. "Brad," McMahon said, "I think you're going to have to relieve me." Bradley did so two days later, replacing him with General Donald Stroh. General Lloyd Brown met the same fate as McMahon when his Twenty-eighth Division failed to live up to expectations. Bradley sent General James Wharton to take over, but he was killed by a sniper six hours into his tenure, so Bradley presented the unit to Dutch Cota as a reward for his good work with the Twenty-ninth Division at Omaha and elsewhere. That was not all. The divisional problem child in Normandy was the Ninetieth Division. After the Ninetieth's miserable baptism of fire, Eisenhower reported to Marshall that Collins and others believed that it was just about the worst-trained division they had ever seen. Bradley fired its first commander, General Eugene Landrum, and then his successor, General Jay MacKelvie, when neither man could fix it. Bradley eventually put General Raymond McLain in charge and gave him carte blanche to overhaul it. Just because a division commander was not removed did not mean he had proved his generalship. Although General Robert Macon's Eighty-third Division was almost as bad as the Ninetieth, Eisenhower and Bradley kept Macon around because they felt he could pull things together. General Leland Hobbs's Thirtieth Division fumbled a crossing of the Vire River when the infantry got mixed up with elements of the Third Armored Division, leading to a shouting match among Hobbs, Corlett, and the Third Armored's assistant commander, General John Bohn. Hobbs, too, managed to survive professionally, but it was hardly an auspicious start for him or the Thirtieth. Small wonder that Eisenhower and Bradley were so discouraged as they looked over their divisional roster. Eisenhower concluded that only Eddy and Huebner showed any potential for corps command, to which Bradley added Ridgway's name. It did not seem to occur to them, though, that there might be a correlation between the results these officers provided and the fact that they all led veteran outfits.

Even at the time some lamented Eisenhower's and Bradley's willingness to so quickly kick the blocks out from under division chiefs. After all, leading 15,000-man divisions into combat for the first time against as formidable an opponent as the Wehrmacht was a daunting task, and it was unsurprising that many commanders and their troops made all sorts of mistakes. Even if action against individuals such as McMahon was justified, Eisenhower's and Bradley's trigger-finger intolerance for failure sent the wrong message. Some commanders became more interested in avoiding mistakes than in taking advantage of opportunities, contributing to a cautiousness that did not serve the army well in northwest Europe. Patton had learned this the hard way in the Mediterranean and wrote in his diary, "Collins and Bradley are too prone to cut off heads. This will make division commanders lose their confidence. A man should not be damned for an initial failure with a new division. Had I done this with Eddy of the 9th Division in Africa, the army would have lost a potential corps commander."[52] Another officer, General James Gavin, who rose to lead the Eighty-second Division later in the conflict, expanded on Patton's thinking:

> Summarily relieving senior officers, it seems to me, makes others pusillanimous and indeed discourages other potential combat leaders from seeking high command. Again, it is not individuals acting against other individuals—it is not a personal matter—it is the way the system works and is expected to work. . . . The shift from peacetime to war footing and then to battle has a tremendous psychological impact on individuals. Summarily relieving those who do not appear to measure up in the first shock of battle is not only a luxury we cannot afford—it is very damaging to the Army as a whole.[53]

Wiser field army commanders such as Patton allowed their division and corps leaders the opportunity to settle down and learn from their mistakes. In Normandy, though, Bradley and his corps commanders often showed little such understanding.[54]

As it was, Bradley's top priority as July wore on was ending the impasse that had taken hold in Normandy. To do so, he developed a plan dubbed "Cobra" to break through the German lines. The stakes were high. Bradley believed that success not only would restore fluidity to the campaign, but also would heal the rifts that the frustrating stalemate had created in the Anglo-American alliance as British and American officers sniped at each other for their mutual lack of progress. On the other hand, failure might cost him and Eisenhower their jobs and convince the Combined Chiefs of Staff to support the air generals' contention that strategic bombing could most easily defeat Germany. Cobra basically called for blowing a hole in the German lines along a straight stretch of road west of the Vire River and St. Lo through which armored units would charge toward the Breton ports and into the French heartland. Bradley assigned the task to Collins, whose aggressiveness in the conquest of Cherbourg had distinguished him from the other corps commanders. An angry Corlett protested because he felt that his occupation of St. Lo had proven his value, but Bradley refused to change his mind. After looking over Collins's final preparations, Bradley said to him, "Anything else we can give you? You've got everything now but my pistol." Collins then extended his hand for the pistol. As Cobra came together, those in the know grew increasingly enthusiastic. Even Patton endorsed Cobra, though he still groused that it was too timid for his tastes. Bradley, however, hoped that Cobra would be the key to victory in France.[55]

Cobra began on the morning of 25 July when 2,500 warplanes pounded German defenses, followed by concentrated fire from over a thousand artillery pieces. Tragically, some of the planes dropped their bomb loads short of their targets and accidentally hit crouching GIs waiting to advance. More than 600 soldiers were killed or wounded by this friendly fire. Among the dead was Lesley McNair, the army's ground forces commander, who had crossed the Atlantic to observe the action. The demoralization and disruption the errant bombing caused was bad enough, but when the Fourth, Ninth, and Thirtieth divisions pushed forward they discovered that the defending Germans seemed as full of fight as ever. Collins, however, surmised that the resistance was unorganized and haphazard, so he decided to commit the First, Second Armored, and Third Armored divisions to exploit the breakthrough he sensed was in the making. He was right; the entire western part of the German line had collapsed, leaving only scattered remnants to keep up the contest. The Seventh Corps, soon joined by Middleton's Eighth Corps to the west along the coast, plunged southward against weakening German opposition. On 30 July General John Wood's Fourth Armored Division seized Avranches at the junction between the Brittany and Cotentin peninsulas, opening the door for further operations against the Breton ports and east toward Paris. The campaign had clearly entered a new phase.

This victory was accompanied by important changes in the army's organizational structure in France. Marshall and Eisenhower had always intended to introduce an American army group into the theater, and soon after he assumed command of Overlord Eisenhower decided that Bradley would lead it. On 20 July Eisenhower raised the issue of establishing the army group to Bradley during a visit to France to discuss Cobra. Eisenhower noted that the First Army now contained too many divisions to easily handle, and added that Patton's Third Army headquarters, as well as the headquarters of two new corps, were already on the continent and ready to go. Bradley agreed in principle, but wanted to wait until after he broke through the German lines because it would be easier for one field army to sort out the inevitable traffic jams than two. Moreover, while Bradley had few qualms about turning the First Army over to Hodges, he did not relish working with the unpredictable Patton again. By way of compromise, Eisenhower and

Bradley agreed to activate the new Twelfth Army Group on 1 August. Eisenhower chose the number not only to differentiate it from the field armies in Europe, but also to preserve the identity of the fictitious First Army Group in England, whose supposed existence as part of Operation Fortitude was still deceiving the Germans into holding back some of their forces just in case the Allies launched an amphibious assault against Pas-de-Calais.

When Bradley finally assumed control of the Twelfth Army Group, he was conscious of the fact that he was breaking new ground. Except for a short period at the end of World War One, the army had never had army groups. Officers had studied the concept in the interwar years at the Command and General Staff School and the Army War College, but there were no firm procedures in place. Bradley therefore figured that he was free to make up the rules as he went along. He claimed that he hoped to operate by issuing broad missions to field armies and letting their commanders find the best way to fulfill them. In reality, Bradley frequently interfered down to the division level, and admitted years later, "In sum, I would exercise the closest control over Hodges and Patton."[56] Considering his willingness to micromanage, it was hardly surprising that his army group headquarters eventually ballooned to nearly a thousand officers. In an effort to stay nimble and keep up with the front lines, Bradley established an advanced army group headquarters called Eagle Tac, but even it grew to 400 people by war's end.[57]

While Bradley, Hodges, their corps commanders, and their tired soldiers slugged it out with the Wehrmacht in the Normandy hedgerows, George Patton remained on the sidelines carrying out his assigned task in Operation Fortitude. Patton's Third Army was slated to enter the campaign eventually, but Bradley did not initially give Patton a firm date. Waiting came hard for Patton, whose impatience was magnified by his fears that the war might end before he got a chance to fulfill his destiny. Nor was his mood helped by a painfully infected toe caused by a dropped blackout curtain. He secretly crossed the English Channel in early July, but proximity to the front did not mean that Bradley was ready to commit him immediately to battle. Patton exclaimed to Collins in frustration, "You know, Collins, you and I are the only people around here who seem to be enjoying this goddamned war!"[58] Not surprisingly, Patton did not like the way the Normandy campaign was shaping up. As far as he was concerned, the continuing stalemate was due to Eisenhower's and Bradley's poor generalship, and he was pretty sure he could break through the German lines quickly if given the chance. He was, however, careful to keep these sentiments to himself because he understood that his military future depended on his staying in Eisenhower's and Bradley's good graces. Ingratiation was an integral part of Patton's character, so he felt no compunction in ladling out insincere compliments to and about both men regarding their military acumen. In the meantime, he girded himself for his hopefully dramatic introduction to the war in France and put the finishing touches to his Third Army staff. Observers noted that although Patton's staff had no individual standouts, it was efficient and devoted to him. In addition, after watching Bradley relieve several division commanders and noting the detrimental impact that had on the rest of them, Patton rededicated himself to displaying more patience and understanding toward his subordinates.[59]

The Allies had big plans for the Brittany peninsula. They hoped to seize its ports, especially Brest, and turn nearby Quiberon Bay into a huge logistical complex to support their campaign. With this in mind, Bradley intended to use Patton's entire Third Army to conquer the peninsula. Even before he officially activated the Third Army, Bradley on 28 July dispatched Patton to Brittany to supervise Middleton's Eighth Corps offensive there. The problem was that events had outrun Bradley's scheme. Crumbling German resistance west of St. Lo presented the Americans with the opportunity not only to clear Brittany, but also to strike deep into central France. Bradley and Patton had not yet recognized this possibility, but some of their subordinates did, especially the Fourth Armored Division's John Wood. Middleton did too, but he was also dealing with innumerable difficulties that made his life complicated that first week of August. He was not worried about the Germans cutting him off from the rest of the army because he knew that Ralph Huebner's First Division was protecting the Avranches bottleneck. Middleton and Huebner had played poker together before the war, and Middleton was confident that Huebner could keep the Germans at bay. Instead, he had other concerns. For one thing, his units were running off in all directions to exploit the hole Collins had blown through the German lines, and coordinating and keeping track of them was not easy. Moreover, Bradley and Patton were sending him sometimes contradictory directives. Although he was now an army group commander, Bradley could not resist interfering at the divisional level. Patton certainly did not want to cross Bradley, so he took his frustrations out on Middleton. On 1 August Patton wrote, "I found that Middleton, in spite of what I had already told him, had failed to send any infantry with the 4th Armored Division but had decided to send one infantry division with the 6th Armored Division on Brest. . . . I cannot make out why Middleton was so apathetic or dumb. I don't know what was the matter with him."[60] In fact, there was nothing wrong with Middleton, whom even Patton usually respected, but rather it was the confused command structure and circumstances that hindered Eighth Corps operations. Patton's overbearing presence irked Middleton, but he had worked with him in Sicily and had a pretty good understanding of the man. Orders being orders, Middleton focused his attention on Brest, and on the evening of 6 August General Robert Grow's Sixth Armored Division reached the city's outskirts. Unfortunately, Grow lacked the strength to storm the place, and by the time reinforcements arrived the Germans were dug in and prepared for the siege that now began. While it is possible that a surer advance toward Brest might have resulted in its early occupation, there is no doubt that mobile warfare was proving as problematic for the American army as the Normandy stalemate.[61]

It did not take Bradley and Patton long to recognize the opportunity to strike out of Avranches deep into France. To lead the attack they turned to General Wade "Ham" Haislip, commander of the newly activated Fifteenth Corps. The Virginia-born Haislip had graduated from West Point in 1912 and after participating in the Veracruz occupation went overseas to France in World War One as a machine gun officer and secretary to the Fifth Corps staff. He returned to the States in 1921 to teach at West Point, and afterward attended the Infantry School from 1923 to 1924, the Command and General Staff School from 1924 to 1925, the French École Superieure de Guerre from 1925 to 1927, and finally the Army War College from 1931 to 1932. He next became an instructor at the Command and General Staff School for four years and then served with an infantry regiment. In 1938 he was assigned to the General Staff in Washington, from where he eventually rose to become assistant chief of staff for personnel. Marshall lauded Haislip for successfully handling "all the matters relating to the operation of the Selective Service System, development of the Training Centers, the Promotion System and the method of appointing commissioned personnel. Prior to that, as head of the Budget and Legislative Branch you rendered equally important service within the War Department and before the Bureau of the Budget and Committees of Congress."[62] Considering his background, Marshall and McNair's decision to assign him first to the Fourth Division and then to organize and train the new Eighty-fifth Division was hardly surprising. The Eighty-fifth was one of the army's first draftee divisions, and its good combat record in Italy was a testament to Haislip's capabilities. McNair certainly thought so, and it was no doubt on his recommendation that Marshall placed Haislip in charge of the Fifteenth Corps. Haislip had not seen any combat in World War Two, but unlike Crittenberger, Reinhardt, and Woodruff he did not have to worry about Eisenhower transferring him elsewhere. Haislip was one of Eisenhower's oldest friends. They had met in Texas before World War One, and in fact Haislip had introduced Eisenhower to his future wife. Shortly after the Japanese attacked Pearl Harbor, Eisenhower labeled Haislip one of the army's ablest officers. Bradley does not appear to have thought much of Haislip one way or another. As for Patton, he was initially skeptical of Haislip when they first met in England, but warmed to him as the spring went on.

Haislip was a short, stout, and peppery man full of enthusiasm and good cheer. His determination, resourcefulness, and good judgment compensated for a contentious streak that manifested itself in his demands for crystal-clear orders. Although sensitive to both criticism and praise, he possessed plenty of confidence in his own abilities. As a result, he was calm and cool under pressure, so that neither the Wehrmacht nor George Patton was likely to rattle him much. As with Collins, years of instructing had enhanced his powers of persuasion and articulation, and sometimes made him prone to exaggeration. Teaching also gave him plenty of time to reflect on military matters such as a corps's role in warfare. His emphasis on teamwork enabled him to put together an excellent and loyal staff. He let his chief of staff run his headquarters so he could visit the front as often as possible. He had a rule that he was the only member of his headquarters with the authority to say no to requests from his combat commanders, which made him very popular among divisional leaders. So did his willingness to give them immediate answers and plenty of autonomy. Haislip believed in making simple plans and sticking to them ruthlessly, a combination that allowed him to generate the kind of driving power superiors such as Patton appreciated. Finally, he possessed that streak of humanity that often differentiated American generals from their colleagues in other armies. When one of his soldiers lost his arm in a training accident in England, Haislip not only visited him in the hospital, but wrote to Patton, "I know how you feel about these matters and am sending you this information in the hope that you may find time to write to him. I know he would appreciate it greatly, as the war is over for him."[63] Haislip's first assignment from Patton was to seize Le Mans, 86 miles from Avranches. Haislip's flanks would be exposed and he had little knowledge of the local terrain or intelligence of enemy activities, but German resistance had practically evaporated in this sector, so the Fifteenth Corps rolled into Le Mans on 8 August without serious opposition.[64]

While Middleton and Haislip were galloping off in opposite directions, big things were also occurring along the First Army's front in Normandy. There the Germans continued to fight hard east of St. Lo, and Corlett's and Gerow's corps made slow progress. In an effort to restore their fast-deteriorating military situation, the Germans decided to launch a counterattack toward the Avranches bottleneck that if successful would sever the Third Army from the rest of the Allied force. Unfortunately for the Germans, Allied code breakers learned of the plan and warned Bradley, so he was able to order in reinforcements even before the offensive got under way. The initial German assault in the Mortain area on the night of 6–7 August still caught Hobbs's Thirtieth Division by surprise, but the Thirtieth was now a veteran outfit and resisted fiercely. The Thirtieth was part of Collins's Seventh Corps, and Collins fought with his usual skill. Bradley had confidence in Collins, as well as in the commanders of the divisions that quickly flooded into the Mortain region, including Barton's Fourth, Eddy's Ninth, and General Edward Brooks's Second Armored. After five days of heavy back-and-forth combat, the Germans broke off the operation to confront a dire threat developing to the southeast.[65]

Haislip's all-but-uncontested occupation of Le Mans presented Bradley with the opportunity not just to defeat the German army in Normandy, but to surround and destroy it altogether. Bradley ordered Haislip's corps to attack north from Le Mans toward Argentan in conjunction with an offensive by the Canadian First Army south to Falaise. Once the Americans and Canadians linked up, German forces in Normandy would be trapped. Having successfully completed his first mission, Haislip was ready and eager to go. His enthusiasm, however, paled compared with Patton's. Patton saw mobile warfare as his forte, and he enjoyed the chance to demonstrate his abilities. His aide remembered:

> Yesterday on the way back to our headquarters we were speeding along through choking dust under a high blue heaven crisscrossed with the vapor contrails of our tactical planes. It was a bad stretch of road from which our bulldozers had recently pushed to either side the reeking mass of smashed half-tracks, supply trucks, ambulances, and blackened German corpses. Encompassing with a sweep of his arms the rubbled farms and bordering fields scarred with grass fires, smoldering ruins, and the swollen carcasses of stiff-legged cattle, the General [Patton] half turned in his seat. "Just look at that, Codman," he shouted. "Could anything be more magnificent?" As we passed a clump of bushes, one of our concealed batteries let go with a shattering salvo. The General cupped both hands. I leaned forward to catch his words. "Compared to war, all other forms of human endeavor shrink to insignificance." His voice shook with emotion. "God, how I love it!"[66]

Haislip got going on 10 August and in three days was on the outskirts of Argentan. Unfortunately, the accompanying Canadian drive to Falaise progressed slowly against stiff German opposition. Patton wanted to cross interallied boundaries and seize Falaise on his own to close the trap. When he called Bradley for permission, he jokingly added that he could push the British back to the sea for another Dunkirk too. Patton's "boastful, supercilious attitude" angered Bradley, and he refused to assent to the proposal. There was more to Bradley's judgment than spite. For one thing, he was worried that American and Canadian troops might fire on one another, leading to unnecessary casualties. In addition, Haislip was a new corps commander isolated from the rest of the Twelfth Army Group. His corps contained divisions in which Bradley had doubts. These included the troubled Ninetieth, the new French Second Armored Division, and Wyche's Seventy-ninth. A German counterattack might shatter the exposed Fifteenth Corps. As Bradley later put it, "I much preferred a solid shoulder at Argentan to the possibility of a broken neck at Falaise."[67] Haislip could see Bradley's point, though he was not happy about it. Bradley shortly afterward dispatched his corps to the Seine River, but not before a French truck hit Haislip and gave him a painful black eye

that required sixteen stitches to repair. As for Patton, he was furious and dismayed, though as usual he vented most of his frustration in his diary while maintaining an ingratiating attitude toward the author of the decision. In the end,
Patton's predictions that Bradley was squandering a magnificent victory proved
true. By the time the First Canadian Army finally closed the gap on 21 August,
some 40,000 Germans had escaped, including a good many headquarters personnel around whom the Germans would reconstitute their units. On the other
hand, the operation killed 10,000 Germans, captured another 40,000, and eliminated the German army in Normandy, thus opening the door for the Allies to
complete the liberation of France.[68]

Eisenhower moved quickly to take advantage of the German army's disarray.
Although the Allies were already outrunning their supply lines, he decided not to
stop at the Seine River as originally planned and instead to continue to advance
eastward. On 19 August elements of Wyche's Seventy-ninth Division in Haislip's
corps crossed the Seine northwest of Paris. Eisenhower hoped to delay occupying
Paris to avoid the burden of feeding its population and sorting out the inevitable
political fallout, but Free French insistence and a Parisian uprising forced his
hand, so he had Bradley send Gerow's Fifth Corps to help the French Second Armored Division free the city. Bradley was irked by the diversion and took his frustrations out on Gerow by yelling at him for not moving fast enough toward Paris.
The French Second Armored entered the city after hard fighting on 24 August,
followed by elements of the Fourth Division the next day. Meanwhile, Patton continued to bypass scattered German opposition in his hurry to get to Germany. He
crossed the upper Seine and plunged toward the Meuse River. He occupied Reims
on 29 August without much trouble, and then the World War One battlefields
where the American Expeditionary Force had shed so much blood a quarter of a
century earlier fell just as easily. To Patton, it appeared that one more hard push
would bring the Third Army into Germany itself. At an early September conference with Eisenhower, Bradley, and Hodges, Patton said he would stake his reputation on it. Eisenhower replied, "Be careful now, that reputation of yours hasn't
been worth very much." Patton laughed and said simply, "Pretty good now."[69]

Two new corps facilitated Patton's rapid advance across France, the Twelfth
and the Twentieth. General Walton Walker led the Twentieth. Born in Texas in
1889, Walker, like Patton, spent a year at the Virginia Military Institute before
transferring to West Point. After receiving his commission in 1912, Walker served
in the Veracruz occupation and along the Mexican border before going overseas
to France in World War One. There he led a machine-gun battalion at St. Mihiel
and the Argonne. In the 1920s he graduated from the Field Artillery School and
taught at the Infantry School and later at the Coastal Artillery School. He attended the Command and General Staff School from 1925 to 1926 and, after a

stint of duty in China, the Army War College from 1935 to 1936. He was assigned to the General Staff's War Plans Division in 1937 and remained there until 1940. When Marshall was put in charge of the War Plans Division in 1938, Walker, who had previously served as Marshall's executive officer, invited him and his wife to stay at his apartment until they found suitable accommodations. Walker struck Marshall as a forceful and competent officer, so upon becoming chief of staff he rapidly moved Walker up through the army's hierarchy. Walker successively commanded a regiment, an armored brigade, an armored division, and finally the Fourth Armored Corps and the Desert Training Center. McNair praised his efforts to organize and systematize the Desert Training Center, and later his work with the Fourth Armored Corps. He took the corps, now relabeled the Twentieth, to England in February 1944. Walker was, like Gerow and Haislip, an old Eisenhower friend from their pre–World War One Mexican border days—he and Eisenhower had been hunting companions and were both nearly killed by the same lightning bolt—so there was little chance of Eisenhower sending him home as he had Woodruff and Reinhardt. Bradley was more circumspect. As for Patton, he initially had doubts about Walker not only because he was untested, but also because his pudgy frame did not convey the hardness of character he valued. But, as with Haislip, Patton gradually warmed to Walker, if not to his physique, so that he wrote in early July, "If he does not blow up, he will do a good job."[70] Walker worked as deputy for the Nineteenth Corps during Corlett's illness before Patton committed the Twentieth Corps to combat in early August.[71]

As Patton eventually realized, Walker's doughy physical appearance belied his combat prowess. To his friends he was "Johnny Walker" because of his fondness for scotch whiskey. Abrasive, reticent, no-nonsense, and unsentimental, Walker was not an especially popular man among his troops. He rarely smiled in public and was not much for small talk. Perhaps to compensate for his short stature, he tended to strut instead of walk. Although no intellectual, he was a cool and forceful leader with plenty of tactical skill. He was willing to fight anytime, anywhere, and with whatever he had on hand, and even Patton respected his aggressive instincts. Indeed, he was one subordinate whom Patton rarely had to prod into action. Walker for his part enjoyed serving in the Third Army because he knew that Patton would back him up if he made a mistake, especially one of commission. His division chiefs disliked him because he limited their autonomy and rode herd on them. Still, he got results and was by the end of the war Patton's favorite lieutenant. Soon after he first took the Twentieth Corps into action, Walker intervened in the Seventh Armored Division's efforts to seize Melun along the Seine. Under Walker's personal leadership, the division successfully stormed the town. Considering his attributes, it was small wonder that Patton called him "my toughest son-of-a-bitch" and gave him some of the Third Army's most difficult assignments.[72]

As for the Twelfth Corps, it was led by General Gilbert "Doc" Cook. Born in 1889, Cook went to the University of Arkansas and the Arkansas Military Academy before transferring to West Point. He graduated in 1912 and was stationed in Texas and then in the Canal Zone before going to France in World War One. After the conflict he taught at the Infantry School on two different occasions, during the second of which he worked closely with Marshall. He also attended the Command and General Staff School from 1924 to 1925, the Tank School from 1930 to 1931, and the Army War College from 1931 to 1932. Stints with the General Staff and at Fort Washington followed, and he was back at the Command and General Staff School before the United States entered World War Two. In addition to making Marshall's acquaintance, Cook and McNair had a mutual admiration society. With such powerful fans, it was therefore not surprising that Cook moved rapidly through the army's hierarchy after Pearl Harbor, becoming successively an assistant division, division, and finally corps commander. Fortunately, Cook also had real ability. He was a gifted instructor who served as a mentor and sounding board for innumerable officers who eventually attained high wartime positions, including Collins, Devers, Middleton, and even Patton. Colleagues frequently labeled Cook "brilliant," not only in their contemporary correspondence, but also in postwar memoirs and interviews. One recalled that Cook told him that an officer loses his effectiveness as soon as he begins to feel sorry for his men. Cook's tact, energy, and astuteness enabled him to put together a first-rate staff for the Twelfth Corps. Unlike the case with Haislip and Walker, Patton had no doubts about Cook's abilities in large part because he knew him well from prewar association. For his sweep across France, Patton assigned Cook the important and dangerous job of protecting the Third Army's exposed right flank. In mid-August, Cook drove his new corps along the Loire River's north bank in such a way as to win Patton's admiration and capture Orleans in the process.[73]

Unhappily, Cook's tenure as a battle commander lasted less than three weeks. He had for years tried to hide the fact that he suffered from a circulatory affliction called Buerger's disease. He was in such poor shape by the time he got to France that he could not walk the length of a football field. His toes had turned black and he had lost the feeling in his hands and feet when Patton found him in a hospital on 18 August. After hearing the details, Patton told Cook that under the circumstances he could not stay with the Twelfth Corps. Patton hated to relieve Cook not only because Cook had gotten off to such an auspicious start, but also because the two men saw eye-to-eye on most issues. Still, it was obviously impossible for such a sick man to have such important responsibilities.

Eisenhower happened to be visiting Bradley's headquarters the next day, and the two men after consulting with Patton opted to give the Twelfth Corps to the Ninth Division's Manton Eddy. They could have asked Marshall for a stateside corps commander, but they wanted to reward one of their division chiefs for his good work. Eddy had led the Ninth in North Africa, Sicily, and now France, and Eisenhower, Bradley, Patton, and Collins all respected his work. Patton used him as a prime example of a division commander who had grown in his job. As for Bradley, he credited Eddy with turning the Ninth Division into a well-disciplined, thoroughly professional, and low-key outfit that fulfilled its missions without the attitude and drama of the more famous Big Red One. Finally, Marshall had confirmed his already positive evaluation of Eddy at a dinner with him the previous year during his visit to North Africa. None of the other division commanders had so far performed as consistently well since D-Day, and indeed Eisenhower had decided back on 22 July to give Eddy the next available corps.[74]

The Illinois-born Eddy did not go to West Point, but instead graduated from the Shattuck Military Academy in Minnesota in 1913. After his efforts to make it in the insurance business failed, at his father's suggestion he entered the army, and he received a commission in 1916. He fought valiantly in World War One in France, receiving a leg wound and rising to lead a machine-gun battalion by the end of the conflict. He returned to the States to take the company commanders' course at Fort Benning, and then taught military science at Riverside Military Academy in Georgia for four years. During a second tour of duty at Benning, this time at the Infantry School, he met and impressed Marshall. He attended the Command and General Staff School from 1932 to 1934 and then remained there as an instructor until 1938. Postings in Kentucky and Maryland followed, and by the time the United States entered World War Two he was running a regiment. Marshall and McNair selected him first as assistant commander and then, just before Operation Torch, as commander of the Ninth Division.[75]

Eddy was a florid and heavyset man with glasses and a permanent squint. Journalists approved of him because of his humility, honesty, down-to-earth manner, and sense of humor. Eddy liked to tell the story of a nighttime encounter with a soldier during a storm in North Africa. The GI was trying without much success to pound a tent peg with his helmet when he caught a glimpse of Eddy's flashlight and yelled, "Hey, bud, come and hold the light for me, will you?" Eddy complied, and when the soldier finished a bemused Eddy asked his name. The soldier suddenly recognized Eddy and exclaimed, "Jesus Christ!"[76] Eddy was also respected by his fellow officers for his balanced, deliberative, professional, and meticulous approach to war. Bradley, for example, later noted, "Manton liked to count his steps carefully before he took them."[77] At the same time, however, Eddy was a nervous and chronic worrier forever fussing about his flanks, his resources, enemy intentions, and so forth. His disposition did little to help his chronic high blood pressure, which he tried to keep secret from his superiors. Bradley eventually learned that Eddy needed constant reassurance, and was willing to take the time to do so because Eddy usually delivered results. One officer remembered that at a high-ranking conference before Cobra a fretful Eddy left the meeting without saying goodbye, even though the other generals called after him. Bradley finally ran after Eddy and repeatedly hollered "Goodbye, General," until Eddy acknowledged him. Patton also respected Eddy, but used a somewhat different strategy to deal with his anxieties. Patton gradually figured out that if he gave Eddy permission to stop his latest offensive, Eddy would interpret this as evidence that Patton lacked confidence in him and would therefore attack even more vigorously to prove his worth. When Eddy arrived to take over the Twelfth Corps, he asked Patton if he should be concerned about his exposed right flank. Patton responded that it depended on how nervous he was. Nor was Eddy reassured by Patton's orders that he advance 50 miles in one day. Eddy was accustomed to the slow progress in Normandy, and was consequently exhilarated when his corps pushed 72 miles on his first twenty-four hours on the job. Indeed, he wryly told Bradley that commanding a corps was easy and that he had been wasting his time with a division.[78]

While the Third Army was racing across central France, Hodges's First Army was, after a slower start and against more opposition, finally making remarkable progress of its own. Hodges possessed none of Patton's flamboyance, but he too had no desire to stop at the Seine and let the Germans catch their breath. Neat and trim and in good form, Hodges had emerged from Bradley's shadow and was coming into his own as a field army commander. Moreover, he had at his disposal three veteran corps led by men tempered in the Norman hedgerows. After mopping up Argentan-Falaise and contributing to the freeing of Paris, First Army elements crossed the Seine on 25 August and struck out for the Belgian border, with Collins on the right, Gerow in the center, and Corlett on the left. A week later Collins and Corlett trapped 25,000 fleeing German soldiers around Mons in Belgium. With scarcely a pause, Collins reached the Meuse River on 5 September and captured Liege two days later. On the First Army's left, the British Twenty-first Army Group also registered significant gains. The British Second Army raced into Belgium and occupied Brussels and Antwerp with scarcely a fight. By early September even Hodges, not normally a man to indulge in optimistic musings, stated that the Allies might well win the war with ten more days of good weather.[79]

Invasion of Southern France

The Anglo-American alliance was the closest military partnership in modern history up to that point. Indeed, such cooperation was a key reason for Allied victory. This did not, however, mean that the relationship was trouble free; far from it. British and American leaders bickered over a variety of military and diplomatic issues ranging from China's role in the conflict to the strategic bombing of Germany to the Royal Navy participation in the Pacific War. Combined Chiefs of Staff conferences were full of table poundings, implied and explicit threats, arm-twisting, and verbal abuse. The invasion of southern France, codenamed first "Anvil" and later "Dragoon," was certainly among the longest and bitterest military disputes between the two countries. Shipping shortages prevented its simultaneous implementation with Overlord, but Eisenhower and the Joint Chiefs pushed for its execution later that summer. Their reasoning was primarily logistical. Eisenhower pointed out that seizing Marseilles in particular would provide him with the port he needed to help supply his growing armies in northwest Europe. Without Marseilles, there was also no way to quickly bring across the Atlantic the backlog of American divisions waiting for deployment to Europe. The British, on the other hand, opposed Anvil-Dragoon because the forces necessary to carry it out would have to come from Italy. Taking these units would be the final nail in the coffin for British efforts to win the war from the Mediterranean. Although Churchill in particular waged a long and bitter rearguard action to kill Anvil-Dragoon, the Americans successfully insisted on the operation and scheduled it for mid-August.

Establishing Anvil-Dragoon's command structure was as difficult and convoluted as its origins. When the initial planning for the operation began, Eisenhower was still in the Mediterranean wrapping up loose ends before he traveled to England to take over Overlord. Personnel for Anvil-Dragoon was one of many last-minute concerns to which he attended, and was the subject of considerable trans-Atlantic discussion between him and Marshall. To be sure, the final decisions were Marshall's, but the chief of staff gave Eisenhower wide discretion, in part because his selections would invariably impact Overlord. Eisenhower first toyed with the idea of assigning Patton to lead the invasion with his Seventh Army. Patton was already in the theater and familiar with it, was currently underutilized, had plenty of experience with amphibious warfare, and got along well with the French. Once Eisenhower realized that Marshall had no objection to his employing Patton in Overlord, though, he changed his mind. Eisenhower now recommended that Clark continue to lead the Fifth Army in Italy and simultaneously oversee the Seventh Army's planning for Anvil-Dragoon. When the time came to implement Anvil-Dragoon, Eisenhower figured that Clark would surrender the Fifth Army to John Lucas and take the Seventh Army into southern France. Eisenhower believed that Clark was the right man because he was an experienced officer with an amphibious warfare background as extensive as Patton's. Moreover, the British were amenable to the idea—though probably as much to get the fractious and chauvinistic Clark out of Italy as for any other reason. Eisenhower optimistically—some would say naively—anticipated that the upcoming Anzio landing would enable Clark to seize Rome quickly and then focus on Anvil-Dragoon by, say, early February 1944. One problem was that Clark was not terribly enthusiastic about the idea. He worried that Anvil-Dragoon would be a small-scale affair and a strategic dead end that would do little to gratify his ego or advance the war effort. He much preferred to stay in Italy with the Fifth Army to conquer Rome. Clark would of course obey orders, but he asked to bring the Fifth Army to southern France instead of the Seventh so it would not lose its identity if all American troops eventually left Italy. Eisenhower refused because he felt that changing armies in the middle of two campaigns would be too complicated. Despite Clark's grumblings, within a few weeks of getting to England Eisenhower thought he had the command structure for Anvil-Dragoon all set up.[80]

Unfortunately for Eisenhower, a combination of circumstances and Jake Devers disrupted and altered his plans for Anvil-Dragoon. There was little Eisenhower could do about the discouraging military situation in the Mediterranean in early 1944, but he had no one to blame but himself for Devers's involvement. Eisenhower had recommended Devers as deputy theater commander and senior American officer in the Mediterranean largely because he did not like the man and did not welcome his participation in Overlord. As soon as Devers reached the Mediterranean and recovered from a bout of the flu, he examined and was dismayed by Eisenhower's command arrangements for Anvil-Dragoon. Devers had little faith in either Patton or Clark, and he had questioned putting Lucas in charge of the Fifth Army even before Anzio. Confidence had never been one of Devers's shortcomings, and he quickly went about rectifying the shortcomings he perceived in his theater. Devers asked Marshall to send one of two stateside field army commanders, Courtney Hodges or General William Simpson, to the Mediterranean to lead the Seventh Army in Anvil-Dragoon. Marshall, however, rejected both requests. For one thing, Eisenhower had already staked tentative claims on both men, and Overlord had priority. In addition, Marshall told Devers that Anvil-Dragoon must have a battle-experienced general at its helm, and neither Hodges nor Simpson had yet seen action in the conflict. In fact, the only two men available in Europe who met Marshall's conditions were Patton and Clark. Fortunately for Devers's peace of mind, circumstances eliminated both men from contention. Devers saw Patton as a loose cannon after the slapping incidents and did not want him in his theater, so he was relieved when Eisenhower eventually ordered Patton to England for Overlord. As for Clark, Devers had declining faith in his military abilities and seriously doubted that he could manage the bitter struggle along the Gustav Line and the Anzio beachhead while simultaneously overseeing the invasion of southern France. In this he and Clark were in rare agreement. Clark was fixated on Rome and did not want to be diverted by a secondary operation elsewhere. He made it clear to Jumbo Wilson, the British theater chief in the Mediterranean, that he did not wish to leave the Fifth Army until Rome had fallen. Wilson and Devers agreed with Clark's logic, and Devers eventually persuaded Marshall of its soundness. Devers may have succeeded in sidelining Clark and Patton from Anvil-Dragoon, but it did not solve his basic problem of finding a leader for the operation. After all his machinations, he remained at square one.[81]

Assigning a qualified American commander for Anvil-Dragoon was merely one of many quandaries Devers tackled that winter. He also was grappling with Clark's Anzio imbroglio and the usual interallied squabbles with the British and French. Devers was ordinarily an optimistic and ebullient man, but he could not help but feel somewhat downcast by the difficulties he inherited when Eisenhower manufactured his transfer to an administrative post in an increasingly backwater theater. Still, Devers prided himself on his problem-solving abilities, and he knew that a solution to the Anvil-Dragoon command conundrum might present itself if he had a little patience. After mulling the issue over with his chief of staff, Devers decided that they both needed a good night's sleep if they were going to find someone, anyone, with the requisite combat experience for Anvil-Dragoon. As Devers knew, the trouble was that the army had not yet produced a big cadre of battle-experienced generals from which to choose, and most of the men who met this standard were with Eisenhower in England preparing for Overlord, were preoccupied in Italy, or were somewhere in the remote Pacific. Next morning Devers read a cable announcing that the Fourth Corps headquarters was on its way from the States to Italy for Clark's use. Devers asked his staff, "Who the hell commands the Fourth Corps?" When someone piped up that it was General Sandy Patch, Devers exclaimed, "That's my man!" Indeed, Patch met Marshall's specifications for an Anvil-Dragoon commander perfectly. He had successfully led a division and then a corps through the Guadalcanal campaign in 1942–1943 before he was invalided home. Marshall was amenable to the idea, so on 2 March Devers issued the orders putting Patch in charge of the Seventh Army for the Anvil-Dragoon operation.[82]

Like Collins and Corlett, Patch was one of the few high-ranking American ground forces commanders to make his mark in both the Pacific and European wars. Although his Fourteenth Corps had successfully cleared Guadalcanal of its Japanese defenders, Patch's caution enabled the Japanese to evacuate their forces to fight another day. Nevertheless, Marshall lauded Patch's efforts in what was still a significant American victory. Unfortunately, Patch's health, never good, broke down even before the fighting ended, so Marshall brought him back to the States in April 1943 to take over the Fourth Corps in the Pacific Northwest. Patch's elevation to Seventh Army command had little to do with Marshall's partiality. In fact, Marshall had never really understood the taciturn and enigmatic Patch and was by

1944 ambivalent toward him at best. During the fighting on Guadalcanal Patch clashed so much with Collins, then leading the Twenty-fifth Division, over the best way to prosecute the campaign that afterward Patch wrote a negative efficiency report on Collins. Marshall had a hard time accepting Patch's evaluation because he and Collins had worked together at Fort Benning and Marshall knew Collins's value. Patch's account convinced Marshall that there was something amiss with *Patch*, not Collins. On the other hand, Patch had just won one of the army's first victories, so Marshall was not inclined to look a gift horse in the mouth.

After Patch returned to the States, though, he committed a more serious sin in Marshall's eyes. In mid-June 1943, Ernest King wrote to Marshall that he had received word that at a recent dinner Patch stated publicly that while in the Pacific he had authorized the killing of Japanese Admiral Isoroku Yamamoto by American warplanes after intelligence reports revealed his itinerary. Marshall was understandably dismayed that Patch might have exposed the fact that the military was decrypting Japanese radio messages, and he dispatched an officer to Fort Lewis to get Patch's side of the story. Patch responded in writing that he did not order the attack or initiate any such conversation. Marshall replied to Patch's vague explanation with a curt note accusing him of evading the question. A bout of pneumonia prevented Patch from answering until 21 July. This time Patch said that he did not believe that there was a need for absolute secrecy on Yamamoto's death because it was well known throughout the Pacific and he had spoken out after the deed was done. Patch either had failed to understand Marshall's point or was deliberately playing dumb. Neither explanation reflected well on him as far as Marshall was concerned. Thoroughly exasperated, Marshall let the matter drop. In a letter to King, Marshall admitted that he was at a loss as to how to proceed because any disciplinary action against Patch might generate unfavorable publicity and further jeopardize American cryptoanalysis secrets. Marshall probably acceded to Devers's request for Patch as head of the Seventh Army because there was no one else available who met his criteria. According to Devers, Patch knew he was on thin ice with Marshall and felt bad about it. Anvil-Dragoon, however, provided him with an opportunity for redemption.[83]

Patch had his work cut out for him. Anvil-Dragoon was an amphibious operation that involved both interservice and international coordination for which he was responsible. Not surprisingly, the Free French posed some of the biggest challenges for him and Devers. The Free French were eager to participate in the liberation of their homeland and planned to use their French Expeditionary Force, currently engaged in Italy, to do so. To lead it, Free French leader Charles de Gaulle placed General Jean de Lattre de Tassigny in charge of French divisions allotted to Anvil-Dragoon instead of current French Expeditionary Corps commander General Alphonse Pierre Juin. Devers much preferred the cooperative and skillful Juin, but guessed that Juin had lost out because he had not jumped on the Free French bandwagon early enough. Although de Lattre was an ambitious and capable man, he was also touchy. He irked Devers by showing up late to meetings and pacing the floor while he talked, like Douglas MacArthur. Devers finally figured out that the best way to deal with de Lattre was to discuss contentious issues with him privately without their staffs, in the presence of two interpreters. On the other hand, Patch and de Lattre initially hit it off. De Lattre saw something sensitive and mystical in Patch that he found appealing, and Patch had a knack for getting along with others. Devers and Patch recognized and sympathized with the Free French fixation with pride and prestige and tried to be accommodating, most notably by giving de Lattre the important jobs of seizing Toulon and Marseilles after the Seventh Army secured its beachhead and moved inland.[84]

In addition to de Lattre's French troops, Patch's Seventh Army also contained an American corps taken from Clark's Fifth Army in Italy. Patch at first hoped to use Geoffrey Keyes's Second Corps, but Devers and Clark insisted that he employ Lucian Truscott's Sixth Corps instead. Both Truscott and Keyes had amphibious experience, but most observers rated Truscott higher as a combat commander, and Devers felt that his skills could be better used in France than in the increasingly secondary Italian campaign. Clark for his part respected Truscott's military talents too, but also believed he was a prima donna who often caused more trouble than he was worth. Under the circumstances, he preferred to hold onto the less gifted but still competent Keyes. Truscott brought with him three of the army's most experienced units: the Third, Thirty-sixth, and Forty-fifth divisions. Whatever doubts Patch may have had about Truscott evaporated after their first meeting. They broke the ice by discussing their wartime experiences, and emerged from the conference in almost complete agreement. Truscott came away with a positive impression of Patch that never diminished. Their staffs on the other hand had a more tempestuous relationship. Seventh Army headquarters contained some holdovers from the Patton era who were very thankful that Clark had not taken over. On the whole, however, the Seventh Army staff was much greener than that of Truscott's veteran Sixth Corps. Its lack of amphibious expertise might explain why Patch traveled to England in mid-May to consult with Corlett about his experiences in the Pacific. Whereas Truscott issued simple, sensible, and fair orders, the Seventh Army headquarters gained a reputation for being more inflexible, amateurish, and by-the-book. Despite these and other difficulties, Patch managed to get his army ready for Anvil-Dragoon, so that a week before the landing Devers wrote Marshall, "Everything seems to be set for Dragoon. Patch has done a remarkably fine piece of work in coordinating the activities of the Americans, the French and the British, the Navy and the Air. He is well-liked by all and his problems have been numerous and difficult."[85]

Devers had never been happy with his assignment to the Mediterranean. He had held a prominent position in England and had expected to participate in Overlord as a field army or army group commander. Then, without much warning, Eisenhower exiled him to an administrative post in an increasingly unimportant theater. Devers was a persistent and ambitious man, though, who knew how to create his own opportunities, and he was not about to accept this fate until he had exhausted all his options. With this in mind, he manufactured one last major organizational change to Anvil-Dragoon, designed to catapult him back into the center of the war. As he saw things, the operation required an army group headquarters and commander. The French had made it clear that they eventually wanted their own field army, and at its current rate of progress Clark's Fifth Army would probably reach France via the Italian west coast by the end of the summer. Obviously someone would have to coordinate this new French army, Clark's Fifth Army, and Patch's Seventh Army. In July Devers asked Marshall for permission to quietly establish an army group headquarters, and with typical bravado he offered to lead it. To bolster his argument, he added that Jumbo Wilson thought Devers was the best man for the job.

As Devers well understood, asking for an army group was not the same as getting it. Since the army group would be fighting in France, establishing it required both Marshall's and Eisenhower's approval. Devers suspected correctly that Eisenhower did not much like him. Not only did Eisenhower find Devers's glib personality off-putting, but Devers had also bureaucratically outmaneuvered Eisenhower on several occasions, most recently in keeping Truscott in the Mediterranean when Eisenhower desperately wanted him for Overlord. For Eisenhower, there were two issues to consider: creating the army group and assigning its chief. He supported an additional army group in France. Such an American army group would retain close control over the French field army's troops, supplies, operations, and civil affairs, which as far as Eisenhower was concerned was all to the good. As for the army group's commander, Eisenhower was surprisingly willing to accept Devers. In his cables to Marshall, he admitted that he had had his doubts about Devers, but noted that all reports from the Mediterranean indicated he was doing a first-rate job there. Devers seemed to possess the strong and forceful character necessary for interallied responsibilities. Eisenhower also pointed out that Devers had been to the front a lot and had demonstrated that he could inspire the troops. Although Eisenhower believed that a combat leader should have as few administrative duties as possible, he felt that Devers could if necessary also continue as Wilson's deputy and senior American officer in the Mediterranean because most of the work there was now routine. Once Eisenhower signaled his approval, Marshall acquiesced as well, in mid-July. He had always had a more positive opinion of Devers than did Eisenhower anyway. Marshall, however, warned

Devers that he had to set up his headquarters quickly, keep it small, staff it with personnel already in the Mediterranean, and make sure not to shirk his duties as Wilson's deputy. Devers was of course pleased with the outcome; indeed, he could not have scripted it better. He got to work with his usual energy, and in less than a month he informed Marshall that the headquarters for what would become the Sixth Army Group was ready to go.[86]

Anvil-Dragoon's target was the French Riviera east of Toulon. Patch planned to land Truscott's Sixth Corps first, followed by de Lattre's French units. Despite extensive amphibious experience dating back to the Dieppe raid two years earlier, Truscott was still nervous and jittery in the days leading up to the big assault. Fortunately, German defenses along France's southern coast were nowhere near as extensive as those Eisenhower had confronted two months earlier in Normandy. When Truscott's three divisions splashed ashore on 15 August, only General John Dahlquist's Thirty-sixth Division faced much resistance. The next day de Lattre's French troops landed and advanced rapidly westward toward Toulon and Marseilles. Their élan compensated for their lack of heavy weapons, and the German garrisons in both cities surrendered on 28 August after sharp fighting. While the French were busy restoring their national honor, Truscott put his three divisions on the road up the Rhone River valley toward Montelimar and Grenoble in an effort to sever the German retreat route from western France. Grenoble fell to the Thirty-sixth Division on 22 August, but confused fighting around Montelimar enabled a good many Germans to break through and elude Truscott's trap. Undaunted, Truscott pushed his tired men northeastward toward the Belfort Gap, the closest escape hatch into Germany. His soldiers marched and drove so rapidly that Patch's Seventh Army headquarters often lost touch with them. This was fine with Truscott; he liked waging war his own way without much supervision from above. As it was, Patch and Devers shared his combative nature and did little to rein him in. Patch was more frustrated with de Lattre than with Truscott. After Toulon and Marseilles capitulated, de Lattre repeatedly badgered Patch for an increased role in the campaign. Devers eventually intervened and calmed troubled interallied waters by assigning the French the job of clearing the west side of the Rhone. On 2 September French partisans seized Lyon ahead of Truscott's charging GIs. Patch originally intended to pause there and regroup, but with the Germans on the run he, Devers, and Truscott opted to keep going. The Germans, however, reached the Belfort Gap first and turned to confront the Seventh Army in early September. At about the same time elements of the Seventh Army linked up with Eisenhower's forces to the north. Although a good many Germans managed to evade Truscott's snares, it was certainly not due to a lack of aggressiveness on Truscott's, Patch's, or Devers's part. Indeed, they demonstrated a killer instinct from start to finish. The Seventh Army succeeded in capturing some 57,000 Germans at the cost of 4,000 French and 2,700 American casualties. In addition to liberating southern France, Devers's troops also occupied the important ports of Toulon and Marseilles, which eventually paid enormous logistical dividends to the Allies. Devers, Patch, Truscott, and de Lattre deserved all the kudos they could get. Patch no doubt took particular pride in a congratulatory message relayed to him via Devers from Marshall. If Patch's first-rate performance did not completely erase the sins the chief of staff believed he had committed, it still went a long way toward the redemption Patch sought.[87]

Conclusions

Overlord gave the army its opportunity to implement its doctrine of strategic concentration against the enemy's heartland. Although the army had already fought in North Africa, Sicily, and Italy, these were secondary campaigns involving a comparatively small number of ground units. In northwest Europe, on the other hand, the army deployed the bulk of its divisions for a climactic battle against the Wehrmacht. Because the stakes were so high, Marshall and Eisenhower tried hard to provide the best possible leadership for the mostly green GIs tossed into the war's maw. The problem was that there were not that many battle-hardened generals available to command the field armies and corps awaiting commitment to northwestern Europe, and most of them had experience only at the divisional level. Marshall and especially Eisenhower valued such men highly and went to considerable lengths to procure them. Doing so, however, often meant weakening the war effort in other theaters and alienating local commanders. Nevertheless, Marshall not only transferred Collins and Corlett over from the Pacific, but also sent a crippled Middleton back from the States. This provided a leavening of experience, but Eisenhower remained unsatisfied, which was why he accepted the troublesome Patton and tried so desperately to secure Truscott's services. Having exhausted the limited pool of veteran commanders, Eisenhower had to rely on untried men. In this case, he was willing to entrust corps to officers he knew and respected from his old army days. Gerow, Haislip, and Walker had not seen action before Overlord, but they were all Eisenhower's friends of more than twenty years, and he had faith that they would all perform well. Conversely, he reassigned the untried Crittenberger, Devers, Reinhardt, and Woodruff because he either did not know them or did not like them as much. Cook and Hodges were the big exceptions to Eisenhower's emphasis on experience or familiarity, and in their cases he took them partly because of their outstanding reputations and partly because they had powerful patrons—Marshall in Hodges's case and Patton for Cook—who vouched for them.

During the Normandy campaign Bradley's corps commanders faced serious problems that went beyond fighting the always dangerous Wehrmacht in the hedgerows. For one thing, all of them were new to their positions. They all discovered that leading a corps was much different from leading a division, just as Bradley realized that a field army was a different animal from a corps. Running a corps required less administration and more thinking than a division, and corps commanders had to learn to let go of some of the minutiae that was part of a division commander's routine. Moreover, most of the divisions they directed were new to war and therefore unwieldy and insufficiently responsive to their direction. Considering such handicaps, it is remarkable that the corps commanders did so well. Although they all failed on occasion to make the kind of progress Bradley wanted, none of them suffered a crushing defeat or a serious reverse. Of the four corps commanders, Collins was the clear standout. He landed at Utah beach, seized Cherbourg, spearheaded the breakout during Operation Cobra, and foiled the German counterattack at Mortain. Corlett, Gerow, and Middleton performed less spectacularly, but still to the satisfaction of Bradley and Eisenhower. After the First Army broke out of Normandy, Bradley activated Patton's Third Army for the exploitation. The Third Army's eastward-driving corps commanders—Cook, Eddy, Haislip, and Walker—all galloped across France with enough aggressiveness to placate the irrepressible Patton. None of them, however, had to face the kind of grinding combat that Collins, Corlett, Gerow, and Middleton confronted in Normandy, so in this respect they remained untested. Nevertheless, as the Allies approached the German border, Bradley's field army and corps commanders displayed increasing deftness in handling their now veteran divisions. They would need these hard-won skills for the difficult winter ahead.

Eisenhower may have faced the cream of the Wehrmacht in the west, but he also had the pick of the army's personnel litter to lead his field armies, corps, and divisions. Jake Devers, on the other hand, had to make do with whomever he could scrounge up for Anvil-Dragoon. Fortunately, Devers used the problem-solving skills of which he was so proud to attain the services of Lucian Truscott and Sandy Patch. Holding onto Truscott required a prolonged bureaucratic battle with Eisenhower, but Patch's appearance in the Mediterranean was a fortuitous event that Devers was smart enough to take advantage of. Securing Patch enabled Devers to avoid giving the Seventh Army to Patton or Clark, neither of whom he much respected. As a result, he undertook the invasion of southern France with two veteran commanders who prosecuted their campaign with aggressiveness and skill. When they were integrated into Eisenhower's force, they joined an increasingly competent group of commanders capable of applying an army doctrine that emphasized firepower and mobility.

6

MacArthur's Return to the Philippines

"I Have Returned"

Shortly after midnight on 20 October 1944, the cruiser USS *Nashville* arrived off the eastern shore of the central Philippine island of Leyte. There was nothing out of the ordinary about *Nashville*; it was merely one of an enormous armada of 738 ships of all shapes and sizes, from aircraft carriers to tugs, transporting or escorting over 160,000 troops and their supplies and equipment from Hollandia and the Admiralties. In fact, the only thing that really differentiated *Nashville* from the other warships of her class was Douglas MacArthur's presence onboard. Thirty-one months earlier MacArthur had promised to liberate the Philippines, and now he was there to redeem his pledge—or anyhow to begin the process. Indeed, soon after he boarded *Nashville* he said to Sutherland in a hoarse voice, "I tell you, Dick, we will destroy them if we have to we will rise up out of the water and destroy them."[1]

That morning, after the usual preliminary bombardment to kill or demoralize any Japanese around, four divisions from Franklin Sibert's Tenth Corps and John Hodge's Twenty-fourth Corps—the First Cavalry and Twenty-fourth divisions for the former and Seventh and Ninety-sixth divisions for the latter—splashed ashore near Tacloban and at Dulag. The scene was so impressive that Hodge called it an "awe-inspiring sight."[2] The soldiers met only scattered and light enemy opposition, so they quickly sorted themselves out and plunged into the jungle while beachmasters began organizing the beachhead for the follow-up waves of supplies, equipment, and reinforcements. In the early afternoon, MacArthur, Philippines president Sergio Osmeña, and a gaggle of staffers, journalists, commanders, and various hangers-on boarded a landing craft that took them to the Twenty-fourth Division's beachhead south of Tacloban. The landing craft drew too much water to reach the beach, so MacArthur and his party had to walk the last yards to the shore through surf up to their waists while photographers and newsreel camera operators recorded the event for posterity. Although Japanese sniper and mortar fire still peppered the area, MacArthur insisted on touring the beachhead and talking to the chief of the Twenty-fourth Division, Fred Irving. One soldier saw MacArthur, nudged his buddy, and said, "Hey, there's General MacArthur." The other GI did not even bother to turn around, but instead snorted, "Oh, yeah? And I suppose he's got Eleanor Roosevelt along with him." When MacArthur returned to the beach, a microphone had been set up for him. He strode over to it and intoned, "People of the Philippines, I have returned! By the grace of Almighty God, our forces stand again on Philippine soil." After he finished his speech, he turned the microphone over to Osmeña to say a few words, and then the two men consulted for a while before MacArthur returned to *Nashville.* He had every right to be satisfied with the day's accomplishments, which had placed some 60,000 GIs on Leyte at the cost of only 157 casualties.[3]

MacArthur had advocated a campaign to free the Philippines ever since the Japanese drove him from the archipelago and he gave his famous "I shall return" speech in Australia in March 1942. But MacArthur did not speak for the Joint Chiefs of Staff. Chief of Naval Operations Ernest King and many naval officers believed that the best way to prosecute the Pacific War was by seizing Formosa, not Luzon. By way of compromise, in March 1944 the JCS authorized the Dual Drive Offensive by SWPA and the POA toward the vaguely defined China-Formosa-Luzon region and placed in abeyance a final decision as to which island it would ultimately target. As MacArthur's and Nimitz's forces raced westward, MacArthur continued to push for liberating the Philippines. Although he effectively pleaded his case with Roosevelt during a late July meeting at Pearl Harbor to review strategy, the president was content to leave the details of Pacific War strategy in the Joint Chiefs' hands. In the end, it was a combination of logistics, opportunism, and misinterpretation that got MacArthur what he so desperately wanted. In mid-September, Admiral William Halsey's Third Fleet conducted a series of almost unopposed air raids against Japanese positions in the central Philippines. The Japanese were actually hoarding their strength for future battles, but Halsey misconstrued his success as evidence of enemy weakness in the area. He recommended taking advantage of this lack of Japanese activity by striking at Leyte immediately. The Joint Chiefs were receptive to the idea because assailing Formosa was logistically unfeasible until early 1945. Rather than let the Pacific War stagnate until then, the JCS opted to seize the opportunity before it to accelerate the Pacific War. After hurried consultations with MacArthur and Nimitz, on 3 October the JCS ordered SWPA and the POA to cancel most of the various intermediate and now unnecessary operations—the notable exception was the bloody and probably superfluous attacks on Peliliu and Angaur islands in the Palaus by the First Marine and Eighty-first divisions—and occupy Leyte preliminary to an assault on Luzon. The Joint Chiefs believed that by cooperating MacArthur and Nimitz would have sufficient resources for the job.

MacArthur assigned Krueger and his Sixth Army the task of seizing Leyte. Krueger in turn had at his disposal Sibert's and Hodge's corps. Sibert's Tenth Corps was a new SWPA outfit, but Nimitz loaned Hodge's corps to MacArthur after the Joint Chiefs canceled its mission against Yap Island. Although all but one of the divisions allotted to the two corps were combat-hardened—the exception was General James Bradley's rookie Ninety-sixth Division in the Twenty-fourth Corps—both Sibert and Hodge were new to their responsibilities. MacArthur and Krueger probably should have used more experienced corps commanders, but there were only two available: Chink Hall and Oscar Griswold. Hall, however, was busy wrapping up the Morotai operation, and GHQ had slated Griswold for the Luzon invasion. Indeed, the Leyte campaign consumed more time and resources than anticipated and was in many respects SWPA's toughest of the war for several reasons. For one, the Japanese decided to make their stand in the Philippines on Leyte instead of Luzon, and ultimately funneled 45,000 reinforcements to the island, mostly through the west coast city of Ormoc, to augment their original 20,000 defenders. The Americans were unable to stop these convoys due to SWPA's insufficient air power in the region. Because MacArthur opted to launch the assault beyond the range of land-based air support, he initially had to rely on navy carriers to control the skies. Unfortunately, the Battle of Leyte Gulf in late October exhausted the navy and diluted its strength in the area. To make things worse, torrential rains and Leyte's soggy terrain not only made fighting on the island a more miserable experience than usual, but also delayed the construction of airfields. As a result, MacArthur often did not have air superiority, let alone air supremacy, over Leyte. Instead of the relatively easy occupation MacArthur hoped for, the Leyte campaign became a grueling and exhausting struggle with the skillful Japanese that lasted more than two months.

Krueger as usual went about the campaign methodically and systematically, but there was nothing easy about it. Although Hodge's Twenty-fourth Corps secured the southern part of Leyte's central valley by the end of October, Sibert's Tenth Corps ran into considerably more trouble to the north. Fred Irving's Twenty-fourth Division occupied the northern coastal town of Carigara on 2 November, but encountered heavy opposition three days later on the road to Ormoc at Breakneck Ridge. It took a week of relentless combat to break the enemy grip on the ridge, and by then the Twenty-fourth Division was so exhausted that Sibert had to bring up Bill Gill's recently arrived Thirty-second Division to continue the drive to Ormoc. Unfortunately, the Thirty-second Division had an equally difficult time as it pushed southward. To the east, Hodge's forces slowly clawed their way toward Ormoc over difficult terrain. Finally, in an effort to break the battle open, Krueger persuaded MacArthur to let him land General Andrew Bruce's Seventy-seventh Division south of Ormoc on 7 December. Ormoc fell on the tenth, but it still took the unit twelve days of fighting to clear the Ormoc valley and link up with the First Cavalry Division moving southward. Krueger turned the campaign over to Eichelberger's Eighth Army on 26 December, and mopping up the remaining 5,000 Japanese defenders continued until the following May. By that time, the Americans had committed seven divisions and suffered 15,500 casualties, including 3,500 dead, on the island. The Japanese for their part lost approximately 60,000 men.

Considering the fierce combat, heavy losses, and terrible terrain and weather, it was not surprising the Leyte campaign was hard on everyone from the rank and file to MacArthur and his field commanders. Leyte was SWPA's biggest and bloodiest campaign to date. Most of the fighting in New Guinea had occurred in small areas at the division and regimental levels, but on Leyte an entire field army containing two corps and eventually seven divisions conducted operations. It was warfare on a completely new scale for SWPA. From this perspective, it was understandable that American ground forces made all sorts of mistakes. Krueger complained that the infantry relied too much on frontal assaults when enveloping maneuvers promised better results, was too dependent on roads and artillery, and lacked initiative. Worst of all, Krueger did not believe that officers took sufficient care of their men, a cardinal sin as far as he was concerned. Such predictable tactics and indifference to the troops' welfare contributed to high casualties and the slowness of the advance to Ormoc.[4]

Sibert liked and respected Krueger, and later referred to him as the finest soldier he ever served under. In fact, Sibert needed the kind of firm direction Krueger was accustomed to providing. Although Krueger publicly praised Sibert's performance at Leyte, he was not as laudatory behind closed doors. The Tenth Corps entered the campaign with understrength units, and Sibert's lack of tactical imagination did little to compensate for this shortcoming. Instead, he attempted to bull his way through Japanese defenses as he had at Lone Tree Hill. Krueger had few complaints about Verne Mudge's First Cavalry Division, which fought with the same professionalism and élan it had displayed in the Admiralties and maintained its reputation as the best outfit in SWPA. Irving's Twenty-fourth Division and Gill's Thirty-second Division were another story. Sibert became increasingly frustrated with the Twenty-fourth Division's slow progress at Breakneck Ridge, and at one point relieved one of Irving's regimental commanders for lack of aggressiveness without consulting Irving. After he pulled the Twenty-fourth Division out of the line, Sibert with Krueger's consent removed Irving from his post. Irving, a battle-hardened general and SWPA's longest-serving divisional commander, was stunned by this development, for which he received no explanation.

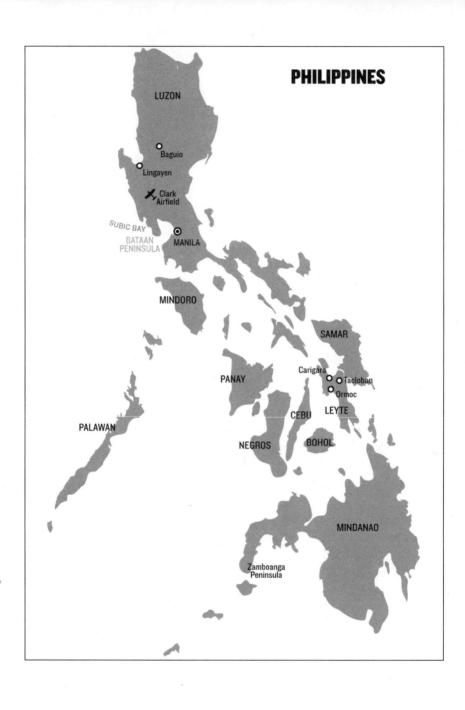

MacArthur, though, later explained to Clovis Byers, "Irving is fine but his staff can't command, he can't eliminate incompetence."[5] No doubt the Twenty-fourth Division had taken more time than anyone expected to overcome the Japanese at Breakneck Ridge, but it also faced formidable obstacles there. Eichelberger for one concluded that Irving actually did better than anyone had a right to expect. Others noted that after Sibert committed it to battle, the Thirty-second Division advanced just as slowly as the Twenty-fourth Division had, but Gill escaped such draconian punishment. Gill and Sibert, however, were old friends who looked out for one another, even though Gill thought he deserved to lead the Tenth Corps more than Sibert. As it was, Gill needed Sibert's support; the stress of the campaign took such a toll on Gill that he was hospitalized after physically abusing several officers and enlisted men.[6]

Hodge's Twenty-fourth Corps, unlike Sibert's, entered the Leyte campaign at full strength, but it was hurriedly and unexpectedly deployed there. As a result, Hodge and his staff had to do much of their own planning without sufficient guidance from or reference to anyone else. Despite such difficulties, Hodge was on the whole proud of his new corps's performance on Leyte. Although he felt that some of his units had difficulty adjusting to combat as part of a corps team on a large battlefield—he noted, for example, that the Seventh Division's men tended to fight shoulder-to-shoulder instead of maneuvering because of their experiences at tiny Attu and Kwajalein—he was pleased that he had put together such a good outfit. Most observers agreed with him. MacArthur and Krueger were both complimentary, as was Nelly Richardson after an inspection trip. Eichelberger later complained that Hodge whined too much about his lack of supplies, but he had nothing critical to say about Hodge's generalship or the quality of his corps. Of Hodge's divisions, Andrew Bruce's Seventy-seventh Division attracted the most positive reviews. Indeed, people rated it as highly as the elite First Cavalry Division, although in all fairness its assignments were not quite as daunting as those of its sister divisions on Leyte. Eichelberger's generous evaluation may have been colored by the fact that he had led the Seventy-seventh back in the States, but Krueger had no such prejudices. Bruce wrote his wife that he almost blushed upon hearing Krueger's effusive and atypical praise. Hodge's satisfaction with the Seventy-seventh Division, however, was somewhat tainted by his suspicion that Bruce might be too ambitious for his own good.[7]

Krueger's admiration for Bruce's division was unusual not only because it was so out of character, but also because of the stress he was under. MacArthur had always leaned on Krueger to complete his operations quickly as part of his effort to get to the Philippines—that "needle from behind"—but now he dramatically increased that pressure because SWPA could not assail Luzon, the archipelago's political and economic heart, until Krueger had crushed Japanese resistance on

Leyte. While MacArthur refrained from giving Krueger direct orders on waging the campaign, he kept close tabs on the fighting and made numerous suggestions. Krueger's efforts to explain the obstacles and problems he faced made little impression on MacArthur. Krueger had been in SWPA for eighteen months, but this was his first time maneuvering entire corps in battle, so he was learning like everyone else. He made frequent trips to the front to consult and prod his subordinates, and tried to profit from lessons learned the hard way. He had hoped to defeat the Japanese and turn the mopping-up duties to Eichelberger's Eighth Army by 24 November, and felt bad that he was unable to meet this deadline. The persistent rain, thick and sticky mud, and determined Japanese opposition made Leyte into a thoroughly wretched experience, although he tried to remain upbeat. One correspondent remembered seeing a weary Krueger in a foxhole after a Japanese air raid, clad only in his underwear, tin hat, and poncho. Whatever his difficulties and frustrations, Krueger was hardly the kind of man to quit, so he remorselessly pushed his subordinates forward. Even Eichelberger, certainly no friend, had to admit, "It seems that [Krueger] is a tough bird. I have been preaching that for a long time but some people seem to be just finding it out. It is one thing to sit hundreds of miles away and settle things on a map but it is different when one gets out in the rain and mud."[8]

Several days after the Sixth Army landed, MacArthur established his headquarters on Tacloban, from where he closely monitored the campaign's progress. As the days went by, he became progressively more frustrated with Krueger's inability to secure the island so SWPA could move on to invade Luzon. Indeed, as October stretched into November and then December, MacArthur started to question Krueger's competence and generalship. Before SWPA invaded Leyte, MacArthur asked Marshall not to retire Krueger when he turned sixty-four because "his services have been superior in every respect and his intimate knowledge of theater conditions and operations make it impossible to adequately replace him."[9] Now, however, MacArthur concluded that perhaps Krueger was no longer the right man for the job as SWPA's primary ground forces commander. If this was the case, his obvious replacement was Eichelberger, whose new Eighth Army was waiting in the wings to mop up on Leyte. After Eichelberger arrived on 21 November, MacArthur repeatedly complained to him about Krueger's apparent lethargy. MacArthur explained to Eichelberger that he had retained Krueger's services despite his age because he thought Krueger was a driver, but his failure to wrap up the campaign in a timely manner boded poorly for future operations on Luzon and elsewhere. That being the case, MacArthur continued, he might have to relieve Krueger from his command. It is unclear whether MacArthur was really serious, or whether he was merely using Eichelberger to prod Krueger into action and blow off steam. At one point, for example, MacArthur in Krueger's presence urged Eichelberger to "come back and see me often," which Eichelberger interpreted as MacArthur's way of reminding Krueger that he was not irreplaceable. As it was, Krueger managed to retain his post, but it was not the last time that MacArthur played his two field commanders off against each other for his own benefit.[10]

Eichelberger had strongly suspected that things were not going according to plan on Leyte, but he was still surprised by conditions there when he arrived on 21 November. His old friend Fred Irving greeted him at the airfield with the startling news that Sibert had relieved him as Twenty-fourth Division commander. Eichelberger was also shocked by the torrential rains, endless mud, and Japanese air raids of a kind rarely seen in SWPA. Although Eichelberger found Krueger friendly and hale, he was obviously under considerable stress. Eichelberger could not help but engage in unseemly schadenfreude over Krueger's difficulties, telling his wife that "my tears dripped off my chin when I listened to excuses such as I would not have been allowed to make myself some time ago."[11] Krueger was vague about when he would be ready to turn the campaign over to the Eighth Army, but Eichelberger was content to let Krueger clean up his own mess. By now Eichelberger so disliked Krueger that he claimed that he would rather be reassigned than serve under him again if, for example, MacArthur made Krueger an army group commander. He explained to his wife, "[Krueger] is as big an ass as I have ever known. He can be pleasant when he wants and be the reverse when he so desires. I dislike him thoroughly and this goes for now and all future years. As far as I am concerned he can choke anytime and the sooner the better."[12] In truth, Eichelberger was well aware that MacArthur was not in the mood to reward Krueger with anything after his performance on Leyte. Eichelberger was happy to listen to and stoke MacArthur's frustrations with Krueger, but he placed little stock in MacArthur's threats to remove him from the Sixth Army. MacArthur, Eichelberger knew, rarely relieved his devoted subordinates, and for all his failings, Krueger had been invariably loyal to his chief.[13]

In addition to undermining and badmouthing Krueger, Eichelberger was busy setting up his Eighth Army headquarters and preparing to take over the Leyte campaign. Doing so required him to make all sorts of often complicated logistical, operational, and personnel decisions. As was often the case, dealing with people presented some of the biggest challenges. Chink Hall and his Eleventh Corps staff were already on Leyte when Hall came down with malaria due to his failure to take his daily atabrine tablets. This violated SWPA protocol, but Eichelberger found Hall's negligence more puzzling than anything else. Of course, he liked Hall and was pleased that the Eighth Army and Eleventh Corps staffs worked together well, so he was not inclined to make an issue of it. Daily doses of quinine restored Hall's health, after which Eichelberger sent him back to Morotai to clean up festering Japanese resistance there. Eichelberger also got along well with General Roscoe Woodruff, Irving's successor as head of the Twenty-fourth Division. Woodruff had been slated to lead a corps in Europe, but Eisenhower and Bradley wanted someone with combat experience, so they shipped him back to the States. Although Eisenhower recommended that Woodruff receive another corps, Mc-Nair for some reason decided that he was not up to the job and gave him a stateside division instead. After he spent some time in the States, Marshall transferred him to SWPA. Woodruff had been sitting around on Leyte without much to do until Krueger tapped him for the Twenty-fourth Division. With his usual bluntness, Krueger said abruptly, "Woodruff, I'm relieving you of your command." Woodruff wondered what sin he had committed because he really had neither responsibilities nor command. Before he could protest his innocence, Krueger sprang the good news that he was getting the Twenty-fourth Division. He had done well with the division and Eichelberger was pleased with his performance. On the other hand, Eichelberger and Byers were annoyed with Bill Gill's tendency to bypass Sibert's corps headquarters and bellyache directly to the Eighth Army, and with John Hodge's "crybaby attitude" toward the allotment of supplies.

As far as Eichelberger was concerned, though, his biggest personnel conundrum was Fred Irving. Eichelberger and Irving were old friends who had served together in Australia and Hollandia. Eichelberger felt sorry for Irving and believed he had been treated unfairly. Moreover, he admired Irving's stoic and uncomplaining attitude in the face of such injustice. While Eichelberger had no immediate opening for Irving commensurate with his rank, he concluded that Irving was a valuable officer whom he could eventually put to good use. Fortunately, Sutherland also sympathized with Irving's plight. Eichelberger did not trust Sutherland one bit, but he was willing to set aside his suspicions for Irving's sake. With Sutherland's approval, Eichelberger made Irving his deputy commander and placed him in charge of the Eighth Army's rear areas for the time being. Irving was very happy to find refuge in Eichelberger's army. Many of these and other personnel issues required a good bit of socializing and schmoozing to smooth out, but this was no difficult task for the genial Eichelberger. His headquarters was as usual a social magnet for high-ranking officers, and Eichelberger noted wryly that people tended to show up around mealtime. He did not mind this much because he was determined to make his Eighth Army a happy military family, not a fearful one like that other SWPA entity.[14]

Sutherland's friendliness toward Eichelberger may or may not have been related to his declining power at GHQ. MacArthur and Sutherland had never been personally close, but they had worked well together professionally until mid-1944. Sutherland had angered MacArthur first by bringing his mistress, Elaine Clarke, to Hollandia against orders, and then by authorizing an invasion of Leyte without MacArthur's explicit approval. MacArthur's rebuke provoked Sutherland into offering his resignation, but MacArthur refused to accept it. MacArthur's doubts about Sutherland's abilities increased as time went on. After Krueger's men seized the Japanese airfield at Tacloban on Leyte, MacArthur and Sutherland inspected it in a jeep. Sutherland several times worried out loud that the Japanese might have mined the airstrip and urged MacArthur to drive elsewhere. Although MacArthur said nothing at the time, later on he repeatedly mentioned the incident to others, asking, "Why do you suppose Dick was so concerned about mines?" The more MacArthur thought about it, the more convinced he became that Sutherland was a man afraid to accept responsibility or face danger. For instance, he remembered that Sutherland had declined the opportunity to take over the First Corps at Buna. In fact, MacArthur's suspicions that there was something wrong with Sutherland were accurate because Sutherland's health was deteriorating under the strains of his position. He was already plagued with chronically high blood pressure and teeth grinding, and at Leyte he contracted an inner ear infection and jungle rot on his feet. Such health problems would have taxed even a young man, and Sutherland was over fifty. As a result, GHQ's deputy chief of staff, Richard Marshall, was doing more and more of Sutherland's work. It was an open secret that Sutherland's grip over GHQ was slipping, and more than one person saw it as just deserts for his abrasive and cold-hearted management style.[15]

A week after MacArthur established his advanced headquarters at Tacloban, Sutherland ordered his mistress brought to Leyte from Brisbane despite MacArthur's direct orders that she remain in Australia. Whatever his motivations for doing so—loneliness, lust, defiance; Sutherland never clearly explained—it was certainly a foolish decision. Sutherland directed General Jack Sverdrup, SWPA's aviation engineer, to construct a cottage for her down the road from Tacloban. Sverdrup did not want to, but he felt he had no choice because Sutherland was his boss. He did, however, ask Roger Egeberg, the GHQ physician, to inform MacArthur about Elaine Clarke's presence. Egeberg did so, and MacArthur responded angrily, "I don't believe it! I don't believe it! I told him not to let her come north of Australia, and he knows that." He asked Richard Marshall to investigate. Marshall knew the truth, but for whatever reason he lied and told MacArthur it was just a rumor. It might have ended there had not Clarke's bossiness and Sutherland's continuing unpopularity prompted several of MacArthur's staffers to persuade Egeberg to raise the issue again. A week before Christmas, Egeberg and MacArthur talked on the porch of GHQ headquarters after dinner. After Egeberg steered the conversation in the proper direction, MacArthur asked, "Say, Doc, whatever happened to that woman?" Egeberg initially feigned ignorance, so MacArthur continued, "Oh, you know, *that woman*." Egeberg replied, "She's in that cottage I told you about down at Tanauan." MacArthur exploded,

"What! Get me Dick!" He stormed into the house and confronted a startled Sutherland at his desk. "Dick Sutherland," MacArthur exclaimed, "I gave you an order. You disobeyed it. You are relieved of your command. You are under arrest." Sutherland belligerently responded, and all the officers milling about in the street outside heard the ensuing altercation, which included MacArthur cussing Sutherland out in a manner that would have done Krueger proud.[16]

Sutherland's personal pilot flew a distraught Clarke back to Brisbane the next day. Everyone at GHQ expected Sutherland to follow her in disgrace at any time, but it did not happen. After his anger had cooled, MacArthur had second thoughts and did not follow up with written orders removing Sutherland as chief of staff. SWPA was preparing for a big and complicated assault on Luzon, and MacArthur may have concluded that Sutherland's services were at that point too indispensable to part with him. Or he may have been resorting to a crueler and more diabolical punishment than relief. By now Sutherland no longer wanted to be chief of staff, partly because of his stress-induced bad health, and partly because he saw it as a dead-end job. By taking away his mistress and publicly humiliating him, MacArthur turned the chief of staff position into a living purgatory and reduced Sutherland to a shell of his former self. He was still chief of staff, but without the authority and power he once wielded. In fact, from that point on Richard Marshall assumed more and more of Sutherland's duties. To what extent these machinations would impact SWPA's future operations remained to be seen, but it was clear that Sutherland's reign of brutal efficiency was over.[17]

To Luzon

Leyte was important because it got MacArthur to his beloved Philippines, but its occupation was merely preparatory to his bigger goal of seizing Luzon, the archipelago's political and economic center. MacArthur had originally promised to assail Luzon on 20 December, but prolonged and unexpected Japanese resistance on Leyte forced him to postpone the assault. Even after Krueger finally got a handle on the situation on Leyte, there were other delays. Weather and tides were part of the problem, but the biggest obstacle was the lack of air support for the invasion. Recent operations had worn out the navy's carrier task forces, and anyway their inability to maintain adequate air cover over Leyte gave MacArthur a jaded view of fighting beyond the range of land-based warplanes under his command. To rectify this deficiency, on 15 December a regiment from the Twenty-fourth Division grabbed Mindoro Island, south of Luzon, without much opposition. American and Australian aviation engineers worked around the clock to carve airfields out of the jungle to support the big attack on Luzon, and fighter planes were flying out of Mindoro in only five days. On 2–4 January 1945, another huge American armada assembled in Leyte Gulf and sailed for Luzon. Although the remnants of the Japanese navy stayed out of the way, the Japanese unleashed their latest innovation on the approaching fleet: kamikazes. Wave after wave of these suicide planes sank or damaged twenty-five vessels, but fortunately neglected the vulnerable transports. Krueger's Sixth Army splashed ashore on 9 January at Lingayen Bay, halfway up Luzon's west coast, the same place the Japanese had landed three years earlier. As at Leyte, the Japanese were unwilling to expose their soldiers to American naval firepower, so Krueger's men waded to the beach without hearing hardly a shot fired in anger, followed by MacArthur on another victory tour. Within a few days, MacArthur had placed 175,000 troops along a 25-mile-wide beachhead within striking distance of Manila.

In retrospect, it might have been wiser for MacArthur to use Eichelberger's fresh Eighth Army on Luzon instead of Krueger's tired Sixth. At the time, though, it made sense to give the job to Krueger. MacArthur's GHQ drew up its plans for Luzon before the Leyte campaign cast doubts on Krueger's generalship. Until Leyte, MacArthur had considerable respect for Krueger, who had successfully overseen every SWPA operation in New Guinea for a year and a half. He and his staff were experienced at integrating and coordinating SWPA's disparate land, sea, and air forces for the complex amphibious warfare prevalent in the Pacific. Whatever Eichelberger's achievements with the First Corps, directing a field army was much more complicated, and his army staff was fresh off the boat from the States. Moreover, initially many assumed that the Eighth Army would be a mopping-up and training entity. Krueger had at his disposal the two best corps in the Pacific, Palmer Swift's First and Oscar Griswold's Fourteenth. Swift may have been a new corps commander, but before that he had led the First Cavalry Division to victory in the Admiralties and turned it into the finest unit in SWPA. His staff, formerly Eichelberger's, had been in SWPA since 1942 and had participated in the Buna and Hollandia operations. As for Griswold's corps, it had become part of SWPA when the Joint Chiefs divided SOPAC's combat resources between MacArthur and Nimitz. Although the Fourteenth Corps's staff had been cobbled together out of the American Division, it had successfully supervised fighting on Guadalcanal, New Georgia, and Bougainville. Griswold had partaken in the latter two battles and now, after six months twiddling his thumbs on Bougainville, was rested and ready to go. Krueger's general plan was for Griswold's corps to drive for Manila while Swift protected his left, or eastern, flank and the Lingayen Bay beachhead.

While MacArthur's and Krueger's staffers pored over their maps, reports, and charts, General Tomoyuki Yamashita, the commander of the Japanese forces in the Philippines, was formulating his own plans for the Luzon campaign. Yamashita had at his disposal approximately 275,000 men, but he had lost his best troops, their equipment, and almost all of his airpower on Leyte. As a military realist, Yamashita recognized that there was little chance he could overcome American firepower and mobility to defeat MacArthur on the battlefield. Instead, he hoped to give his compatriots in the Home Islands time to prepare for an American invasion by holding out as long as possible on Luzon. To do so, he chose not to defend Manila and the Luzon plains, but rather to deploy his soldiers in well-placed strongholds throughout the island. He put 152,000 men in the Cordillera Central Mountains surrounding the fertile Cagayan valley in central Luzon (the Shobu Group), another 30,000 soldiers in the Zambales Mountains overlooking Clark Field between Manila and Lingayen Bay (the Kembu Group), and 50,000 troops in the Sierra Madre Mountains east of Manila to control the city's water supplies (the Shimbu Group). Yamashita gambled that the Americans would exhaust themselves pounding on these tough defenses.

Because of Yamashita's deployments, the first days of the campaign went very well for the Americans. Swift's corps pushed eastward while Griswold's troops thrust southward toward the Agno River against minimal opposition. Ironically enough, however, the very absence of Japanese resistance undermined and almost destroyed the relationship between MacArthur and Krueger. SWPA planners had not drawn up a detailed timetable for the Sixth Army to seize its objectives because no one was certain to what extent the Japanese would fight. Krueger knew that there were tens of thousands of Japanese in the Cordillera Central Mountains, and he worried that they might plunge into the gap between Griswold's and Swift's corps and storm Lingayen Bay if the Fourteenth Corps moved southward too quickly. Ever methodical, Krueger insisted on a measured advance that kept the two corps in contact with each other. MacArthur disagreed. He wanted to get on the road to reach Manila as quickly as possible, preferably by his—and Krueger's—birthday on 26 January, and doubted that the Japanese would assume the offensive anywhere. Just a few days after the landing, on 12 January, MacArthur and Krueger met on MacArthur's flagship, the cruiser USS *Boise*. MacArthur pointed out the gratifyingly low casualties the Sixth Army had suffered so far and urged Krueger to drive as rapidly as possible for Manila. Krueger in response alluded to all the Japanese in the hills to the east as the reason for his cautious pace. The exchange grew heated as Krueger dug in his heels and argued back. MacArthur as usual refused to override Krueger's orders, but the discussion reinforced his growing belief, first expressed on Leyte, that Krueger might be too old and timid to wage his kind of war. On 21 January, after both MacArthur and Krueger had moved ashore, MacArthur drove to Krueger's headquarters near Dagupan to renew the debate. On his way over, MacArthur explained to his personal physician, Roger Egeberg:

You know, I want to talk to Walter to see if I can persuade him to go down the plain a little bit faster. I think he feels that every side valley on our east is full of Japanese ready to come storming out. Well, there are plenty of Japanese back there, but they're defending the Cagayan Valley where they hope to make their last big stand, and they are not going to come charging down into the plain with all that we have here.[18]

MacArthur and Krueger chatted in a screened porch full of the books that Krueger took with him everywhere, but once again MacArthur failed to bend Krueger to his will. On their way back to his headquarters, MacArthur said somewhat ominously to Egeberg, "Walter is pretty stubborn. Maybe I'll have to try something else."[19]

Removing Krueger from the Sixth Army was one obvious way to change the dynamics of the advance on Manila. Indeed, MacArthur seriously contemplated doing so during the long frustrating weeks in front of the Philippine capital. Many of his staffers and subordinates urged him to make the change. General George Kenney, SWPA's aggressive air forces chief, bluntly told MacArthur that he would not get the celerity he sought until Krueger was out of the way. Sutherland agreed, arguing that Krueger was simply too old for his job. To replace Krueger, Sutherland recommended either Eichelberger or Chink Hall. Eichelberger was of course an obvious choice because he already led his own army and was a proven winner. Hall, on the other hand, had not so far done anything to differentiate himself from the other corps commanders. In the end, however, MacArthur opted to keep Krueger where he was. He had told Marshall on several occasions that Krueger was an outstanding general and had recently recommended his promotion to the four-star rank, so he may have been too embarrassed to suddenly relieve him of his command. MacArthur may also have recognized that supplanting Krueger would open up another slot he had to fill, and none of SWPA's division commanders had proven himself capable of waging war at that higher level. Or it may have been simpler than either of these explanations. MacArthur and Krueger had known and respected each other for forty years, during which they had built up a bond of trust not easily torn down. MacArthur firmly believed in rewarding and respecting loyalty, which was something that Krueger had shown in spades during his time in SWPA, and MacArthur may not have wanted to humiliate him. Perhaps this was what MacArthur meant when he said to Kenney, "I would hate to have to retire an old man like that and send him home."[20]

Krueger may or may not have realized that his head was on the chopping block, but he knew full well that MacArthur wanted greater results from him. As usual, Krueger responded to MacArthur's pressure by exerting some of his own on his subordinates. Of his two corps commanders on Luzon, Swift was more susceptible to Krueger's heavy-handed form of persuasion. After all, Swift was indebted to Krueger for his current position, and was in many ways Krueger's protégé. Moreover, Swift had great respect for high-ranking positions, regardless of his feelings for the men who filled them. Swift had at his disposal two divisions, the Sixth and Forty-third. Both were veteran outfits, the former having cut its teeth at Lone Tree Hill and the latter at New Georgia. The First Corps's initial objective was to seize the road junction near Rosario that connected Baguio in the Cagayan valley with Manila. Once in American hands, it would be extremely difficult for the Japanese to pour into the Luzon plain. Unhappily, the Forty-third Division ran into considerable resistance and suffered heavy casualties in its first attempts to occupy the town and crossroads. Even after Krueger reinforced Swift with the hard-hitting Twenty-fifth Division, the First Corps was unable to clear the area until the end of January. As the days went by, with MacArthur breathing down his neck, Krueger grew increasingly frustrated with Swift and decided that he had to do something to improve his corps's poor performance. Although Krueger of course chewed Swift out, he refrained from relieving him of his post. Instead, Krueger without Swift's foreknowledge or approval removed the First Corps's chief of staff and operations officer. The tight-knit First Corps staffers had thought they were doing a good job under difficult circumstances, so they were shocked, angered, and demoralized by Krueger's unexpected purge. They felt especially bad for Swift. A humiliated Swift was equally stunned and interpreted Krueger's action as the vote of no confidence it was. But, as one staffer later remembered, "Nevertheless, the operation went on, as though losing a first-rate Chief of Staff and a first rate G-3 [operations officer] were an every day occurrence."[21]

Nor did Krueger neglect Oscar Griswold. Griswold's two divisions, the Thirty-seventh and Fortieth, at first encountered almost no opposition as they worked their way southward toward Manila. Indeed, Griswold's biggest problem—besides being hit by a rock churned up by a passing truck—was rebuilding the destroyed bridges so he could resupply his advancing troops. On 23 January, however, the Fourteenth Corps ran into the 30,000 Japanese soldiers of the Kembu Group defending Clark Field, about halfway down the road to Manila. Initial attacks by elements of the Fortieth Division made little headway, so Griswold boldly wheeled almost his entire force to the east and threw it at Clark Field, even though doing so exposed his left flank. Seizing the airfield and the surrounding heights took until the end of the month and cost a good many injuries all around. Despite this triumph, Griswold felt little jubilation. For one thing, he was perplexed with MacArthur's premature announcement of the fall of Fort Stotsenburg, a prewar army base adjacent to Clark Field. With a surprisingly quaint naiveté, Griswold asked himself, "*Why does he do this?*"[22] More disconcerting, though, was Krueger's anger at the Fourteenth Corps's slow progress toward Manila. Krueger seemed to blame Griswold not only for the time it took him to overcome Japanese defenses, but also for the existence of those defenses in the first place. After the Thirty-seventh Division successfully stormed Fort Stotsenburg, Griswold invited Krueger to a ceremony marking its recapture. This thoughtful gesture did not placate Krueger one bit, prompting Griswold to write, "[Krueger] raised flag over Stotsenburg. Was nasty and critical about things in general. Nothing seemed to please him. Refused to meet the men who saved the flag!"[23] Nine days later, Griswold expanded on his feelings about Krueger, noting that he was the "damndest man to serve with I ever saw!"[24] Unlike the equally beleaguered Swift, Griswold was more inclined to argue back, especially in defense of his subordinates. The Thirty-seventh Division was a National Guard unit from Ohio led by guardsman General Robert Beightler. Although Griswold and Beightler were friends, Krueger liked neither guard units nor guard officers, so he was very critical of Beightler. He was just as hard on General Rapp Brush and his Fortieth Division. Griswold, though, risked Krueger's wrath by defending both men and their outfits. And so, with Krueger breathing down his neck, Griswold left the Fortieth Division behind to deal with the remaining Japanese around Clark Field and got the Thirty-seventh Division back on track for Manila.[25]

While Krueger made life difficult for Swift and Griswold, MacArthur continued to seek ways to prod the Sixth Army forward toward Manila. For example, MacArthur moved his headquarters south of the Sixth Army's back at Bonuan Boquig, placing him considerably closer to the fighting than Krueger. Doing so not only served as an unsubtle reminder to Krueger of his sluggishness, but also enabled MacArthur to range along the front lines to keep personal tabs on the advancing troops. He was unhappy to discover the Thirty-seventh Division moving so slowly, and on 30 January he issued a sharp order to Krueger condemning Beightler's apparent lethargy. On 27 January, the first substantial reinforcements arrived on Luzon, including Verne Mudge's elite First Cavalry Division. MacArthur saw the outfit as the ideal instrument for reaching Manila quickly. Bypassing Krueger, on 1 February MacArthur told Mudge, "Go to Manila. Go around the Nips, bounce off the Nips, but go to Manila."[26] Although still 70 miles from Manila, Mudge hurriedly formed two flying columns and sent them southward with orders to avoid enemy contact and get to the Philippine capital as rapidly as possible.[27]

MacArthur left no stone unturned in his determination to get to Manila quickly. If Krueger was unwilling or unable to reach the city in a timely manner, then MacArthur was prepared to give someone else a chance to do so. MacArthur already knew that he could play Krueger and Eichelberger off against each other, but now he took the competition to a whole new level by injecting the Eighth

Army into the campaign. GHQ planned to land General Joseph Swing's Eleventh Airborne Division at Nasugbu on Luzon's coast about 50 miles southeast of Manila. MacArthur not only placed Eichelberger in charge of the operation over Krueger's protests, but also gave him verbal orders to push on to the capital as soon as he secured the beachhead. Eichelberger was thrilled by the opportunity to enter the fray and get to Manila ahead of his detested rival. Eichelberger's opinion of Krueger had not improved much since the Sixth Army moved on to Luzon; quite to the contrary. Eichelberger questioned Krueger's generalship and courage, and snidely observed that he could not even handle the divisions he already had, let alone the Eleventh Airborne. He went so far as to hope that Krueger would fail, adding, "If I never see him again it will be too soon."[28] Eichelberger's words were so strident and venomous that even Clovis Byers, his loyal and reverential chief of staff, wished that his boss would stop publicly denigrating Krueger so much. MacArthur and his staffers, on the other hand, deliberately encouraged Eichelberger's prejudices by freely criticizing Krueger in his presence. On 31 January, two regiments of the Eleventh Airborne splashed ashore at Nasugbu without much opposition, and three days later the balance of the division parachuted onto nearby Tagaytay Ridge. A high-spirited Eichelberger hurriedly deployed Swing's men on the road to Manila, determined to win the MacArthur-sponsored race to the city. Eichelberger figured that the odds were in his favor because if Krueger was anywhere near Manila he would already be crowing about it. On 4 February the Eleventh Airborne ran into strong Japanese defenses along the Parañaque River outside of the city. Although the paratroopers managed to push into Nichols Field, they lacked the firepower to force their way into the capital, thus depriving Eichelberger of the laurels he sought. MacArthur terminated Eichelberger's mission on 10 February and incorporated the Eleventh Airborne into Griswold's corps, but Eichelberger was still proud of his performance, noting, "I think our coming here has definitely put the Eighth Army on the map."[29]

Eichelberger may have impressed MacArthur with his élan, but the fact was that Krueger won the race to Manila. On 3 February, elements of the First Cavalry Division reached the northern outskirts of the city and rescued some 4,000 Allied prisoners held at Santo Tomas University. The next day MacArthur insisted that Griswold and Mudge accompany him on a drive into the capital. He did not expect the Japanese to fight hard for the city, and figured it would fall more or less intact. Griswold thought otherwise, and believed that the dead American and Japanese soldiers littering the road were evidence in his favor. He breathed a sigh of relief when they returned to the safety of American lines. Griswold labeled the trip "foolhardy" and could not understand MacArthur's obsessive behavior. In fact, Yamashita had not planned to defend Manila, but the local naval commander decided differently and dug in with his 16,000 troops for a struggle to the bitter end. Consequently, Griswold's First Cavalry and Thirty-seventh divisions had to battle the enemy in vicious street-to-street and house-to-house fighting that lasted a month and completely wrecked the city. Manila contained 800,000 inhabitants at the beginning of the siege, of whom 100,000 died in the crossfire or by Japanese atrocities. MacArthur outraged Griswold by forbidding airstrikes on the city in an effort to preserve lives and property, but the massive amounts of artillery Griswold employed rendered such issues moot. From a sand trap on a golf course at Grace Park, Griswold systematically and professionally prosecuted the offensive into Manila and gradually pushed the Japanese into the old walled enclave of Intramuros. American artillery blew the walls apart and beat down remaining Japanese opposition. Although Griswold again complained that MacArthur had prematurely declared an objective captured ("the one weakness of a really great man—publicity"), he was in high spirits when on 3 March he informed Krueger that Japanese resistance had ended. Indeed, Griswold had good reason to be satisfied with his generalship. In a month of sharp urban combat, and at the cost of 6,575 casualties, he had skillfully destroyed the Japanese garrison and freed Manila. Of equal importance, at least as far as Griswold's career was concerned, he had won MacArthur's respect and admiration in the process. Indeed, MacArthur subsequently referred to Griswold as his best corps commander.[30]

Whatever its symbolic or psychological value to MacArthur, Manila's strategic importance was limited as long as the Japanese controlled its harbor. MacArthur worried that the Japanese might emulate his example in 1941–1942 by withdrawing to the Bataan peninsula for a drawn-out last stand. To prevent this, GHQ decided to use SWPA's amphibious mobility to land General Henry Jones's rookie Thirty-eighth Division and a regiment from the battle-tested Twenty-fourth Division on the Zambales coast northwest of Bataan, from where they could drive eastward and seal the peninsula off from any Japanese trying to retreat there. Because Jones had no experience in amphibious warfare, Krueger persuaded MacArthur to insert Chink Hall's Eleventh Corps headquarters into the operation. The Eleventh Corps was the only army corps in the Pacific War that had not yet seen significant action in the Philippines, but Hall had successfully led it along the Driniumor River and at Morotai. On 29 January, 40,000 GIs landed unopposed at Zambales, seized Subic Bay, and then plunged toward Bataan. Unluckily, on 1 February they ran into heavy resistance from the Japanese still in the Zambales Mountains at ZigZag Pass. Initial efforts to push through failed miserably. Troops were poorly deployed, units got lost, and attacks were uncoordinated. Considering the Thirty-eighth Division's greenness, this should not have been surprising, but Hall showed little patience for the outfit's circumstances. He had already been disappointed with the division's staff during the planning for the invasion, and his anger mounted rapidly when Jones was unable to press his assaults home. Hall criticized Jones's lack of aggressiveness, improper deployments, failure to communicate effectively, and, most importantly, inability to produce results. Jones was an odd fellow anyway—Eichelberger called him a "queer genius"—and perhaps this played a role in Hall's diminishing confidence in him. The Thirty-eighth Division, Hall said, was the worst division he had ever seen. All of this may have been true, but Jones and his men had the excuse of inexperience. Hall, on the other hand, was a SWPA veteran, but he demonstrated little understanding of the terrain, communications problems, Japanese strength and dispositions, and the caliber of the troops he commanded. Although he relieved Jones on 6 February, there was little improvement in the division's performance. The Americans did not seize the pass until 15 February, by which time they had lost 1,400 men. By then there were few Japanese left in the area, so Hall easily occupied the Bataan peninsula. Despite his lackluster generalship at ZigZag Pass, Hall escaped Krueger's and MacArthur's censure, probably because they were too busy overseeing the fight for Manila to notice that Hall was as guilty as Jones. Indeed, MacArthur and Krueger both later praised Hall's actions on Luzon.[31]

Unhappily for Krueger's tired GIs, Manila's conquest and the opening of its harbor did not end the fighting on Luzon, but was instead merely the beginning. Although the Kembu Group around Clark Field had been severely battered, Yamashita's other two strongholds, the Shobu Group in northern Luzon and the Shimbu Group east of Manila, remained intact. Several factors, however, hindered Krueger's efforts to eliminate them. For one thing, the Japanese had had months to dig formidable defenses on the ridges and mountainsides in northern and eastern Luzon, and were comparatively well supplied. To make things worse, Krueger lacked sufficient strength to quickly reduce the Japanese fortresses because MacArthur stripped the Sixth Army of several of its divisions and gave them to Eichelberger for his campaign in the central and southern Philippines. Krueger therefore not only was outnumbered by the defenders, but also had to repeatedly commit tired divisions, some of which had not rested and refitted since before the Leyte campaign. First Griswold's Fourteenth Corps, and then after 15 March Hall's Eleventh Corps, battled the Shimbu Group in the Sierra Madre Mountains east of Manila for control of the reservoirs providing water to the wrecked city. After some fierce combat, what was left of the Japanese retreated eastward and northward in late May. At the same time, Swift's First Corps was locked in a protracted struggle with Yamashita's Shobu Group in northern Luzon. The Thirty-third and Thirty-seventh divisions seized the important resort town of Baguio on 27 April, but the Japanese continued to hold out in the mountains until the end of the war. By skillfully dragging out the campaign, Yamashita accomplished his primary objective of delaying and wearing out American units that might have spent the time preparing for a climactic assault on the Japanese homeland. Indeed, the Americans suffered some 37,870 casualties on Luzon, nearly half of whom fell fighting the Shobu Group in northern Luzon.

On 12 February, Krueger moved his headquarters to San Fernando, north of Manila Bay, where it remained for the rest of the war. The place had nostalgic value for Krueger; he had taken his examination for his commission there in 1901. While there Krueger got word on 5 March of his promotion to full general. Marshall was reluctant to appoint field army commanders to that rank, but he decided that Krueger's record and approaching retirement merited it. It was quite an achievement for someone who had not attended West Point, but had instead started out as a lowly enlisted man and clawed his way up. Krueger was justifiably proud of this accomplishment, which placed him at the very pinnacle of his profession. Not that Krueger took much time to celebrate. He believed that generals should get out into the field as much as possible, and set a personal example with frequent trips to see various corps and divisions. As usual, he paid particular attention to the rank and file that did the bulk of the fighting and dying. When he was not on the road, he tried to relax and forget about the war for awhile. Observers noted that by the time he got to Luzon, Krueger did not read as much history as he used to, but instead plowed his way through spy novels and mystery stories.[32]

The protracted fighting on Luzon was as hard on the generals as on the enlisted men, but in different ways. Burdened with the responsibility for the lives of thousands of men, the war was always with combat generals regardless of their personal circumstances and the privileges of their rank. In addition, the Sixth Army's corps and division commanders had to contend with the crusty Krueger. For all his talents as a general, Krueger's people skills left much to be desired. Krueger treated all his generals the same—directly, roughly, and bluntly. Tact, discretion, diplomacy, and ingratiation simply were not part of his interpersonal baggage. Although some of his subordinates responded well to his particular brand of communication, an increasing number did not. As a result, by the end of the summer Krueger had alienated almost all of his chief lieutenants, and most looked forward to the day when Eichelberger would take over the mopping-up duties on Luzon so Krueger could concentrate on planning the invasion of the southern Japanese island of Kyushu. Even so, they were also uncomfortably aware that they might have to serve under him again in an assault on Japan.

Of the Sixth Army's corps commanders, Oscar Griswold was probably the unhappiest with Krueger. Not only was Griswold new to SWPA and unaccustomed to Krueger's leadership style, but he was also more inclined to fight back. Griswold resented Krueger's browbeating and felt unappreciated for his efforts in seizing Manila. Griswold had always spoken his mind and stood up for himself, and he had no intention of changing for Krueger or anyone else. For example, he refused to relieve Rapp Brush, commander of the Fortieth Division, when Krueger pressured him to do so. He also recommended the Thirty-seventh Division's Robert Beightler for a Distinguished Service Medal against Krueger's wishes. Finally, Griswold spoke positively of Fred Irving in Krueger's presence. Although there is no evidence that Krueger retaliated against Griswold for his defiance and attitude, Griswold remained stressed and miserable. He was further distressed when he was not promoted to lead the Tenth Army after its commander, Simon Buckner, was killed on Okinawa. His health, never good, declined so much that he was hospitalized for a week in May. Thereafter he looked worn out and tired, but maintained a busy schedule, perhaps buoyed by the knowledge that his time under Krueger's tutelage was coming to an end. On 1 July, the Fourteenth Corps became part of Eichelberger's Eighth Army. Griswold was glad to work for his old friend Eichelberger, writing, "It is a relief to belong no longer to Sixth Army, where one is ever heckled and hampered. I think the Corps will be much happier in its new role."[33]

Palmer Swift and Chink Hall felt much the same way. Hall, for example, resented Krueger's unsuccessful efforts to pressure *him* to fire Rapp Brush after the Fortieth Division came under his control. Hall had served in both the Sixth Army and Eighth Army, and he made it clear to Eichelberger that he preferred to work with him. Swift, on the other hand, was in a more delicate situation because he was beholden to Krueger for his appointment as First Corps commander. However, Krueger had not only browbeaten Swift, but also humiliated him by unilaterally replacing the First Corps's chief of staff and operations officer. Eichelberger noticed that although Swift refrained from criticizing Krueger, he did not go out of his way to defend him either. Swift bore the brunt of the fighting in northern Luzon, but he seemed to withstand the pressure quite well. Eichelberger stated that he looked better than he had in New Guinea. Although some criticized his cautiousness, there was nothing wrong with Swift's personal courage. One day his jeep came under fire from Japanese snipers, so he ordered the driver to stop and take cover while he rounded up a half dozen straggling infantrymen and led them into the bush in a successful effort to "get those goddam bastards." Despite this evidence of vigor, Swift was so tired that in July he confessed to Eichelberger that he was ready to go home. For Swift, as with so many GIs in northern Luzon, the war had gone on for too long.[34]

Disaffection with Krueger was by no means limited to the corps level; many division commanders were also unhappy with him. The Fortieth Division's Rapp Brush opted to retire when he learned that his outfit was returning to the Sixth Army after a stint with Eichelberger. He got some measure of revenge on Krueger by venting his spleen to Marshall during a long meeting after he returned to the

States. Robert Beightler was dissatisfied with both Swift and Krueger, the former for not using the Thirty-seventh Division aggressively enough, and the latter for failing to give his outfit sufficient credit for its efforts at Manila and elsewhere. Beightler missed Griswold, who had respected him and treated him well despite his National Guard background. When Eichelberger gave a complimentary speech to the Thirty-seventh Division, Beightler's eyes welled up as he explained that no one had praised his hard-fighting unit since it left the Solomons. Beightler was not the only division commander who appreciated Griswold at Krueger's expense; Bill Gill did too. Griswold had stood by Gill despite his erratic behavior on Leyte, and Gill in return supported Griswold and embraced his hostile attitude toward Krueger. In fact, when Eichelberger took control of operations on Luzon, Gill swore he would never serve another day under Krueger. The Thirty-third Division's General Perk Clarkson also hoped to escape Krueger. Joe Swing and General William Arnold, commanders of, respectively, the Eleventh Airborne Division and the American Division, were already Eichelberger fans. Swing worried that Krueger would relieve him if he came under the Sixth Army's authority, and Griswold speculated that Arnold would meet the same fate. In August, MacArthur gave Fred Irving the Thirty-eighth Division, and Irving could hardly have relished the thought of more time with Krueger. To be sure, Krueger had his adherents, but they were few and far between. The Sixth Division's General Edwin Patrick, for example, got along with Krueger right up to the time of his death by Japanese machine-gun fire in northern Luzon. SWPA generals were soldiers accustomed to obeying orders, but their hostility toward Krueger was hardly conducive to the construction of an effective and trusting command team.[35]

MacArthur was aware of the general discontent within the Sixth Army toward Krueger, but, except for occasional expressions of sympathy to the afflicted, he did little about it. As it was, MacArthur had bigger problems closer to home. MacArthur had retained Sutherland as his chief of staff despite their falling out on Leyte. Regrettably, Sutherland continued to disappoint him. Soon after the Sixth Army landed on Luzon, Sutherland asked MacArthur for permission to fly to Brisbane to see a dentist about his aching teeth. MacArthur approved the request and empathized with his pain, but after Sutherland left MacArthur exclaimed to his personal physician, "Brisbane! Four thousand miles away! Dick must be sick. What's wrong with him, Doc? Is he off his rocker? The Luzon campaign [is] right in front of him. A pinnacle of his career, and he goes off to Brisbane."[36] While Down Under, Sutherland not only got his teeth examined and his jungle rot treated, but also spent time with his mistress. When he returned to the Philippines in early February, however, he discovered that not much had changed for him. The politeness that he and MacArthur displayed toward one another did not completely hide the underlying tension between them, and Sutherland wanted out from under MacArthur's thumb more than ever. His attempt to take advantage of MacArthur's anger with Krueger to secure command of the Sixth Army failed, as did his belated efforts to be kinder to those around him. By summer, his blood pressure was so elevated that he had to travel to the States for tests. He returned in time for the ceremonies surrounding Japan's surrender, but by then he was a mere shadow of his former self.[37]

Despite his various problems and numerous efforts to escape, Sutherland remained at his post until the war's end primarily because MacArthur could not find a suitable replacement. When MacArthur became aware of Sutherland's shattered health, he actively searched for a new chief of staff, but finding one was more easily said than done. Good chiefs of staff were hard to come by. The job required considerable work and little glory because MacArthur tended to delegate the former and monopolize the latter. Generally speaking, MacArthur had not recruited strong-willed and independent men for GHQ, so the pool there was pretty shallow. Richard Marshall, Sutherland's deputy, was an obvious candidate. He had been shouldering an increasingly heavy load due to Sutherland's illness and was thoroughly familiar with SWPA plans, personalities, and limitations. Unfortunately, Marshall lacked the force of personality for the post, and he was reluctant to assume it anyway. MacArthur considered General Daniel Sultan and General Joseph Stilwell, but neither panned out. Mulling things over, MacArthur concluded that Eichelberger would be a good chief of staff. After all, he had a proven track record in SWPA, and was just then impressing almost everyone with his successful campaign in the central and southern Philippines. On 4 June, MacArthur broached the subject with Eichelberger, stating, "I may have to make you my Chief of Staff. I have looked over the list and you are the only one who can do it. Dick has been sick . . . but was up again and at work and that may explain the crazy things he has been doing for the last six months. Think this over and so shall I."[38] Eichelberger did so, and not surprisingly rejected the offer. Although serving as chief of staff would give him a broader view of the war, it would also take him away from his prestigious and important combat command just before the climactic invasion of Japan. Besides, Eichelberger had little respect for GHQ staffers, as a group, and did not want to join MacArthur's sycophantic band. After Eichelberger turned him down, MacArthur figured that the lackluster Sutherland/Marshall team would have to suffice.[39]

Eichelberger's Amphibious Blitzkrieg

One of the reasons for the Sixth Army's long and exhausting ordeal on Luzon was that Krueger lacked sufficient resources to prosecute it effectively. Instead of reinforcing Krueger, MacArthur opted to embark on another concurrent campaign to occupy the central and southern Philippines. This region had little strategic value, but MacArthur insisted on liberating it even though the Joint Chiefs had not explicitly authorized him to do so. His reasoning is unclear. He may have wanted to protect American prisoners and Filipino civilians from Japanese retribution, or to provide airbases for planned Australian operations in nearby Borneo, or to restore American prestige by freeing the entire archipelago. Whatever MacArthur's motives, conducting the campaign required all or parts of five divisions—the Americal, Twenty-fourth, Thirty-first, Fortieth, and Forty-first—as well as plenty of air and naval power that he might have committed to Luzon. He put Eichelberger in charge, and in a series of brilliant operations that included fourteen major and twenty-four minor amphibious assaults in just forty-four days, often on a logistical shoestring, the Eighth Army fulfilled its mission. Eichelberger's amphibious blitzkrieg included landings on Palawan on 28 February, the Zamboanga Peninsula on 10 March, Panay on 18 March, Cebu on 26 March, Los Negros on 29 March, Sanga-Sanga on 2 April, Jolo on 9 April, Bohol on 11 April, and, finally, eastern Mindanao on 17 April. In most cases, the Japanese did not fight on the beaches, but instead retreated inland to make their last stands against the Americans and Filipino guerrillas. Most of the combat ended that summer, but significant numbers of Japanese continued to hold out until the end of the war. The tactically brilliant but strategically barren campaign cost the United States some 9,000 casualties and the Japanese a little over 50,000.

Eichelberger was not surprisingly very proud of his achievement. He saw the campaign as an opportunity to get out from Krueger's shadow and show the world what he and his army could do on their own. He never questioned the strategic utility of his blizzard of landings, but instead wrote of them, "Personally I do not think anyone else has equaled them for brilliance in this theater or faintly approached them."[40] GHQ staffers stroked his ego by noting that he did more with less than anyone else in SWPA—meaning Krueger. In this they merely took their cue from MacArthur, who showered Eichelberger with praise not only because he sincerely admired his generalship, but also as part of his continuing effort to play him off against Krueger. "You run an army in combat just like I would have liked to have done it," MacArthur stated, adding that Eichelberger was SWPA's equivalent to famed Confederate cavalry leader Jeb Stuart.[41] On the other hand, MacArthur compared Krueger to plodding Union general George Meade. From now on, he promised Eichelberger, GHQ would treat the Sixth Army and the Eighth Army equally in the allocation of resources, promotions, and assignments. Although Eichelberger was embarrassed by MacArthur's gushing, he thought it no more than his due.[42]

Eichelberger's leadership style in the central and southern Philippines stood in marked contrast to Krueger's. He could have used Hall's Eleventh Corps headquarters, but instead opted to work only through Sibert's Tenth to avoid complicating the chain of command any more than necessary. Eichelberger believed in giving a man a job to do and letting him do it, so he interfered as little as possible in his subordinates' tactical dispositions. The Americal Division's William Arnold, for example, recalled that he rarely saw anyone from the Eighth Army's and Tenth Corps's headquarters during his operations in the Visayan Islands. For most division commanders accustomed to Krueger's rough and heavy-handed methods, Eichelberger was like a breath of fresh air because he motivated by encouragement. This autonomy and implied confidence no doubt contributed to the Eighth Army's success. Krueger had pawned Rapp Brush's Fortieth Division off on Eichelberger because he disliked the outfit and its leader, but Eichelberger was happy with Brush's actions on Panay. Indeed, Eichelberger proved adept at making use of the human materiel at his disposal. He had placed Fred Irving in charge of the Eighth Army's rear areas after Krueger and Sibert removed him from the Twenty-fourth Division, and was so pleased with his performance that he gave him the responsibility for mopping up Leyte and Samar. At the same time, he talked Irving up to MacArthur until MacArthur admitted that relieving him had been a mistake and promised to give him the next available division. Eichelberger's mainstay during the campaign, however, was Roscoe Woodruff, Irving's successor as head of the Twenty-fourth Division. Eichelberger was very impressed with Woodruff's efforts on Mindanao and increasingly saw him as his right-hand man. Woodruff fought doggedly and skillfully even though he had cracked several ribs after falling into a neck-deep Japanese spider hole. He was in so much pain that he scarcely slept for two weeks, but he soldiered on because he did not want to be declared unfit for duty and sent home.[43]

The only general who disappointed Eichelberger during his campaign in the central and southern Philippines was Franklin Sibert. Sibert had impressed Eichelberger in New Guinea, and Eichelberger had been happy to present Sibert with a Distinguished Service Medal for his efforts on Leyte. During the fighting on Mindanao, however, Eichelberger grew increasingly disenchanted with Sibert. In May, Eichelberger complained that Sibert's new supply base at Parang was vulnerable to monsoons and that Sibert had failed to devote sufficient manpower to rebuilding bridges. He was also frustrated by his inability to get Sibert to assail Sarangani Bay. In June, General Joe "Vinegar Joe" Stilwell visited Eichelberger. There was bad blood between Stilwell and Sibert from their days together in the China-Burma-India theater earlier in the war. With the directness and acidity that had caused him no end of trouble in China, Stilwell told Eichelberger that Sibert's problem was that he was just plain stupid. The more Eichelberger thought about it, the more convinced he became that Stilwell was right. That being the case,

Eichelberger decided that he would ask MacArthur to relieve Sibert if the two had to work together during the invasion of Japan. By way of replacement, Eichelberger quickly settled on Woodruff, whom Eichelberger credited for most of the successes on Mindanao. Before he took such drastic action, though, on 1 July Eichelberger ordered Sibert to his headquarters for a blunt discussion of his shortcomings. As Byers explained, "Sibert has an uncanny knack of leaving the main task and chasing off on a side issue. There is also a run of stubbornness which is unfortunate because he is so darned friendly."[44] Happily for everyone, the war ended before Eichelberger had to make a final determination of Sibert's fate. In fact, Eichelberger's analysis of Sibert was not fair. Unlike, say, Griswold, Sibert worked best under close supervision, which was one reason why he so respected Krueger. He was also sick with a heart condition that kept him from keeping up with his responsibilities.[45]

Conclusions

The army deployed more combat divisions to the liberation of the Philippines than it did to the Italian campaign. Unfortunately, MacArthur's ground forces team did not exactly shine there. At the field army level, Krueger as usual fought systematically and relentlessly on Leyte and Luzon, but he was hindered by a lack of imagination, insufficient resources, and often unreasonable pressure from MacArthur. Although his most successful operation was the amphibious landing near Ormoc that knocked the blocks out from under the Japanese on Leyte, his tactics rarely deviated from the orthodox. Worse still, his leadership style alienated most of his chief lieutenants, so that by the end of the campaign almost no one wanted to serve with him. This certainly did not bode well for the planned assault of Japan. Eichelberger, on the other hand, performed with considerably more operational flair in the central and southern Philippines, and did so in part by winning the confidence and support of his subordinates. MacArthur, however, wasted his talents in a strategically worthless campaign that did not advance the war effort much. Indeed, it probably would have been better if Eichelberger had led the invasion of Luzon.

As for MacArthur's corps commanders, their performances in the Philippines ranged from competent to poor. Sibert and Hodge fought conventionally and predictably on Leyte, but they were hindered by rugged terrain, poor weather, insufficient air support, and their inexperience leading troops at the corps level. Of the two, most observers rated Hodge more highly. Sibert did not win any laurels on Mindanao either, and in fact by the end of the operation Eichelberger seriously contemplated relieving him. On Luzon, Griswold showed the most talent with his assaults on Clark Field and Manila, both of which required considerable tactical skill. Hall did not cover himself with any glory at ZigZag Pass, but he improved while fighting the Shimbu Group east of Manila. Finally, Swift's unexpected caution made him perhaps the most disappointing corps commander because he failed to live up to the potential he demonstrated leading the First Cavalry Division on New Guinea. He was no doubt outnumbered in northern Luzon, but he failed to take advantage of opportunities later in the campaign to rout the Japanese in their mountain stronghold. Although none of MacArthur's corps commanders made any major mistakes that seriously derailed the war effort, Griswold was the only one who did much to set himself apart from the rest.

7
Long Bloody Winter

Autumn Stalemate

Eisenhower hoped that ordering his armies across the Seine River without pausing to regroup would propel them into Germany by the end of the year before logistical constraints curtailed offensive operations. Unfortunately, his gambit failed. Although the Germans lost 300,000 soldiers in the west that summer—as well as another 900,000 on the Eastern Front—they frantically created and reconstituted units in a remarkably short time to man their West Wall along Germany's western border. Proximity to Germany eased their logistical burdens, and the region's villages, rivers, hills, marshes, and forests provided ideal positions from which to repel Allied assaults. On the other hand, gasoline shortages in particular were bringing the Allied advance to a halt. Part of the problem was that the Allies lacked a usable, undamaged deepwater port near the front lines to succor their troops. The British had fortuitously seized Antwerp on 4 September with its wharves, cranes, marshaling yards, and elevators intact, but they were so focused on pushing on toward Germany that they neglected to clear the enemy from the Scheldt Estuary's banks leading into the city. Until they did so, Antwerp was logistically useless. In addition, the Allies could not easily move the stores they had already unloaded on the continent because their bombers had destroyed so much of France's railroad network in the weeks leading up to D-Day. In an effort to surmount these difficulties, Eisenhower's logisticians resorted to air transport and a system of round-the-clock truck convoys called the Red Ball Express to deliver gasoline to the fast-moving front. But it was not enough; the Red Ball Express alone consumed 300,000 gallons of precious gasoline a day. In early September Allied armies began grinding to a standstill due to insufficient gasoline. Patton's Third Army, now along the upper Meuse River, felt the impact first and worst. The Third Army required over 275,000 gallons of gasoline a day, but throughout late August it received on average only about 202,000 gallons a day. At the end of the month the supply dried up almost completely. To continue advancing, Patton relied on captured German gasoline and sidelined an entire corps, but this was no way to wage offensive war. Patton understood this as well as anyone and exclaimed, "My men can eat their belts, but my tanks have gotta have gas."[1]

These growing logistical challenges compelled Eisenhower to make some difficult strategic decisions. There were two traditional invasion routes into Germany from the west, one in the north through the Low Countries to Germany's industrial heartland in the Ruhr, and the other in the south from Metz to the coal-rich Saar region. Eisenhower's earliest inclination was to attack Germany from both directions with Montgomery's British Twenty-first Army Group advancing to the north and Bradley's Twelfth Army Group moving to the south. Unfortunately, gasoline shortages forced Eisenhower to prioritize. Montgomery argued that he should get all available supplies, as well as Hodges's entire First Army, for a single offensive thrust around the West Wall into Germany while Patton remained quiescent along the Meuse. Bradley and Patton for their part wanted to conduct their own full-fledged offensive. Conscious as always of Anglo-American relations, Eisenhower opted for a compromise that favored Montgomery's drive because he felt that Germany could not continue the war without the Ruhr's factories. Eisenhower agreed to give Montgomery the bulk of the available supplies, but he did not place Hodges's First Army under his command or stop Patton altogether. Instead, he ordered Hodges to advance in a northeasterly direction to cover the British right flank and authorized Patton to keep going if he had the means to do so. As with most compromises, Eisenhower's plan pleased no one completely.

The key to Montgomery's offensive was Operation Market-Garden. Market-Garden called for using General Lewis Brereton's Allied First Airborne Army to seize and hold onto a series of bridges in the Netherlands over the Rhine River, its distributaries, and nearby canals until British General Brian Horrocks's Thirtieth Corps arrived to relieve them. If successful, Market-Garden would enable Montgomery to skip across the Rhine, outflank the West Wall, and descend on the Ruhr before winter. It was a bold plan that failed due to a combination of skilled German opposition, bad luck, and false and unrealistic assumptions. On 17 September nearly 20,000 troops transported by 1,545 planes and 478 gliders from the British First Airborne Division, General James Gavin's Eighty-second Airborne Division, and General Maxwell Taylor's 101st Airborne Division landed with little difficulty and set about capturing their assigned bridges. Unfortunately, the operation began to unravel almost immediately. The airborne units alighted practically atop two refitting German armored divisions, whose presence Montgomery was aware of but chose to downplay. Worse yet, the Thirtieth Corps ran into heavy resistance as it pushed northward and quickly fell behind schedule. Horrocks managed to reach the two American airborne divisions, which had attained most of their objectives, but by the time the Thirtieth Corps got to the Lower Rhine River in strength on 25 September the Germans had practically destroyed

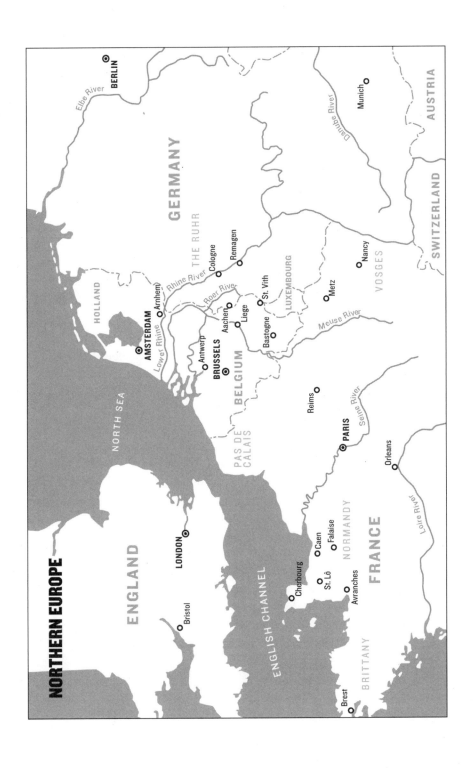

NORTHERN EUROPE

ENGLAND

NORTH SEA

ENGLISH CHANNEL

Bristol

LONDON

Cherbourg

St. Lô

Avranches

Brest

BRITTANY

Caen

Falaise

NORMANDY

FRANCE

Orleans

PARIS

Reims

Seine River

Loire River

PAS DE CALAIS

BELGIUM

BRUSSELS

Antwerp

Aachen

Liege

Bastogne

St. Vith

LUXEMBOURG

Meuse River

Metz

Nancy

VOSGES

HOLLAND

AMSTERDAM

Arnhem

Lower Rhine

Rhine River

Roer River

Cologne

Remagen

THE RUHR

GERMANY

Elbe River

BERLIN

Danube River

Munich

SWITZERLAND

AUSTRIA

the British First Airborne Division at Arnhem. Fewer than 2,200 men managed to make it across the river to safety. Although Market-Garden succeeded in getting the British Second Army to the Lower Rhine, it cost the Allies some 17,000 casualties and failed to achieve its primary purpose.

While Montgomery's troops struggled along the canals and over the bridges in Holland, Hodges's First Army was getting into position to cover the British Second Army's right flank. Doing so placed the First Army in a poor location from which to launch its own offensive. Situated in its front were the German city of Aachen and the Huertgen Forest, both defended by the increasingly formidable West Wall. The Germans could be expected to fight hard for their homeland, whereas Hodges's tired troops were handicapped by continuing supply problems. Initial attacks by Gerow's Fifth Corps and Collins's Seventh Corps in mid-September made some progress, but Hodges lacked the reserves to exploit the few opportunities that developed. During the remainder of September Hodges brought up Corlett's Nineteenth Corps and accumulated as many supplies as he could. On 2 October, following the usual preliminary bombardment by aircraft and artillery, Corlett assailed the West Wall around Aachen. After heavy fighting Hobbs's Thirtieth and Harmon's Second Armored divisions succeeded in linking up with Collins's Seventh Corps to encircle the city on 16 October. Fierce house-to-house combat followed, but on 21 October Huebner's First Division managed to clear Aachen of its diehard German defenders and capture the first city in Germany to fall to the Allies.

Pete Corlett's career was one of the casualties of the fighting around Aachen. Corlett disliked the remote and austere Hodges and resented his obvious partiality toward Collins. Hodges and Corlett did not see much of each other during the race across France, but after the front congealed they had to work together more closely. Familiarity did little to improve their relationship. At one point Corlett complained to Hodges that his front was too long, but Hodges's only response was to ask him to do more to support Collins. Hodges for his part did not appreciate Corlett's abrasive, complaining, and opinionated personality. Hodges was dismayed that Corlett used so much of the First Army's scarce artillery ammunition supply during his preliminary bombardment on 2 October, and then that it took so long for the Nineteenth Corps to seal off Aachen. Nor did Hodges welcome Corlett's incessant demands for additional men and ammunition when he knew full well that these things were not immediately available. To Hodges, Corlett seemed like an increasingly pessimistic and negative officer who demonstrated little of Collins's can-do attitude. He was also disturbed by Corlett's poor health. Hodges addressed these concerns by exerting more pressure on Corlett to wrap up the Aachen operation, which did little to endear him to Corlett and in fact merely confirmed Corlett's suspicions that Hodges did not understand the problems the Nineteenth Corps faced. When Bradley and Hodges visited Corlett's command post after the Nineteenth Corps's attack began, Hodges lit into Corlett for wasting ammunition. Corlett felt that he had done a good job under difficult circumstances, so he lost his temper and yelled back at Hodges. Not long after this incident, Corlett returned to his command post one day and learned that some First Army staffers had said that the Nineteenth Corps's comparatively low casualties indicated that Corlett's units were not fighting very hard. An infuriated Corlett immediately jumped into his jeep and drove to First Army headquarters to set them straight. Hodges was not there, but chief of staff Bill Kean was. "If you don't think we are fighting," Corlett exclaimed to Kean, "I will take you down and show you. It would only take an hour and a half."[2] Although Corlett later noted virtuously that Kean and his staffers did not take him up on his offer, there is little doubt that their report of the incident to Hodges put Corlett in the worst possible light.

Corlett's increasingly strident, erratic, and insubordinate behavior convinced Hodges to relieve him of his command. On 18 October Corlett visited Hobbs at his command post in a rundown German building north of Aachen to discuss the continuing battle. Corlett was in a comparatively good mood because he had recently heard that Bradley was transferring the Nineteenth Corps to General William Simpson's new Ninth Army, giving him the opportunity for a fresh start under a more amiable superior. He learned of Hodges's decision when he returned to his headquarters. Despite the stress he had been under, Corlett was devastated to lose his corps and later wrote, "I was tired and run-down and perhaps sick. My temper was short. My marvelous and loyal staff had suffered from my scolding. Perhaps because it was augmented by these conditions, leaving the XIX Corps, every man and officer of which I loved, was just plain heartbreak."[3] After a perfunctory and awkward meeting with Hodges, Corlett drove to Luxembourg City to confer with Bradley at Twelfth Army Group headquarters. Bradley knew and approved of Hodges's action, but did his best to soften the blow by officially informing Eisenhower that Hodges removed Corlett because of his poor health and adding that he would be happy to take Corlett back as corps commander once he had recovered. Bradley did so not only because of his kind nature, but also because Corlett's aides had complained bitterly to him of the insensitive and public manner in which Hodges had fired Corlett. Corlett's aides were not the only ones unhappy with Hodges. Hobbs cried when he received word of Corlett's relief because he feared he had let Corlett down, and Ernie Harmon wrote to Bradley that he had been pleased with Corlett's leadership and was sorry to see him go. Bradley, however, had never particularly cared for Corlett and he was not about to interfere with Hodges's resolution of the problem. In a message to Marshall, Eisenhower conveyed and seconded Bradley's willingness to take Corlett back. Once Corlett was safely out of the theater, though, Eisenhower in early December told Marshall that he had no real desire to reemploy Corlett. Marshall for his part appreciated Corlett's efforts and was solicitous of his feelings. When Marshall learned that Corlett was returning to the States by boat, he had an aide contact Corlett's wife in Santa Fe, New Mexico, and arrange for her to fly to New York City and stay at the Waldorf-Astoria Hotel. As soon as Corlett disembarked an officer met him with a car and drove him to the hotel for a surprise reunion with his wife. Marshall eventually put Corlett in charge of a stateside corps, and he did not serve overseas again during the war.[4]

Ernie Harmon and the other division commanders in the Nineteenth Corps all hoped to replace Corlett, but Bradley instead gave the post to General Raymond McLain. Although merit no doubt played an important role in Bradley's decision, there was in this particular case also a political angle. McLain was not a Regular Army officer, but rather a member of the Oklahoma National Guard. Born in Kentucky in 1890, McLain left school after the sixth grade, started selling real estate, and eventually became a prominent Oklahoma City banker. He enlisted in the Oklahoma National Guard in 1912, earned a commission, and spent World War One patrolling the Mexican border. After the conflict he remained in the National Guard and rose steadily through its ranks. Unlike some of his National Guard colleagues, he took his job seriously. He studied military history and theory, and in 1938 took an abbreviated course at the Command and General Staff School designed for National Guard officers such as himself.

After the United States entered World War Two, McLain became the Forty-fifth Division's artillery commander. He accompanied the division to the Mediterranean and fought with it in Sicily, southern Italy, and Anzio. His performance there won the praise and respect of Bradley, Clark, Lucas, Middleton, and Patton. Lucas, for example, wrote, "He is an exceptionally capable field artilleryman and a very gallant soldier."[5] Lucas's only concern was that McLain might not survive the war because he put himself in the line of fire so often that he had already had two jeeps shot out from under him. McLain's biggest and most important booster, however, was George Marshall. Marshall heard good things about McLain during his inspections to the Mediterranean and thereafter kept a close watch on his career and sought ways to advance him through the ranks. He did so partly because he was always looking for talented officers to promote to responsible posts, but also because he wanted to placate National Guard supporters who complained that Regular Army officers monopolized all the important combat positions. When Marshall learned that Clark had given the Forty-fifth Division to William Eagles instead of McLain after Middleton's knee rendered him unfit for combat, he was sufficiently concerned to ask Clark for an explanation. Clark assured Marshall that he had nothing against McLain and believed he would make a fine division chief, but Eagles was more deserving and had been immediately available. At Marshall's suggestion, Eisenhower transferred McLain to England and put him in charge of the Thirtieth Division's artillery. The Ninetieth Division's miserable record in Normandy gave McLain his opportunity to shine. Patton figured that McLain was the man to turn the outfit around and recommended his appointment to lead it. When Hodges demurred and offered several alternatives, Patton said, "Now, well look here. This division is going to be in my Army. I'd like to have McLain. Why can't you let me have him?" Bradley said, "All right, he gets it."[6] Bradley warned McLain that the Ninetieth had already chewed up two previous commanders, but entrusted him with full authority to act as he saw fit to reform the unit. McLain purged the Ninetieth of underperforming officers, made himself visible to the rank-in-file, and challenged the troops with increasingly difficult assignments to restore their self-confidence. By the end of the summer McLain had transformed the Ninetieth into one of the best American divisions in the theater. Eisenhower and Bradley both suggested McLain for promotion, and Patton talked him up to Marshall during one of the chief of staff's visits. Marshall told Patton— and probably Eisenhower and Bradley as well—that he really hoped that McLain would receive a corps. Considering McLain's record and Marshall's keen interest in him, it was hardly surprising that Eisenhower and Bradley appointed him to run the Nineteenth.

As a national guardsman without much formal education, McLain was an anomaly in an army that valued professionalism, experience, and training. This did not mean that McLain was any less capable than his Regular Army colleagues after the United States entered the war. He once said to Bradley, "In the army I learned organization—it was all I knew and I used it as best I could."[7] He was in fact a natural soldier, leader, and fighter. Shrewd and articulate, he could relate to the citizen soldiers who made up most American units during the war and get the best out of them. William Simpson, McLain's field army commander during his time with the Nineteenth Corps, later identified McLain's greatest strength as his ability to apply common-sense solutions to the most complicated problems. Although some officers resented his meteoric rise because they rightly attributed it in part to his National Guard background, McLain eventually won the respect of almost everyone with whom he worked. This included Joe Collins, who grew to appreciate McLain's friendship, combativeness, and cooperation. McLain was also fortunate that he did not have to serve under the unforgiving Hodges. Marshall was very pleased with McLain's selection and wrote to him a couple months later, "You have displayed [the] outstanding characteristics of a leader and it is my earnest hope that you will find the same opportunities for your talents in Corps command that you did with a Brigade and Division."[8]

McLain was fortunate not only in escaping Hodges's clutches, but also in avoiding the fighting in the Huertgen Forest. The Huertgen Forest was a dense and spooky wooded area south of Aachen that the Germans had filled with camouflaged pillboxes, barbed wire, bunkers, mines, and other accouterments designed to kill GIs. It reminded some of World War One's Argonne or the Civil War's Wilderness. Although waging war there completely contradicted the army's emphasis on mobility, Hodges decided to clear it out to protect his right flank. In early October two regiments of General Louis Craig's crack Ninth Division from Collins's Seventh Corps marched into Huertgen and within three weeks had suffered 4,500 casualties and seized little ground. Hodges pulled them out, readjusted his lines, and gave the Huertgen job to Gee Gerow. In early November Gerow sent Dutch Cota's Twenty-eighth Division charging into Huertgen. After some initial successes, the Twenty-eighth stalled and ultimately lost over 6,100 men there. Interlocking fields of fire and shrapnel from shells bursting among the trees turned the woods into a charnel house for the cold and disoriented soldiers. Undaunted, Hodges and Gerow fed Tubby Barton's Fourth Division, elements of General Lunsford Oliver's Fifth Armored Division, and part of General Donald Stroh's Eighth Division into the Huertgen maelstrom. Barton's troops endured 4,000 battle and 2,000 noncombat casualties, and the Eighth and Fifth Armored divisions added another 5,100 men to the butcher's bill. Worse yet, Hodges and Gerow had only a few miles of blasted woods to show for their investment. Concurrent offensives to the north spearheaded by Collins's Seventh Corps managed to grind their way to the Roer plain, but it was a far cry from the breakthrough the First Army wanted. From mid-September to mid-December, the First Army sustained 7,000 killed, 35,000 wounded, and 4,800 missing or captured along the West Wall.

The long dreary autumn was hard on Hodges and his subordinates too. In mid-September Hodges predicted that the First Army could push through the West Wall to the Rhine with little trouble, but after two months before the West Wall he worried that the Allies might still lose the war. His strenuous schedule took a toll on his health. He contracted a bad cold he could not shake and eventually admitted that he was exhausted. Illness did little to enhance his limited imagination or sweeten his sour disposition. Although he tried various tactical approaches to the Huertgen conundrum, he did not grasp that the place was simply not worth the effort. As far as Hodges was concerned, though, many of the First Army's problems were due to bad leadership at the division and corps level. This did not of course include Collins, whose optimistic and can-do attitude that autumn was all the more pronounced in comparison to the gloomy weather and circumstances around him. Unlike his attitude toward his other corps commanders, Hodges placed considerable faith in Collins and gave him wide latitude to act as he saw fit. Corlett was not the only general with whom Hodges quarreled. He seriously contemplated relieving Cota for allegedly mishandling the Twenty-eighth Division, and he did fire Stroh for not living up to expectations. It was the staid and upright Gerow, however, who bore the brunt of Hodges's dissatisfaction. On several occasions that autumn Hodges chewed out Gerow for improperly deploying and not keeping track of his men.[9]

Gerow's difficulties that autumn went beyond Hodges's inability to recognize the futility of waging war in the Huertgen Forest with tired and disoriented troops. Gerow had some extended family members in France who were accused of collaborating with the Germans, and he got sucked into the resulting drama. In addition, in mid-September Gerow had to fly back to the States to testify before a congressional committee about his actions as Marshall's chief of war plans in the days leading up to the surprise Japanese attack on Pearl Harbor. He did not immediately realize that events were transpiring that would ultimately redound to his benefit. Marshall and Eisenhower were planning to bring a new field army, the Fifteenth, to France. The previous July Eisenhower had told Marshall that he preferred Truscott to lead it, but if it proved impossible to pry Truscott away from Devers then he hoped to give it to McNair or Gerow. Marshall mentioned Clark as a possibility, but by the time Marshall and Eisenhower made their final decision Clark had been elevated to lead the Fifteenth Army Group. Eisenhower probably included McNair's name to placate Marshall because in the following sentences of his message he all but disqualified him by noting his deafness and his lack of combat experience in the war. Eisenhower might have saved his breath; a week later his own bombers took McNair out of the war and out of the world during Operation Cobra. On the other hand, Eisenhower had no doubts about Gerow's proven competence. He praised Gerow to Marshall, writing, "Gerow has shown all the qualities of vigor, determination, reliability and skill that we are looking for. If he continues as at present both Bradley and I believe he will be an excellent army commander."[10] In truth, though, Gerow had not done much to distinguish himself from the other corps commanders. He had fought competently, but not brilliantly, and Collins's record was clearly superior. Gerow, however, had the advantage of Eisenhower's and Bradley's longstanding friendship, and it was that as much as anything that made him their leading candidate for the Fifteenth Army. Eisenhower himself admitted this, at least implicitly, by writing his brother in mid-September, "Gerow is doing a splendid job. He is one of our finest commanders and all of us are very keen on him. Personally I always knew he would make good but it is a delight to have my convictions proved before the world. As you know, Gerow has always been my best friend in the Army."[11]

Unlike Eisenhower and Bradley, Marshall had his doubts about Gerow's drive and determination. When in September Marshall and Eisenhower next corresponded on the issue, Marshall noted that Truscott's performance at Anzio and during the advance through Rome had been so outstanding that he clearly deserved the next available field army. Moreover, Truscott was, unlike Gerow, already a lieutenant general. Marshall reminded Eisenhower that he himself had long wanted Truscott and this was his chance to get him. Eisenhower could hardly argue with Marshall's logic, so he agreed to take Truscott for the Fifteenth Army. In the end, though, Truscott ended up returning to Italy to lead the Fifth Army after Marshall appointed Clark to run the Fifteenth Army Group. This opened the door for Eisenhower not only to renew his lobbying for Gerow, but also to use Marshall's logic against *him*. Eisenhower once again lauded Gerow's record, and added that Gerow was senior to the other corps commanders, so his advancement was, like Truscott's, less likely to cause discord among the generals than if they were to elevate, say, the relatively junior Collins. Marshall chose not to make an issue of the matter, perhaps because he knew that Eisenhower and Bradley intended to use the Fifteenth Army mostly as an administrative entity to oversee rear areas. Gerow certainly had done little to separate himself from the other corps chiefs that autumn, and in fact he was in the process of failing in Huertgen Forest. There had been lots of scuttlebutt in the army about Gerow's promotion, so he could scarcely have been surprised when he got the word on 12 December that he would command the Fifteenth Army as soon as its headquarters was established in Europe.[12]

The Fifteenth Army was the fifth and last field army the United States deployed in northwestern Europe, and it saw very little combat. The fourth one—after Hodges's First, Patton's Third, and Patch's Seventh—was General William Simpson's Ninth Army. When Simpson and his headquarters staff arrived in England in May 1944, their army was labeled the Eighth. Eisenhower, however, did not want another field army to compete with the famous British Eighth Army, so he asked Marshall to renumber it. As for its leader, William "Big Bill" Simpson was one of the unsung heroes of the war. Tall, completely bald—Patton introduced him to Third Army staffers by saying, "Gentlemen, this is General Simpson. When he isn't commanding Ninth Army, he acts as an advertisement for hair tonic"[13]—long-faced, and slender, Simpson reminded one observer of an ascetic monk. He was widely admired in the prewar army by officers such as Devers and Harmon for his integrity, earthy sense of humor, intelligence, and kindness. He was also an astute and self-confident man with plenty of ability and a thorough understanding of both warfare and those who wage it. His energetic, clear, and balanced approach to tactics yielded some of the army's most impressive victories in the European War. Although Patton concluded that Simpson relied too much on his staff, Simpson did so because he knew how to create a first-rate headquarters. He and his chief of staff, General James Moore, worked so closely and well together that some compared their relationship to that of German generals Paul von Hindenburg and Erich Ludendorff during World War One. Simpson's warm smile and knack for making everyone feel important motivated his staffers to exert themselves to please him. Simpson also got the best out of his corps and division commanders by giving them plenty of autonomy, keeping in constant touch with them with frequent visits to the front, supporting their decisions, and sympathizing with their problems. He even made sure to send each of his corps commanders to London at least once during the campaign on his plane for a few days of rest away from the front. His considerate attitude enabled him to cooperate with all kinds of people, including even the ill-mannered Montgomery. He suffered throughout the war from a painful ulcer, but this did not seem to inhibit his effectiveness. Indeed, Eisenhower later wrote, "If Simpson ever made a mistake as an army commander, it never came to my attention."[14] Taken together, Simpson was perhaps the best all-around field army commander the United States produced during the war because he possessed none of Eichelberger's hypersensitivity, Hodges's sourness, Krueger's brusqueness, Patton's unruliness, Patch's inscrutability, or Gerow's staidness. Indeed, it was a shame that Marshall and Eisenhower did not appoint him head of the First Army instead of the retiring and difficult Hodges.[15]

Like several of his contemporaries, as a youth Simpson had given little indication of military prominence. He was born in Texas in 1888, the son of a rancher and former Confederate soldier, and read military biographies to learn generalship. He secured an appointment to West Point even though he had not finished high school, and matriculated when he was scarcely seventeen. Considering his age, he not surprisingly struggled academically, and he graduated in 1909 at the bottom of his class. He was stationed in the Philippines, North Dakota, California, and Texas before participating in Pershing's Punitive Expedition into Mexico. During World War One he fought at St. Mihiel and the Argonne as a division commander's aide and then as his chief of staff. After occupation duty he returned to the States and attended the Infantry School in 1924, the Command and General Staff School from 1924 to 1925, and, after a stint at the head of a battalion, the Army War College from 1927 to 1928. He worked on the General Staff for a couple years, taught military science at Pomona College from 1932 to 1936, and returned to the Army War College as an instructor. He moved rapidly through the ranks after World War Two broke out in Europe, serving successively as a regimental, assistant division, division, corps, and field army commander.

Simpson was a prime example of a capable general who almost missed out on a prominent role in the war because he spent so much time stateside training troops. Although McNair only reluctantly suggested Simpson for division command in July 1941, he became more enthusiastic about him the more he saw and heard of him. In fact, Simpson was so effective that he, like Bradley, received the rare responsibility of training two different divisions. His old friend Bob Eichelberger was also impressed with Simpson. Just before Eichelberger went overseas in the summer of 1942 to fight the Japanese he called a stenographer into his office and in Simpson's presence recommended Simpson to McNair for a corps. McNair put Simpson in charge of the Twelfth Corps and was sufficiently pleased with his performance that he persuaded Marshall to give him the Fourth Army in October 1943. Running the army and taking it into action, however, were two different things, and at this point Simpson's lack of battle experience began to tell. Devers asked for Simpson for Anvil-Dragoon, but Marshall turned him down because Simpson was untried in combat. In March 1944 Marshall offered Eisenhower either Lloyd Fredendall's Second Army or Simpson's Fourth Army—subsequently renumbered first the Eighth and then the Ninth—and added that McNair felt that Fredendall was the better candidate. Eisenhower was not about to subject himself again to Fredendall, who had caused him considerable grief in North Africa, so he opted for Simpson. At the same time, Eisenhower noted that he really hoped to eventually reward a deserving corps commander for his work in the upcoming campaign by assigning him to lead this field army. Simpson did not realize it, but he was threatened with the same fate that had befallen Crittenberger, Reinhardt, and Woodruff. He passed his first test with Bradley during a meeting at Bradley's Bristol headquarters in May 1944. Simpson and Bradley had never met, so Bradley was understandably wary of the newcomer. Bradley said, "You're a much older man than I am. I hope you don't mind serving under me." Simpson responded, "None whatsoever. I assure you of my full cooperation."[16] Eisenhower had no personal problems with Simpson either, but in late August he told Marshall that he was seriously thinking of giving the Ninth Army to a veteran such as Corlett or Gerow. Happily for Simpson, on 1 October Eisenhower informed Marshall that he had changed his mind not because of anything Simpson did or did not do, but simply because preparations for committing the Ninth Army under Simpson had progressed so far that it would be counterproductive to remove him now. With that, the way was finally clear for Simpson to join the war.[17]

The Ninth Army's first combat assignment was to seize Brest. After the rest of Patton's Third Army plunged eastward across France, Troy Middleton's Eighth Corps remained behind in Brittany to reduce the city. Middleton had three divisions and some armor at his disposal, or about 80,000 men. Although American intelligence placed German strength at about 16,000 troops, there were actually nearly 40,000 die-hard defenders in Brest. Middleton was an astute man—in fact, he was just about the closest thing the army had to an intellectual at the corps level—and he recognized that storming the city was not worth the effort. Not only would American casualties be heavy, but the Germans would certainly wreck the port and render it useless for Allied logistical needs. Bradley and Patton agreed with Middleton's analysis, but also believed that the army for prestige purposes needed to see the operation through to its successful conclusion. Middleton was not persuaded by this argument, and he became increasingly angry and depressed with the situation. It was bad enough to wage war for pride's sake, but Middleton also complained that he lacked sufficient air support, supplies, and ammunition, and that infantrymen were not pressing their attacks home. Indeed, Middleton grew so discouraged and querulous that Patton contemplated removing him from his command. He did not, but instead resorted to a different strategy. Patton told Bradley that he was too busy racing across France to oversee Middleton's backwater campaign against Brest and asked him to give the job to someone else. As it was, Bradley had been thinking along the same lines. He sympathized with Middleton, telling him during a 26 August visit, "You're running a private war of your own over here. Fighting here has been tougher than anywhere else on the front."[18]

To help him out, Bradley sent Simpson and his Ninth Army headquarters to supervise Middleton's assault on the city. Simpson was elated to receive his first important job, even though Middleton continued to do most of the planning and thinking. Middleton conducted his war with his usual dispassion. General Charles Gerhardt, head of the Twenty-ninth Division, remembered that Simpson and Middleton came to his command post to watch one of his regiments go into action. Simpson was very interested and watched intently, but a seemingly apathetic Middleton sat down and did something else. Nevertheless, Simpson respected Middleton's ability and did not interfere much. Not until Bradley diverted supplies and air support from eastern France did the Eighth Corps make much progress. On 20 September the last Germans in and around Brest surrendered, finally giving the Allies a shattered port that they no longer needed. Taking the city cost the army 9,800 casualties.[19]

After Brest fell, Bradley initially sent Simpson and Middleton to the Ardennes, a heavily forested region in northern Luxembourg and southeastern Belgium, to fill the gap between Hodges's First Army and Patton's Third Army. Simpson did not much like the look of things in the Ardennes because he had so few troops to cover such a large area, so he was relieved when Bradley suddenly shifted him again. This time Bradley redeployed the Ninth Army headquarters, but not Middleton's Eighth Corps, to the Netherlands-Belgium border between the British Twenty-first Army Group and Hodges's First Army. Bradley did so because he worried that Montgomery might eventually persuade Eisenhower to give him the nearest American field army. If he did so, Bradley preferred that Montgomery get the untried Ninth Army rather than the battle-hardened First Army and its capable corps commanders Collins, Gerow, and now Middleton.[20]

Simpson's mission was to push toward the Roer plain in conjunction with

Hodges's offensive to the south. To do so, Bradley assigned him McLain's Nineteenth Corps and General Alvan Gillem's new Thirteenth Corps. Simpson planned for Ernie Harmon's veteran Second Armored Division to play a key role in the operation. Harmon had traveled to the States after Clark relieved him from the First Armored Division in Italy the previous July. Although Marshall had once angrily told Harmon that he was unfit for higher command, the chief of staff was all sweetness and light when the two men met at the Pentagon. Marshall first ordered Harmon and his wife to White Sulphur Springs for a month of rest and recreation after his long tour of duty in the Mediterranean, and then appointed him to lead the stateside Twenty-third Corps. Before Harmon reached the corps headquarters in Texas, however, he received a message to return to Washington immediately. Next morning Marshall told Harmon that Eisenhower and Bradley wanted him to take over the Second Armored Division now that its previous commander, General Edward Brooks, had been promoted to the corps level. Marshall stated that Harmon had earned his new corps and was free to reject the offer, but Harmon decided that it was his duty to obey Eisenhower's and Bradley's summons. He served in the First Army before moving over to the Ninth Army with McLain's Nineteenth Corps. Harmon was deeply concerned when he received his assignment in Simpson's offensive. He knew it would be a tough fight and, after his experience in Hodges's First Army, worried that he would be removed from his new job if he failed. When Simpson learned from McLain of Harmon's unease, he invited Harmon to Ninth Army headquarters for lunch. After Harmon expressed his concerns, Simpson said, "Ernie, I just want you to know that I think you're the finest Armored Division Commander in Europe, and that includes my classmate, George Patton. So if anybody can take this objective you can do it. If you don't take it, I know nobody else could have done it." For Harmon the contrast between the cutthroat First Army and Simpson's Ninth Army was like night and day. Small wonder he later wrote, "Simpson, though little known outside military circles, was one of the truly great leaders of the European theater, a real general's general."[21]

The Ninth Army's attack began on 16 November. Whereas the tense First Army's headquarters sweated out their preliminary bombardments at their desks, Simpson's staffers passed the opening hours of their offensive watching a movie. McLain's Nineteenth Corps encountered heavy opposition from Germans defending the innumerable villages dotting the countryside, and Harmon's tanks fought a series of seesaw battles in the fields and streets. The Germans fed reinforcements into the region, sparking a brutal war of attrition. The Nineteenth Corps made slow progress, but by the end of the month had closed in on the Roer River. The Thirteenth Corps came up shortly thereafter, bringing the operation to a close. Although the Ninth Army achieved no breakthroughs and advanced less than twenty miles, its troops and staffers made no major mistakes and displayed a calm professionalism that won Bradley's regard. At the cost of 1,133 killed, 6,864 wounded, and 2,059 missing, the Ninth had demonstrated to everyone that it was a force to be reckoned with.[22]

The Thirteenth Corps played a secondary role in the Ninth Army's offensive, but this was not because of any lack of confidence in its commander, General Alvan Gillem. Indeed, Gillem was so qualified that it was odd that Marshall had not sent him overseas earlier. Although he had been born into a prominent army family in Nashville in 1888, Gillem did not make it to West Point. He went to the University of Arizona and the University of the South before enlisting in the army in 1910 and receiving a commission only a year later. Instead of serving in France in World War One, he, like Eichelberger, wound up spending eight months in Siberia as part of President Woodrow Wilson's futile attempts to manage the Russian Revolution. He attended the Command and General Staff College from 1922 to 1923 and the Army War College two years later. He also taught at the Infantry School even though he had never graduated from there, led a battalion for two years, and then an infantry regiment. Although initially a reluctant supporter of armored warfare—he once told Patton that he had no desire to learn to drive or even ride in a tank—he eventually changed his mind and committed himself to the branch. He commanded an armored brigade and an armored division during the American military buildup before the Japanese attacked Pearl Harbor. After the United States entered the conflict, Marshall successively put Gillem in charge of an armored corps, the Desert Training Center, all armored forces, and finally a corps slated for overseas deployment. Considering his impressive resume, it was hardly surprising that Gillem had a wide circle of admirers and supporters who vouched for him. Patton praised his work, and Devers recommended him as his successor as head of army armor. McNair, on the other hand, could not seem to make up his mind about Gillem. At one point he rated Gillem as the best available stateside corps commander, but a few months later placed him nineteenth out of the twenty-three corps commanders. Fortunately for Gillem, Eisenhower had no such doubts about him. Upon taking over Overlord, Eisenhower told Marshall that after preliminary conversations with Bradley and others he could almost guarantee that he would eventually ask for Gillem because of his obvious ability. He reiterated his desire for Gillem's services in the following months, and worried that Marshall might send him elsewhere. When in May Simpson and Eisenhower had their first meeting, they quickly agreed that Gillem's corps should join the Ninth Army as soon as possible. A few days later, Eisenhower finally asked Marshall to send Gillem and his Thirteenth Corps headquarters across the Atlantic.[23]

Gillem was a natural corps commander. In fact, he was the kind of consummate military professional that the American army strove to produce. Dignified, upright, and well-mannered, Gillem's calm demeanor and level-headedness reassured superiors and subordinates alike. His self-confidence and shrewd understanding of battle enabled him to formulate sound plans and implement them in a forceful and determined manner. Although somewhat starchy, he was also capable of changing and adapting to the new circumstances in which the army found itself. He and Simpson got along very well, and he never caused Simpson a moment of worry. Small wonder Simpson wrote to him a few years after the war, "I wish to assure you that I have never regretted my choice of you and always considered myself most fortunate to have you with me in my Ninth Army. I have always appreciated the splendid and outstanding job that you did and will always appreciate it. I want you to know that I do have the highest regard for you professionally."[24] Simpson praised all his corps commanders, but Gillem became his mainstay for the remainder of the conflict. Gillem for his part recognized and was grateful for the opportunity he had to serve with Simpson and generously gave him much of the credit for whatever successes he enjoyed.[25]

To the south of Simpson and Hodges, George Patton was having an equally frustrating autumn in the Lorraine region. Geography and gasoline shortages had brought Patton's charge across France to a halt along the Moselle River well short of the West Wall. Aggressive as always, Patton hoped to seize Metz and Nancy and push on through the West Wall to the Rhine River. Unfortunately, not only was he at the end of a long logistical chain, but also the British and Hodges had priority over the limited supplies available. That he was able to assume the offensive at all was due in part to Bradley's support. Montgomery's efforts to sideline the Twelfth Army Group brought Patton and Bradley closer together, and Bradley was willing to bend the rules by sending the Third Army additional supplies and men in order to show Eisenhower what his army group could accomplish. Eddy's Twelfth Corps jumped off toward Nancy on 4 September and took the city eleven days later. After that, however, Eddy got bogged down in heavy fighting east of the city. This included some of the army's biggest tank battles of the war, in which John Wood's Fourth Armored Division distinguished itself. Meanwhile, on 27 September Walker's Twentieth Corps assailed Metz. Unlike Nancy, Metz was well defended and surrounded by an elaborate series of fortresses that stymied the Twentieth Corps, so the operation sputtered to a halt in mid-October. Patton responded by bringing in reinforcements made available by Bradley and retooling his tactics. Walker and Eddy launched new attacks in a driving rain on 8 November. Despite inclement weather, stout German resistance, and difficult terrain, Metz's last fortress fell on 22 November and Eddy reached the Saar River. Patton entered Metz in triumph on 25 November, but the fact remained that Patton had been no more successful at breaking through the German lines and reaching the Rhine than Hodges or Simpson.

As far as Patton was concerned, his superiors and subordinates were as big a problem as the Germans, bad weather, and limited supplies. Although Bradley encouraged Patton in both word and deed to advance further than Eisenhower had authorized, Patton often did not always appreciate his help. He instead complained when Bradley withheld or withdrew supplies and units from his army. At one point Patton confided in his diary that Bradley was not much of a general and it would perhaps be best if he were killed—presumably by the Germans. Patton even speculated that he would be better off serving in Devers's Sixth Army Group because Devers interfered less and was more aggressive than Bradley.

As for his subordinates, Patton frequently lamented their timidity. He wrote to a friend, "Commanding an Army is not such a very absorbing task except that one has to be ready at all hours of the day and night . . . to make some rather momentous decision, which frequently consists of telling somebody who thinks he is beaten that he is not beaten."[26] Patton spent the long dreary autumn prodding, pushing, cajoling, encouraging, and threatening his corps and division commanders to complete their missions. He congratulated himself on the patience he felt he displayed toward them, but he was never satisfied for long with their labors. Manton Eddy was his biggest challenge. Like Bradley before him, Patton discovered that the nervous, worrisome, and tense Eddy needed constant reassurance. Patton was willing to provide it because Eddy usually got results, but he found Eddy's attitude wearying. Patton urged Eddy to relax more by taking a couple of stiff drinks before retiring to bed early. After Eddy fumbled his response to a German counterattack, Patton scribbled in his diary in late September, "Eddy was very manly in assuming full responsibility for the withdrawal order, but I cannot understand his frame of mind. He worries too much. I will do all the worrying necessary. The Corps commanders must fight. I would get rid of him but I do not know of any other better except possibly Harmon now commanding the 2nd Armored Division."[27] Two months later Patton concluded that Eddy was so overwrought from the pressures of the campaign that he needed a temporary rest, but refrained from ordering him to take one because he feared that the psychological impact on Eddy would be worse than keeping him at his post.

On the other hand, Patton had far fewer complaints with Walker. Dressed in pink breeches and shiny boots, with a pistol belt wrapped tightly around his large frame, Walker possessed a pugnacious streak wide enough to suit even Patton's tastes, and proved it by seizing Metz after a long and grim struggle. Patton defused Walker's occasional doubts by threatening to take away some of his units and give them to someone who would use them effectively, such as Eddy. Walker usually responded by redoubling his efforts. Nor did Patton have many concerns about Haislip, whose aggressiveness Patton respected. Unfortunately for Patton, Devers persuaded Eisenhower and Bradley to transfer the Fifteenth Corps to Patch's Seventh Army on 29 September because Patch could better supply it through Marseilles. Patton was as unhappy to part with Haislip as Haislip was to leave the Third Army. Losing the Fifteenth Corps deprived Patton not only of a capable corps commander, but also of a unit that would have helped his offensive toward the Rhine.[28]

Jake Devers's Sixth Army Group operated to Patton's south in the Alsace region. On 15 September it officially became part of Eisenhower's force, and four days later Jean de Lattre de Tassigny's French First Army became operational. Along with Sandy Patch's Seventh Army, this gave Devers two field armies under his control. By the time these organizational changes occurred, Devers's swift advance across France had, like Bradley's and Montgomery's, ground to a halt due to supply shortages and increasing German resistance. Devers, however, confronted some difficulties uniquely his own. Although Patch and de Lattre did not face large numbers of German troops, they had to fight in the wooded Vosges Mountains, which gave the Germans geographic advantages every bit as significant as those enjoyed by their comrades defending Aachen, the Huertgen Forest, or Metz. Moreover, whereas Eisenhower and Bradley were close friends who worked well together, Eisenhower's relationship with Devers was far more strained. Eisenhower disliked Devers's bombastic and cocky attitude and remained angry that Devers had previously bested him in several bureaucratic battles. As a result, Eisenhower and his staffers treated the Sixth Army Group like the Twelfth Army Group's unwanted and ugly stepsister to whom nothing was given and of whom nothing was expected. In fact, Eisenhower would have preferred to send Patch's entire Seventh Army to the Twelfth Army Group, but, as he explained to Bradley, recognized that it had to stay with Devers to "preserve an American complexion to the Southern [Sixth Army] Group for reasons you will understand"—meaning to control the French.[29] Eisenhower rarely visited Devers's headquarters, and often neglected the Sixth Army Group in ways big and small. For example, he established the Fifteenth Army to oversee the Twelfth Army Group's rear areas so Bradley could focus on the fighting, but he did nothing to relieve Devers's equally heavy responsibilities behind his lines. Devers was aware of Eisenhower's hostility and was puzzled by it because he felt he had always been friendly and supportive. He resented that his army group did not get the respect, credit, and support it deserved. In late November Devers had a long meeting with Eisenhower's operations chief, General Harold "Pinky" Bull, during which he explained that the Sixth Army Group was not the Twelfth Army Group's useless appendage, but a full partner in the war that deserved the resources it needed to do its job. Unfortunately, this did not seem to make much of an impression on Eisenhower.[30]

Marshall's continuing support had gone a long way toward protecting Devers from Eisenhower's retribution, but another problem unique to Devers's army group undermined it. While Bradley's Twelfth Army Group was an overwhelmingly American entity, Devers had a strong French component in his. Devers recognized French sensitivities and bent over backward to accommodate them by, for instance, giving them the job of storming Toulon and Marseilles during Anvil-Dragoon. Unhappily, his efforts never seemed to satisfy the temperamental de Lattre. Devers grumbled that de Lattre heard only what he wanted to hear and remembered only what he wanted to remember. In October Marshall crossed the Atlantic on an inspection trip that included Devers's army group. During a briefing at the French First Army headquarters, de Lattre suddenly and angrily criticized Patch for withholding supplies. Marshall's patience with the French was by this stage of the war just about exhausted, so he quickly lost his temper and told de Lattre he did not want to hear such talk. Although Devers explained to Marshall afterward that de Lattre's accusations were without merit, Marshall interpreted the whole incident as evidence that Devers did not have sufficient control over his command.[31]

Considering the difficulties under which he labored, it was remarkable that Devers did as well as he did that fall. The key to his success was his knack for placing himself squarely on the side of common sense and reason. This ability had already enabled him to wrangle his way out of an administrative post in the Mediterranean and into one of the two or three most prominent combat commands in northwestern Europe. He established his army group headquarters in Lyon, and was far more successful at keeping it small and manageable than was Bradley. He used the supply shortage and Sixth Army Group's access to the port of Marseilles not only to persuade Eisenhower to give him additional divisions, but also to transfer Haislip's Fifteenth Corps to Patch's Seventh Army over Patton's strident objections. Patton's anger, though, cooled somewhat when Devers proved so cooperative and supportive that Patton wished he were part of Devers's army group. Despite his problems with de Lattre, Devers succeeded in keeping the French in the war and under American control through the skillful use of American logistical support. Finally, he maintained a command team that contained some of the best officers in the European theater.[32]

When the Sixth Army Group resumed the offensive in earnest in November, it did so without Lucian Truscott's services. Truscott had maintained his sterling reputation by spearheading the Seventh Army's drive through southern France toward the Belfort Gap. Marshall and Eisenhower initially rewarded him for his performance there and elsewhere by tapping him to take over the Fifteenth Army, but he eventually ended up with the Fifth Army in Italy instead. To replace him at the head of the Sixth Corps, Eisenhower sent over General Edward Brooks. Brooks had been born in New Hampshire in 1893 and graduated from Norwich University in 1916. He enlisted in the Vermont National Guard and saw service in

France in World War One as a battery commander and operations chief for an artillery brigade. After occupation duty he became an artillery instructor at Fort Sill, Oklahoma, from 1922 to 1926, and then led an artillery battery in the Philippines and at Fort Riley, Kansas. He attended the Command and General Staff School from 1932 to 1934 and the Army War College from 1936 to 1937 before returning to teach at the Command and General Staff School. He worked with Marshall as chief of the statistics branch in the General Staff from 1939 to 1941. Several months before the United States entered World War Two, Devers as head of the armored forces brought Brooks over to his staff. He became commander of the Eleventh Armored Division in 1942 and crossed the Atlantic to England before D-Day to take over the Second Armored Division. He and the Second Armored saw extensive action in Normandy and the Low Countries. Brooks was an enthusiastic man with a reputation for fairness. He once lugged a heavy pack for twenty miles to get some idea of what his men could do. Some of his troops nicknamed him "Standing Eddie" because of his habit of standing in his jeep while reviewing them so he could see them better. In fact, he had a special railing welded onto this jeep so he could more easily remain upright. Others called him "Great Balls of Fire" because he invariably uttered that phrase when excited. Whatever his nickname, no one questioned his courage and aggressiveness. One officer remembered that Brooks was standing in the middle of a crossroads in Marchiennes, France, when a German column came barreling down the street at them. Brooks grabbed a machine gun and blazed away at the Germans until they escaped. Smart, clear-headed, and concise, Brooks made his points without elaboration or gesturing, and impressed everyone with his competence and his quality staff.[33]

Eisenhower's decision to appoint Brooks as Truscott's successor was by process of elimination because at that point very few other division commanders had been as consistently stellar. He had repeatedly impressed the right people at the right time. Although McNair had initially been concerned with Brooks's inexperience with large formations, by January 1944 he rated Brooks third out of the twelve armored division commanders available for Overlord. Patton listed Brooks as one of four officers he would consider for the Second Armored Division, and Eisenhower put his name at the top of his preferences. Marshall obliged them by dispatching Brooks overseas, and Brooks ably led the Second Armored through the tough fighting in Normandy and the race across France. Bradley labeled him among his best division commanders and assigned him to temporarily replace Gerow at the head of the Fifth Corps when Gerow returned to the States to testify about his actions regarding the Japanese attack on Pearl Harbor. After Truscott left the Sixth Corps, Eisenhower and Bradley offered Brooks to Devers. Devers responded that if he could pick anyone in the Twelfth Army Group for the post, it would be Brooks. The two men had served together earlier in the conflict and Devers had enormous respect for Brooks's ability. On the other hand, some in the Sixth Corps noted that the outfit was never quite the same after Truscott left. Truscott inspired the rank and file by frequently visiting the front and making his presence known. Brooks did not get out of his headquarters as often, and he lacked Truscott's personal magnetism. Fortunately for Brooks, Devers understood and accepted that it would be impossible for anyone to completely fill Truscott's big shoes. Devers himself was perfectly happy with Brooks. As soon as Brooks took over the Sixth Corps on 18 October, Devers had dinner with him so they could renew their friendship and review the military situation. Afterward Devers wrote, "He is in great shape and the usual Ted. I have great confidence that he will adequately replace Truscott who has been a brilliant commander ever since he has been under my command."[34]

Devers also had plenty of confidence in Sandy Patch, head of the Seventh Army. Patch had led the Seventh Army through southern France with an aggressiveness that almost matched Truscott's, and he was eager to resume the offensive as soon as possible. Devers greatly admired Patch's leadership, flexibility, and staff. The view from below was, on the other hand, not as laudatory. The Seventh Army headquarters was for all practical purposes a new organization that not surprisingly made rookie mistakes. One observer noted that it was too by-the-book and unresponsive to the needs of its combat leaders compared to Clark's Fifth Army in Italy. Moreover, Patch did not get out into the field as often as he should have. This did not, however, prevent Patch from exercising his authority over his corps commanders or recognizing their limitations. For example, he had a remarkably astute understanding of Haislip's strengths and weaknesses even though the two men were not personally close. There were reasons for Patch's apparent lassitude. For one thing, his health was never good. Not only did he have weak lungs vulnerable to pneumonia, but he was also laid up in early September with a bad back. Finally, Patch received terrible news in late October that would have sapped the enthusiasm of even the most gung-ho commander. His son had been wounded while leading a company in the Seventy-ninth Division and had convalesced at Seventh Army headquarters. Four days after he returned to his outfit, Patch's friend General Robert Spragins, commander of the Forty-fourth Division, phoned Patch while Patch was waiting for his daily briefing. Patch took the call and then went through the meeting. Afterward he asked his aide if he knew what the call was about. When the aide pleaded ignorance, Patch said, "He told me that Mac was killed today." Indeed, Mac Patch was cut down by a German tank round and died instantly. Patch was not much for words, and at his son's funeral he said simply, "So long, son." Although Bradley later noted that the psychological impact of his son's death was so great as to impair Patch's military effectiveness, there was little direct evidence of this. Only a few days later Devers found Patch ready and willing to attack the Germans, and in the ensuing weeks and months Devers gave no indication that he was dissatisfied with Patch's performance. Even so, there can be little doubt that his son's death weighed heavily on Patch, as it would on any father.[35]

Eisenhower's expectations for Devers's army group were limited to tying down German troops by pushing toward Mulhouse and Strasbourg while Bradley's Twelfth Army Group delivered the important blows that would hopefully bring American forces to the Rhine River. Unlike Patton, Devers sensibly waited until the heavy autumn rains slackened before launching his attack on 13 November. The French First Army broke through German lines and seized Belfort Gap on 16 November before reaching the Rhine River four days later. To the north, Patch's Seventh Army also made significant progress. Both Brooks's and Haislip's corps breached the German defenses, which enabled Haislip to commit the French Second Armored Division to exploit the opening and charge toward Strasbourg. French tanks entered the city on 23 November and crushed the last vestiges of resistance within three days. Devers and Patch wanted to cross the Rhine, but Eisenhower instead directed the Sixth Army Group northward toward the Saar. At that point Devers's offensive began to falter. The French First Army became preoccupied not only with battling a stubborn pocket of German strength around Colmar, but also with integrating native and colonial units. The Seventh Army for its part came up against the West Wall and stalled amidst the stout German defenses.[36]

Devers and his chief subordinates were proud of their victory. Despite limited expectations and resources, they had advanced all the way to the Rhine River over rough terrain and against skilled German opposition. Devers was as pleased with his army and corps commanders as he was with their accomplishments. He praised Patch and Brooks in particular for having the foresight to anticipate Eisenhower's orders to swing to the north toward the West Wall. At the same time, though, Devers, Patch, Brooks, and Haislip all regretted that Eisenhower had denied them permission to cross the Rhine and had failed to provide them with sufficient resources to breach the West Wall. After noting the other Allied armies' lack of progress that autumn compared with his army group's promising start, Devers commented, "It would seem to me that strength should be reinforced, not weakness."[37] Indeed, Devers speculated that the Sixth Army Group's unexpected success may have embarrassed Eisenhower's headquarters, but noted that he only did what he thought he was supposed to do.

As for Haislip, his happiness was somewhat tempered by other factors. For one thing, he felt unappreciated by his superiors. Haislip was accustomed to Patton's rough oversight and was slow to adjust to Devers's and Patch's lighter touches. He lamented that neither Devers nor Patch bothered to congratulate him after he broke through the German lines. Moreover, he had a close call during the offensive. On 24 November Eisenhower and Bradley visited the Fifteenth Corps on an inspection trip just as a strong local German counterattack threatened to overrun its headquarters. When Eisenhower and Bradley's motorcade drove up, Haislip ran out to greet them and yelled, "For God's sake, sir, I was just on my way down to tell you not to come. Please go on. We don't want you." Eisenhower, however, would not hear of it and replied, "Dammit, Ham, you invited me here for lunch and I'm not going until I get it." Haislip rushed them through their meal while his headquarters personnel hurriedly prepared to defend themselves. Fortunately the Germans did not materialize, but at such a crucial time Haislip hardly enjoyed devoting his attention toward protecting the supreme commander, old friend or not.[38]

After the heady days of the previous summer, the Allies had good reason to be dissatisfied with their campaign along the West Wall that fall. They achieved no decisive breakthroughs such as Cobra, made no spectacular advances across the Rhine, and saw little evidence of the chaos and confusion that marked the German retreat across France. Instead, the Allies repeatedly encountered a determined and skilled enemy who bent but did not break. Hodges's performance was perhaps the most disappointing because he received a disproportionate share of the available resources and expectations. Hodges never understood the limitations the poor terrain imposed on his tired troops. His poor relationship with his subordinates also contributed to his difficulties. Although Hodges continued to get along well with Collins, he treated Gerow, Corlett, and most of his division chiefs poorly. Corlett was no doubt a truculent officer, but Hodges's bullying brought out the worst in him and contributed to his relief. By fostering an atmosphere of blame, mistrust, and intolerance for any failure, Hodges sucked much of the initiative out of many of his chief lieutenants. As a result, his operations degenerated into a brutal war of attrition that resulted in thousands of casualties but little gain. To be sure, Eisenhower deployed the First Army in a cramped sector that was not conducive to army doctrine, but this was hardly a satisfactory excuse—and not one that Hodges himself would have tolerated from his generals.

Patton's and Simpson's operations that autumn were marginally more successful than Hodges's. Neither the Third Army nor the Ninth Army achieved any breakthrough, but both armies gained ground and escaped the dissension that characterized the First Army. Unlike Hodges, Simpson created a supportive and trusting relationship with his corps and division commanders that made the Ninth Army a much happier organization than the First Army. No doubt Simpson's corps commanders, Gillem and McLain, were much easier to get along with than the staid Gerow, cocky Collins, and abrasive Corlett, but Simpson understood that he had to make allowances for the personal friction inevitable in war.

Patton recognized this as well. Although he was frequently frustrated with the timidity he felt many of his corps and division commanders displayed, he tried to counter it with rough encouragement. If he yelled at and browbeat them, it was because he saw their potential and wanted to bring it out. He refrained from relieving them unless absolutely necessary and was willing to give them second chances to succeed. He displayed remarkable patience toward Eddy in particular, exactly because he had such confidence in him.

Ironically enough, the most successful army that autumn was Patch's distant and unappreciated Seventh. Although Eisenhower had comparatively little interest or faith in Devers's Sixth Army Group operations, they came closest to unraveling the German line. The French First Army and the Seventh Army bulled their way through difficult terrain to the Rhine River and probably could have crossed had not Eisenhower directed Devers toward the West Wall instead. There were several reasons for the army group's accomplishments, but a big one was the good working relationship Devers established with his field army and corps commanders. He continued to display an astute sensitivity toward the French that kept them in the war and obeying his orders. He thought the world of Patch and gave him an autonomy to conduct operations that Bradley would have thought strange. If Patch was somewhat remote from his corps and division commanders, this did not prevent him from skillfully maneuvering the Seventh Army through the Vosges Mountains. Devers, Patch, Haislip, and Brooks all displayed a dexterity often lacking in the other field armies that autumn. Although they faced less opposition than Patton, Hodges, and Simpson did, this was a good reason to reinforce instead of neglect them.

Battle of the Bulge

By mid-December 1944 Eisenhower's American armies were stretched thin from the Low Countries to the Vosges Mountains. Not only did Eisenhower lack enough divisions to adequately man his long line, but those divisions that were available were often in woeful shape. Heavy combat along the West Wall had reduced once proud units such as the First, Ninth, and Twenty-eighth divisions to shells of their former selves. Replacements were slow in arriving, especially the precious riflemen who did the vast majority of the fighting and dying. Moreover, the Allies were only now getting a handle on the logistical problems that had caused them so much grief that autumn, and there were still shortages of some critical materiel. Finally, the cloudy winter weather prevalent in western Europe limited the air support upon which the army so heavily relied. These and other difficulties forced Eisenhower and Bradley to make some hard decisions. One of

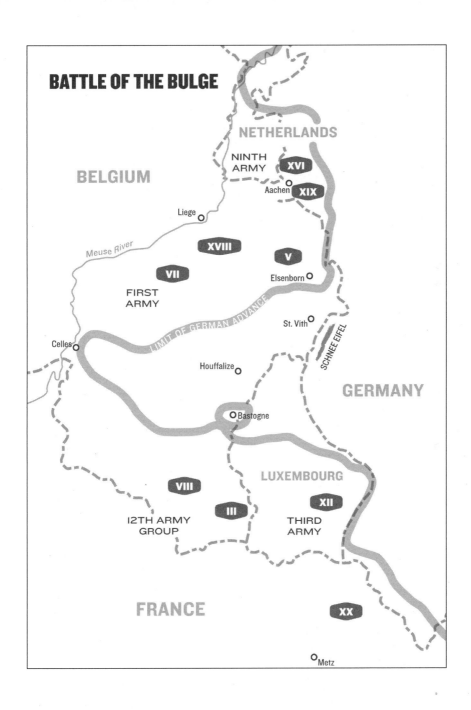

BATTLE OF THE BULGE

NETHERLANDS

BELGIUM

NINTH ARMY

XVI

Aachen

XIX

Liege

Meuse River

XVIII

V

VII

Elsenborn

FIRST ARMY

St. Vith

SCHNEE EIFEL

LIMIT OF GERMAN ADVANCE

Celles

Houffalize

GERMANY

Bastogne

LUXEMBOURG

VIII

XII

III

THIRD ARMY

12TH ARMY GROUP

FRANCE

XX

Metz

them was to conserve manpower by lightly screening the Ardennes, that forested region along the German-Belgium-Luxembourg border. Indeed, Bradley turned the Ardennes into a big rest and rehabilitation center for divisions that had been badly mauled in the Huertgen to recover and for new divisions fresh from the States to acclimate. Bradley gambled that there was little chance of the Germans attacking through such a heavily timbered area with so few roads, even though they had done exactly that in 1940. The American high command was slow to respond to scattered intelligence reports of a German buildup in the Ardennes and was therefore caught completely by surprise when on 16 December some 250,000 German troops organized into twenty-five divisions assailed the 83,000 tired or green GIs there. The German objective was to cross the Meuse River, seize Antwerp, and cut the British Twenty-first Army Group in the Low Countries off from the Americans to the south. This would hopefully turn the tide of the war in Germany's favor. The ensuing six-week-long Battle of the Bulge was the biggest engagement in American military history, and served as a test for both the American soldiers and their commanders involved in the action.

The German offensive squarely struck Troy Middleton's Eighth Corps. Middleton had only three and a half divisions with which to cover his 85-mile-long sector and had been deeply concerned about his vulnerable position for some time. When Jim Moore, the Ninth Army's chief of staff, observed that Middleton's headquarters at Bastogne, Belgium, was awfully far behind the front, Middleton responded, "Jim, as far as I can see there's nothing between me and the Germans but terrain, and I aim to have plenty of that."[39] Unfortunately, Middleton received little sympathy from his superiors, who were focusing on important operations to the north and south. When Middleton expressed his qualms to Bradley, Bradley assured him that the Germans would not attack him. Bradley was at least kind and sympathetic. Patton on the other hand bluntly told Middleton, "Oh, you're always disturbed about these wide fronts. . . . Oh, but don't you worry."[40] But Middleton did worry. If he did not prepare his units as much as he should have for the eventuality he foresaw, he did at least put some thought into the proper response.

Middleton was asleep at his Bastogne headquarters when a guard knocked on his van to inform him that German artillery fire was blanketing his entire front. Soon after daybreak messengers began arriving with reports, and by midmorning Middleton knew that sixteen different German divisions were assailing his corps. General Alan Jones's new 106th Division had been in the line for only five days, and two of its regiments were deployed along a high and exposed ridge, called the Schnee Eifel, jutting toward the West Wall. Middleton left it up to the inexperienced Jones to decide whether to stay and fight or withdraw, but noted that a combat command from General John Leonard's Ninth Armored Division was on the way to help. Jones opted to hold his ground and wait for the American armor.

Unfortunately, retreating GIs clogged the roads leading to the front, so the tanks were unable to reach Jones's beleaguered men. The Germans quickly surrounded the two exposed regiments and compelled their surrender on 19 December. At least 7,000 American soldiers marched off into captivity.

To the south, the Germans also hit Dutch Cota's Twenty-eighth Division. The Twenty-eighth was still recovering from its horrific ordeal in the Huertgen Forest, but it was a tough outfit and did not give up. Although the Germans destroyed one of its regiments and drove the other one off, the remainder of Cota's men, with the help of Tubby Barton's Fourth Division, managed to hold on and prevent the Germans from widening their breach. Back at Bastogne, gloom and uncertainty pervaded Eighth Corps headquarters. Communications with forward units were tentative at best, reserves were limited, and timely and accurate information was hard to come by. Middleton, however, kept a clear head and relied on the dispassion and intellect that had characterized his career. He knew he was facing a major German onslaught, and he also recognized that controlling the limited Ardennes road network was a key to stemming the German tide. In particular, he zeroed in on road hubs of St. Vith and Bastogne and opted to make his stands there by committing his remaining reserves and arriving reinforcements to their defense. He got part of General Robert Hasbrouck's Seventh Armored Division, the remnants of the 106th, and the retreating regiment from the Twenty-eighth Division into St. Vith. For Bastogne, Middleton sent a combat command from General William Morris's Tenth Armored Division and the 101st Airborne Division. Middleton had by now been in touch with Patton, who did not much like Middleton's plan to hold on to Bastogne and told him, "You're just [the] damnest fool I've ever seen."[41] Bradley, though, agreed with Middleton, so the troops stayed put and were surrounded. By the time all these pieces were in place, Eisenhower had redrawn the organizational boundaries in the Ardennes and reduced Middleton's responsibilities to simply protecting Bastogne as part of Patton's Third Army. Despite this temporary marginalization, Middleton had done much to shape the course of the battle. While he admitted to Bradley that the Germans had shattered his corps, he added quite accurately that doing so had cost them more than they could afford.[42]

To Middleton's north, the German juggernaut hit Gerow's Fifth Corps with equal ferocity. Despite Eisenhower's and Bradley's fervent support, Gerow's record as a corps commander had been up to then decidedly mediocre. Hodges rode herd over Gerow and had on several occasions yelled at him for improperly handling his units. The Battle of the Bulge, however, gave Gerow the opportunity to demonstrate his worth. When the German attack began Gerow had four divisions at his disposal, one of which—General Walter Robertson's veteran Second—was engaged in offensive operations. Gerow's southernmost outfit, General

Walter Lauer's new Ninety-ninth Division, caught the brunt of the German assault along Elsenborn Ridge. Although almost as green as Jones's unlucky 106th, Lauer's men fought hard and gave a good account of themselves. Gerow swiftly recognized that he was facing a major German threat, but his biggest initial challenge was getting Hodges to see it. Hodges did not approve of Gerow's request to cancel the Second Division's eastward drive until next morning, 17 December. Fortunately, Gerow's informal deputy commander, Clarence Huebner, had told Robertson the evening before to start planning his withdrawal, so the Second Division managed to get away quickly and without significant losses for its redeployment along Elsenborn Ridge. It arrived just in time to bolster the beleaguered Ninety-ninth and stave off defeat. In the following days of vicious combat the Second and Ninety-ninth divisions held their positions, even though they became so intermingled that Gerow eventually placed Robertson in charge of them both. Gerow also used the reinforcements he received—the First, Thirtieth, and Eighty-second Airborne divisions—to extend his right flank and keep pace with the German advance. In holding Elsenborn Ridge, Gerow's Fifth Corps limited the German breach and helped constrict their offensive.

Middleton's and Gerow's professional responses to the German attack contrasted sharply with Hodges's more controversial performance. Hodges's declining health throughout the autumn had certainly limited his effectiveness and contributed to the First Army's difficulties in breaking through the West Wall—and would continue to play a role during the Battle of the Bulge. Although Hodges went to bed with a bad cold on the night of 15–16 December, the next morning he seemed okay. He was neither alarmist about nor dismissive of the German offensive, but instead adopted a wait-and-see attitude while his staffers accumulated information about the extent of the enemy assault. On the morning after that, though, he was so seriously ill that he could barely function. One aide remembered seeing him at his desk, semiconscious, with his head cradled in his arms. How long he remained in this condition is unclear, but in the following days he did little to inspire his army or take firm control of the battle. It was small wonder that outside observers remarked on the chaos, disorganization, and lack of direction that initially permeated First Army headquarters. During this critical time Hodges's chief of staff, the strong-willed Bill Kean, stepped in to fill the command void. Kean worked closely with Hodges and issued orders in his name. In fact, Kean ran the First Army as much as Hodges did during those dark days. Nevertheless, Bradley for one later opined that Hodges's inability to get a grip on First Army operations contributed to the unnecessarily pessimistic outlook that some people at first embraced.[43]

Despite Hodges's woes, the American high command's response to the German breakthrough was amazingly swift. In fact, the Seventh Armored Division arrived in the Ardennes as early as 17 December. This was partly attributable to the army's mechanization that enabled troops to reach their destinations quickly, but more so the supple thinking Eisenhower and his lieutenants displayed. The reinforcements they dispatched not only helped Middleton and Gerow slow and constrain the German drive, but also set the stage for the American counteroffensive that won the battle. Bradley was at Eisenhower's headquarters at Versailles when they received word of the German assault. Bradley figured that it was just a spoiling attack, but Eisenhower sensed that there was more to it than that. He acted on his hunch by ordering two refitting armored divisions, the Seventh and Tenth, to the Ardennes to help Middleton. Next day, in response to pleas from Hodges and a now anxious Bradley, he released to them the theater reserve, the Eighty-second and 101st Airborne divisions. There was equal flexibility within the Twelfth Army Group. Simpson traveled to First Army headquarters when he learned of Hodges's ordeal. There he was shown a captured map that revealed the outlines of the German plan. After taking a long look at it, Simpson said to Hodges, "Well, I think from what we see here I don't feel too much alarmed. We're going to have to do some hard fighting, but I think eventually we'll stop this thing."[44] This was of course easy for Simpson to say because he was not in the direct path of the German juggernaut. Fortunately, Simpson was willing to offer more than bland reassurance. When Hodges complained that he was having trouble contacting Eisenhower and Bradley to ask for their permission to tap into the Ninth Army's resources, Simpson replied, "Hell, you don't have to do that. What do you want?"[45] Soon Hobbs's Thirtieth Division and Ernie Harmon's Second Armored Division were on their way to bolster Gerow's right flank.[46]

Hodges no doubt appreciated Simpson's assistance, but these and other reinforcements on their way to the Ardennes were still in *response* to the German onslaught. Eisenhower, however, increasingly saw the German attack as an opportunity to take the initiative and destroy the Wehrmacht out in the open. Doing so required a strong and well-organized counteroffensive, not dispatch of troops willy-nilly to threatened parts of the front. Fortunately, Bradley and Patton were thinking along the same lines and discussed the matter at a 18 December meeting at Bradley's advanced headquarters in Luxembourg City. Despite his previous dismissal of Middleton's concerns, Patton had not been especially surprised by the German sally, having several weeks earlier predicted that Middleton was asking for trouble by sitting still in the Ardennes. He was initially unhappy with Bradley's orders suspending his current operations, but upon further reflection he concluded that fighting in the Ardennes offered him as much glory and action as assailing the West Wall—or, as he put it, he could kill Germans just as well in the Ardennes as anywhere else. He and Bradley sketched a plan for a Third Army drive into the Ardennes, so he was well prepared for a conference with Eisenhower, Bradley, Devers, and other high-ranking officers the next day at the Twelfth Army Group's main headquarters at Verdun. Eisenhower emphasized the opportunities before them and urged everyone to remain positive and upbeat. In response to Eisenhower's question, Patton stated that he could strike in three days with three divisions. Many in the room questioned whether he could disengage his divisions from their current positions in the face of the enemy, turn them 90 degrees to the north, march them over bad roads in the winter weather, and redeploy them in the Ardennes in seventy-two short hours. Patton assured them that he had already begun preparations and simply had to give the word to put the selected units in motion. Enjoying the attention, he said, "This time the Kraut has stuck his head in a meat grinder, and this time I've got hold of the handle."[47] Thus, only three days after the German assault, the army had authorized a major counteroffensive to turn the tide.

After the meeting broke up, Eisenhower made one more important—and, as things turned out, controversial—decision that impacted the battle. His chief of staff, Beetle Smith, suggested placing the First and Ninth armies temporarily under Montgomery's command. Smith noted that the German intrusion in the center of his lines made it difficult for Bradley to keep in touch with Hodges and Simpson, so he could hardly manage all three of his armies well. Smith was also aware of Hodges's health problems, and probably concluded that he needed firm direction that Bradley could not at present provide. Eisenhower realized that making the change would upset Bradley and give Montgomery the chance to further alienate the Americans, but he decided that military logic trumped personal and national pride and agreed to the proposal.[48]

Patton opted to conduct his offensive with the Twenty-sixth, Eightieth, and Fourth Armored divisions. To lead these units, Patton gave the job to General John Millikin and his Third Corps. Patton's selection of Millikin for such an important mission was puzzling for several reasons. Most obviously, Millikin and his corps headquarters were brand new and untried in combat, having arrived in the theater the previous October. Moreover, Patton had never liked Millikin much and opposed his appointment to corps command. Patton believed that corps should go to experienced and proven division commanders, not greenhorns from the States. Placing such inexperienced generals over skilled division chiefs, he felt, lowered morale and was not fair. In fact, Patton had lobbied Bradley to assign the Third Corps to John Wood, but Bradley concluded that although Wood was a hard fighter, division level was probably his limit. Finally, Patton had two perfectly capable corps commanders at his disposal in Manton Eddy and Johnny Walker. Circumstances, however, limited Patton's options and persuaded him to go with Millikin. Patton intended to use Eddy's Twelfth Corps to attack the base of the bulge the Germans had created in the American line with the follow-up divisions he wanted to deploy there. As for Walker, Patton decided that he needed to stay behind to watch over the divisions that had recently established a vulnerable bridgehead over the Saar River. Besides, Patton hoped that Millikin's ambition and freshness would compensate for his rawness. Just to make sure, though, Patton planned to ride herd on him to make sure he did things right.[49]

Millikin's background provides evidence that Marshall did not hold an officer's position in the army's innumerable cliques against him. Millikin was born in Indiana in 1888, the son of a barber. He graduated from West Point in 1910 and was subsequently stationed in Hawaii, Arizona, and Virginia. In 1917 he married the eldest daughter of General Peyton March, army chief of staff from 1918 to 1921. While Millikin served as executive officer at the General Staff School in France during World War One, March and John Pershing waged an increasingly bitter bureaucratic battle over who controlled the army. Pershing and his supporters ultimately prevailed and dominated the army throughout much of the interwar years, while March sank into obscurity. None of this, however, had much impact on Millikin's career. After occupation duty with the provost marshal, he returned to Washington and played a part in defusing the racial tension there in 1919. He attended the Cavalry School in 1924, the Command and General Staff School from 1924 to 1925, and the Army War College from 1930 to 1931. He also taught at the Command and General Staff School and the Cavalry School. After World War Two broke out in Europe he commanded successively a cavalry regiment, a cavalry brigade, and finally the Second Cavalry Division. In August 1942 he took over the Thirty-third Division, but after it was deployed overseas Marshall assigned him to lead the Third Corps. Aloof, sharp-eyed, and full of nervous energy, Millikin possessed a cavalryman's build. One officer described him as "a very forceful, level headed man, cold and stern but conscientious. An efficient officer, better liked by his superiors than his subordinates but respected by all."[50] While certainly competent, Millikin lacked both the drive and that deftness of touch that a good commander needed to smooth out rough edges and ruffled feathers in order to get things done. Nor was he very good at inspiring the rank and file to exert itself on his behalf.[51]

As with Sandy Patch, Millikin owed his presence in the European theater to neither Marshall nor Eisenhower. McNair had been impressed with Millikin's job with his cavalry regiment and recommended his promotion to division command. Neither McNair nor Marshall knew Millikin very well, so it is unclear why they elevated him to the corps level. McNair approved of the way Millikin handled the Third Corps, but Marshall did not seem to think much of him one way or another. In January 1944 Marshall sent Eisenhower a list of long-standing—comparatively, of course—stateside corps commanders available for deployment to Europe, ranked in order of efficiency by McNair. Millikin was at the bottom of the list of four. When Eisenhower received the message, he literally drew a line through Millikin's name to indicate that he did not want him, though he never explained his reasoning. When Eisenhower met with Bill Simpson in May 1944 to determine the Ninth Army's corps commanders, Simpson asked for Millikin because he respected his abilities. Eisenhower was not so sure, but gave in not only to please Simpson but also because he doubted the quality of the other remaining stateside corps commanders. Although Millikin was slated for Simpson's Ninth Army, Eisenhower and Bradley decided to place him in the Third Army instead because Patton was down to two corps after Middleton's and Haislip's transfers.[52]

Both Bradley and Patton worried about giving Millikin such an important first assignment, which was why Patton closely supervised his actions. Bastogne's surrounded defenders were barely holding on in the face of ferocious German assaults and needed rescuing as soon as possible. Patton had wanted to assail the southwestern base of the bulge to cut the Germans off from their homeland, but saving Bastogne forced him to operate further to the west. Millikin's Third Corps jumped off on 22 December and made good progress the first day. Patton urged Millikin to go to the front and get a feel for the battle, and was pleased with his performance. After that, though, the advance bogged down. Part of the problem was the usual fierce German resistance, but the unimaginative tactics Patton and Millikin employed also played a role. In their efforts to rescue Bastogne, they resorted to frontal assault because Patton in particular was interested more in celerity than in finesse. The brilliance Patton demonstrated in organizing his offensive did not continue through its implementation. Not until 26 December did the Fourth Armored Division muscle its way into Bastogne. Saving the garrison did not put an end to the operation; the Germans continued to hammer both the town and the vulnerable corridor the Fourth Armored had carved out. Patton fed reinforcements into the fray, including the Thirty-fifth, Ninetieth, and Sixth Armored divisions. Throughout the fighting in December and January, Patton's opinion of Millikin fluctuated. He lamented that he had to repeatedly push the cautious Millikin to keep moving, but also noted that Millikin was probably doing as well as could be expected under the difficult circumstances into which he was thrust. After the battle, however, Patton concluded that Millikin's tactics were too amateurish compared to those of his other corps commanders.[53]

The other corps commanders Patton referred to were Manton Eddy and Troy Middleton. However, neither of them performed significantly better than Millikin in the Third Army's initial counteroffensive. Eddy began his attack near the southwestern base of the bulge on 24 December with elements of the Fourth, Fifth, Ninth Armored, and Tenth Armored divisions. Eddy was his usual fussy and worrisome self, but German resistance, tired troops, broken terrain, and the limited road network initially prevented him from achieving his customary success.

To the west of Millikin's Third Corps, Middleton's Eighth Corps began probing the Germans as early as 27 December. Patton's admission to Middleton that he had been right about defending Bastogne did not prevent him from exerting heavy pressure on the reluctant Middleton to assail the Germans as soon as possible. To do so, Patton placed at Middleton's disposal three new divisions: the Eighty-seventh, Eleventh Armored, and Seventeenth Airborne. Although Middleton as usual appeared complacent and uninvolved, he was actually deeply concerned about pushing such raw outfits so quickly into intense combat. Patton interpreted Middleton's reservations as another example of the timidity he abhorred and ordered him to commit the units at once. In this case Middleton was correct; the Germans chewed up all three divisions. Indeed, the Seventeenth Airborne suffered so heavily that Middleton had to pull it out of the line for two days for refitting. In the end, though, Middleton, Millikin, and Eddy all made progress through brute attrition and gradually pushed the Germans northward and eastward. Patton continued to grumble about the excessive caution of his commanders, but he was heartened by Middleton's and Eddy's upbeat attitude toward the end of the battle, and even stated that Middleton was a great soldier.[54]

While Patton's counteroffensive was getting under way, Hodges's First Army struggled to get a grip on the dangerous situation in the northern part of the bulge. St. Vith fell on 23 December after a stubborn battle, giving the Germans access to the local road network. German armored columns continued to push westward toward the Meuse River as the Americans tried desperately to deploy their forces to cut them off. There were vicious skirmishes at remote and snowy crossroads throughout the northern Ardennes. Fighting without their customary air and artillery support, and often without much guidance from any headquarters, ad hoc American detachments still gave good accounts of themselves by delaying and hindering the German advance. On the afternoon of 20 December, Bernard Montgomery strode into First Army headquarters like, as one of his officers put it, "Christ come to cleanse the temple."[55] Montgomery and his staffers were shocked by the confusion and lack of control they found there. Montgomery traced much of the problem back to Hodges, who was still clearly ill. Indeed, Montgomery worried that Hodges might succumb to a heart attack under the strain of command and conveyed as much to Eisenhower's headquarters. Eisenhower figured that Montgomery did not understand Hodges's personality and replied, "I know that you realize that Hodges is the quiet reticent type and does not appear as aggressive as he really is. Unless he becomes exhausted he will always wage a good fight." Just in case the various reports of Hodges's infirmity were true, however, Eisenhower added, "You will of course keep in touch with your important subordinates and inform me instantly if any change needs to be made on United States side."[56] Despite his arrogance, First Army staffers admired

Montgomery's obvious professionalism and were more amused than annoyed with his peculiar mannerisms. They really resented the laudatory press Patton was receiving more than Montgomery's presence. Montgomery made some common-sense suggestions for straightening out the tangled American lines and did not interfere much with First Army tactical operations. He erred though in asserting that the First Army would be unable to assume the offensive for several weeks. As it was, the First Army was steadily imposing order on the battlefield as reinforcements flowed to the Ardennes. Hodges's health was also improving, and with it the tone and tenor of his headquarters. By Christmas week, First Army headquarters was convinced that the worst was over and looked forward to going on the attack.[57]

The deployment of General Matthew Ridgway's Eighteenth Airborne Corps was one big reason for the optimism among First Army staffers. Although Bradley had initially offered Hodges General John B. Anderson's new Sixteenth Corps headquarters, Hodges insisted on the more experienced Ridgway. The forty-nine-year-old Ridgway was born in Fort Monroe, Virginia, the son of an army officer. He graduated from West Point in 1917, but instead of going to France in World War One, he spent the conflict teaching languages at his alma mater. He was disappointed that he did not see active service in the war and worried that it might inhibit his career. However, the proficiency in Spanish he developed would become a key to his professional success. After working as West Point's athletic director during Douglas MacArthur's tenure as superintendent, Ridgway was stationed in China in Marshall's regiment. He then served in Nicaragua during the turmoil there as part of an American team overseeing elections before attending the Infantry School while Marshall was assistant commandant. Marshall was impressed with Ridgway's performance and made a mental note of it. Ridgway subsequently put in his time at the Command and General Staff School from 1933 to 1935 and the Army War College from 1936 to 1937. His and Marshall's paths crossed for a third time when Ridgway accompanied Marshall on a diplomatic mission to Brazil in the spring of 1939. He was part of the War Plans Division when the Japanese attacked Pearl Harbor and soon after became Marshall's operational briefer too. Ridgway wanted a combat command, though, and repeatedly badgered Marshall's staff secretary, the irascible Beetle Smith, for news of a transfer. Finally one day Smith told him, "This morning General Marshall said, and I quote, 'Tell Ridgway I'm tired of seeing him hanging around out there every time my door opens. When I have something for him, I'll send for him.'"[58] Ridgway's persistence, as well as his prior relationship with Marshall, paid off when Marshall appointed him assistant commander of the Eighty-second Division under Ridgway's old friend Omar Bradley. When Bradley moved on to another division, Ridgway took over the Eighty-second. It was Ridgway's good fortune that the Eighty-second became the army's first airborne division, giving Ridgway the inside track to a prominent role in the war and making him a leading expert on airborne operations.[59]

Ridgway led the Eighty-second Airborne with distinction in Sicily, Italy, and especially Normandy, where for the first time he parachuted into action. The Eighty-second not only played an important role on D-Day, but remained in Normandy until early July because Bradley so valued its services. Ridgway's performance won the respect and admiration of Marshall, Eisenhower, and Bradley. Indeed, Ridgway was already in line for a corps when Bradley finally returned his bled-down division to England. As soon as the Eighty-second settled in the Midlands, Ridgway traveled to Eisenhower's headquarters and talked with his old friend Beetle Smith. Smith informed him that Eisenhower planned to organize the British and American airborne divisions into the First Airborne Army under General Lewis Brereton. Brereton's responsibilities would be primarily training and organizational; the real fighting would be conducted by the army's two component corps, one British and one American. Eisenhower authorized two different corps mostly to placate national sensibilities because the Americans in particular disliked some of the more prominent British airborne commanders. When Bradley learned about these discussions, he said, "Christ, why don't they use Ridgway. He's a fighter and knows more about airborne than all of them."[60] As a reward for jobs well done, Eisenhower acted on Bradley's thinking by giving Ridgway the new Eighteenth Airborne Corps. He was the logical choice; there were no other American airborne commanders available with his rank and experience. Ridgway accepted the offer immediately, though he regretted leaving the Eighty-second. Although Ridgway fought through Market-Garden, British General F. A. M. "Boy" Browning's First Airborne Corps actually oversaw the British-organized operation. Like a good soldier, Ridgway did not complain about his lack of authority, but it clearly rankled and perhaps contributed to the Allied setback. Two of his American airborne divisions, the Eighty-second and 101st, were recovering from their Market-Garden ordeal at Reims when Eisenhower dispatched them to the Ardennes. Ridgway and most of his new Eighteenth Corps headquarters were in England when they got the news. He immediately got them on board planes and flew with them to the continent, and they entered the lines on 19 December.[61]

Lean, hawkish, and ramrod straight, Ridgway was the embodiment of the can-do American general and one of the best combat commanders the army produced during the conflict. He was a superb leader who inspired his men through his frequent visits to the field, his charismatic personality, and his obvious courage. For Ridgway, war was an intensely personal affair in which setbacks required immediate rectification. He possessed a religious streak and believed that God and the

United States of America were working together for humanity's betterment. Indeed, he was convinced that God would not gather him to heaven until Germany was defeated. His zealousness and single-mindedness were almost intimidating; one observer later remembered, "The force that emanated from him was awesome. It reminded me of Superman. You had the impression he could knock over a building with a single blow, or stare a hole through a wall, if he wanted to. It was a powerful *presence*."[62] Ridgway combined this intensity with intelligence, a phenomenal memory, aggressiveness, and a ruthless intolerance for failure that sometimes made him overbearing and unsympathetic. Some complained that he was moody, self-centered, and prone to jump to conclusions based on hunches instead of evidence. The fact that his hunches were usually correct did not preclude this impulsive streak. He was in many respects cut from the same cloth as Collins, whose battle instincts he shared. Another officer elaborated:

> General Ridgway, from the moment I first set eyes on him, had extraordinary daring, magnetism, and strength of character, and looked like my idea of a leader and an officer. When he walked into the officers' mess you could feel his presence. He had this look of eagles in his eyes. There was a certain vibrancy that exuded from him. He was broad chested and square shouldered. He walked with a bounce, and had a wonderful jaw and aquiline nose. He just looked like a fantastic officer. He spoke in lofty terms and said the right things. He was physically fit. He exercised, and he had a demeanor and a bearing that was very inspiring.[63]

The fact that women were attracted to him was not as surprising as his two divorces in an era and an institution that frowned on such things.[64]

Hodges assigned Ridgway's Eighteenth Airborne Corps the important task of extending the First Army's line through the northern Ardennes and preventing the Germans from turning its right flank. To do so, Hodges initially gave Ridgway parts of Hobbs's Thirtieth Division and General Maurice Rose's Third Armored Division, as well as the Eighty-second Airborne Division, now under Jim Gavin. Wearing his usual full web of equipment, including a grenade strapped to his harness, Ridgway repeatedly visited the front to get a feel for the action. Despite the paucity of resources at his disposal, he was confident that he could do the job. Fighting crackled up and down his sketchy and impromptu line as he dispatched his units to defend the innumerable crossroads for which he was responsible. Ridgway also authorized the extraction of the heavily outnumbered troops battling at St. Vith. This cost the Americans the valuable road junction, but it gave the defenders the opportunity to fight another day. Although he obeyed Montgomery's orders to consolidate his lines, Ridgway was unhappy surrendering any ground. However, Montgomery's reasonable instructions, the continued stubbornness of beleaguered GIs, and the timely arrival of reinforcements all enabled the Eighteenth Airborne Corps to stymie or deflect repeated German attacks westward.[65]

While Ridgway struggled to shore up his tatterdemalion line, Montgomery and Hodges were already thinking about an eventual First Army counterattack. To implement it, Montgomery directed Hodges to assemble troops near the Meuse River that would serve as a "savage rabbit" by assailing the Germans from a secure defensive position preparatory to a full-scale offensive. To lead these GIs, Montgomery asked Hodges for his most aggressive and skilled combat commander: Joe Collins. Collins had been Hodges's mainstay throughout the fighting in northwest Europe, so Hodges was perfectly comfortable giving him another starring role. Collins and his Seventh Corps headquarters deployed near the Meuse on 23 December and set about bringing some sort of order to the prevailing chaos in their sector. Collins was his usual vigorous and forceful self in part because of the confidence he had in the outfits Hodges provided. Collins rated Ernie Harmon's Second Armored Division and Rose's Third Armored Division as the two best in the entire army. Moreover, Harmon and Rose both shared Collins's aggressive instincts and were eager to enter the fight. Collins was unfamiliar with the new Eighty-fourth Division, but its commander, General Alexander Bolling, seemed full of quiet self-assurance. When an exuberant Harmon informed Collins that the German armored spearhead approaching the Meuse was exposed and low on fuel near Celles, Collins was all in favor of unleashing the Second Armored Division on them. Unfortunately, Montgomery's instructions called for the Seventh Corps to remain on the defensive for the time being. Collins, however, opted to stretch and twist Montgomery's orders by committing Harmon into action on Christmas. Harmon exclaimed, "The bastards are in the bag!" when he got the news. Over the course of the next few days, the Second Armored completely demolished the Germans, bringing their offensive to an abrupt halt and ending whatever hopes they still harbored of reaching the Meuse. For Hodges, who received initial reports of Harmon's success just before his Christmas dinner, it was about the best gift he could have asked for.[66]

Hodges, Collins, Ridgway, and Harmon were eager to go over on the attack now that the Germans had shot their bolt. Unfortunately, Montgomery did not think that the First Army was ready to do so. Moreover, he believed that when it did, its goal should be limited to shoving the Wehrmacht out of its bulge back to Germany. Eisenhower and his American commanders, on the other hand, wanted to trap and destroy enemy forces in the bulge, not simply see them off. Montgomery's attitude, as well as the limited road network at the base of the bulge, shaped First Army planning along Montgomery's line of thinking. As a result, when the First Army finally launched its counteroffensive on 3 January, its target was the center of the bulge. Collins's Seventh Corps assailed Houffalize while Ridgway's Eighteenth Airborne Corps aimed at St. Vith. Although German fortunes were clearly waning, there was nothing easy about it. Cloud cover limited American air support, snow fostered trench foot, and wooded terrain that had facilitated the American defense now helped the Germans. Collins and Ridgway pushed their subordinates hard, but the battle still degenerated into a brutal war of attrition in which the First Army made slow progress. Ridgway, for example, recommended the relief of the new Seventy-fifth Division's commander, General Fay Prickett, for his uninspiring and tentative attitude. Not until 16 January did the First Army and Third Army finally establish contact near Houffalize, which enabled Eisenhower to return the First Army to Bradley's control at midnight on 17–18 January. The Seventh Armored seized St. Vith on 23 January, and by the end of the month the Americans had erased the bulge and reestablished the front lines more or less where they were in mid-December.[67]

The Battle of the Bulge was the largest engagement in American military history. For forty-one days nearly a million GIs suffered 81,000 casualties in repelling the ferocious German offensive. Twenty-nine American divisions were ultimately involved in the fighting, or nearly half of all the divisions the army deployed against the Germans in the entire war. There was, however, more to the Battle of the Bulge than mere scale. In their high-stakes gamble to turn the war's tide, the Germans expended almost all of their remaining reserves in the Ardennes. This enabled the Allies to push to the Rhine and into Germany the following spring more easily than would have been the case had the Germans possessed all the infantry and tanks lost in the Ardennes. Finally, the Battle of the Bulge was a great and successful test of the American army. Even at the time some observers criticized the army's excessive reliance on artillery and air support to overcome the enemy and compensate for the infantry's shortcomings. Indeed, the fighting in Normandy and elsewhere seemed to indicate that American infantrymen lacked the ability and fortitude to come to grips with the Wehrmacht on their own. There is some truth to this, but it is important to remember that the army was the sum of all its parts. Moreover, the vast majority of the GIs in France were new to war and confronted tough German troops skilled in defensive warfare. In the Ardennes most American soldiers fought capably even when outnumbered and outgunned. To be sure, there were some untried units that stumbled in their first actions, but others did not. The veteran outfits for their part consistently performed well even without their accustomed air and artillery support.

The army's senior commanders at the Battle of the Bulge also fought effectively. They refused to be stampeded by the surprise German attack, but instead responded with cool professionalism. If their tactics were often pedestrian, this was due in part to the geographical limitations under which they operated. At the highest level, Eisenhower and Bradley deserved credit for accurately grasping the situation and rushing help to the threatened sector. Indeed, the first reinforcements reached the Ardennes the day after the German assault began and played a major role in slowing down the German juggernaut. Eisenhower also made the politically difficult but militarily sound decision to give Montgomery control over the First and Ninth armies. As for the field army leaders, Patton's brilliant operational response was somewhat counterbalanced by the unimaginative tactics he employed in his Third Army counteroffensive. Even so, his willingness to aggressively enter the fray helped wrest the initiative away from the Germans. Hodges's performance was more problematic. He was a remote and uninspiring figure to begin with, and his inopportune sickness exacerbated these traits. Considering his illness and personality, it is remarkable that the First Army did so well.

The corps commanders were creatures of the strategies their superiors crafted, but within those limits they ably carried out their duties. Gerow and Middleton successfully delayed, stymied, and deflected the German onslaught with the limited resources at their disposal until reinforcements arrived. Middleton in particular merited praise for outlining and defining the battle by standing fast at St. Vith and Bastogne. Millikin and Eddy prosecuted their missions competently enough in the face of skilled German opposition and Patton's overbearing attitude. On the other side of the bulge, Ridgway and especially Collins brought the German advance to a standstill with their aggressive actions. Mopping up the Ardennes produced no decisive breakthroughs and trapped few Germans, but considering the handicaps under which the corps commanders labored—poor terrain, exhausted troops, and the unconducive strategy Montgomery insisted upon—they waged an efficient war of attrition.

8

Conquest of Germany

To the Rhine

Events in the winter of 1944–1945 further eroded Jake Devers's already tenuous relationship with Eisenhower. In an effort to divert American resources away from the Ardennes during the Battle of the Bulge, on 1 January 1945 the Germans launched an offensive against Patch's Seventh Army called Operation Nordwind. Allied intelligence picked up on German intentions beforehand, giving Devers plenty of time to prepare for the onslaught. Although Devers was very short of riflemen and ammunition because Eisenhower was redirecting everything he could to the Ardennes, he was still confident that he could repel the German attack. He had consulted his subordinates, carefully inspected his lines, and ordered his troops to brace themselves. Moreover, he had considerable confidence in Patch, Haislip, and Brooks, all of whom were experienced commanders who had taken the Wehrmacht's measure before and were willing to do so again. As far as Devers was concerned, his biggest problem was not the Germans but rather Eisenhower. Eisenhower had instructed the Seventh Army to take over much of Patton's line so the Third Army could fight in the Battle of the Bulge, and now he worried that Patch was too thinly spread to withstand the German assault. Nor did he trust Devers's generalship. Eisenhower believed that Patch should withdraw his army to the Vosges Mountains and make his stand there. Neither Devers nor Patch thought such drastic action was necessary. They doubted the need to give up ground for which they had battled so hard the previous autumn. Doing so would also mean abandoning Strasbourg, and there was no guarantee that the French would willingly surrender such a symbolically important city.

While the attack was expected, the ferocity of the German onslaught caught Devers and his subordinates off guard. The Germans ultimately threw seventeen divisions at the Seventh Army and at the French First Army to the south containing the Colmar Pocket. Eisenhower responded by ordering Devers to abandon Strasbourg and fall back to the Vosges as planned, but was outraged when Devers seemed to drag his feet. Fortunately, in this case French intransigence benefited the Allied cause; French leader Charles de Gaulle adamantly refused to give up Strasbourg. After a tense 3 January meeting with de Gaulle, Eisenhower relented and in effect told Devers to fight the battle as he saw fit. The Germans pushed part of Haislip's Fifteenth Corps back to the Moder River, but it rallied and with some opportune help from the French Second Armored Division managed to counterattack and restore its line. By the time Haislip and his entire headquarters came down with dysentery on 8 January, the crisis in their sector had passed. On the other hand, Brooks's Sixth Corps waged a longer and more difficult struggle along the Rhine. Although Devers had no doubts about Brooks's abilities, he questioned the aggressiveness of some of the Sixth Corps's division commanders. After the Germans mauled General Roderick Allen's new Twelfth Armored Division, Devers and Patch reluctantly directed Brooks to withdraw to the Moder to make his stand there. Brooks settled in behind the Moder on 20–21 January, and three days later the Germans came up and renewed their assault. Despite heavy fighting, the new American line held, and several days later the Germans broke off the engagement, bringing Nordwind to an end. Devers attributed the Sixth Corps's success primarily to Brooks's tenaciousness, fine judgment, and vigorous tactics. He also had nothing but praise for Patch's and Haislip's performances. Once again, this time at the cost of approximately 17,000 casualties, the Sixth Army Group and its commanders did a fine job without much support, resources, or positive attention from Eisenhower's headquarters.[1]

As far as Eisenhower was concerned, Devers's mishandling of the Colmar Pocket was the source of many of the Sixth Army Group's problems that winter. The Colmar Pocket was a 1,200-square-mile German-held protuberance on the Rhine's west bank south of Strasbourg. Eisenhower had the previous fall urged Devers to send Brooks's Sixth Corps to eliminate the pocket, but Devers successfully argued that the French First Army could take care of the problem. As things turned out, the French lacked the strength to do so, so the Germans remained ensconced behind the Seventh Army. As the weeks went on, Eisenhower developed an odd obsession with the Colmar Pocket and repeatedly overrated its significance. He fixated on it as much because it seemed like conclusive evidence of Devers's military incompetence as for any other reason. Although he told Marshall that he did not believe that the Sixth Army Group's failure to eradicate the pocket was Devers's fault, he clearly felt differently. When the Germans launched Operation Nordwind, Devers had to repel the offensive with Patch's Seventh Army only because the French were busy containing the Germans in the pocket. Had Devers squashed the Germans there in a timely manner, Eisenhower felt, Devers would have had the French First Army available to reinforce and assist the Seventh Army in coping with Nordwind. Moreover, not only had the Colmar Pocket inhibited past operations, but it also had the potential to cripple future ones as well by interfering with Allied efforts to reach the Rhine. As Eisenhower saw things, he could not undertake a broad front advance to the Rhine as long as the Germans could use the Colmar Pocket as a springboard for attacks into France. He therefore wanted the pocket destroyed as soon as possible. Devers believed that Eisenhower overestimated German strength in the pocket, but he would of course obey orders. He had already directed the French First Army to assail the pocket when he met with Eisenhower on 27 January. Eisenhower reiterated his desire to neutralize this "sore" in his lines quickly. Devers said he would do his best, but warned that it would probably take longer than Eisenhower hoped because of the poor weather. In response, Eisenhower diverted several divisions from the Twelfth Army Group to Devers's Sixth. This unsurprisingly angered and dismayed Bradley and Patton, both of whom were all too willing to condemn Devers for their inconvenience. For this reason Eisenhower explained to Marshall about Devers: "The overall results he and his organization produce are generally good, sometimes outstanding. But he has not, so far, produced among the seniors of the American organization here the feeling of trust and confidence that is so necessary to continued success."[2]

Devers assigned General Frank "Shrimp" Milburn and his new Twenty-first Corps the job of helping the French lance the Colmar Pocket boil with the American divisions Eisenhower sent to the Sixth Army Group. Born in Indiana in 1892, Milburn graduated from West Point in 1914. He spent World War One in the Canal Zone, and then had a series of mundane jobs with various infantry regiments in the interwar years. Indeed, he had few of the staff and teaching positions that marked the biographies of many World War Two corps commanders. He did well at the Command and General Staff School, ranking eighteenth of 125, but never attended the Army War College. He was assistant commander of the Sixth Division when the United States entered World War Two, and Marshall subsequently put him in charge of the Eighty-third Division in September 1942 and then the Twenty-first Corps in December 1943. Milburn had been a famous athlete at West Point and still maintained a lean and muscular look. He was also a pleasant and quiet man who was easily overlooked. Although he rarely spoke up at meetings, colleagues respected him for his energy, steadiness, and clarity. He gave his officers considerable autonomy to act as they saw fit and generally supported them in their decisions. There was nothing outstanding about Milburn, but he was still a thoroughly competent and capable officer.[3]

By the end of 1944 there were plenty of high-ranking experienced officers available to lead the Twenty-first Corps, so Eisenhower's willingness to accept Milburn, who had never heard a shot fired in anger, was surprising. Milburn had done well training the Twenty-first in the States, and in June 1944 McNair rated him as the best of the eight stateside corps commanders. Indeed, Marshall had twice offered him to Douglas MacArthur for service in the Pacific. When Marshall and Eisenhower discussed the Twenty-first Corps in July, Eisenhower noted that although most of his advisers found Milburn perfectly acceptable, he preferred to give the unit to some deserving division commander such as Manton Eddy or Clarence "Ralph" Huebner. He did not know Milburn well and was in any case reluctant to employ an untested man in such an important post. In mid-September, however, Eisenhower changed his mind for a couple of reasons. For one thing, few of his current division commanders had shown much potential for corps command, and those who had—Eddy, Huebner, Ridgway, and Brooks, most prominently— either already had been elevated or would soon be. The remainder were either too new to their responsibilities or had not demonstrated the necessary qualifications for the corps level. In addition, Eisenhower had recently received a letter from General Benjamin Lear, McNair's successor as Army Ground Forces chief, calling Eisenhower's attention to Milburn's qualities. Lear noted Milburn's exemplary record with the Twenty-first so far and added that he would make a superior combat leader. Lear's persuasiveness, as well as the apparent thinness of his European theater's divisional bench just then, convinced Eisenhower that Milburn should accompany his corps to Europe and take it into battle. After Milburn arrived in December, Eisenhower dispatched him and his headquarters to Devers's Sixth Army Group to bring the Seventh Army up to three corps. Devers liked almost everyone, so he not surprisingly warmly welcomed Milburn and expected him to fit in well with his Sixth Army Group family.[4]

Devers assigned Milburn five divisions—the Third, Twenty-eighth, Seventy-fifth, Twelfth Armored, and French Fifth Armored—and placed him in de Lattre's French First Army, making him the only corps commander to serve under French control during the conflict. De Lattre deployed Milburn on the north side of the Colmar Pocket between his two French corps and sent him into action on 28 January. The French had assailed the pocket beginning on 20 January, but had made little progress in the face of bad weather and stiff German resistance. Once the Twenty-first Corps added its weight, though, German defenses began to crumble. Colmar fell on 3 February, and the French snuffed out the final bridgehead six days later. The frustrating and perhaps unnecessary campaign cost the Allies 21,000 men, of whom 8,000 were American. German casualties were at least 22,000. As for Milburn, he turned in a solid performance that won de Lattre's praise and paved the way for more impressive successes later.[5]

Once the Battle of the Bulge was over and Devers got to work on the Colmar Pocket, Eisenhower was free to resume the Allied drive to the Rhine River. Doing so, however, resurrected his old strategic dispute with Montgomery over the best way to get there. Montgomery continued to favor a single thrust to the Rhine by his British Twenty-first Army Group that included significant American forces under his command. Eisenhower and Bradley, on the other hand, preferred a broad front advance by all the Allied armies. As usual, Eisenhower compromised to preserve Anglo-American harmony. He gave Montgomery top priority, including authority over Simpson's Ninth Army, for an advance to the Rhine, but also permitted Bradley and Devers to attack eastward to the river as well. Montgomery's offensive, codenamed "Veritable," called for the Canadian First Army and British Second Army to push toward the Rhine on 8 February, followed by Simpson's Ninth Army two days later in an operation dubbed "Grenade." Before Simpson could get under way by crossing the Roer River, the Americans had to seize the dams that controlled the river's water levels to make sure the Germans did not attempt to flood the Ninth Army at the start of its operation. This job went to Hodges's First Army—or, more specifically, to General Ralph Huebner's Fifth Corps.

Huebner took over the Fifth Corps in mid-January after Gerow moved up to the Fifteenth Army. The change had been in the works for some time, which was why Huebner was Gerow's assistant commander when the Battle of the Bulge began. Eisenhower had marked Huebner down as a potential corps chief the previous July because of Huebner's stellar performance in Normandy as head of the First Division. Huebner had been born in Kansas in 1888 and enlisted in the army in 1910. After receiving his commission, he went overseas to France in World War One. Huebner began the conflict leading a company and worked his way up to a regiment despite sustaining three wounds along the way. He graduated from the Command and General Staff School in 1925 sixth out of his 258 classmates, a ranking surpassed among future European War corps commanders only by Omar Bradley's. He subsequently met and impressed Marshall as an instructor at the Infantry School, attended the Army War College from 1928 to 1929, and returned to teach at the Command and General Staff School. He was chief of the Training Branch when the United States entered World War Two. Marshall eventually transferred him to the Mediterranean as British General Harold Alexander's deputy chief of staff. However, Alexander fired him in the summer of 1943 because he was too outspoken in defense of American interests. Fortunately for Huebner, he fell right into one of the army's most coveted posts. Patton and Bradley had recently relieved Terry Allen as head of the famous First Division after the Sicily campaign, and they appointed Huebner to take his place. They figured that Huebner could instill some discipline into that prima donna outfit. Huebner led the Big Red One in Normandy, across France, and in the fighting around Aachen before ascending to the Fifth Corps.[6]

Huebner benefited enormously in leading one of the army's most famous and proficient divisions, but there was more to his success than that. When Huebner took over the Big Red One, Patton and Bradley concluded that the outfit had become too proud and out of control, and they counted on Huebner to fix it. Fortunately, Huebner had just the personality to do so. He was a flinty and hard-boiled disciplinarian who knew how to train everything from squads to corps. He had his work cut out for him; the First Division's GIs had loved Terry Allen and deeply resented an outsider taking his place. Moreover, they were convinced that they were the best soldiers in the army with the record to prove it, and felt little need to change their behavior to suit anybody. Huebner responded by cracking down hard and deliberately making himself hated as a way to rally the men around their officers. He also gave them plenty of ammunition and set them loose on firing ranges because he believed that they would enjoy nothing more than the opportunity to shoot without much supervision. Later he claimed that he had the "shootinest" division in the army. As a result of these and other actions, Huebner gradually won the respect of the Big Red One and gave it the necessary discipline to excel in its next campaign. In France the First Division lived up to its reputation in spearheading the assault on Omaha beach and then in fighting its way to the German border. The combative Huebner bragged to Bradley that there was no no-man's-land in front of his outfit, and that his men disliked taking prisoners. By the time the First Division assailed Aachen, however, it had suffered so many casualties that it was barely battle-worthy. When one officer expressed his concerns about the unit's viability, Huebner, whose jeep had been destroyed by enemy fire a short time earlier, puffed his pipe for a long minute and replied, "If higher authority decides that this is the place and the time that the 1st Division is going to cease to exist, I guess this is where we cease to exist."[7] As things turned out, the battered Big Red One survived and took the city, but by then its skeletonized regiments were in terrible shape. The remaining cadre managed to acclimatize replacements quickly and sufficiently enough for the First to turn in a credible performance at the Battle of the Bulge, for which Huebner's training was partially responsible. Small wonder that one officer later remembered, "He was the greatest soldier there ever was, I think. He was a wonderful division commander."[8]

Whatever Huebner's undeniable qualities as the head of a division, he still had to prove himself at the corps level. Moreover, he had to demonstrate his worth to Courtney Hodges, who distrusted any corps commander whose surname was not Collins. Hodges's health may have improved since the Battle of the Bulge, but his temperament had not. Indeed, two weeks after Huebner took over the Fifth Corps Hodges complained to him about his new outfit. Hodges focused his attention on the poor performance he detected in Walter Robertson's Second Division, with which he had a long-standing grudge dating back to Normandy. Despite these disheartening harbingers, Hodges gave Huebner the important task of seizing the Roer River dams so Simpson could undertake his part of Montgomery's offensive to the Rhine. Huebner in turn assigned the job to General Arthur Parker's new

Seventy-eighth Division. Delegating the mission to the green Seventy-eighth was only one part of Huebner's plan that Hodges disliked. The Seventy-eighth initially made good progress after its 5 February assault, but inexperience, washed-out roads, heavy rains, and the detritus of previous battles soon bogged it down. Conscious that he had to have the dams in hand by 10 February so Simpson's operation could begin on schedule, Hodges exerted increasing pressure on Huebner and Parker that included the usual threats of dismissal if better results were not forthcoming. Hodges also reinforced Huebner with Louis Craig's Ninth Division to jump-start the attack. With Craig's help, the Fifth Corps seized the last of the dams on 9 February. Unfortunately, the Germans destroyed the dams' machinery, so the Americans could not shut off the flow of water, which soon inundated the Roer River valley and forced Simpson to delay his drive to the Rhine. For Huebner, it was an uncomfortable introduction to Hodges's leadership methods, but he did not let Hodges's badgering dampen his combativeness and enthusiasm.[9]

It took two weeks for the Roer River waters to sufficiently stabilize so that the Ninth Army could risk a crossing. During the delay a frustrated and anxious Simpson frequently toured the front and consulted his corps and division commanders while his chief of staff, Jim Moore, put the final touches on Operation Grenade. The long wait gave the Ninth Army plenty of time to accumulate an enormous stockpile of supplies and ammunition for the big assault. Bradley was greatly impressed with the energy, competence, and enthusiasm he discovered during a visit to Ninth Army headquarters. Indeed, he believed that the Ninth Army was much easier to work with than Hodges's fractious First Army and Patton's boisterous Third Army. Simpson even got along well with and won the respect of Montgomery. As a result, there was plenty of optimism in the Ninth Army about the upcoming offensive. One of Ray McLain's staffers opined, "Wherever the Nineteenth Corps attacks, it will go through the Boche like shit through a tin horn."[10] On the morning of 23 February, Gillem's Thirteenth Corps and McLain's Nineteenth Corps, supported upstream to the south by Collins's Seventh Corps, charged across the Roer. Gillem and McLain succeeded in reaching the other side against moderate opposition, but Collins did not get a firm foothold until the next day. Once across, Simpson committed his armor to the battle and ordered Gillem and McLain to drive for the Rhine. Collins made a similar decision even sooner. The Ninth Army reached the Rhine on 1 March, but by then Simpson had raised his expectations by setting his sights on grabbing a bridge over the big river. Although McLain almost got the span at Krefeld, the Germans blew it up in the face of the attacking GIs. Undaunted, Simpson believed he could still cross the Rhine without a bridge because the Germans on the other side seemed so disorganized. McLain felt the same way and assured Simpson that his men could quickly get over to the east bank. Unfortunately, Montgomery refused. He was focused on implementing a massive and methodical set-piece crossing by the British Second Army and did not want to risk a fly-by-night ad hoc effort that might encounter unforeseen difficulties. This put a somewhat downbeat coda on what was otherwise a very successful operation. Simpson and Collins had captured 30,000 Germans, killed another 6,000, and reached the Rhine River with only 7,300 casualties. Simpson and the Ninth Army had once again demonstrated an unruffled efficiency without the interpersonal drama that often characterized Patton's and especially Hodges's armies. Bradley for one later called the operation "one of the most perfectly executed of the war."[11]

Simpson ordered the new Sixteenth Corps to clean up the remaining pockets of German resistance in his sector west of the Rhine. Led by General John B. "Andy" Anderson—not to be confused with General John W. Anderson, a stateside corps commander and former head of the Third Division during Operation Torch—the Sixteenth was the last corps committed to the European theater that saw significant action during the war. There was nothing unusual about Anderson's career trajectory. Born in Iowa in 1891, he graduated from West Point in 1914 and served in France in World War One. After the conflict he attended the Command and General Staff School from 1924 to 1925 and the Army War College three years later. He subsequently worked for the General Staff from 1928 to 1932, and then for the chief of artillery. After the United States entered World War Two, Marshall put him in charge of the 102nd Division, from which he ascended to the Sixteenth Corps in December 1943. Anderson owed his presence in Europe primarily to Simpson. Simpson had asked for him as one of his three Ninth Army corps commanders in his first meeting with Eisenhower the previous May. Although McNair rated Anderson as second only to Milburn among the remaining eight stateside corps commanders, Eisenhower did not seem to have a strong opinion of him. By the time Simpson and Eisenhower discussed the issue, however, there were not many unallotted stateside corps commanders left whom Eisenhower really liked except for Gillem. Moreover, none of Eisenhower's division chiefs had yet had the opportunity to prove themselves worthy of promotion to the corps level. The Battle of the Bulge delayed the Sixteenth Corps's activation, and Anderson spent the engagement serving as Ridgway's deputy in the Eighteenth Airborne Corps. Whatever Eisenhower's reservations, Simpson was happy with Anderson from the start. He easily grafted Anderson and his headquarters into the Ninth Army's happy military family, and the two men worked well together for the remainder of the conflict. Indeed, after the war Anderson called his time with Simpson and the Ninth Army "the most pleasant service of my career."[12] Eisenhower and Bradley both eventually approved of him, though they were more inclined to attribute his success to Simpson's tutelage. Anderson was a pleasant, dedicated, and self-effacing man with no hobbies or interests outside of the army. Like Gillem and Milburn, he performed well from the get-go and carried out his first assignment thoroughly and competently.[13]

Bradley was eager to begin his own offensive toward the Rhine with his two field armies lest Montgomery marginalize him right out of the war. Some important personnel changes occurred before he did so. As the Battle of the Bulge was winding down, Eisenhower appointed Ernie Harmon to lead the new Twenty-second Corps, whose headquarters had arrived in Europe the previous November. Harmon had on several occasions been in line for a corps of his own, and had in fact taken over one in the States earlier in the year until Eisenhower asked him to return to Europe to run the Second Armored Division. Now, with another corps in the offering, Harmon had second thoughts. He loved the Second Armored and had no desire to leave it, and he doubted that the Twenty-second would see much action because the war would soon end. When he expressed his reservations to Bradley, Bradley told him that he had earned the promotion and should accept it. Besides, Bradley continued, the Twenty-second Corps might go to the Pacific to fight the Japanese after Germany succumbed. Harmon took Bradley's advice and assumed command of the corps. He was disappointed with the inexperienced and overage officers he found at corps headquarters, whom he had to weed out, and as he expected the Twenty-second saw almost no action. On 30 March Maurice Rose, head of the Third Armored Division, was killed in action. Hodges with Bradley's approval sent Harmon to replace him. Collins, in whose corps the Third Armored belonged, believed that assistant commander General Doyle Hickey was perfectly capable of running the outfit. Harmon felt the same way after looking things over and with Bradley's permission returned to the Twenty-second Corps for the remainder of the war.[14]

Once the Battle of the Bulge ended, Eisenhower decided to withdraw Ridgway's Eighteenth Airborne Corps headquarters and refit its airborne divisions. This left Hodges's First Army with only two corps with which to conduct the extensive operations Bradley planned for it. Bradley believed that the common-sense solution was to return Troy Middleton's Eighth Corps from Patton's Third Army to the First Army, which would give Hodges and Patton three corps apiece. Patton, however, protested the order. He did not mind surrendering a corps headquarters because he preferred three big corps to four smaller ones, but he did not want to give up Middleton. Although Patton occasionally groused about Middleton's dispassion, he highly respected his generalship and did not want to lose his services. Middleton for his part told Patton he wanted to stay in the Third Army. He added, probably disingenuously, that he had no strong feelings about Hodges one way or another. Instead, Patton offered to yield Millikin's Third Corps. Patton believed that Millikin had done a good job relieving Bastogne during the Battle of the Bulge, but since then had found his tactics amateurish. Moreover, Patton did not much like Millikin personally. Bradley agreed to Patton's request. After listening to this discussion during a meeting at Bastogne, Eisenhower added that a general ought to keep an officer he trusted, and snidely referenced Devers as the unhappy result of departing from this principle.[15]

During a mid-February visit to First Army headquarters, one of Bradley's aides remarked on the unhappy changes that had occurred there since Hodges assumed command: "First Army has lost some of the cohesive quality General Bradley managed to give it as commander. Hodges has found it difficult to do this, lacking the warmth and personality of General Bradley. Hodges is essentially a brittle impersonal general to the bulk of his staff. Even though appearing as a temperate quiet minded leader similar to Bradley, subordinates suggest that his grasp is not as great as that of Bradley."[16] Additionally, by then the First Army staffers had a well-deserved reputation as a surly and independent-minded group that condescended to other organizations and monopolized resources. Despite such characterizations, Eisenhower and Bradley still had great confidence in Hodges and looked upon the First Army as the best field army, man for man and unit for unit, on the Western Front. The First Army certainly had the track record to back up Eisenhower's and Bradley's confidence, having borne the brunt of the war effort from Normandy on. Much of its success was due in no small part to Joe Collins. Collins's performance with his Seventh Corps, while by no means flawless, had been outstanding. In late January Collins returned from a short vacation at Cannes more energetic than usual and ready to play his assigned role in Operation Grenade. After he finished supporting the Ninth Army's drive over the Roer, he immediately spearheaded the First Army's attack to the Rhine. Pivoting to the southeast, Collins pushed rapidly toward Cologne, whose 800,000 inhabitants made it one of Germany's largest cities. As Collins's divisions left the Roer, Hodges had his other corps cross the river and join the offensive, codenamed "Lumberjack." Millikin's Third Corps went over on 25 February, and Huebner's Fifth Corps followed on 2 March. Cologne fell to Collins's men three days later, and soon afterward the other corps reached the Rhine. Collins could take pride not only in another fine display of generalship, but also in some encouraging words from Eisenhower. Eisenhower visited Collins during his march to Cologne to personally explain his rationale for promoting Gerow instead of him to take over the Fifteenth Army. He owed Collins as much, said Eisenhower, because he had been the star corps commander since D-Day. As it was, Collins was more interested in leading the Seventh Corps into Germany than in running an administrative army, so he was not terribly disappointed at being passed over. Although he succumbed to a bad cold as soon as Cologne fell, he was still ready and willing to jump across the Rhine whenever Hodges gave him the go-ahead.[17]

Patton had further to go to get to the Rhine than Eisenhower's other field army commanders, but this was due far more to geography than to any lack of drive on his part. As usual, he was eager to assume the offensive and chafed at Eisenhower's decision to give Montgomery's efforts priority. Although Eisenhower's orders limited him to an aggressive defense, Patton with Eisenhower's and Bradley's tacit approval used this ambiguity to assail the West Wall. Bradley's willingness to let Patton employ William Morris's Tenth Armored Division longer than Eisenhower wanted did not prevent Patton's continued criticisms of Bradley's timidity in his diary. Whatever Patton's problems with his superiors, he displayed considerable skill in his dealings with his corps commanders. Eddy wanted to begin his attack on 6 February, but Patton insisted that he start two days earlier. When Eddy complained bitterly to Patton that he did not understand the need for proper preparation, Patton responded that they would still be on the Seine River if he had taken such things into account. As it was, Eddy became increasingly optimistic as his forces crossed the Sauer River and pushed southeastward. Indeed, he even declined Patton's offer to let him temporarily suspend his operations due to poor weather. Nor did Patton have much trouble with Middleton, whose success in driving toward the Moselle River and supplying his comparatively isolated divisions over poor roads won Patton's admiration. Oddly enough, Patton was initially most disappointed with the usually aggressive Walker. Walker and Morris fumbled an initial effort to cross the Saar River because Morris lost track of his bridge train. Fortunately, Walker got matters straightened out and seized Trier on 1 March. Six days later, elements of the Fourth Armored Division reached the Rhine near Coblenz. Patton could take pride both in his tactics and in the manner with which he handled his subordinates. Unlike his heavy-handed and counterproductive interpersonal methods in North Africa, he showed the right amount of encouragement, forgiveness, and prodding. As he noted in his diary, "Walker . . . told me that . . . the corps of the Third Army did better than in other Armies because the corps commanders have had the confidence that if they made a mistake, they would still be backed up."[18]

At the southern end of the Allied line in the Saar region, Devers came up with an uninspired plan, codenamed Undertone, for the Sixth Army Group to breach the West Wall and drive to the Rhine. Simply put, Undertone called for Patch's Seventh Army to push straight through the German defenses. Patton's successes to the northwest, though, opened up more sophisticated possibilities. Patton proposed to slice behind the Germans confronting Patch along the West Wall in an effort to cut them off from the Rhine. Neither Bradley nor Patton was very enthusiastic about working with Devers, whose military abilities they questioned because of the Sixth Army Group's difficulties in solving the Colmar Pocket puzzle. Still, the advantages of coordination were so obvious that everyone from Eisenhower down recognized them. As things turned out, Devers and especially Patch proved so cooperative as to remove many of Patton's doubts. Despite very different personalities—Patch was as self-effacing and diffident as Patton was flamboyant and boastful—Patton and Patch were old friends who understood one another. When they met to discuss the operation, Patch teased Patton by saying, "George, I forgot to congratulate you for being the last man to reach the Rhine." Patton, remembering Patch's retreat during Nordwind, responded puckishly, "Let me congratulate you on being the first man to leave it."[19] Getting down to business, the two men agreed to let their corps commanders communicate with each other over boundaries without reference to army headquarters. Later on Patch permitted Patton to intrude on his sector for the simple reason that he believed it was the logical thing to do. On 15 March, Patch's three corps—from west to east, Milburn's Twenty-first, Haislip's Fifteenth, and Brooks's Sixth—jumped off against the West Wall. Whatever difficulties Patch may have faced the previous winter, he was in fine spirits and health now. Although the Germans resisted stoutly, on 19 March one of Milburn's divisions broke through, followed by one of Haislip's the next day. Patton's approaching troops accelerated the German withdrawal. Patton had opened up his offensive the day before Patch's with Eddy's and Walker's corps. While Eddy and Walker pushed eastward, Middleton seized Coblenz on 19 March in another display of generalship that impressed Patton. Impatient as ever, Patton told Walker that he was doing well, but not well enough. Soon, however, Patton's and Patch's armor were racing each other for the Rhine. Patch's men got there first, on 24 March, the same day they linked up with the Third Army. A good many Germans escaped the American net and retreated across the Rhine, but the Third Army and Seventh Army still captured 90,000 prisoners between them. By way of casualties, the Third Army suffered 5,200 and the Seventh Army another 12,000. With that, organized German opposition along the Rhine's west bank came to an end.[20]

Into Germany

By the time Eisenhower's forces closed in on the Rhine, Nazi Germany's days were clearly numbered. On the Eastern Front, the Soviets had overrun most of East Prussia and were approaching Berlin. The Nazi empire, which had once stretched from France to the outskirts of Moscow, was now limited to northern Italy, parts of the Balkans, chunks of Austria and Czechoslovakia, northern Holland, Denmark and Norway, and of course the German heartland. Germany's economy, once the most powerful in Europe, was wrecked. The Soviet capture of the Romanian oilfields and the Anglo-American strategic bombing campaign had contributed to a logistical paralysis in which it was extremely difficult to find the fuel to operate the planes, tanks, and other vehicles upon which the Wehrmacht relied. German losses after more than five years of war were astronomical. Approximately 3.5 million German soldiers had died in the conflict so far, in addition to another 1.5 million civilians. Nor could Germany rely on its allies for salvation or even assistance. Its European friends—Italy, Bulgaria, Hungary, Finland, and Romania—had surrendered or been conquered. American bombers and submarines had isolated and were systematically burning up the Japanese Home Islands, and it was increasingly clear that an American invasion was in the offing. Finally, the Allied coalition continued to hold despite strains over Poland and eastern Europe. By any objective and reasonable assessment, Hitler's Germany was coming to an end.

The Rhine served as a giant moat protecting the German heartland from the full fury of the Allied onslaught. To the north, Montgomery was preparing for a massive crossing of the big river, codenamed Operation Plunder, that was in many respects a miniature version of Overlord. Since Montgomery had priority, the Twelfth Army Group was more or less left to its own devices to find its way across the river with whatever equipment it had on hand. Seizing an intact bridge over the Rhine before the Germans destroyed it was another option, but Simpson had discovered the difficulties in doing so during Grenade. Nevertheless, American commanders kept their eyes and ears open in case an opportunity presented itself. On the morning of 7 March, elements of John Leonard's Ninth Armored Division, tough veterans of some of the worst fighting in the Ardennes, approached the German town of Remagen on the Rhine's west bank. Just before 1 P.M., the lead platoon emerged from some woods onto a cliff overlooking Remagen and discovered that the Ludendorff Bridge was still intact. After fighting their way through the town, the Americans began crossing the bridge just as the Germans detonated the explosives on it. Unfortunately for the Germans, the full charge did not ignite, leaving the bridge damaged but usable. The Americans swarmed to the other side and secured the bridge. Through this combination of luck and initiative, the First Army had breached the Rhine.

Hodges had just returned to his headquarters from visiting Collins's command post in Cologne when he got word of Leonard's coup. He phoned Bradley and said matter-of-factly, "Brad, we've gotten a bridge." Bradley immediately grasped the opportunities presented and replied enthusiastically, "Hot dog, Courtney. This will bust him wide open." When Bradley called Eisenhower's headquarters to tell them of the good news, however, he met a surprisingly chilly reception from Eisenhower's operations officer, Pinky Bull, who did not believe it would be easy to exploit a crossing in such a remote area. After several attempts to explain the potentialities before them, a frustrated Bradley finally exclaimed, "What in hell do you want us to do, pull back and blow it up?" Fortunately, Eisenhower was more excited than Bull and directed Bradley to secure the bridgehead.[21]

Remagen was in John Millikin's sector, so his Third Corps got the responsibility for protecting and expanding the bridgehead Leonard had gained. There was nothing easy about it. For one thing, the Germans made persistent but ultimately unsuccessful efforts with air power, artillery, and even sabotaging frogmen to destroy the Ludendorff Bridge and prevent engineers from building accompanying spans. In addition, considerable congestion developed on the west side of the bridge as various units jockeyed for their turn to cross the Rhine. Hodges visited the bridgehead on 8 March and barely escaped injury or death when the Germans shelled a divisional command post right after he entered it. Although he later joked with Patton that his front lines resembled an intestinal tract, he was actually highly displeased with Millikin's apparent lack of control over the situation. Indeed, Hodges had been singularly unimpressed with Millikin ever since he joined the First Army. During the drive to the Rhine, Hodges condemned Millikin for resting the Seventy-eighth Division instead of committing it to action, for sending the Ninth Division to storm Bonn instead of bypassing the city, and for not providing sufficient infantry to the Ninth Armored Division. There was in fact some truth to Hodges's criticisms; Millikin lacked the force of personality to really assume responsibility for the situation at Remagen and straighten out the disorder. Many at First Army headquarters openly lamented that Collins was not in charge there. Collins, brash as ever, even told Hodges that he could get better results. On 15 March Bradley called on First Army headquarters and talked with Hodges for an hour and a half about exploiting their good fortune across the Rhine. By the end of the conversation they agreed that whatever his attributes, Millikin simply was not the right man for the job of leading the Third Corps. Hodges explained, "Mind you, I have only the greatest admiration and respect for the GIs doing the fighting out there, but I think they have had bad leadership in this bridgehead battle."[22]

Hodges asked for Ernie Harmon as Millikin's replacement, but Bradley doubted that he could be spared from the Twenty-second Corps right then. Instead, Bradley suggested General James Van Fleet, the former chief of the Ninetieth Division, who had recently assumed command of the new Twenty-third Corps headquarters in England. Hodges readily agreed, and Bradley sent for him immediately after clearing it with Eisenhower. Van Fleet was not terribly surprised to learn that Millikin was in trouble. He recalled Patton criticizing him for a lack of aggressiveness during the Battle of the Bulge, and rumor had it that Hodges was not happy with him either. Van Fleet flew to the continent and drove to Hodges's headquarters. After Hodges officially informed him that he would take over the Third Corps, Van Fleet asked if Millikin knew yet of the impending change. Hodges said, "No, you tell him; tell him to report back to Army headquarters." This disturbed Van Fleet not only because it placed him in an uncomfortable and embarrassing position, but also because it violated army protocol. Van Fleet found the situation distasteful, improper, and not necessarily justified. Orders were orders though, so Van Fleet traveled to Millikin's command post and broke the bad news to him. Millikin was so shocked that he did not know what to say. When he regained his composure, he asked Van Fleet for the reason for his relief, and Van Fleet responded that he did not know. Millikin then phoned Hodges for verification and upon receiving it said, "Well, I have bad news for you too, sir. The railroad bridge at Remagen has collapsed." This was true enough, but by then engineers had constructed three other spans as well as a ferry service. Millikin did not return to the States like Corlett before him, but instead ended up leading the Thirteenth Armored Division in the last weeks of the war after its commander had been wounded. Although his demotion was no doubt painful, Patton for one remarked on Millikin's excellent attitude in awkward circumstances.[23]

After a slow start, Van Fleet's rise through the ranks during the war was remarkable. Born in New Jersey in 1892, Van Fleet graduated from West Point in 1915 in the same class as Eisenhower and Bradley. Unlike them, though, Van Fleet went overseas to France in World War One and was wounded at the head of a machine-gun battalion in the Argonne. After occupation duty he worked as a Reserve Officer Training Corps instructor and football coach at several universities for six years and then as a battalion commander in Panama from 1925 to 1927. Van Fleet subsequently served as both a student and teacher at the Infantry School before returning to the University of Florida from 1929 to 1933. Unlike every other overseas World War Two corps commander, Van Fleet attended neither the Command and General Staff School nor the Army War College. Instead, he spent the remainder of the decade with the troops and training reservists, and was leading a regiment in the Fourth Division when the United States entered World War Two. While most of his colleagues were rapidly promoted to increasingly responsible posts, Van Fleet remained with his regiment. Many noticed and commented upon this anomalous career stagnation, but Van Fleet tried to be philosophical about it and focus on the job at hand. According to Bradley and Collins, Marshall refused to elevate Van Fleet because he confused him with an alcoholic officer with a similar name. Van Fleet himself later doubted this story because Marshall knew that Van Fleet was a teetotaler from their time together at Fort Benning, but Van Fleet may not have been aware of Marshall's tendency to forget and confuse names.

Whatever the truth, Van Fleet began to attract attention after his regiment shipped to England. Collins noticed Van Fleet's qualities even before D-Day and with Bradley's encouragement made a mental note to keep an eye on him. Van Fleet fought so well in Normandy that Collins recommended his promotion to brigadier general, and Bradley later compared him to Ridgway and noted that he earned about three medals a day. At one point Van Fleet was wounded in the stomach, but after getting bandaged up at a field hospital he opted to return to the front. Bradley found him there and said, "I came here to decorate you, but I ought to court martial you. You are AWOL; you left that hospital without being discharged."[24] Considering his record and his new patrons, it was hardly surprising that Eisenhower and Bradley elevated Van Fleet first to assistant commander of the Second Division, and then to lead the Ninetieth Division after McLain left to take over the Nineteenth Corps. Van Fleet's performance with the unit in Lorraine and the Ardennes won Patton's admiration. Patton, however, also concluded that Van Fleet was tired, so he sent him to England to run the Twenty-third Corps, but he promised to bring him back as soon as possible. Unfortunately for Patton, Bradley and Hodges secured his services first for the Third Corps. Van Fleet was a straight-up fighter who led from the front. While not much of an intellectual, he was a superb trainer who inspired confidence. Reticent and something of a loner, he was also brusque and frank. He established order at the Remagen bridgehead, but in the ensuing weeks he angered Hodges on more than one occasion by losing touch with First Army headquarters.[25]

Remagen was the first and the most difficult Allied crossing of the Rhine that month. On 23 March, after much preparation and with considerable hoopla, Montgomery's Twenty-first Army Group stormed over the big river at Wesel in Operation Plunder. The attack included a massive 21,000-man airdrop by the British Sixth Airborne and American Seventeenth Airborne divisions coordinated, as in Market-Garden, by the British First Airborne Corps. This time the airborne assault went much more smoothly, though it probably was not necessary for Plunder's success. Simpson's Ninth Army also participated in the big push. Anderson's Sixteenth Corps crossed the Rhine upstream from Wesel near Rheinberg at the same time as the British Second Army. Simpson had been prepared to cross the Rhine for a month, and had chafed under what he believed to be needless delays. Despite his frustrations, he still managed to maintain a good working relationship with Montgomery. The day before Plunder, Eisenhower showed up unannounced at Simpson's headquarters. Eisenhower discovered that the Ninth Army staffers had plenty of time on their hands because they had completed their preparations long ago, so he chatted with an old friend while he waited for Simpson to return from the front. Simpson gave Anderson the responsibility for spearheading the charge over the Rhine because he wanted to save his more experienced corps commanders, Gillem and McLain, for the breakout he envisioned. Anderson got Leland Hobbs's Thirtieth and Ira Wyche's Seventy-ninth divisions over without too much trouble, but he had to wait on the British to get access to good highways inland. When he got permission from the British on 26 March, Anderson committed the Eighth Armored Division too soon, resulting in considerable congestion in the narrow bridgehead and preventing the Sixteenth Corps from exploiting its success. It also provoked Simpson's one postwar criticism of Anderson's generalship. This setback, however, did not stop both Eisenhower and Bradley from praising Simpson for another well-planned and well-conducted operation.[26]

With both Hodges and Simpson across the Rhine, Bradley took aim at the Ruhr, the German industrial heartland. Rather than directly assail the rubble-strewn and densely populated region, Bradley opted to use the First Army and Ninth Army to encircle it in an operation that began on 25 March. Collins's Seventh Corps of course spearheaded the First Army's drive from the south, while McLain's Nineteenth Corps rounded the Ruhr's northern boundaries. The two armies linked on 1 April, trapping in the resulting pocket more than 300,000 German soldiers, who did not give up until 18 April. Three days later, Bradley officially regained complete control over the Ninth Army, placing at his disposal four field armies containing forty-six divisions for his final offensive. Bradley left Van Fleet's Third Corps, Middleton's Eighth Corps, Anderson's Sixteenth Corps, and Ridgway's Eighteenth Airborne Corps to contain and reduce the Ruhr Pocket while his remaining units plunged into central Germany. Simpson, delighted to be back in the Twelfth Army Group, directed Gillem and McLain to push toward the Elbe River, which they reached against scattered opposition on 11 April. Simpson believed he could easily get to Berlin in a couple of days, so he was deeply disappointed when Eisenhower decided to let the Soviets have the honor—and casualties—of storming the German capital. As a result, Simpson spent the remaining four weeks of the war marking time along the Elbe.

To the south, the substantial progress Hodges made toward Leipzig and Dresden did not sweeten his typically ill-tempered mood. He criticized Van Fleet's slowness in eliminating the Ruhr Pocket and even snapped at Collins for advancing too cautiously. Collins, however, ignored Hodges's petulant messages. He figured that the war was almost over, so there was no need for him to take unnecessary risks that might needlessly jeopardize the lives of his GIs. Like the Ninth Army, the First Army ended the conflict along the Elbe. On 27 April, about seventy miles southwest of Berlin, its troops were the first to encounter the Red Army.[27]

Instead of seizing Berlin, Eisenhower chose to focus on southern Germany. Rumors—mostly false, as things turned out—had it that the Germans planned to make their final stand there in the so-called National Redoubt, and Eisenhower wanted to preclude any last-ditch German effort in the region that might prolong the war. He had plenty of resources available for the job now that he had surrendered Berlin to the Soviets. Patton slipped across the Rhine on 22 March with General Leroy "Red" Irwin's Fifth Division from Eddy's corps. Patton took even more pleasure in beating Montgomery over the river than he did in drawing historical parallels between this accomplishment and those of previous conquerors. Haislip's corps from Patch's Seventh Army crossed over at Worms on 26 March, followed by the French First Army at Speyer five days later. Haislip later noted proudly that within sixty-eight hours after the first boat left the Rhine's west bank for the far shore, the Fifteenth Corps sent 120,000 troops and 30,000 vehicles over the big river. From there the three field armies plunged southward and southeastward toward the National Redoubt. Whatever chagrin Devers felt toward Patton for beating his Sixth Army Group across the Rhine paled in comparison to his subsequent difficulties with the always troublesome French. As part of their campaign to reclaim their national glory, de Lattre's French First Army sought to seize as much German territory as possible. Unhappily, the French often disregarded the field army boundaries that Devers drew and clogged roads allotted to Brooks's Sixth Corps. Devers's attempts to keep the French in line were only partially successful. As for Patch, he left the problems with the French to Devers and focused on his mission. He continued to cooperate wholeheartedly with the Third Army, but did not relish the idea of sharing the laurels of securing the Danube with the attention-seeking Patton. He could, however, take pride in his three corps commanders—Brooks, Haislip, and Milburn—who fought skillfully in difficult terrain against German opposition ranging from nonexistent to fierce as they rolled southward. Haislip's Fifteenth Corps occupied Nuremburg on 21 April and Munich fourteen days later. Milburn's Twenty-first Corps reached the Danube before Patton on 22 April, and Brooks's Sixth Corps established contact with the Fifth Army in Italy at the Brenner Pass on 4 May. Considering the anonymity with which the Seventh Army had waged war, it made perfect sense for it to end the conflict in one of the more remote parts of Germany.[28]

Patton's Third Army advanced to the east of Patch's. Although Patton as usual grumbled in his diary about Bradley's supposed timidity, he continued to get along with Patch and had no problems cooperating with the Seventh Army as his GIs pushed toward the Czechoslovak border. Unlike the Seventh Army, the Third Army underwent two major organizational changes in the last month of the conflict. Bradley transferred the Eighth Corps to the First Army to help Hodges contain the Ruhr Pocket in order to spare Middleton unnecessary pain in his arthritic knee from driving around too much by jeep. To take its place, Bradley sent Patton Van Fleet's Third Corps. Unlike Middleton, who had indicated that he wanted to return to Louisiana State after the conflict ended, Van Fleet had a promising postwar career to look forward to, and Bradley wanted to give him as much high-level combat experience as possible before the Germans surrendered. Patton regretted parting with Middleton, but he was pleased that Van Fleet proved as hard-driving at the corps level as when he was leading the Ninetieth Division.

Patton also lost Manton Eddy's services. On 17 April Patton lunched with Eddy and found him noticeably apathetic, tired, and nervous. Two days later Eddy's chief of staff phoned Patton to tell him that Eddy was so sick that he had to surrender his post. Eddy had kept his high blood pressure secret for years, but now his affliction caught up with him and rendered him unfit for duty. While Eddy's worrisome nature often tried his patience, Patton had come to respect and appreciate his abilities and was sorry to give him up. When Patton flew with Eddy to Paris to see him off to the States, he found Eddy surprisingly placid about his condition. To replace him as chief of the Twelfth Corps, Patton recommended Ernie Harmon, Hugh Gaffey, or Red Irwin to Eisenhower and Bradley. Eisenhower and Bradley did not want to take Harmon and Gaffey away from their current jobs with, respectively, the Twenty-second Corps and the Fourth Armored Division. Instead of settling on Irwin, though, Eisenhower suggested Ira Wyche, commander of the Seventy-ninth Division. Patton speculated that Eisenhower threw Wyche's name into the mix because he did not want to look prejudiced in favor of an old West Point classmate like Irwin. Patton, however, successfully argued that Irwin deserved the position because he had more combat experience than Wyche. The war was all but over by the time Irwin took over the Twelfth Corps, so he had no opportunity to make much of a mark at the head of his new outfit.[29]

Conclusions

Stability and continuity characterized the last months of the war for the American Army's high command in northwest Europe. Eisenhower added only three officers—Anderson, Milburn, and Van Fleet—to his stable of active corps commanders. Another one—Millikin—was relieved from his post. Moreover, the performances of the field army and corps commanders were superior to those from the previous year. The drive to the Rhine and the conquest of Germany were marked by considerable deftness, skill, and self-confidence. The decline in the Wehrmacht's fighting power certainly enabled the army to do things it had not been able to before the Battle of the Bulge, but there was more to it than that. After more than ten months of war in northwest Europe, the army now contained a large number of experienced divisions led by battle-hardened commanders. Field army and corps commanders used this expertise to undertake the kind of sophisticated operations that contributed to Germany's defeat.

9
Closing In on Japan

Okinawa Bloodletting

While MacArthur and SWPA were busy liberating the Philippines, Nimitz and the POA had not been idle. In late September 1944, Nimitz journeyed to San Francisco to persuade Ernest King to forgo an assault on Formosa and instead seize the islands of Iwo Jima and Okinawa. Nimitz explained that assailing Formosa would be too costly in time and blood, but that the POA had the resources to attack Iwo Jima and Okinawa. King agreed and got the Joint Chiefs of Staff to go along with the idea. Nimitz wanted Iwo Jima, part of the Bonin Islands chain, to provide protection and refuge for the big B-29 bombers that had already begun raiding Japanese cities from the Marianas. Three marine divisions stormed the island in mid-February and took it after six weeks of brutal combat that killed or wounded nearly 27,000 marines and practically wiped out the entire 21,000-man Japanese garrison. Nimitz sought Okinawa, located in the Ryukyu Islands only 350 miles south of Kyushu, as a staging and jumping-off point for the final invasion of Japan itself. Because of its obvious strategic importance, the Japanese placed 100,000 troops there, and planned to support them with thousands of kamikazes flying from Japan and Formosa against the American vessels transporting and supporting the operation. The ensuing Okinawa campaign would be the bloodiest and fiercest of the Pacific War and would stretch POA resources to its limits.

By the spring of 1945, massive American amphibious assaults were hardly unusual, but the enormous fleet that arrived off of Okinawa's western shore in late March was still impressive for all sorts of reasons. It contained 1,200 vessels of all sizes and shapes, including 433 transport ships holding 183,000 soldiers and marines, which staged from embarkation points as far away as Seattle, Hawaii, Guadalcanal, Leyte, the Marianas, and Espiritu Santo in the New Hebrides Islands. Organizing, coordinating, supplying, and shepherding this huge armada was, despite the usual snafus and delays, a testament to the logistical expertise of POA planners, most of whom were by now well-practiced at this sort of thing. Indeed, experience was, with one big exception, a prominent characteristic of the personnel involved. The invading Tenth Army consisted of two corps, John Hodge's Twenty-fourth and marine General Roy Geiger's Third Amphibious. Hodge's three divisions—the Seventh, Seventy-seventh, and Ninety-sixth—were all battle-hardened units, as were Geiger's marine outfits. Hodge had seen as much combat as any general in the Pacific War, having fought on Guadalcanal, New Georgia, Bougainville, and Leyte. Most of his division and regimental commanders were also familiar with the challenges and obstacles that lay ahead.

Considering the plethora of combat-experienced leaders available in the Pacific, it was odd and ironic that the Tenth Army's commander, General Simon Bolivar "Buck" Buckner, had never heard a shot fired in anger. Other than this, there was nothing unusual about Buckner's career trajectory. Born in Kentucky in 1886, the son of the Confederate general who surrendered Fort Donelson to Ulysses Grant during the Civil War, Buckner went to the Virginia Military Institute for two years before transferring to West Point, from which he graduated in 1906. He tried to get into World War One as a pilot, but a medical board turned him down because of a minor eye defect, so he remained stateside during the conflict, training troops. He spent most of the interwar years as a student, teacher, and administrator. He attended the Infantry School in 1924, the Command and General Staff School from 1924 to 1925, and the Army War College from 1928 to 1929. He also taught at West Point and the Command and General Staff School, and served as executive officer at the Army War College. In 1932 he returned to West Point first as assistant commandant of cadets and then as the commandant. At the end of the decade he took over a regiment before becoming chief of staff for the Sixth Division. In July 1940, Marshall put him in charge of the Alaska Defense Force, a remote but important post, especially after the Japanese seized two islands in the Aleutians chain. He did a good job, but in 1942 he got into trouble by quarreling with the navy's commander in Alaskan waters, Admiral Robert Theobald. During a staff meeting with Theobald, Buckner read aloud a derogatory poem circulating among army officers that poked fun at Theobald's supposed timidity. Theobald was predictably outraged, and for awhile Marshall seriously considered removing Buckner from his post because he so damaged interservice relations, but he ultimately decided against it. Fortunately, Buckner got along well and formed a strong working relationship with Theobald's successor, Admiral Thomas Kinkaid. Kinkaid, though, often jokingly observed to Buckner that he was in no position, career-wise, to bicker with him.[1]

Although he was one of the army's most educated officers, Buckner cultivated an image of action and bravado, and seemed devoid of nuance and subtlety. One journalist who met him in Alaska described him as "a big bear of a man, ruddy-faced, with a hunter's sharp eyes, a roaring voice and a thatch of snowy hair, he is like that rugged land: huge, uninhabited, hard."[2] Indeed, Buckner was a strict disciplinarian who drove his men relentlessly to get things done. Alaska suited him and his penchant for physical fitness so well that he planned on moving there after the war. Every morning he walked his dog over the muskeg and bogs to keep in shape. Later, while in Hawaii, he exercised by spear fishing. With his fellow officers he was witty and entertaining, even flippant. Ever the optimist, Buckner preferred to look on the bright side and downplayed or ignored obstacles. Despite his dispute with Theobald, he generally got along well with people, even those in the navy. His difficulties with Theobald were no doubt traceable to his fierce commitment to taking the war to the enemy and never flinching in the face of adversity. He always remembered and tried to live by a piece of Victorian-era advice his father gave him: "Do your duty in whatever field it may lie and never forget that you are a gentleman."[3]

Marshall's decision to appoint Buckner to command the Tenth Army was puzzling because he had neither seen combat nor led a corps or even a division. Marshall, however, had his reasons. For one thing, he had always liked and respected Buckner. In July 1941 he secured Buckner's promotion to major general because he felt that Buckner had done a "splendid job" in Alaska. The following March he considered bringing Buckner home to give him a corps preparing for overseas deployment, but concluded that his services were still needed in Alaska. Although disappointed with Buckner's unnecessary quarrel with Theobald, Marshall rationalized that Buckner's poor judgment grew out of his aggressive and direct nature, attributes Marshall valued and encouraged. Despite the damage that Buckner caused to interservice relations in Alaska, Marshall still recommended his elevation to lieutenant general in March 1943. Marshall toyed with the idea of assigning Buckner to lead a field army after the Americans and Canadians wrested the Aleutian Islands from the Japanese and Alaska became a military backwater in the spring of 1943, but he did not make his move until the following summer, when he dispatched Buckner to Hawaii to take over the new Tenth Army. Marshall and Nelly Richardson had by then made it clear to King and Nimitz that the army did not want marines controlling large army units; with the army and marines both deploying corps in the POA, it was obvious by the summer of 1944 that the army needed a field army in the theater for the major operations under consideration. Richardson was a potential candidate for the job, but his unpopularity among naval and marine officers made him an unwise choice. Moreover, Marshall had doubts about Richardson that made his selection unlikely. Hodge was another possibility, but he was busy preparing for the invasion of Leyte, and anyway he had yet to prove himself at the corps level. While there were by now numerous talented and veteran generals capable of taking the Tenth Army into action, Eisenhower's campaign in northwest Europe was sucking up almost all of these men

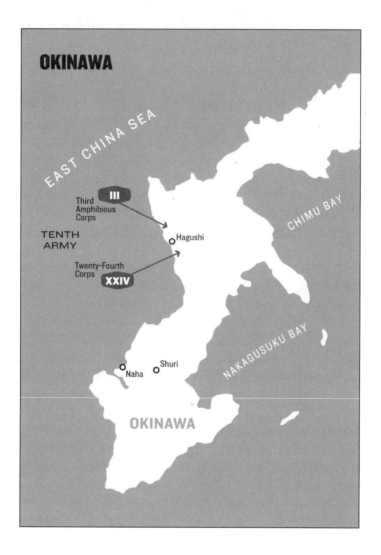

for the huge forces the army was using there. Those whom Eisenhower did not want were mostly the bottom of the barrel and hence unlikely to have impressed Marshall. Buckner, on the other hand, had considerable administrative experience, had with the exception of Theobald gotten along well with his navy counterparts, and met Marshall's usual requirements for important combat positions. Besides, Marshall disliked denying proficient officers their chance to lead men into battle when they had performed well in noncombat assignments.[4]

As things turned out, Buckner's first battle in the POA was bureaucratic. The POA was a navy-dominated theater in which Nimitz called the shots, so he would determine where, or even whether, the Tenth Army would see action. Buckner's professional fate, therefore, was dependent upon Nimitz's attitude toward him. To complicate matters further, Richardson was unhappy with Buckner's presence in the theater. Richardson had ambitions of his own to lead men into combat and knew full well that Buckner's Tenth Army would dilute his already limited authority in the POA. Soon after Buckner arrived in Hawaii, Richardson handed him a job tailor-made to wreck his prospects in the Pacific. On 5 July, Richardson placed Buckner in charge of the board he constituted to investigate Holland Smith's decision to remove Ralph Smith as Twenty-seventh Division commander on Saipan. For Buckner, it was a thankless and seemingly no-win assignment. A report favorable to the army might anger Nimitz and ruin his chances of taking the Tenth Army into battle. On the other hand, he would antagonize his immediate superior, Richardson, if he sided with the navy and marines. In his effort to square this circle, Buckner worked hard to moderate the board's findings so that it would generate as little interservice conflict as possible. The board concluded that while Holland Smith had the right to relieve Ralph Smith, he did so without full knowledge of the facts. By now Buckner recognized Richardson's unpopularity and powerlessness, so he moved to cozy up to Nimitz. Buckner was, unlike Richardson, a friendly man, and he managed to win over Nimitz with his charm and openness. In his meetings with the POA chief he lamented Richardson's attempts to make hay out of the report by disseminating it far and wide, and assured Nimitz that there were no interservice problems in the Tenth Army's staff. Richardson was not at all pleased with Buckner's efforts to ingratiate himself with Nimitz, but Buckner was willing to pay that price to get an active role in the Pacific War. The result spoke for itself; on 7 October, Buckner scrawled in his diary, "Adm. Nimitz after sounding out my attitude on the Smith vs. Smith controversy and finding that I deplored the whole matter and harbored no interservice ill feelings, announced that I would command the new joint project."[5] The Tenth Army would conduct the invasion of Okinawa.[6]

Securing a predominant role in the Okinawa operation was of course important for Buckner, but it did not end his bureaucratic struggles, which went beyond the usual logistical wrangling that accompanied any major military undertaking. Richardson and Buckner remained leery of one another and skirmished over matters such as who would command the Okinawa garrison after the Tenth Army occupied the island. A bigger problem for Buckner was wresting Hodge's Twenty-fourth Corps away from SWPA in sufficient time for the Okinawa invasion. The Twenty-fourth belonged to the POA, but Nimitz had lent it to MacArthur to use on Leyte. Unfortunately, Buckner's efforts to gain its release ran into one SWPA roadblock after another. Part of the reason was that the fighting on Leyte lasted longer than anyone had anticipated, requiring the continued commitment of Hodge's divisions. In addition, GHQ was in the habit of expropriating anything that came into its theater, regardless of previous ownership. In January, Buckner prevailed upon Nimitz to send MacArthur a message insisting that he live up to his promise to return the corps to the POA. When Buckner flew to Leyte to work out the details, he learned that the Sixth Army had stripped the corps of much of its equipment for the assault on Luzon. Moreover, the corps's three divisions had had little time to rest and refit for the upcoming campaign. Ever the optimist, Buckner comforted himself with the knowledge that whatever its condition, the Twenty-fourth Corps was a battle-tested outfit full of veterans who would no doubt acquit themselves well on Okinawa. Although Buckner did not know it, his annoying persistence in freeing Hodge's corps, as well as his alliance with the navy, had angered some at GHQ, including MacArthur. MacArthur told Eichelberger that Buckner had sold out to the navy, and he vowed to bust him for his disloyalty if he ever had the opportunity. This did not bode well for Buckner. The planned final attack on Japan would no doubt necessitate a reorganization of the Pacific War's command structure, after which Buckner might well find himself under MacArthur's authority and subject to his retribution.[7]

Despite these and other problems, Buckner remained confident and upbeat, and looked forward to the "great adventure" awaiting him on Okinawa. When Admiral Kelly Turner, commander of the fleet shepherding the Tenth Army to the island, took Buckner aside and expressed concern about the enormous obstacles they would confront, Buckner refused to be downcast and instead tried to buck Turner up until Turner admitted that he was just testing Buckner's resolve. Buckner had confidence in his battle-experienced units and their leaders, and wryly remarked that he was just about the only combat virgin in the Tenth Army. He got along well with Hodge, and was especially impressed with the Seventy-seventh Division's General Andrew Bruce. On 31 March, the day before the big attack, Buckner attended a shipboard Easter service and then retired early to get some sleep. Before bedding down for the night, he noted that his baptism of fire would coincide not only with Easter, but also with his father's birthday. He saw this as a good sign, writing, "I hope that I shall be able to look back upon it [the landing] with the same degree of enthusiasm with which I anticipate it."[8] Buckner arose at 4:30 the next morning, ate the navy's traditional battle breakfast of hotcakes and coffee, and was pleased with the calm and clear weather. Like most observers, he was impressed and awed by the navy's massive preliminary bombardment, and watched with equal satisfaction the orderly way with which the landing waves from the four assault divisions—the First Marine, Sixth Marine, Seventh, and Ninety-sixth—splashed ashore on Okinawa's Hagushi beaches on its western shore. To everyone's utter amazement, the Americans met almost no resistance and quickly established their beachhead. Buckner breathed a sigh of relief, feeling that the Japanese had missed their greatest opportunity to defeat the Tenth Army.

In the following days, the marines and soldiers pushed northward and southward against little opposition. Buckner planned to go about the reduction of Japanese defenses systematically and gradually, and initially believed he could do so in plenty of time and with minimal casualties. He was wrong.[9]

Like their comrades on Luzon, the Japanese on Okinawa had no expectation of victory against overwhelming American materiel superiority. Instead, they hoped to delay the Americans for as long as possible to buy time for their compatriots back home to prepare for the seemingly inevitable invasion of Japan itself. To carry out their strategy, the Japanese had two arrows in their quiver. The first called for the extensive use of kamikazes flying from airfields on Formosa and Kyushu against the American armada supporting the Tenth Army on Okinawa. Kamikazes were not new to the Pacific War, but in this case the Japanese planned to throw 4,000 of them at the American vessels off of Okinawa. Indeed, the day before the Tenth Army landed on the island, a kamikaze so injured the cruiser USS *Indianapolis* that it had to return to the West Coast for repairs. In the weeks that followed, wave after wave of kamikazes, sometimes hundreds at a time, assailed the American fleet. Although American fighter planes and antiaircraft guns shot the kamikazes down in large numbers, a few almost always got through to crash into the frantically maneuvering ships. By the time the campaign was over, kamikazes killed 4,900 sailors, wounded almost as many, sank 26 vessels, and damaged an astonishing 368 more.

For naval officers, the problem was that they could not leave Okinawa's waters until the Tenth Army secured the island, but Buckner's slow and cautious tactics left them exposed to the kamikazes for a lot longer than they wanted. The kamikaze threat became so serious that on 23 April Nimitz and several of his lieutenants met with Buckner to urge him to accelerate his efforts. Buckner, however, frostily responded that ground operations were none of the navy's business. Nimitz did not like this one bit and responded, "Yes, but ground though it may be, I'm losing a ship and a half a day. So if this line isn't moving within five days, we'll get someone here to move it so we can all get out from under these stupid attacks."[10] In the end, Nimitz did not carry out his threat. Removing Buckner would cause an interservice row dwarfing the one at Saipan the previous year, and Nimitz did not want to rupture the army-navy relationship during the penultimate battle for Japan. Like it or not, the navy had to live and die with Simon Bolivar Buckner.

Although Buckner of course wanted to oblige the navy, he was having an incredibly difficult time overcoming the second arrow in Japan's Okinawa quiver. The Japanese had decided to cede the majority of Okinawa to the invading Americans—hence the Tenth Army's unopposed landing—and instead concentrate their forces on the hills and ridges on the southern third of the island. There they had constructed three strong defensive lines honeycombed with hundreds of deep, mutually supporting, and interconnected tunnels. Overcoming the first line along Kakazu Ridge took Hodge three weeks, three divisions, and thousands of casualties, but the Japanese still managed to withdraw to the more formidable Shuri Line. In response to the heavy Japanese resistance and the pressure the navy was exerting on him, Buckner brought in from the north Geiger's marines and the Seventy-seventh Division to help Hodge crack the Shuri Line. After repulsing a large and unwise counterattack that cost the Japanese some 5,000 men, Buckner launched an all-out assault on 10 May. The marines and soldiers, accompanied by tanks, pushed forward after an enormous preliminary bombardment from land, sea, and air. The intensity of the combat surpassed anything previously seen in the Pacific War. The Japanese used their artillery effectively from the reverse sides of hills to disrupt American assaults, destroy armor, and inflict losses. Intense fighting occurred in dozens of locales with innocuous-sounding names such as Sugar Loaf Hill, Conical Hill, Chocolate Drop, and Strawberry Hill. In late May, however, heavy rains turned the battlefield into a quagmire that made life even more miserable for the combatants huddling in their foxholes and bunkers. Worse yet for the Americans, the deluge provided sufficient cover for the Japanese to evacuate their Shuri Line and retreat unscathed to their final position at the southern tip of the island. The downpour did not stop until 5 June, and three days later Buckner had his men ready for another major attack. More bloody fighting ensued as the Americans gradually blasted the Japanese out of their fortifications, and by the middle of the month it was increasingly clear that the end of the campaign was in sight.

Buckner decided early in the campaign to go about destroying the Japanese systematically in an attempt to keep American casualties to a minimum. Buckner's tactics, though, were often as slow and unimaginative as they were methodical. He frequently called for frontal assaults following massive preliminary bombardments designed to kill or wound most of the targeted Japanese before the soldiers and marines left their lines of departure. Unhappily, the Japanese usually rode out the shelling and airstrikes in their underground sanctuaries before emerging to repulse the American charges and inflict heavy losses. Instead of reexamining his tactics, Bucker responded to these setbacks by leaning on his corps and divisional leaders to accelerate their operations. Hodge resented the pressure Buckner exerted, but more or less agreed with his underlying philosophy, writing in mid-April:

> It is going to be really tough. There are 65,000 to 70,000 fighting Japs holed up in the south end of the island and I see no way to get them out except to blast them out yard by yard. . . . I know the Navy is saying that I am not pushing

but I do not intend to take Marine style casualties if I can help it unless the situation demands all-out speed where men alone have to face weapons.[11]

But there were alternative solutions. For example, both naval officers and General Andrew Bruce, commander of the Seventy-seventh Division, recommended breaking the campaign open by an amphibious landing behind Japanese lines. Buckner, however, rejected the idea because he concluded that doing so would just complicate the Tenth Army's already difficult resupply efforts.

In any event, Bruce was just about the only high-ranking army officer on Okinawa who demonstrated much tactical creativity. In addition to suggesting an amphibious end-run, Bruce conducted nighttime attacks and refrained from assailing enemy positions until he situated his artillery to hit the Japanese on the reverse sides of hills. Buckner's other generals displayed far less tactical finesse, though no one could deny their dogged determination. General James Bradley's Ninety-sixth Division carried out some of the Tenth Army's most difficult assignments, so it was small wonder that the stress impaired Bradley's health. While Buckner was privately critical of General George Griner's Twenty-seventh Division after it arrived, he praised the unit to others to avoid reigniting the controversy the outfit and the marines had on Saipan. Buckner worked hard to get along with the marines, but he was disturbed by the wanton destruction they left in their wake, and was unhappy with the Sixth Marine Division's performance. As far as Buckner was concerned, the Seventh Division's General Archibald Arnold was the standout among his lieutenants, though it is hard to see that Arnold was any more proficient than anyone else. Whatever his problems with terrain, tactics, personnel, and the navy, Buckner remorselessly prosecuted his campaign to its gory conclusion, so that by mid-May he was able to write, "We are making slow but steady progress and killing lots of Japs. It is tough going and will continue to be for some time, but I feel that we have control of the situation."[12]

Buckner was unaware that a good many of his army colleagues shared the navy's frustrations with his way of doing things. On 3 June, General Joseph "Vinegar Joe" Stilwell, the army's Ground Forces chief, arrived unannounced on Okinawa on an inspection trip. Stilwell stayed for four days observing the battle and conferring with Buckner and some of his lieutenants. Stilwell was an acerbic and critical man trying to wheedle his way into a combat command, so it was hardly surprising that he found much to criticize in Buckner's performance. He interpreted Buckner's efforts to get along with the navy as kowtowing, and did not like it one bit. He sardonically summarized Buckner's attitude in his diary: "Nimitz is perfect. His staff is perfectly balanced. Cooperation is magnificent. The Marine divisions are wonderful. In fact, everything is just dinky."[13] He was equally disturbed with Buckner's costly and unimaginative frontal assaults. Andrew Bruce agreed. During a meeting between the two men, Bruce expressed his frustrations with Buckner's tactics. Stilwell responded sympathetically, and before he left he took Bruce aside and said to him, "Keep up your crazy tactics, Bruce, kid. I wish we had more of you out here. You have shown more initiative than anyone else."[14] Stilwell's efforts to raise his concerns with Buckner elicited little more than a few flippant and dismissive wisecracks. Not surprisingly, Stilwell badmouthed Buckner during the rest of his Pacific tour. His denunciations to MacArthur in Manila merely reinforced MacArthur's determination to get rid of Buckner one way or another when the opportunity presented itself. Other SWPA generals such as Eichelberger and Joe Swing were equally troubled with Buckner's conduct on Okinawa, although in all fairness they were not present on the scene to see the obstacles the Tenth Army confronted. The upshot was that Buckner's Okinawa victory, when it came, was likely to prove pyrrhic for his career.[15]

As it was, the Japanese ended Buckner's life before MacArthur ended his career. On 18 June, Buckner and a gaggle of staff officers visited the First Marine Division's front. Some of the marines worried that his presence would attract enemy fire, so they asked him to replace his three-starred helmet with one less conspicuous. Buckner refused until the marines at a nearby battalion command post radioed that he was clearly visible. This concession to good sense, though, failed to prevent him from standing at the crest of a hill, arms akimbo, surveying the scene. Shortly thereafter, Japanese artillery opened fire, sending everyone scurrying for cover. Unfortunately, Buckner had little chance to react because an exploding shell sent a rock fragment into his chest, knocking him to the ground. As the marines hurriedly carried him off in a poncho, he asked if anyone else had been hurt, and was relieved to learn that no one else had. He died a few minutes after he reached the battalion aid station, unaware of the marine private who held his hand and said over and over, "You are going home, General, you are homeward bound."[16]

Ten weeks before Buckner's death, on 3 April, the Joint Chiefs of Staff had decided that MacArthur would lead all army forces in the Pacific in the planned invasion of Japan. The Tenth Army was therefore slated to come under MacArthur's authority as soon as the Okinawa campaign ended. After he learned the sad news about Buckner, Marshall radioed MacArthur and asked him to designate a new Tenth Army commander. By way of recommendation, Marshall mentioned that Joe Stilwell was still in the Pacific on his way home from his inspection tour. In addition, Marshall noted that now that the European War was over there was an abundance of experienced generals stateside who could leave for Okinawa immediately. Specifically, Marshall identified the Seventh Army's Alexander Patch, the Fifth Army's Lucian Truscott, and the Third Army's George Patton. If MacArthur was willing to wait a few days, Marshall continued, he could have the Ninth

Army's William Simpson or the Sixth Army Group's Jacob Devers. MacArthur countered by proposing Oscar Griswold for the job. Griswold had impressed MacArthur with his performance at Manila, and in fact was the only corps commander who distinguished himself in the Philippines. Griswold, MacArthur explained, was well qualified, had served extensively in the Pacific, understood amphibious operations, and was familiar with many of the Tenth Corps's personnel from his time in the Solomon Islands. If Griswold was unacceptable, MacArthur said he would favor Stilwell, Patch, and Truscott in that order. Marshall responded in such a way that indicated that the matter really was not open to negotiation. "For several rather important reasons," Marshall stated, "I would much prefer Stilwell's assignment to Griswold's." Marshall assured MacArthur that he had no doubts about Griswold's ability or MacArthur's judgment, but felt that Stilwell deserved the post. To preclude any further discussion, Marshall concluded, "Therefore, Stilwell is placed immediately at your disposal." MacArthur in this case got the hint and agreed to the appointment.[17]

Joe Stilwell had had an active but frustrating war. Born in Florida in 1883, Stilwell was such a precocious and difficult child that his father sent him to West Point to straighten him out. He graduated in 1904 and decided to make a career out of the army. Except for a stint in the Philippines fighting the Moros, he spent most of his time before World War One back at West Point teaching languages and history. He served as an intelligence officer in France during World War One, and after the conflict went on the first of three tours of duty in China that lasted a total of thirteen years. There he learned the Chinese language and culture and developed a deep respect and empathy for the country's peasantry. During his time stateside, he gained a reputation as a gifted tactician and trainer at the Infantry School and the Command and General Staff School. Marshall recognized Stilwell's abilities, and after becoming chief of staff he rapidly moved Stilwell upward from brigade to division to corps commander.

Marshall had considered assigning Stilwell to fight in North Africa, but he and Secretary of War Henry Stimson decided in January 1942 to dispatch him to the China-Burma-India theater instead. There Stilwell had the overlapping and sometimes contradictory jobs of serving as deputy theater commander, Chinese leader Chiang Kai-shek's chief of staff, head of American forces, and distributor of lend-lease materials. With his wealth of experience in China, Stilwell was on paper the ideal man for the mission. His determination, single-mindedness, raw intelligence, and personal example seemed an ideal combination for training and equipping Chiang's armies to fight the Japanese. Regrettably, in the flesh Stilwell was utterly miscast for his role. His job required considerable diplomacy, sophistication, patience, and discretion, none of which Stilwell possessed. Indeed, Stilwell was a tactless, caustic, sullen, and contentious man with a monochrome view of the world. He once said to a group of cavalry officers and cadets, "The only value of the horse cavalry is that you have horses and you can eat them when you need to."[18] He never forgave a slight or let go of an argument. He quarreled with almost everyone of importance in the theater, including especially Chiang, whom Stilwell repeatedly denigrated publicly and privately. Although he managed to reopen the Burma Road to China in the summer of 1944, he was completely over his head in the intrigue and backbiting that swirled around Chiang and his sycophantic court. That he lasted as long as he did in the theater was due primarily to Stimson's and Marshall's stalwart support and understanding. In October 1944, though, Chiang successfully manufactured Stilwell's recall. After he returned to the States, Marshall appointed him Ground Forces commander, from which he migrated to the Tenth Army.[19]

The "several important reasons" that Marshall alluded to, but did not specify, in his message to MacArthur favoring Stilwell's assignment to lead the Tenth Army were both personal and professional. Marshall and Stilwell were old friends. In fact, Stilwell was one of the few people who called Marshall by his first name. Of equal importance, Marshall had enormous respect for Stilwell's abilities and had on several occasions been willing to go the extra mile to protect and promote him. For example, as assistant commandant of the Infantry School, Marshall had three times dissuaded the commandant from relieving the outspoken and caustic Stilwell as an instructor. He performed a similar service with the president, albeit less successfully, during Stilwell's difficult tenure in China. Marshall appreciated Stilwell's sacrifices in the China-Burma-India theater and rewarded him for his services by appointing him head of the Army Ground Forces in January 1945. Stilwell unsurprisingly did not enjoy his desk job, so in May he asked Marshall for field command. Marshall explained that there were no openings in the Pacific available for someone with Stilwell's rank. However, Marshall continued, he had been thinking about sending Stilwell to the Pacific to check up on the training of replacements, and he had no objection if Stilwell tried to work out something with MacArthur during his inspection tour. Stilwell's harsh criticisms of Buckner's performance were therefore motivated as much by opportunism as objective assessment. Since MacArthur's opinion of Buckner was as low as Stilwell's, it was no wonder that the two men quickly came to a meeting of minds. MacArthur told Stilwell that he would relieve Buckner at the first opportunity and put Stilwell in his place. Stilwell was in Guam on his way home when he learned of Buckner's death, and immediately he radioed MacArthur to offer his services. MacArthur's lobbying for Griswold, though, indicated that he either had forgotten his pledge to Stilwell or did not take it seriously. Fortunately for Stilwell, Marshall's intervention got him the job. MacArthur put the best face on things and later lied to Stilwell that he had been his number-one choice to command the Tenth Army. As for

Stilwell, he was thrilled by this sudden change of fortune that placed him in charge of a field army on the eve of the invasion of Japan.[20]

Stilwell's joy was matched by the regret and chagrin of his competitors for the post. Griswold knew that MacArthur had recommended him as Buckner's replacement and was crushed when the job went to Stilwell instead. As usual, though, Griswold tried to be philosophical and summarized his feelings in his diary: "A little hard luck for me—'C'est la guerre.'" Robert Richardson was equally disappointed. Richardson recognized his unpopularity with the navy and had been trying to ingratiate himself with MacArthur in the hopes of securing a combat position. When he learned of Buckner's death, he hurried to Manila to lobby MacArthur for the position. "I must ask Doug to give me a field command," he said to Stilwell before he left, unaware that he was not even under consideration. Like Griswold, he was deeply disheartened to be passed over, his career ambitions another casualty of the bureaucratic war within the war.[21]

Unfortunately for Stilwell, though happily for the soldiers and marines on Okinawa, he took over the Tenth Army at the very end of the difficult campaign and therefore had little opportunity to distinguish himself. By the time the fighting was officially declared over on 2 July, the Tenth Army had suffered 7,374 men killed, 31,807 wounded, and 239 missing. Including the navy's heavy losses, American casualties at Okinawa totaled almost 50,000. As for the Japanese, more than 110,000 of their troops perished on the island. Despite all the bloodshed, the strategic benefits were well worth the effort, or so it seemed at the time. Okinawa provided the United States with a base for the planned invasion of Kyushu and underscored for the Japanese their dire circumstances. Even before the campaign ended, the army and navy began stuffing the island with airfields, warehouses, port facilities, and all the other paraphernalia required for the final assault on Japan. And for all this Simon Bolivar Buckner deserved a good deal of the credit.

Planning for the Invasion of Japan

The American counteroffensive against Japan began in August 1942 with the marine landing at Guadalcanal. After that the Americans had pushed northward and westward like an enormous steamroller, isolating and obliterating hapless Japanese strongpoints in its way. The massive American military machine seemed impervious to the laws of entropy because it increased in violence, strength, and speed as it relentlessly progressed. It is easy to pity those bypassed Japanese soldiers reduced to a squalid hand-to-mouth existence on their fetid jungle-filled islands, but their fate was certainly preferable to that of their compatriots who found themselves in the direct path of the American juggernaut that destroyed all resistance and turned the local geography into a barren, death-filled moonscape. While the American counteroffensive rolled toward Japan, the American submarine war gradually paralyzed the Japanese empire by sinking its merchant marine. This made it increasingly difficult for the Japanese to resupply and reinforce their overseas garrisons and import the raw materials their industry needed to produce the war materiel upon which the Japanese military depended. Finally, the American strategic bombing campaign burned Japanese cities to ashes one by one, including a raid on Tokyo in March 1945 that leveled much of the metropolis and killed approximately 85,000 inhabitants. Most horrifying of all from the Japanese perspective was that the Americans had hitherto conducted the Pacific War with only a fraction of their available resources. Germany's surrender, though, freed up a wealth of additional manpower, equipment, talent, and supplies that the Joint Chiefs of Staff could now deploy against faltering Japan.

After Okinawa, the next obvious American objective was the final assault on the Home Islands to force Japan's capitulation and end the war. However, things were not as clear as they appeared. Many high-ranking officers felt that an invasion of Japan to compel its surrender might not be necessary. These men, including Army Air Force chief Henry Arnold and JCS chair William Leahy, believed that the naval blockade and strategic bombing would persuade resource-poor and isolated Japan to lay down its arms sooner or later. Although Marshall favored an attack, Ernest King, Nimitz, and MacArthur were more ambivalent. King advocated the encirclement of Japan by seizing bases on the Chinese coast and elsewhere to better conduct the naval blockade. In May, MacArthur encouraged Sutherland to take his time in formulating a plan to assail Japan, telling him that it would probably not be required. A month later, though, MacArthur had changed his tune, perhaps in response to reports from Okinawa. Eichelberger wrote, "Some people think that the Japs will quit and at one time the BC [Big Chief, meaning MacArthur] thought so also but when I asked him the other day he said 'no' very emphatically. The little fellow is a mean enemy because he does not surrender."[22] Whatever their perspectives, everyone recognized the need to draw up plans for an invasion if the JCS ordered one. Almost everyone also agreed that the campaign, dubbed Operation Downfall, would be very bloody. After all, if the Japanese were willing to fight to the death for small or remote locales such as Peleliu and Tarawa and Okinawa, they would certainly sell their lives dearly for their homeland, regardless of the circumstances surrounding their resistance. Estimates of probable American casualties varied, but SWPA and POA both agreed that approximately 50,000 men would fall in the first month of Downfall alone. Japanese losses of course would be astronomical.[23]

The Joint Chiefs of Staff's 3 April decision placing MacArthur in charge of all army forces in the Pacific gave him not only primary responsibility for planning the final assault on Japan, but also the task of integrating the army units and commanders on their way from Europe. Although the rank-in-file from Europe were hardly enthusiastic about risking their lives one more time against a new enemy, many of their generals clamored for prominent roles in the invasion. They wanted to be in on the action for both personal and professional reasons, and lobbied Marshall and his staffers for permission to do so. Lucian Truscott, for example, wrote to Thomas Handy, "I don't know what your plans are, but just keep in mind that I am a pretty good fighting man, and I am by no means wedded to my present position or rank. I am not asking for anything, you understand; I am merely suggesting that I am yours to command, in any capacity, if there is some fighting to be done."[24] Marshall was sympathetic to such pleas, and on 6 April he radioed MacArthur that they should not waste this pool of talented generals who had successfully taken the Wehrmacht's measure in some of the world's greatest battles. He believed that the experience these men possessed would prove invaluable in delivering the coup de grace against Japan. Unfortunately, there were not enough slots for everyone. Marshall wanted to arrange things so that only the most capable generals and their staffs went to the Pacific, but in such a way as to spare the feelings of those left behind.[25]

Neither MacArthur nor his generals were very enthusiastic about Marshall's idea. The generals feared that their higher-ranking and more famous European theater counterparts might supersede them. They believed that they deserved the right to command the units invading Japan because they were familiar with the situation and had proven their worth in innumerable operations and campaigns. As for MacArthur, he was very loyal to his subordinates, felt that they had done a good job, and knew their strengths and weaknesses. He did not want to interfere with a formula that, whatever its faults, had enabled the Americans to drive the Japanese all the way across the Pacific. Moreover, MacArthur could hardly have been happy at the thought of celebrated generals from Europe horning in on his limelight. Still, Marshall was his superior and MacArthur wanted to at least appear cooperative. He said he was willing to take the best generals from Europe, but insisted that they not supplant his senior people. As he explained to Marshall,

The absorption of the highest officers of the European front presents certain difficulties because of their rank and because the size of the force here will be smaller than that which existed in Europe and hence there will be a scarcity of posts. In general the troops here are admirably officered and need no general influx which should be mainly absorbed in the new increments to come and in the new commands and staffs. Concur most heartily that proven merit and ability alone should be the criterion of assignment. Believe the problem can be readily resolved without offense to anyone.[26]

In fact, dealing with the generals from Europe proved more complicated than MacArthur promised and Marshall hoped. One problem was ego. MacArthur's could of course be taken for granted, but it also manifested itself in an unlikely source. Omar Bradley, commander of the Twelfth Army Group, had after D-Day in Normandy asked Marshall to transfer him to the Pacific as soon as the Germans surrendered. As his army group fought across Europe, he frequently commented that he hoped his last amphibious assault was against Japan. Marshall greatly respected Bradley, who had amassed an enviable combat record, and in April 1945 offered him to MacArthur to lead an army group in the invasion of Japan. MacArthur, however, did not much like the idea. If Bradley came over as an army group commander, he would supersede Krueger, who MacArthur believed was a better general because of his wealth of amphibious experience. MacArthur could have given Krueger and Bradley each his own army group, but that would have required completely retooling early thinking for Operation Downfall—and alienating the touchy and Krueger-hating Eichelberger in the process. MacArthur instead intended to be his own army group commander. By way of compromise, MacArthur proposed that Bradley take a field army consisting of the divisions and corps on their way from Europe. Marshall relayed the suggestion to Bradley's superior, Dwight Eisenhower. Eisenhower, though, did not like the idea at all. Eisenhower responded disingenuously that appointing Bradley to a mere field army would hurt his postwar army career, denigrate his previous accomplishments in Europe, and come across to the public as a demotion. Eisenhower's implication was that asking Bradley to step down a level would be humiliating for him. Although Bradley stated that he would go wherever the army sent him, Eisenhower's views mirrored his own. As a result, Bradley did not go to the Pacific in any capacity, but in August reluctantly accepted President Harry Truman's request that he run the Veterans Administration.[27]

Instead of Bradley, Courtney Hodges got the big prize of leading all the ground units deploying from Europe to the Pacific. Hodges was a shy and retiring man who had commanded Eisenhower's workhorse First Army during the fighting in northwest Europe. The First Army took more ground, suffered heavier losses, and sustained higher casualties than any other American field army during the war. It was the First Army that spearheaded the breakthrough in Normandy and fought at the Battle of the Bulge. Although some argued that Hodges was overrated, Marshall and Eisenhower thought a lot of him. Marshall had cultivated his career, and at the end of the European War Eisenhower lauded him as a "scintillating star." Like most of his colleagues, Hodges was eager to combat the Japanese, and Marshall selected him over others not only for his seemingly stellar record, but no doubt also because he was the one least likely to clash with or threaten MacArthur. Indeed, MacArthur accepted him without much fuss, and Eichelberger speculated that he did so because Hodges was "the most innocuous of them all."[28] Regardless of the reason, Hodges was delighted with his good fortune.[29]

The other European War army group and field army commanders, for their part, were correspondingly disappointed to be shut out of the invasion of Japan. Marshall tried to find them responsibilities commensurate with their ranks, but it was not easy because few such posts were available, and they lacked the excitement and prestige of combat positions. In May, Marshall had an idea. He suggested to General Albert Wedemeyer, Stilwell's replacement in China, that perhaps some of the high-ranking European War generals and their staffs could go to China and lead Chinese armies against the Japanese there. He specifically mentioned the Ninth Army's William Simpson, the Fifth Army's Lucian Truscott, the Sixth Army Group's Jacob Devers, and the Third Army's George Patton for the jobs, though he wryly noted that the Chinese probably would not understand Patton's profanity. Wedemeyer was agreeable to the proposal, and Simpson and Truscott even flew to China to investigate its practicality. Marshall's other assignments were equally unsatisfactory. In June, for example, he appointed a disappointed Patch to lead the stateside Fourth Army. Patton's and Mark Clark's ambitions of going to the Pacific failed to pan out either. Clark was hardly surprised that MacArthur showed no interest in him, and he ended up as military governor of Austria. On the other hand, Patton had higher hopes. Of all the European War generals, he had lobbied the most aggressively to fight the Japanese after Germany surrendered, and he was not picky about where or how he did it. He and his friends sounded out both Marshall and MacArthur, but nothing came of their efforts. MacArthur unsurprisingly did not ask for the glamorous Patton's services, and Marshall did not offer them. As for Marshall's China experiment, the Japanese capitulated before anything came of it.[30]

Marshall used a different strategy to choose the generals to lead the corps destined for the Pacific from Europe. Instead of asking for MacArthur's approval and opinion, he opted to simply inform him who would be commanding the corps and gambled that MacArthur would not complain. Marshall left the actual selection of the men to Hodges. Hodges in turn picked the Third Corps's James Van Fleet, the Fifth Corps's Clarence Huebner, the Seventh Corps's J. Lawton Collins, the Thirteenth Corps's Alvan Gillem, and the Eighteenth Airborne Corps's Matthew Ridgway. Four of the five had fought under Hodges in Europe, so it was not surprising that Hodges decided to bring them to the Pacific with him. Indeed, Hodges considered Collins and Ridgway in particular two of the army's best soldiers. Gillem, on the other hand, had served in Simpson's Ninth Army. However, since two of the divisions slated for the Pacific were armored, it made sense to have an armored expert such as Gillem, who had performed consistently well. Ernie Harmon of the Twenty-second Corps was another option, but his abrasive and profane personality hardly meshed well with Hodges's reticent demeanor. As Marshall hoped, MacArthur accepted all five men without complaint.[31]

MacArthur's willingness to defend the interests of his subordinates from outside interference did not mean that he had his military house in order. In fact, he had personnel problems serious enough to intrude on the planning for Operation Downfall. For example, Sutherland caused so much trouble during negotiations with Nimitz's staff at Guam over reorganizing Pacific forces and planning the assault on Japan that Marshall seriously contemplated telling MacArthur that Sutherland should not participate in any further such discussions. Eichelberger was not surprisingly another source of discontent. By now Eichelberger so detested Krueger that he bluntly told MacArthur that he would rather be relieved than serve under Krueger again. As usual, MacArthur deflected Eichelberger's anger with manipulative conciliation. He praised Eichelberger's generalship, promised to help secure his promotion, guaranteed him a prominent role in the invasion of Japan, and assured him that he would not have to take orders from Krueger. MacArthur also agreed with Eichelberger that Krueger's slow and cautious tactics left much to be desired, and added that from now on he would give Krueger assignments befitting his limited abilities. Although MacArthur probably always intended to be his own army group commander, Eichelberger's hostility certainly destroyed any intention MacArthur may have had of elevating Krueger to that level.[32]

MacArthur also had trouble fitting the Tenth Army into Operation Downfall. Although Buckner had before he died hoped to play a part in the invasion of Japan, MacArthur had planned to replace him at the first opportunity because he disapproved of both Buckner's unimaginative and costly assaults on Okinawa and his cozy relationship with the navy. Stilwell was more to MacArthur's liking, but this did not end MacArthur's problems. Nimitz tried to hold onto the Tenth Army despite the Joint Chiefs of Staff's directive that placed all army forces in the Pacific under MacArthur's control. In response, MacArthur decided that if Nimitz continued to be difficult, he would simply bring in another field army headquarters, fill it with army units stripped from the Tenth Army, and leave Stilwell a commander without any troops. Later, MacArthur resorted to the simpler expedient of denying the Tenth Army any role in the final assault on Japan and assigning Downfall to Hodges's, Krueger's, and Eichelberger's armies only. Stilwell was unhappy to be victimized by more of the bureaucratic warfare that had caused him so much trouble in China, and wrote morosely in his diary, "Apparently, Tenth Army is cut out of any part in [the invasion of Japan]. Result of the Doug-Nimitz hate."[33]

Downfall proposed two successive invasions of the Japanese Home Islands. The first, Operation Olympic, called for Krueger's Sixth Army to land on the southern island of Kyushu on 1 November. His objective was to seize the southern third of the island for the construction of airbases and port facilities to support the main effort, slated for the following March. With its comparatively large size and mountainous terrain, Kyushu promised to be a bigger and bloodier version of the Luzon campaign. Indeed, it would be the largest Pacific War operation to date. To wage it, MacArthur allotted Krueger fourteen divisions, 427,000 men, and 626,000 tons of equipment carried on 1,318 transports and landing craft. The Sixth Army would consist of four corps: Swift's First, Hall's Eleventh, General Harry Schmidt's all-marine Fifth Amphibious, and Doc Ryder's recently arrived Ninth. All four corps commanders had considerable combat experience, though Ryder had come by his while leading the Thirty-fourth Division in Italy. Krueger had worked with Swift and Hall in New Guinea and the Philippines, but he was unfamiliar with Ryder and Schmidt. MacArthur explained to Eichelberger that the campaign was tailor-made for Krueger's methodical and unimaginative nature, but it was equally true that it required someone with Krueger's tenacity and determination, especially since the Japanese were staking almost everything they had on its outcome.

If the occupation of Kyushu did not force Japan's capitulation, MacArthur would implement the second part of Downfall: Operation Coronet. Coronet called for a massive amphibious assault on Honshu near the Japanese capital of Tokyo with twenty-five divisions on 1 March 1946. It would easily be the largest undertaking of the Pacific War. MacArthur's original plan envisioned the Eighth Army and Tenth Army landing first, followed by the First Army. MacArthur's squabbling with Nimitz over the Tenth Army, however, persuaded him to cut it out of Coronet altogether. Instead, MacArthur opted to proceed with Eichelberger's Eighth Army and Hodges's First Army only. The Eighth Army would come ashore at Sagami Bay southwest of Tokyo, while the First Army simultaneously attacked the east side of the Boso Peninsula. Eichelberger would initially have at his disposal three corps: Sibert's Tenth, Gillem's Thirteenth, and Griswold's Fourteenth. Hodges for his part would use Geiger's Third Amphibious Corps of marines and Hodge's Twenty-fourth Corps. Later, after each army had established a solid bridgehead, the remaining corps from Europe would reinforce them. All the field army and corps commanders were veterans with the records to prove it, but their competence varied. Eichelberger had shown considerable tactical flair in New Guinea and the Philippines, but despite his reputation Hodges was an unoriginal and conventional general more in the Krueger mode. Eichelberger and Griswold were old friends with impressive records who would undoubtedly have worked well together. On the other hand, Eichelberger had been so disappointed with Sibert's performance on Mindanao that he had seriously considered replacing him with Roscoe Woodruff, though it is unclear whether he would have done so had Coronet proved necessary. As for Gillem, he could provide the armored expertise that Eichelberger lacked and, since Eichelberger generally gave his subordinates considerable leeway, probably would have functioned well in the Eighth Army. Hodges was of course familiar with the four remaining corps commanders from Europe, but not with Hodge and Geiger. Although Van Fleet, Huebner, Collins, and Ridgway were new to the Japanese way of war, there is little doubt that they would have fought with considerable professionalism accumulated from their experiences with the Germans. Hodge and Geiger had served together on Okinawa, and if their performances had been more adequate than brilliant, they were certainly familiar with the kind of opposition they would face on Honshu.

In August 1945 Bill Simpson and his chief of staff and close friend, James Moore, were on their way to the States from their visit to China to investigate the possibility of their leading Chinese armies against the Japanese. Simpson was his usual charming self, but he noticed that Chiang Kai-shek's ruling Kuomintang seemed much more interested in the Chinese communist threat than in fighting the Japanese. He and Moore flew to Manila and then Guam, where they had dinner with Nimitz. On Guam Moore wondered why there were so many journalists and brass milling around. Something big seemed to be in the making. As they prepared to fly to Hawaii, General Carl "Tooey" Spaatz, commander of the Army Air Force's strategic bombing campaign in the Pacific, sent word that he was eager to see them. Simpson, however, responded, "Oh, the hell with that. Tooey just wants me to get down there and get tight [drunk] with him. This eye is bothering me, and I'm going back to . . . Hawaii to get it fixed." As a result, he and Moore missed the hoopla and drama surrounding the dropping of atomic bombs on Hiroshima on 6 August and Nagasaki three days later. These two events, as well as the Soviet Union's declaration of war on Japan, persuaded the Japanese to surrender and rendered Operation Downfall mercifully academic.[34]

Conclusions

The operations in the last months of the war were an unwelcome indicator of what would have happened had the Americans implemented Operation Downfall. On Okinawa in particular the Japanese fought tenaciously even though victory was almost impossible, and they inflicted heavy casualties on the invading Tenth Army. To win the campaign, Buckner and his lieutenants resorted to costly frontal assaults that usually displayed little tactical imagination. Operation Olympic promised to replicate Okinawa on a much larger scale. The Japanese recognized that Kyushu would probably be the Americans' first target and had concentrated their best forces there. Although Krueger and his chief subordinates were, unlike Buckner, experienced veterans, they tended to fight in an orthodox and methodical manner. Finally, the mountainous terrain would have provided the Japanese plenty of places from which to skillfully defend themselves. Considering the geography and personnel involved, Olympic would have been Okinawa writ large. This, however, does not mean that MacArthur's decision to use the Sixth Army was necessarily wrong. Kyushu's difficult topography probably precluded anything other than straightforward combat. Waging war there required the single-minded determination, stamina, and remorselessness that Krueger and Swift in particular possessed. On the other hand, it is equally fortunate that MacArthur assigned Eichelberger such a prominent role in Coronet. By that time, the Japanese would have had little left over after the fighting in Kyushu, and there was more room for the Americans to maneuver. Under these circumstances, Eichelberger's tactical flair, as well as that of Gillem and Ridgway and Collins in particular, might have produced a quicker victory than if Krueger were in charge. Downfall would no doubt have been enormously bloody, but in this instance MacArthur married the right men to the right missions.

Conclusions

Gaining and Losing Command

In World War Two the army deployed overseas eight field armies and twenty corps that saw significant action. There were also five army groups in which Americans participated but did not necessarily command. In the European War, one corps operated in North Africa, a corps and a field army in Sicily, three corps and a field army in Italy, and four field armies and thirteen corps in northwestern Europe. As for the war against Japan, the army used three field armies and five corps. Thirty-eight officers, some of whom served at more than one level, led these units in major combat operations. These men were important not only because they directed thousands of troops, but also because their choices changed history. For example, Lucas's decision to hunker down at Anzio, Clark's to strike directly for Rome, Bradley's to push into Brittany, Collins's to commit his armor during Cobra, Krueger's to assail the Japanese at Ormoc, and Middleton's to fight for Bastogne and St. Vith all altered the course of the conflict in important ways. It was the army group, field army, and corps commanders who ran the army machinery that won the war against Germany and Japan.

Successfully leading army groups, field armies, and corps required stamina, nerve, a certain kind of charisma, drive, ability, intelligence, and a willingness to accept responsibility for decisions that might result in the deaths of hundreds and even thousands of people. Nevertheless, there was no shortage of ambitious officers who aspired to these posts. Attaining these senior commands was a great professional achievement for officers because they were among the most important positions in the army, especially during wartime. Although failure could result in demotion and ignominy—not to mention lost lives and defeat—the rewards could include promotion, fame and glory, the rare opportunity to ply one's trade in its purest form, and the patriotic satisfaction of contributing to the war effort. Bradley, for instance, parlayed his accomplishments in North Africa and Sicily into command of the Twelfth Army Group, and Patton used his victories to become a household name. Many of the others commented later on the professional pride they felt in a job well done. The war demonstrated that there was no magic formula to attaining army group, field army, or corps command, but most of those who secured these coveted roles shared certain commonalities.

Although the United States' institutionalized racism and sexism in the late nineteenth and early twentieth centuries essentially limited the army's officer corps to white males, an officer's family background did not play much of a role in his chances of attaining a senior combat command in World War Two. Those who gained these posts came from a wide variety of socioeconomic and geographic circumstances. Patton's family was as wealthy and prominent as Bradley's was poor and undistinguished. Most of these men, though, grew up in middle- or lower-class families scattered throughout the country. Some—Clark, Fredendall, Keyes, Patch, Ridgway, Sibert, and Swift—were army brats following in their fathers' footsteps. Brooks's father was a New Hampshire salesman, Devers's a Pennsylvania jeweler, Gerow's a Virginia railroad conductor, Hodges's a Georgia newspaper publisher, Millikin's an Indiana barber, and Eddy's an Illinois insurance man. The big exception was the foreign-born Krueger. What mattered was not birthplace or birthright, but rather *birthday*. Because of Marshall's emphasis on comparative youth and the years in which the war occurred, most of the war's senior combat commanders were born within relatively few years of one another. Their average age at the conflict's start was the early fifties. Krueger was at sixty the oldest, and Collins the youngest at forty-five. There were some talented and capable older officers available for these positions, but Marshall generally frowned on giving them responsible combat posts because he felt they lacked the necessary stamina.

Climbing through the army's educational system was of far greater importance than family background and circumstances in achieving a high combat command. How a man gained access to the Regular Army's officer corps was not as significant as getting there in the first place. West Point was the most common, but not only, way of doing so. Eddy, Fredendall, Gillem, Hodges, Hodge, Huebner, Krueger, Middleton, and Truscott were all commissioned from the ranks, and Brooks and Gerow from other military schools. McLain, an anomaly in all sorts of ways, rose through the Oklahoma National Guard. Those who graduated from West Point tended to rank somewhere in the middle of their classes, indicating that attaining high combat posts required more than mere academic prowess—or that some officers did a considerable amount of maturing after they left the military academy. The Command and General Staff School and Army War College were far more important than West Point in determining an officer's career trajectory. Theoretically, only the best and brightest younger officers were selected for these schools, so they served as institutional gatekeepers that screened out all but the most accomplished and promising men. It was therefore no coincidence that almost all of the war's army group, field army, and corps commanders attended at least one of them. Eddy, McLain, Milburn, and Truscott missed out on the Army War College, and Van Fleet was unique in never darkening the doors of either place. However, everyone else graduated from both schools. These schools introduced the army's elite to each other and to a common way of operating. Although the Army War College did not rate its graduates, the Command and General Staff School did. Corlett, Griswold, and Swift ranked in the bottom half of their class, whereas Anderson, Bradley, Huebner, Hodge, and Middleton ended up in the top ten percent of theirs. The rest were somewhere in between.

Taking full advantage of the army's educational system was an important factor in achieving a senior combat command, but there was more to it than that. Performance there and elsewhere mattered little if no one noticed, so successful officers sought patrons to look after their careers. One reason for Patton's obsessive and flamboyant behavior on interwar polo fields was to impress and be noticed by his superiors. Others confined themselves to the diligent fulfillment of their regular duties. Although having multiple sponsors was helpful, Marshall and to a lesser extent McNair were the ones who mattered the most during World War Two. The two men worked together in assigning officers to stateside division, corps, and field army commands based on their evaluation of an officer's record and character. Marshall in particular had closely tracked the careers of promising young officers for years. Once he became chief of staff, he moved these men rapidly up the army's hierarchy to increasingly important posts. Many, if not most, of the war's highest commanders were Marshall men, including Bradley, Clark, Collins, Cook, Devers, Eddy, Eichelberger, Eisenhower, Hodges, Huebner, Middleton, Ridgway, and Walker. He was also open to promoting officers whom others he trusted vouched for. For example, he was unfamiliar with Corlett and Fredendall, but secured their services for Eisenhower upon receiving glowing reports about them. Marshall looked for officers with integrity, initiative, a sense of duty, a can-do attitude, aggressiveness, and drive, which was a big reason why so many combat leaders shared so many of these traits—they were all cut from the same Marshall cloth.

On the other hand, there were things that might have mattered to Marshall but that he did not care much about. These included not only family background, but also an officer's previous role in the army's innumerable cliques. When a Kentucky woman expressed concern about Krueger's German background, for example, Marshall defended Krueger's loyalty and noted, "It is nothing remarkable to have high ranking officers in our Army of German stock."[1] Marshall was a Pershing man, but he did nothing to prevent Millikin from rising to corps command despite his marriage to Peyton March's daughter. Although Marshall placed great emphasis on an officer's character, he was willing to tolerate eccentric men who he felt were capable of delivering victory. Marshall and the maverick Patton were poles apart in personality, but Marshall still promoted Patton's career because he believed that Patton possessed the aggressiveness, sturdiness, determination, and drive that Marshall valued. Finally, and perhaps most surprisingly, Marshall was not terribly concerned about an officer's lack of combat experience. Bradley, Collins, Crittenberger, Devers, Eisenhower, Keyes, Milburn, Ridgway, and Truscott never left the Americas during World War One, and Eichelberger and Gillem ended the conflict in Siberia. Nevertheless, all these men managed to attain senior combat posts in the next war. In fact, Marshall generally did not even consider combat experience in World War Two as a necessary prerequisite for senior positions. This made sense early on when everyone was green, but he usually maintained this pretence even as the war progressed and the army accumulated more and more battle-hardened officers. Marshall did not want to punish men who had proven themselves in stateside training assignments by denying them the opportunity to lead troops into battle in commands commensurate with their ranks. For instance, he pushed successfully for Hodges's appointment to the First Army, Simpson's to the Ninth Army, and Buckner's to the Tenth Army even though none of these men had taken a division or corps into action and there were by then several veteran corps commanders available for promotion. When Marshall did act to procure battle-experienced officers, he did so mostly at Eisenhower's behest.

As president and commander-in-chief, Franklin Roosevelt had authority over all the country's armed forces, but after the United States entered the war he never interfered with Marshall's personnel decisions at the army group, field army, and corps levels. In fact, when one aggrieved general asked Marshall's permission to appeal his case to the president, Marshall agreed but warned him that Roosevelt would just laugh at him.[2] Although Marshall could have used his power as chief of staff to unilaterally assign army personnel wherever he saw fit, he did not because he firmly believed that his theater commanders in particular should if possible have lieutenants of their own choosing. Determining army group, field army, and corps leaders for overseas deployment therefore resulted from discussions between Marshall and his theater chiefs. The extent of these negotiations varied depending on the theater's importance and Marshall's rapport with its leader. Because most of the field armies and corps sent overseas ended up in Eisenhower's and MacArthur's theaters, Marshall's relationship with these men was most relevant to the selection process. Eisenhower was a Marshall protégé, so the conversations between them over personnel were extensive, freewheeling, and open. Marshall gave Eisenhower increasing autonomy over personnel decisions, but he still had his opinions and expected Eisenhower to consider them carefully. Eisenhower did so because of the enormous respect he had for Marshall, even if he did not always concur with his recommendations. Marshall, for example, persuaded Eisenhower to jettison Hartle as Central Task Force commander for Operation Torch, to accept Hodges and Simpson for the First and Ninth armies, and to take on Collins and Corlett for Overlord. Marshall for his part deferred to Eisenhower's appointment of Keyes to run the Second Corps and Gerow to lead the Fifteenth Army despite the doubts he harbored toward both men.

Marshall's relationship with MacArthur was, on the other hand, more formal and restrained, but even here there was still a give-and-take in assigning personnel. Marshall usually made recommendations for corps and field army commands that MacArthur was free to accept or reject. MacArthur went along with Marshall's suggestion to use Eichelberger and Hall as corps commanders, but picked his own people—Krueger, Swift, and Sibert, most obviously—for other important combat posts. Indeed, Marshall's insistence on Stilwell as Buckner's successor as head of the Tenth Army was the only instance in which Marshall forced a field army or corps commander on MacArthur. Marshall's willingness to defer to his theater commanders on personnel matters meant that as the war progressed ambitious high-ranking combat officers had an additional hurdle to surmount before they could take their units into action.

It is difficult to overestimate Eisenhower's role in European War personnel decisions. In consultation with Marshall, Eisenhower chose or endorsed every single army group, field army, and corps commander deployed to combat against the Wehrmacht except for Patch and Crittenberger. Eisenhower and Marshall both emphasized character, but there were some important differences between the two men in their selection criteria. Eisenhower placed less stock in an officer's educational accomplishments and more in his combat experience than did Marshall. Throughout the conflict, and especially in the lead-up to Overlord, Eisenhower strove to secure as many veteran commanders as possible. He lobbied strenuously for Truscott, and willingly accepted Collins, Corlett, and Middleton because they had seen previous action. It was largely their greenness that cost Crittenberger, Reinhardt, and Woodruff their corps, and Anderson, Milburn, and Millikin probably would have met similar fates had not others vouched for them to Eisenhower. In addition, Eisenhower was more susceptible to political pressure than Marshall. For example, he let public opinion influence his thinking toward Patton during the Knutsford incident. Finally, although Eisenhower aspired and claimed to share Marshall's dispassionate and almost cold-blooded evaluation of an officer's qualities, he was actually more likely to let personal feelings interfere with his judgment. He willingly accepted Haislip, Walker, and especially Gerow as corps commanders, even though none of them had led units in combat, because they were trusted old friends. He also tolerated Fredendall longer than was prudent out of a misplaced sense of loyalty. Most damningly, he consistently devalued and denigrated Devers simply because he disliked him.

MacArthur's selection process for his field army and corps commanders was different from Eisenhower's. Most obviously, he did not want anyone who might horn in on his limelight. MacArthur for instance relegated Eichelberger to training duties in Australia after Eichelberger's victory at Buna made him famous enough to threaten to overshadow MacArthur's role in the war against Japan. Indeed, MacArthur procured Krueger for the Sixth Army in part because he knew that the no-nonsense and publicity-averse Krueger would stay in the background. Other than this peculiarly MacArthurian standard, MacArthur tended to choose his senior ground forces commanders strictly on the basis of his firsthand observation of their performance. He cared little about an officer's educational attainments, World War One combat experience, character, or personality. Instead, he and Krueger looked to elevate to the corps level aggressive division commanders within their theater who had proven themselves in independent missions. Although MacArthur accepted Marshall's offer of Eichelberger and Hall to lead the First and Eleventh corps early in the war, he did so because he did not yet have any division commanders who met his criteria. Once he possessed a cadre of battle-experienced division leaders, though, MacArthur put the best ones in charge of his corps. Marshall probably would not have considered promoting Swift and Sibert, but MacArthur gave them their own corps because he felt that they had fought well, respectively, in the Admiralties and at Lone Tree Hill. Similarly, MacArthur was willing to give Eichelberger the Eighth Army as a reward for his fine performances at Hollandia and Biak. On the other hand, Bill Gill's timidity at Aitape convinced MacArthur and Krueger to leave him with the Thirty-second Division. Later on, before the intended invasion of Japan, MacArthur acquiesced to all the European War generals Marshall suggested, except for Bradley, because doing otherwise would have thoroughly disrupted planning.

Considering the collaborative nature of these personnel decisions, it was not surprising that the men who received these assignments came from a variety of places and circumstances. Although all three of the army group commanders were promoted from within their theaters, only Bradley had previously led a corps and field army in combat. Clark had experience at the field army level, but Devers had held only administrative posts—albeit important ones—before he moved up to the Sixth Army Group. Of the ten men who led field armies into action, only four of them—Bradley, Eichelberger, Patton, and Truscott—had battle experience with corps. Buckner, Hodges, Krueger, and Simpson all came directly from assignments in the western hemisphere. Clark was already in the Mediterranean theater when Eisenhower put him in charge of the Fifth Army, but he had never led a corps or division. A similar situation prevailed with the corps commanders. Fifteen of them deployed overseas without ever seeing action with divisions: Anderson, Cook, Crittenberger, Dawley, Eichelberger, Fredendall, Gerow, Gillem, Griswold, Haislip, Hall, Milburn, Millikin, Patton, and Walker. Indeed,

Marshall sent Milburn and Millikin overseas in late 1944 because Eisenhower did not believe he had enough quality division commanders to do the job. Three others—Bradley, Keyes, and Lucas—were elevated to corps from within the Mediterranean theater after serving as deputies first. None of them, though, had commanded a division in combat. Only fourteen cut their teeth with divisions before taking over corps. Of these, ten were promoted from within their theater: Brooks, Eddy, Huebner, McLain, Patch, Ridgway, Sibert, Swift, Truscott, and Van Fleet. The other four—Collins, Corlett, Hodge, and Middleton—were transferred from divisions in one theater to corps in another.

Of the thirty-eight officers who led army groups, field armies, and corps into significant action during the war, fourteen of them, or more than a third, were removed from their commands for one reason or another. Although this might seem like evidence that American generals performed poorly in the conflict, a closer look at the details indicates that this was not the case. Of the fourteen who lost their jobs, six of them—Bradley, Clark, Eichelberger, Gerow, Patton, and Truscott—were promoted to more important posts. Cook, Eddy, and Patch succumbed to illness, and Buckner was killed at Okinawa. This left five officers who were relieved because of perceived failure on the battlefield: Corlett, Fredendall, Dawley, Lucas, and Millikin. However, a case can be made that wartime politics and personality conflicts rather than bad generalship were more responsible for Corlett's, Dawley's, Lucas's, and Millikin's woes. This means that Fredendall's relief was the only clear-cut example of battlefield defeat. Most of this turnover occurred in the European War partly because the large number of units deployed there provided greater opportunity for advancement, and because the prickly Clark and Hodges were there. On the other hand, seventeen officers led their units from their deployment to combat to the end of the war. For all the personality drama in SWPA, MacArthur did not replace a single field army or corps commander. There was, in short, considerably more stability to the American high command than the numbers would initially indicate.

Evaluating American Commanders

Evaluating the record of the army's World War Two corps, field army, and army group commanders is a thorny and subjective task. The playing field for these men was by no means even and fair. For one thing, there were wide differences in the terrain upon which the officers campaigned and the enemy they faced. The Germans were the more militarily sophisticated and technologically advanced opponent, but they also were willing to surrender when the situation warranted doing so. On the other hand, the Japanese emphasis on fighting to the death made even mopping-up duties inordinately dangerous. While European War generals impressed the public by capturing thousands of German soldiers in the spring of 1945 as they rolled to and beyond the Rhine, a couple of months later Buckner sparked criticism because he had to practically destroy the Japanese garrison on Okinawa in an enormously costly effort to secure the island. In each case it was pretty clear that the enemy had lost the war, but the contrast between the German and the Japanese response to this reality clearly impacted the performance of the American generals involved. Moreover, waging war under adverse topographical conditions also limited the chances of reputation-enhancing victory. Those generals operating in New Guinea's jungles, the Italian mountains, or Okinawa's cramped spaces had much less room to maneuver and gain spectacular and eye-catching triumphs than those clashing in the North African desert or central France. These geographic factors partly explain Patton's success and subsequent fame and Krueger's problems and historical anonymity. In addition, chronology mattered. Those generals who took their units into combat earlier in the conflict, when the enemy was stronger and American troops greener, obviously had a more difficult time than those who deployed later in the war with combat-hardened divisions against a weakened opponent. It is unfair to compare Gerow's and Corlett's experience in Normandy in June 1944 with Van Fleet's in Germany the following spring. Finally, a general's commander helped determine his achievements. It did not matter how accomplished a field army or corps commander was if his superior failed to use him properly and give him chances to excel. Krueger's and Hodges's pedestrian tactics at, respectively, Leyte and the West Wall gave Corlett, Gerow, Hodge, and Sibert little opportunity to shine. Devers and Patch, though, provided their corps commanders with free rein to conduct their battles creatively. These limitations do not excuse a general's poor record—after all, a sign of greatness in any endeavor is overcoming counterproductive circumstances—but they do help to explain them.

Assessing the army's high-ranking combat commanders' World War Two records was more than just an academic exercise because the army needed its best and brightest to lead it into the uncertain postwar era. Marshall certainly saw things that way, and on several occasions and in several ways asked Eisenhower for his opinion of his chief lieutenants. Each time Eisenhower consulted his conscience and various subordinates before rendering his opinion. On 19 January 1945 he explained to Marshall that based on both present performance and future potential, Collins was his best combat commander, with Walker, Eddy, Ridgway, Middleton, and Brooks close seconds. In this instance, Eisenhower gave extra points for youthfulness because Marshall was interested in men who would be around to steer the army through the inevitable problems associated with demobilization and retrenchment. On 1 February 1945, after a meeting with Marshall five days earlier, Eisenhower elaborated and expanded on his evaluation by numerically ranking his chief Army Air Force officers, staffers, logisticians, and combat commanders and writing a short description about each man. This time he gave past performance and future potential equal weight. He rated Bradley first, Patton fourth, Clark fifth, Truscott sixth, Gerow eighth, Collins ninth, Patch tenth, Hodges eleventh, Simpson twelfth, Ridgway sixteenth, Brooks seventeenth, Walker eighteenth, Haislip twenty-second, Devers twenty-fourth, Eddy twenty-fifth, McLain thirty-second, Huebner thirty-fifth, Harmon thirty-sixth, and Van Fleet thirty-seventh. Except for some snide remarks about Devers, almost all his accompanying comments were positive. On 26 March Eisenhower gave Marshall another appraisal, this one limited to his American field army commanders. He placed Patton first but added unhelpfully,

> Patton is a particularly warm friend of mine and has been so over a period of 25 years. Moreover, I think I can claim a proprietary interest in him because of the stand I took in several instances, well known to you, in this war. In certain situations he has no equal, but by and large it would be difficult indeed to choose between him, Hodges and Simpson for army command, while Patch is little, if any, behind the others.[3]

Eisenhower's various assessments were both extensive and problematic. For one thing, they were inconsistent, incomplete, and methodologically hazy. He placed Patch ahead of Hodges and Simpson on his 1 February evaluation, but less than two months later rated him as his least effective field army commander. Walker and Eddy also declined dramatically between these two appraisals, but, as with Patch, Eisenhower offered no reason why. He also failed to mention Gillem, Anderson, and Milburn, probably because he lacked sufficient information to make an informed judgment about them. Indeed, he tended to value most highly those with whom he was in daily contact. Nor did he devote any time to Corlett and Millikin now that they had been relieved. On the other hand, Clark and Truscott got scored even though they were in the Mediterranean theater, but not Keyes and Crittenberger. Eisenhower claimed that he based his estimations on past performance and future potential, but beyond that he never clearly explained exactly what criteria he used. Instead, he offered a brief description of each officer that was, with the exception of Devers, invariably positive. It is unclear why Eisenhower felt that Brooks was a better corps commander than Haislip when the former was a "magnetic; courageous; balanced corps commander" and the latter was a "fine Corps CG [commanding general], fighter, cool." Moreover, Eisenhower's thinking was hardly objective and considered; his prejudices and personal preferences came through loud and clear. He scored Gerow ahead of all other corps commanders except for Collins and put Devers at twenty-fourth with some accompanying unkind words. Finally, it is likely that Eisenhower was simply too far removed from the field army and corps commanders to make accurate pronouncements. This is not to say that Eisenhower's reviews are worthless, but rather that they should be taken with a grain of salt.

Eisenhower was not the only high-ranking general who fought in northwestern Europe to assess his subordinates. On 1 December 1944, before the Battle of the Bulge and the drive to and beyond the Rhine, Bradley at Eisenhower's behest ranked his chief lieutenants in the following order: Hodges third, Truscott fifth, Patton sixth, Collins seventh, Gerow eighth, Clark ninth, Middleton fourteenth, Patch fifteenth, Simpson sixteenth, Eddy eighteenth, Haislip nineteenth, Corlett twentieth, Devers twenty-first, Walker twenty-third, Brooks twenty-fourth, McLain twenty-fifth, Huebner twenty-ninth, Harmon thirtieth, Ridgway thirty-first, and Van Fleet thirty-second. As with Eisenhower's calculations, Bradley provided no justifications for his rating system. It was also filled with some of the same prejudice and illogic that marked Eisenhower's appraisals. Most obviously, Bradley evaluated Devers, Clark, and Patch even though these men had never served under him, meaning that his observations were based mostly on reputation and hearsay. As the war came to an end in Europe, Eisenhower and Bradley discussed personnel with some of their field army chiefs. Patton rated Walker as his finest combat commander at the corps level, but added that Middleton was a better all-around soldier. It was no secret that Hodges valued Collins over his other corps commanders. Simpson placed Gillem first among his corps commanders, with McLain and Anderson a close second and third. Patch told Eisenhower that although Haislip had the most exemplary record of his corps commanders, Milburn during his comparatively short tenure with the Seventh Army had impressed him more. All the field army commanders, though, believed that they had the best corps commanders in the army, which is perhaps the greatest tribute they could have given.[4]

Marshall seemed less interested in personnel in other theaters, perhaps because the bulk of the army's high-ranking combat leaders were deployed to northwestern Europe. Nevertheless, some of these commanders voiced their opinions about their chief lieutenants. Clark never clarified which of his corps commanders he preferred—or, more accurately, his evaluations fluctuated depending on the battlefield situation—but Truscott did so after he took over the Fifth Army. Toward the end of the conflict he noted that although he valued both Keyes and Crittenberger, he rated the latter as the better corps commander. MacArthur's frequent denunciations of Krueger's generalship to Eichelberger did not prevent him from giving Krueger the toughest assignments. If he played Krueger and Eichelberger off against each other, he could do so and still continue to win battles only because he recognized that both men were accomplished officers. In all likelihood, MacArthur understood that Krueger and Eichelberger each performed best under certain circumstances and increasingly tailored his plans to accommodate their strengths. As for his corps commanders, MacArthur was more forthcoming. He told Marshall that he rated Griswold first and Hall second. Eichelberger seemed to prefer Griswold first, and made it clear that he ranked Sibert last. Krueger by and large appeared to dislike all his corps commanders. Ironically, the only one he praised much was Eichelberger; he commended him for his performances at Hollandia and especially Biak, and recommended his promotion to lead the Eighth Army.

The army produced two clearly outstanding corps commanders: J. Lawton Collins and Lucian Truscott. Collins's case is the more obvious. He fought skillfully in both defensive and offensive operations during his eventful tenure as head of the Seventh Corps. Under Collins's determined leadership the Seventh Corps landed at Utah beach, stormed Cherbourg, spearheaded Cobra, stymied the German counterattack at Mortain, marched across France, battled with more success than any other First Army outfit along the West Wall, shattered the tip of the German counteroffensive toward the Meuse at the Battle of the Bulge, seized Cologne during its push to the Rhine, and helped seal the Ruhr Pocket. Marshall, Eisenhower, Bradley, Ernie Harmon, Middleton, Richardson, and of course Hodges all praised him. Even those who denigrated him—Patch and Patton, most prominently—did so because they disliked his brash and cocky personality, not because they questioned his generalship. Truscott's record was almost as impressive. Truscott fought adroitly with his Sixth Corps at Anzio and the capture of Rome, the invasion of southern France, and the drive to the Belfort Gap. Throughout it all he displayed an aggressive and can-do attitude that won the praise of Marshall, Eisenhower, Bradley, Devers, and Lucas. Truscott had his detractors too—Clark called him a prima donna and Patton thought he was somewhat overrated—but most observers regarded him as a superb combat officer.

There were also several corps commanders who fought very well for a comparatively long time under both predictable and adverse circumstances, but did not quite rise to Collins's and Truscott's level. These include Eddy, Eichelberger, Middleton, and Walker. Eichelberger led the First Corps to victory in miserable circumstances at Buna, and then went on to success at Hollandia and Biak. He was one of the few high-ranking Pacific War generals who showed much tactical finesse. MacArthur, Sutherland, and even Krueger praised his actions, overlooked the bitterness and paranoia and self-pity he occasionally displayed, and recommended his promotion to lead the Eighth Army. Brooks, Eddy, Haislip, Middleton, and Walker all had long track records too, and all saw their share of desperate combat—Eddy and Middleton at the Battle of the Bulge, Eddy and Walker in Lorraine, and Brooks and Haislip in Alsace during Operation Nordwind. Neither Eisenhower nor Bradley rated them especially highly, but Devers, Patton, and Patch were closer to the scene and knew better.

The majority of corps commanders fought capably, but either did not have the chance to display the consistent brilliance that characterized Collins and Truscott or made at least one mistake that blighted their records. Some promising officers, such as Cook and Van Fleet, did not lead their corps long enough to demonstrate their abilities. Although others performed well in an operation or even two, they did not have the time or opportunity to build sufficiently impressive résumés as corps commanders to merit a high rating. This was especially true of Ridgway. The Battle of the Bulge was his only occasion to show what he could do at the corps level, and after that his assignments were comparatively simple or unimportant because of the difficulties in employing airborne units. Others saw plenty of combat, but not in the desperate circumstances that characterized and distinguished Collins at Mortain, Truscott at Anzio, and Middleton in the Battle of the Bulge. Anderson, Bradley, Crittenberger, Gillem, Griswold, Huebner, Keyes, McLain, and Milburn all carried out most of their offensive operations effectively, but did so against an outnumbered and outgunned enemy. For example, it is hard to criticize Griswold's actions at New Georgia, Bougainville, and even Luzon, but in each instance victory was mostly a matter of time due to overwhelming American materiel superiority. This was also the case with Crittenberger and Keyes in Italy, Bradley in North Africa and Sicily, and Anderson and Gillem and McLain in the drive to the Rhine River. There was nothing easy about their engagements, but success required mostly the kind of calm professional competence that these men possessed. Finally, there were several corps commanders who, while not losing any battles, made serious errors or simply did not consistently live up to their billing. These include Corlett, Gerow, Hall, Hodge, Lucas, Patch, Patton, Sibert, and Swift. Hall, Hodge, Patch, Sibert, and Swift attained their objectives, but demonstrated little tactical imagination in doing so. Indeed, Sibert was unique in that his efficiency seemed to decline as time went on, perhaps due to poor health. For all his subsequent fame and glory, in Tunisia Patton failed to achieve any important breakthroughs and alienated a good many of his officers and men with his abusive and bizarre behavior. Corlett, Gerow, and Lucas had not exactly set the world on fire even before they ran afoul of the West Wall and Anzio.

Lastly, there were a small number of corps commanders who failed at their jobs: Dawley, Fredendall, and Millikin. Fredendall's case is the most obvious. No doubt Fredendall faced enormous problems in Tunisia—green troops, logistical constraints, interallied squabbles, etc.—but his abrasive personality exacerbated these difficulties. The subsequent Kasserine Pass fiasco cost him the Second Corps and ended his active participation in the conflict. Dawley and Millikin were also relieved of their commands at, respectively, Salerno and the Remagen bridgehead. Both Patton and Hodges had been dissatisfied with Millikin even before the Ninth Armored Division crossed the Rhine, so his relief was the result of accumulated sins compounded by a starchy personality. Although many have argued that Dawley was not responsible for the close call at Salerno, it is equally true that he did not display much dynamic leadership there either.

In the field army category, Patton and Eichelberger stand out as the army's best in, respectively, the European and Pacific wars. It is, however, important to differentiate between Patton's unpredictable and counterproductive behavior with the Seventh Army in Sicily and his more disciplined and beneficial actions in northwestern Europe with the Third Army. As Bradley later noted, the slapping incidents and the resulting consequences forced Patton to take a good hard look at himself and reevaluate his conduct. The Patton that emerged in northwestern Europe in 1944 was a far more mature, self-controlled, reflective, and thoughtful version of the one in the Mediterranean. Fortunately, he retained his old aggressiveness, intelligence, and resourcefulness. Patton exploited the Cobra breakthrough, drove across central France, clawed his way through Lorraine, launched a counterattack to stop the Germans at the Battle of the Bulge, and pushed to the Rhine and into Germany. In these operations he exhibited ample amounts of initiative, forcefulness, and dexterity. Indeed, he never took counsel of his fears. With the possible exception of Simpson, no field army commander got more out of his subordinates. Whereas intimidation, accusation, and abuse characterized his interpersonal relations with his lieutenants in Sicily, in northwestern Europe he used praise, forgiveness, and encouragement to inculcate his war-making philosophy in others. He assured his corps commanders that he would not punish them for sins of commission, so they did not fear losing their jobs because of one well-intentioned mistake. It is therefore no coincidence that some of the army's best corps commanders—Eddy, Haislip, Middleton, and Walker—served under him.

As for Eichelberger, his success at the field army level rested upon his virtuoso performance in liberating the central and southern Philippines in 1945 in an amphibious blitzkrieg. If the campaign was strategically worthless, this was not Eichelberger's fault. Like Patton, Eichelberger waged his war with considerable tactical flexibility, often operated on a logistical shoestring, and showed no fear of enemy intentions or capabilities. He also used his genial and freewheeling personality with his subordinates—as opposed to the paranoia he often displayed toward Krueger and GHQ—to create and instill loyalty among his combat commanders and staffers so that the Eighth Army became one of the happiest units in SWPA. Small wonder that so many of the Pacific War division commanders looked forward to working with him.

Bradley, Krueger, Patch, Simpson, and Truscott were all capable field army commanders who amassed solid, though not brilliant, records during the war. Bradley led the First Army from D-Day to Cobra. Patch and his Seventh Army landed in southern France, pushed rapidly to the German border, engaged in heavy combat in Alsace with minimal assistance from Eisenhower's headquarters, and then participated in the offensive to the Rhine and into southern Germany. Truscott's Fifth Army shattered the German Gothic Line in Italy, and Simpson's Ninth Army saw extensive action at Brest and in the Rhineland before spearheading the Allied offensive into central Germany. As for Krueger, his Sixth Army fought in complicated amphibious operations in New Guinea, Leyte, and Luzon. Eisenhower lauded Patch, Simpson, Truscott, and especially Bradley for their performances. Clark, on the other hand, was more subdued about Truscott's role as Fifth Army commander, but this was mostly due to personality clashes. MacArthur undermined his public praise for Krueger by damning his alleged timidity behind closed doors as a Machiavellian ploy to play Krueger and Eichelberger off against one another.

Military success aside, these five officers were very different men in personality, character, and methods. Patch was enigmatic and shy, Krueger abrasive and outspoken, Bradley folksy and reassuring, Simpson balanced and friendly, and Truscott forceful and forthright. Although Patch exhibited excessive caution with the Fourteenth Corps at Guadalcanal, as a field army commander he was perhaps the most aggressive of the five. Krueger for his part waged war carefully, but he had the additional burden of serving under MacArthur in complex assaults that required considerable interservice coordination against die-hard Japanese defenders in the most primitive parts of the globe. Indeed, Krueger probably faced greater and more varied challenges than any other field army commander. This mitigates some of the criticisms MacArthur and others leveled against him. Bradley, Simpson, and Truscott used encouragement to motivate and inspire their subordinates, which won their loyalty and paid big dividends on the battlefield. Patch was more distant, and by the end of the war Krueger's bluntness and criticism had alienated practically everyone who worked under him. Despite their dissimilarities, all these generals shared a thorough understanding of army doctrine, willingly subordinated their egos for the greater good, and recognized the capabilities of the troops they controlled.

Finally, Buckner, Clark, and Hodges all emerged from the war with average records as field army commanders. They were not failures by any means; all three completed most of their missions and possessed an aggressiveness and sturdiness that enabled them to deal with crises at Salerno, during the Battle of the Bulge, and on Okinawa. Unfortunately, they also had some shortcomings that limited their effectiveness. While on Okinawa, an inexperienced Buckner resorted to unimaginative frontal assaults that contributed to the Tenth Army's heavy casualties in the campaign. There may have been no way to seize the island without excessive losses, but Buckner was unwilling to experiment with alternative tactics. By the time he was killed he had lost the confidence of MacArthur, Stilwell, and other high-ranking officers in the Pacific, though in all fairness these men were hardly objective in their evaluations.

Clark was a prima donna who often seemed interested more in furthering his own career than in attaining victory. He sacrificed Dawley and Lucas at Salerno and Anzio rather than accept some responsibility for the Allied problems in these landings, threw away the chance to destroy the German army in Italy in order to gain glory from seizing Rome, undermined the Allied coalition by repeatedly denigrating the British contribution to the Italian campaign, and displayed considerable fickleness toward his corps commanders. Although Eisenhower and Marshall were aware of some of Clark's less admirable traits, they chose to focus on his forcefulness, organizational skills, and administrative ability instead. Clark's corps and division commanders were also cognizant of his weaknesses, and most of them never really warmed to him.

As for Hodges, his tactics were, like Buckner's, relatively straightforward. His poor health and sour disposition hindered his efficiency, especially during the fighting along the West Wall and in the first days of the Battle of the Bulge. With the exceptions of Collins and Ridgway, he treated his subordinates poorly. It is no coincidence that some of the war's more mediocre corps commanders—Corlett, Gerow, Millikin—served under Hodges. Marshall, Eisenhower, and Bradley thought the world of Hodges, but their personal affinity seemed to blind them to his flaws. Whatever the First Army's accomplishments as Eisenhower's workhorse outfit, it deserved a better commander.

Of the three American army group commanders, Bradley emerged from the conflict with the greatest reputation. Marshall praised his virtues, Eisenhower rated him as his best subordinate, and almost all of his field army, corps, and division commanders respected his abilities. Bradley was in many respects the quintessential American army World War Two general in that he practiced the American way of war, with all its attributes and flaws, as well as anyone. In his campaigns he waged war professionally, dispassionately, thoughtfully, practically, and flexibly. It was his Twelfth Army Group that oversaw the most powerful field armies, operated in the center of Eisenhower's long line during the fighting in northwestern Europe, and engaged in the army's greatest battles. He broke new ground as the first American army group commander of the war. In this role he built an enormous headquarters and interfered down to the division level. Despite his willingness to relieve subordinates for their failings, he brought to his post a humanity, modesty, and intelligence that made his lieutenants eager to do their best for him. As for Clark, by the time he became the head of the Fifteenth Army Group, the Italian campaign had become peripheral to the war effort. Moreover, most of the important combat in Italy had ended by the time he ascended to the Fifteenth Army Group, making his tenure somewhat anticlimactic and of less importance than his service with the Fifth Army. Finally, Devers has often been unfairly denigrated as an army group commander in large part because of Eisenhower's and Bradley's hostility. In fact, he was just as capable and amassed just as impressive a record as Bradley with an army group. No doubt Devers was glib and supremely confident, but it is hard to argue with the results he achieved in northwestern Europe. Devers led his Sixth Army Group through the invasion of southern France, the drive to the Belfort Gap, the bitter struggle in Alsace, the German counteroffensive in Operation Nordwind, and the push to and beyond the Rhine into southern Germany. The war might have ended sooner had Eisenhower taken advantage of the opportunity Devers developed to cross the Rhine in the autumn of 1944. Devers attained his objectives despite limited resources, a small staff, the indifference and hostility of his superior, and the presence within his command of an occasionally recalcitrant French field army that interpreted orders as requests. He succeeded in part because he acquired talented lieutenants, such as Brooks, Haislip, Milburn, Patch, and Truscott, in whom he had unlimited confidence. Although Eisenhower criticized him for not reducing the Colmar Pocket quickly enough, he also exaggerated its danger as a way of discrediting Devers. Devers's aggressiveness, common sense, and insight enabled him to perform just as ably as Bradley.

Although the record of the army's corps, field army, and army group commanders was largely good, it is possible to criticize their performance in the conflict. The army's combat leaders often seemed excessively cautious and overly reliant on materiel superiority to achieve victory. Such criticisms, though, must be placed in context; army officers labored under innumerable limitations. The army had to share scarce resources with the navy and marines, the Army Air Force, and industry and agriculture. As a result, the army fielded only eighty-nine divisions to wage war across two oceans. The infantry in particular received the least-educated people to bear the brunt of the fighting and dying. Small wonder that observers on both sides noted that American riflemen seemed reluctant to take the initiative, but instead relied on artillery and air support to destroy the Germans and Japanese. However, the army must be viewed holistically, not by its individual components. Whatever its shortcomings in the infantry, the army compensated for them with its superb artillery, air power, logistical support, and firepower. Taken together, the United States fielded the greatest and most powerful army the world had ever seen, one that won its war only three years after committing large forces to action. The army did not need brilliant generals who performed miracles on the battlefield, but rather competent men capable of taking advantage of American economic power to apply army doctrine effectively and with minimal losses. Fortunately, Marshall and his lieutenants succeeded in identifying and using these men to win the war.

Biographical Afterword

John B. Anderson retired from the army in 1946, but had trouble adjusting to civilian life until he got a job with some Washington investment bankers. In the summer of 1947 he wrote to Simpson, "Since my retirement I have found time hanging rather heavy on my hands and it was a great relief to again be occupied with something that is both interesting and instructive. If at any time you are in the market for securities of any kind, I shall be happy to have an opportunity to handle your purchases and sales."[1] He died in 1976.

Omar Bradley, after overhauling and reforming the Veterans Administration, succeeded Eisenhower as army chief of staff in 1948 and was a year later appointed chairman of the Joint Chiefs of Staff. He stayed in that position throughout the Korean War and retired in 1953. In 1950 he became the last officer promoted to the rank of general of the army. Bradley subsequently served as one of the "wise men" who advised President Lyndon Johnson on the Vietnam War, and was also a consultant for the film *Patton.* He died in 1981.

Edward Brooks found victory bittersweet because his only son died in an airplane crash in Germany shortly after the European War ended. Brooks returned to the States and served successively as head of the Fourth Service Command from 1945 to 1947, as assistant chief of staff for personnel from 1949 to 1951, and finally as commander of the Second Army from 1951 until his retirement in 1953. He died in 1978.

Mark Clark served as high commissioner for Austria from 1945 to 1947, commander of Sixth Army from 1947 to 1949, and head of the Army Field Forces from 1949 to 1952. He then succeeded Matthew Ridgway as supreme commander in East Asia for the last year of the Korean War before retiring in 1953. He subsequently became president of the Citadel from 1954 to 1960, and died in 1984.

J. Lawton Collins became the army's director of information from 1945 to 1947, deputy chief of staff from 1947 to 1949, and finally chief of staff from 1949 to 1953, during the Korean War. Afterward he served as the United States representative to the North Atlantic Treaty Organization's military committee and a special representative to South Vietnam from 1954 to 1955. He retired in 1956 and died in 1987.

Charles Corlett retired in 1946 and eventually wrote his memoirs, which according to

Bradley indicated that he still had a chip on his shoulder years after the war ended. He died in 1971.

Gilbert Cook served on a variety of army boards after the war and retired in 1948. The army periodically called him back to help critique war games in the late forties and early fifties. He died in 1963.

Willis Crittenberger was appointed head of the Caribbean Defense Command from 1945 to 1948. He subsequently served as American representative to the Inter-American Defense Board and then First Army commander before he retired in 1952. Crittenberger not only lost a son along the Rhine, but another one was killed in a helicopter crash in the Vietnam War. Crittenberger died in 1980.

Ernest Dawley commanded the Tank Destroyer Center until the end of the European War, after which he became head of the Ground Force Reinforcement Command. He retired in 1947 and died in 1973.

Jacob Devers was appointed commander of army ground forces after the war. He retired in 1949 and died thirty years later.

Manton Eddy managed to get his high blood pressure under sufficient control to succeed Gerow as commandant of the Command and General Staff School in 1948. Two years later he became first deputy of the American European Command and then commander of the Seventh Army. He retired in 1953 and died in 1962.

Robert Eichelberger oversaw the military occupation of Japan as Eighth Army commander until his retirement in 1948. In subsequent years he became increasingly embittered with MacArthur, Krueger, and Sutherland, scribbling his grievances down in copious notes. He died in 1961.

Dwight Eisenhower worked as army chief of staff from 1945 to 1948, president of Columbia University from 1948 to 1950, and supreme Allied commander in Europe from 1950 to 1952 before returning to America to run as the Republican candidate for president in 1952. After defeating Adlai Stevenson, Eisenhower served two terms in an administration characterized by restraint and moderation. He published his memoirs after leaving office and died in 1969.

Lloyd Fredendall served as deputy commander, and then commander, of the stateside Second Army after Eisenhower sent him home from North Africa. He led the Second Army until the end of the European War and retired in 1946. Fredendall died in 1963.

Leonard Gerow was appointed commandant of the Command and General Staff School after the war, and also chaired a board that studied and made recommendations on army education. In 1948 he became commander of the Second Army. He retired in 1950 and died in 1972.

Alvan Gillem commanded the Seventh Corps from 1945 to 1946 and the Third Army from 1947 until his retirement in 1950. He also chaired the 1945 Gillem Board that recommended giving black Americans greater opportunities in the army. After his retirement to Georgia he served four years as executive director of the National Foundation for the March of Dimes. He died in Atlanta in 1973.

Oscar Griswold commanded the Fourth Division from 1945 until his retirement in 1947. He died in 1959.

Wade Haislip subsequently served as commander of the Seventh Army in 1945, president of the secretary of war's personnel board from 1945 to 1946, senior member of the chief of staff's advisory group from 1946 to 1948, deputy chief of staff for administration from 1948 to 1949, and finally vice chief of staff from 1949 to 1951. After he retired he became governor of the Soldier's Home in Washington for fifteen years and died in 1971.

Charles Hall retired in 1948 and died three years later.

Ernest Harmon led the army constabulary in Europe after the war and then became deputy commander of Army Ground Forces from 1947 until his retirement in 1948. He subsequently became president of Norwich University from 1950 to 1965. He died in 1979.

Millard Harmon, after the Solomons campaign, became Army Air Force commander in the Pacific Ocean Area until his plane disappeared over the Marshall Islands in February 1945.

John Hodge received the unenviable job of occupying southern Korea and overseeing its transition from Japanese protectorate to divided country, a task for which he was temperamentally unsuited. He left the peninsula in 1948 and subsequently became commander of the Fifth Corps from 1948 to 1950, the Third Army from 1950 to 1952, and finally the Army Field Forces from 1952 to 1953. He retired in 1953 and died in Washington, D.C., ten years later.

Courtney Hodges remained in command of the First Army after it returned to the States until his retirement in 1949. He died in 1966 in Texas.

Clarence Huebner served as chief of staff of American forces in the European Theater from

1946 to 1947 and then deputy commander of the European Command until his retirement in 1950. He died in 1972.

Geoffrey Keyes commanded the Third Army in 1946–1947 and then became American high commissioner on the Allied council for Austria. He retired in 1950 and died in 1967.

Walter Krueger retired in 1946 to San Antonio, Texas. Unhappily, his last years were full of strife and woe. Because he owed back taxes from the war, he and his wife were able to afford a house only through the financial generosity of friends. His son was dismissed from the army for drunkenness, and his daughter suffered a mental breakdown and killed her husband, an army colonel, with a ten-inch knife. These events, as well as his wife's death in 1956, shattered Krueger. When one officer complained that he had not been promoted, Krueger wrote to him:

> I wish you would compare your situation with mine for a moment. You are fortunate in having a loving wife by your side and three wonderful children. I, on the other hand, have lost my precious wife, my son Jimmie's career ended in disgrace and my only daughter's tragic action broke my heart. All the promotions and honors that have come to me cannot possibly outweigh these heartaches and disappointments. If true happiness is the aim of life—and I believe it is—then you are more fortunate than I and I would gladly trade with you.[2]

He eventually found solace in work and travel, and died in 1967.

John Lucas served as deputy commander of the Fourth Army after returning to the States. As time went on he became increasingly bitter about Clark's actions at Anzio. He was chief of the Army Advisory Group in Nanking, China, when he died in 1949.

Douglas MacArthur oversaw Japan's surrender, occupation, and rehabilitation with an imperiousness that appealed to the Japanese character. When communist North Korea invaded South Korea in June 1950, MacArthur became supreme commander of all United Nations forces sent to defend South Korea. He turned the war's tide with his daring amphibious assault at Inchon, but was caught by surprise when the Chinese intervened in the war and drove the United Nations troops out of North Korea. MacArthur's public and strident calls to expand the war into China conflicted with President Harry Truman's desire to limit the conflict and concentrate on the Soviet threat in Europe. Truman relieved him of his command in May 1951 because MacArthur refused to keep his opinions to himself. MacArthur returned home to a tumultuous welcome from an American public sympathetic to his simple and dramatic solutions. He gave a famous speech before Congress in which he said, "Old soldiers don't die, they just fade away." In subsequent congressional hearings, however, the American military establishment lined up against MacArthur and discredited his ideas. He died in 1964.

George Marshall retired as chief of staff in 1945, but his career as a reluctant public servant was just beginning. President Truman shortly thereafter dispatched him to China in a long and ultimately unsuccessful effort to negotiate a peace between the Chinese Nationalists and Communists. Upon his final return in 1947, Truman appointed him secretary of state. During his tenure at Foggy Bottom the United States enacted the Truman Doctrine and the Marshall Plan to rehabilitate Western Europe and protect it from communism. When Truman needed a strong secretary of defense to meet the challenges posed by the Korean War, he turned to Marshall. An increasingly ill and tired Marshall held the post for a year. In 1953 President Dwight Eisenhower sent Marshall to England as the United States representative to Queen Elizabeth II's coronation. As Marshall walked up the aisle at Westminster Abbey and took his seat, the audience stood up in a spontaneous sign of respect. A puzzled Marshall looked around to see what dignitary had entered, unaware that the crowd was honoring him. He died in 1959.

Raymond McLain stayed in the army after the war as assistant chief of information and then as chief of information from 1946 to 1949. He subsequently served as the army's comptroller until his retirement in 1952. He died two years later.

Troy Middleton returned to Louisiana State University after the war first as comptroller from 1945 to 1950 and then as president from 1951 to 1962. He also served on innumerable federal and state advisory boards. He died in 1976.

Frank Milburn led the Fifth Corps from 1945 to 1946 and the First Division from 1946 to 1949, and was deputy commander of American forces in Europe from 1949 to 1950. He then commanded the First Corps through some of the worst fighting in the Korean War from 1950 to 1951 before retiring a year later. Counting stateside assignments during World War Two, Milburn had the distinction of commanding five different corps during his career. After retirement he coached basketball and football at Rocky Mountain College in Colorado for a time, and he died in 1962.

John Millikin ended the war as commander of the Thirteenth Armored Division. He retired in 1948 and died in 1970.

Alexander Patch was appointed commander of the Fourth Army in Texas at the end of the war. His poor health was aggravated by excessive drinking, and he died of pneumonia in November 1945.

George Patton paid for his outspokenness at the cost of his Third Army command when he embarrassed Eisenhower by defending the use of former Nazis to help govern occupied Germany. He died in an automobile accident in December 1945.

Robert Richardson retired in 1946 and died while visiting Rome in 1954.

Matthew Ridgway served as military adviser to the American delegation to the United Nations from 1946 to 1948 and then as deputy chief of staff for administration. He replaced Walton Walker as Eighth Army commander in Korea in December 1950 after Walker's death. He became the unsung hero of the war by restoring Eighth Army morale and stopping the Chinese offensive. He replaced Douglas MacArthur as supreme American commander in East Asia in May 1951 and became supreme commander of Allied forces in Europe the following year. President Eisenhower appointed Ridgway army chief of staff in 1953, but Ridgway clashed repeatedly with the Eisenhower administration over military policy and retired in 1955. In the 1960s he warned against deep military involvement in Vietnam and wrote his memoirs. He died in 1993 at age ninety-eight.

Franklin Sibert retired in 1946, moved to Florida, and died in 1980.

William Simpson took over the Second Army at the end of the war until his retirement in 1946. He and his wife were unable to have children, so after the war they adopted a ten-year-old girl. He died in 1980.

Walter Bedell Smith had a distinguished postwar career that included serving as ambassador to the Soviet Union from 1946 to 1949 and director of the Central Intelligence Agency from 1950 to 1953. He retired in 1954 and died seven years later.

Joseph Stilwell led the Western Defense Command and then the Sixth Army right after the war. He died of stomach cancer in 1946.

Innis Palmer Swift retired in 1946 and died seven years later.

Richard Sutherland retired from the army in 1946. He reconciled with his wife after confessing his affair to her. He died in 1966.

Lucian Truscott took over the Third Army after Patton's relief and remained in Germany until his retirement. He died in 1965.

James Van Fleet served first as deputy commander of the First Army and then as deputy chief of staff for the European Command. In 1948 he was appointed head of the military advisory mission to Greece and Turkey as part of the new Truman Doctrine. Van Fleet played a decisive role in helping the Greek government defeat the communist insurgency. For this reason he was selected to succeed Ridgway as Eighth Army commander in Korea. He ably repelled the ferocious Chinese attack in the spring of 1951 and then pushed northward into North Korea before truce talks brought his offensive to a halt. He retired in 1953, served as a counterinsurgency consultant to the Kennedy administration, and died in 1992.

Walton Walker served as head of the Eighth Service Command from 1945 to 1946 and then the Fifth Army from 1946 to 1948. In 1948 he assumed command of the Eighth Army in Japan. When communist North Korea invaded South Korea two years later, Walker led the American forces sent to defend South Korea. Despite an unhappy relationship with MacArthur, the supreme commander in East Asia, Walker successfully defended the Pusan Perimeter in late summer 1950 from North Korean assault. After the Inchon landing changed the course of the conflict, the Eighth Army pushed into North Korea. Walker was killed in a jeep accident near Seoul in December as his troops retreated southward in response to Chinese intervention in the war.

Notes

ABBREVIATIONS

ASOOH	*Armed Forces Oral Histories: Army Senior Officer Oral Histories*
DDEL	Dwight D. Eisenhower Library, Abilene, Kansas
DMMA	Douglas MacArthur Memorial Archives, Norfolk, Virginia
EP	*The Papers of Dwight David Eisenhower, The War Years*
MP	*The Papers of George Catlett Marshall*
USAHEC	United States Army Heritage and Education Center, Carlisle, Pennsylvania

INTRODUCTION

1. Most of the information about Roanoke during the war comes from Clare White, *Roanoke: 1740–1982* (Roanoke, VA: Roanoke Valley Historical Society, 1982), 104–107.

2. The students of Lillian Craig's class to George Marshall, 2 March 1944, *MP*, vol. 4, 345n.

3. For good discussions of Roosevelt's selection of Marshall, see Mosley, *Marshall,* 125–128; Mark A. Stoler, *Marshall: Soldier–Statesman of the American Century* (Boston: Twayne Publishers, 1989), 60–67. For Marshall's view of his appointment, see Marshall, interview by William Spencer, 9 July 1947, George C. Marshall Foundation, 3–4.

4. Omar Bradley and Clay Blair, *A General's Life: An Autobiography by General of the Army Omar N. Bradley and Clay Blair* (New York: Simon and Schuster, 1983), 63.

5. The quote is from ibid., 205. For Marshall's daily routine and habits, see Marshall to Henry Woodring, 8 October 1941, *MP*, vol. 2, 633; Marshall to Roy Keehn, 2 February 1941, *MP*, vol. 3, 96. For other evaluations, both good and bad, of Marshall by his contemporaries, see J. Lawton Collins, *Lightning Joe: An Autobiography* (Baton Rouge: Louisiana State University Press, 1979), 48–50; Bradley and Blair, *General's Life,* 65; Lucian Truscott, *Command Missions: A Personal Story* (New York: E. P. Dutton, 1954), 22, 383; George Patton diary, 7 October 1944, *The Patton Papers, 1940–1945,* vol. 2, ed. Martin Blumenson (Boston: Houghton Mifflin, 1974), 563; Dwight Eisenhower to Spencer Ball Akin, 19 June 1942, *EP,* vol. 1, 338–339; Albert Wedemeyer, interview by Anthony Deskis, 7 February 1973, USAHEC, section 4, 41–42; Harry Butcher, 7 September 1972, *Three Years with Eisenhower: The Personal Diary of Captain Harry C. Butcher, USNR, Naval Aide to General Eisenhower, 1942 to 1945* (London: William Heinemann, 1946), 79; William Gill, as told to Edward Jaquelin Smith, *Always a*

Commander: The Reminiscences of Major General William H. Gill (Colorado Springs: Colorado College, 1974), 30–31; Dwight Eisenhower, *Crusade in Europe* (New York: Doubleday, 1948), 40; Dwight Eisenhower, *At Ease: Stories I Tell to Friends* (Garden City, NY: Doubleday, 1967), 248; Jacob Devers, interview by Maclyn Burg, 2 July 1975, DDEL, 33; Roscoe Woodruff, interview by Maclyn Burg, 16 March 1972, DDEL, 48; Thomas Handy, interview by Maclyn Burg, 22 May 1973, DDEL, 148–154; Handy interview, 18 December 1975, DDEL, 232; John Edwin Hull, interview by James Wurman, 4 December 1973, *ASOOH,* section 3, 35; Hull interview, 22 February 1974, *ASOOH,* section 6, 37; John Edwin Hull, *The Autobiography of General John Edwin Hull, 1895–1975* (M. Anderson, 1978), 110–111; Henry Matchett, interview by Thomas Soapes, 22 July 1976, DDEL, 33; Maxwell Taylor, *Swords and Plowshares* (New York: W. W. Norton, 1972), 37, 40; Chester Hansen diary, 7 October 1944, Hansen Papers, USAHEC, box 4; Katherine Tupper Marshall, *Together: Annals of an Army Wife* (New York: Tupper Love, 1946), 9, 67–68, 109–110; Troy Middleton, interview by Orley B. Caudill, 1975, An Oral History with Troy H. Middleton, Mississippi Oral History Collection, University of Southern Mississippi, 54; William Leahy, *I Was There: The Personal History of the Chief of Staff to Presidents Roosevelt and Truman Based on His Notes and Diaries Made at the Time* (New York: McGraw-Hill, 1950), 191–192; Johnson Hagood, "General George Catlett Marshall," in *These Are the Generals* (New York: Alfred A. Knopf, 1943), 17; Charles H. Corlett, *The Autobiography of Major General Charles H. Corlett*, ed. William Farrington (Santa Fe, NM: Sleeping Fox Enterprises, 1974), 106–107; Leonard Gerow, interview by Forest Pogue, 24 March 1958, Marshall Foundation, 41.

6. Marshall, 21 June 1943, "Transcript of Off-The-Record Remarks to the Governors' Conference," *MP,* vol. 4, 33.

7. Marshall to the students of Miss Craig's class, 15 March 1944, *MP,* vol. 4, 345; Eisenhower, *Crusade in Europe,* 34–35; Katherine Tupper Marshall, *Together,* 9; George Marshall, interview by Forest Pogue, 14 February 1957, *George C. Marshall Interviews and Reminiscences for Forest C. Pogue* (Lexington, VA: George C. Marshall Research Foundation, 1991), 452.

8. Marshall to the students of Miss Craig's class.

9. The quote is from Eisenhower, *Crusade in Europe,* 35. See also Katherine Tupper Marshall, *Together,* 9.

10. Eisenhower, *Crusade in Europe,* 317.

11. Matthew Ridgway, *Soldier: The Memoirs of Matthew B. Ridgway* (New York: Harper and Brothers, 1956), 27.

12. For a critique of the Command and General Staff School in particular, see Timothy Nenninger, "Leavenworth and Its Critics: The U.S. Army Command and General Staff School, 1922–1940," *Journal of Military History* 58 (April 1994): 199–231. See also Gary Wade, *CSI Report No. 5: Conversations with General J. Lawton Collins* (Fort Leavenworth, KS: Combat Studies Institute), 2; Henry Stimson diary, 27 October 1941, Henry Lewis Stimson Diaries, Yale University Library, reel 7, vol. 35, 165–166; Frank James

Price, *Troy H. Middleton: A Biography* (Baton Rouge: Louisiana State University Press, 1974), 91–92; Hull interview, 4 December 1973, *ASOOH*, 8.

13. Marshall to Kenyon Joyce, 30 March 1942, *MP*, vol. 3, 152–153.

14. Gill, *Always a Commander*, 30. As things turned out, Gill beat the odds and ended up leading the Thirty-second Division in the Pacific War.

15. Marshall to Ralph Immell, 14 September 1939, *MP*, vol. 2, 57; Marshall to George Lynch, 19 July 1940, ibid., 272; Marshall to Walter Grant, 7 July 1941, ibid., 561; Marshall to Walter Wilson, 7 October 1941, ibid., 632; Marshall to Theater Commanders, 16 January 1942, *MP*, vol. 3, 67; Marshall to Lesley McNair, 1 October 1942, ibid., 377–378; Stimson diary, 27 October 1941, Stimson Diaries, reel 7, vol. 35, 165–166; Joseph Stilwell diary, 21 January 1942, *The Stilwell Papers,* ed. Theodore White (New York: William Sloane, 1948), 27; Mark Skinner Watson, *Chief of Staff: Prewar Plans and Preparations* (Washington, DC: Government Printing Office), 245–246; Marshall to McNair, 1 December 1942, Marshall Foundation, National Archives Project, Verifax 3334.

16. Marshall to Douglas MacArthur, 14 April 1943, DMMA, RG-4, reel 594.

17. Marshall to Eisenhower, 20 March 1944, *MP*, vol. 4, 356–357.

18. Marshall to McNair, 1 December 1942, Marshall Foundation, National Archives Project, Verifax 3334.

19. Ridgway, *Soldier*, 18.

20. Although there are biographies for several corps, field army, and army group commanders, most of them have not been studied in depth.

21. Eisenhower, *At Ease*, 253.

22. For example, see John Ellis, *Brute Force: Allied Strategy and Tactics in the Second World War* (New York: Viking, 1990) and Max Hastings, *Overlord: D-Day and the Battle for Normandy* (New York: Simon and Schuster, 1984).

CHAPTER 1: STOPPING THE JAPANESE OFFENSIVE

1. Handy, interview by D. Clayton James, 8 September 1971, James Collection, DMMA, RG-49, box 3, 25–26.

2. Robert W. Coakley and Robert M. Leighton, *Global Logistics and Strategy, 1943–1945* (Washington, DC: Government Printing Office, 1968), 836.

3. Walter Krueger to MacArthur, 30 May and 2 July 1944, DMMA, RG-4, reel 593; Robert Eichelberger to his wife, 18 December 1944, *Dear Miss Em: General Eichelberger's War in the Pacific, 1942–1945,* ed. Jay Luvaas (Westport, CT: Greenwood Press, 1972), 179.

4. For accounts of MacArthur's trip from Corregidor to Australia, see William Manchester, *American Caesar: Douglas MacArthur, 1880–1964* (New York: Dell Publishing, 1978), 296–313; Geoffrey Perret, *Old Soldiers Never Die: The Life of Douglas MacArthur* (New York: Random House, 1996), 276–284. For MacArthur's demeanor, see Paul P. Rogers, *The Good Years: MacArthur and Sutherland* (New York: Praeger, 1990), 198–202.

5. Joseph Swing, interview by James, 26 August 1971, James Interviews, USAHEC, 27–28.

6. Quoted in Michael Schaller, *Douglas MacArthur: The Far Eastern General* (New York: Oxford University Press, 1989), 74. For some views on MacArthur's character and personality, both positive and negative, see Eichelberger to his wife, 24 November 1942, 24 January, 17 November, and 18 December 1944, *Dear Miss Em,* 31–32, 90, 168, 179; Eichelberger's dictations, *Dear Miss Em,* 64–65; George Marshall, 29 October 1956, *George C. Marshall Interviews and Reminiscences for Forest C. Pogue* (Lexington, VA: George C. Marshall Research Foundation, 1991), 608–609; William Gill, as told to Edward Jaquelin Smith, *Always a Commander: The Reminiscences of Major General William H. Gill* (Colorado Springs: Colorado College, 1974), 46–49; Dwight Eisenhower, *At Ease: Stories I Tell to Friends* (Garden City, NY: Doubleday, 1967), 213–214; Hull interview, 21 February 1974, *ASOOH,* section 6, 10; John Edwin Hull, *The Autobiography of General John Edwin Hull, 1895–1975* (M. Anderson, 1978), 103; Barksdale Hamlett, interview by Jack Ridgway and Paul Water, 23 January 1976, *ASOOH,* section 1, 69–70; Griswold diary, 3 March 1945, Griswold Papers, USAHEC, box 1; Handy, interview by Edward Knoff Jr., 22 April 1974, Handy Papers, USAHEC, vol. 2, section 4; George Decker, interview by Dan H. Ralls, 9 November 1972, USAHEC, interview 2, 20–21; Wedemeyer interview, USAHEC, section 4, 41–42; Harold Riegelman, *Caves of Biak: An American Officer's Experiences in the Southwest Pacific* (New York: Dial Press, 1955), 51; Daniel Barbey, *MacArthur's Amphibious Navy: Seventh Amphibious Force Operations, 1943–1945* (Annapolis, MD: United States Naval Institute, 1969), 21–22, 24–25; George C. Kenney, *General Kenney Reports: A Personal History of the Pacific War* (Washington, DC: Air Force Historical Studies Office, 1997), 31; Rogers, *Good Years,* 203; Bonner Fellers, interview by James, 26 June 1971, D. Clayton James Interviews, Mitchell Memorial Library, Mississippi State University, 10–11, 23.

7. Richard Marshall, interview by James, 27 July 1971, James Interviews, 8.

8. The quote is from Kenney, *Kenney Reports,* 26. See also Eisenhower to MacArthur, 9 April 1942, *EP,* vol. 1, 235. For views of Sutherland, see Eichelberger to his wife, 30 December 1942, 30 December 1944, 15 January 1945, *Dear Miss Em,* 49, 188, 195; Roger Olaf Egeberg, *The General: MacArthur and the Man He Called "Doc"* (New York: Hippocrene Books, 1983), 40–41; Paul P. Rogers, *The Bitter Years: MacArthur and Sutherland* (New York: Praeger, 1990), 148, 150; Rogers, *Good Years,* 231, 233–237; Weldon E. (Dusty) Rhoades, *Flying MacArthur to Victory* (College Station: Texas A&M University Press, 1987), 202–203, 262–264; MacArthur to Marshall, 3 February 1944, DMMA, RG 4, reel 594; Clyde Eddleman, interview by L. G. Smith and M. G. Swinder, 28 January 1975, USAHEC, section 2, 23–24; Swing interview, 26 August 1971, James Interviews, USAHEC, 23; Richard Marshall interview, 27 July 1971, James Interviews, 8–12; Woodruff, 8 September 1971, ibid., 26; Thomas Kinkaid, 10 July 1961, *The Reminiscences of Thomas Cassin Kinkaid* (Columbia University: Oral History Research Office, 1961), 365.

9. Eichelberger, "Some Thoughts about Sutherland and Krueger," Robert L. Eichelberger Papers, Perkins Library, Duke University, box 73, 570–577.

10. Henry Stimson diary, 22 November 1944, The Henry Lewis Stimson Diaries, Yale University Library, reel 9, vol. 49, 44.

11. Omar Bradley and Clay Blair, *A General's Life: An Autobiography by General of the Army Omar N. Bradley and Clay Blair* (New York: Simon and Schuster, 1983), 70; Marshall to MacArthur, 10 August 1942, *MP,* vol. 3, 296–297; Marshall to MacArthur, 8 September 1944, ibid., vol. 4, 578; Marshall, 21 November 1956 and 11 April 1957, *Marshall Interviews and Reminiscences,* 244–245, 376–377; Hull interview, 21 February and 8 April 1974, *ASOOH,* sections 6–7, 23, 34; Rogers, *Bitter Years,* 61; Rogers, *Good Years,* 230; Handy interview, 22 April 1974, Handy Papers, USAHEC, vol. 2, section 4, 37–39; Perret, *Old Soldiers,* 108–111; Clovis Byers diary, 26 January 1944, Clovis Byers Collection, Hoover Institution Archives, Stanford University, box 36, folder 1.

12. Kinkaid, 10 April 1961, *Kinkaid Reminiscences,* 85–86.

13. Marshall to McNair, 6 October 1942, *MP,* vol. 3, 388–389; Eisenhower to Robert Richardson, 16 May 1942, DMMA, RG-4, reel 593; MacArthur to Marshall, 2 and 7 July 1942, ibid., reel 593; Marshall to MacArthur, 7, 22, and 30 July 1942, ibid., reel 593; MacArthur to Richardson, 7 July 1942, ibid., reel 593; Richardson to MacArthur, 10 July, 3 and 9 August 1942, ibid., reel 593.

14. The quote is from Eichelberger to his wife, 15 August 1942, *Dear Miss Em,* 26. See also Marshall to McNair, 27 March 1942, *MP,* vol. 3, 151–152; Marshall to Eichelberger, 25 June 1942, ibid., 250–251; Eisenhower to George Patton, 29 July 1942, *EP,* vol. 1, 426–427; Robert L. Eichelberger, with Milton MacKaye, *Our Jungle Road to Tokyo* (New York: Viking Press, 1950), xv–xvi; Rogers, *Good Years,* 317; Marshall to MacArthur, 7 and 30 July, 1 and 3 August 1942, DMMA, RG-4, reel 593; Joseph Stilwell diary, 16 January 1942, *The Stilwell Papers,* ed. Theodore White (New York: William Sloane, 1948), 26; Byers diary, 3 August 1942.

15. Byers diary, 17 March 1944.

16. For views of Eichelberger, see Gill, *Always a Commander,* 51; Riegelman, *Caves of Biak,* 171–172, 274; James Collins, interview by Wade Hampton, 1983, USAHEC, section 2, 8, 39; Douglas MacArthur, *Reminiscences: General of the Army Douglas MacArthur* (New York: McGraw-Hill, 1964), 157; Barbey, *MacArthur's Amphibious Navy,* 27; William Arnold, interview by Warren Stumpe, August and September 1975, *ASOOH,* 146–147, 250–251; Clovis Byers to Emma Eichelberger, 30 May 1944, Eichelberger Papers, Duke University, reel 45, correspondence 1943–1944; Rogers, *Bitter Years,* 47; Griswold diary, 3 March 1945, Griswold Papers, USAHEC, box 1; Richard Marshall interview, 27 July 1971, James Interviews, 7–8; Eddleman interview, 29 June 1971, ibid., 25; Charles Willoughby, interview by James, 30 July 1971, ibid., 11–12; Woodruff interview, 8 September 1971, ibid., 20; Roscoe Woodruff, "The World War Two," Roscoe Woodruff Papers, DDEL, 3.

17. Willoughby interview, 20 July 1971, James Interviews, 11–12.

18. Eichelberger to his wife, 3, 9, 22, 24 November 1942, *Dear Miss Em,* 28–32; MacArthur, *Reminiscences,* 157; Rogers, *Good Years,* 326; Richard Marshall interview, 27 July 1971, James Interviews, 14; Byers diary, 1 October and 16 November 1942.

19. Rogers, *Good Years,* 336.

20. For some various accounts of the meeting, see Eichelberger, dictations, *Dear Miss Em,* 32–33; Eichelberger to V. L. Peterson (unsent), 19 January 1943, ibid., 62; Eichelberger, *Jungle Road,* 20–22; Eichelberger to Chauncy Fenton (unsent), 20 October 1943, Eichelberger Papers, Duke University, reel 45, correspondence 1943–1944. See also Rogers, *Good Years,* 336; Kenney, *Kenney Reports,* 157–158; Byers diary, 30 November 1942.

21. Eichelberger to Peterson (unsent), 19 January 1943, *Dear Miss Em,* 62.

22. Ibid., 61; Eichelberger to his wife, 5, 29, and 31 December 1942, 1 January 1943, ibid., 40, 49–50; Eichelberger to Fenton (unsent), 20 October 1943, Eichelberger Papers, Duke University, reel 45, correspondence 1943–1944; Rogers, *Bitter Years,* 48–49, 56, 198; Rogers, *Good Years,* 431.

23. Eichelberger, *Dear Miss Em,* 65.

24. Barbey, *MacArthur's Amphibious Navy,* 27.

25. Ibid., 169–170; Rogers, *Bitter Years,* 48–49; MacArthur to Marshall, 23 August 1943, DMMA, RG-4, reel 494; Marshall to MacArthur, 25 August 1943, ibid., reel 594; MacArthur to Eichelberger, 8 January 1943, *Dear Miss Em,* 51–53; Peterson to Eichelberger, 10 February 1943, Eichelberger Papers, Duke University, reel 44, correspondence 1943–1944; Eddleman interview, 28 January 1975, USAHEC, section 2, 20.

26. The quote is from Byers to Emma Eichelberger, 9 February 1944, Eichelberger Papers, Duke University, reel 45, correspondence 1943–1944. For examples of Eichelberger's frame of mind, see Eichelberger to his wife, 22 March, 11 April, 30 May, 15 and 18 July, 4 and 10 August, 22 September, 26 November , 11–12 December 1943, 7 January 1944, *Dear Miss Em,* 67–68, 70–72, 74, 80, 82–83, 87; Barbey, *MacArthur's Amphibious Navy,* 169–170; Eichelberger to his wife, 30 September and 28 October 1943, Eichelberger Papers, Duke University, reel 44, correspondence 1943–1944; Rogers, *Bitter Years,* 77–78.

27. MacArthur to Marshall, 26 August 1943, DMMA, RG-4, reel 594.

28. For the Marshall/MacArthur debate over Eichelberger's future, see Marshall to John DeWitt, 17 March 1943, *MP,* vol. 3, 590; Eichelberger to his wife, 15 May, 10 August, 23 and 29 December 1943, *Dear Miss Em,* 68, 84–85; Eichelberger to his wife, 1 June, 19 and 30 August, 22 October 1943, Eichelberger Papers, Duke University, reel 44, correspondence 1943–1944; Eichelberger to Fenton (unsent), 20 October 1943, Eichelberger Papers, Duke University, reel 45, correspondence 1943–1944; Eichelberger to his wife, 26 January 1944, Eichelberger Papers, Duke University, reel 45, correspondence 1943–1944; Marshall to MacArthur, 25 August and 20 December 1943, DMMA, RG-4, reel 594; MacArthur to Marshall, 21 December 1943, ibid., reel 594; Byers diary, 18 May, 29 September, and 22 December 1943; McNair to Marshall, 30 March 1943, Marshall Foundation, reel 305, item 4646.

29. Egeberg, *MacArthur and the Man He Called "Doc,"* 126–127.

30. MacArthur, *Reminiscences,* 170; Rogers, *Bitter Years,* 17–18; MacArthur to Marshall, 11 and 16 January 1943, DMMA, RG-4, reel 594; Eddleman interview, 29 June 1971, James Interviews, 24.

31. Bruce Palmer, interview by James Shelton and Edward Smith, 1976, USAHEC, 326.

32. Byers diary, 10 June 1944.

33. For views of Krueger, see Marshall, *Marshall Interviews and Reminiscences,* 578; Decker interview, 9 November 1972, USAHEC, interview 2, 10–11, 19–21, 31–32; J. Lawton Collins, *Lightning Joe: An Autobiography* (Baton Rouge: Louisiana State University Press, 1979), 112; Gill, *Always a Commander,* 38, 84; James Collins interview, 1983, USAHEC, 40; Dwight D. Eisenhower, *Crusade in Europe* (New York: Doubleday, 1948), 11; William Chase, *Front Line General: The Commands of Maj. Gen. Wm. C. Chase* (Houston: Pacesetter Press, 1975), 26–27; Barbey, *MacArthur's Amphibious Navy,* 27, 151; Malin Craig to Eichelberger, 7 May 1943, Eichelberger Papers, Duke University, reel 44, correspondence 1943–1944; Eichelberger to his wife, 1 June 1943, ibid.; William Arnold interview, July and August 1975, *ASOOH,* 190; Eisenhower to Eichelberger, 3 January 1944, Eichelberger Papers, Duke University, reel 45, correspondence 1943–1944; Rogers, *Bitter Years,* 34–35, 93; Eddleman interview, 15 April 1975, USAHEC, section 4, 10; William Gill interview, n.d., Gill Papers, USAHEC, box 1, tape 3, 11; Swing interview, 26 August 1971, Swing Papers, James Interviews, USAHEC, 22–23, 28; Fellers interview, 26 June 1971, James Interviews, 20–21; Richard Marshall interview, 27 July 1971, ibid., 9; Eddleman interview, 29 June 1971, ibid., 26; Willoughby interview, 30 July 1971, ibid., 11; Woodruff interview, 8 September 1971, ibid., 18–20, 22; Eichelberger dictations, Eichelberger Papers, box 73, 570–577; Gerow interview, 24 August 1958, Marshall Foundation, 61; Robert S. Allen, *Lucky Forward: The History of Patton's Third U.S. Army* (New York: Vanguard Press, 1947), 9–14.

34. Marshall to Stanley Embrick, 1 May 1940, *MP,* vol. 2, 206; Marshall to Woodring, 22 May 1940, ibid., 219–220; Marshall to Krueger, 14 April 1941, ibid., 473–474; Krueger to Marshall, 20 April 1941, ibid., 474n; Marshall to Henry Stimson, 3 May 1941, ibid., 492–493; Marshall, *Marshall Interviews and Reminiscences,* 578; Alfred Gruenther, interview by Ed Edwin, 20 April 1967, DDEL, 2–4; Eisenhower to Gruenther, 20 February 1943, *EP,* vol. 2, 995; Stimson diary, 19 January 1943, Stimson Diaries, reel 8, vol. 41; Walter Krueger, *From Down Under to Nippon: The Story of the Sixth Army in World War II* (Washington, DC: Combat Forces Press, 1953), 3–4; Eddleman interview, 28 January 1975, USAHEC, section 2, 20–21; McNair to Marshall, 7 October 1941, George Marshall Papers, Marshall Foundation, box 76, folder 31.

35. Eichelberger to his wife, 6 March 1944, *Dear Miss Em,* 94–95.

36. The quote is from MacArthur, *Reminiscences,* 170. See also Decker interview, 9 November 1972, USAHEC, interview 2, 18, 20–21, 31–32; Krueger, *From Down Under,* 10; Rogers, *Bitter Years,* 17–18, 34–35, 55, 153, 245; Eddleman interview, 11 February

1975, USAHEC, section 3, 11; Eddleman interview, 29 June 1971, James Interviews, 24; Eichelberger to his wife, 31 May, 21 August 1943, 1 June 1944, *Dear Miss Em,* 70, 74, 118.

37. Marshall to Millard Harmon, 14 September 1942, Marshall Papers, Marshall Foundation, Pentagon Office, box 70.

38. Henry Arnold diary, 16 September 1942, *American Airpower Comes of Age: General Henry H. "Hap" Arnold's World War II Diaries,* ed. John Huston (Maxwell Air Force Base, AL: Air University Press, 2002), vol. 1, 380; Henry Arnold, *Global Mission* (New York: Harper and Brothers, 1949), 337; Memorandum for Franklin Roosevelt, 8 February 1943, Marshall Foundation, reel 305, item 4646.

39. Stimson diary, 11 May 1943, Stimson Diaries, reel 8, vol. 43, 33–34.

40. The quote is from Lucian Truscott, *Command Missions: A Personal Story* (New York: E. P. Dutton, 1954), 383. For other opinions of Patch, see William K. Wyant, *Sandy Patch: A Biography of Lt. Gen. Alexander M. Patch* (New York: Praeger, 1991), 58–59; Collins, *Lightning Joe,* 145–147; Marshall, 21 November 1956, *Marshall Interviews and Reminiscences,* 370; Stimson diary, 11 May 1943, Stimson Diaries, reel 8, vol. 43; J. Lawton Collins, interview by Charles Sperow, 1972, USAHEC, 113–114; Devers interview, 18 August 1974, DDEL, 43; Jean Joseph Marie Gabriel De Lattre de Tassigny, *The History of the French First Army*, trans. Malcolm Barnes (London: George Allen and Unwin, 1952), 53; Devers diary, 27 September and 1 November 1944, 6 June 1945, Devers Papers, USAHEC; George Patton, *War As I Knew It* (Boston: Houghton Mifflin, 1947), 255.

41. Wyant, *Sandy Patch,* 40–44, 62; Marshall to Alexander Patch, 19 March 1943, *MP,* vol. 3, 596; Stimson diary, 22 July 1942, Stimson Diaries, reel 7, vol. 39; Arnold, 24 September 1942, *Arnold Diaries,* vol. 1, 392; McNair to Marshall, 10 September 1941, Marshall Papers, Marshall Foundation, Pentagon Office, box 76, folder 31; John Miller Jr., *Guadalcanal: The First Offensive* (Washington, DC: Historical Division, Department of the Army, 1949), 213.

42. Millard Harmon to Marshall, 25 November 1942, Marshall Papers, Marshall Foundation, Pentagon Office, box 70, folder 6.

43. Collins, *Lightning Joe,* 145–147.

44. The quote is from William Halsey and J. Bryan III, *Admiral Halsey's Story* (New York: Da Capo Press, 1976), 148. See also Marshall to Patch, 19 March 1943, *MP,* vol. 3, 596.

45. Quoted in Wyant, *Sandy Patch,* 58–59.

46. Ibid., 64, 71–72; Marshall to Patch, 19 March 1943, *MP,* vol. 3, 596; Marshall, 21 November 1956, *Marshall Interviews and Reminiscences,* 370; J. Lawton Collins interview, 1972, USAHEC, 113–114; Devers interview, 2 July 1975, DDEL, 181; Eichelberger to his wife, 20 May 1943, Eichelberger Papers, Duke University, reel 44, correspondence 1943–1944; Millard Harmon to Marshall, 25 November 1942, Marshall Papers, Marshall Foundation, Pentagon Office, box 70; Marshall, interview with Sidney Matthews, et al., 25 July 1949, Marshall Foundation, interview 3, part 2, 3; Richard B. Frank, *Guadalcanal*

(New York: Random House, 1990), 571; Devers, interview by Pogue, 12 August 1958, Marshall Foundation, 59–60.

47. Wyant, *Sandy Patch,* 71–72; Marshall to Patch, 19 March 1943, *MP,* vol. 3, 596; Patch to Marshall, 2 April 1943, ibid., 596n.

48. For information on Griswold and Marshall's decision to appoint him Fourteenth Corps commander, see John Kennedy Ohl, *Minuteman: The Military Career of General Robert S. Beightler* (Boulder, CO: Lynne Rienner Publishers, 2001), 120–121; Eichelberger, *Jungle Road,* 91; William Arnold interview, July and August 1975, *ASOOH,* 204; James Van Fleet, interview by Bruce Williams, 20 January 1973, Van Fleet Papers, USAHEC, vol. 1, box 1, 44–45; McNair to Marshall, 10 July and 7 October 1941, Marshall Papers, Marshall Foundation, Pentagon Office, box 76, folder 31; Gill, *Always a Commander,* 84, 106; Marshall to MacArthur, 7 and 30 July 1942, DMMA, RG-5, reel 593; Memorandum for Roosevelt, 20 October 1945, Marshall Foundation, reel 349, item 5226; Millard Harmon to Handy, 10 September 1943, Marshall Foundation, National Archives Project, Verifax 2054.

49. John Miller Jr., *Cartwheel: The Reduction of Rabaul* (Washington, DC: Historical Division, Department of the Army, 1959), 76.

50. Griswold diary, 24 July 1943, Griswold Papers, USAHEC, box 1.

51. William Arnold interview, July and August 1975, *ASOOH,* 111–112; Griswold diary, 25 April, 7–8 May, 25 July 1943, Griswold Papers, USAHEC, box 1; Harold R. Winton, *Corps Commanders of the Bulge: Six American Generals in the United States Army* (Lawrence: University Press of Kansas, 2007), 55.

52. The quote is from Eichelberger to his wife, 14 December 1943, Eichelberger Papers, Duke University, reel 45, correspondence 1943–1944. See also Griswold diary, 4–9, 16–19, 23 November 1943, Griswold Papers, USAHEC, box 1; Byers diary, 6 and 9 November 1943; Marshall to Millard Harmon, 6 August 1943, Marshall Papers, Marshall Foundation, Pentagon Office, box 70, folder 7; Millard Harmon to Handy, 10 September 1943, Marshall Foundation, National Archives Project, Verifax 2054.

53. William Arnold interview, July and August 1975, *ASOOH,* 123–124, 129.

54. Millard Harmon to Handy, 17 May 1944, Marshall Foundation, National Archives Project, Verifax 2184.

55. MacArthur to Marshall, 9 July 1944, DMMA, RG-4, reel 594.

56. Marshall to William Halsey, 3 April 1944, *MP,* vol. 4, 385; Marshall to Joseph Stilwell, 4 September 1944, ibid., 570–571; Marshall to MacArthur, 5 July 1944, DMMA, RG-4, reel 594.

CHAPTER 2: THE NORTH AFRICAN CAMPAIGN

1. Eisenhower to his son, 31 January 1944, *EP,* vol. 3, 1700.

2. Dwight Eisenhower, *At Ease: Stories I Tell to Friends* (Garden City, NY: Doubleday, 1967), 248–249. However, Eisenhower told his son that he said, "I don't care what you do. You broke my heart when you pulled me away from troops and brought me to

Washington. You can't do anything more to me." See John Eisenhower, *General Ike: A Personal Reminiscence* (New York: Free Press, 2003), 82.

3. Quoted in Leonard Mosley, *Marshall: Hero for Our Times* (New York: Hearst Books, 1982), 188.

4. George C. Marshall, 29 October 1956 and 15 February 1957, *Marshall Interviews and Reminiscences for Forest C. Pogue* (Lexington, VA: George C. Marshall Research Foundation, 1991), 470, 611; Walter Krueger, *From Down Under to Nippon: The Story of the Sixth Army in World War II* (Washington, DC: Combat Forces Press, 1953), 4; McNair to Marshall, 7 October 1941, Marshall Papers, George C. Marshall Foundation, Pentagon Office, box 76, folder 31; Mark Clark, *Calculated Risk* (New York: Harper and Brothers, 1950), 16–17; Gerow interview, 24 February 1958, Marshall Foundation, 31.

5. Eisenhower, *At Ease,* 248.

6. Ibid., 195, 224, 238; Eisenhower to Akin, 19 June 1942, *EP,* vol. 1, 338–339.

7. Eisenhower to Marshall, 3 June 1942, *EP,* vol. 1, 327; Eisenhower notes, 8 June 1942, ibid., 333; Eisenhower to Akin, 19 June 1942, ibid., 338–339; Harry Butcher, 26 January 1943, *Three Years with Eisenhower: The Personal Diary of Captain Harry C. Butcher, USNR, Naval Aide to General Eisenhower, 1942 to 1945* (London: William Heinemann, 1946), 213–214; Henry Stimson diary, 15 June 1942, The Henry Lewis Stimson Diaries, Yale University Library, reel 7, vol. 39, 151–152; Dwight Eisenhower, *Crusade in Europe* (New York: Doubleday, 1948), 50; Clark, *Calculated Risk,* 20.

8. For impressions of Eisenhower, see J. Lawton Collins, *Lightning Joe: An Autobiography* (Baton Rouge: Louisiana State University Press, 1979), 114; Omar Bradley and Clay Blair, *An Autobiography by General of the Army Omar N. Bradley and Clay Blair* (New York: Simon and Schuster, 1983), 131–133; Charles H. Corlett, *Cowboy Pete: The Autobiography of Major General Charles H. Corlett,* ed. William Farrington (Santa Fe, NM: Sleeping Fox Enterprises, 1974), 88; Lucian Truscott, *Command Missions: A Personal Story* (New York: E. P. Dutton, 1954), 21–22, 24; Marshall, 15 November 1956, *Marshall Interviews and Reminiscences,* 346; Butcher, 10 December 1942 and 13 May 1943, *Three Years with Eisenhower,* 189–190, 259; Francis De Guingand, *Generals at War* (London: Hodder and Stoughton, 1964), 192–193; Omar Bradley, *A Soldier's Story* (New York: Henry Holt, 1951), 206; William Simpson, interview by Maclyn Burg, 15 March 1972, DDEL, 13; Gruenther interview, 20 April 1967, ibid., 2–4, 20, 35; Woodruff interview, 16 March 1972, ibid., 1, 16–17; Lyman Lemnitzer, interview by David Berliner, 21 November 1972, Columbia University, 24; James Gavin, interview by Ed Edwin, 20 January 1967, Columbia University (at DDEL), 17; Hobart Gay, interview by Willard Wallace, 1981, *ASOOH,* 59; Thomas Betts, interview by Maclyn Burg, 18 October 1973, DDEL, 35–36; Troy Middleton interview, interview by Orley B. Caudill, 1975, An Oral History with Troy H. Middleton, Mississippi Oral History Collection, University of Southern Mississippi, 52–54; William M. Hoge, *Engineer Memoirs* (Washington, DC: Office of History, U.S. Army Corps of Engineers, 1993), 45.

9. Eisenhower to Patton, 29 July 1942, *EP*, vol. 1, 426–427; Eisenhower, *At Ease,* 252; Handy interview, 22 April 1974, USAHEC, vol. 2, section 4, 31.

10. Marshall to Eisenhower, 28 September 1942, Marshall Papers, Marshall Foundation, Pentagon Office, box 66, folder 43.

11. Eisenhower to Vernon Prichard, 27 August 1942, *EP*, vol. 1, 505–506.

12. Eisenhower notes, 10 December 1942, *EP*, vol. 2, 824; Eisenhower to Gerow, 24 February 1943, ibid., 987; Eisenhower to his son, 22 May 1943, ibid., 1152; Eisenhower, *Crusade in Europe,* 40–41; Bradley, *Soldier's Story,* 100; Gavin interview, 20 January 1967, Columbia University (at DDEL), 117.

13. Marshall to Clark, 16 February 1940, *MP*, vol. 2, 160; Marshall to Lloyd Fredendall, 1 July 1942, *MP*, vol. 3, 264; Marshall, 14 February 1957, *Marshall Interviews and Reminiscences,* 465; Eisenhower to Marshall, 3 June 1942, *EP*, vol. 1, 327; Clark, *Calculated Risk,* 20; Devers interview, 4 February 1975, DDEL, 119–120; Clark, interview by John Luter, 4 January 1970, ibid., 2–3; Second Corps War Diary, n.d., Clark Diaries and Correspondence, Mark W. Clark Papers, Daniel Library, The Citadel, vol. 1; Devers interview, 12 August 1958, Marshall Foundation, 70–71.

14. Collins, *Lightning Joe,* 102; Bradley and Blair, *General's Life,* 203–204; Carl McCardle, "Lieutenant General Mark Wayne Clark," in *These Are the Generals* (New York: Alfred A. Knopf, 1943), 89; George Patton's diary, 28 September and 21 October 1942, *The Patton Papers, 1940–1945*, vol. 2, ed. Martin Blumenson (Boston: Houghton Mifflin, 1974), 87, 92–93; Eisenhower to Patton, 29 July 1942, *EP*, vol. 1, 425–426; Eisenhower to Marshall, 17 August, 3 and 29 October 1942, ibid., 478, 591–592, 639–642; Butcher, 19 July 1942, *Three Years with Eisenhower,* 20; Eisenhower, *Crusade in Europe,* 76; Clark, *Calculated Risk,* 39–40, 58; Devers interview, 4 February 1975, DDEL, 119–120, 183; Handy interview, 22 May 1973, ibid., 147; Robert Wood, interview by William Naras Jr., 21 February 1974, *ASOOH,* section 3, 30, 39–41; Second Corps War Diary, 5 July, 11, 12, 13 August 1942, Clark Diaries and Correspondence, vol. 1; Roscoe Woodruff, "The World War Two," Woodruff Papers, DDEL, 8; Eisenhower, 11 June 1943, Memorandum for Personal File, A-472, ibid.

15. Bradley and Blair, *General's Life,* 84; Handy interview, 22 May 1973, DDEL, 158–162.

16. Eisenhower to Charles Kenon Gailey Jr., 19 September 1942, *EP*, vol. 1, 568.

17. For information about Smith, see Lord Alanbrooke, 27 July 1944, *War Diaries, 1939–1945,* ed. Alex Danchev and Daniel Todman (Berkeley: University of California Press, 2001), 575; Bradley and Blair, *General's Life,* 69; Marshall to Ernest King, 3 September 1942, *MP*, vol. 3, 342; Patton diary, 9 October 1944, *Patton Papers,* vol. 2, 564; Marshall, 13 November 1956, *Marshall Interviews and Reminiscences,* 627; Charles Bonesteel III, interview by Robert St. Louis, 1973, USAHEC, 136–137; Eisenhower to Walter Bedell Smith, 11 November 1942, *EP*, vol. 2, 693; Butcher, 7, 15, 27, and 30 September 1942, *Three Years with Eisenhower,* 78, 90, 103–104; Eisenhower, *Crusade in Europe,* 54–55; De Guingand, *Generals at War,* 195–196; Bradley, *Soldier's Story,* 30–31;

Ray Barker, interview by Maclyn Burg, 15 July 1972, DDEL, 18–19; Maxwell D. Taylor, *Swords and Plowshares* (New York: W. W. Norton, 1972), 38.

18. Eisenhower to Gerow, 16 July 1942, *EP,* vol. 1, 386; Eisenhower to Marshall, 3 October 1942, ibid., 591; Devers interview, 4 February 1975, DDEL, 143; Second Corps War Diary, 26 September 1942, Clark Diaries and Correspondence, vol. 2; Marshall to Eisenhower, 26 September 1942, *MP,* vol. 3, 367; Marshall to Eisenhower, 28 September 1942, Marshall Papers, Marshall Foundation, Pentagon Office, box 66, folder 43; Gerow interview, 24 September 1958, Marshall Foundation, 33–34; Devers interview, 12 August 1958, Marshall Foundation, 35.

19. McNair to Marshall, 10 September 1941, Marshall Foundation, Pentagon Office, box 76, folder 31.

20. Marshall to Fredendall, 5 May and 1 July 1942, *MP,* vol. 3, 181n, 264; Marshall, 29 October 1956, *Marshall Interviews and Reminiscences,* 616; Eisenhower, *Crusade in Europe,* 83; McNair to Marshall, 7 October 1941, Marshall Foundation, Pentagon Office, box 76, folder 31; Butcher diary, 29 January 1944, Papers Relating to the Allied High Command—1943–45, David Irving Collection, reel 3; Second Corps War diary, 1 and 6 October 1942, Clark Diaries and Correspondence, vol. 2.

21. Marshall to Fredendall, 1 July 1942, *MP,* vol. 3, 264.

22. Mark Murphy, 20 March 1943, "These Are the Generals—Fredendall," *Saturday Evening Post* 215, no. 38:22, 110; Truscott, *Command Missions,* 144–145; Marshall, 29 October 1956, *Marshall Interviews and Reminiscences,* 616.

23. J. Lawton Collins interview, 1972, USAHEC, 161.

24. For views of Patton, see Truscott, *Command Missions,* 60; Marshall, 29 October and 19 November 1956, *Marshall Interviews and Reminiscences,* 547, 607; Bonesteel interview, *ASOOH,* 30–31; Butcher, 9 and 17 August 1942, *Three Years with Eisenhower,* 40–41, 54; Stimson diary, 27 August 1942, Stimson Diaries, reel 7, vol. 40; Ernest N. Harmon, with Milton MacKaye and William Ross MacKaye, *Combat Commander: Autobiography of a Soldier* (Englewood Cliffs, NJ: Prentice-Hall, 1970), 69; Eisenhower, *Crusade in Europe,* 40–41, 82; William Chase, *Front Line General: The Commands of Maj. Gen. Wm. C. Chase* (Houston: Pacesetter Press, 1975), 24; Handy interview, 22 May 1973, DDEL, 54–55; Wood interview, 21 February 1974, *ASOOH,* section 3, 29; Henry Cabot Lodge, *The Storm Has Many Eyes: A Personal Narrative* (New York: W. W. Norton, 1973), 44; Hobart Gay, interview by Willard Wallace, 1981, *ASOOH,* 62; Hull interview, 5 December 1973, *ASOOH,* section 4, 58; John Edward Hull, *The Autobiography of General John Edward Hull, 1895–1975* (M. Anderson, 1978), 67; Hamlett interview, 4 February 1976, *ASOOH,* section 3, 14; Katherine Tupper Marshall, *Together: Annals of an Army Wife* (New York: Tupper Love, 1946), 57; Middleton interview, 1975, Middleton Oral History, 32; Hoge, *Engineer Memoirs,* 227; Matthew Ridgway, interview by John Blair, 15 September 1971, Ridgway Papers, USAHEC, box 89, vol. 1, session 2, 105–106.

25. Collins, *Lightning Joe,* 114; Marshall to Patton, 26 January 1942, *MP,* vol. 3, 85; Patton to Eisenhower, 1 October 1940 and 18 February 1942, *Patton Papers,* vol. 2, 15,

55–56; Marshall, 19 November 1956, *Marshall Interviews and Reminiscences,* 547; Eisenhower to Patton, 20 July 1942, *EP,* vol. 1, 399–400; Eisenhower to Marshall, 17 August 1942, ibid., 478; Butcher, 9 August 1942, *Three Years with Eisenhower,* 40–41; Stimson diary, 26 March 1941, Stimson Diaries, reel 6, vol. 32, 115; Stimson diary, 26 August 1942, Stimson Diaries, reel 7, vol. 40, 33; Eisenhower, *Crusade in Europe,* 40–41, 82; Clark, *Calculated Risk,* 40; McNair to Marshall, 7 October 1941, Marshall Foundation, Pentagon Office, box 76, folder 31; Second Corps War Diary, 11 August 1942, Clark Diaries and Correspondence, vol. 1; Devers interview, 12 August 1958, Marshall Foundation, 57–58.

26. The quote is from Patton diary, 3 November 1942, *Patton Papers,* vol. 2, 97–98. See also Patton diary, 9 and 17 August, 28 September, 21 October 1942, 2 June 1943, ibid., 81–82, 84, 87, 92–93, 258; Patton to Hugh Scott, n.d., ibid., 86; Truscott, *Command Missions,* 59; Butcher, 17 August and 3 October 1942, *Three Years with Eisenhower,* 54, 109; Stimson diary, 26 August 1942, Stimson Diaries, reel 7, vol. 40; Harmon, *Combat Commander,* 66; Eisenhower, *Crusade in Europe,* 82.

27. Robert D. Murphy, *Diplomat among Warriors* (Garden City, NY: Doubleday, 1964), 132.

28. Eisenhower to Marshall, 11 November 1942, *EP,* vol. 2, 690.

29. Patton to Eisenhower, 14 November 1942, *Patton Papers,* vol. 2, 114; Patton diary, n.d., ibid., 126; Eisenhower to Marshall, 10, 11, 17 November 1942, *EP,* vol. 2, 688, 690, 731; Eisenhower to Smith, 11 November 1942, ibid., 693; Eisenhower to his son, 20 November 1942, ibid., 747.

30. Hamilton E. Howze, *A Cavalryman's Story: Memoirs of a Twentieth-Century Army General* (Washington, DC: Smithsonian Institution Press, 1996), 52.

31. For criticisms of Eisenhower and his response, see Alanbrooke, 7 and 28 December 1942, 3 and 20 January 1943, *War Diaries,* 346–347, 351, 355–356, 365; Bradley and Blair, *General's Life,* 133; Marshall to Eisenhower, 22 December 1942, *MP,* vol. 3, 488; Patton to his wife, 3 December 1942, *Patton Papers,* vol. 2, 133; Patton diary, n.d. and 15 January 1943, ibid., 138, 154; Eisenhower notes, 10 December 1942, *EP,* vol. 2, 824–825; Butcher, 26 and 28 January 1943, *Three Years with Eisenhower,* 213–214, 216; Eisenhower, *At Ease,* 261; Marshall interview with Matthews, et al., 25 July 1949, Marshall Foundation, interview 3, part 2, 2; Hughes diary, 24 January 1943, Irving Collection, reel 5.

32. Eisenhower memo, 11 June 1943, Memorandum for Personal File, A-472, Eisenhower Papers, DDEL.

33. Alanbrooke, 3 January 1943, *War Diaries,* 355–356; Patton's diary, 8 and 10 January 1943, *Patton Papers,* vol. 2, 150, 152–153; Eisenhower to Operations Division, 20 November 1942, *EP,* vol. 2, 743; Eisenhower notes, 10 December 1942, ibid., 824–825; Eisenhower to Marshall, 31 December 1942, ibid., 880–881; Eisenhower to Clark, 6 January 1943, ibid., 898–899; Eisenhower to Marshall, 17 January 1943, ibid., 908; Eisenhower memo, 25 February 1943, ibid., 989–990; Eisenhower memo, 22 May 1944,

EP, vol. 3, 1880; Butcher, 1 January 1943, *Three Years with Eisenhower,* 199; Second Corps War diary, 31 December 1942, Clark Diaries and Correspondence, vol. 2; Second Corps War diary, 19 January 1943, Clark Diaries and Correspondence, vol. 3; Eisenhower to Marshall, 27 January 1943, Marshall Papers, Marshall Foundation, Pentagon Office, box 66, folder 47.

34. The quote is from Eisenhower to Marshall, 15 February 1943, *EP,* vol. 2, 956. See also Bradley and Blair, *General's Life,* 135; Patton's diary, 22 November 1942, *Patton Papers,* vol. 2, 128; Truscott, *Command Missions,* 144–146, 151; Eisenhower to Fredendall, 4 February 1943, *EP,* vol. 2, 939–941; Hamilton Howze, interview by Robert Reed, 20 November 1972, *ASOOH,* section 2, 56–57.

35. Truscott, *Command Missions,* 146, 169; Eisenhower to Fredendall, 20 and 22 February 1943, *EP,* vol. 2, 968–969, 982; Fredendall to Eisenhower, 20 February 1943, ibid., 969n; John Waters, interview by William Parnell III, 1980, USAHEC, 590–591; Harmon, *Combat Commander,* 120.

36. Howze interview, 5 February 1973, *ASOOH,* section 3, 48–49.

37. Bradley and Blair, *General's Life,* 135; Harmon, Personal Memoirs of Major General E. N. Harmon, Kreitzberg Library, Norwich University, 45; Eisenhower to Fredendall, 20 and 22 February 1943, *EP,* vol. 2, 968, 982; Howze, *Cavalryman's Story,* 65–66; Corlett, *Cowboy Pete,* 102; Truscott, *Command Missions,* 547–548; William S. Triplet, *A Colonel in the Armored Divisions: A Memoir, 1941–1945,* ed. Robert H. Ferrell (Columbia: University of Missouri Press, 2001), 122–123; Howze interview, 5 February 1973, *ASOOH,* section 3, 48–50.

38. Harmon, *Combat Commander,* 111–119; Howze interview, 5 February 1973, *ASOOH,* section 3, 8–9; Harmon, Personal Memoirs, 70–71, 75.

39. Bradley and Blair, *General's Life,* 128.

40. Ibid., 130–131; Patton diary, 2 March 1943, *Patton Papers,* vol. 2, 177–178; Eisenhower to Marshall, 3 March 1943, *EP,* vol. 2, 1006; Eisenhower to Ernest Harmon, 12 March 1943, ibid., 1026; Butcher, 15 and 16 February 1943, *Three Years with Eisenhower,* 224, 226; Harmon, *Combat Commander,* 120; Bradley, *Soldier's Story,* 31–32.

41. Harmon, *Combat Commander,* 120.

42. Bradley and Blair, *General's Life,* 134.

43. Eisenhower to Gerow, 24 February 1943, *EP,* vol. 2, 987.

44. For criticisms of Fredendall and Eisenhower's decision to remove him, see Eisenhower, *Crusade in Europe,* 150; Bradley and Blair, *General's Life,* 135–137; Truscott, *Command Missions,* 173; Eisenhower to Fredendall, 22 February and 2 March 1943, *EP,* vol. 2, 980–981, 1002–1003; Eisenhower to Marshall, 3 and 4 March 1943, ibid., 1006–1007; Harmon, *Combat Commander,* 120; Bradley, *Soldier's Story,* 39–42; Handy interview, 29 March 1979, DDEL, 298; Eisenhower to Marshall, 3 March 1942, Marshall Papers, Marshall Foundation, Pentagon Office, box 66, folder 49.

45. Truscott, *Command Missions,* 173; Eisenhower to Patton, 6 March 1943, *EP,* vol. 2,

1011; Eisenhower to Marshall, 8 March 1943, ibid., 1016–1017; Butcher, 7 March 1943, *Three Years with Eisenhower,* 234–235; Harmon, *Combat Commander,* 120.

46. Patton diary, 30 November, 2 December 1942, 10, 14, 16, 26 January, 4 March 1943, *Patton Papers,* vol. 2, 129–130, 132, 150, 154, 156, 161–162, 173; Patton to his wife, 3 and 20 December 1942, 19 February 1943, ibid., 133, 141, 172; Patton to Nina Patton, 22 December 1942, ibid., 143; Patton to James Harbord, 30 December 1942, ibid., 144; Butcher, 4 February and 7 March 1943, *Three Years with Eisenhower,* 219, 235.

47. Bradley, *Soldier's Story,* 19–20.

48. The quote is from Collins, *Lightning Joe,* 179–180. See also Marshall, 19 November 1956, *Marshall Interviews and Reminiscences,* 542; Decker interview, 3 November 1972, USAHEC, interview 1, 45–46; Donald Bennett, interview by Smith and Hatcher, 1976, USAHEC, section 1, 71; Waters interview, 1980, USAHEC, 672–674; J. Lawton Collins interview, 1972, USAHEC, 161; Matchett interview, 22 July 1976, DDEL, 27–28; Hamlett interview, 4 February 1976, *ASOOH,* section 3, 15; Theodore Parker, interview by Robert Bavis III, 1983, *ASOOH,* 41; Middleton interview, Middleton Oral History, 52–54; Ernie Pyle, *Brave Men* (New York: Grosset and Dunlap, 1944), 306–312; Hoge, *Engineer Memoirs,* 45, 205, 227; Fred Walker, 25 August 1943, *From Texas to Rome: A General's Journal* (Dallas: Taylor Publishing, 1969), 225.

49. Bradley and Blair, *General's Life,* 63.

50. Ibid., 63, 82–83, 112–113, 131–133, 137–138; Marshall to Hugh Drum, 3 November 1941, *MP,* vol. 2, 661; Marshall to Omar Bradley, 23 December 1942, *MP,* vol. 3, 491; Marshall to Eisenhower, 7 March 1943, ibid., 580; Marshall, 28 September 1956, *Marshall Interviews and Reminiscences,* 578; Eisenhower to Marshall, 11 February 1943, *EP,* vol. 2, 951; Eisenhower to Patton, 6 March 1943, ibid., 1010; Bradley, *Soldier's Story,* 15–20, 31–32, 45.

51. The quote is from Bradley and Blair, *General's Life,* 139. See also ibid., 58–59, 137, 151; Patton to Bradley, 18 February 1942 and 5 May 1943, *Patton Papers,* vol. 2, 55, 242; Patton to his wife, 13 March and 8 April 1943, ibid., 189, 215; Patton diary, 15 March 1943, ibid., 191; Bradley, *Soldier's Story,* 52.

52. Harmon, *Combat Commander,* 125.

53. Ibid., 77–78.

54. Bradley and Blair, *General's Life,* 143, 148–149; Patton diary, 15, 17, 18, 21, 23, 24, 27, 28, and 30 March, 4 and 15 April 1943, *Patton Papers,* vol. 2, 191, 193, 196–199, 201, 211, 221; Patton to his wife, 24 and 25 March, 8 April 1943, ibid., 198, 215; Harmon, *Combat Commander,* 123–124; Bradley, *Soldier's Story,* 64–65; Hughes diary, 7 March 1945, Irving Collection, reel 5; Stanley P. Hirshson, *General Patton: A Soldier's Life* (New York: HarperCollins, 2002), 316–317.

55. Bradley, *Soldier's Story,* 74.

56. Bradley and Blair, *General's Life,* 154; Hansen diary, 1 May 1943, Hansen Papers, USAHEC, box 4; Eisenhower to Marshall, 3 March 1943, Marshall Papers, Marshall Foundation, Pentagon Office, box 66, folder 49.

57. Bradley and Blair, *General's Life,* 151, 154, 169–170; Marshall to Eisenhower, 8 May 1943, *MP,* vol. 3, 685; Marshall to Alexander Surles, 8 May 1943, ibid., 686; Patton diary, 14 April, 8 and 20 May 1943, *Patton Papers,* vol. 2, 220, 245, 253–254; Eisenhower to Marshall, 13 May 1943, *EP,* vol. 2, 1129–1130; Butcher, 10 and 13 May 1943, *Three Years with Eisenhower,* 253, 259.

58. Patton diary, 17 April 1943, *Patton Papers,* vol. 2, 223.

59. Eisenhower, 11 June 1943, Memorandum for Personal File, A-472, DDEL.

60. Bradley and Blair, *General's Life,* 151; Patton to Alexander Surles, 10 April 1943, *Patton Papers,* vol. 2, 216; Patton diary, 14 April and 7 May 1943, ibid., 220, 244; Eisenhower to Patton, 14 April 1943, ibid., 220; Marshall to Patton, 4 May 1943, ibid., 232; Eisenhower to Handy, 20 March 1943, *EP,* vol. 2, 1048.

61. Eisenhower, 11 June 1943, Memorandum for Personal File, A-472, DDEL.

62. Handy to Marshall, 7 May 1943, Marshall Foundation, National Archives Project, Verifax 1947; Patton to his wife, 10 May 1943, *Patton Papers,* vol. 2, 248; Clark to his wife, 24 May 1943, Clark Diaries and Correspondence, vol. 10.

63. Eisenhower to Marshall, 16 April 1943, Marshall Papers, Marshall Foundation, Pentagon Office, box 66, folder 50; Truscott's aide's diary, 10 May 1943, Truscott Papers, Marshall Foundation, box 18, folder 2; William R. Buster, *Time On Target: The World War II Memoir of William R. Buster,* ed. Jeffrey Suchanek and William J. Marshall (Frankfort: Kentucky Historical Society, 1999), 57.

64. Walker, 5 July 1943, *From Texas to Rome,* 208–209.

65. Patton diary, 2 June 1943, Patton Papers, vol. 2, 258; Eisenhower to Marshall, 24 August 1943, *EP,* vol. 2, 1354; Harmon, *Combat Commander,* 142–143; Howze interview, 5 February 1973, *ASOOH,* section 3, 49–50; Walker, 10 June 1943, *From Texas to Rome,* 203.

66. Bradley and Blair, *General's Life,* 158; Eisenhower to Marshall, 11 May 1943, *EP,* vol. 2, 1123; Eisenhower to Surles, 17 May 1943, ibid., 1137; Bradley, *Soldier's Story,* 81, 88, 100–101; Howze interview, 5 February 1973, *ASOOH,* section 3, 12–13; Hansen diary, 9 February 1945, box 5.

Chapter 3: The Long and Frustrating Italian Campaign

1. Lord Alanbrooke, *War Diaries: 1939–1945,* ed. Alex Danchev and Daniel Todman (Berkeley: University of California Press), 351.

2. Eisenhower notes, 10 December 1942, *EP,* vol. 2, 824–825.

3. Marshall to Eisenhower, 15 May 1943, *MP,* vol. 3, 694–695; Eisenhower to Marshall, 17 May 1943, *EP,* vol. 2, 1141.

4. Omar Bradley, *A Soldier's Story* (New York: Henry Holt, 1951), 69–70.

5. Omar Bradley and Clay Blair, *A General's Life: An Autobiography by General of the Army Omar N. Bradley and Clay Blair* (New York: Simon and Schuster, 1983), 169; Marshall to Eisenhower, 26 September 1942, *MP,* vol. 3, 367; Patton to Bradley, 23 April 1943, *The Patton Papers, 1940–1945,* vol. 2, ed. Martin Blumenson (Boston: Houghton

Mifflin, 1974), 232; Patton, n.d., ibid., 231; Patton to his wife, 10 May 1943, ibid., 248; Patton diary, 17 May 1943, ibid., 252; Eisenhower to Marshall, 11 May and 27 June 1943, *EP,* vol. 2, 1123, 1217; Marshall, interview by Matthews, et al., 25 July 1949, George C. Marshall Foundation, interview 3, part 1, 5; Marshall to Eisenhower, 26 June 1943, Marshall Foundation, National Archives Project, Xerox 292.

6. Eisenhower to Marshall, 1 July 1943, *EP,* vol. 2, 1233.

7. Fred Walker, 14 May 1943, *From Texas to Rome: A General's Journal* (Dallas: Taylor Publishing, 1969), 196; Marshall to Eisenhower, 7 March 1943, *MP,* vol. 3, 580; Patton to Bradley, n.d., *Patton Papers,* vol. 2, 231; Patton to his wife, 10 May 1943, ibid., 248; Patton diary, 17 May 1943, ibid., 251; Lucian Truscott, *Command Missions: A Personal Story* (New York: E. P. Dutton, 1954), 124–125; Eisenhower to his son, 27 June 1942, *EP,* vol. 1, 365; Eisenhower to Marshall, 21 February and 30 April 1943, *EP,* vol. 2, 979, 1104; Harry Butcher, 1 July 1943, *Three Years with Eisenhower: The Personal Diary of Captain Harry C. Butcher, USNR, Naval Aide to General Eisenhower, 1942 to 1945* (London: William Heinemann, 1946), 287; Frank James Price, *Troy H. Middleton: A Biography* (Baton Rouge: Louisiana State University Press, 1974), 135, 144; Gay interview, 1981, *ASOOH,* 22; Eisenhower, 11 June 1943, Memorandum for Personal File, A–472, DDEL; Bradley and Blair, *General's Life,* 170; Bradley interview, n.d., McCarthy Collection, Marshall Foundation, box 17, folder 3.

8. The quote is from Patton to Handy, 5 July 1943, *Patton Papers,* vol. 2, 271. See also Bradley and Blair, *General's Life,* 170, 174; Patton diary, 16 and 17 April, 22 and 28 May, 2, 8, 10, 20, 21 June, 5 July 1943, *Patton Papers,* vol. 2, 222–223, 254, 256, 258, 263–264, 264, 266–267, 272; Patton to his wife, 23 April and 13 May 1943, ibid., 231, 250; Lucas diary, 9 July 1943, Lucas Papers, USAHEC, box 1, 6; Hughes diary, 17 April and 7 May 1943, Papers Relating to the Allied High Command—1943–45, David Irving Collection, reel 5.

9. For Bradley's unhappiness, see Bradley and Blair, *General's Life,* 170–174. See also Patton diary, 17 May 1943, *Patton Papers,* vol. 2, 252; Bradley interview, n.d., McCarthy Collection, Marshall Foundation, box 17, folder 3.

10. Hansen diary, 10 July 1943, Hansen Papers, USAHEC, box 4.

11. The quote is from Hughes diary, 20 July 1943, Irving Collection, reel 5. See also Patton diary, 12 and 13 July 1943, *Patton Papers,* vol. 2, 283; Eisenhower to Marshall, 5 July 1943, *EP,* vol. 2, 1258; Butcher, 13 July 1943, *Three Years with Eisenhower,* 304–305; Lucas diary, 12 and 14 July 1943, box 1; Eisenhower to Marshall, 17 July 1943, Marshall Papers, Marshall Foundation, Pentagon Office, box 66, folder 52.

12. Truscott's aide's diary, 23 July 1943, Truscott Papers, Marshall Foundation, box 18, folder 3.

13. Patton diary, 22 July 1943, *Patton Papers,* vol. 2, 296.

14. Bradley and Blair, *General's Life,* 192; Patton diary, 20 and 22 July 1943, *Patton Papers,* vol. 2, 294, 296; Patton to Eisenhower, 24 July 1943, ibid., 299; Patton to his wife, 24 July 1943, ibid., 300.

15. Patton diary, 30 and 31 July, 10 and 17 August 1943, ibid., 307–308, 318–319, 323; Patton to his wife, 2, 9, 15 August 1943, ibid., 311, 317, 321; Truscott, *Command Missions,* 228, 234–235, 243; Butcher, 2 and 14 August 1943, *Three Years with Eisenhower,* 319, 330; Robert Coffin, interview by Sidney Yateman, 25 July 1980, *ASOOH,* 65–66.

16. Patton diary, 24 June 1943, McCarthy Collection, Marshall Foundation, box 17, folder 5; Bradley and Blair, *General's Life,* 179, 183, 195; Hansen diary, 10 and 21 July 1943, box 4l; Robert Porter Jr., interview by John Sloan, 1981, *ASOOH,* 302.

17. Bradley and Blair, *General's Life,* 199; Hansen diary, 21 and 22 July 1943, box 4; Bradley, *Soldier's Story,* 51–52, 145–146, 159–160, 473; Lucas diary, 14 August 1943, box 1, 114–116, 118.

18. Eisenhower to Marshall, 24 August 1943, *EP,* vol. 2, 1353.

19. Marshall to Eisenhower, 17 August and 1 September 1943, *MP,* vol. 4, 92, 108; Eisenhower to Patton, 2 August 1943, *Patton Papers,* vol. 2, 310; Patton to his wife, 9 August 1943, ibid., 317; Patton to McNair, 10 August 1943, ibid., 317; Patton to Eisenhower, 24 July 1943, ibid., 299; Eisenhower to Marshall, 18, 24, and 27 August 1943, *EP,* vol. 2, 1341, 1354, 1357–1358; Henry Stimson, 28 July 1943, The Henry Lewis Stimson Diaries, Yale University Library, reel 8, vol. 44, 59; Lucas diary, 21 July 1943, box 1.

20. Butcher, 20 and 21 August 1943, *Three Years with Eisenhower,* 335–336, 338–339; Hansen diary, 4 September 1943, box 4; Eisenhower to Patton, 17 August 1943, *Patton Papers,* vol. 2, 329–330; Eisenhower to Marshall, 6 September 1943, ibid., 349; Eisenhower to Marshall, 24 November 1943, *EP,* vol. 3, 1571–1573; Eisenhower to Patton, 1 December 1943, ibid., 1576; Stimson, 22, 23–24, 25 November 1943, Stimson Diaries, reel 8, vol. 45, 50, 56, 59; Lucas diary, 19 and 21 August, 2 September 1943, box 1, 125–127, 136.

21. Patton diary, 25 November 1943, *Patton Papers,* vol. 2, 378.

22. Bradley and Blair, *General's Life,* 208; Patton diary, 31 July, 20 August, 2, 4, 6, 7 September, 27 October, 25 November 1943, *Patton Papers,* vol. 2, 308, 332–333, 345, 346–347, 350, 366, 378; Patton to his wife, 10 September, 22 October, 20 and 25 November, 20 December 1943, ibid., 351, 365, 374, 379, 390; Patton to McNair, 27 September 1943, ibid., 358; Patton to Stimson, 27 November 1943, ibid., 380–381; Eisenhower to Patton, 30 September 1943, *EP,* vol. 3, 1473; Lucas diary, 7 September 1943, box 1, 139.

23. Eisenhower to Marshall, 5 December 1942, 5 January, 8 May, 24 and 27 August 1943, *EP,* vol. 2, 800, 897, 1118, 1354, 1357–1358; Eisenhower notes, 10 December 1942, ibid., 824–825; Eisenhower memo, 22 May 1944, *EP,* vol. 3, 1880; Eisenhower to Gruenther, 10 October 1944, *EP,* vol. 4, 2217–2218; Eisenhower to Clark, 5 May 1945, ibid., 2685; Mark Clark, *Calculated Risk* (New York: Harper and Brothers, 1950), 141, 165; Wood interview, 21 February 1974, *ASOOH,* section 3, 30; Lucas diary, 30 August 1943, box 1, 132–133; Clark, 18 June 1943, Clark Diaries and Correspondence, Mark W. Clark Papers, Daniel Library, The Citadel, vol. 3; Eisenhower, 11 June 1943, Memorandum for Personal File, A–472, DDEL; Bradley and Blair, *General's Life,* 204–205.

24. Bradley and Blair, *General's Life,* 169; Marshall to Eisenhower, 26 September 1942, *MP,* vol. 3, 367; Patton to Bradley, n.d., *Patton Papers,* vol. 2, 231; Eisenhower to Marshall, 15 May and 24 August 1943, *EP,* vol. 2, 1136, 1354; Clark, *Calculated Risk,* 175; McNair to Marshall, 7 October 1941, Marshall Foundation, Pentagon Office, box 76, folder 31; Marshall, interview by Matthews, et al., 25 July 1949, Marshall Foundation, interview 3, part 1; Clark, 20 September 1943, Clark Diaries and Correspondence, vol. 5; Marshall to Eisenhower, 26 June 1943, Marshall Foundation, National Archives Project, Xerox 292.

25. Butcher, 16 September 1943, *Three Years with Eisenhower,* 358.

26. Ibid., 6 September 1943, 47; Patton diary, 16 September 1943, *Patton Papers,* vol. 2, 353; Truscott, *Command Missions,* 249–250, 252; Eisenhower to Marshall, 16 and 20 September 1943, *EP,* vol. 3, 1428, 1439–1440; Clark, 7, 10, 11, 14, and 16 September 1943, Clark Diaries and Correspondence, vol. 5.

27. Clark, 20 September 1943, Clark Diaries and Correspondence, vol. 5.

28. Walker, 20 September 1943, *From Texas to Rome,* 257.

29. Eisenhower to Marshall, 16, 19, and 20 September 1943, *EP,* vol. 3, 1428, 1436, 1439; Eisenhower to Ernest Dawley, 22 September 1943, ibid., 1447–1448; Clark, *Calculated Risk,* 206, 208; Clark to Eisenhower, 16 September 1943, Irving Collection, reel 3; Clark, 15, 17, and 20 September 1943, Clark Diaries and Correspondence, vol. 5; Walker, 20 September 1943, *From Texas to Rome,* 257–258.

30. Walker, 20 September 1943, *From Texas to Rome,* 258.

31. For Dawley's relief and the controversy surrounding it, see Patton diary, 22 September 1943, *Patton Papers,* vol. 2, 356; Truscott, *Command Missions,* 253; Marshall, interview by Matthews, et al., 25 July 1949, Marshall Foundation, interview 3, part 1, 5; Gavin interview, 20 January 1967, Columbia University (at DDEL), 15–16; Wood interview, 21 February 1974, *ASOOH,* section 3, 48; Walker, 14 September 1943, *From Texas to Rome,* 250–251.

32. Eisenhower to Marshall, 24 August 1943, *EP,* vol. 2, 1354.

33. Bradley, *Soldier's Story,* 10; Lucas diary, 24 May, 30 August, 2, 7, 8, 24 September 1943, box 1, 1, 133, 135–136, 139–140, 152; Hansen diary, 6 September 1943, box 4; Marshall to Eisenhower, 1 September 1943, *MP,* vol. 4, 108; Eisenhower to Marshall, 24 August and 2 September 1943, *EP,* vol. 2, 1354, 1380–1381; Walker, 8 October 1943, *From Texas to Rome,* 268.

34. Marshall to Eisenhower, 26 September 1943, *MP,* vol. 3, 367; Truscott, *Command Missions,* 319–320; Ben Harrell, interview by Robert Hayden, n.d., USAHEC, section 2, 55; James Gavin, *On to Berlin: Battles of an Airborne Commander, 1943–1946* (New York: Viking Press, 1978), 77–78; Devers diary, 19 January 1944, Devers Papers, USAHEC; McNair to Marshall, 7 October 1941, Marshall Foundation, Pentagon Office, box 76, folder 31; Roscoe Woodruff, "The World War Two," Woodruff Papers, DDEL, 32.

35. Bradley and Blair, *General's Life,* 170; Marshall to Eisenhower, 7 March 1943, *MP,* vol. 3, 580; Patton diary, 28 September and 30 November 1942, 2 June, 22 July, 18

September, 6 October 1943, *Patton Papers,* vol. 2, 87, 129–130, 258, 296, 354, 261; Patton to Eisenhower, 24 July 1943, ibid., 299; Patton to his wife, 24 July 1943, ibid., 300; Patton to Geoffrey Keyes, 24 August 1944, ibid., 528; Eisenhower to Patton, 29 July 1942, *EP,* vol. 1, 426–427; Eisenhower to Marshall, 18 and 24 August 1943, *EP,* vol. 2, 1341, 1354; Eisenhower to Marshall, *EP,* vol. 3, 1436; Eisenhower to Patton, 20 September 1943, ibid., 1438; Eisenhower to Keyes, 27 September 1943, ibid., 1465–1466; Lucas diary, 18 November 1943, box 1, 233; Clark, 13 November 1943, Clark Diaries and Correspondence, vol. 5.

36. The story is from James C. Fry, *Combat Soldier* (Washington, DC: National Press, 1968), 202–203. See also Patton diary, 28 September 1942, *Patton Papers,* vol. 2, 87; Patton to Keyes, 24 August 1944, ibid., 528; Truscott, *Command Missions,* 453; Harrell interview, n.d., USAHEC, section 3, 26–27; Wood interview, 22 February 1974, *ASOOH,* section 4, 7; Porter interview, 1981, *ASOOH,* 317; Charles Bolte, interview by Arthur Zoebelein, 20 January 1972, *ASOOH,* section 2, 5–6; Lucas diary, 10 July and 8 September 1943, box 1, 41, 140.

37. Clark to his wife, 14 November 1943, Clark Diaries and Correspondence, vol. 10.

38. Henry Lemley, interview by Gerald Feeney, 5 April 1974, *ASOOH,* section 1, 32.

39. Patton diary, 14 November 1943, *Patton Papers,* vol. 2, 372; Truscott, *Command Missions,* 284, 547; Gavin interview, 20 January 1967, Columbia University (at DDEL), 18; Wood interview, 21 February 1974, *ASOOH,* section 3, 26–27, 29, 40–41; Wood interview, 22 February 1974, *ASOOH,* section 4, 8; Bolte interview, 9 December 1971, *ASOOH,* section 1, 97; Lucas diary, 26 September and 2 October 1943, box 1, 158, 167; Clark to Eisenhower, 16 September 1943, Irving Collection, reel 3; Clark, 13 November 1943, Clark Diaries and Correspondence, vol. 5; Clark to his wife, 7 November 1943, Clark Diaries and Correspondence, vol. 10; Walker, 17 December 1943, *From Texas to Rome,* 287.

40. Lucas diary, 25 October 1943, box 1, 206–207.

41. Patton diary, early November 1943, *Patton Papers,* vol. 2, 368; Patton to his wife, 7 November 1943, ibid., 369–370; Truscott, *Command Missions,* 284; Wood interview, 22 February 1974, *ASOOH,* section 4, 8; Lucas diary, 2 and 3 October, 26 December 1943, box 1, 166–167, 170, 276; Clark, 4 and 6 December 1943, Clark Diaries and Correspondence, vol. 5; Woodruff, "The World War Two," 33; Walker, 18 November and 19 December 1943, *From Texas to Rome,* 275–276, 288.

42. Lucas diary, 9 November 1943, box 1, 225.

43. For examples of the thinking of Clark's subordinates, see Patton diary, early November 1943, *Patton Papers,* vol. 2, 368; Patton to his wife, 7 November 1943, ibid., 369–370; Truscott, *Command Missions,* 284, 547; Ernest N. Harmon, with Milton MacKaye and William Ross MacKaye, *Combat Commander: Autobiography of a Soldier* (Englewood Cliffs, NJ: Prentice-Hall, 1970), 150–152; Price, *Troy H. Middleton,* 168–169; Lucas diary, n.d., 19 October, 9, 19, 26 November 1943, box 1, 191, 197, 225, 234; Clark, 18 September, 13, 24, and 29 November, 10 December 1943, Clark Diaries and Correspondence, vol. 5; Woodruff, "The World War Two," 32; Walker, 8 and 12

November, 17 December 1943, *From Texas to Rome,* 275–276, 287; Truscott's aide's diary, 3 November, 6 and 7 December 1943, box 18, folder 3; Patton diary, 9 January 1944, McCarthy Collection, Marshall Foundation, box 17, folder 6, 119.

44. J. Lawton Collins, *Lightning Joe: An Autobiography* (Baton Rouge: Louisiana State University Press, 1979), 333; Bradley and Blair, *General's Life,* 210, 217; Marshall to Eisenhower, 23 and 28 December 1943, *MP,* vol. 4, 202, 210; George C. Marshall, 13 November 1956, *Marshall Interviews and Reminiscences for Forest C. Pogue* (Lexington, VA: George C. Marshall Foundation, 1991), 627; Eisenhower to Marshall, 23, 25, 27, 29 December 1943, *EP,* vol. 3, 1609–1610, 1612–1614, 1622–1623, 1631–1632; Eisenhower to Devers, 29 December 1943, ibid., 1632–1633; Stimson, 11 December 1941, Stimson Diaries, reel 7, vol. 36, 98–99; Eisenhower, *Crusade in Europe* (New York: Doubleday, 1948), 216; Bradley, *Soldier's Story,* 171–172, 210; Devers interview, 18 November 1974, DDEL, 70–71; Second Corps War Diary, 26 September 1942, Clark Diaries and Correspondence, vol. 2; Marshall to Devers, 19 March 1941, Marshall Papers, Marshall Foundation, Pentagon Office, box 43, folder 50; Orlando Ward to Devers, 25 March 1941, ibid., box 63, folder 50.

45. Bradley and Blair, *General's Life,* 210.

46. Ibid.; Patton to his wife, 9 August 1941, 9 January 1943, 9 February 1944, *Patton Papers,* vol. 2, 41–42, 149, 413; Patton to Devers, 22 August 1942, ibid., 84; Patton diary, n.d., 12 and 16 February, mid-October 1944, ibid., 149, 414–415, 565; Eisenhower to Devers, 4 April 1942, *EP,* vol. 1, 227; Butcher, 3 August 1943, *Three Years with Eisenhower,* 322–323; Eisenhower to Marshall, 25 December 1943, 18 January, and 9 February 1944, *EP,* vol. 3, 1612–1614, 1665–1666, 1715–1716; Butcher diary, 20 January and 8 February 1944, Irving Collection, reel 3.

47. Collins, *Lightning Joe,* 333; Marshall, 13 November 1956, *Marshall Interviews and Reminiscences,* 627; Harmon, *Combat Commander,* 61; J. Lawton Collin interview, n.d., USAHEC, 271; Devers interview, 19 August 1974, DDEL, 4, 15–16, 20, 33–34, 41–42; Devers interview, 18 November 1974, DDEL, 69; Matchett interview, 22 July 1976, DDEL, 27; Wood interview, 21 February 1974, *ASOOH,* section 3, 46; Lodge, *The Storm Has Many Eyes: A Personal Narrative* (New York: W. W. Norton, 1973), 44; Eichelberger to his wife, 8 May 1943, Robert L. Eichelberger Papers, Perkins Library, Duke University, reel 44, correspondence 1943–1944; William M. Hoge, *Engineer Memoirs* (Washington, DC: Office of History, U.S. Army Corps of Engineers, 1993), 108; David Wittels, 10 July 1943, "These Are the Generals: Devers," *Saturday Evening Post* 216, no. 2:15, 102.

48. Hughes diary, 10 January, 16 February, and 16 March 1944, Irving Collection, reel 5; Devers interview, 4 February 1975, DDEL, 153–154; Devers interview, 2 July 1975, DDEL, 182–183; Patton to his wife, 9 and 26 February 1944, *Patton Papers,* vol. 2, 413, 418; Clark, *Calculated Risk,* 400; Wood interview, 21 February 1974, *ASOOH,* section 3, 44–45; Devers diary, 19 January and 1 November 1944; Butcher diary, 8 February 1944, Irving Collection, reel 3; Devers interview, 12 August 1958, Marshall Foundation, 33, 65–66, 70–71, 73.

49. Clark, *Calculated Risk,* 258.

50. Quoted in Robert Wallace, *The Italian Campaign* (Chicago: Time-Life Books, 1981), 131. See also Clark, *Calculated Risk,* 254; Price, *Troy H. Middleton,* 169–170; Clark, 2, 9, and 19 January 1944, Clark Diaries and Correspondence, vol. 6; Harold Alexander, *The Alexander Memoirs, 1940–1945* (New York: McGraw-Hill Book, 1962), 126.

51. Lucas diary, 10 January 1944, 295–296.

52. Ibid., n.d., 305.

53. Patton diary, 6 January 1944, *Patton Papers,* vol. 2, 396; Truscott, *Command Missions,* 298, 304, 306, 309, 311; Galvan, *On to Berlin,* 77–78; William Rosson, interview by Douglas Burgess, 1981, *ASOOH,* 83; Lucas diary, n.d., 10 and 24 January 1944, box 1, 281, 285–286, 295–296, 305, 328; Patton diary, 9 January 1944, McCarthy Collection, Marshall Foundation, box 17, folder 6.

54. Clark, 23 January 1944, Clark Diaries and Correspondence, vol. 6.

55. Quoted in Carlo D'Este, *Fatal Decision: Anzio and the Battle for Rome* (New York: HarperCollins, 1991), 277.

56. Alanbrooke, *War Diaries,* 522; Marshall to Devers, 18 February 1944, *MP,* vol. 4, 311; Devers to Marshall, 19 February 1944, ibid., 312n; Patton diary, 16 and 17 February 1944, *Patton Papers,* vol. 2, 415–416; Eisenhower to Marshall, 16 February 1944, *EP,* vol. 3, 1730–1731; Clark, *Calculated Risk,* 306; Lucas diary, 16 February 1944, box 1, 380–381; Hughes diary, 6 January 1944, Irving Collection, reel 5; Butcher diary, 17 February 1944, Irving Collection, reel 3; Clark, 27 January, 1, 16, and 17 February 1944, Clark Diaries and Correspondence, vol. 6; Alexander, *Alexander Memoirs,* 126; Marshall to Eisenhower, 1 March 1944, Marshall Papers, Marshall Foundation, Pentagon Office, box 67, folder 4; Devers interview, 12 August 1958, Marshall Foundation, 63–64.

57. Alexander, *Alexander Memoirs,* 126.

58. Devers to Marshall, 19 February 1944, *MP,* vol. 4, 312n; Truscott, *Command Missions,* 319–320, 324, 327–328; Clark, *Calculated Risk,* 296, 306, 309, 327; Lucas diary, 30 and 31 January, 18 February 1944, box 1, 348–349, 351, 389, 394; Clark, 27, 28, 30 January, 1, 9, 16, 17, 18, and 24 February 1944, Clark Diaries and Correspondence, vol. 6.

59. Lucas diary, 16 February 1944, box 1, 380–381.

60. Marshall to McNair, 20 February 1944, *MP,* vol. 4, 312–313; Truscott, *Command Missions,* 327–328; Gavin interview, 20 January 1967, Columbia University (at DDEL), 16; Wood interview, 21 February 1974, *ASOOH,* section 3, 48; Lucas diary, 29 and 30 January, 1, 15, 16, 17, 18 February 1944, box 1, 344, 348–349, 353, 379–381, 385, 389, 394; Hughes diary, 20 March 1944, Irving Collection, reel 5; Marshall to Eisenhower, 1 March 1944, Marshall Papers, Marshall Foundation, Pentagon Office, box 67, folder 4.

61. Clark, *Calculated Risk,* 306.

62. Truscott, *Command Missions,* 547–548; Eisenhower to Marshall, 24 August 1943, *EP,* vol. 2, 1354; Eisenhower to Marshall, 16 February 1944, *EP,* vol. 3, 1730–1731; Devers interview, 2 July 1975, DDEL, 174; Clark, 8 March 1944, Clark Diaries and Correspondence, vol. 6; Harmon, *Combat Commander,* 152; Howze interview, 5 February

1973, *ASOOH,* section 3, 48–50; Wood interview, 22 February 1974, *ASOOH,* section 4, 7; Devers interview, 12 August 1958, Marshall Foundation, 63.

63. The quote is from Eisenhower to Marshall, 5 December 1944, *EP,* vol. 4, 2336. See also Truscott, *Command Missions,* 540; Walters interview, n.d., USAHEC, 681; Harmon, *Combat Commander,* 181; Harrell interview, n.d., USAHEC, section 3, 18; Devers interview, 2 July 1975, DDEL, 174; Wood interview, 22 February 1974, *ASOOH,* section 4, 7; Howze interview, 5 February 1973, *ASOOH,* section 3, 33.

64. Truscott, *Command Missions,* 312, 546–548; Clark, 7 February 1944, Clark Diaries and Correspondence, vol. 6; Harmon, *Combat Commander,* 166, 181; Wood interview, 21 February 1974, *ASOOH,* section 3, 47; Lemley interview, *ASOOH,* section 2, 43; Truscott's aide's diary, 22 and 30 January, 11 February 1944, box 18, folder 4.

65. Truscott, *Command Missions,* 324, 331, 339–340; Clark, 28 February, 2, 8, 24 March 1944, Clark Diaries and Correspondence, vol. 6.

66. Devers interview, 4 February and 2 July 1975, DDEL, 158–159, 178–180, 183; Devers diary, 19 January 1944; Clark, 17 and 28 February, 1 and 22 March 1944, Clark Diaries and Correspondence, vol. 6.

67. Marshall to Devers, 18 February and 22 April 1944, *MP,* vol. 4, 311, 430; Clark, *Calculated Risk,* 299; Devers interview, 4 February and 2 July 1975, DDEL, 158–159, 183; Porter interview, 1981, *ASOOH,* 317, 326; Clark, 6 and 17 December 1943, Clark Diaries and Correspondence, vol. 5; Clark, 11 and 30 January, 2 and 7 February 1944, Clark Diaries and Correspondence, vol. 6; Walker, 8, 13, 16, 20, 21, 22, 23, 29 January, 6 February 1944, *From Texas to Rome,* 296–297, 300–301, 308–310, 313, 316, 322–323, 325; Devers to Marshall, 13 June 1944, Marshall Papers, Marshall Foundation, Pentagon Office, box 63, folder 57.

68. Marshall to Devers, 22 April 1944, *MP,* vol. 4, 430.

69. Alexander, *Alexander Memoirs,* 126.

70. Howze interview, 5 February 1973, *ASOOH,* section 3, 37.

71. Clark, *Calculated Risk,* 357–358; Rosson interview, 1981, *ASOOH,* 91; Clark, 31 May 1944, Clark Diaries and Correspondence, vol. 7; Truscott, *Command Missions,* 375; D'Este, *Fatal Decision,* 369; Marshall interview by Matthews, et al., 25 July 1949, Marshall Foundation, interview 3, part 2, 9.

72. Clark, *Calculated Risk,* 357, 367; Clark, 14, 15, 22, 30 May, 12 June 1944, Clark Diaries and Correspondence, vol. 7.

73. Bradley and Blair, *General's Life,* 223; Marshall to Willis Crittenberger, 4 May 1942, *MP,* vol. 3, 180–181; Truscott, *Command Missions,* 453; Harmon, Personal Memoirs of Major General E. N. Harmon, Kreitzberg Library, Norwich University, 44; Walker, 2 March 1944, *From Texas to Rome,* 335; Devers interview, 12 August 1958, Marshall Foundation, 59–60; Memorandum for Roosevelt, 18 June 1945, Marshall Foundation, reel 349, item 5228.

74. Eisenhower to Marshall, 29 January 1944, *EP,* vol. 3, 1695–1696. Eisenhower's reasoning is deleted from the printed volume, but is available from the DDEL.

75. Devers diary, 10 July 1944.

76. Marshall to Devers, 19 January 1944, *MP,* vol. 4, 238; Eisenhower to Smith, 2 October 1943, *EP,* vol. 3, 1479–1480; Eisenhower to Devers, 1 February 1944, ibid., 1701; Clark, *Calculated Risk,* 367; Bolte interview, 20 January 1972, *ASOOH,* section 2, 5–6; Edward Almond, interview by Thomas Fergusson, 27 March 1975, *ASOOH,* section 3, 17; Devers diary, 22 February, 27 June, 9 September 1944; Butcher diary, 29 January 1944, Irving Collection; Clark, 22 March 1944, Clark Diaries and Correspondence, vol. 6; Clark, 12 and 30 June 1944, Clark Diaries and Correspondence, vol. 7; Clark, 14 December 1944, Clark Diaries and Correspondence, vol. 8; Woodruff, "The World War Two," 41; Devers to Marshall, 13 June 1944, Marshall Papers, Marshall Foundation, Pentagon Office, box 63, folder 57; Crittenberger to Lucian Truscott, 13 April 1945, Truscott Papers, Marshall Foundation, box 5, folder 20.

77. Harmon, *Combat Commander,* 202–203; Clark, *Calculated Risk,* 367; Devers diary, 7 July 1944; Clark, 12 June 1944, Clark Diaries and Correspondence, vol. 7; Clark, 10 and 16 July 1944, Clark Diaries and Correspondence, vol. 8; Truscott's aide's diary, 12 February 1944, box 18, folder 4; ibid., 19 February 1944, box 18, folder 4.

78. The quote is from Clark, *Calculated Risk,* 402. For Clark's discontent, see also Truscott, *Command Missions,* 382; Clark, *Calculated Risk,* 367–368; Devers diary, 7 July 1944; Clark to his wife, 18 September 1944, Irving Collection, reel 3; Clark, 13 and 19 June 1944, Clark Diaries and Correspondence, vol. 7; Clark, 9 November 1944, Clark Diaries and Correspondence, vol. 8; Clark to his wife, 30 July and 5 October 1944, Clark Diaries and Correspondence, vol. 10.

79. The quote is from Clark, *Calculated Risk,* 367–368. See also Clark, 15 September and 9 October 1944, Clark Diaries and Correspondence, vol. 8.

80. Devers diary, 19 September 1944.

81. Ibid., 9 September 1944; Devers to Marshall, 1 July 1944, Marshall Papers, Marshall Foundation, Pentagon Office, box 63, folder 58; Devers interview, 12 August 1958, Marshall Foundation, 104.

82. Devers to Handy, 9 September 1944, Marshall Foundation, National Archives Project, Verifax 2241.

83. Smith to Handy, 9 February 1945, Handy Papers, Marshall Foundation, box 1, folder 7.

84. Marshall to John Dill, 21 September 1944, *MP,* vol. 4, 596–597; Stimson diary, 20 October 1944, Stimson Diaries, reel 9, vol. 48, 171; Marshall interview by Matthews, et al., 25 July 1949, Marshall Foundation, interview 3, part 2, 9; Clark, *Calculated Risk,* 423; Devers diary, 15 September and 1 November 1944; Hughes diary, 8 February 1945, Irving Collection, reel 5; Devers interview, 12 August 1958, Marshall Foundation, 16.

85. Winston Churchill to Clark, 23 November 1944, Irving Collection, reel 3; Clark, 9 January 1944, Clark Diaries and Correspondence, vol. 6.

86. Chandler, ed., *EP,* vol. 4, 2315n; Marshall interview by Matthews, et al., 25 July

1949, Marshall Foundation, interview 3, part 2, 9; Clark, *Calculated Risk,* 404; Hansen diary, 27 November 1944, box 5; Clark, 9 January 1944, Clark Diaries and Correspondence, vol. 6; Clark to his wife, 7 and 11 December 1944, 1 January 1945, Clark Diaries and Correspondence, vol. 10; Marshall to Eisenhower, 21 November 1944, Smith Files, Irving Collection, reel 4, file 8; Truscott to Handy, 8 March 1945, Handy Papers, Marshall Foundation, box 1, folder 8.

87. Much of the story of Truscott's appointment to the Fifth Army, including the quotes, is from Truscott, *Command Missions,* 383, 446–448. See also Marshall to Eisenhower, 21 September 1944, *MP,* vol. 4, 595; Chandler, ed., *EP,* vol. 4, 2315n; Eisenhower to Marshall, 22 and 27 November, 5 December 1944, ibid., 2315–2316, 2320–2321, 2336; Clark, *Calculated Risk,* 404; Devers diary, 25 October 1944; Churchill to Clark, 23 November 1944, Irving Collection, reel 3; Marshall to Eisenhower, 21 November 1944, Smith Files, Irving Collection, reel 4, file 8; Hull to Eisenhower, 21 November 1944, Marshall Foundation, reel 124, item 3208; Truscott to Marshall, 15 January 1945, Truscott Papers, Marshall Foundation, box 6, folder 16.

88. Patton diary, 28 November 1944, McCarthy Collection, Marshall Foundation, box 17, folder 8; Devers diary, 28 November 1944.

89. Truscott to Handy, 8 May 1945, Handy Papers, Marshall Foundation, box 1, folder 8.

90. Almond to Truscott, 24 September 1945, Truscott Papers, Marshall Foundation, box 5, folder 1.

91. Truscott, *Command Missions,* 453; Patton diary, 26 November 1944, *Patton Papers,* vol. 2, 567; Bolte interview, 20 January 1972, *ASOOH,* section 2, 5; Arnold interview, 27 March 1975, *ASOOH,* section 3, 17; Devers diary, 28 November 1944; Hansen diary, 27 November 1944, Hansen Papers, USAHEC, box 5; Clark, 6 December 1944, Clark Diaries and Correspondence, vol. 8; Clark to his wife, 7 December 1944, Clark Diaries and Correspondence, vol. 10; Hughes diary, 8 February 1945, Irving Collection, reel 5; Devers to Marshall, 1 July 1944, Marshall Papers, Marshall Foundation, Pentagon Office, box 63, folder 58; Devers interview, 12 August 1958, Marshall Foundation, 65; Memorandum for Roosevelt, 12 April 1945, Marshall Foundation, reel 349, item 5228; Truscott to Handy, 8 March 1945, Handy Papers, Marshall Foundation, box 1, folder 8; Crittenberger to Truscott, 9 January 1945, Truscott Papers, Marshall Foundation, box 5, folder 20; Keyes to Truscott, 26 June 1945, ibid., box 6, folder 7.

92. Clark to his wife, 16 February 1945, Clark Diaries and Correspondence, vol. 10.

93. Clark interview, 4 January 1970, DDEL, 22–24.

CHAPTER 4: THE DUAL DRIVE OFFENSIVE

1. Quoted in Wesley Frank Craven and James Lea Cate, eds., *The Army Air Forces in World War II: The Pacific,* vol. 4: *Guadalcanal to Saipan: August 1942 to July 1944* (Chicago: University of Chicago Press, 1950), 615.

2. The quote is from Robert Eichelberger to his wife, 23 March 1944, *Dear Miss Em:*

General Eichelberger's War in the Pacific, 1942–1945, ed. Jay Luvaas (Westport, CT: Greenwood Press, 1972), 96. See also Eichelberger to his wife, 17 November 1943, 6 February 1944, ibid., 79, 91–92; Eichelberger to his wife, 20 November 1943, Eichelberger Papers, Perkins Library, Duke University, reel 45, correspondence 1943–1944; Byers to Emma Eichelberger, 9 February 1944, ibid.

3. Eichelberger to his wife, 11 February 1944, *Dear Miss Em,* 92–93.

4. Eichelberger to his wife, 30 May, 4, 10, and 21 August, 17 and 22 November 1943, ibid., 70, 72, 74, 79; Eichelberger to his wife, 14 June 1943, Eichelberger Papers, reel 44, correspondence 1943–1944; Eichelberger to his wife, 6 January and 12 February 1944, Eichelberger Papers, reel 45, correspondence 1943–1944; Eddleman interview, 28 January 1975, USAHEC, section 2, 25–26; Byers diary, 6 February, 19 May, and 20 August 1943, Clovis Byers Collection, Hoover Institution, Stanford University, box 36, folder 1.

5. Eichelberger to his wife, 11–12 December 1943, 26 January, 17 February, 13 and 29 March, 17 April 1944, *Dear Miss Em,* 82–83, 90, 93, 95, 97, 99; Byers diary, 26 January 1944.

6. Byers diary, 22 April 1944.

7. Eichelberger to his wife, 22–23 April, 3 August 1944, *Dear Miss Em,* 106–107, 150; MacArthur to Eichelberger, 2 May 1944, Eichelberger Papers, reel 45, correspondence 1943–1944; Eichelberger to his wife, 25 July and 18 August 1944, Eichelberger Papers, reel 46, correspondence 1943–1944; Byers diary, 15 June 1944.

8. Eddleman comments, Walter Krueger Papers, United States Military Academy, box 40, 5.

9. Eichelberger to his wife, 17 May, 5 July 1944, *Dear Miss Em,* 115, 141; Roger Olaf Egeberg, *The General: MacArthur and the Man He Called "Doc,"* (New York: Hippocrene Books, 1983), 53; Eichelberger to his wife, 24, 28, and 30 May 1944, Eichelberger Papers, reel 45, correspondence 1943–1944; Byers diary, 28 May, 5 and 8 June 1944.

10. Eichelberger to his wife, 25 July and 11 October 1944, Eichelberger Papers, reel 46, correspondence 1943–1944; Byers diary, 10 June 1944.

11. MacArthur to Krueger, 14 June 1944, DMMA, RG-4, reel 593.

12. Eichelberger to his wife, 13 June 1944, *Dear Miss Em,* 120; Decker interview, USAHEC, interview 2, 22–23; MacArthur to Krueger, 5 June 1944, DMMA, RG-4, reel 595; Krueger to MacArthur, 5, 8, and 14 June 1944, ibid., reel 593.

13. Robert Eichelberger, with Milton MacKaye, *Our Jungle Road to Tokyo* (New York: Viking Press, 1950), 144.

14. Ibid., 156–157; Eichelberger to his wife, 9, 13, 14, 18, 28, and 30 June, 3 August 1944, *Dear Miss Em,* 120–121, 130, 138, 140, 150; Eichelberger to his wife, 16 June and 25 July 1944, Eichelberger Papers, reel 45, correspondence 1943–1944; Eichelberger to his wife, 29 July 1944, Eichelberger Papers, reel 46, correspondence 1943–1944; Decker interview, USAHEC, interview 2, 22–23; Harold Riegelman, *Caves of Biak: An American Officer's Experiences in the Southwest Pacific* (New York: Dial Press, 1955), 138–139;

Krueger to MacArthur, 16 June 1944, DMMA, RG-4, reel 593; MacArthur to Marshall, 9 July 1944, DMMA, RG-4, reel 594; Eddleman interview, 28 January 1975, USAHEC, section 2, 18–19; Byers diary, 15 and 18 June 1944.

15. Clyde Eddleman, Krueger's operations officer, later claimed that Krueger never opposed the creation of the Eighth Army. See Eddleman to William M. Leary, 13 August 1985, Krueger Papers, box 40, 2. See also Eichelberger to his wife, 26 January and 17 and 22 April, 25 June 1944, 24 March 1945, *Dear Miss Em,* 90, 99, 106, 136–137, 237; Decker interview, USAHEC, interview 3, 6–7; Walter Krueger, *From Down Under to Nippon: The Story of the Sixth Army in World War II* (Washington, DC: Combat Forces Press, 1953), 135; Krueger to MacArthur, 2 July 1944, DMMA, RG-4, reel 593.

16. For Eichelberger's long and tedious musings about field army command, see Eichelberger, 8, 25, 30 June, 1, 4, 5, 6, 20, 21, 24, 26, 29, 30 July, 2, 16, 22 August 1944, 24 March 1945, *Dear Miss Em,* 120, 136–137, 140–142, 146–149, 151, 237; Eichelberger to his wife, 3 May, 1 and 26 June 1944, Eichelberger Papers, reel 45, correspondence 1943–1944; Eichelberger to his wife, 3, 13, 17, 19 July, 11 and 13 September, 21 October 1944, Eichelberger Papers, reel 46, correspondence 1943–1944; See also Byers to Emma Eichelberger, 30 May 1944 Eichelberger Papers, reel 45, correspondence 1943–1944; Byers diary, 12, 27, 28 August, 1 September 1944.

17. The quote is from Paul B. Rogers, *The Bitter Years: MacArthur and Sutherland* (New York: Praeger, 1990), 149. See also Eichelberger to his wife, 10 May 1944, Eichelberger Papers, reel 45, correspondence 1943–1944; Eichelberger to his wife, 22 June 1945, Eichelberger Papers, reel 47, correspondence 1945; Eichelberger to his wife, 11 and 12 December 1943, 4 and 5 April 1944, *Dear Miss Em,* 82–83, 97–98; Rogers, *Bitter Years,* 56, 82; Paul B. Rogers, *The Good Years: MacArthur and Sutherland* (New York: Praeger, 1990), 231; MacArthur to Marshall, 3 February 1944, DMMA, RG-4, reel 594; Byers diary, 4 April 1944.

18. Rogers, *Bitter Years,* 91.

19. Ibid., 67–69, 80–83, 91, 162–164; Egeberg, *MacArthur and the Man He Called "Doc,"* 59, 61; Rogers, *Good Years,* 207; Weldon E. (Dusty) Rhoades, *Flying MacArthur to Victory* (College Station: Texas A&M Press, 1987), 194–195, 262–264, 283–284; Eddleman interview, 15 April 1975, USAHEC, section 4, 4–5; Eichelberger to his wife, 30 September 1943, Eichelberger Papers, reel 44, correspondence 1943–1944.

20. The quote is from McNair to Marshall, 7 October 1941, George C. Marshall Foundation, Pentagon Office, box 76, folder 31. See also Eichelberger to his wife, 6 July and 21 August 1944, *Dear Miss Em,* 141–142, 151; Eichelberger to his wife, 29 July and 5 August 1944, Eichelberger Papers, reel 46, correspondence 1943–1944; Riegelman, *Caves of Biak,* 174; James Collins interview, 1982, USAHEC, section 2, 39; Krueger, *From Down Under,* 135; William Chase, *Front Line General: The Commands of Maj. Gen. Wm. C. Chase* (Houston: Pacesetter Press, 1975), 29–30, 37; MacArthur to Krueger, 20 March 1944, DMMA, RG-4, reel 593; Krueger to MacArthur, 19 June, 2 July 1944, ibid.; MacArthur to Marshall, 1 May 1944, DMMA, RG-4, reel 594; Handy interview, 2

November 1973, USAHEC, vol. 1, section 3, 28; Swing interview, 26 August 1971, James Interviews, USAHEC, 15; Byers diary, 28 July 1943.

21. Riegelman, *Caves of Biak,* 174.

22. James Collins interview, 1982, USAHEC, section 2, 40.

23. The quote is from Byers diary, 20 August 1944. For evaluations of Swift, see Eichelberger to his wife, 21 August 1944, *Dear Miss Em,* 151; Riegelman, *Caves of Biak,* 274; Palmer interview, USAHEC, 67; James Collins interview, 1982, USAHEC, section 2, 39; Chase, *Front Line General,* 37, 39.

24. Krueger to MacArthur, 2 July 1944, DMMA, RG-4, reel 593.

25. Palmer interview, USAHEC, 40.

26. Krueger, *From Down Under,* 135; Marshall to MacArthur, 23 April 1944, DMMA, RG-4, reel 594; MacArthur to Marshall, 1 May 1944, ibid.; McNair to Marshall, 10 September and 7 October 1941, Marshall Foundation, Pentagon Office, box 76, folder 31.

27. Stilwell, 9 and 27 May 1942, *The Stilwell Papers,* ed. Theodore White (New York: William Sloane, 1948), 100, 110; Stilwell to Franklin Sibert, 12 September 1942, *Stilwell's Personal File: China-Burma-India, 1942–1944,* ed. Riley Sunderland and Charles F. Romananus (Wilmington, DE: Scholarly Resources, 1976), 267; Sibert to Stilwell, 14 September 1942, Eyes Alone Correspondence of General Joseph W. Stilwell, January 1942—October 1944, National Archives and Records Administration, reel 1; Stilwell to Marshall, 29 September 1942, Stilwell Correspondence, reel 1.

28. Frank James Price, *Troy H. Middleton: A Biography* (Baton Rouge: Louisiana State University Press, 1974), 82; Palmer interview, USAHEC, 93; William H. Gill, as told to Edward Jaquelin Smith, *Always a Commander: The Reminiscences of Major General William H. Gill* (Colorado Springs: Colorado College, 1974), 106; Eichelberger to his wife, 20 June 1945, Eichelberger Papers, reel 47, correspondence 1945; Woodruff interview, 8 September 1971, James Interviews, 25–26; Byers diary, 1 June 1945.

29. Eichelberger to his wife, 29 June and 9 August 1944, Eichelberger Papers, reel 46, correspondence 1943–1944; Krueger to MacArthur, 19 June and 2 July 1944, DMMA, RG-4, reel 593; Eddleman interview, USAHEC, section 5, 9–10.

30. Marshall to MacArthur, 18 January 1944, DMMA, RG-4, reel 594; MacArthur to Marshall, 19 January 1944, ibid.

31. Gill, *Always a Commander,* 64.

32. Ibid., 63–64, 84; Eichelberger to his wife, 21 March 1944, Eichelberger Papers, reel 45, correspondence 1943–1944; Eichelberger to his wife, 29 July 1944, Eichelberger Papers, reel 46, correspondence 1943–1944; Eddleman interview, 15 April 1975, USAHEC, section 4, 2; Krueger, *From Down Under,* 297; Charles Hall, interview by Robert Ross Smith, 27 March 1947, USAHEC, 1–5.

33. McNair to Marshall, 7 October 1941, Marshall Foundation, Pentagon Office, box 76, folder 31.

34. Patton diary, 23 January 1944, *The Patton Papers, 1940–1945,* ed. Martin Blumenson (Boston: Houghton Mifflin, 1974), vol. 2, 402.

35. J. Lawton Collins, *Lightning Joe: An Autobiography* (Baton Rouge: Louisiana State University Press, 1979), 105–106.

36. Eichelberger to his wife, 8 September 1944, *Dear Miss Em,* 154; Stimson diary, 23 January 1941, The Henry Lewis Stimson Diaries, Yale University Library, reel 6, vol. 32, 80; John Edwin Hull, *The Autobiography of General John Edwin Hull, 1895–1975* (M. Anderson, 1978), 107–108; Eichelberger, 13 September 1944, "Memorandum of Interview with General MacArthur," Eichelberger Papers, reel 46, correspondence 1943–1944; Andrew Bruce to his wife, 20 August 1944, Bruce Papers, USAHEC, box 2; McNair to Marshall, 7 October 1942, Marshall Foundation, Pentagon Office, box 82, folder 43.

37. Marshall to McNair, 6 October 1942, *MP,* vol. 3, 388–389.

38. Marshall to Eisenhower, 26 September 1942, ibid., 367; Marshall to McNair, 6 October 1942, ibid., 388–389; McNair to Marshall, 7 October 1942, Marshall Foundation, Pentagon Office, box 82, folder 43; Holland M. Smith and Percy Finch, *Coral and Brass* (New York: Charles Scribner's Sons, 1949), 115–116; Stilwell, 16 January 1942, *Stilwell Papers,* 26.

39. Richardson to Marshall, 16 August 1944, Marshall Foundation, Pentagon Office, box 82, folder 46.

40. Richardson to Marshall, 16 August 1944, *MP,* vol. 4, 553n; Eichelberger to his wife, 29 August and 29 December 1944, *Dear Miss Em,* 153, 187; Eichelberger, 12 September 1944, "Memorandum of Interview with General MacArthur," ibid., 156; Henry Arnold, 9 June 1945, *American Airpower Comes of Age: General Henry H. "Hap" Arnold's World War II Diaries,* ed. John Huston (Maxwell Air Force Base, AL: Air University Press, 2002), vol. 2, 322–323; Hull, *Hull Autobiography,* 107–108; E. B. Potter, *Nimitz* (Annapolis, MD: Naval Institute Press, 1976), 302–305, 346–347; Frank Midkiff to Marshall, 21 March 1944, Marshall Foundation, Pentagon Office, box 82, folder 45; Richardson to Marshall, 16 December 1944, ibid., folder 47; Chester W. Nimitz, 27 January 1965, *The Reminiscences of Chester W. Nimitz,* Columbia University Oral History Collection and New York Times Oral History Program, no. 153 (Sanford, NC: Microfilming Corporation of America, 1979), 70; Smith, *Coral and Brass,* 115–116; Eichelberger to his wife, 27 June 1945, Eichelberger Papers, reel 37, correspondence 1945; Richardson to Handy, 22 February 1945, Handy Papers, Marshall Foundation, box 5, folder 5.

41. Marshall to Richardson, 25 December 1944, Marshall Foundation, Pentagon Office, box 82, folder 47.

42. Marshall to Handy, 3 August 1944, ibid., folder 46; Handy to Richardson, 12 August 1944, ibid.; Handy to Marshall, 30 August 1944, ibid.; Richardson to Marshall, 16 December 1944, ibid.

43. Potter, *Nimitz,* 302–305, 317, 320–321, 346–347; Richardson to Marshall, 12 August 1943, Marshall Foundation, Pentagon Office, box 82, folder 43; Smith, *Coral and Brass,* 126, 128, 142, 170; Richardson to Marshall, 27 December 1943, Marshall Foundation, National Archives Project, Verifax 2081.

44. Marshall to Charles Corlett, 6 October 1941, *MP,* vol. 2, 631; Marshall to McNair,

27 March 1942, *MP*, vol. 3, 151–152; Marshall to John De Witt, 17 March 1943, ibid., 591; Marshall to Eisenhower, 17 and 25 February 1944, *MP*, vol. 4, 306, 317; Charles H. Corlett, *Cowboy Pete: The Autobiography of Major General Charles H. Corlett,* ed. William Farrington (Santa Fe, NM: Sleeping Fox Enterprises, 1974), 85; Potter, *Nimitz,* 320–321, 346–347; Richardson to Marshall, 9 February 1944, Marshall Foundation, Pentagon Office, box 82, folder 44; Marshall to Richardson, n.d., Marshall Foundation, Pentagon Office, box 82; Eisenhower to Marshall, 9 February 1944, *EP,* vol. 3, 1715–1716.

45. J. Lawton Collins interview, 1972, USAHEC, 95; Bruce to his wife, 29 April 1944, Bruce Papers, USAHEC, box 2; Marshall to Richardson, 19 February 1944, Marshall Foundation, National Archives Project, Verifax 1284; Marshall to Millard Harmon, 21 February 1944, ibid.

46. Joseph Stilwell was a conspicuous exception to the overwhelmingly positive evaluations of Hodge. He thought Hodge was "dumb." See Stilwell, 2 September 1945, *Seven Stars: The Okinawa Battle Diaries of Simon Bolivar Buckner, Jr., and Joseph Stilwell,* ed. Nicholas Evan Sarantakes (College Station: Texas A&M University Press, 2004), 112. For more generous evaluations, see Gary Wade, *CSI Report No. 5: Conversations with General J. Lawton Collins* (Fort Leavenworth, KS: Combat Studies Institute, 1983), 4; J. Lawton Collins interview, USAHEC, 65; Chase, *Front Line General,* 160; Woodruff interview, 16 March 1972, Woodruff Papers, DDEL, 49; Eddleman interview, 28 January 1975, USAHEC, section 2, 10; Bruce to his wife, 2 May 1944, Bruce Papers, USAHEC; Richardson to Marshall, 18 January 1945, Marshall Foundation, Pentagon Office, box 82, folder 49; Thomas Kinkaid, 9 October 1961, *The Reminiscences of Thomas Cassin Kinkaid* (Columbia University: Oral History Research Office, 1961), 421; Memorandum for Roosevelt, 25 October 1945, Marshall Foundation, reel 349, item 5226.

47. The quote and Holland Smith's reasoning are in Smith, *Coral and Brass,* 171–175.

48. Ibid., 176–177.

49. For a good discussion of the Buckner Board, see Philip A. Crowl, *Campaign in the Marianas* (Washington, DC: Government Printing Office, 1959), 191–201, with the board's conclusions on 194. See also Buckner diary, 5, 17, 18, 19, 26 July 1944, Buckner Papers, DDEL, part 2.

50. Buckner diary, 23 September 1944, Pre-part 2; Eichelberger to his wife, 29 August and 29 December 1944, *Dear Miss Em,* 153, 187; Eichelberger, 12 September 1944, Memorandum of Interview with General MacArthur, ibid., 156; Nimitz, 27 January 1965, *Reminiscences,* 70; Smith, *Coral and Brass,* 201–202; Crowl, *Marianas,* 195–196; Marshall to King, 30 August 1944, Marshall Foundation, National Archives Project, Verifax 2190.

CHAPTER 5: LIBERATION OF FRANCE

1. Lord Alanbrooke, 15 June, 7 July, 15 August 1943, *War Diaries, 1939–1945,* ed. Alex Danchev and Daniel Todman (Berkeley: University of California Press, 2001), 420, 427,

441–442; Stimson, August 1943, "My Visit to Quebec," The Henry Lewis Stimson Diaries, Yale University Library, reel 8, vol. 4, 95; Stimson diary, 18 December 1943, ibid., vol. 45, 129–130; Dwight Eisenhower, *Crusade in Europe* (New York: Doubleday, 1948), 197.

2. Stimson diary, 16 December 1943, Stimson Diaries, reel 8, vol. 45, 121.

3. Omar Bradley and Clay Blair, *A General's Life: An Autobiography by General of the Army Omar N. Bradley and Clay Blair* (New York: Simon and Schuster, 1983), 210; Roosevelt to John Pershing, 20 September 1943, *MP*, vol. 4, 129n; Marshall, 15 November 1956, *George C. Marshall Interviews and Reminiscences for Forest C. Pogue* (Lexington, VA: George C. Marshall Research Foundation, 1991), 345; Harry Butcher, 23 November 1943, *Three Years with Eisenhower: The Personal Diary of Captain Harry C. Butcher, USNR, Naval Aide to General Eisenhower, 1942 to 1945* (London: William Heinemann, 1946), 382, 384–385; Stimson to Eisenhower, 24 December 1943, *EP*, vol. 3, 1639n; Stimson, 10 August, 7 and 15 September 1943, "My Visit to Quebec," Stimson Diaries, reel 8, vol. 4, 95, 105, 119–120; Stimson diary, 28 September 1943, ibid., vol. 44, 153–154; Stimson diary, 17 and 18 December 1943, ibid., vol. 45, 126, 129–130; Eisenhower, *Crusade in Europe,* 196–197; Marshall interview with Matthews, et al., 25 July 1949, George C. Marshall Foundation, interview 3, part 2, 7; Katherine Tupper Marshall, *Together: Annals of an Army Wife* (New York: Tupper Love, 1946), 142; William D. Leahy, *I Was There: The Personal Story of the Chief of Staff to Presidents Roosevelt and Truman Based on His Notes and Diaries Made at the Time* (New York: McGraw-Hill, 1950), 191–192.

4. Pershing to Roosevelt, 16 September 1943, *MP*, vol. 4, 129.

5. J. Lawton Collins, *Lightning Joe: An Autobiography* (Baton Rouge: Louisiana State University Press, 1979), 175; Alanbrooke, 8 November 1943, *War Diaries,* 467; Marshall to Robert Sherwood, 25 February 1947, *MP*, vol. 4, 103; Marshall, 15 November 1956, *Marshall Interviews and Reminiscences,* 345; Stimson diary, 15 and 28 September, 7 October 1943, Stimson Diaries, reel 8, vol. 44, 119–120, 122, 153–154, 177; Stimson to Roosevelt, 16 September 1943, ibid., 122; Stimson to Hopkins, 10 November 1943, ibid., reel 8, vol. 45, 38; Stimson diary, 17, 18, and 23 December 1943, ibid., 126, 129–130, 140; Marshall interview by Matthews, et al., 25 July 1949, Marshall Foundation, interview 3, part 2, 7; Leahy, *I Was There,* 191–192; Eisenhower, *Crusade in Europe,* 197.

6. Alanbrooke, 4 December 1943 and 29 January 1944, *War Diaries,* 491, 516; Eisenhower memo, 6 December 1943, *EP*, vol. 3, 1585–1588; Stimson diary, 16 December 1943, Stimson Diaries, reel 8, vol. 45, 121; Eisenhower, *Crusade in Europe,* 197; Handy interview, 22 April 1974, USAHEC, vol. 2, section 4, 31.

7. Butcher, 10 December 1943, *Three Years with Eisenhower,* 392.

8. For Eisenhower's attitude, see Butcher, 25 July, 16 September, 5 and 19 October, 6 and 10 December 1943, ibid., 314, 360, 366, 369, 388–390; Eisenhower memo, 6 December 1943, *EP*, vol. 3, 1585–1588; Eisenhower, *Crusade in Europe,* 197, 206–207; Butcher diary, 5 December 1943 and 16 January 1944, Papers Relating to the Allied High Command—1943–45, David Irving Collection, reel 3.

9. Bradley and Blair, *General's Life,* 226; Charles H. Corlett, *Cowboy Pete: The Autobiography of Major General Charles H. Corlett,* ed. William Farrington (Santa Fe, NM: Sleeping Fox Enterprises, 1974), 88; Patton diary, 1 March 1944, *The Patton Papers, 1940–1945,* ed. Martin Blumenson (Boston: Houghton Mifflin, 1974), vol. 2, 419–420; Butcher, 11 and 28 May 1944, *Three Years with Eisenhower,* 462, 471; Stimson diary, 20 December 1943, Stimson Diaries, reel 8, vol. 45, 133.

10. Eisenhower to his son, 31 January 1944, *EP,* vol. 3, 1700; Eisenhower to Marshall, 9 February and 15 March 1944, ibid., 1715–1716, 1769; Marshall to Eisenhower, 26 January 1944, DDEL, Pre-Presidential Papers, Principal File, Box 132; Butcher diary, 29 January and 7 February 1944, Irving Collection, reel 3.

11. Bradley and Blair, *General's Life,* 204–205, 206–207, 211–212; Marshall to Eisenhower, 25 August, 1 September 1943, *MP,* vol. 4, 93, 108; Eisenhower to Marshall, 24 and 27 August, 6 September 1943, *EP,* vol. 2, 1353, 1357–1358, 1388; Eisenhower to Marshall, 17, 23, and 27 December 1943, *EP,* vol. 3, 1605–1606, 1609, 1622–1623; Stimson diary, 16 September 1943, Stimson Diaries, reel 8, vol. 44, 124; Eisenhower, *Crusade in Europe,* 215; Omar Bradley, *A Soldier's Story* (New York: Henry Holt, 1951), 1–8; James McNarney to Eisenhower, 21 December 1943, Marshall Foundation, reel 109, item 2594.

12. W. H. S. Wright, 2 June 1944, "Report to the Secretary of War," Irving Collection, reel 3.

13. The quote is from Corlett, *Cowboy Pete,* 97. See also ibid., 88; Collins, *Lightning Joe,* 179–180; Bradley and Blair, *General's Life,* 212–213, 241; Eisenhower to his son, 31 January 1944, *EP,* vol. 3, 1700; Bradley, *Soldier's Story,* 173, 222; Hansen diary, 3 June 1944, Hansen Papers, USAHEC, box 4; Parker interview, 1983, *ASOOH,* 45.

14. Marshall to Eisenhower, 28 December 1943, *MP,* vol. 4, 210.

15. Marshall to Courtney Hodges, 15 January 1941, *MP,* vol. 2, 389; Marshall to McNair, 27 March 1942, *MP,* vol. 3, 151–152; Marshall to Eisenhower, 26 September 1942, ibid., 367; Marshall to Eisenhower, 29 December 1943, *MP,* vol. 4, 215; Marshall to Handy, 29 December 1943, *MP,* vol. 4, 216; Eisenhower to Marshall, 17, 23, 27, 29, 30 December 1943, 18 and 20 January 1944, *EP,* vol. 3, 1605–1606, 1609, 1622–1623, 1630–1632, 1641, 1664–1665, 1669; McNarney to Eisenhower, 21 December 1943, Marshall Foundation, reel 109, item 2594.

16. Bradley, *Soldier's Story,* 225–226.

17. For evaluations of Hodges, pro and con, see Bradley and Blair, *General's Life,* 94–95, 218, 359–360, 363; Corlett, *Cowboy Pete,* 97; Patton diary, early Nov. 1943, *Patton Papers,* vol. 2, 367; Patton to his wife, 18 August 1944, ibid., 517; Marshall, 4 February 1957, *Marshall Interviews and Reminiscences,* 387; Eisenhower memo, 1 February 1945, *EP,* vol. 4, 2466–2447; Eisenhower to Hodges, 26 May 1945, ibid., 2545; Bennett interview, n.d., USAHEC, 71–72; Ernest N. Harmon, with Milton MacKaye and William Ross MacKaye, *Combat Commander: Autobiography of a Soldier* (Englewood Cliffs, NJ: Prentice-Hall, 1970), 207–208, 248–249; J. Lawton Collins interview, 1972,

USAHEC, 59, 268–269; James Gavin, *On to Berlin: Battles of an Airborne Commander, 1943–1946* (New York: Viking Press, 1978), 205; David W. Hogan, *A Command Post at War: First Army Headquarters in Europe, 1943–1945* (Washington, DC: Center of Military History, 2000), 288–289; Hansen diary, 11–12 February 1945, box 5; Charles Broshous, interview with Thomas Soapes, 17 March 1976, DDEL, no. 2, 93; Wright, 2 June 1944, "Report to the Secretary of War," Irving Collection, reel 3; First Army War Diary, 30 July 1944, Papers Relating to the Allied High Command—1943–45, David Irving Collection, reel 8, file 35; Robert S. Allen, *Lucky Forward: The History of Patton's Third U.S. Army* (New York: Vanguard Press, 1947), 11–15.

18. Eisenhower to Devers, 16 January 1944, *EP*, vol. 3, 1660–1661.

19. Bradley and Blair, *General's Life*, 223; Eisenhower to Marshall, 24 August 1943, *EP*, vol. 2, 1354; Eisenhower to Devers, 16 January 1944, *EP*, vol. 3, 1660–1661; Devers to Eisenhower, 18 January 1944, ibid., 1661n; Eisenhower to Marshall, 23 and 27 December 1943, 18 and 28 January, 29 April 1944, ibid., 1609–1610, 1623, 1665–1666, 1694, 1840–1841; Marshall to Devers, 19 January 1944, *MP*, vol. 4, 238; Devers to Marshall, 18 January 1944, ibid., 238n; Butcher diary, 20 and 29 January 1944, Irving Collection, reel 3; Lucian Truscott, *Command Missions: A Personal Story* (New York: E. P. Dutton, 1954), 383.

20. Collins, *Lightning Joe*, 134, 142–143, 175–179; Bradley and Blair, *General's Life*, 223–224; Eisenhower to Marshall, 18 January 1944, *EP*, vol. 3, 1665–1666; Eichelberger to his wife, 23 December 1943, *Dear Miss Em: General Eichelberger's War in the Pacific, 1942–1945,* ed. Jay Luvaas (Westport, CT: Greenwood Press, 1972), 84; Marshall, 21 November 1956, *Marshall Interviews and Reminiscences,* 370; J. Lawton Collins interview, 1972, USAHEC, 68–61, 115; Bradley, *Soldier's Story,* 228; Hull interview, 4 December 1973, *ASOOH,* section 3, 28; Marshall to MacArthur, 20 December 1943, DMMA, RG-4, reel 594; MacArthur to Marshall, 21 December 1943, ibid., reel 594.

21. Collins, *Lightning Joe,* 166; Collins interview, 1972, USAHEC, 63–64.

22. First Army War Diary, 19 November 1944, reel 8, file 35.

23. Collins, *Lightning Joe,* 46, 181; Bradley and Blair, *General's Life,* 224; Gary Wade, *CSI Report No. 5: Conversations with General J. Lawton Collins* (Fort Leavenworth, KS: Combat Studies Institute, 1983), 3; Maxwell Taylor, interview with Richard Manion, 8 December 1972, USAHEC, section 3, 21; Eisenhower memo, 1 February 1945, *EP*, vol. 4, 2466–2467; Eisenhower to Marshall, 11 April 1945, ibid., 2598–2599; Palmer interview, n.d., USAHEC, 60, 66; Bradley, *Soldier's Story,* 228; Devers interview, 2 July 1975, DDEL, 181; J. Milnor Roberts Jr., interview by Kenneth Bouldin, 18 October 1982, *ASOOH,* 86–89; Maxwell D. Taylor, *Swords and Plowshares* (New York: W. W. Norton, 1972), 71; Hansen diary, 9 and 15 June, 27 July 1944, box 4; Troy Middleton, interview by Orley B. Caudill, 1975, An Oral History with Troy H. Middleton, Mississippi Oral History Collection, University of Southern Mississippi, 46–47; Devers interview, 12 August 1958, Marshall Foundation, 59–60; Patton diary, 3 February, 6 and 9 July 1944, McCarthy Collection, Marshall Foundation, box 17, folder 7, 20, 85, 88.

24. Bradley and Blair, *General's Life,* 224; Marshall to Corlett, 6 October 1941, *MP,* vol. 2, 631; Marshall to McNair, 27 March 1942, *MP,* vol. 3, 151–152; Marshall to Eisenhower, 17 February 1944, *MP,* vol. 4, 306; Corlett, *Cowboy Pete,* 85, 87–88; Patton diary, 18 February 1944, *Patton Papers,* vol. 2, 416–417; Eisenhower to Marshall, 19 February and 27 March 1944, *EP,* vol. 3, 1736, 1795; Bradley, *Soldier's Story,* 228; Richardson to Marshall, 9 February 1944, Marshall Foundation, box 82, folder 44; Eisenhower to Marshall, 24 February 1944, Marshall Foundation, Pentagon Office, box 67, folder 3; Hull to Marshall, 3 September 1943, Marshall Foundation, National Archives Project, Verifax 2066; Marshall to Richardson, 19 February 1944, Marshall Foundation, National Archives Project, Verifax 1284.

25. Bradley and Blair, *General's Life,* 224; Corlett, *Cowboy Pete,* 88–89, 97; Patton diary, 18 February 1944, *Patton Papers,* vol. 2, 416–417; Hansen diary, 2 July 1944, box 4.

26. William M. Hoge, *Engineer Memoirs* (Washington, DC: Office of History, U.S. Army Corps of Engineers, 1993), 204.

27. Bradley and Blair, *General's Life,* 263; Marshall to Richardson, 19 January 1944, *MP,* vol. 4, 242; Marshall to Eisenhower, 25 February 1944, ibid., 317; Patton to Bradley, n.d., *Patton Papers,* vol. 2, 231; Patton to McNair, 10 August 1943, ibid., 317; Eisenhower to Marshall, 24 August 1943, *EP,* vol. 2, 1354; Frank James Price, *Troy H. Middleton: A Biography* (Baton Rouge: Louisiana State University Press, 1974), 73, 135, 170–172, 175–176; Devers diary, 18 January 1944, Devers Papers, USAHEC; Eisenhower to Marshall, 24 February 1944, Marshall Foundation, Pentagon Office, box 67, folder 3; Patton diary, 8 March 1944, McCarthy Collection, Marshall Foundation, box 17, folder 6; Eisenhower to Marshall, 25 February 1944, Marshall Foundation, National Archives Project, Verifax 1284.

28. Price, *Troy H. Middleton,* 91–92, 121, 137; Lucas diary, n.d., 19 October, 19 November 1943, Lucas Papers, USAHEC, box 1, 191, 197, 234.

29. The quote is from Middleton interview, Middleton Oral History, 30–32. See also Patton diary, 30 July 1943, *Patton Papers,* vol. 2, 307; Gay journal, 5 April 1945, ibid., 680; Eisenhower to Marshall, 5 July 1944, *EP,* vol. 3, 1972; Eisenhower to Marshall, 11 April 1945, *EP,* vol. 4, 2599; James Moore, interview by Larry F. Paul, 1984, *ASOOH,* 108; Paul Dewitt Adams, interview by Irving Monclov and Marlin Lang, 5 May 1975, *ASOOH,* section 1, 8–9; Gay interview, 1981, *ASOOH,* 22; Hull interview, 4 December 1973, *ASOOH,* section 3, 13; Hansen diary, 26 August 1944, box 4; Hansen diary, 13 November 1944, 10 January 1945, ibid., box 5; Simpson interview, 26 January 1972, Simpson Papers, USAHEC, box 15, 340; Patton, *War As I Knew It* (Boston: Houghton Mifflin, 1947), 259; Middleton interview, Middleton Oral History, 29; Roscoe Woodruff, "The World War Two," Woodruff Papers, DDEL, 32; Hoge, *Engineer Memoirs,* 204; Fred Walker, 25 March 1942, *From Texas to Rome: A General's Journal* (Dallas: Taylor Publishing, 1969), 70–71; Patton diary, 13 April 1944, McCarthy Collection, Marshall Foundation, box 17, folder 6, 49.

30. Woodruff interview, 16 March 1972, DDEL, 42–44.

31. Collins, *Lightning Joe,* 179; Bradley and Blair, *General's Life,* 223–224; Eichelberger to his wife, 3 April 1944, *Dear Miss Em,* 97; Eisenhower to Marshall, 29 January and 9 February 1944, *EP,* vol. 3, 1695–1696, 1715–1716; Bradley, *Soldier's Story,* 227; Woodruff interview, 16 March 1972, DDEL, 42–44; Woodruff, "The World War Two," 40; Eisenhower to Marshall, 24 February 1944, Marshall Foundation, Pentagon Office, box 67, folder 3; Eisenhower to Marshall, 21 and 25 February 1944, Marshall Archives, National Archives Project, Verifax 1284; Marshall to Eisenhower, 24 and 28 February 1944, Marshall Foundation, National Archives Project, Verifax 1284; Marshall to Devers, 5 July 1943, Marshall Foundation, National Archives Project, Xerox 293.

32. Eisenhower notes, 16 February 1942, *EP,* vol. 1, 109.

33. Bradley and Blair, *General's Life,* 223; Eisenhower to Marshall, 19 September 1942, *EP,* vol. 1, 566–567; Eisenhower to Marshall, 18 January 1944, *EP,* vol. 3, 1665–1666; Marshall to Drum, 3 November 1941, *MP,* vol. 2, 661; Butcher, 26 January 1943, *Three Years with Eisenhower,* 213–214; Woodruff interview, 16 March 1972, DDEL, 42–44; Dwight Eisenhower, *At Ease: Stories I Tell to Friends* (Garden City, NY: Doubleday, 1967), 202–203; Bradley, *Soldier's Story,* 227; McNair to Marshall, 7 October 1941, Marshall Foundation, Pentagon Office, box 76, folder 31; Butcher diary, 7 February 1944, Irving Collection, reel 3; Ray S. Cline, *Washington Command Post: The Operations Division* (Washington, DC: Center of Military History, 1951), 294; Gerow interview, 24 February 1958, Marshall Foundation, 33–34, 61; Devers interview, 12 August 1958, Marshall Foundation, 35; Marshall, 29 October 1956, *Marshall Interviews and Reminiscences,* 614.

34. Roberts interview, 18 October 1982, *ASOOH,* 86–89.

35. Bradley and Blair, *General's Life,* 223; Eisenhower to Marshall, 19 September 1942, *EP,* vol. 1, 566–567; Handy interview, 22 May 1973, DDEL, 59; Butcher diary, 28 April 1944, Irving Collection, reel 3; Bradley, *Soldier's Story,* 227; Matchett interview, 22 July 1976, DDEL, 4–5; Roberts interview, 18 October 1982, *ASOOH,* 91; Hansen diary, 11 September 1943, box 4; Van Fleet interview, 20 January 1973, Van Fleet Papers, USAHEC, vol. 1, box 1, 45; Hughes diary, 10 April 1944, Irving Collection, reel 5; Gerow interview, 24 February 1958, Marshall Foundation, 11.

36. Middleton interview, Middleton Oral History, 37.

37. Devers interview, 12 August 1958, Marshall Foundation, 59; Bradley and Blair, *General's Life,* 218–219, 220–223; Marshall to Eisenhower, 28 December 1943, 19 January 1944, *MP,* vol. 4, 210, 239; Marshall to Handy, 29 December 1943, ibid., 216; Marshall to Devers, 19 January 1944, ibid., 238; Eisenhower to Patton, 17 August 1943, *Patton Papers,* vol. 2, 330; Eisenhower to Marshall, 6 September 1943, ibid., 349; Marshall, 19 November 1956, *Marshall Interviews and Reminiscences,* 545, 547; Butcher, 29 December 1943, *Three Years with Eisenhower,* 397–398; Eisenhower to Marshall, 20 September, 23 October, 17, 27, and 29 December 1943, 18 January 1944, *EP,* vol. 3, 1439–1440, 1524, 1604–1606, 1622–1623, 1630–1632, 1664–1665; Eisenhower to Smith, 2 October 1943, ibid., 1480; Eisenhower to Stimson, 26 December 1943, ibid., 1617; Eisenhower to

Eichelberger, 3 January 1944, Robert L. Eichelberger Papers, Perkins Library, Duke University, reel 45, correspondence 1943–1944; Hughes diary, 9 January 1944, Irving Collection, reel 5; Butcher diary, 12 December 1943, Irving Collection, reel 3.

38. Bradley and Blair, *General's Life,* 208, 211, 218–219; Patton diary, 7 September 1943, *Patton Papers,* vol. 2, 350; Eisenhower, *Crusade in Europe,* 215–216; Bradley, *Soldier's Story,* 229–230; Bradley interview, n.d., McCarthy Collection, Marshall Foundation, box 17, folder 3.

39. Patton diary, 18 January 1944, *Patton Papers,* vol. 2, 398–399.

40. Patton diary, 7 November 1943, ibid., 370.

41. Patton to his wife, 20 December 1943, 12 and 19 January, 9 and 26 February, 12 April 1944, ibid., 390, 397, 400, 413, 418, 435; Patton diary, 27 October 1943, 1 and 26 January, 18 and 23 February, 1 March, 7 July 1944, ibid., 366, 394, 407, 416–420, 478; Patton to Eisenhower, 29 December 1943, ibid., 392; Eisenhower, *Crusade in Europe,* 223–225; Bradley, *Soldier's Story,* 357; Hughes diary, 2 January 1944, Irving Collection, reel 5; Butcher diary, 27 January 1944, Irving Collection, reel 3; Patton for History: Talk with Lieutenant General G. S. Patton, 19 June 1944, Irving Collection, reel 4, file 9.

42. Quoted in Stanley Hirshson, *General Patton: A Soldier's Life* (New York: HarperCollins, 2002), 460.

43. Marshall to Eisenhower, 1 May 1944, *MP,* vol. 4, 445.

44. The quote is from Patton diary, 3 May 1944, *Patton Papers,* vol. 2, 452. See also Bradley and Blair, *General's Life,* 220–223; Marshall to Eisenhower, 26 and 29 April, 1 May 1944, *MP,* vol. 4, 437, 442–443, 445; Patton diary, 26, 27 April, 1 May 1944, *Patton Papers,* vol. 2, 441, 444, 450–451; Patton to his wife, 27 and 30 April, 2 May 1944, ibid., 444, 448, 451–452; Patton to Everett Hughes, 30 April 1944, ibid., 448; Eisenhower to Marshall, 29 April and 3 May 1944, *EP,* vol. 3, 1837–1841, 1846; Stimson to Eisenhower, May 1944, ibid., 1854n; Eisenhower, *Crusade in Europe,* 223–225; Eisenhower, *At Ease,* 269; Bradley, *Soldier's Story,* 231; Hughes diary, 29 April 1944, Irving Collection, reel 5.

45. Collins, *Lightning Joe,* 190, 196; Bradley and Blair, *General's Life,* 243–244; Butcher, 11 May 1944, *Three Years with Eisenhower,* 462; Taylor, *Swords and Plow-shares,* 74–75; Hansen diary, 2 and 3 June 1944, box 4; Butcher diary, 12 May 1944, Irving Collection, reel 3; Wright, 2 June 1944, "Report to the Secretary of War," Irving Collection, reel 3.

46. Butcher, 28 April 1944, *Three Years with Eisenhower,* 453; Matchett interview, 22 July 1976, DDEL, 11–14; Roberts interview, 18 October 1982, *ASOOH,* 102; Hansen diary, 7 and 12 June 1944, box 4; Handy interview, 2 November 1973, USAHEC, vol. 1, section 1, 16.

47. Collins, *Lightning Joe,* 221; J. Lawton Collins interview, 1972, USAHEC, 171; Eisenhower, *Crusade in Europe,* 260; Bradley, *Soldier's Story,* 301; Hansen diary, 6, 9, and 29 June 1944, box 4.

48. Bradley, *Soldier's Story,* 321.

49. Eisenhower to Marshall, 5 July 1944, *EP,* vol. 3, 1972.

50. Collins, *Lightning Joe,* 220; Corlett, *Cowboy Pete,* 92; Marshall to Roosevelt and Stimson, 14 June 1944, *MP,* vol. 4, 480; Marshall to Bradley, 12 July 1944, ibid., 524; Eisenhower to Bradley, 18 June and 8 July 1944, *EP,* vol. 3, 1935, 1986; Eisenhower to Marshall, 19 June and 5 July 1944, ibid., 1936, 1972; Eisenhower, *Crusade in Europe,* 262; Hansen diary, 17, 20, 28, and 29 June, 2 and 19 July 1944, box 4; First Army War Diary, 14 June 1944, reel 8, file 35, 6.

51. Bradley, *Soldier's Story,* 65.

52. Patton diary, 7 July 1944, *Patton Papers,* vol. 2, 478.

53. Gavin, *On to Berlin,* 232–233.

54. For information of Bradley's and Eisenhower's view of divisional commanders, see Bradley and Blair, *General's Life,* 270; Eisenhower to Marshall, 5 and 22 July 1944, *EP,* vol. 3, 1972, 2022–2023; Hansen diary, 24 June, 13 July 1944, box 4; First Army War Diary, 5, 10, 13, and 19 July 1944, reel 8, file 35, 19; Bradley, *Soldier's Story,* 228–229.

55. Bradley and Blair, *General's Life,* 278; Corlett, *Cowboy Pete,* 95; Patton to his wife, early July 1944, *Patton Papers,* vol. 2, 478; Patton diary, 23 July 1944, ibid., 486; Bradley, *Soldier's Story,* 332; Butcher diary, 20 July 1944, Irving Collection, reel 3; Bradley interview, n.d., McCarthy Collection, Marshall Foundation, box 17, folder 3.

56. Bradley and Blair, *General's Life,* 284.

57. Ibid., 283–284; Eisenhower to Marshall, 6 July 1944, *EP,* vol. 3, 1978–1979; Bradley, *Soldier's Story,* 355–356, 358–359.

58. Collins, *Lightning Joe,* 247–248.

59. Patton diary, 6 June, 10, 12, 14 July 1944, *Patton Papers,* vol. 2, 465, 480–481; Patton to his wife, 9 June, 6, 10 July 1944, ibid., 465, 473, 480; Patton to Bradley, 15 June 1944, ibid., 467; Patton to Eisenhower, 14 July 1944, ibid., 481; Paul Harkins, interview by Jacob Couch Jr., 28 April 1974, USAHEC, 28; Wood interview, 21 February 1974, *ASOOH,* section 3, 26–27; Gay interview, 1981, *ASOOH,* 57; Hansen diary, 5 July 1944, box 4; Patton diary, 17 June 1944, McCarthy Collection, Marshall Foundation, box 17, folder 6, 77; Patton diary, 12 July 1944, ibid., folder 7, 90.

60. Patton diary, 1 August 1944, *Patton Papers,* vol. 2, 495–496.

61. Price, *Troy H. Middleton,* 186–187; Hansen diary, 1 August 1944, box 4; Middleton, interview, Middleton Oral History, 32, 49.

62. Marshall to Haislip, 30 January 1942, Haislip Papers, Hoover Institution Archives, Stanford University, box 1.

63. Haislip to Patton, 6 April 1944, ibid.

64. For information on Haislip and his appointment to the Fifteenth Corps, see William K. Wyant, *Sandy Patch: A Biography of Lt. Gen. Alexander M. Patch* (New York: Praeger, 1991), 183; Collins, *Lightning Joe,* 36; Eisenhower note, 5 January 1972, *EP,* vol. 1, 39; Eisenhower memo, 1 February 1945, *EP,* vol. 4, 2466–2468; Eisenhower to Marshall, 11 April 1945, ibid., 2599; J. Lawton Collins interview, 1972, USAHEC, 317; Eisenhower, *At Ease,* 288–289; Devers diary, 1 October 1944; Haislip, "Corps in Combat," Haislip Papers, USAHEC, 1–4, 6–7, 25–26; Russel F. Weigley, *Eisenhower's Lieutenants: The*

Campaign of France and Germany, 1944–1945 (Bloomington: Indiana University Press, 1981), 758–759; Hansen diary, 24 November 1944, box 5; Patton, *War As I Knew It,* 383–384; Patton diary, 2 April 1944, McCarthy Collection, Marshall Foundation, box 17, folder 6, 45; Patton diary, 16 August 1944, ibid., folder 7, 136; Haislip to Eisenhower, 14 May 1945, Haislip Papers, Hoover Institution, box 1; Haislip to McNair, 27 April 1944, ibid.

65. Bradley and Blair, *General's Life,* 292.

66. Charles R. Codman, 8 August 1944, *Drive* (Boston: Little, Brown, 1957), 159.

67. Bradley and Blair, *General's Life,* 298–299.

68. Ibid., 296; Patton diary, 14 and 15 August 1944, *Patton Papers,* vol. 2, 510–511; Patton to Marshall, 17 August 1944, ibid., 517; Patton diary, 16 August 1944, McCarthy Collection, Marshall Foundation, box 17, folder 6, 136; Weigley, *Eisenhower's Lieutenants,* 205.

69. The exchange is from Hansen diary, 3 September 1944, box 4. See also Gerow interview, 24 February 1958, Marshall Foundation, 8; Bradley and Blair, *General's Life,* 318; Patton diary, 2 September 1944, *Patton Papers,* vol. 2, 537.

70. Patton diary, 3 July 1944, McCarthy Collection, Marshall Foundation, box 17, folder 7, 85.

71. Marshall to McNair, 27 March 1942, *MP,* vol. 3, 151–152; Patton to his wife, 6 March 1944 and 1 March 1945, *Patton Papers,* vol. 2, 421, 649; Weigley, *Eisenhower's Lieutenants,* 758–759; Harkins interview, n.d., USAHEC, 28; Waters interview, n.d., USAHEC, 712–713; John Eisenhower, *General Ike: A Personal Reminiscence* (New York: Free Press, 2003), 2; Patton diary, 3 July 1944, McCarthy Collection, Marshall Foundation, box 17, folder 7, 85; McNair to Walton Walker, 9 March and 2 August 1943, Walker Collection, Marshall Foundation, box 6, folder 19.

72. Patton's characterization of Walker is from Joseph C. Goulden, *Korea: The Untold Story of the War* (New York: McGraw-Hill, 1982), 111. See also Wade, *Conversations with Collins,* 6; Patton diary, 2 March 1945, *Patton Papers,* vol. 2, 651; Gay journal, 5 April 1945, ibid., 680; Eisenhower memo, 1 February 1945, *EP,* vol. 4, 2466–2467; Eisenhower to Marshall, 11 April 1945, ibid., 2599; Harkins interview, n.d., USAHEC, 28; Waters interview, 1980, USAHEC, 712–713; Hansen diary, 5 July, 11 October, and 5 November 1944, box 4; Patton, *War As I Knew It,* 305; Clay Blair, *The Forgotten War: America in Korea, 1950–1953* (New York: Times Books, 1987), 34–35.

73. Collins, *Lightning Joe,* 136–137; Patton diary, 12 August 1944, *Patton Papers,* vol. 2, 507; Eisenhower to Marshall, 18 August 1944, *EP,* vol. 4, 2073; J. Lawton Collins interview, 1972, USAHEC, 54, 58, 241; Devers interview, 19 August 1974, DDEL, 41–42; Hull interview, 22 October 1973, *ASOOH,* section 1, 24–25; Hull interview, 4 December 1973, *ASOOH,* section 3, 15; Patton, *War As I Knew It,* 110; Middleton to Gilbert Cook, 6 July 1942, Cook Papers, DDEL, box 3; McNair to Cook, 10 April 1941, 6 April 1942, ibid.; Cook to McNair, 7 April 1941, ibid.; Patton to Cook, 10 December 1944, ibid.; Cook to Patton, 3 May 1945, ibid.; Manton Eddy to Cook, 6 January 1945,

ibid.; Ralph Canine to Cook, 3 October 1944, ibid.; Patton to Lear, 18 August 1944, ibid.

74. Bradley and Blair, *General's Life,* 308; Patton diary, 2 June 1943 and 18 August 1944, *Patton Papers,* vol. 2, 258, 519; Eisenhower to Marshall, 22 July 1944, *EP,* vol. 3, 2022–2023; Eisenhower to Marshall, 18 August 1944, *EP,* vol. 4, 2073; Patton, *War As I Knew It,* 110; Patch to Cook, 6 October 1944, Cook Papers, DDEL, box 3; H. G. Rudner to Cook, 14 October 1944, ibid.; Bradley, *Soldier's Story,* 301; Hansen diary, 24 June 1944, box 4; Collins, *Lightning Joe,* 221.

75. Much of this information about Eddy came from Harold R. Winton, *Corps Commanders of the Bulge: Six American Generals and Victory in the Ardennes* (Lawrence: University Press of Kansas, 2007), 48–50.

76. Ernie Pyle, *Brave Men* (New York: Grosset and Dunlap, 1944), 396.

77. Bradley, *Soldier's Story,* 100–101.

78. Ibid., 88, 298; Bradley and Blair, *General's Life,* 136, 158; Patton to his wife, 20 August 1944, *Patton Papers,* vol. 2, 522; Patton diary, 26 August 1944, ibid., 529; Gay journal, 5 April 1945, ibid., 680; Eisenhower memo, 1 February 1945, *EP,* vol. 4, 2466–2468; Harkins interview, n.d., USAHEC, 26–27; Gay interview, 1981, *ASOOH,* 28; Hansen diary, 9 June 1944, box 4; Patton, *War As I Knew It,* 242; Canine to Cook, 3 October 1944, Cook Papers, DDEL, box 3; Patton diary, 20 April 1945, Irving Collection, reel 4, file 10; Pyle, *Brave Men,* 394–396; Allen, *Lucky Forward,* 117.

79. First Army War Diary, 6 September 1944, reel 8, file 35.

80. Eisenhower to Marshall, 17, 23, 25, 27, 29 December 1943 and 18 January 1944, *EP,* vol. 3, 1604–1605, 1609–1610, 1612–1614, 1623, 1631–1632, 1664–1665; Marshall to Eisenhower, 28 December 1943, *MP,* vol. 4, 210; Marshall to Devers, 19 January 1944, ibid., 238; Butcher, 29 December 1943, *Three Years with Eisenhower,* 397–398; Mark W. Clark, *Calculated Risk* (New York: Harper and Brothers, 1950), 250–251, 256; Butcher diary, 16 December 1943, Irving Collection, reel 3; Clark, 26 and 31 December 1943, Clark Diaries and Correspondence, Clark Papers, Daniel Library, The Citadel, vol. 5.

81. Marshall to Devers, 17 January 1944, *MP,* vol. 4, 238n; Devers to Marshall, 18 and 23 January 1944, *MP,* vol. 4, 238n, 239n; Truscott, *Command Missions,* 382; Clark, *Calculated Risk,* 289–290; Devers interview, 2 July 1975, DDEL, 176–179; Clark interview, 4 January 1970, DDEL, 17–18; Hughes diary, 6 and 9 January 1944, Irving Collection, reel 5; Butcher diary, 20 January 1944, Irving Collection, reel 3; Clark, 9 and 27 January, 17 and 29 February 1944, Clark Diaries and Correspondence, vol. 6; Devers interview, 12 August 1958, Marshall Foundation, 59.

82. Devers interview, 2 July 1975, DDEL, 178–179; Devers interview, 12 August 1958, Marshall Foundation, 59–60; Marshall to Devers, 28 February 1944, Marshall Foundation, National Archives Project, Verifax 1284.

83. Wyant, *Sandy Patch,* 77–80; Marshall to Patch, 29 June 1943, *MP,* vol. 4, 39; Pogue, 25 July 1949, *Marshall Interviews and Reminiscences,* 10–11; Devers interview, 12 August 1958, Marshall Foundation, 59–60.

84. Jean Joseph Marie Gabriel De Lattre de Tassigny, *The History of the French First Army,* trans. Malcolm Barnes (London: George Allen and Unwin, 1952), 53, 75, 173; Devers interview, 12 August 1958, Marshall Foundation, 89–93, 98–99, 108–109, 116.

85. The quote is from Devers to Marshall, 9 August 1944, Marshall Papers, Marshall Foundation, Pentagon Office, box 63, folder 59. See also Truscott, *Command Missions,* 382–383; Harrell interview, n.d., USAHEC, section 3, 59–69; Wood interview, 21 February 1974, *ASOOH,* section 3, 28; Rosson interview, 1981, *ASOOH,* 96; Lemley interview, 5 April 1974, *ASOOH,* section 2, 32–33; De Lattre de Tassigny, *French First Army,* 135; Clark, 12 and 13 June 1944, Clark Diaries and Correspondence, vol. 7; Clark, 10 July 1944, Clark Diaries and Correspondence, vol. 8; Walker, 13 July 1944, *From Texas to Rome,* 407; Devers to Marshall, 22 March 1944, Marshall Papers, Marshall Foundation, Pentagon Office, box 63, folder 55; Devers to Marshall, 9 May and 13 June 1944, Marshall Papers, Marshall Foundation, Pentagon Office, box 63, folder 57; Truscott's aide's diary, 30 June 1944, Truscott Papers, Marshall Foundation, box 18, folder 4.

86. For Devers's campaign for army group command, see Marshall to Devers, 16 July 1944, *MP,* vol. 4, 523–524; Devers to Marshall, 13 July 1944, ibid., 524n; Eisenhower to Marshall, 12 and 15 July 1944, *EP,* vol. 3, 2000, 2009–2010; Butcher diary, 13 July 1944, Irving Collection, reel 3; Marshall to Eisenhower, 17 July 1944, Irving Collection, Smith Files, reel 4, file 8; Devers to Marshall, 1 July 1944, Marshall Papers, Marshall Foundation, Pentagon Office, box 63, folder 58; Devers to Marshall, 9 August 1944, ibid., folder 59.

87. Marshall to Devers, 18 August 1944, *MP,* vol. 4, 556; Devers diary, 27 and 28 August, 12 September 1944; Truscott's aide's diary, 12 August 1944, box 18, folder 5.

CHAPTER 6: MACARTHUR'S RETURN TO THE PHILIPPINES

1. Paul B. Rogers, *The Bitter Years: MacArthur and Sutherland* (New York: Praeger, 1990), 180.

2. John Hodge to Richardson, 2 November 1944, George C. Marshall Foundation, Pentagon Office, box 82, folder 47.

3. For some descriptions of MacArthur's landing, see George C. Kenney, *General Kenney Reports: A Personal History of the Pacific War* (Washington, DC: Air Force Historical Studies Office, 1949), 447–448; Ronald H. Specter, *Eagle against the Sun: The American War with Japan* (New York: Free Press, 1985), 427–428; Geoffrey Perret, *Old Soldiers Never Die: The Life of Douglas MacArthur* (New York: Random House, 1996), 421–423.

4. For Krueger's criticisms, see M. Hamlin Cannon, *Leyte: The Return to the Philippines* (Washington, DC: Government Printing Office, 1954), 244–248.

5. Byers diary, 22 November 1944, Clovis Byers Collection, Hoover Institution, Stanford University, box 36, folder 1.

6. William H. Gill, as told to Edward Jaquelin Smith, *Always a Commander: The*

Reminiscences of Major General William H. Gill (Colorado Springs: Colorado College, 1974), 106; Walter Krueger, *From Down Under to Nippon: The Story of the Sixth Army in World War II* (Washington, DC: Combat Forces Press, 1953), 187–188; Eichelberger to his wife, 22–23 November and 1–2 December 1944, Robert L. Eichelberger Papers, Perkins Library, Duke University, reel 46, correspondence 1943–1944; Eichelberger to his wife, 20 January, 18 February, 30 April 1945, ibid., correspondence 1945; Robert Hackett, interview by Carey Livingston, 1983, *ASOOH,* 128; Byers diary, 21 November 1944; Cannon, *Leyte,* 213; Palmer to Leary, 26 August 1985, Walter Krueger Papers, box 40, 1.

7. Eddleman interview, n.d., USAHEC, section 5, 10–11; Bruce to his wife, 19 December 1944, Bruce Papers, USAHEC, box 2; Hodge to Richardson, 2 November 1944, Marshall Foundation, Pentagon Office, box 82, folder 47; Richardson to Marshall, 30 December 1944, ibid.; Richardson to Marshall, 18 January 1945, ibid., folder 49; Byers diary, 23 November, 26 December 1944, 1 January 1945; Eichelberger to his wife, 12 February 1945, *Dear Miss Em: General Eichelberger's War in the Pacific, 1942–1945,* ed. Jay Luvaas (Westport, CT: Greenwood Press, 1972), 215; Memorandum for Roosevelt, 18 June 1945, Marshall Foundation, reel 349, item 5228.

8. The quote is from Eichelberger to his wife, 23–24 November 1944, Eichelberger Papers, reel 46, correspondence 1943–1944. See also Eichelberger to his wife, 12 and 29 November 1944, *Dear Miss Em,* 164, 172; Eichelberger diary, 12 December 1944, ibid., 176–177; Roger Olaf Egeberg, *The General: MacArthur and the Man He Called "Doc"* (New York: Hippocrene Books, 1983), 76, 84.

9. MacArthur to Marshall, 10 October 1944, DMMA, RG-4, reel 594.

10. Eichelberger to his wife, 22 October, 12, 18, and 27 December 1944, *Dear Miss Em,* 162, 176–177, 186; Egeberg, *MacArthur and the Man He Called "Doc,"* 76, 84; Byers diary, 15 December 1944.

11. Eichelberger to his wife, 23 November 1944, *Dear Miss Em,* 170.

12. Eichelberger to his wife, 27 December 1944, Eichelberger Papers, reel 46, correspondence 1943–1944.

13. Eichelberger to his wife, 21 and 24 November, 8, 18, and 21 December 1944, 13 January 1945, *Dear Miss Em,* 169, 171, 175, 179–180, 195; Eichelberger diary, 12 December 1944, ibid., 176–177; Eichelberger to his wife, 21–22, 27–28 November, 13–14 December 1944, Eichelberger Papers, reel 46, correspondence 1943–1944.

14. For Eichelberger's personnel problems, see Eichelberger to his wife, 5 and 21 November, 8, 29, and 30 December 1944, 13 January and 12 February 1945, *Dear Miss Em,* 164, 169, 175, 187–188, 195, 215; Eichelberger to his wife, 22–23, 23–24, 27–28 November, 17 and 27 December 1944, Eichelberger Papers, reel 46, correspondence 1943–1944; Eichelberger to his wife, 7 January 1945, ibid., correspondence 1945; Byers diary, 16 January 1945, box 36, file 1; Woodruff interview, 8 September 1971, D. Clayton James Interviews, Mitchell Memorial Library, Mississippi State University, 19; Marshall to Eisenhower, 24 February 1944, Marshall Papers, Marshall Foundation, National Archives Project, Verifax 1284.

15. Eichelberger to his wife, 18 December 1944, *Dear Miss Em,* 179; Eichelberger to his wife, 29–30 November and 18–19 December 1944, Eichelberger Papers, reel 46, correspondence 1943–1944; Egeberg, *MacArthur and the Man He Called "Doc,"* 70, 90–93; Rogers, *Bitter Years,* 162–164, 198, 236; Weldon E. (Dusty) Rhoades, *Flying MacArthur to Victory* (College Station: Texas A&M University Press, 1987), 304; Byers diary, 13 November 1944.

16. Egeberg, *MacArthur and the Man He Called "Doc,"* 90–93; Rogers, *Bitter Years,* 211, 216; Rhoades, *Flying MacArthur,* 325, 333.

17. Rogers, *Bitter Years,* 216; Rhoades, *Flying MacArthur,* 333–338.

18. Egeberg, *MacArthur and the Man He Called "Doc,"* 114–115.

19. Eichelberger to his wife, 18 January, 9, 21, and 22 February 1945, *Dear Miss Em,* 197, 214, 225; Decker interview, *ASOOH,* interview 2, 20–21; Egeberg, *MacArthur and the Man He Called "Doc,"* 114–115, 117; Rogers, *Bitter Years,* 240, 248–249; MacArthur to Krueger, 30 January 1945, DMMA, RG-4, reel 593; Griswold diary, 14 January and 17 February 1945, Griswold Papers, USAHEC, box 1; Eddleman interview, 28 January 1975, USAHEC, section 2, 32–33; Eddleman interview, 29 January 1971, James Interviews, 24; Byers diary, 21 February 1945.

20. The quote is from Eichelberger to his wife, 14 February 1945, *Dear Miss Em,* 216. See also Eichelberger to his wife, 22 February 1945, ibid., 225; Rogers, *Bitter Years,* 248–249; Byers diary, 14 and 21 February 1945; Marshall to MacArthur, 16 January 1945, DMMA, RG-4, reel 594; MacArthur to Marshall, 17 January 1945, ibid.

21. The quote is from Harold Riegelman, *Caves of Biak: An American Officer's Experiences in the Southwest Pacific* (New York: Dial Press, 1955), 231. See also Riegelman, *Caves of Biak,* 274; Eichelberger to his wife, 31 March 1945, *Dear Miss Em,* 242; Freeman interview, n.d., USAHEC, 72–73; James Collins interview, 1982, USAHEC, section 2, 43–44; Eddleman interview, 29 June 1971, James Interviews, 26.

22. Griswold diary, 26 January 1945, Griswold Papers, USAHEC, box 1.

23. Ibid., 31 January 1945.

24. Ibid., 9 February 1945.

25. Eichelberger to his wife, 31 March 1945, *Dear Miss Em,* 242; John Kennedy Ohl, *Minuteman: The Military Career of General Robert S. Beightler* (Boulder, CO: Lynne Rienner Publishers, 2001), 140–141; Griswold diary, 15–18, 19–20, 28, 30 January 1945, Griswold Papers, USAHEC, box 1; Eddleman interview, 29 June 1971, James Interviews, 26.

26. Quoted in John Costello, *The Pacific War* (New York: Quill, 1982), 532.

27. MacArthur to Krueger, 30 January 1945, DMMA, RG-4, reel 593.

28. Eichelberger to his wife, 5 February 1945, Eichelberger Papers, reel 46, correspondence 1945.

29. The quote is from Eichelberger to his wife, 8 February 1945, *Dear Miss Em,* 213. For Eichelberger's view of the operation, see Eichelberger to his wife, 19 January, 4, 6, 8, 9, 21 February, 24 March 1945, ibid., 197, 209, 212–214, 225, 237; Eichelberger to his

wife, 19 January and 9 February 1945, Eichelberger Papers, reel 46, correspondence 1945. See also Robert White to Emma Eichelberger, 21 June 1945, Eichelberger Papers, reel 47, correspondence 1945; Swing to Peyton March, 24 February 1945, *Dear General: World War II Letters,* ed. Dale F. Yee (Palo Alto, CA: 11th Airborne Division Association, 1987), 19; Byers diary, 27 February 1945.

30. Griswold diary, 28 January, 7, 11–17, 23 February 1945, Griswold Papers, USAHEC, box 1; Eichelberger to his wife, 4 March 1945, Eichelberger Papers, reel 46, correspondence 1945; Byers diary, 3 March 1945; Memorandum for Roosevelt, 12 April 1945, Marshall Foundation, reel 349, item 5228.

31. Krueger to MacArthur, 15 January 1945, DMMA, RG-4, reel 593; William Chase, *Front Line General: The Commands of Maj. Gen. Wm. C. Chase* (Houston: Pacesetter Press, 1975), 100; Eichelberger to his wife, 18 and 26 February 1945, Eichelberger Papers, reel 46, correspondence 1945; Byers diary, 25 January 1945; Krueger, *From Down Under,* 297, 319; MacArthur to Marshall, 11 April 1945, DMMA, RG-4, reel 594; Robert Ross Smith, *Triumph in the Philippines* (Washington, DC: Government Printing Office, 1963), 319; Memorandum for Roosevelt, 18 June 1945, Marshall Foundation, reel 349, item 5228.

32. Kevin C. Holzimmer, *General Walter Krueger: Unsung Hero of the Pacific War* (Lawrence: University Press of Kansas, 2007), 221, 231; Krueger, *From Down Under,* 282; Marshall to MacArthur, 16 January 1945, DMMA, RG-4, reel 594.

33. The quote is from Griswold diary, 1 July 1945, Griswold Papers, USAHEC, box 1. See also Eichelberger diary, 20 March 1945, *Dear Miss Em,* 251n; Eichelberger to his wife, 15, 21, and 30 June 1945, ibid., 282–283, 286; Eichelberger dictations, 6 July 1945, ibid., 290; Griswold to Eichelberger, 28 April 1945, Eichelberger Papers, reel 46, correspondence 1945; Eichelberger to his wife, 25 May, 22 June, 16 July, and 8 August 1945, Eichelberger Papers, reel 47, correspondence 1945; Swing to March, 28 May 1945, *Dear General,* 35; Byers diary, 16 June 1945.

34. Eichelberger's diary, 20 March 1945, *Dear Miss Em,* 251n; Eichelberger to his wife, 30 June 1945, ibid., 286; Eichelberger to his wife, 25 May and 8, 9, 16, 26 July 1945, Eichelberger Papers, reel 47, correspondence 1945; Riegelman, *Caves of Biak,* 256; Ohl, *Minuteman,* 199–200.

35. Eichelberger to his wife, 7, 21, and 30 June, 6 July 1945, *Dear Miss Em,* 279, 283, 286, 290; Gill, *Always a Commander,* 106; Eichelberger to his wife, 13 and 25 March 1945, Eichelberger Papers, reel 46, correspondence 1945; Swing to Eichelberger, 9 February 1945, ibid.; Eichelberger to his wife, 1 June, 1, 3 and 11 August 1945, Eichelberger Papers, reel 47, correspondence 1945; Byers diary, 7 July 1945; Ohl, *Minuteman,* 199–200; Swing to March, 3 July 1945, *Dear General,* 37; Perk Clarkson to Richardson, 29 April 1945, Marshall Foundation, Pentagon Office, box 82, folder 49.

36. Egeberg, *MacArthur and the Man He Called "Doc,"* 114.

37. Ibid.; Eichelberger to his wife, 14 and 21 February, 6 April, 8 June 1945, *Dear Miss Em,* 216, 225, 246, 280; Eichelberger to his wife, 22 January and 22 February 1945,

Eichelberger Papers, reel 46, correspondence 1945; Rogers, *Bitter Years,* 236, 244, 267; Rhoades, *Flying MacArthur,* 346, 349, 388, 391; Byers diary, 21 February 1945.

38. Eichelberger to his wife, 4 June 1945, *Dear Miss Em,* 278.

39. Rogers, *Bitter Years,* 244; Eichelberger to his wife, 1 July 1945, *Dear Miss Em,* 286–287; Eichelberger to his wife, 10 June 1945, Eichelberger Papers, reel 47, correspondence 1945; Stilwell diary, 18 June 1945, *Seven Stars,* 82.

40. Eichelberger to his wife, 19 June 1945, Eichelberger Papers, reel 47, correspondence 1945.

41. Eichelberger to his wife, 28 April 1945, Eichelberger Papers, reel 46, correspondence 1945.

42. Eichelberger to his wife, 1, 2, 24 March, 10 April, 31 May 1945, *Dear Miss Em,* 228–229, 237–238, 248, 273; Simon Buckner to his wife, 26 March 1945, *Seven Stars,* 27; Eichelberger to his wife, 21, 26, and 31 March 1945, Eichelberger Papers, reel 46, correspondence 1945; Eichelberger to his wife, 22 May 1945, Eichelberger Papers, reel 47, correspondence 1945.

43. Eichelberger to his wife, 24 and 29 March, 6 and 27 April, 19, 26, 29, and 31 May 1945, *Dear Miss Em,* 238, 240, 246–247, 259–260, 268, 271–273; Robert Eichelberger, with Milton MacKaye, *Our Jungle Road to Tokyo* (New York: Viking Press, 1950), 219; William Arnold interview, July and August 1975, *ASOOH,* 150–151; Eichelberger to his wife, 30 March, 1 and 10 April 1945, Eichelberger Papers, reel 46, correspondence 1945; Eichelberger to his wife, 1 and 22 May 1945, Eichelberger Papers, reel 47, correspondence 1945; Roscoe Woodruff, "The World War Two," Woodruff Papers, DDEL, 69, 78–79.

44. Byers diary, 1 July 1945.

45. Eichelberger to his wife, 18 and 25 May, 9 June, 1 July 1945, *Dear Miss Em,* 259–260, 271, 280, 286; Eichelberger to his wife, 5 August 1944, 23 and 30 April 1945, Eichelberger Papers, reel 46, correspondence 1944 and 1945; Eichelberger to his wife, 20 June and 1 July 1945, Eichelberger Papers, reel 47, correspondence 1945; Woodruff interview, 8 September 1971, James Interviews, 25–26; Woodruff, "The World War Two," 78; Byers diary, 3 May 1945; Palmer to Leary, 26 August 1985, Krueger Papers, United States Military Academy, box 40, 1.

Chapter 7: Long Bloody Winter

1. The quote is from Martin Blumenson, *Liberation* (Alexandria, VA: Time-Life Books, 1978), 172. The statistics come from Russell F. Weigley, *Eisenhower's Lieutenants: The Campaign of France and Germany, 1944–1945* (Bloomington: Indiana University Press, 1981), 266.

2. Charles H. Corlett, *Cowboy Pete: The Autobiography of Major General Charles H. Corlett,* ed. William Farrington (Santa Fe, NM: Sleeping Fox Enterprises, 1974), 103.

3. Ibid., 105.

4. The information on Corlett's problems and his relief is from ibid., 102–107; J.

Lawton Collins, *Lightning Joe: An Autobiography* (Baton Rouge: Louisiana State University Press, 1979), 277; Omar Bradley and Clay Blair, *A General's Life: An Autobiography by General of the Army Omar N. Bradley and Clay Blair* (New York: Simon and Schuster, 1983), 337; Eisenhower to Marshall, 20 October and 5 December 1944, *EP*, vol. 4, 2233–2234, 2336; Ernest N. Harmon, with Milton MacKaye and William Rose MacKaye, *Combat Commander: Autobiography of a Soldier* (Englewood Cliffs, NJ: Prentice-Hall, 1970), 216; J. Lawton Collins interview, 1972, USAHEC, 230; Corlett, *Cowboy Pete* (original manuscript), Hoover Institution Archives, Stanford University, 260–261, 267–270; Hansen diary, 19 October and 2 November 1944, Hansen Papers, USAHEC, box 4; First Army War Diary, 14 October 1944, Papers Relating to the Allied High Command—1943–45, David Irving Collection, reel 8, file 35.

5. Lucas diary, 14 December 1943, Lucas Papers, USAHEC, 264.

6. Simpson interview, 26 January 1972, Simpson Papers, USAHEC, box 15, 454–456.

7. Hansen diary, 23 November 1944, box 5.

8. The quote is from Marshall to Raymond McLain, 19 December 1944, *MP*, vol. 4, 701–702. For information on McLain's appointment, background, and character, see Collins, *Lightning Joe,* 277; Bradley and Blair, *General's Life,* 269; Corlett, *Cowboy Pete,* 105; Gary Wade, *CSI Report No. 5: Conversations with General J. Lawton Collins* (Fort Leavenworth, KS: Combat Studies Institute, 1983), 6; Marshall, 29 October 1956, *George C. Marshall Interviews and Reminiscences for Forest C. Pogue* (Lexington, VA: George C. Marshall Research Foundation, 1991), 613–614; Eisenhower to Marshall, 27 March 1944, *EP*, vol. 3, 1796; Eisenhower to Marshall, 19 and 25 August 1944, *EP*, vol. 4, 2080, 2096; Eisenhower memo, 1 February 1945, ibid., 2466–2468; Harmon, *Combat Commander,* 216; J. Lawton Collins interview, 1972, USAHEC, 178, 230; Wilson A. Heefner, *Patton's Bulldog: The Life and Service of General Walton H. Walker* (Shippensburg, PA: White Mane Books, 2001)*,* 100; Omar Bradley, *A Soldier's Story* (New York: Henry Holt, 1951), 297–298; William Depuy, interview by Bill Mullin and Les Brownlee, 19 March 1979, *ASOOH,* section 2, 6, 30; Corlett, *Cowboy Pete* (original manuscript), Hoover Institution, 271; Lucas diary, 14 December 1943, box 1, 264; Hansen diary, 2 and 23 November 1944, box 5; Simpson interview, 26 January 1972, Simpson Papers, USAHEC, box 15, 454–456; Marshall to Eisenhower, 26 March 1944, Irving Collection, Smith Files, reel 4, file 8; Marshall to Devers, 20 March 1944, Marshall Papers, George C. Marshall Foundation, Pentagon Office, box 63, folder 55; Devers to Marshall, 22 March 1944, ibid.

9. Corlett, *Cowboy Pete,* 103; David W. Hogan, *A Command Post at War: First Army Headquarters in Europe, 1943–1945* (Washington, DC: Center of Military History, 2000), 185–186, 193–194; Butcher diary, 16 September 1944, Irving Collection, reel 3; First Army War Diary, 7, 11, and 14 September, 18, 20, and 27 November, 6 and 14 December 1944, reel 8, file 35.

10. Eisenhower to Marshall, 22 July 1944, *EP*, vol. 3, 2022–2023.

11. Eisenhower to his brother, 14 September 1944, *EP*, vol. 4, 2140.

12. Collins, *Lightning Joe,* 303; Bradley and Blair, *General's Life,* 340; Marshall to Eisenhower, 21 September 1944, *MP,* vol. 4, 595; Marshall, 29 October 1956, *Marshall Interviews and Reminiscences,* 614; Marshall to Eisenhower, 26 July 1944, *EP,* vol. 3, 2023n; Eisenhower to Marshall, 22 July 1944, ibid., 2022–2023; Eisenhower to Marshall, 19 and 31 August, 18 September, 27 November 1944, 19 January 1945, *EP,* vol. 4, 2079, 2108, 2159, 2321, 2442; Eisenhower to Bradley, 25 September 1944, ibid., 2192; Hansen diary, 27 July 1944, box 4; George Patton, *War As I Knew It* (Boston: Houghton Mifflin, 1947), 172; Hughes diary, 21 September, 16 October, 3, 4, and 12 November 1944, Irving Collection, reel 5.

13. Robert S. Allen, *Lucky Forward: The History of Patton's Third U.S. Army* (New York: Vanguard Press, 1947), 159n.

14. Dwight Eisenhower, *Crusade in Europe* (New York: Doubleday, 1948), 376.

15. Ibid.; Bradley and Blair, *General's Life,* 219, 340–341; Patton diary, 29 May 1944, *The Patton Papers, 1940–1945,* vol. 2, ed. Martin Blumenson (Boston: Houghton Mifflin, 1974), 461; Wedemeyer interview, n.d., USAHEC, section 2, 32; Thomas R. Stone, "General William Hood Simpson: Unsung Commander of U.S. Ninth Army," *Parameters,* June 1981, 44–52; Moore interview, 1984, *ASOOH,* 103, 100, 120–122, 136–138; Eisenhower memo, 1 February 1945, *EP,* vol. 4, 2466–2467; Waters interview, 1980, USAHEC, 713; Harmon, *Combat Commander,* 211–212; William S. Triplet, *A Colonel in the Armored Divisions: A Memoir, 1941–1945,* ed. Robert H. Ferrell (Columbia: University of Missouri Press, 2001), 45; Simpson interview, 15 March 1972, DDEL, 59–60; Devers interview, 19 August 1974, DDEL, 43; Matchett interview, 22 July 1976, DDEL, 26–27; Hansen diary, 18 and 24 July 1944, box 4; Simpson interview, 22 April 1971 and 22 January 1972, Simpson Papers, USAHEC, box 15, 199, 411–412.

16. Simpson interview, 15 March 1972, DDEL, 64.

17. Bradley and Blair, *General's Life,* 217–218; Marshall to Eisenhower, 26 September 1942, *MP,* vol. 3, 367; Marshall to Devers, 17 January 1944, *MP,* vol. 4, 238n; Eisenhower to Marshall, 23 December 1943, 27 March 1944, *EP,* vol. 3, 1609, 1795; Eisenhower to Marshall, 31 August and 1 October 1944, *EP,* vol. 4, 2108, 2204; Simpson interview, 15 March 1972, DDEL, 1–2; McNair to Simpson, 23 January 1943, Simpson Papers, USAHEC, box 14; Simpson interview, 22 April 1971 and 26 January 1972, Simpson Papers, USAHEC, box 15, 161–165, 287–288, 301–302; McNair to Marshall, 10 July, 10 September, and 7 October 1941, Marshall Papers, Marshall Foundation, Pentagon Office, box 76, folder 31; Marshall to Eisenhower, 22 March 1944, Irving Collection, Smith Files, reel 4, file 8; McNair to Marshall, 23 April 1942, Marshall Foundation, reel 306, item 4650.

18. Hansen diary, 26 August 1944, box 4.

19. Patton diary, 22 August 1944, *Patton Papers,* vol. 2, 525; Moore interview, 1984, *ASOOH,* 108, 101–102, 125; Hansen diary, 31 August, 1 and 3 September 1944, box 4; Simpson interview, 22 April 1971 and 26 January 1972, Simpson Papers, USAHEC, box 15, 134, 340, 436–437; Charles Gerhardt manuscript, Gerhardt Papers, USAHEC, box 1, 77; Patton, *War As I Knew It,* 121, 127–128.

20. Bradley and Blair, *General's Life,* 340; Simpson interview, 15 March 1972, DDEL, 77–79.

21. The quote is from Harmon, *Combat Commander,* 211–212. For the story of Simpson reassuring Harmon, see Moore interview, 1984, *ASOOH,* 101–102. See also Harmon, *Combat Commander,* 204–207; Bradley, *Soldier's Story,* 437.

22. The casualty figures are from Weigley, *Eisenhower's Lieutenants,* 431. See also Bradley, *Soldier's Story,* 422; Parker interview, 1983, *ASOOH,* 45–46; Hansen diary, 15 November 1944, box 5.

23. Patton to Adna Chaffee, 22 March 1941, *Patton Papers,* vol. 2, 24–25; Eisenhower to Patton, 29 July 1942, *EP,* vol. 1, 426–427; Eisenhower to Marshall, 29 January, 27 March, 21 May 1944, *EP,* vol. 3, 1695–1696, 1796, 1878; Marshall to Eisenhower, 26 January 1944, Eisenhower's Pre-Presidential Papers, DDEL, Principal File, Box 132; Devers interview, 18 November 1974, DDEL, 89, 105; Simpson to Alvan Gillem, 24 August 1954, Gillem Papers, USAHEC, box 6; Devers to Gillem, 9 April 1943 and 24 May 1943, ibid., box 7; World War Two Corps Commanders Data Sheet, n.d., ibid., box 16; McNair's Efficiency Reports on Gillem, 1 January and 1 July 1944, ibid.; Hansen diary, 30 October 1944, box 4; Simpson interview, 26 January 1972, Simpson Papers, USAHEC, box 15; Handy to Marshall, 13 February 1944, Marshall Papers, Marshall Foundation, Pentagon Office, box 63, folder 3; Stanley Hirshson, *General Patton: A Soldier's Life* (New York: HarperCollins, 2002), 227.

24. Simpson to Gillem, 24 August 1954, Gillem Papers, USAHEC, box 6.

25. Eisenhower to Marshall, 11 April 1945, *EP,* vol. 4, 2599–2560; World War Two Corps Commanders Data Sheet, n.d., Gillem Papers, USAHEC, box 16; Simpson's Efficiency Report on Gillem, 18 June 1945, ibid.; Simpson interview, 26 January 1972, Simpson Papers, USAHEC, box 15, 454; Van Fleet interview, 20 January 1973, Van Fleet Papers, USAHEC, box 1, vol. 1, 45; Memo for Roosevelt, 23 October 1945, Marshall Foundation, reel 349, item 5226; Stone, "Simpson," 48.

26. Patton to Walter Dilingham, 11 October 1944, *Patton Papers,* vol. 2, 563–564.

27. Patton diary, late September 1944, ibid., 558–560.

28. For information about Patton's relationships with Eddy, Haislip, and Walker that fall, see Marshall to Beatrice Patton, 25 October 1944, *MP,* vol. 4, 637; Patton diary, 15, 16, 22, 28 September, 8 October, 11 and 19 November, 7, 14 December 1944, *Patton Papers,* vol. 2, 548–549, 553, 555, 563–564, 573, 575, 588, 591; Heefner, *Patton's Bulldog,* 93; Patton to Wade Haislip, 29 September 1944, Haislip Papers, USAHEC; Hansen diary, 11 October 1944, box 4; Hansen diary, 5 November 1944, box 5; Patton, *War As I Knew It,* 126–127, 133–134, 188; Bradley, *Soldier's Story,* 427–428; Hughes diary, 13 September 1944, Irving Collection, reel 5; Patton diary, 16 December 1944, McCarthy Collection, Marshall Foundation, box 17, folder 8, 213.

29. Eisenhower to Bradley, 15 September 1944, *EP,* vol. 4, 2147.

30. Patton diary, 21 September and mid-October 1944, *Patton Papers,* vol. 2, 552, 565; Devers diary, 25 October, 23 and 25 November, 14 December 1944, Devers Papers,

USAHEC; Hansen diary, 5 October 1944, box 4; Devers interview, 12 August 1958, Marshall Foundation, 44–46.

31. Stimson diary, 16 October 1944, The Henry Lewis Stimson Diaries, Yale University Library, reel 9, vol. 48, 151; Jean Joseph Marie Gabriel De Lattre de Tassigny, *The History of the French First Army,* trans. Malcolm Barnes (London: George Allen and Unwin, 1952), 194; Devers diary, 11 October and 7 November 1944; Devers interview, 12 August 1958, Marshall Foundation, 87–88.

32. Patton diary, 22 September, 5 November, and 7 December 1944, *Patton Papers,* vol. 2, 553, 568, 588; Devers diary, 22 September, 5 and 14 December 1944.

33. Devers diary, 17 November 1944; Hansen diary, 24 November 1944, box 5; William R. Buster, *Time on Target: The World War II Memoir of William R. Buster,* ed. Jeffrey Suchanek and William J. Marshall (Frankfort: Kentucky Historical Society Foundation, 1999), 71, 107.

34. The quote is from Devers diary, 18 October 1944. See also Lemley interview, 24 April 1974, *ASOOH,* section 3, 31; Marshall to Eisenhower, 26 January 1944, DDEL, Pre-Presidential Papers, Principal File, Box 132; Devers interview, 12 August 1958, Marshall Foundation, 65; Patton diary, 8 March 1944, McCarthy Collection, Marshall Foundation, box 17, folder 6, 35; McNair to Marshall, 6 April 1943, Marshall Foundation, National Archives Project, Xerox 2294; Eisenhower to Marshall, 4 April 1943, ibid.

35. Bradley and Blair, *General's War,* 396–397; William K. Wyant, *Sandy Patch: A Biography of Lt. Gen. Alexander M. Patch* (New York: Praeger, 1991), 149–151; Lemley interview, 5 April 1974, *ASOOH,* section 2, 32–33; Devers diary, 7, 12, 21, 27 September, 11 and 26 October, 1, 4, 19 November 1944; First Army War Diary, 29 October 1944, reel 8, file 35.

36. Eisenhower to the Combined Chiefs of Staff, 29 September 1944, *EP,* vol. 4, 2200.

37. Devers diary, 14 December 1944.

38. Haislip's exchange with Eisenhower is from Hansen diary, 24 November 1944, box 5. For Patch's and Haislip's views, see also Patton diary, 20 November and early December 1944, *Patton Papers,* vol. 2, 576, 583; Devers diary, 1 October, 11, 17, 19, 20, 26 November, 5, 14, 17 December 1944; Devers to Marshall, 11 December 1944, Marshall Papers, Marshall Foundation, Pentagon Office, box 63, folder 59; Devers interview, 12 August 1958, Marshall Foundation, 45–46; Devers to Haislip, 29 November 1944, Haislip Papers, Hoover Institution, box 1.

39. Moore interview, 1984, *ASOOH,* 108–109.

40. Middleton interview, An Oral History with Troy H. Middleton, Mississippi Oral History Collection, University of Southern Mississippi, 34.

41. Ibid., 44.

42. Ibid., 34, 44; Matthew Ridgway, *Soldier: The Memoirs of Matthew B. Ridgway* (New York: Harper and Brothers, 1956), 49–50; Patton diary, about 21 December 1944, *Patton Papers,* vol. 2, 602; Frank James Price, *Troy H. Middleton: A Biography* (Baton

Rouge: Louisiana State University Press, 1974), 214, 227; Bradley, *Soldier's Story,* 453–454, 475; First Army War Diary, 2 November 1944, reel 8, file 35.

43. Bradley and Blair, *General's War,* 359–360; Hogan, *Command Post at War,* 212–213; James Gavin, *On to Berlin: Battles of an Airborne Commander, 1943–1946* (New York: Viking Press, 1978), 205; Betts interview, 16 August 1976, DDEL, no. 4, 263; First Army War Diary, 16 December 1944, reel 8, file 35.

44. Simpson interview, 15 March 1972, DDEL, 89–90.

45. Ibid., 69–70.

46. For Eisenhower's response, see Weigley, *Eisenhower's Lieutenants,* 457–458.

47. Quoted in William K. Goolrick and Ogden Tanner, *Battle of the Bulge* (Alexandria, VA: Time-Life Books, 1979), 111.

48. For a discussion of these decisions, see Patton diary, late November 1944, *Patton Papers,* vol. 2, 582; Bradley and Blair, *General's Life,* 363; Betts interview, 16 August 1976, DDEL, no. 4, 263.

49. Heefner, *Patton's Bulldog,* 109; Bradley and Blair, *General's Life,* 368; Patton diary, 22 December 1944 and 7 February 1945, *Patton Papers,* vol. 2, 604, 637–638; Patton diary, 17 December 1944, McCarthy Collection, Marshall Foundation, box 17, folder 8; Hansen diary, 2 November 1944, box 5; Patton, *War As I Knew It,* 155.

50. Quoted in Harold R. Winton, *Corps Commanders of the Bulge: Six American Generals and Victory in the Ardennes* (Lawrence: University Press of Kansas, 2007), 46.

51. Part of Millikin's biography comes from ibid., 44–48. See also Hansen diary, 19 December 1944, box 5; Hogan, *Command Post at War,* 253.

52. Marshall to Eisenhower, 26 January 1944, Eisenhower's Pre-Presidential Papers, DDEL, Principal File, Box 132; Marshall to MacArthur, 18 January 1944, DMMA, RG-4, reel 594; McNair to Marshall, 7 October 1941, Marshall Foundation, Pentagon Office, box 76, folder 31; Simpson to Millikin, 18 October 1944, Simpson Papers, USAHEC, box 6; Simpson interview, 26 January 1972, ibid., box 15; McNair to Marshall, 27 June 1944, Marshall Foundation, RG-165, box 427.

53. Bradley and Blair, *General's Life,* 368; Patton diary, 22 December 1944, 6, 11, 17 January, 7 February 1945, *Patton Papers,* vol. 2, 604, 616, 622, 625, 637–638; Paul F. Braim, *The Will To Win: The Life of General James A. Van Fleet* (Annapolis, MD: Naval Institute Press, 2001), 137; Hansen diary, 19 December 1944 and 10 January 1945, box 5.

54. Patton diary, 4, 6, 8, 17, 27 January 1945, *Patton Papers,* vol. 2, 615–616, 619–620, 625, 630; Hansen diary, 10 January 1945, box 5; Middleton interview, Middleton Oral History, 35, 44; Patton diary, 7 and 24 January 1945, McCarthy Collection, Marshall Foundation, box 17, folder 9, 217, 253.

55. Quoted in Weigley, *Eisenhower's Lieutenants,* 505.

56. Eisenhower to Montgomery, 22 December 1944, *EP,* vol. 4, 2369.

57. Bradley and Blair, *General's Life,* 367; Harry Butcher, 11 January 1945, *Three Years with Eisenhower: The Personal Diary of Captain Harry C. Butcher, USNR, Naval Aide to*

General Eisenhower, 1942 to 1945 (London: William Heinemann, 1946), 628; Gavin, *On to Berlin,* 243–244; Hogan, *Command Post at War,* 220, 229; Montgomery to Eisenhower, 23 December 1944, Irving Collection, Smith Files, reel 4, file 8; First Army War Diary, 23 and 27 December 1944, reel 8, file 35.

58. Ridgway, *Soldier,* 49–50.

59. Ibid., 27–28, 47; part of Ridgway's biography comes from Winton, *Corps Commanders of the Bulge,* 40–41. See also First Army War Diary, 17 December 1944, reel 8, file 35; Bradley and Blair, *General's Life,* 50.

60. Hansen diary, 19 June 1944, box 4.

61. Bradley and Blair, *General's Life,* 269; Marshall to Bradley, 12 July 1944, *MP,* vol. 4, 517; Ridgway, *Soldier,* 17; Eisenhower to Marshall, 11 February 1943, *EP,* vol. 2, 951; Eisenhower to Henry Arnold, 13 July 1944, *EP,* vol. 3, 2001; Hansen diary, 19 and 24 June 1944, box 4; Hansen diary, 5 November 1944, box 5; Butcher diary, 13 July 1944, Irving Collection, reel 3.

62. Quoted in Clay Blair, *The Forgotten War: America in Korea, 1950–1953* (New York: Times Books, 1987), 559.

63. Melvin Zais, interview by William Golden and Richard Rice, 1977, *ASOOH,* vol. 1, 229.

64. Bradley and Blair, *General's Life,* 50, 263; Ridgway, *Soldier,* 31; J. Lawton Collins interview, 1972, USAHEC, 5; Eisenhower memo, 1 February 1945, *EP,* vol. 4, 2466–2467; Gavin, *On to Berlin,* 143, 221; Maxwell D. Taylor, *Swords and Plowshares* (New York: W. W. Norton, 1972), 44; Hansen diary, 28 September 1944, box 4; Triplet, *Colonel in the Armored Divisions,* 195.

65. Collins, *Lightning Joe,* 284; Gavin, *On to Berlin,* 221; J. Lawton Collins interview, 1972, USAHEC, 233; Hansen diary, 7 February 1945, box 5; Blair, *Forgotten War,* 449–462.

66. Collins, *Lightning Joe,* 283–285; Gavin, *On to Berlin,* 247–248; First Army War Diary, 21, 23, and 25 December 1944, reel 8, file 35.

67. First Army War Diary, 29 December 1944 and 9 January 1945, reel 8, file 35.

CHAPTER 8: CONQUEST OF GERMANY

1. For a view of Devers's thinking, see Devers diary, 20, 21, 25, 26, 29 December 1944, 1, 6, 8, 9, 10, 17, 18 January 1945, Devers Papers, USAHEC. See also Betts interview, 16 August 1976, DDEL, no. 4, 263–264; Patton diary, 5 February 1945, Papers Relating to the Allied High Command—1943–45, David Irving Collection, reel 4, file 10.

2. The quote is from Eisenhower memo, 1 February 1945, *EP,* vol. 4, 2466–2468. See also Eisenhower to Marshall, 12 January 1945, ibid., 2425; Dwight Eisenhower, *Crusade in Europe* (New York: Doubleday, 1948), 331–332; Omar Bradley and Clay Blair, *A General's Life: An Autobiography by General of the Army Omar N. Bradley and Clay Blair* (New York: Simon and Schuster, 1983), 390, 403; Patton diary, 23 January 1945, *The Patton Papers, 1940–1945,* vol. 2, ed. Martin Blumenson (Boston: Houghton Mifflin,

1974), 628; Devers diary, 23 January 1945; George Patton, *War As I Knew It* (Boston: Houghton Mifflin, 1947), 221–222, 225–226.

3. Jean Joseph Marie Gabriel De Lattre de Tassigny, *The History of the French First Army,* trans. Malcolm Barnes (London: George Allen and Unwin, 1952), 365; Roscoe Woodruff, "The World War Two," Woodruff Papers, DDEL, 43; Clay Blair, *The Forgotten War: America in Korea, 1950–1953* (New York: Times Books, 1987), 279–280, 572.

4. Eisenhower to Marshall, 22 July 1944, *EP,* vol. 3, 2022–2023; Eisenhower to Marshall, 18 September 1944, *EP,* vol. 4, 2161; Marshall to MacArthur, 18 January and 23 April 1944, DMMA, RG-4, reel 594; Devers diary, 24 December 1944; Marshall to Eisenhower, 22 and 25 July 1944, Irving Collection, Smith Files, reel 4, file 8; Marshall to Eisenhower, 26 January 1944, DDEL, Pre-Presidential Papers, Principal File, Box 132; McNair to Marshall, 27 June 1944, George C. Marshall Foundation, Records of the General Staff, Box 427, RG-165; Hull to Marshall, 17 September 1944, Marshall Foundation, National Archives Project, Verifax 2239.

5. De Lattre de Tassigny, *French First Army,* 365.

6. Marshall, 19 November 1956, *George C. Marshall Interviews and Reminiscences for Forest C. Pogue* (Lexington, VA: George C. Marshall Research Foundation, 1991), 543; Eisenhower to Marshall, 22 July 1944, *EP,* vol. 3, 2022–2023; Bradley and Blair, *General's Life,* 195; Lucas diary, 27 and 28 July 1943, Lucas Papers, USAHEC, box 1; Hughes diary, 27 July 1943, Irving Collection, reel 5.

7. James Woolnough, interview by W. D. MacMillan and William Stevenson, 18 February 1971, USAHEC, vol. 1, 18.

8. The quote is from ibid., 16. See also J. Lawton Collins, *Lightning Joe: An Autobiography* (Baton Rouge: Louisiana State University Press, 1979), 235; Harry Butcher, 29 October 1944, *Three Years with Eisenhower: The Personal Diary of Captain Harry C. Butcher, USNR, Naval Aide to General Eisenhower, 1942 to 1945* (London: William Heinemann, 1946), 587–588; Omar Bradley, *A Soldier's Story* (New York: Henry Holt, 1951), 156–157, 529; Matchett interview, 22 July 1976, DDEL, 14; Porter interview, 1981, *ASOOH,* 307–308; Van Fleet interview, 3 March 1973, Van Fleet Papers, USAHEC, box 1, interview 3, 6; First Army War Diary, 19 and 25 June, 13 November 1944, Papers Relating to the Allied High Command—1943–45, David Irving Collection, reel 8, file 35, 9, 14.

9. Bradley and Blair, *General's Life,* 395; First Army War Diary, 31 January, 8 February, 14 March 1945, reel 8, file 35.

10. First Army War Diary, 21 February 1945, reel 8, file 35.

11. The quote is from Bradley and Blair, *General's Life,* 399–400. See also ibid., 395; Patton diary, 24 February 1945, *Patton Papers,* vol. 2, 647; Eisenhower to Marshall, 2 March 1945, *EP,* vol. 4, 2504; Francis De Guingand, *Generals at War* (London: Hodder and Stoughton, 1964), 164; Moore interview, 1984, *ASOOH,* 157; Thomas R. Stone, "General William Hood Simpson: Unsung Commander of U.S. Ninth Army," *Parameters,* June 1981, 50; Hansen diary, 17 February, 1 and 2 March 1945, box 5.

12. Quoted in Stone, "Simpson," 52n.

13. Eisenhower to Marshall, 21 May 1944, *EP,* vol. 3, 1878; Simpson interview, 15 March 1972, DDEL, 55–58; Stone, "Simpson," 48; Simpson to John B. Anderson, 9 April 1945, Simpson Papers, USAHEC, box 6; Anderson to Simpson, 15 July 1947, ibid., box 14; Simpson interview, 22 April 1971 and 1 June 1974, ibid., box 15, 160, 286, 896; Marshall to Eisenhower, 26 January 1944, DDEL, Pre-Presidential Papers, Principal File, Box 132; McNair to Marshall, 27 June 1944, Marshall Foundation, Records of the General Staff, Box 427, RG-165.

14. Ernest N. Harmon, with Milton MacKaye and William Ross MacKaye, *Combat Commander: Autobiography of a Soldier* (Englewood Cliff, NJ: Prentice-Hall, 1970), 248–252; Collins, *Lightning Joe,* 316–317.

15. Patton diary, 7 February 1945, *Patton Papers,* vol. 2, 637–638; Patton, *War As I Knew It,* 237; Patton diary, 5 and 10 February 1945, Irving Collection, reel 4, file 10; First Army War Diary, 8 February 1945, reel 8, file 35.

16. Hansen diary, 11–12 February 1945, box 5.

17. Collins, *Lightning Joe,* 303; Bradley and Blair, *General's Life,* 400, 405; Hansen diary, 4, 5, 11–12 February, 2 and 28 March 1945, box 5; First Army War Diary, 3 February and 7 March 1945, reel 8, file 35.

18. The quote is from Patton diary, 2 March 1945, *Patton Papers,* vol. 2, 651. See also ibid., 6, 12, 22, 24, 27 February 1945, 637–638, 644–645, 647–649; Bradley and Blair, *General's Life,* 394; Butcher, 3 March 1945, *Three Years with Eisenhower,* 650; Wilson A. Heefner, *Patton's Bulldog: The Life and Service of General Walton H. Walker* (Shippens-burg, PA: White Mane Books, 2001), 111; Patton, *War As I Knew It,* 226–227, 234, 238, 247; Patton diary, 20 February 1945, Irving Collection, reel 4, file 10.

19. Quoted in Russell F. Weigley, *Eisenhower's Lieutenants: The Campaign of France and Germany, 1944–1945* (Bloomington: Indiana University Press, 1981), 636.

20. Bradley and Blair, *General's Life,* 403; Patton diary, 3 and 23 January, mid-March 1945, *Patton Papers,* vol. 2, 614, 628, 657; Devers diary, 17 March 1945; Patton, *War As I Knew It,* 259; Patton to Cook, 15 May 1945, Cook Papers, DDEL, box 3; Patton diary, 11, 14, and 20 March 1945, Irving Collection, reel 4, file 10; Eisenhower to Marshall, 17 March 1945, *EP,* vol. 4, 2531.

21. For the story of Hodges's, Bradley's, Bull's, and Eisenhower's responses, see First Army War Diary, 7 March 1945, reel 8, file 35; Bradley, *Soldier's Story,* 510; Weigley, *Eisenhower's Lieutenants,* 628–629.

22. The quote is from First Army War Diary, 15 March 1945, reel 8, file 35. See also Bradley and Blair, *General's Life,* 408; David W. Hogan, *A Command Post At War: First Army Headquarters in Europe, 1943–1945* (Washington, DC: Center of Military History, 2000), 253; First Army War Diary, 8, 9, 11, 12 March 1945, reel 8, file 35; William M. Hoge, *Engineer Memoirs* (Washington, DC: Office of History, U.S. Army Corps of Engineers, 1993), 148.

23. Paul F. Braim, *The Will To Win: The Life of General James A. Van Fleet* (Annapolis, MD: Naval Institute Press, 2001), 137–138; Van Fleet interview, 20 January 1973, Van

Fleet Papers, USAHEC, vol. 1, box 1, 71–72; Hughes diary, 20 March and 12 April 1945, Irving Collection, reel 5; Patton diary, 10 April 1945, Irving Collection, reel 4, file 10; First Army War Diary, 17 March 1945, reel 8, file 35.

24. Quoted in Braim, *Will To Win,* 89.

25. Ibid., 61, 89, 93, 132–133, 141; Collins, *Lightning Joe,* 182, 224; Bradley and Blair, *General's Life,* 263, 408; Gary Wade, *CSI Report No. 5: Conversations with General J. Lawton Collins* (Fort Leavenworth, KS: Combat Studies Institute, 1983), 3–4; Marshall, 28 September 1956, *Marshall Interviews and Reminiscences,* 578; Eisenhower to Smith, 16 June 1944, *EP,* vol. 3, 1928; Waters interview, 1980, USAHEC, 695–696; J. Lawton Collins interview, 1972, USAHEC, 152–154; Depuy interview, 19 March 1979, *ASOOH,* section 2, 30; Hansen diary, 18 June 1944, box 4; Van Fleet interview, 20 January 1973, Van Fleet Papers, USAHEC, vol. 1, box 1, 46, 70; Patton, *War As I Knew It,* 187, 311; First Army War Diary, 5 April 1945, reel 8, file 35; Hoge, *Engineer Memoirs,* 148; Blair, *Forgotten War,* 805–806.

26. Bradley and Blair, *General's Life,* 424; Bradley, *Soldier's Story,* 528; Moore interview, 1984, *ASOOH,* 158–159; Simpson interview, 26 January 1972, Simpson Papers, USAHEC, box 15, 456–457, 881–882; Eisenhower to Marshall, 26 March 1945, Marshall Foundation, Pentagon Office, box 67, folder 21.

27. Collins, *Lightning Joe,* 322; First Army War Diary, 5 April 1945, reel 8, file 35; Weigley, *Eisenhower's Lieutenants,* 699.

28. Bradley and Blair, *General's Life,* 430–431; Patton diary, 23 March 1945, *Patton Papers,* vol. 2, 659; Bradley, *Soldier's Story,* 543; Patton, *War As I Knew It,* 273–274; Patton diary, 23 April 1945, Irving Collection, reel 4, file 10; Haislip to Eisenhower, 14 May 1945, Haislip Papers, Hoover Institution Archives, Stanford University, box 1.

29. Bradley and Blair, *General's Life,* 430–431; Patton, *War As I Knew It,* 303–305; Patton to Cook, 19 April 1945, Cook Papers, DDEL, box 3; Patton diary, 17, 19, 20, 21 April 1945, Irving Collection, reel 4, file 10.

CHAPTER 9: CLOSING IN ON JAPAN

1. Marshall to De Witt, 3 September 1942, *MP,* vol. 3, 334–335; Robert Theobald to Marshall, 20 August 1942, ibid., 341n; Thomas Kinkaid, 12 June 1961, *The Reminiscences of Thomas Cassin Kindaid* (Columbia University: Oral History Research Office, 1961), 224, 243–244.

2. David Wittels, 8 May 1943, "These Are the Generals: Buckner," *Saturday Evening Post* 215, no. 45:17, 102.

3. The quote is from Buckner diary, 19 June 1944, Buckner Papers, DDEL, 1944, part 1. See also ibid., part 2; Marshall to McNair, 27 March 1942, *MP,* vol. 3, 151–152; Frederick J. Clark, *Engineer Memoirs: Interviews with Lieutenant General Frederick J. Clark* (Washington, DC: Historical Division, Office of Administrative Services, Chief of Engineers Office, 1979), 30–31; Kinkaid, 12 June 1961, *Kinkaid Reminiscences,* 224, 243–244.

4. Marshall to De Witt, 22 July 1941, *MP,* vol. 2, 575; Marshall to McNair, 27 March 1942, *MP,* vol. 3, 151–152; Marshall to De Witt, 3 September and 2 October 1942 and 17 March 1943, ibid., 334–335, 379–380, 591; Omar Bradley, *A Soldier's Story* (New York: Henry Holt, 1951), 175; Eichelberger to his wife, 17 July 1944, Robert L. Eichelberger Papers, Perkins Library, Duke University, reel 46, correspondence 1943–1944; Marshall, 15 April 1943, Memorandum for the AC of S, G-1, George C. Marshall Foundation, Pentagon Office, box 65, folder 47; Richardson to Marshall, 10 August 1944, ibid., box 82, folder 46; Richardson to Marshall, 28 February 1945, Marshall Foundation, reel 119, item 2930; Marshall to Richardson, 24 May 1944, ibid., reel 124, item 3214; Hull to Handy, 26 August 1944, ibid., reel 124, item 3214; DeWitt to Marshall, 28 August 1943, Marshall Foundation, National Archives Project, Verifax 2062; Handy to Cooke, 2 May 1944, ibid., Verifax 2188.

5. Buckner diary, 7 October 1944, Buckner Papers, DDEL, 1944, part 2.

6. Buckner diary, 13 September 1944, 17 January, 7 February 1945, *Seven Stars: The Okinawa Battle Diaries of Simon Bolivar Buckner, Jr., and Joseph Stilwell,* ed. Nicholas Evan Sarantakes (College Station: Texas A&M University Press, 2004), 17, 19; Stilwell, 19 June 1945, *Seven Stars,* 87; Eichelberger to his wife, 9 October 1944, Eichelberger Papers, reel 46, correspondence 1943–1944; Buckner diary, 19 July, 23 September 1944, Buckner Papers, DDEL, 1944, part 2; Buckner diary, 17 February 1945, ibid., 1945, part 1; Byers diary, 11 August 1944, Clovis Byers Collection, Hoover Institution Archives, Stanford University, box 36, folder 1.

7. Eichelberger to his wife, 4 March 1945, *Dear Miss Em: General Eichelberger's War in the Pacific, 1942–1945,* ed. Jay Luvaas (Westport, CT: Greenwood Press, 1972), 230; Buckner diary, 17 January 1945, *Seven Stars,* 19; Eichelberger to his wife, 2 January 1945, Eichelberger Papers, reel 46, correspondence 1945; Richardson to Marshall, 30 December 1944, Marshall Foundation, Pentagon Office; Buckner diary, 9, 17, 26, 27, and 28 January 1945, Buckner Papers, DDEL, 1945, part 1; Byers diary, 21 December 1944 and 14 February 1945.

8. Buckner diary, 31 March 1945, *Seven Stars,* 28–29.

9. For information on Buckner's attitude, see Buckner diary, 12, 13, 20, 31 March, 1 April 1945, *Seven Stars,* 21–22, 24, 28–29; Buckner to his wife, 14 April 1945, ibid., 39; Eichelberger to his wife, 16 March 1945, Eichelberger Papers, reel 46, correspondence 1945; Buckner diary, 19 September 1944, Buckner Papers, DDEL, 1944, part 2; Buckner diary, 20 March 1945, ibid., 1945, part 1.

10. Quoted in E. B. Potter, *Nimitz* (Annapolis, MD: Naval Institute Press, 1976), 375.

11. Hodge to Richardson, 17 April 1945, Marshall Foundation, Pentagon Office, box 82, folder 49.

12. The quote is from Buckner to his wife, 13 May 1945, *Seven Stars,* 57. See also Buckner to his wife, 14 April and 3 May 1945, ibid., 39, 51; Buckner diary, 19 April, 10 May 1945, *Seven Stars,* 42, 55; Bruce to his wife, 5 June 1944, Bruce Papers, USAHEC, box 2; Richardson to Marshall, 5 July 1945, Marshall Foundation, Pentagon Office, box

82, folder 51; Buckner diary, 14, 15, 20, 22, 29 April 1945, Buckner Papers, DDEL, 1945, part 2.

13. Stilwell diary, 6 June 1945, *Seven Stars,* 74–75.

14. Bruce to his wife, 5 June 1945, Bruce Papers, USAHEC, box 2.

15. Stilwell diary, 3 5, 6, 18 June 1945, *Seven Stars,* 72–75, 82; Eichelberger to his wife, 3 June 1945, Eichelberger Papers, reel 47, correspondence 1945; Bruce to his wife, 27 June 1945, Bruce Papers, USAHEC, box 2; Swing to March, 20 May and 17 August 1945, *Dear General: World War II Letters,* ed. Dale F. Yee (Palo Alto, California: 11th Airborne Division Association, 1987), 33, 39–40; Buckner diary, 20 May 1945, *Seven Stars,* 59.

16. The account of Buckner's death is from Sarantakes, *Seven Stars,* 82.

17. For discussion of Buckner's replacement, see Marshall to MacArthur, 19 and 20 June 1945, DMMA, RG-4, reel 595; MacArthur to Marshall, 19 and 20 June 1945, ibid.

18. Walters interview, 1980, USAHEC, 703–704.

19. For views of Stilwell, see Devers interview, 12 August 1958, Marshall Foundation, 74–75; Lord Alanbrooke, 14 May 1943, *War Diaries: 1939–1945,* ed. Alex Danchev and Daniel Todman (Berkeley: University of California Press, 2001), 403; Omar Bradley and Clay Blair, *A General's Life: An Autobiography by General of the Army Omar N. Bradley and Clay Blair* (New York: Simon and Schuster, 1983), 65–66; Eichelberger to his wife, 22 June 1945, *Dear Miss Em,* 283; Taylor interview, 10 November 1972, USAHEC, section 2, 9; Albert Wedemeyer, *Wedemeyer Reports!* (New York: Henry Holt, 1958), 197–202.

20. Marshall to Stilwell, 13 January 1945, *MP,* vol. 5, 30; Marshall to Handy, 10 May 1945, *MP,* vol. 5, 176; Eichelberger to his wife, 1 July 1945, Eichelberger Papers, reel 47, correspondence 1945; Stilwell diary, 18, 19, and 24 June, 13 August 1945, *Seven Stars,* 82, 87–88, 105; Marshall, 29 October 1956, *George C. Marshall Interviews and Reminiscences for Forest C. Pogue* (Lexington, VA: George C. Marshall Research Foundation, 1991), 605–606.

21. Eichelberger to his wife, 21 June 1945, *Dear Miss Em,* 283; Stilwell diary, 19 and 24 June 1945, *Seven Stars,* 87–88; Griswold diary, March–May 1945, Griswold Papers, USAHEC, box 1.

22. Eichelberger to his wife, 8 June 1945, Eichelberger Papers, reel 47, correspondence 1945.

23. For a good analysis of the various views and anticipated casualties, see John Ray Skates, *The Invasion of Japan: Alternative to the Bomb* (Columbia: University of South Carolina Press, 1994), 21–32, 74–82. See also Weldon E. (Dusty) Rhoades, *Flying MacArthur to Victory* (College Station: Texas A&M Press, 1987), 386.

24. Truscott to Handy, 29 March 1945, Handy Papers, Marshall Foundation, box 1, folder 8.

25. Marshall to MacArthur, 6 April 1945, *MP,* vol. 5, 134; Marshall to Henry Conger Pratt, 14 May 1945, ibid., 187–188; Marshall to Wedemeyer, 16 June 1945, ibid., 228–229.

26. The quote is from MacArthur to Marshall, 7 April 1945, DMMA, RG-4, reel 594. See also Eichelberger to his wife, 16 February 1945, *Dear Miss Em,* 217; Pogue, 14 February 1957, *Marshall Interviews and Reminiscences,* 429; Buckner to his wife, 2 June 1945, *Seven Stars,* 66–67; Eichelberger to his wife, 8 April 1945, Eichelberger Papers, reel 46, correspondence 1945; Rhoades, *Flying MacArthur,* 405.

27. Bradley and Blair, *General's Life,* 435–436; Marshall to MacArthur, 6 April 1945, *MP,* vol. 5, 134; Eichelberger to his wife, 13 June 1945, *Dear Miss Em,* 281; Eisenhower to Marshall, 26 April 1945, *EP,* vol. 4, 2647–2648; Eichelberger to his wife, 28 April 1945, Eichelberger Papers, reel 46, correspondence 1945; Eichelberger to his wife, 6 June 1945, Eichelberger Papers, reel 47, correspondence 1945; Marshall to MacArthur, 24 April 1945, DMMA, RG-4, reel 594; MacArthur to Marshall, 24 April 1945, ibid.; Hansen diary, 1 September 1944, box 4.

28. Eichelberger to his wife, 31 May 1945, Eichelberger Papers, reel 47, correspondence 1945.

29. Bradley and Blair, *General's Life,* 435–436; Harry Butcher, 1 May 1945, *Three Years with Eisenhower: The Personal Diary of Captain Harry C. Butcher, USNR, Naval Aide to General Eisenhower, 1942 to 1945* (London: William Heinemann, 1946), 677–678; Eisenhower to Marshall, 26 and 30 March, 26 April 1945, *EP,* vol. 4, 2544, 2564, 2647; Marshall to MacArthur, 24 April and 1 May 1945, DMMA, RG-4, reel 594; MacArthur to Marshall, 24 April 1945, ibid., reel 594; Marshall to Eisenhower, 25 April 1945, Smith Files, Papers Relating to the Allied High Command, 1943–45, David Irving Collection, reel 4, file 8.

30. William K. Wyant, *Sandy Patch: A Biography of Lt. Gen. Alexander M. Patch* (New York: Praeger, 1991), 207–210; Bradley and Blair, *General's Story,* 435–436; Lucian Truscott, *Command Missions: A Personal Story* (New York: E. P. Dutton, 1954), 504; Patton to Marshall, 1 September 1944, *The Patton Papers, 1940–1945,* ed. Martin Blumenson (Boston: Houghton Mifflin, 1974), vol. 2, 536; Patton to his wife, 8 October 1944, ibid., 563; Patton to Eichelberger, 25 May 1945, ibid., 707; Marshall to Wedemeyer, 16 May 1945, *MP,* vol. 5, 192–193; Wedemeyer, *Wedemeyer Reports!,* 332; Butcher, 1 May 1945, *Three Years with Eisenhower,* 677–678; Eisenhower to Marshall, 26 April 1945, Eisenhower Papers, vol. 4, 2648; Moore interview, 1984, Army Senior Officer Oral Histories, 169–171; Eichelberger to his wife, 1 and 31 May 1945, Eichelberger Papers, reel 47, correspondence 1945; Hughes diary, 16 February 1945, Irving Collection, reel 5; Clark to Eisenhower, 12 May 1945, Irving Collection, reel 3; Clark to his wife, 20 December 1944, Clark Papers, Clark Diaries and Correspondence, 1942–1950, Daniel Library, The Citadel, vol. 10; Cook to Patton, 3 May and 27 June 1945, Cook Papers, DDEL, box 3, Cook–Patton Correspondence; Cook to Stephen Chamberlin, 2 June 1945, ibid.

31. J. Lawton Collins, *Lightning Joe: An Autobiography* (Baton Rouge: Louisiana State University Press, 1979), 303, 331–332; Matthew Ridgway, *Soldier: The Memoirs of Matthew B. Ridgway* (New York: Harper and Brothers, 1956), 150; Paul F. Braim, *The Will To Win: The Life of General James A. Van Fleet* (Annapolis, MD: Naval Institute

Press, 2001), 147–148; First Army War Diary, 17 December 1944 and 31 January 1945, reel 8, file 35.

32. Eichelberger to his wife, 24 March, 10 April, 13, 14, and 30 June 1945, *Dear Miss Em,* 237, 248–249, 281, 285; Eichelberger dictations, 11 December 1952, ibid., 287n; Skates, *Invasion of Japan,* 153–154.

33. The quote is from Stilwell diary, 5 August 1945, *Seven Stars,* 102. See also Buckner to his wife, 14 June 1945, ibid., 80; Stilwell diary, 22 July and 5 August 1945, ibid., 98, 102; Byers diary, 5 July 1945.

34. The story is from Moore interview, 1984, *ASOOH,* 169–171. See also Wedemeyer, *Wedemeyer Reports!,* 332.

CONCLUSIONS

1. Marshall to Woodring, 22 May 1940, *MP,* vol. 2, 219–220.

2. Marshall, 29 October 1956, *George C. Marshall Interviews and Reminiscences for Forest C. Pogue* (Lexington, VA: George C. Marshall Research Foundation, 1991), 614.

3. The quote is from Eisenhower to Marshall, 26 March 1945, *EP,* vol. 4, 2544. See also Eisenhower to Marshall, 19 January, 11 April 1945, ibid., 2442, 2596–2597; Eisenhower memo, 1 February 1945, ibid., 2466–2469.

4. Bradley's ranking is in Russell F. Weigley, *Eisenhower's Lieutenants: The Campaign of France and Germany, 1944–1945* (Bloomington: Indiana University Press, 1981), 758–759. See also Eisenhower to Marshall, 9 and 11 April 1945, *EP,* vol. 4, 2595–2597; Simpson interview, 1 June 1974, USAHEC, box 15, 896.

BIOGRAPHICAL AFTERWORD

1. Anderson to Simpson, 15 July 1947, Simpson Papers, USAHEC, box 14.

2. Quoted in Kevin C. Holzimmer, *General Walter Krueger: Unsung Hero of the Pacific War* (Lawrence: University Press of Kansas, 2007), 251.

Bibliography

ARCHIVAL SOURCES

The Citadel, Daniel Library, Charleston, South Carolina
  Mark W. Clark Papers
Duke University, Perkins Library, Durham, North Carolina
  Robert L. Eichelberger Papers
Dwight D. Eisenhower Library, Abilene, Kansas
  Oral Interviews of Henry Aurand, Ray Barker, Thomas Betts, Charles Bolte, Charles Broshous, Mark Clark, Jacob Devers, James Gavin, Alfred Gruenther, Thomas Handy, Lyman Lemnitzer, John Leonard, Leroy Lutes, Henry Matchett, William Simpson, Roscoe Woodruff
  Papers of Simon Buckner, Gilbert Cook, Roscoe Woodruff
Douglas MacArthur Memorial Archives, Norfolk, Virginia
George C. Marshall Foundation, Lexington, Virginia
  George C. Marshall Interviews with L. M. Guyer and C. H. Donnelly; Sidney Matthews, Howard Smyth, Roy Lemison, David Hamilton; Harry Price and William Foulke; William Spencer; John Sutherland
  Oral Interviews of Omar Bradley, Jacob Devers, Leonard Gerow
  Papers of Thomas Handy, George Marshall, Frank McCarthy, Lucian Truscott, James Van Fleet, Walton Walker
Mississippi State University, Mitchell Memorial Library, Mississippi State, Mississippi
  D. Clayton James's Interviews
National Archives and Records Administration, Washington, D.C.
  Eyes Alone Correspondence of General Joseph W. Stilwell, January 1942–October 1944
Norwich University, Kreitzberg Library, Northfield, Vermont
  Personal Memoirs of Major General E. N. Harmon
Papers Relating to the Allied High Command—1943–45, David Irving Collection
Stanford University, Hoover Institution Archives, Stanford, California
  Clovis Byers Collection, Charles Corlett Manuscript, Wade Haislip Papers
United States Army Heritage and Education Center, Carlisle, Pennsylvania
  Oral Histories of Donald Bennett, Charles Bonesteel III, James Collins, J. Lawton Collins, George Decker, Clyde Eddleman, Thomas Handy, Ben Harrell, Paul Freeman, Paul Harkins, Bruce Palmer Jr., Williston Palmer, Matthew Ridgway, Maxwell Taylor, John Waters, Albert Wedemeyer, James Woolnough

Papers of Andrew Bruce, Willis Crittenberger, Jacob Devers, Charles Gerhardt, William Gill, Alvan Gillem, Oscar Griswold, Wade Haislip, Thomas Handy, Chester Hansen, Geoffrey Keyes, John Lucas, Matthew Ridgway, William Simpson, Joseph Swing, James Van Fleet

United States Military Academy, West Point, New York

Walter Krueger Papers

University of Southern Mississippi, Mississippi Oral History Collection, Hattiesburg, Mississippi

An Oral History with Troy H. Middleton

Yale University Library, Boston, Massachusetts

The Henry Lewis Stimson Diaries

PRIMARY SOURCES

Alanbrooke, Lord. *War Diaries: 1939–1945.* Ed. Alex Danchev and Daniel Todman. Berkeley: University of California Press, 2001.

Alexander, Harold. *The Alexander Memoirs, 1940–1945.* New York: McGraw-Hill, 1962.

Allen, Robert S. *Lucky Forward: The History of Patton's Third U.S. Army.* New York: Vanguard Press, 1947.

Armed Forces Oral Histories: Army Senior Officer Oral Histories. Frederick, MD: University Publications of America, 1989.

Arnold, Henry. *American Airpower Comes of Age: General Henry H. "Hap" Arnold's World War II Diaries.* 2 vols. Ed. John Huston. Maxwell Air Force Base, AL: Air University Press, 2002.

———. *Global Mission.* New York: Harper and Brothers, 1949.

Barbey, Daniel E. *MacArthur's Amphibious Navy: Seventh Amphibious Force Operations, 1943–1945.* Annapolis, MD: United States Naval Institute, 1969.

Bradley, Omar. *A Soldier's Story.* New York: Henry Holt, 1951.

Bradley, Omar, and Clay Blair. *A General's Life: An Autobiography by General of the Army Omar N. Bradley and Clay Blair.* New York: Simon and Schuster, 1983.

Buster, William R. *Time On Target: The World War II Memoir of William R. Buster.* Ed. Jeffrey Suchanek and William J. Marshall. Frankfort: Kentucky Historical Society, 1999.

Butcher, Harry. *Three Years with Eisenhower: The Personal Diary of Captain Harry C. Butcher, USNR, Naval Aide to General Eisenhower, 1942 to 1945.* London: William Heinemann, 1946.

Chase, William. *Front Line General: The Commands of Maj. Gen. Wm. C. Chase.* Houston: Pacesetter Press, 1975.

Clark, Frederick J. *Engineer Memoirs: Interviews with Lieutenant General Frederick J. Clark.* Washington, DC: Historical Division, Office of Administrative Services, Chief of Engineers Office, 1979.

Clark, Mark W. *Calculated Risk.* New York: Harper and Brothers, 1950.

Codman, Charles R. *Drive.* Boston: Little, Brown, 1957.

Collins, J. Lawton. *Lightning Joe: An Autobiography*. Baton Rouge: Louisiana State University Press, 1979.

Conquer: The Story of the Ninth Army, 1944–1945. Washington, DC: Infantry Journal Press, 1947.

Corlett, Charles H. *Cowboy Pete: The Autobiography of Major General Charles H. Corlett*. Ed. William Farrington. Santa Fe, NM: Sleeping Fox Enterprises, 1974.

De Guingand, Francis. *Generals at War*. London: Hodder and Stoughton, 1964.

De Lattre de Tassigny, Jean Joseph Marie Gabriel. *The History of the French First Army*. Trans. Malcolm Barnes. London: George Allen and Unwin, 1952.

Egeberg, Roger Olaf. *The General: MacArthur and the Man He Called "Doc."* New York: Hippocrene Books, 1983.

Eichelberger, Robert. *Dear Miss Em: General Eichelberger's War in the Pacific, 1942–1945*. Ed. Jay Luvaas. Westport, CT: Greenwood Press, 1972.

——— with Milton MacKaye. *Our Jungle Road to Tokyo*. New York: Viking Press, 1950.

Eisenhower, Dwight. *At Ease: Stories I Tell to Friends*. Garden City, NY: Doubleday, 1967.

———. *Crusade in Europe*. New York: Doubleday, 1948.

———. *The Papers of Dwight David Eisenhower: The War Years*. 4 vols. Ed. Alfred D. Chandler Jr. Baltimore: Johns Hopkins Press, 1970.

Eisenhower, John. *General Ike: A Personal Reminiscence*. New York: Free Press, 2003.

Fauntleroy, Barbara Gavin, ed. *The General and His Daughter: The Wartime Letters of General James M. Gavin to His Daughter Barbara*. New York: Fordham University Press, 2007.

Fry, James C. *Combat Soldier*. Washington, DC: National Press, 1968.

Gavin, James. *On to Berlin: Battles of an Airborne Commander, 1943–1946*. New York: Viking Press, 1978.

Gill, William H., as told to Edward Jaquelin Smith. *Always a Commander: The Reminiscences of Major General William H. Gill*. Colorado Springs: Colorado College, 1974.

Halsey, William, and J. Bryan III. *Admiral Halsey's Story*. New York: Da Capo Press, 1976.

Harmon, Ernest N., with Milton MacKaye and William Ross MacKaye. *Combat Commander: Autobiography of a Soldier*. Englewood Cliffs, NJ: Prentice-Hall, 1970.

Headquarters, X Corps Artillery. *Pacific Diary*. Washington, DC: National Government Publication, 1963–1983.

Hoge, William M. *Engineer Memoirs*. Washington, DC: Office of History, U.S. Army Corps of Engineers, 1993.

Howze, Hamilton E. *A Cavalryman's Story: Memoirs of a Twentieth-Century Army General*. Washington, DC: Smithsonian Institution Press, 1996.

Hull, John Edwin. *The Autobiography of General John Edwin Hall, 1895–1975*. M. Anderson, 1978.

Kenney, George C. *General Kenney Reports: A Personal History of the Pacific War*. Washington, DC: Air Force Historical Studies Office, 1949.

Kinkaid, Thomas. *The Reminiscences of Thomas Cassin Kinkaid*. Columbia University: Oral History Research Office, 1961.

Koch, Oscar W., with Robert G. Hays. *G-2: Intelligence for Patton.* Atglen, PA: Schiffer Military History, 1999.

Krueger, Walter. *From Down Under to Nippon: The Story of the Sixth Army in World War II.* Washington, DC: Combat Forces Press, 1953.

Leahy, William D. *I Was There: The Personal Story of the Chief of Staff to Presidents Roosevelt and Truman Based on His Notes and Diaries Made at the Time.* New York: McGraw-Hill, 1950.

Lodge, Henry Cabot. *The Storm Has Many Eyes: A Personal Narrative.* New York: W. W. Norton, 1973.

MacArthur, Douglas. *Reminiscences: General of the Army Douglas MacArthur.* New York: McGraw-Hill, 1964.

Marshall, George Catlett. *George C. Marshall Interviews and Reminiscences for Forest C. Pogue.* Lexington, VA: George C. Marshall Research Foundation, 1991.

———. *The Papers of George Catlett Marshall.* Vols. 2–5. Ed. Larry I. Bland. Baltimore: Johns Hopkins University Press, 1986, 1991, 1996, 2003.

Marshall, Katherine Tupper. *Together: Annals of an Army Wife.* New York: Tupper Love, 1946.

Murphy, Robert D. *Diplomat among Warriors.* Garden City, NY: Doubleday, 1964.

Nimitz, Chester W. *The Reminiscences of Chester W. Nimitz.* Columbia University Oral History Collection and New York Times Oral History Program, no. 153. Sanford, NC: Microfilming Corporation of America, 1979.

Patton, George. *The Patton Papers, 1940–1945.* Vol. 2. Ed. Martin Blumenson. Boston: Houghton Mifflin, 1974.

———. *War As I Knew It.* Boston: Houghton Mifflin, 1947.

Polk, James H. *World War II Letters and Notes of Colonel James H. Polk, 1944–1945.* Ed. James H. Polk III. Oakland, OR: Red Anvil Press, 2005.

Pyle, Ernie. *Brave Men.* New York: Grosset and Dunlap, 1944.

Rhoades, Weldon E. (Dusty). *Flying MacArthur to Victory.* College Station: Texas A&M University Press, 1987.

Ridgway, Matthew. *Soldier: The Memoirs of Matthew B. Ridgway.* New York: Harper and Brothers, 1956.

Riegelman, Harold. *Caves of Biak: An American Officer's Experiences in the Southwest Pacific.* New York: Dial Press, 1955.

Rogers, Paul P. *The Bitter Years: MacArthur and Sutherland.* New York: Praeger, 1990.

———. *The Good Years: MacArthur and Sutherland.* New York: Praeger, 1990.

Sarantakes, Nicholas Evan, ed. *Seven Stars: The Okinawa Battle Diaries of Simon Bolivar Buckner, Jr., and Joseph Stilwell.* College Station: Texas A&M Press, 2004.

Smith, Holland M., and Percy Finch. *Coral and Brass.* New York: Charles Scribner's Sons, 1949.

Smith, Walter Bedell. *Eisenhower's Six Great Decisions: Europe 1944–1945.* New York: Longmans, Green, 1956.

Stilwell, Joseph. *The Stilwell Papers*. Ed. Theodore White. New York: William Sloane, 1948.

———. *Stilwell's Personal File: China-Burma-India, 1942–1944*. Ed. Riley Sunderland and Charles F. Romananus. 5 vols. Wilmington, DE: Scholarly Resources, 1976.

Taylor, Maxwell D. *Swords and Plowshares*. New York: W. W. Norton, 1972.

Triplet, William S. *A Colonel in the Armored Divisions: A Memoir, 1941–1945*. Ed. Robert H. Ferrell. Columbia: University of Missouri Press, 2001.

Truscott, Lucian. *Command Missions: A Personal Story*. New York: E. P. Dutton, 1954.

Wade, Gary. *CSI Report No. 5: Conversations with General J. Lawton Collins*. Fort Leavenworth, KS: Combat Studies Institute, 1983.

Walker, Fred. *From Texas to Rome: A General's Journal*. Dallas: Taylor Publishing, 1969.

Wedemeyer, Albert. *Wedemeyer Reports!* New York: Henry Holt, 1958.

Yee, Dale F., ed. *Dear General: World War II Letters*. Palo Alto, CA: 11th Airborne Division Association, 1987.

SECONDARY SOURCES

Ambrose, Stephen E. *Eisenhower: Soldier, General of the Army, President-Elect, 1890–1952*. Vol. 1. New York: Simon and Schuster, 1983.

Ancell, R. Manning, with Christine M. Miller. *The Biographical Dictionary of World War II Generals and Flag Officers*. Westport, CT: Greenwood Press, 1996.

Astor, Gerald. *Terrible Terry Allen: Combat General of World War II—the Life of an American Soldier*. New York: Ballantine Books, 2003.

Atkinson, Rick. *An Army at Dawn: The War in North Africa, 1942–43*. New York: Henry Holt, 2002.

Belote, James, and William Belote. *Typhoon of Steel: The Battle for Okinawa*. New York: Harper and Row, 1970.

Bergerud, Eric. *Touched with Fire: The Land War in the South Pacific*. New York: Viking, 1996.

Berlin, Robert H. "U.S. Army World War II Corps Commanders: A Composite Biography." U.S. Army Combined Arms Center. www.cgsc.edu/carl/resources/csi/berlin2/berlin2 .asp.

Blair, Clay. *The Forgotten War: America in Korea, 1950–1953*. New York: Times Books, 1987.

Blumenson, Martin. "America's World War II Leaders in Europe: Some Thoughts." *Parameters* 19 (December 1989): 2–13.

———. *Liberation*. Alexandria, VA: Time-Life Books, 1978.

———. *Mark Clark*. New York: Congdon and Weed, 1984.

Blumenson, Martin, and James L. Stokesbury. *Masters of the Art of Command*. Boston: Houghton Mifflin, 1975.

Bonn, Keith E. *When the Odds Were Even: The Vosges Mountains Campaign, October 1944–January 1945*. Novato, CA: Presidio Press, 1994.

Braim, Paul F. *The Will To Win: The Life of General James A. Van Fleet*. Annapolis, MD: Naval Institute Press, 2001.

Breur, William B. *Feuding Allies: The Private Wars of the High Command.* New York: John Wiley and Sons, 1995.

Cannon, M. Hamlin. *Leyte: The Return to the Philippines.* Washington, DC: Government Printing Office, 1954.

Chwialkowski, Paul. *In Caesar's Shadow: The Life of General Robert Eichelberger.* Westport, CT: Greenwood Press, 1993.

Cline, Ray S. *Washington Command Post: The Operations Division.* Washington, DC: Center of Military History, 1951.

Coakley, Robert W., and Robert M. Leighton. *Global Logistics and Strategy, 1943–1945.* Washington, DC: Government Printing Office, 1968.

Costello, John. *The Pacific War.* New York: Quill, 1982.

Craven, Wesley Frank, and James Lea Cate, eds. *The Army Air Forces in World War II: The Pacific.* Vol. 4: *Guadalcanal to Saipan: August 1942 to July 1944.* Chicago: University of Chicago Press, 1950.

Cray, Ed. *General of the Army: George C. Marshall, Soldier and Statesman.* New York: W. W. Norton, 1990.

Crowl, Philip A. *Campaign in the Marianas.* Washington, DC: Government Printing Office, 1959.

D'Este, Carlo. *Decision in Normandy.* New York: Dutton Books, 1994.

———. *Eisenhower: A Soldier's Life.* New York: Henry Holt, 2002.

———. *Fatal Decision: Anzio and the Battle for Rome.* New York: HarperCollins, 1991.

———. *Patton: A Genius for War.* New York: HarperCollins Publishers, 1995.

Ellis, John. *Brute Force: Allied Strategy and Tactics in the Second World War.* New York: Viking, 1990.

Falk, Stanley L. *Decision at Leyte.* New York: W. W. Norton, 1966.

Frank, Richard B. *Guadalcanal.* New York: Random House, 1990.

Gabel, Christopher R. *The US Army GHQ Maneuvers of 1941.* Washington, DC: Center of Military History, 1992.

Gailey, Harry A. *Bougainville, 1943–1945: The Forgotten Campaign.* Lexington: University Press of Kentucky, 1991.

———. *Howlin' Mad vs. the Army: Conflict and Command, Saipan 1944.* Novato, CA: Presidio Press, 1986.

Goolrick, William K., and Ogden Tanner. *The Battle of the Bulge.* Alexandria, VA: Time-Life Books, 1979.

Goulden, Joseph C. *Korea: The Untold Story of the War.* New York: McGraw-Hill, 1982.

Hastings, Max. *Overlord: D-Day and the Battle for Normandy.* New York: Simon and Schuster, 1984.

Heefner, Wilson A. *Patton's Bulldog: The Life and Service of General Walton H. Walker.* Shippensburg, PA: White Mane Books, 2001.

Hill, James R. "A Comparative Analysis of the Military Leadership Styles of George C. Marshall and Dwight D. Eisenhower." MA thesis, U.S. Army Command and General Staff College, 2008.

Hirshson, Stanley P. *General Patton: A Soldier's Life.* New York: HarperCollins, 2002.

Hogan, David W. *A Command Post at War: First Army Headquarters in Europe, 1943–1945.* Washington, DC: Center of Military History, 2000.

Holzimmer, Kevin C. *General Walter Krueger: Unsung Hero of the Pacific War.* Lawrence: University Press of Kansas, 2007.

Hoyt, Edwin P. *Backwater War: The Allied Campaign in Italy, 1943–1945.* Westport, CT: Praeger, 2002.

———. *The Glory of the Solomons.* New York: Stein and Day, 1983.

Irving, David. *The War between the Generals.* New York: Congdon and Lattes, 1981.

James, D. Clayton. *The Years of MacArthur.* 2 vols. Boston: Houghton Mifflin, 1970, 1975.

Larger Units: Theater Army—Army Group—Field Army. Fort Leavenworth, KS: Combat Studies Institute, 1985.

Manchester, William. *American Caesar: Douglas MacArthur, 1880–1964.* New York: Dell Publishing, 1978.

Miller, John, Jr. *Cartwheel: The Reduction of Rabaul.* Washington, DC: Historical Division, Department of the Army, 1959.

———. *Guadalcanal: The First Offensive.* Washington, DC: Historical Division, Department of the Army, 1949.

Morris, Eric. *Salerno: A Military Fiasco.* New York: Stein and Day, 1983.

Mosley, Leonard. *Marshall: Hero for Our Times.* New York: Hearst Books, 1982.

Murray, Williamson, and Allan R. Millett. *A War To Be Won: Fighting the Second World War.* Cambridge, MA: Belknap Press, 2000.

Nenninger, Timothy K. "Leavenworth and Its Critics: The U.S. Army Command and General Staff School, 1922–1940." *Journal of Military History* 58 (April 1994): 199–231.

Ohl, John Kennedy. *Minuteman: The Military Career of General Robert S. Beightler.* Boulder, CO: Lynne Rienner Publishers, 2001.

Perret, Geoffrey. *Old Soldiers Never Die: The Life of Douglas MacArthur.* New York: Random House, 1996.

Phillips, Henry Gerard. *The Making of a Professional: Manton S. Eddy, USA.* Westport, CT: Greenwood Press, 2000.

Pogue, Forrest C. "GC Marshall and His Commanders." In *Essays in Some Dimensions of Military History,* 4:80–90, ed. B. F. Cooling III. Carlisle Barracks, PA: U.S. Army Military Research Collection, 1976.

———. *George C. Marshall: Ordeal and Hope, 1939–1942.* New York: Viking Press, 1966.

———. *George C. Marshall: Organizer of Victory, 1943–1945.* New York: Viking Press, 1973.

Potter, E. B. *Nimitz.* Annapolis, MD: Naval Institute Press, 1976.

Price, Frank James. *Troy H. Middleton: A Biography.* Baton Rouge: Louisiana State University Press, 1974.

Reardon, Mark J. *Victory at Mortain: Stopping Hitler's Panzer Counteroffensive*. Lawrence: University Press of Kansas, 2002.

Schaller, Michael. *Douglas MacArthur: The Far Eastern General*. New York: Oxford University Press, 1989.

Skates, John Ray. *The Invasion of Japan: Alternative to the Bomb*. Columbia: University of South Carolina Press, 1994.

Smith, Robert Ross. *Triumph in the Philippines*. Washington, DC: Government Printing Office, 1963.

Specter, Ronald H. *Eagle against the Sun: The American War with Japan*. New York: Free Press, 1985.

Stoler, Mark A. *George C. Marshall: Soldier-Statesman of the American Century*. Boston: Twayne Publishers, 1989.

Stone, Thomas R. "General William Hood Simpson: Unsung Commander of U.S. Ninth Army." *Parameters* (June 1981): 44–52.

Taaffe, Stephen R. *MacArthur's Jungle War: The 1944 New Guinea Campaign*. Lawrence: University Press of Kansas, 1998.

These Are The Generals. New York: Alfred A. Knopf, 1943.

Tuchman, Barbara W. *Stilwell and the American Experience in China, 1911–45*. New York: MacMillan, 1971.

Wallace, Robert. *The Italian Campaign*. Chicago: Time-Life Books, 1981.

Watson, Mark Skinner. *Chief of Staff: Prewar Plans and Preparations*. Washington, DC: Government Printing Office, 1950.

Weigley, Russell F. *Eisenhower's Lieutenants: The Campaign of France and Germany, 1944–1945*. Bloomington: Indiana University Press, 1981.

Weintraub, Stanley. *15 Stars: Eisenhower, MacArthur, Marshall: Three Generals Who Saved the American Century*. New York: Free Press, 2007.

White, Clare. *Roanoke: 1740–1982*. Roanoke, VA: Roanoke Valley Historical Society, 1982.

Winton, Harold R. *Corps Commanders of the Bulge: Six American Generals and Victory in the Ardennes*. Lawrence: University Press of Kansas, 2007.

Wishnevsky, Stephan T. *Courtney Hicks Hodges: From Private to Four-Star General in the United States Army*. London: McFarland, 2006.

Wyant, William K. *Sandy Patch: A Biography of Lt. Gen. Alexander M. Patch*. New York: Praeger, 1991.

Index

Bizerte, Tunisia, 67, 77, 78, 79, 82, 83, 105
Blamey, Thomas, 35
Bohn, John, 188
Bohol, Philippines, 233
Boise, USS, 222
Bolero, Operation, 165
Bolling, Alexander, 273
Bonin Islands, 295
Bonn, Germany, 289
Bonuan Boquig, Luzon, 225
Boso peninsula, Honshu, 313
Bougainville campaign, 45–46, 154, 221, 296, 327
Bradley, James, 212, 303
Bradley, Omar
   aftermath of war, 333
   and Allen, Terry, 83, 86, 87, 90
   background and character, 74–76
   and Battle of the Bulge, 260, 262, 263, 264, 265, 266, 268, 270, 274, 275
   and Brest, 248–49
   and Brooks, 325
   and Clark, 60, 325
   and Cobra, 189–90
   and Collins, 171, 172, 185, 189–90, 194, 249, 325, 326
   command style, 75, 77, 79, 81, 167, 169, 183, 187–88, 191
   and Corlett, 173, 187, 190, 209, 241, 325
   and Devers, 107, 108, 278, 286, 325, 331
   and Eddy, 81, 198, 199–200, 253, 325
   and Eisenhower, 76, 80
   evaluation of, 327, 329, 330–31
   evaluation of commanders, 325
   and Fredendall, 73, 76
   and Gerow, 177, 178, 185, 187, 196, 245, 325
   and Haislip, 193, 325
   and Harmon, Ernest, 79, 81, 250, 284, 325
   and Hodges, 168, 169, 191, 249, 285, 325
   and Huebner, 325
   and invasion of Italian mainland, 95
   and invasion of Japan, 310
   and Kasserine Pass, 72
   and Marshall, 3, 5, 76
   and McLain, 188, 242, 243, 325
   and Middleton, 87, 175, 176, 249, 262, 263, 325
   and Normandy campaign, 184–96
   and Overlord preparations, 93, 99, 160, 166, 167, 183
   and Patch, 325
   and Patton, 77, 80–81, 87, 90–91, 179–80, 190, 195, 252, 325
   and Rhine crossing, 288, 289
   and Ridgway, 188, 271, 290, 325
   and Ruhr, 292
   and Ryder, 81
   selected as First Army commander, 165–66
   selected as Second Corps commander, 76–77
   and Sicily campaign, 85, 89, 90, 132
   and Simpson, 248, 251, 283, 292, 325
   and Smith, Walter Bedell, 60
   and Truscott, 325
   and Tunisian campaign, 78–79, 81
   and Twelfth Army Group, 166, 191
   and Van Fleet, 289, 290–91, 293, 325
   and Walton Walker, 197, 325
   and Wood, 266
   and Woodruff, 176–77
Breakneck Ridge, Leyte, 212, 213, 215
Brenner Pass, 293
Brereton, Lewis, 238, 271
Brest, France, 192, 193, 248–49, 329
Brisbane, Australia, 14, 28, 35, 135, 137, 142, 219, 220, 231
Brittany peninsula, 190, 192, 248, 316
Brooke, Alan, 67, 84, 112, 159, 162
Brooks, Edward
   aftermath of war, 333
   background and character, 255–56
   evaluation of, 326–27
   and Mortain, 194
   and Nordwind, 276–77
   selected as Sixth Corps commander, 256–57
Brown, Allen, 120

Clark, Mark (*continued*)
    selected as Fifteenth Army Group
        commander, 128–29
    selected as Fifth Army commander, 66,
        68, 83
    and southern Italy campaign, 102–06
    and Truscott, 105, 114, 115, 117, 121,
        124, 130–31
    and Walker, Frederick, 99, 100, 119
Clarke, Elaine, 141–42, 218
Clark Field, Philippines, 222, 224, 225, 228,
    236
Clarkson, Perk, 231
Coblenz, Germany, 286, 287
Cobra, Operation, 189–90
Collins, J. Lawton
    and advance to the Rhine, 282–83, 285
    aftermath of war, 333
    background and character, 171–72
    and Battle of the Bulge, 273–74, 275
    and Cherbourg, 185
    and Cobra, 189–90
    and Cologne's fall, 285
    and D-Day, 183, 185
    and Devers, 108
    and drive across France, 200
    and Eddy, 199
    evaluation of, 326
    and Guadalcanal campaign, 38, 39, 40,
        41
    and Hodge, 153
    and Hodges, 169, 259, 273, 281, 292, 311,
        330
    and Huertgen Forest, 244
    and invasion of Japan, 311, 314, 315
    and MacArthur, 170
    and Marshall, 161, 170, 172
    and McLain, 243
    and Mortain, 194
    and New Georgia campaign, 43, 44
    and Normandy campaign, 186, 209
    and Richardson, 149
    Ruhr, 292
    selected as Seventh Corps commander,
        170–71

    and Van Fleet, 190
    and West Wall, 240, 244
Colmar Pocket, 258, 276, 277–78, 279, 286,
    331
Cologne, Germany, 285, 288
Combined Chiefs of Staff, 84, 94, 106, 162,
    189, 201
Command and General Staff School, 6
Conical Hill, Okinawa, 302
Connor, Fox, 54, 55
Cook, Gilbert
    aftermath of war, 334
    background and character, 198
    evaluation of, 327
    and liberation of France, 198
    relieved as Twelfth Corps commander,
        198
    selected as Twelfth Corps commander,
        198
Coral Sea, Battle of, 25
Cordillera Central Mountains, Luzon, 222
Corlett, Charles
    and Aachen, 240
    aftermath of war, 333–34
    background and character, 173–74
    and drive across France, 200
    evaluation of, 327
    and Hodges, 240, 241
    and Kwajalein, 152, 153, 173
    and Normandy campaign, 184, 186, 187,
        188, 190, 194, 209
    relieved as Nineteenth Corps
        commander, 240–42
    selected as Nineteenth Corps
        commander, 173
    selected as Twenty-fourth Corps
        commander, 153, 173
Coronet, Operation, 313
Corps, 10–11
Corregidor, Philippines, 19, 20, 134
Cota, Norman, 184, 188, 244, 245, 263
Cotentin Peninsula, France, 185, 190
Craig, Lillian, 1, 5, 6, 9
Craig, Louis, 144, 146, 244, 282
Craig, Malin, 2, 3, 28

Eddy, Manton (*continued*)
and North African campaign, 78, 81
relieved as Twelfth Corps commander, 293–94
and Rhine crossing, 292
selected as Twelfth Corps commander, 198–99
and Sicily campaign, 89
Egeberg, Roger, 219, 222, 223
Eichelberger, Robert
aftermath of war, 334
asked to be MacArthur's chief of staff, 232
background and character, 27–28
and Biak operation, 139–40
and Buckner, 304
and Buna-Gona, 28, 29–31
evaluation of, 326, 328
exiled by MacArthur, 31–33
and Fuller, 136, 139
and Gill, 218
and Hall, 217
and Hodge, 218
and Hodges, 310–11
and Hollandia operation, 135–38
and invasion of Japan, 308, 310, 312, 313, 314, 315
and Irving, 136, 217, 218, 234
and Krueger, 136, 138, 140–41, 141–42, 217, 226, 233, 312
and Leyte campaign, 217–18
and Luzon campaign, 225–26
and MacArthur, 29–30, 31, 33, 135, 136–37, 217, 233
Marshall's efforts to secure services for Europe, 32–33, 170
relieved as First Corps commander, 141
and Richardson, 149
selected as Eighth Army commander, 140
selected as First Corps commander, 27
and Sibert, 234–35
and Simpson, 248
and southern Philippines campaign, 232–35
and Sutherland, 28–29, 30, 31, 33, 136, 141, 218

and Swift, 144, 230
and Woodruff, 218, 234, 235
Eisenhower, Dwight
and advance to the Rhine, 279–80
aftermath of war, 334
and Anderson, John B., 283, 324
and Anzio operation, 106, 110, 112
background and character, 53, 54–56
and Battle of the Bulge, 260, 263, 265, 266, 273, 275
and Bradley, 81, 92, 95, 166, 187, 190, 310, 324, 329, 330
and Brooks, 256, 323, 324
and Clark, 60, 66, 68–69, 83, 95, 97, 132, 201, 324, 330
and Collins, 170, 285, 324, 326
and Colmar Pocket, 277–78
concerns about Overlord leadership, 169–70
and conquest of Germany, 292
considered as chief of staff, 160, 162–63
and Cook, 208
and Corlett, 173, 187, 209, 242, 324
criteria for assigning officers, 11, 51–52, 57, 165, 208, 320, 323–25
and Crittenberger, 123, 124, 131, 176, 208, 324
and Dawley, 96, 97, 98
and Devers, 107–08, 112, 124, 170, 206, 208, 254, 260, 276–77, 278, 285, 324, 331
and drive across France, 196, 237
and Eddy, 198–99, 323, 324
evaluation of commanders, 323–25
and Fredendall, 62, 66, 69, 70, 73, 83, 248
and Gerow, 177, 178, 187, 208, 209, 245, 246, 263, 324
and Gillem, 251, 283, 324
and Haislip, 193, 208, 259, 324
and Harmon, Ernest, 71–72, 73, 81–82, 115, 250, 294, 324
and Hodges, 167, 208, 269, 285, 310, 324, 330
and Huebner, 280, 324

and Clark, 104, 119, 131
evaluation of, 133, 327
and Gustav Line, 118, 119, 120, 121
and invasion of North Africa, 65
and invasion of southern France, 205
and northern Italian campaign, 129
selected as Second Corps commander,
101
and Sicily campaign, 85, 87, 89, 90, 92,
101
and southern Italy campaign, 104
and Truscott, 131
King, Ernest, 15, 23, 37, 56, 156, 157, 159,
160, 162, 204, 211, 295, 297, 308
Kinkaid, Thomas, 296
Kiriwina Island, 36
Knox, William Frank, 162
Kokoda Trail, New Guinea, 25
Kolombangara Island, 44
Krefeld, Germany, 282
Krueger, Walter
aftermath of war, 336
and Aitape, 145
background and character, 33–34
and Biak operation, 139
command style, 138, 229
criteria for corps commanders, 18
and Eichelberger, 136, 137, 138, 139–40,
326
and Eisenhower, 53
evaluation of, 235, 329
and Gill, 145–46
and Griswold, 42, 224–25, 229–30
and Hall, 146–47
and Hodge, 215
and Hollandia, 135, 137
and invasion of Japan, 310, 312–13
and Irving, 213
and Leyte campaign, 212–13, 215–16,
217
and Luzon campaign, 221, 222, 224, 228,
229
and MacArthur, 35, 136, 215–16, 222
MacArthur's doubts about, 216–17, 221,
223

and Marshall, 34–35
and New Guinea campaign, 36
officers' unhappiness with, 229–31, 234
selected as Sixth Army commander,
34–35
and Sibert, 138, 144, 213
and Sutherland, 36
and Swift, 142–43, 224, 230
Kwajalein, Marshall Islands, 152, 153,
173
Kyushu, Japan, 229, 295, 301, 307, 313,
314, 315

Landrum, Eugene, 188
De Lattre de Tassigny, Jean, 204–05, 207,
208, 254, 255, 279, 293
Lauer, Walter, 264
Leahy, William, 15, 161, 308
Lear, Benjamin, 279
Leipzig, Germany, 292
Le Mans, France, 194, 195
Leonard, John, 262, 288, 289
Leyte campaign, 210–19
Leyte Gulf, Battle of, 212
Licata, Sicily, 88
Liege, Belgium, 200
Lingayen Bay, Luzon, 20, 221, 222
Liri Valley, Italy, 119
Liscome Bay, USS, 151, 152
Loire River, France, 198
Lone Tree Hill, Battle of, 144, 145
Longstop Hill, Battle of, 67
Los Negros, Philippines, 233
Lucas, John
aftermath of war, 336
and Anzio operation, 110, 111, 112, 113,
114
background and character, 100–101
and Clark, 104, 110, 111, 113, 114
evaluation of, 327
and McLain, 242
and Middleton, 104, 175
and Patton, 93, 111
relieved as Sixth Corps commander,
112–14

New Georgia campaign, 42–44
New Guinea campaign, 134–48
New Zealand, 14
Nichols Field, Luzon, 226
Nimitz, Chester, 17, 148, 150, 151, 152, 153, 156, 211, 212, 221, 295, 297, 298, 299, 300, 301, 303, 308, 312, 313, 314
Nordwind, Operation, 276–77
Normandy campaign, 184–96
North Africa, invasion of, 65–66
North African campaign, 67–79
Northern Italy campaign, 121–31
Nuremberg, Germany, 293

Okinawa campaign, 295–307
Oliver, Lunsford, 244
Olympic, Operation, 312
Omaha beach, Normandy, 184–85
Oran, Algeria, 56, 61, 66, 162
Orleans, France, 198
Ormoc, Leyte, 212, 213
Osmeñia, Sergio, 210, 211
Oujda, Morocco, 68, 95
Overlord, Operation, 159–85
Owen Stanley Mountains, 25, 26, 30

Pacific Ocean Area (POA), 17
Pacific War, 13–19
Palawan, Philippines, 233
Palermo, Sicily, 89, 101
Panay, Philippines, 233, 234
Parañaque River, Luzon, 226
Parang, Mindanao, 234
Paris, France, 196
Parker, Arthur, 281–82
Pas-de-Calais, France, 179, 191
Patch, Alexander
    and advance to the Rhine, 286–87
    aftermath of war, 337
    and Alsace, 254, 257, 258, 260
    background and character, 38–39
    and Collins, 40, 172
    and conquest of Germany, 293
    and Corlett, 174
    evaluation of, 327, 329

and Guadalcanal campaign, 38, 39, 40
    and Haislip, 257, 258
    health, 39, 40–41, 257
    and invasion of Japan, 311
    and invasion of southern France, 204, 205, 207, 208
    and Keyes, 205
    and de Lattre, 205
    and Nordwind, 276, 277
    and Patton, 38, 287
    relieved as Fourteenth Corps commander, 41
    and Rhine crossing, 293
    selected as Fourteenth Corps commander, 39
    selected as Fourth Corps commander, 124
    selected as Seventh Army commander, 203
    suggested as Bucker's replacement, 304, 305
    in trouble with Marshall, 204
    and Truscott, 205
Patrick, Edwin, 231
Patton, George
    and advance to the Rhine, 285–87
    aftermath of war, 338
    and Allen, Terry, 78, 90
    and Anzio operation, 112–13
    and Argentan-Falaise, 193, 195–96
    background and character, 63–64
    and Battle of the Bulge, 263, 265, 266, 267, 268, 269, 275
    and Bradley, 76, 77, 81, 85, 90, 93, 180–81, 183, 191, 252, 253, 286
    in Brittany peninsula, 192
    and Brooks, 256
    changed attitude, 180–81
    and Clark, 59, 69, 74, 80
    and Cobra, 190
    and Collins, 172
    command style, 78, 87, 90–91, 189, 192, 253, 260, 286
    and conquest of Germany, 293
    and Cook, 198, 208

and marines and navy, 150, 152, 157–58, 297

and Marshall, 61, 150–51

and Nimitz, 150

and Patch, 39

rejected as First Corps commander, 26

rejected as Tenth Army commander, 307

selected as army's central Pacific commander, 149–50

and Smith, Holland, 156

Ridgway, Matthew

aftermath of war, 338

background and character, 270–72

and Battle of the Bulge, 272, 273, 274, 275

evaluation of, 327

and importance of corps, 10–11

and invasion of Japan, 311, 314, 315

and Market-Garden, 271

and Normandy campaign, 187, 188

and Salerno, 98

selected as Eighteenth Corps commander, 271

and Sicily campaign, 86

Roanoke, Virginia, 1

Robertson, William, 263, 264, 281

Rockhampton, Australia, 28, 135, 136

Roer River region, 244, 249, 250, 280, 281, 282, 285

Roi, Kwajalein, 152

Rome, Italy, 94, 102, 103, 105, 106, 107, 110, 111, 112, 113, 114, 115, 118, 120, 121, 122, 124, 126, 132, 162, 202, 203

Roosevelt, Franklin

and Eisenhower, 160, 162, 163

and invasion of North Africa, 56, 159

and MacArthur, 20, 23, 160, 211

and Marshall, 3, 5, 160, 161

and Overlord commander, 159–63

Rosario, Luzon, 224

Rose, Maurice, 272, 273, 284

Roundup, Operation, 54

Rowell, Frank, 3

Ruhr region, 238, 292, 293

Ryder, Charles

health of, 104–05

and invasion of Japan, 313

and invasion of North Africa, 61, 66

recommended as corps commander, 124–25

and seizure of Rome, 121

and southern Italy campaign, 102, 104, 105, 119

and Tunisian campaign, 73, 79, 81

Ryukyus Islands, 295

Saar region, 238, 252, 258, 286

Saar River, 267, 286

Sagami Bay, Honshu, 313

Saidor, New Guinea, 36

Saipan, Marianas, 154, 155, 156, 157

Salerno, Italy, 94, 96, 97, 98, 99, 100

Samar, Philippines, 234

Sanananda, New Guinea, 30

San Fernando, Luzon, 229

Sanga Sanga, Philippines, 233

Sansapor-Mar, New Guinea, 144

Santo Tomas University, Manila, 226

Sarangani Bay, Mindanao, 234

Sarmi, New Guinea, 144

Sauer River, 286

Scheldt Estuary, Netherlands, 237

Schmidt, Harry, 313

Schnee Eifel, 262

Scoglitti, Sicily, 88

Sea Horse, Guadalcanal, 39

Seine River, France, 195, 196, 200, 237

Sele River, Italy, 96

Shimbu Group, 222, 228, 236

Shingle, Operation, 106

Shobu Group, 222, 228, 229

Shuri Line, Okinawa, 302

Sibert, Franklin

aftermath of war, 338

background and character, 144–45

evaluation of, 327

and Gill, 215

health, 235

and invasion of Japan, 313

Veritable, Operation, 280
Versailles, France, 130, 265
Vire River, France, 188, 189
Volturno River, Italy, 102
Vosges Mountains, 254, 260, 276

Wakde, New Guinea, 137, 144
Walker, Frederick
  and Clark, 99, 105, 119
  and Keyes, 105, 119
  and Patton, 86
  and Rapido River operation, 118, 119
  and Salerno, 96, 98, 99
  and southern Italy campaign, 105
Walker, Walton
  and advance to the Rhine, 286
  aftermath of war, 339
  background and character, 196–97
  as Corlett's deputy, 187
  and drive across France, 209
  evaluation of, 326–27
  and Metz, 252, 253
  and Patton, 286
  selected as Twentieth Corps commander, 196–97
Ward, Orlando, 69, 70, 71, 72, 73, 78
Watchtower, Operation, 37
Watson, Edwin, 28, 32

Wedemeyer, Albert, 311
Wesel, Germany, 291
Wharton, James, 188
Wilkinson, Gerald, 21
Wilson, Henry, 107, 108, 118, 126, 127, 128, 202, 203, 206, 207
Wood, John, 190, 192, 252, 266
Wood, Walter, 1
Woodlark Island, 36
Woodring, Henry, 3
Woodruff, Roscoe
  on Leyte, 218
  removed as Overlord participant, 169, 176, 177
  and southern Philippines campaign, 234, 235
Worms, Germany, 293
Wyche, Ira, 185, 195, 196, 291, 294

Yalta Conference, 131
Yamamoto, Isoroku, 204
Yamashita, Tomoyuki, 221, 222, 226, 228
Yap Island, 212

Zambales Mountains, Luzon, 222, 227
Zamboanga peninsula, Philippines, 233
Zanana, New Georgia, 43
ZigZag Pass, Luzon, 227–28, 236